Navegando 1

Annotated Teacher's Edition

James F. Funston

Contributing Writers

Rolando Castellanos

Paul J. Hoff

Keith Mason

EMCParadigm Publishing, Saint Paul, Minnesota

ISBN 0-8219-2799-X

Published by EMC/Paradigm Publishing
875 Montreal Way
St. Paul, Minnesota 55102
800-328-1452
www.emcp.com
E-mail: educate@emcp.com

Printed in the United States of America
3 4 5 6 7 8 9 10 XXX 08 07 06 05 04

CONTENTS

Scope and Sequence

	Objectives	Topics	Dialog	Cultura viva

Lección A	• ask for and give names
	• ask or tell where someone is from
	• ask for and state age
	• ask and tell how someone is feeling
	• express courtesy
	• ask for and state the time
		greetings
		farewells
		alphabet
		names
		numbers 0–20
		Spanish-speaking countries
		benefits of learning Spanish
			¡Hola!
			¿De dónde eres,
			  Hugo?
				Saludos y
				  despedidas
				Los cumpleaños

Lección B		greetings farewells health formal and informal time numbers 21–100 courtesy Spanish-speaking countries	Buenos días ¿Cómo te llamas?	Más sobre los saludos Con cortesía

Tú lees: Estrategia: *Using cognates to understand Spanish*
El mundo hispanohablante

Tú escribes: Estrategia: *Using the dictionary*

	Objectives	Topics	Dialog	Cultura viva

Lección A	• identify people and classroom objects
	• ask for and give names
	• ask or tell where someone is from
	• discuss school schedules and daily activities
	• describe classroom objects and clothing
	• say some things people do
	• state location
	• talk about how someone feels
		identifying people
		where a person is from
		Spanish influence in the
		  United States
		classroom objects
			¿Cómo se llama
			  ella?
			La nueva estudiante
			  de Los Ángeles
				La influencia
				  hispana en los
				  Estados Unidos
				El español en los
				  Estados Unidos

Lección B		school subjects
		class schedule
		days of the week
		colors
		clothing
		school life in the United
		  States and in
		  Spanish-speaking
		  countries
		technology
			El horario de clases
			¿Cuál es tu
			  dirección de
			  correo
			  electrónico?
				Los colegios en el
				  mundo hispano
				Las notas

Tú lees: Estrategia: *Activating background knowledge*
Puentes y fronteras

Tú escribes: Estrategia: *Writing a dialog journal*

Capítulo 3 ¡Vamos a la ciudad!

 México

	Objectives	Topics	Dialog	Cultura viva

Lección A	• talk about places in the city
	• make introductions and express courtesy
	• ask and answer questions
	• discuss how to go somewhere
	• say some things people do
	• say where someone is going
	• talk about the future
	• order food and beverages
		places in a city
		Mexico City
		courtesy
		transportation
			En la Ciudad de
			  México
			¿Qué?
				De visita en la Ciudad
				  de México
				¿Cómo viajamos en
				  el D.F.?

Lección B		places in a city
		Mexico
		foods
		restaurant dining
			Vamos al museo
			¿Qué van a comer?
				El Distrito Federal
				  (el D.F.)
				Salir a comer en
				  México

Tú lees:	Estrategia: *Anticipating special vocabulary* Frida Kahlo, una artista universal			
Tú escribes:	Estrategia: *Combining images to build word pictures*			

Capítulo 4 Mi familia y mis amigos

 Puerto Rico República Dominicana

	Objectives	Topics	Dialog	Cultura viva
Lección A	• talk about family and relationships • seek and provide personal information • express possession • say some things people do • express an opinion • state likes and dislikes • describe people and things	family relationships possession descriptions Puerto Rico	En la fiesta del abuelo ¿Por qué estás triste?	Puerto Rico ¿Cómo se llama?

Lección B		leisure-time activities
		relationships with
		  friends
		Dominican Republic
		likes and dislikes
		descriptions
			Me gusta mucho
			¿Cómo es ella?
				La República
				  Dominicana
				El merengue

Tú lees:	Estrategia: *Skimming* El béisbol y la familia Martínez			
Tú escribes:	Estrategia: *Creating an outline*			

Idioma	Estrategia	Oportunidades	¡Extra!	Readings
Making introductions: *te, le, les* *Repaso rápido:* question-asking words Asking questions Saying where someone is going: *ir*			Títulos de cortesía En otras palabras En la ciudad	El metro de la Ciudad de México es fantástico
Talking about the future: *ir a* + infinitive Saying what someone does: present tense of *-er* verbs	The importance of reviewing	Se habla español en México y en tu ciudad	Está en la internet Más bebidas y comidas Para ser natural	Grupo musical La Ola

Idioma	Estrategia	Oportunidades	¡Extra!	Readings
Repaso rápido: adjectives Expressing possession: possessive adjectives Saying what you do: present tense of *-ir* verbs Describing people and things with *estar*		¿Quieres ser au pair?	Los papás o los padres Exclamaciones Otros miembros de la familia	¿Qué es la familia?
Using *gustar* to state likes and dislikes Using *a* to clarify or emphasize what you are saying *Ser* vs. *estar*	Using contextual cues			Grupo musical La Ola

Capítulo 5 Una semana típica

 Costa Rica

 Nicaragua

	Objectives	Topics	Dialog	Cultura viva
Lección A	• describe everyday activities • say what someone is going to do • seek and provide personal information • write about everyday life • say what someone likes or dislikes • express strong feelings • talk about dates and holidays	electronic equipment Costa Rica weekly schedule leisure-time activities	Me gustan las tiendas ¡Qué semana!	Costa Rica ¡Pura vida!

Lección B		dates
		special days
		Nicaragua
		numbers
		  (101–999,999)
		months
			¿Cuándo es tu
			  cumpleaños?
			¡Feliz cumpleaños!
				Nicaragua
				Los días de fiesta

Tú lees: Estrategia: *Scanning for details before reading*
Hacer un viaje a Costa Rica

Tú escribes: Estrategia: *Brainstorming*

Capítulo 6 En casa

Venezuela

Colombia

	Objectives	Topics	Dialog	Cultura viva

Lección A	• identify items in the kitchen and at the dinner table
	• express obligations, wishes and preferences
	• talk about everyday activities
	• state an opinion
	• discuss food and table items
	• point out people and things
	• describe a household
	• tell what someone says
	• say how someone is doing
		objects in a kitchen
		table setting and
		  cleanup
		foods
		Venezuela
		at the dinner table
			¿Me vas a ayudar?
			¿Te gusta la sopa?
				Explorando Venezuela
				Las arepas
				  venezolanas

Lección B		rooms and floors of a house describing a home Colombia how someone is doing	La casa de Elisa Tengo mucho calor	Colombia ¡Hogar, dulce hogar!

Tú lees: Estrategia: *Using graphics to understand a reading*
La casa de mis sueños

Tú escribes: Estrategia: *Connecting phrases*

Idioma	Estrategia	Oportunidades	¡Extra!	Readings
Saying what someone has: *tener* Expressing strong feelings with *¡Qué (+ adjective/noun)!* Direct object pronouns	Avoiding interference with English	¿Trabajar en Costa Rica?	Tipos de música ¿Cómo son los días de la semana?	Los chicos ticos
Telling where someone is coming from: *venir* *Repaso rápido:* present tense to indicate the future Using the numbers 101–999,999 Asking for and giving the date			El pretérito de *ser*	Grupo musical La Ola

Idioma	Estrategia	Oportunidades	¡Extra!	Readings
Expressing obligations with *tener que* and *deber* Stem-changing verbs: $e \rightarrow ie$ Pointing out someone or something: demonstrative adjectives		¿Piensas viajar a otro país?	Más comida	Una deliciosa tradición
Telling what someone says: *decir* Expressing wishes with *querer* or *gustaría* *Repaso rápido:* regular present-tense verbs Stem-changing verbs: $e \rightarrow i$	Recognizing words in context		Altos y bajos Las palabras *e* y *u* Con permiso y perdón	Grupo musical La Ola

Capítulo 7 El tiempo libre

 Argentina   **Chile**

	Objectives	Topics	Dialog	Cultura viva
Lección A	• talk about leisure-time activities • discuss sports • say what someone can do • discuss length of time • describe what is happening • talk about the seasons and weather • indicate order	leisure-time activities entertainment sports Argentina time expressions	¿No quieres jugar al ajedrez? Quiero alquilar una película	Argentina Che, bailá conmigo...
Lección B		seasons weather sports leisure-time activities Chile ordinal numbers	¡Vamos a esquiar! ¿Qué temperatura hace?	Chile ¿Farenheit o centígrados?

Tú lees: Estrategia: *Previewing*
El mundo de los deportes

Tú escribes: Estrategia: *Questioning*

Capítulo 8 Mis quehaceres

 España

	Objectives	Topics	Dialog	Cultura viva
Lección A	• talk about household chores • say what just happened • ask for and offer help • talk about the past • identify and describe foods • discuss food preparation • make comparisons	household chores Spain	¿Me ayudas? Hay mucho por hacer	España: país multicultural Los quehaceres en una casa española
Lección B		foods shopping in a market comparisons preparing *paella* eating in Spain	¿Qué nos hace falta comprar? Comprando chorizo	La paella ¡Cómo se come en España!

Tú lees: Estrategia: *Gathering meaning from context*
Ir de tapas y a merendar

Tú escribes: Estrategia: *Using graphic organizers*

Idioma	Estrategia	Oportunidades	¡Extra!	Readings
Stem-changing verbs: $o \rightarrow ue$ and $u \rightarrow ue$ Expressions with *hace* Saying what is happening: present progressive *Repaso rápido:* direct object pronouns Using the present progressive with direct object pronouns	Clarifying meaning by asking questions	El español y los deportes	La fiebre del gol ¿Damas en los baños? Comparando inglés y español	El juego del pato
Verbs that require special accentuation Present tense of *dar* and *poner* Describing people using *-dor* or *-ista* Using ordinal numbers			¿Cuándo es verano?	Grupo musical La Ola

Idioma	Estrategia	Oportunidades	¡Extra!	Readings
Repaso rápido: direct object pronouns Indirect object pronouns Saying what just happened with *acabar de* Present tense of *oír* and *traer* Talking about the past: preterite tense of *-ar* verbs	Increasing your vocabulary	Estudiante de intercambio	El verbo *colgar* El uso de *vosotros* El cambio de $g \rightarrow j$	¿Quién lo hace?
Making comparisons *Repaso rápido:* preterite tense of regular *-ar* verbs Preterite tense of *dar* and *estar*			*Hacer falta, importar y parecer* ¿Cuánto pesa? El euro	Grupo musical La Ola

Capítulo 9 La ropa

 Panamá   **Ecuador**

	Objectives	Topics	Dialog	Cultura viva

Lección A	• describe clothing
	• identify parts of the body
	• express disagreement
	• talk about the past
	• discuss size and fit
	• discuss price and payment
		clothing
		shopping in a
		  department store
		parts of the body
		Panama
		bargaining
			¿Cuál prefieres?
			Un vestido de seda
				Panamá, el cruce del
				  mundo
				También se dice

Lección B		shopping in a
		  department store
		gift ideas
		jewelry
		size and fit
		Ecuador
		at the cash register
			Busco un regalo
			¿Cómo va a pagar?
				Ecuador, país de
				  maravillas naturales
				De compras en
				  Guayaquil

Tú lees:	Estrategia: *Using visual format to predict meaning* La tienda por departamentos Danté			
Tú escribes:	Estrategia: *Indicating sequence*			

Capítulo 10 Un año más

 Perú   **Guatemala**

	Objectives	Topics	Dialog	Cultura viva
Lección A	• discuss past actions and events • talk about everyday activities • express emotion • indicate wishes and preferences • write about past actions • talk about the future • make polite requests • describe personal characteristics	school likes and dislikes Peru travel	Fue un año divertido	El Perú, centro del imperio inca

Lección B		plans for the future
		vacations
		Guatemala
		careers
			¿Adónde van de
			  vacaciones?
				Guatemala, tierra
				  maya

Tú lees:	Estrategia: *Applying your skills* Es sólo una cuestión de actitud			
Tú escribes:	Estrategia: *Defining your purpose for writing*			

Idioma	Estrategia	Oportunidades	¡Extra!	Readings

Adjectives as nouns
Talking about the past:
  preterite tense of
  -er and -ir verbs
Preterite tense of ir
  and ser
Affirmative and negative
  words
	Developing language
	  survival skills: regatear
		Regatear	¿Recuerdas?	Las molas: símbolo de la
				  cultura kuna

Diminutives
Preterite tense of leer,
  oír, ver, decir, hacer and
  tener
Repaso rápido:
  prepositions
Using prepositions
			En otras palabras	Grupo musical La Ola

Idioma	Estrategia	Oportunidades	¡Extra!	Readings

	The importance of
	  reviewing
		En otro país
		Pensando en el futuro,
		  las carreras y el
		  español
				Machu Picchu

			Me gustaría	Grupo musical La Ola

INTRODUCTION

Navegando is a comprehensive Spanish language series that was designed and written to make teaching and learning Spanish an exciting and rewarding experience. The 21st century is a time of innovation and change in which knowledge of a world language is more important than ever before. Information-based technologies and an international marketplace require a workforce with specific competencies and knowledge in the area of interpersonal communication. Such a dynamic environment calls for a global mind-set, cultural understanding and a personal commitment to ongoing self-development to participate effectively with diverse populations.

The series was created to support and advance the vision of the National Standards for Foreign Language Learning. *Navegando* combines the five Cs of communication, cultures, connections, comparisons and communities with interesting content, varied and effective methodology, interactive activities and an ongoing discussion of the wealth of opportunities available to students through the study of Spanish. The program empowers students to learn to speak, read, write and comprehend Spanish and to do so in a culturally authentic manner. Chapter activities and readings motivate students to look beyond the classroom at real life in the Spanish-speaking world. Clear and concise grammar explanations guide students to understand and use Spanish with increasing accuracy, while communicative activities

allow students to use Spanish in meaningful, everyday situations. In addition, the many text-related photographs and illustrations provide attractive, authentic visual support for the thematic content.

The extensive components of the series that complement the textbook are described in this Annotated Teacher's Edition (ATE) and have been carefully developed to provide instructors with an effective and flexible program for teaching students to communicate in Spanish. Whether a teacher wants to provide Web-based learning, listening practice, additional grammar and vocabulary activities, video, CD-ROM software or some other means of addressing student learning, materials are available to reinforce, recycle and expand upon the textbook content, thus allowing the teacher to decide which components and activities to use in a given lesson.

One of the greatest challenges that educators face today is the need to reach a large number of students, each with individual interests and learning styles. *Navegando* is a comprehensive, flexible instructional program that allows teachers and students to meet the challenge together. The series offers exciting opportunities to address the multiple intelligences, career skills, critical thinking, cross-curricular learning, creative problem solving and the ability to work effectively with others. With *Navegando*, students will enjoy using Spanish in meaningful ways while becoming familiar with the fascinating cultures of the Spanish-speaking world.

PHILOSOPHY AND GOALS

Learning a language has always meant more than merely memorizing words and structures and then putting them together with the hope of actually being able to communicate. Just as language is inseparable from culture, so is it inseparable from the authentic communication of thoughts and emotions. The culture of the Spanish-speaking world varies from moment to moment and from one place to the next. Language and culture cannot be segmented and learned out of context if students are ever going to

become proficient. As students use *Navegando*, they will have exciting opportunities to learn about culture and to use language for obtaining and communicating information. In *Navegando*, students will cross several disciplines and will use a wide variety of resources, including the Internet, newspapers, magazines and libraries, for obtaining and sharing information, ideas and feelings. These authentic learning experiences will introduce them to and expand their knowledge of language, math and science, social sciences and the arts and humanities. In *Navegando,* students will learn not only academic skills but also problem solving, survival and employment skills, so that when they walk out of the classroom, they will be able to communicate confidently using authentic Spanish.

Navegando is a reflection of extensive research and the work of many dedicated professionals in foreign-language education and related fields. Focus-group research and extensive feedback from teachers have been applied to every component to make it better. In addition, a variety of important initiatives in language teaching and learning influenced the writing and design of the series. Many of the key principles and guiding forces in the creation of both the textbook and the supplemental materials are summarized on the following pages.

NATIONAL STANDARDS

The *Goals 2000: Educate America Act* of 1994 provided funding for improving education. One result of this funding was the establishment of content standards in foreign-language education as determined by a K–12 Student Standards Task Force. The task force represented people involved in various languages, levels of instruction, geographic regions and curricular models. They defined a national framework of content standards in foreign-language education, which was published in 1996. This document was revised and expanded in 1999. The new framework, *Standards for Foreign Language Learning in the 21st Century including Chinese, Classical Languages, French, German, Italian, Japanese, Portuguese, Russian, and Spanish,* includes information about standards application in specific languages. An executive summary of the National Standards can be obtained from the American Teachers of Foreign Languages, a collaborator in the project, at www.actfl.org. Following are the main points of the National Standards.

Communication

Communicate in Languages Other Than English

Standard 1.1: Students engage in conversations, provide and obtain information, express feelings and emotions and exchange opinions.

Standard 1.2: Students understand and interpret written and spoken language on a variety of topics.

Standard 1.3: Students present information, concepts and ideas to an audience of listeners or readers on a variety of topics.

Cultures

Gain Knowledge and Understanding of Other Cultures

Standard 2.1: Students demonstrate an understanding of the relationship between the practices and perspectives of the culture studied.

Standard 2.2: Students demonstrate an understanding of the relationship between the products and perspectives of the culture studied.

Connections

Connect with Other Disciplines and Acquire Information

Standard 3.1: Students reinforce and further their knowledge of other disciplines through the foreign language.

Standard 3.2: Students acquire information and recognize the distinctive viewpoints that are only available through the foreign language and its cultures.

Comparisons

Develop Insight into the Nature of Language and Culture

Standard 4.1: Students demonstrate understanding of the nature of language through comparisons of the language studied and their own.

Standard 4.2: Students demonstrate understanding of the concept of culture through comparisons of the cultures studied and their own.

Communities

Participate in Multilingual Communities at Home and around the World

Standard 5.1: Students use the language both within and beyond the school setting.

Standard 5.2: Students show evidence of becoming lifelong learners by using the language for personal enjoyment and enrichment.

PERFORMANCE ASSESSMENT

A standards-based instructional program is characterized by meaningful communication in the target language as opposed to simply learning about the language. Given that it is important to test not only what we teach but also how we teach, two logical implications of the National Standards for Foreign Language Learning are that assessments should be meaningful in terms of content and purpose and that they should be a reflection of regular classroom practices. For example, the activities in each chapter of *Navegando* offer numerous opportunities for communicative performance assessments that engage students in the interpersonal, interpretive and presentational modes. Through such assessments students can showcase their abilities and also gain an appreciation of the many practical purposes for which they can use the target language.

CROSS-CURRICULAR LEARNING

The National Standards for Foreign Language Learning illustrate that the foreign-language classroom provides a powerful opportunity for connecting language study with other academic disciplines. Such connections make language learning interesting and meaningful via relevant topics and a wide variety of resources for obtaining and sharing information. Students can understand and enjoy the real-life application of their language learning as they relate the study of Spanish to art, geography, history, literature, mathematics, music, social studies and science.

Navegando offers many activities for connecting Spanish with other disciplines. The student textbook includes cross-curricular activities titled *Conexión con otras disciplinas* and the margins of the ATE provide cross-curricular activities titled "Connections."

CAREER AWARENESS/ WORKPLACE READINESS SKILLS

In the Spanish classroom it is important to develop an awareness of the many benefits of learning another language. For example, today there are more opportunities than ever to apply language skills on the job and elsewhere outside the classroom. The global economy has made it more important than ever for graduates from high schools and colleges in the United States to develop their language skills to be able to compete in the international marketplace. Moreover, the growing Hispanic population in the United States has created the need for employees with Spanish proficiency in a wide variety of jobs.

Navegando uses a strand approach to career awareness to address employment opportunities. While students are learning the skills and knowledge that are necessary for them to become proficient in Spanish, they also explore how Spanish language skills can be beneficial when looking for employment. Career awareness is integrated regularly through the *Oportunidades* features in *Navegando*. Activities for introducing students to this significant benefit of learning another language also can be found in the margins of the ATE.

SERVICE LEARNING/ MENTOR PROGRAMS

Service learning and mentor programs are avenues through which students can contribute to their communities and utilize their Spanish skills in real-life settings. Service learning is volunteering one's time to learn about an organization, gain experience and make a positive contribution. A mentor is a person with considerable experience who is willing to work with and help a student learn about an organization. Young people benefit by gaining firsthand experience while learning about themselves, certain types of organizations and their communities. The organization and the community benefit by involving future leaders, saving resources and generating new ideas.

Educators interested in promoting such programs should encourage students to talk with their parents about their desire to volunteer in the community. For example, students may wish to work with an organization where they are able to use Spanish with customers, such as at a library or a museum. Brainstorm with the class other ways students might participate in community service or find a mentor.

Teachers can offer certain practical suggestions to students who would like to pursue service-learning opportunities or mentor programs for school-aged volunteers: 1) Explore the available options; 2) select a job that is interesting; 3) talk with people in several possible organizations to obtain additional information; 4) be realistic about the time available to volunteer; 5) consider whether transportation to the site will be a problem; 6) visit the organization and talk with its members to answer concerns; 7) make a decision.

PARENTAL INVOLVEMENT

Parental involvement in a student's education is a topic of considerable interest. The benefits of having students, parents, teachers and the community involved in supporting one another are undeniable. Teachers can do many things to encourage parents to take on a positive role in their child's education, both in and beyond the classroom. The margins of the *Navegando* ATE and accompanying ancillaries offer suggestions for encouraging parental support for classroom learning, for strengthening communication and for improving parental awareness of student progress and goals.

SPANISH FOR SPANISH-SPEAKING STUDENTS

One result of the growing Hispanic population in the United States is that it is increasingly common to have students who are native or heritage speakers of Spanish in the Spanish classroom. These students may present special needs as they formally study a language that they already have acquired or experienced to varying degrees. At the same time, such students can be a positive presence and a unique resource for other students in the classroom. To address these realities, the *Navegando* ATE includes a variety of activities and suggestions for teaching Spanish to Spanish-speaking students.

THE MULTIPLE INTELLIGENCES

Many factors affect learning. For years, classroom teachers have recognized that intelligence, social environment and motivation all need to be considered when teaching. All students do not learn in the same way and students' diverse learning styles need to be addressed in different ways to maximize individual potential.

Research on how the brain works has provided language teachers with additional information about intelligence and the learning process. One study that has drawn wide attention is Howard Gardner's theory of multiple intelligences. The theory suggests that people have different abilities in many different areas of thought and learning, and that these varying abilities affect their interests and how quickly they assimilate new information and skills. This pluralistic view of intelligence suggests that all people possess at least eight different intelligences, which operate in varying degrees depending on each person's individual profile. The eight intelligences identified by Gardner are the following: bodily-kinesthetic, interpersonal, intrapersonal, linguistic, logical-mathematical, musical, naturalist and spatial (visual) intelligence.

The general characteristics associated with each of these intelligences are described below, along with suggested teaching strategies:

- **Bodily-Kinesthetic:** Students who are athletic may demonstrate bodily-kinesthetic intelligence. They learn best by doing what they enjoy, want to learn through movement and touch and express their thoughts with body movement. They are good with hands-on activities such as woodworking, dancing, athletics and crafts.
  Teaching Strategies:
  Perform an activity as directed by a classmate or the teacher (TPR)
  Create artwork that represents some aspect of the Spanish-speaking world
  Act out a part from a play
  Perform a dance from a Spanish-speaking country
  Build a housing structure that is reminiscent of one that appears in the textbook
- **Interpersonal:** Students with interpersonal intelligence are natural leaders. They communicate well, empathize with others and often know what someone is thinking or feeling without having to hear the person speak.

Teaching Strategies:
Lead a discussion
Debate an issue
Organize and direct a survey
Role-play
Negotiate a settlement

- **Intrapersonal:** People with intrapersonal intelligence may appear to be shy. They are self-motivated and are very aware of their own thoughts and feelings about a given subject.

  Teaching Strategies:
  Create a list of favorite activities
  Write a poem expressing feelings
  Write answers to questions about personal life
  Prepare a written plan for a career path
  Determine the pros and cons of an issue

- **Linguistic:** This type of student demonstrates a strong appreciation for and fascination with words and language. People who display linguistic intelligence enjoy writing, reading, word searches, crossword puzzles and storytelling.

  Teaching Strategies:
  Write to a key pal on the Internet
  Tell a story
  Summarize a magazine or newspaper article
  Discuss the meaning of a song
  Write a poem
  Do a crossword puzzle

- **Logical-Mathematical:** This type of student likes establishing patterns and categorizing words and symbols. Students with logical-mathematical intelligence enjoy mathematics, experiments and games that involve strategy or rational thought.

  Teaching Strategies:
  Tabulate the total cost of a shopping trip
  Calculate the temperature in degrees Fahrenheit and in Celsius equivalents
  Figure changes in ingredient amounts to double or triple a recipe
  List the reasons why something happened
  Write an analysis of an event

- **Musical:** These students can be observed singing or tapping out a tune on a desk or other object. They are discriminating listeners who may be able to hear a song once and then play or sing the tune. Students who demonstrate musical intelligence catch what is said the first time, whereas others around them may need to hear the same thing repeated a number of times.

  Teaching Strategies:
  Perform a song
  Write a song
  Identify musical styles from the Spanish-speaking world
  Listen to and describe a musical piece
  Prepare a comparison of the music of two or more musicians

- **Naturalist:** Students with naturalist intelligence might have a special ability to observe, understand and apply learning to the natural environment. For example, students with naturalist intelligence might collect data about environmental conditions for a particular place and instinctively know what crop would grow best there.

  Teaching Strategies:
  Draw or photograph nature scenes
  Present to the class an object found in nature
  Collect and categorize objects from the natural world
  Do research and present findings about a wildlife protection project
  Keep a notebook of observations of nature
  Go on a nature hike or field trip

- **Spatial (Visual):** These students think in pictures and can conceptualize well. They often like complicated puzzles and may be seen drawing a picture, constructing something from the objects that surround them or daydreaming. They are able to imagine how something would look from a verbal description.

  Teaching Strategies:
  Write a description or comparison of two paintings
  Compare the artistic styles of two painters
  Draw the ideal house
  Design a building
  Identify a shape based on a classmate's description
  Prepare a Cad-Cam design

Benefits of Using the Multiple Intelligences: All students possess different combinations of intelligences. The multiple intelligences theory reflects a way of thinking about people that allows for both similarities and differences. It fosters inclusion, increases opportunities for enrichment, builds self-esteem and develops respect for individuals and the gifts they bring to the classroom. Teachers who utilize multiple intelligences research create an environment that allows all students to learn through their strengths and to share their abilities with others.

Gardner's research has provided important information and a clear message: Educational designers should develop teaching materials that motivate a greater number of students and, in turn, teachers should select teaching and assessment materials that are geared to maximizing student potential. To this end, *Navegando* has been created to address the benefits of teaching to students' multiple intelligences.

COMPONENTS

Navegando consists of a comprehensive three-level Spanish-language program. The first-level program includes the following components:

- Textbook
- Annotated Teacher's Edition (ATE)
- ATE on CD-ROM
- Program Manager
- Workbook
- Workbook Teacher's Edition
- Grammar and Vocabulary Exercises Manual (includes answer key)
- Listening Activities (includes Listening Activities Manual, Listening Activities Manual answer key and Listening Activities Audio CDs)
- Testing/Assessment Program (includes Quizzes with answer key, Test Booklet, Portfolio Assessment and Listening Comprehension Audio CDs)
- Test Generator
- Audio CD Program (includes manual)
- Video/DVD Program (includes manual)
- Overhead Transparencies
- Communicative Activities Manual
- TPR Storytelling Manual
- Activities for Proficiency Manual
- *Materiales para hispanohablantes nativos*
- Spanish Reader
- CD-ROM Software (includes program guide)
- EMC/Paradigm Web site (includes Internet Activities, i-Catcher Video and News Ticker)

TEXTBOOK

The textbook consists of a front section providing maps and the Table of Contents, ten numbered chapters and a handy reference section at the end of the book consisting of appendices, a Spanish–English and English–Spanish glossary and an index. Each thematic chapter is divided into four parts: the two-page chapter opener with objectives, *Lección A, Lección B* and *¡Viento en popa!* The chapters all are structured in a similar manner so that students will become accustomed to the various sections and, therefore, know what to expect. Chapter 10 is intended as a review chapter. It contains no new vocabulary or grammar. Teachers may select from the interesting and varied review activities and readings the chapter offers or may skip the chapter if they choose. **Note:** Instructions for activities in *Navegando* are given in the *tú* form. By requiring that students use the *usted* form of verbs with you and by suggesting that they use *tú* with their peers, you will increase students' exposure to both formal and informal forms. The subject pronoun *vosotros* is introduced, but students are not required to actively use the *vosotros* form of verbs. If you decide to teach using *vosotros,* modify activities to include practice with both *ustedes* and *vosotros.*

Two-page Chapter Opener

Each chapter of *Navegando* opens with two photo-illustrated pages that visually prepare students for the cultural and communicative content of the thematic lessons that follow. Each chapter opener depicts life in the distinct Spanish-speaking places featured in that chapter. Functional and communicative objectives that students will be learning in the chapter are also listed here.

Lección A and Lección B

Both lessons follow the same organizational pattern:

Vocabulario I—Lessons begin with a contextualized, colorful two-page presentation of new and review vocabulary and grammatical structures in a meaningful context. New active vocabulary is presented only in *Vocabulario I* and *II*. Inform students that they are responsible for learning the new words and expressions on these pages and that they should try to guess the meaning of the new vocabulary based on visual cues. You may wish to add that any words they do not recognize can be found in the Spanish–English vocabulary list that appears at the end of each chapter and in the glossary at the end of the book. Accompanying activities help students learn the new words and expressions right where they are first introduced. Vocabulary is recycled in subsequent lessons to further improve student mastery of the material. **Note:** The first activity after *Vocabulario I* (and *Vocabulario II*) is always a listening comprehension activity. The recorded activity is included both in the Listening Activities Program and in the Audio CD Program. (The ATE margins provide icons indicating which components offer additional supporting activities for the contents of the students' textbook.) Reproducible answer sheets for these activities are located at the end of the Audio CD Program Manual.

Diálogo I—Lessons continue with a short thematic dialog that uses new vocabulary and expressions in interesting and authentic depictions of everyday life in the Spanish-speaking world. The people involved in the conversations represent a cross section of age groups, although the emphasis is on the lives of young people. The dialog is followed by three activities: One checks comprehension of the content of the dialog *(¿Qué recuerdas?)*; a second serves as a realistic and natural motivation for students to apply the vocabulary and content of the dialog to their own lives by answering open-ended personalized questions *(Algo personal)*, while concentrating on the communicative aspect of offering opinions and solving problems in Spanish; the third is an additional listening comprehension activity. **Note:** This last recorded activity is included both in the Listening Activities Program and in the Audio CD Program. Reproducible answer sheets for these activities are located at the end of the Audio CD Program Manual.

Cultura viva—The *Cultura viva* section expands the cultural theme of the lesson and provides historical, geographical and political information about the country or countries featured in the chapter. These interesting narratives are intended to heighten students' appreciation of the target culture and to provide insight into daily aspects of Hispanic life. Additional ideas for expanding on the core content may be suggested in the accompanying activities or annotations that appear in the margins of the ATE. The section often presents the opportunity for creative out-of-class projects. Topics covered in the *Cultura viva* include history, geography, nonlinguistic behavioral cues, the arts and culture—relevant information that students will find appealing and useful.

Idioma—The *Idioma* section summarizes the main grammatical points of *Navegando,* which are presented as individual *Estructuras.* The clear and concise explanations (often with the addition of colorful charts for easy reference) are followed by activities that increase in difficulty and scope from mechanical to meaningful to communicative. These activities practice key grammatical structures and vocabulary and are categorized as either *Práctica* or *Comunicación.* In addition, the activities allow for maximum flexibility because they may be done orally or in writing. For easy identification, activities with answers recorded on the audio CD are indicated in the ATE by a compact disc icon.

Vocabulario II—Lessons continue with a second two-page presentation of new and review vocabulary followed by activities.

Diálogo II—A second thematic dialog in the lesson provides additional exposure to authentic Spanish.

Cultura viva—A second, more personal, *Cultura viva* follows, offering a glimpse into some aspect of everyday life in the Spanish-speaking world and providing balance to the more historical *Cultura viva* in the first half of the lesson.

Idioma—A second *Idioma* section follows. Breaking the grammar content for the lesson into two manageable chunks makes it easier for students to digest the information.

Lectura cultural—*Lección A* concludes with a Spanish reading titled *Lectura cultural,* in which students learn about life in the Spanish-speaking world. *Lección B* concludes with a Spanish reading titled *Lectura personal,* in which members of a singing group *(La Ola)* reflect on their surroundings and experiences as they travel throughout the Spanish-speaking world. These personalized readings are written to appeal to the interests and abilities of students. Both readings are followed by comprehension questions *(¿Qué recuerdas?)* and open-ended personalized questions in Spanish *(Algo personal).*

¿Qué aprendí?—The end-of-lesson feature *¿Qué aprendí?* offers students an opportunity to reflect upon what they have learned in the lesson. The section provides a self-test covering important content from the lesson, giving students the opportunity to review the content before having to take the lesson test. Students can access activity answers to the *Autoevaluación* by visiting the EMC/Paradigm Web site at www.emcp.com. The section also provides a list of active vocabulary from the lesson in *Palabras y expresione*s. The list of active vocabulary includes only the words that students must be able to speak, read, write and understand. Words from the list are included in other components of this Spanish program (workbook, testing/assessment, videos, etc.).

Make sure students understand how to use the *Vocabulario* by reviewing with them the *Estrategia* that appears on page 37 of *Capítulo 1:* "Try to learn new vocabulary...." Students may review the list, quizzing themselves to see how many words and expressions they recall. The list also helps teachers hold students accountable for their own learning. English translations are not given here since the list is for reference only. English equivalents may be found in the *Vocabulario* at the end of the chapter and in the glossary at the end of the textbook.

¡Viento en popa!

Tú lees—The end-of-chapter section *¡Viento en popa!* (Full speed ahead!; literally, Wind to the stern!) begins with a formal opportunity for students to improve their ability to read in Spanish. There are a variety of possible techniques for teaching the section. For example, you might wish to begin by having students read the *Estrategia* that accompanies every *Tú lees* in *Navegando.* Then have students complete the warm-up activity titled *Preparación.* Next, you may might want to play the audio CD recording of the first paragraph of the reading. As an alternative, you might choose to read the first paragraph yourself. Read the paragraph again, with students following along in the book. Give students a moment to look over the paragraph silently on their own and to ask questions. Ask for a student to volunteer to read the paragraph aloud. Continue in this way for subsequent paragraphs. Choose the technique that is most effective.

Explain to students that it is not essential to understand every word to read in Spanish. Equivalents for most unknown words have been provided to help students enjoy the content of the readings without having to look up important but passive vocabulary. **Note:** All footnoted vocabulary within the reading is intended to expand student receptive skills and is not intended for active use at this point.

The reading is followed by two activities: One checks comprehension of the content of the reading *(¿Qué recuerdas?)* and the second encourages students to connect the content to their own lives by answering open-ended personalized questions *(Algo personal).*

Tú escribes—The section *Tú escribes* consists of a writing strategy, which is followed by an activity that encourages students to apply what they learned in the chapter. The *Tú escribes* provides a formal opportunity for students to improve their Spanish skills by providing developmental practice in creative writing.

Proyectos adicionales—This section consists of projects that you may choose to use or not, depending on your needs and your students' needs. Many of the activities involve cooperative learning, in which students work in pairs or small groups to accomplish a task. Other activities allow students to work independently. Projects address the five National Standards (see the section on the National Standards in this ATE Introduction) and provide additional opportunities for students to use technology. Furthermore, the *Proyectos adicionales* feature helps students develop their ability to use the functions, grammar, vocabulary and cultural content of the preceding lesson in a manner that is consistent with the instructional intent of the textbook. For example, in *Capítulo 1,* writing and reading skills are emphasized less than speaking and understanding Spanish and acting in a culturally authentic manner in real-life situations. Reading, writing and a broader understanding of the cultural nuances of the Spanish-speaking world are developed in greater depth beginning in *Capítulo 2*; this depth is then reflected in the culminating activities of the *Proyectos adicionales.*

Consider using some of the activities from the *Proyectos adicionales* as a quiz or for prescriptive testing to determine deficiencies in student understanding of the lesson content. This allows for remediation before end-of-lesson testing/assessment. The section also may be used in place of, or along with, the Testing/Assessment Program as part of a portfolio for end-of-lesson summative assessment. (See the Testing/Assessment Program description in this ATE Introduction for information about portfolio assessment.)

Repaso—The section *Repaso* consists of a checklist of the communicative functions taught in the chapter, along with additional objectives that students can use as a self-check to evaluate their own progress. Before beginning a chapter, have students read the list of objectives in the chapter opener. Then, after completing the chapter, have students review what they have learned by reading the *Repaso* (see, for example, page 36).

Trabalenguas—The *Trabalenguas* (tongue twister) is intended as a lighthearted and fun activity to challenge even the best students.

Vocabulario—The *Vocabulario* provides students with an easy-to-find reference in Spanish with English equivalents for all new active vocabulary that students must know from the chapter. Word meaning is confined strictly to the context in which the words are used in that particular chapter. Explain to students that the vocabulary listed in the sections *Palabras y expresiones,* and again in the *Vocabulario,* is vocabulary they need to know for tests, for subsequent chapters of the textbook and for becoming fluent Spanish speakers.

Additional Sections and Special Activities

Conexión con otras disciplinas—These cross-curricular activities (highlighted in blue in the student textbook) require students to apply Spanish skills while focusing attention on another curricular area (mathematics, geography, music, art, history, culinary arts, etc.).

Estrategia—This section offers strategies for learning. Included are pointers on topics such as how to be successful learning Spanish vocabulary and how to improve skills in reading, speaking, writing and listening.

¡Extra!—The *¡Extra!* section provides additional related vocabulary, notes, tips and suggestions to help students feel successful. The section gives students extra information, much like the side notes for teachers in the ATE. The content of the *¡Extra!* features is not required and thus is not addressed in the accompanying Testing/Assessment Program.

Oportunidades—To make learning real for students, teachers try to show how knowledge learned in the classroom translates to real life. The section titled *Oportunidades* provides thoughtful insights about the advantages students will have because they know Spanish and are familiar with the cultures of the Spanish-speaking world. The section addresses issues such as careers, travel, college and lifelong study in the field of languages and cultures.

Repaso rápido—This section offers a quick review of previously taught grammar. The abbreviated explanations are followed by an activity that practices the content of the *Repaso.* You may skip the section anytime you feel students do not need the extra practice.

Appendices

Grammar Review—The grammar introduced in the textbook has been summarized in this end-of-book section for convenient reference.

Verbs—This reference tool offers a summary of the verb conjugations presented in chapters of the textbook.

Numbers—This appendix summarizes the numbers for quick reference.

Syllabification—Syllabification is explained here for teachers who may wish to introduce students to the concept.

Accentuation—This summary is provided for teachers who may choose to teach how words are accentuated in Spanish.

Vocabulary—All active words introduced in the textbook appear in this end glossary. The number and letter following an entry indicate the lesson in which an item is first actively used. Additional words and expressions are included for reference and have no number. Obvious cognates and expressions that occur as passive vocabulary for recognition only have been excluded from this end vocabulary.

Index—The Index lists grammar presented in the textbook, along with an easy reference to where the point was introduced.

ANNOTATED TEACHER'S EDITION (ATE)

This Annotated Teacher's Edition, or ATE, contains a front section and an annotated version of the student textbook. The teacher's notes serve as a guide for using the textbook and accompanying ancillaries, including the following.

ATE Introduction—This ATE Introduction contains a scope and sequence chart for each chapter; the philosophy and goals of the series; a description of all components; a summary explanation of the methodology used in the textbook; a section on using video; a section on using the Internet and computers; a section offering teaching suggestions; a comprehensive section providing suggestions for additional activities and games; a list of useful classroom expressions; and a transcript of the recorded listening comprehension activities that appear in the student textbook, for teachers who wish to read the activities aloud instead of using the recorded version in the Audio CD Program.

Margin Icons—The ATE is an annotated, reduced-size version of the student textbook. Located at the

top of each page of the ATE, the following icons denote additional ancillaries that support the contents of that page.

 Activities for Proficiency Manual

 Audio CD Program

 CD-ROM Software

 Communicative Activities Manual

 Grammar and Vocabulary Exercises Manual

 Listening Activities

 Materiales para hispanohablantes nativos

 Overhead Transparencies

 Quiz

 Spanish Reader

 TPR Storytelling Manual

 Video/DVD Program

Workbook

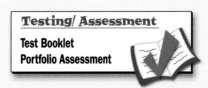

Margin Notes—Bottom margins of ATE pages provide additional teaching suggestions and cultural notes that expand on the lesson content.

Margin Activity Answers—The left- and right-hand margins of the ATE contain answers to close-ended activities.

Margin Activities—Activities described in the left- and right-hand margins of the ATE pages offer additional opportunities to address individual learner needs. Each of the activities falls into one of the following categories:

- **Communities.** These activities connect students to the community through Spanish and provide students with suggestions on how they may participate in service learning.
- **Connections.** Cross-curricular activities included here are opportunities to use Spanish in conjunction with other subject areas.
- **Cooperative Learning.** These activities offer students additional opportunities for cooperative learning beyond the textbook content. The activities require students to cooperate with one another in pairs or small groups, using Spanish for authentic communication.
- **Critical Listening.** These activities promote listening comprehension. They require that students learn not only the sounds of the language, but also the meaning behind them. Ultimately, students will reach a point where they are able to correct their own errors.
- **Critical Thinking.** These activities enhance higher-order thinking skills. Critical thinking is an essential part of the total academic development of students. *Navegando* includes a thorough and systematic program of higher-order thinking activities that address comprehension, application, analysis, synthesis and evaluation.
- **Expansion.** Expansion activities offer enrichment opportunities. They allow students' personal interests and creativity to take over, empowering them to discover a wealth of information about the language and the cultures studied in *Navegando*.
- **Language through Action.** These activities require students to combine Spanish-speaking or listening skills with physical movement. The suggestions enhance student learning while relieving the teacher of the time required to prepare such activities.
- **Multiple Intelligences.** The multiple intelligences are addressed through activities focused on the eight areas identified by brain research: linguistic intelligence, logical-mathematical intelligence, spatial intelligence, bodily-kinesthetic intelligence, musical intelligence, interpersonal intelligence, intrapersonal intelligence and naturalist intelligence.

- **Prereading Strategy.** These questions about the subject matter prepare students for what they are about to read. Students might be asked to look at an illustration and guess what the theme of that dialog is. Students are encouraged to guess the meanings of words they do not recognize and are taught that they need not understand all the vocabulary to discern the main theme of an activity.
- **Pronunciation.** These activities allow students to practice pronunciation. Have students break down sentences into individual words and sounds and then have them use the words you have practiced in meaningful sentences. In addition, after presenting the initial dialog (or other expository material) and accompanying activities, have students work in pairs practicing the activity and focusing on the new pronunciation point. Circulate and assist with pronunciation and intonation.
- **Spanish for Spanish Speakers.** These activities are designed especially for students who are native speakers of Spanish. They allow students to examine their cultural heritage and to increase their Spanish skills.
- **Students with Special Needs.** These activities are for students who need extra help. They allow students to practice areas in which they are having difficulty and facilitate the acquisition of new skills and the comprehension of various subject matters.
- **Technology.** These activities require students to use the Internet, e-mail or another electronic medium in combination with their knowledge of Spanish to complete an activity.
- **TPR.** These activities involve Total Physical Response (TPR). Whereas many teachers have used TPR either extensively or on a limited basis, these activities often require an extra effort on the part of the teacher to prepare for and use TPR in the classroom.

ATE ON CD-ROM

The complete Annotated Teacher's Edition on CD-ROM offers a convenient alternative medium for displaying the wealth of information contained in the ATE. It also contains pop-up versions of the ancillaries indicated by icons in the ATE margins.

PROGRAM MANAGER

The Program Manager provides suggestions for using *Navegando* and the program ancillaries in day-to-day instruction. Refer to the content for helpful hints that will help you determine which content you wish to include in lessons and which activities you wish to omit due to your particular circumstances and time limitations. The end-of-chapter section ¡*Viento en popa!* (consisting of the reading section *Tú lees,* the writing activity *Tú escribes,* the national standards and technology projects, the *Trabalenguas* and the reference section *Vocabulario*) is optional, thus offering you additional flexibility in matching content to the needs, interests and curriculum requirements of your own particular situation.

Dialogs, narratives and many activities from the textbook have been included as audio recordings. This gives you additional choices about how to present or review chapter content. For example, you may choose to have students listen to a recorded activity before going to the textbook, or you may choose instead to use the audio CD as additional reinforcement after having completed the activity in the textbook. Recorded activities are indicated by icons in the margins of the ATE, according to the activity type.

In addition, the many ancillaries described in this ATE Introduction can be used to supplement the textbook. These program components provide an abundance of textbook-related activities to enable you to customize your teaching to the many and varied learning styles and needs of your students.

Because every teacher has his or her own approach to the subject of homework, and because of the extensive variety offered by the *Navegando* support materials, specific homework assignments are not provided in the Program Manager. However, suggestions for including activities from the accompanying ancillaries have been offered to give you an idea of the possible variations the teaching program offers. You should try to include an assortment of different activities, choosing some from the textbook and others from the ancillaries (such as the Workbook, the ATE, etc.).

WORKBOOK

The Workbook activities reinforce and expand student understanding of the functions, grammar, readings and cultural points presented in the textbook. Interesting written activities emphasize both communication and structural production. The Workbook includes a variety of practice in several different formats to maintain student interest. The level of difficulty of the activities ranges from rote practice of vocabulary and basic activities emphasizing receptive skills in reading to more challenging, open-ended items that emphasize productive writing skills.

Reading, writing, grammar, vocabulary and culture are all given thorough attention in the Workbook. Specifically, the Workbook presents an assortment of activities: reading passages taken from actual newspaper and magazine articles with follow-up questions and exercises; sentence-completion exercises; guided compositions; matching activities; practice in geography in mapping activities; word searches; crossword puzzles; and more.

WORKBOOK TEACHER'S EDITION

The Teacher's Edition of the Workbook includes an overprint with answers to activities.

GRAMMAR AND VOCABULARY EXERCISES

The Grammar and Vocabulary Exercises offer additional written practice correlated to the textbook presentation of grammar and vocabulary. Grammar activities are each preceded by a summary explanation of the new structures introduced in the textbook. Vocabulary activities consist of word games, puzzles and other practice that will help students assimilate new words and expressions that are taught in the textbook.

GRAMMAR AND VOCABULARY EXERCISES TEACHER'S EDITION

The Grammar and Vocabulary Exercises Teacher's Edition includes an overprint with answers to activities.

LISTENING ACTIVITIES

- **Listening Activities Manual.** The Listening Activities Manual provides worksheets to be used in conjunction with audio CDs. The activities offer additional listening comprehension practice using the structures and vocabulary of corresponding textbook lessons. Using the activities will help students improve their listening skills and, therefore, their ability to communicate in Spanish. In addition, the activities serve as an excellent preparation for the listening comprehension and oral-proficiency portions of the Testing/Assessment Program. The answer key is included at the end of the manual.

- **Listening Activities Audio CDs.** These audio CDs have been recorded by native speakers and are to be used with the Listening Activities Manual.

TESTING/ASSESSMENT PROGRAM

A proficiency-based curriculum requires testing or assessing an individual's attainment of specific objectives. The *Navegando* Testing/Assessment Program offers comprehensive means for evaluating student performance. Elements of the Testing/Assessment Program are available as a part of the Test Generator for teachers wishing to format customized assessment. The basic program consists of the following components.

- **Quizzes.** Quizzes provide a convenient and flexible means of ongoing written assessment. Ranging in number from ten to thirteen per lesson, quizzes determine the level of student comprehension of the vocabulary, grammar and cultural content of the textbook. They may be used individually, point by point throughout each lesson or combined as a test after completing an entire lesson.
- **Test Booklet.** Tests evaluate students' listening, writing, reading and speaking skills. Each chapter of the booklet contains two sections: 1) the student answer sheets for the listening comprehension and written portion of the test; 2) a separate section that evaluates oral proficiency. For convenience and ease of scoring, each section is worth 100 points. The tests should be given after each chapter. Students use the answer sheets while listening

to the audio CDs, which direct them step by step through specific tasks. The tests include true/false, multiple choice, matching and fill-in-the-blank questions based on the recorded material. Wherever appropriate, picture cues further assist students in selecting their answers as directed by the speakers.

The written tests are intended to measure students' understanding of the language and cultural content of each chapter. They allow students to demonstrate their ability to read and write with accuracy. The oral-proficiency section of each chapter test can be used in an informal and flexible manner and includes three kinds of activities: communicative interaction between teacher and student, paired activities calling for student-to-student interaction and illustrations with related questions students must answer orally in Spanish.

The Test Booklet contains tests for each of the ten chapters. In addition, there are comprehensive midyear and year-end achievement tests. The answers to all the tests are included in the back of the manual.

- **Listening Comprehension Audio CDs.** The listening portion of the *Navegando* Testing/Assessment Program has been recorded by native speakers and is included on audio CDs.
- **Portfolio Assessment.** Intended as an alternative to traditional evaluation tools and as an extension of the Testing/Assessment Program, the Portfolio Assessment includes a variety of activities for monitoring student progress. The communicative objectives that appear on the first pages of each chapter can be used as goals against which the students' progress can be measured. This manual provides valuable tips and guidance for evaluating student performance.

TEST GENERATOR

The Test Generator has several benefits. It allows teachers to test exactly what they have taught, allowing for differences in instructional emphasis, teaching approaches and student learning styles. The teacher can select and modify sections from the existing Testing/Assessment Program, including quizzes and chapter tests, to generate tests that reflect what has been taught. The Test Generator also allows teachers to add their own test questions, as well as edit existing questions. Finally, the Test Generator allows teachers to create A and B versions of tests.

AUDIO CD PROGRAM

The Audio CD Program is an integral part of *Navegando*. It exposes students to a variety of native speakers' voices with different accents and variations in pronunciation and intonation. All content that has been recorded on audio CDs is indicated in the ATE by a compact disc icon. Although the text for many of these activities is contained in the textbook itself, a separate manual provides an exact transcript of the recordings, many of which have been modified so they are more appropriate for speaking and listening practice.

In addition, activities located after *Vocabulario I, Vocabulario II, Diálogo I* and *Diálogo II* that are indicated in the student textbook by the icon 🔊))) have been recorded specifically for listening comprehension practice and are part of the Audio CD Program. For teacher convenience, reproducible answer sheets have been provided for these activities and can be found at the end of the Audio CD Program Manual. The recording transcript of all the listening comprehension activities is provided at the end of this ATE Introduction for teachers wishing to read the activities instead of using the audio CDs.

VIDEO/DVD PROGRAM

Coordinated with each chapter of the *Navegando* textbooks, the three-level Video/DVD Program— titled *El cuarto misterioso*—is an exciting and motivational tool for recombining and reinforcing the content of the series. The mystery was filmed on location in various parts of the Spanish-speaking world using professional actors. The ten episodes, which vary in length from five to eight minutes per chapter, consist of a continuous story line that is carefully coordinated with each chapter of the textbook. The videos depict native speakers in authentic situations that reflect the content of textbook chapters, thus allowing students to see and hear Spanish used in a carefully controlled but realistic and enjoyable context. The few unknown words that are used can be easily understood by the context

(motion, action, gestures, background). Available either as a videocassette or as a DVD, *El cuarto misterioso* allows students to follow along and identify with the characters as they solve the mystery.

Video Program Manual. An accompanying Video/DVD Program Manual contains a transcript of the videos, notes about using the program and numerous pre- and post-viewing activities.

OVERHEAD TRANSPARENCIES

A set of sixty-eight full-color overhead transparencies, coordinated with the ten chapters, is available for use with *Navegando*. The transparencies can be used for a variety of activities, including rote vocabulary and grammar review, map identification of featured countries and conversation over comprehensive scenes that encourage creative self-expression. Use the transparencies to review and expand on the cultural content, grammar, vocabulary and functions that are presented in the textbook and to encourage students to apply their knowledge of Spanish and the Spanish-speaking world.

COMMUNICATIVE ACTIVITIES MANUAL

Effective communicative activities are integral to the success of a Spanish-language program. The Communicative Activities Manual is designed to provide additional communicative practice for students. The manual provides information gap activities and situation cards that promote student-to-student interaction, a communicative functions checklist that reviews the functions introduced in each chapter and postcards that develop writing skills.

TPR STORYTELLING MANUAL

The TPR Storytelling Manual has everything teachers need to incorporate this movement-oriented technique in their classrooms. First, teachers are instructed to present new vocabulary (provided in the manual) through gestures. Then students practice this vocabulary in short situations before finally using it to tell and act out a story. The front portion of the manual explains the TPR Storytelling philosophy and teaching techniques for instructors who have little or no experience with this strategy. Then step-by-step instructions guide teachers through the presentation of basic and advanced stories, one of which is correlated to every chapter in the textbook. Gestures are given for new words and phrases to help teachers convey meaning as they present the situation and the stories. Numerous illustrations guide students as they re-create the stories. Additional teaching suggestions, strategies and assessment options are also provided for each story.

ACTIVITIES FOR PROFICIENCY MANUAL

This manual contains general forms facilitating games, mapmaking, and activities that can be used throughout the year. Also included are chapter-by-chapter blackline masters with supplemental activities that correspond to the content of the chapters. The activities in this manual are fun and engaging, and expose students to a variety of real, everyday language.

MATERIALES PARA HISPANOHABLANTES NATIVOS

The *Materiales para hispanohablantes nativos* manual expands upon the content of *Navegando.* The manual offers additional opportunities for native speakers of Spanish to improve their language skills and knowledge in classrooms in which the majority of students are learning Spanish as a second language. Although the manual is intended to increase student success in class, it also may serve as an independent skill-building activity book that provides opportunities for portfolio assessment, at the discretion of the teacher.

Activities in the manual give native Spanish-speaking students an opportunity to demonstrate their abilities and knowledge in Spanish using the vocabulary, structures and cultural themes in the textbook. In addition, excerpts have been included from the classic Spanish novel *Marcelino pan y vino,* by José María Sánchez-Silva, which students will enjoy reading while improving their skills.

The Appendices at the end of the manual offer additional reinforcement of essential skills. For example, Appendix A offers a list of suggestions for projects requiring students to think creatively and to apply what they learned while reading. Appendix B is a guide for students to use to improve their skills in studying, researching, speaking, reading and writing. Appendix C provides forms to facilitate student and project evaluation.

The activities contained in this manual may be used beginning on the first day of class. Schools may purchase copies for individual students or photocopy pages as they are needed. Native Spanish-speaking students then may read the introductory pages and begin to work on activities that are appropriate to their needs and that are related to the content of the lessons in the textbook. In this way, they will be able to affectively and cognitively connect with the content.

The activities and suggestions contained in the *Materiales para hispanohablantes nativos* offer both students and teachers an alternate means of assessment. Simultaneously, the manual will challenge native Spanish-speaking students to improve their skills and knowledge by offering them interesting and worthwhile practice using their native language.

SPANISH READER

A Spanish reader, *La familia Miranda/El viaje a Guatemala,* is available for teachers wishing to increase student reading opportunities. The first episode, *La familia Miranda,* is coordinated with the first five chapters of *Navegando 1,* and the second episode, *El viaje a Guatemala,* is coordinated with the last five chapters of the textbook.

CD-ROM SOFTWARE

This interactive adventure in multimedia is designed to enhance language acquisition within a functional and cultural context. As publishing interns, students enter a futuristic world where they must solve problems using technology and their Spanish-language skills. In each module, students are faced with the challenge of communicating with colleagues throughout the world, using an online atlas, dictionary and encyclopedia. Included are learner and teacher reports that are used to assess student progress and to determine promotions. The program contains authentic video clips in which native Spanish speakers interact verbally with students on a variety of topics. Students will enjoy applying the vocabulary, grammar and cultural content they are learning to the real-life problems they face in the business world. An abundance of geographic, historic and cultural information further expands the students' understanding of the Spanish-speaking world.

EMC/PARADIGM WEB SITE

Internet Activities—The *Navegando* Internet Activities Web site features activities that are constantly updated to provide students with practice that expands the cultural content of the textbook chapters. These interesting and enriching activities are based on current events, up-to-the-moment information and research data. There are three activities for each chapter of *Navegando*. Students practice using their language skills as they explore authentic realia in Spanish and read contemporary information about Hispanic culture. They combine the use of technology and Spanish in real-life situations as they develop their Internet research skills. Students are carefully guided through the various links to complete each activity. Teachers receive a password to allow them to access all the activities' answers. To view these activities, visit www.emcp.com and follow the on-screen menus and links until you reach the activities.

News Ticker—The News Ticker features five scrolling news articles every day in Spanish. Students click on these articles to read about current events throughout the Spanish-speaking world, chosen to appeal to teenagers. An audio feature allows students to hear the articles recorded by professional native speakers. These articles are archived so that they are accessible by date or by topic. Reach the News Ticker by visiting www.emcp.com and follow the on-screen menus and links.

i-Catcher—These interactive Internet video clips in Spanish showcase young adults who talk about and demonstrate their interests and hobbies. One young Spanish speaker is featured each month. Students can choose the subtitled version to check their listening comprehension skills. The site promotes real-life communication through a monthly monitored chat with the video star simply by logging on. Not only is the site fun, but it has a strong educational foundation. The i-Catcher offers another opportunity for students to check their listening skills with an on-line multiple-choice comprehension quiz. Students develop their writing skills with related Internet links and Web-based activities. Access i-Catcher by going to www.emcp.com and following the on-screen menus and links.

METHODOLOGY

Language-teaching methodology has undergone significant changes over the years. One of the most dramatic changes has been the shift from a sometimes rigid focus on *what* and *how* an instructor would teach to a more flexible and varied approach that focuses on what students can *do* with the language. The *Standards for Foreign Language Learning* are a clear manifestation of this important change. It is exciting to see the increased emphasis on improving students' abilities to use authentic language in real-life contexts.

The methods and techniques found in *Navegando* reflect this student-centered approach to teaching and the authors' commitment to providing the best possible Spanish program to meet the needs of teachers and students in the 21st century. As teachers deal with an ever more diverse student population, there is a greater demand for teaching materials that address varied learning styles and interests. There also is an ever-increasing need for educational materials that enable students to function using Spanish in a variety of practical situations. By presenting meaningful content and by putting students in real-life contexts, *Navegando* creates a positive learning spiral. The activities are structured to allow students to apply immediately what they have learned. The resulting feeling of accomplishment leads them back into the textbook, where they acquire more skills and information and are then able to draw upon their own personal experience to communicate information, ideas, feelings and opinions.

The following methods and techniques reflect the approaches to language instruction found in *Navegando* and will help maximize the effectiveness of both the textbook and ancillary materials.

Learning Styles—Students learn through three main modes: visual, auditory and kinesthetic. Whereas many students learn through a combination of these modes, some students learn mainly through one mode. For example, a visual learner likely benefits from seeing the written language in the textbook, on the board and on an overhead, and also by seeing pictures or a video. Auditory learners benefit from hearing the language spoken by the teacher, by other students and in audiovisual media including music and song lyrics. Kinesthetic learners benefit from making handicrafts such as Mexican paper folding, creating a floor plan of a house or playing games.

Another approach to learning styles, known as 4MAT, outlines four types of learners based on left- and right-brain dominance.

- **Type 1.** Innovative ("why?") learners are mainly interested in personal meaning. This includes connecting new information to personal experience and making it useful in daily life. A number of strategies work with Type 1 learners, such as cooperative learning, brainstorming and integrating content areas (interdisciplinary learning).
- **Type 2.** Analytic ("what?") learners enjoy acquiring facts to deepen their understanding of concepts and processes. They learn best from lectures, independent research, expert commentary and analysis of data.
- **Type 3.** Commonsense ("how?") learners want to know how things work. They enjoy rolling up their sleeves and trying. Concrete and experiential activities are preferred: hands-on tasks, kinesthetic experiences and demonstrations.
- **Type 4.** Dynamic ("if") learners are primarily interested in self-directed discovery. They rely on intuition and enjoy teaching themselves and others. Independent study, simulations, role-plays and games are ideal for dynamic learners.

Knowledge of learning styles helps teachers plan lessons that accommodate all students. Projects, in particular, support learning styles because of the infinite variety that may be used over time to better develop the five Cs of the National Standards: communication, cultures, connections, comparisons and communities. Project types include the following:

Visual and Performing Arts	Media/Technology	Hands-on/Kinesthetic
artwork	advertisement	collage
cartoon	commercial	collection
dance	computer graphic	construction
greeting card	computer program	craft
jewelry	filmstrip	demonstration
mask	infomercial	diorama
mural	magazine	environmental study
music	marketing campaign	field trip
pantomime	movie	flash card
photograph	news report	floor plan
poster	newsletter	game
pottery	newspaper	invention
puppet show	opinion poll	learning center
role-play	radio program	model
sculpture	slide show	sewing
skit	television show	sport
song	video	tool
weaving	Web home page	treasure hunt

Specific examples of projects could include the following:

- Students create a papier-mâché model of the Andes Mountains accompanied by text in the target language about Andean music, geography, plant life, animals, customs, cuisine and history.
- Students create a school newspaper written in Spanish, including pictures and captions.
- Students give a demonstration, preparing a food from the Spanish-speaking world, such as flan, tacos or paella, and then share the food with the class.
- Students learn one or more dances from the Spanish-speaking world and perform them for the class. They could also teach classmates how to do the dance.

Recognition versus Production—It is natural that students are able to recognize new vocabulary and structures before they are able to produce them. The transition from recognition to production may cause errors, but this is an accepted occurrence in the language-learning process. *Navegando* presents new material and then recycles it in a number of different ways in each of the components of the program, thus aiding the transition from recognition to active use of the language. Some activities dealing with structures, for example, promote recognition more than production (especially in the activities immediately after concept presentation). Students will feel more comfortable at the productive levels of communication as they continue in the program and use materials that recycle and build upon previously learned material.

Augmenting the textbook with the many supplementary materials in the series will enable teachers to help students produce Spanish in communicative contexts. In particular, paired and group activities, cooperative activities and the textbook section *¡Viento en popa!* are intended to stimulate production on a communicative level. As a general homework assignment, have students scan each lesson for new vocabulary, grammar and the cultural theme. This will facilitate recognition and, hence, production.

Critical Listening—Perhaps the most basic of all language-learning skills is listening, first for recognition of sounds that convey meaning and later for error correction in pronunciation and structure.

Students can develop this skill by listening to the teacher, to the *Navegando* audio and video components, to themselves and to one another. (At this level, students are able to use critical listening skills such as identification of structures and self-correction.)

Language through Action and Total Physical Response (TPR)—The use of physical action in response to verbal stimuli is considered by many educators to be an asset to language acquisition. One popular technique is Total Physical Response (TPR). Since TPR involves a student's physical memory, it aids in internalizing new concepts and vocabulary and in recycling those already learned. In a typical TPR activity, the instructor first prepares a series of commands that are contextualized and based on material to be presented or practiced in class. The instructor then models and gives a series of commands to the students, who demonstrate comprehension by dramatizing the physical actions corresponding to the language they hear. A variation of TPR involves storytelling. In this approach, spoken language is linked to physical actions and visual images that tell a story. Over time, students go from input (comprehension) to language production as they develop and tell stories.

Many teachers have experimented successfully with TPR but found that it requires an extra effort to prepare activities. For this reason, *Navegando* includes numerous TPR activities to help the instructor incorporate this effective learning technique on a regular basis. The activities will enhance student learning while relieving the teacher of the preparation of materials.

Critical Thinking—It is imperative to help develop higher-order thinking skills in our students if they are to succeed in school and later in life. For this reason, many activities in *Navegando* involve critical thinking. The cognitive abilities and their associated critical thinking skills included in the program are: knowledge acquisition (locate, define, describe, identify, list, match, name, recite, recall); comprehension (explain, summarize, rewrite, convert, translate, rearrange, paraphrase); analysis (compare and contrast, interpret, outline, subdivide, order, categorize, distinguish); evaluation (criticize, conclude, support, justify); synthesis (associate, combine, compile, plan, generalize); and application (compose, create, design, produce).

Communicative Activities (Pair and Group Work)—Pair work and group work help encourage the internalization and application of the target language by providing students with authentic communicative settings with real communicative goals. Numerous activities in every lesson are structured for role-playing or for open-ended practice in pairs; others are designed for groups of no more than five members. Such activities encourage proficiency in a number of ways: more students can use the target language for a longer period of time than is possible in a teacher-centered activity; students feel a sense of accomplishment in this atmosphere because they are interacting successfully; the teacher is able to meet the needs of more students by circulating among students and correcting or directing where necessary; and most important, learning with one's peers results in a nonthreatening learning atmosphere, since the object is communication and not only the correction of errors.

Cooperative Learning—To many, cooperative learning involves merely having students work in pairs or small groups to practice material that has been presented in class. This is one important aspect of cooperative learning and it is extensively utilized in *Navegando.* However, cooperative learning at a more significant level requires that one student relate or share information with another student (or with a small group, or even the entire class) that the student has acquired through personal experience or from recent study. Numerous activities in the textbook and in the ATE include this aspect of cooperative learning and provide teachers with extensive opportunities to include this practice as a regular classroom experience.

Portfolio Assessment—Given the many changes in foreign-language education in recent years, it is apparent that a variety of tools for assessing and documenting student performance is required. One such tool is the portfolio: a systematic, organized method of collecting data that offers teachers the ability to develop a composite record of a student's performance.

Portfolios that document student growth and performance consist of a variety of items that reflect the dynamic experience of studying a foreign language. Such items may include:

- videotaped skits that show students conversing and using appropriate paralinguistic behavior
- an oral interview
- results from listening-comprehension activities
- a recorded audiocassette/audio CD containing a sample of the student speaking Spanish
- compositions about selected themes in Spanish
- a written diary
- art projects (such as a poster) depicting some aspect of a Spanish-speaking part of the world
- peer or self-assessment

The *Navegando* Portfolio Assessment Manual offers a number of ways to collect, record and evaluate student work. The manual is described in this ATE Introduction in the section titled Testing/Assessment Program. Activities in the textbook and supplemental activities in the CD-ROM, the Testing/Assessment Program and the Video Program (and its accompanying manual) provide opportunities for documenting listening comprehension. Paired, group and cooperative learning activities in the textbook, as well as questions taken from the section *Algo personal,* are ideal for developing a portfolio with speaking samples. In addition to content questions that appear after the reading selections in the textbook, the Workbook, CD-ROM and Reader provide samples of a student's reading comprehension. Portfolio writing samples can be taken from a number of different activities that occur throughout the program, including the section *Tú escribes*. Finally, activities to document a student's cultural awareness abound in the textbook and in the program ancillaries.

The portfolio is a multifaceted assessment tool with many benefits. It encourages growth, monitors and records progress and promotes individual self-expression. In addition, portfolios improve data collection, showcase student performance and help improve articulation between levels of a program of instruction.

These are but a few of the approaches to teaching and assessment integrated into *Navegando.* A glance at the textbook, the Annotated Teacher's Edition and the wide array of ancillaries for each level of the program will indicate that every effort has been made to provide a comprehensive and effective program of instruction based on up-to-date language-teaching methods and techniques.

VIDEO IN THE CURRICULUM

Using Video

Video in the language curriculum offers opportunities to visit other lands and locales and to learn about interdisciplinary themes tied to language and culture. Technological advances and expanded cable programming provide teachers in all fields with a variety of special programs to use with students. Educators of world languages are no exception, as more and more programs focusing on target countries and cultures are debuting all the time. It can almost be a full-time job to find and choose educational programming for integration in the foreign-language curriculum. Indeed, the careful selection of video segments in language learning can be a gargantuan task. Fortunately, such efforts can be well worth it. High-quality video selections used in the classroom can become a platform for many successful content-based activities and projects. Video also offers opportunities for curricular enrichment that does not rely solely on teachers.

Advocates of interdisciplinary curriculum initiatives support exposing students of one subject area to related subject matter in other disciplines. Because Spanish-speaking people, countries and cultures have contributed greatly to humanity in so many areas, quality programming has been produced that explores these contributions. From art to cuisine, from music to automobiles, from cinema to fashion, today's cable and public television programming allows people and themes of the target culture to shine in the spotlight.

The National Standards for Foreign Language Learning promote the five Cs: Communication, Cultures, Connections, Comparisons and Communities. All five Cs can be supported by the use of videos and video-inspired activities, especially Connections. The National Standards for the English Language Arts promote "viewing" as a worthy educational goal. While students benefit greatly from viewing high-quality video programs, teachers can fully exploit video viewing through related activities, projects and units.

English versus Target Language—Videos are available with language dialog and narration in English or in Spanish. Some programs offer English with occasional dialog in the Spanish language with English subtitles. Some educators might question the use of "in English" videos in language classes. However, segments in English can be effective learning tools, especially when they encourage Spanish-language activities, projects, discussions or writing or promote the target culture. For example, students of Spanish can watch a segment in English about the Andes that enriches a chapter about a South American Andean nation and then do one or more activities in the target language, such as a collage, a written summary, a handout, an oral report, a discussion, or a reading in the target language about a similar topic. Of course, a balance between videos in English and in Spanish is key. Both English and Spanish videos can be educationally beneficial. Videos in the target language must not be too difficult, following Stephen Krashen's $i + 1$ theory. He theorized that the level must not be more than one level above students' current level of ability, or frustration and lack of comprehension among students will result. Foreign films often have subtitles, which help compensate for comprehension challenges.

Videos: A Variety from Which to Choose—The following types of videos can be used to enrich language instruction:

- **Movies.** Both Spanish-language films with subtitles and traditional native-language films can be used to support the goals of your curriculum. Musical films such as *Man of La Mancha, Evita* and *Selena* can enhance topics such as Don Quixote de la Mancha, Argentina and the Mexican-American singer, respectively. School plays or musicals can be utilized as well to enhance language learning through projects tied to the school's cast and crew, as well as themes, characters, settings and music from the stage plays. Full-length films can be analyzed as literature is analyzed, by discussing plot, setting, characters, conflicts and themes in the target language.

- **Music Specials.** It can be useful to expose students to concerts or other music specials by artists who sing in Spanish. If time is limited, one or a few song performances could be utilized. Students could dig deeper by finding out more about a specific song (e.g., "La Bamba"). Documentaries about a specific genre of music such as Spanish flamenco, Caribbean salsa or Spanish zarzuela could also enhance learning. Select chapters in *Navegando* feature vocabulary and readings tied to target-culture music and names of musical instruments. This could be an ideal time to utilize music-related videos.

- **Documentaries and Travel Segments.** Information-based segments describing background about a topic can be interesting and educational. A segment about Spanish architecture, for example, is ideal. Other possible topics include ecotourism in Costa Rica, archaeological digs in Peru and railroad development in central Mexico.
- **Cooking Shows.** Segments that detail the cuisine, ingredients, cultural aspects of food and actual food preparation can easily enhance the study of cuisine in Spanish-speaking cultures.
- **Visual and Decorative Arts Programs.** Target-culture art including painting, sculpting, architecture, ceramics, glassblowing and woodworking are of interest. Segments from Home and Garden Television feature appropriate programs such as *The Best of Spanish Design* or *The Best of Mexican Design* that can easily complement a unit treating the rooms and appliances of the house.
- **Biographies.** Segments about famous actors, musicians, authors, politicians, scientists and historical figures can enrich the curriculum. Well-known individuals help make up popular culture, an area supported by curriculum integration. Reacting to the facts about these individuals' lives can also help promote students' social and emotional learning.
- *Navegando* **Video/DVD Program.** The ancillary video materials that accompany the *Navegando* series are also valuable educational tools, linking video stories to the material in the textbooks. They offer appropriate materials that can enhance comprehension for both visual and auditory learners.

Activities and Projects

Create a Video—Students can create their own video, making a commercial, preparing a skit using the current chapter's theme and vocabulary, recording a news story about your school or developing a documentary about the sports or drama program. Students could interview other students in Spanish or in English, providing a dubbed translation or subtitles with the translation as is done on television and in movies.

A Movie Review—Students can view a film and write a review of it in Spanish. Students could also do the review orally, live or on videotape.

Art-based Project—Students can create a calendar, brochure or collage about a topic featured in a video that they viewed.

TV/Cable Guide—Students can create a television guide that gives blurbs about various programs tied to Spanish. They can include a magazine cover and even several feature articles about a few of the programs. This project could easily be completed using technology and could be done as a cooperative effort.

Learning Scenarios for Video-Inspired Lessons

Political Issues—Students view the film version of *Selena* and learn about the southwestern United States, Mexican Americans and Tejano music. They explore the U.S.–Mexico border issue historically, learn about Chicano social issues, explore the cuisine of the region and learn more about Selena and her genre of music, Tejano.

Biographies—Another video-inspired activity involves viewing a biography segment about a Spanish-speaking celebrity or historical figure. The students could then read an article about the individual and write a summary of the article. Students could also discuss the segment orally, thus gaining speaking and listening practice.

Foods—You might consider having students view a segment about Spanish, Latin American or Caribbean desserts. Students then replicate one recipe in

Spanish, prepare it and sample it. Students could also create their own menu, do a role-play in a Spanish restaurant or café or create a collage about desserts in the Spanish-speaking world.

Homes—Have students view a video about house design in one of the Spanish-speaking countries and then create a floor plan of their own home, with rooms and objects labeled in Spanish. Students could also learn about how to decorate their homes for holidays.

Arts and Crafts—Students might enjoy viewing a segment about a well-known artist or artisan and then create a work of art or a piece of pottery with the help of the art teacher. If this is not feasible, students could create a drawing that is reflective of an artist's work and color it by hand.

Summary

Videos vary in length, and it is not always necessary to show an entire video. For example, if the textbook features a specific recipe, you could find a cooking segment and use just the part about that recipe. A video segment can be a few seconds to a few class sessions in length, depending on your goals.

Video can enrich our curriculum. Activities, lessons and units can be implemented by the creative teacher to explore themes from videos. You can carefully select programming that will bring many topics and people to life for your students. Such programming can accommodate both visual learners, who must see to learn, and auditory learners, who must hear to learn. Hands-on projects inspired by video segments can also accommodate students who learn through touch.

Tips for Selecting Video Formats—Videotapes and DVDs cannot be played on all types of equipment. VHS videos will not play on European PAL systems and vice versa. Additionally, six DVD zones exist throughout the globe, making DVDs from one zone unplayable in the other five zones. The United States and Canada comprise zone one. Multizone players have been made available over the Internet to provide flexibility. In comparison to videotapes, DVDs and laser discs have several advantages: they generally have superior sound and picture quality and are easier to use in terms of finding a specific scene, because they are encoded in chapters. Many DVDs and laser discs include additional footage or documentaries about the making of the film and frequently have alternate sound tracks, some in Spanish or other languages.

USING THE INTERNET: SUGGESTIONS AND IDEAS

Because of its widespread and instantaneous nature, the Internet holds much promise as a tool for teaching and learning. In foreign-language instruction, the Internet can help teachers meet the challenge of providing students with materials that are up to date and culturally authentic. With scarcely a trace of lag time, information from the target culture can be accessed and utilized in a variety of ways. For example, in a lesson about Madrid, you and your students can:
- visit online museums and see famous paintings
- obtain news from Spanish newspapers
- participate in discussion groups on Spanish culture and civilization
- obtain current weather information and forecasts
- access city and subway maps

- view photographs of major landmarks of the city
- locate tourist information
- exchange e-mail correspondence

By using the Internet as a supplement to *Navegando,* you will create exciting new opportunities for students. Internet-related activities are limited only by your imagination. What follows are sample activities and a variety of supplementary materials that illustrate the vast possibilities of the Internet.

E-MAIL PROJECTS

Consider arranging e-mail (electronic mail) exchanges to complement the use of *Navegando.* For example, have students participate in a number of exchanges that allow them to apply the concepts, vocabulary and cultural information studied in a given lesson. Sample exchanges include the following:

1. After studying weather, students write a weather report for their state/city and send it to a collaborating class or key pals. They also inquire about the weather and climate in the region where the collaborating class is located or where the key pals live. Subsequent exchanges could deal with:
   - sports and activities related to different seasons of the year
   - outdoor activities that the students enjoy
   - the school calendar and how the local climate may affect it
   - weather conditions in different Spanish-speaking countries

2. In relation to a food unit, students develop an e-mail exchange sharing the following information about their culture/family:
   - a typical meal schedule at home
   - a traditional meal schedule in their country
   - a menu for a typical day and for a special celebration

3. After learning about leisure-time activities, students share with their collaborating partners what they do on a typical weekend or during vacation.

4. Students write a description of a well-known individual in sports, music, politics or movies. Send the description to your collaborating classroom with an invitation to guess who the person is.

5. Students conduct surveys to explore cultural comparisons. Topics of interest include:
   - the amount of independence given to adolescents
   - the access and admittance to dance clubs
   - the legal age for driving
   - the number of students who work
   - the minimum wages paid to adolescents who work

6. Examples of other possible exchange topics include school, daily life, family, friends, travel, sports, clothing and popular music. More complex topics of interest might include current events, politics, household rules, curfew and educational aspirations.

A Model Unit for an E-Mail Exchange: Mi familia

This unit allows students to share information about their families and learn about the families of their classmates and key pals. Whereas the unit is appropriate for learners at various levels of proficiency, teacher expectations and student performance will vary accordingly.

Academic Goals—Students will be able to:
1. Use vocabulary related to the family.
2. Use possessive and descriptive adjectives and appropriate verb structures.

Social Goals—Students will be able to:
1. Share information about their families.
2. Find out about the families of their key pals.
3. Recognize similarities and differences between families in the United States and families in cultures where Spanish is spoken.

Procedures for a Beginning Language Class

1. Teach and practice specific vocabulary pertaining to family members. For example, the teacher shows pictures and begins by describing his/her real family or a fictitious family in terms of members, roles, names, ages, likes, dislikes and professions. After the description, the teacher checks to see what students are able to remember. This questioning gives students a chance to use basic expressions.

2. The next step is for students to describe their own families. As preparation for class, students prepare notes about their families (real or imagined) according to the specifications given in advance.

3. After further practice in class, students write descriptions of their families. Possible information includes:
   - family name
   - number of people in the family (family makeup)
   - description of each member of the family (name, age, occupation, personality)
   - family activities and traditions

4. Once the documents are completed and revised using peer editing and student/teacher editing,

the descriptions are sent to collaborating classes abroad and students wait for the responses from their key pals describing their families. When the correspondence is received, students compare families in both cultures and find similarities and/or differences.

Locating Collaborating Colleagues and Key Pals

Possible collaborating partners can be found in the same school building or district, in another city or around the world. Here are some strategies for locating key pals:

- Place ads in professional organization newsletters and journals.
- Attend professional conferences and technology workshops to network with colleagues.
- Search the Internet for Collaborating Classrooms, Cultural Classroom Connection or Exchanges.
- Post messages in Spanish news groups.
- Subscribe to listservs pertinent to Spanish or countries where Spanish is spoken.
- Check related WWW home pages or Internet Guides (a listing is included in the section titled Teacher Resources on the World Wide Web).
- Write to American Schools Abroad (a listing may be obtained from the Department of State in Washington, D.C.).

Tips for Using E-Mail

- Have students avoid tabs and foreign characters unless both groups are using compatible software.
- Write your introductory remarks for the collaborating teacher and then paste the letters of each student/group after your message. Separate each individual message using a line, a symbol or a character.

  This will make it easier for your collaborating teacher to separate the messages and distribute them to his/her students.
- Specify the font and size to use on a project.
- Clearly specify project checkpoints and deadlines.
- Give clear directions for minimum length and content to be included.
- Explain how you will evaluate a project.
- Explain how and where to save a project, including how to name it before saving.

E-Mail Projects: Overcoming E-Mail Limitations

Hardware Limitations—When a limited number of computers are available, students can work in pairs, or individual students can access computers at other times (for example, while others in class are working on an assignment, after completing a test or during lunch periods, study hall or before and after school). Assignments made well in advance of their due date will allow students to manage their work time and produce final products of high quality.

Time Limitations—When computer lab time is limited, schedule individuals or groups in such a way that at least one exchange can be completed per quarter, trimester or semester.

Access Limitations—If you have only one computer with a modem and access to the Internet, get the project ready and transmit it when the line is available. A designated student can be the mailer. If there is no access in school, a teacher or student who has access to the Internet can be the mailer for the group.

Students with computers at home can do their work on their own time. Today's computers allow texts created on one platform to be read by computers on another. For example, using Microsoft Word 5.0 or later, you can open just about any type of text file. In addition, software programs such as Access PC and PC Exchange allow the exchange of files written using computers of different platforms.

INTERNET SEARCH

To search the Internet, use the latest version available of the Web browser of your choice. Web browsers provide a harmonious interface for text and graphics.

You have different options for search engines. Some of them search titles or headers of documents, others search the documents themselves, and still others search indexes or directories. The following are some popular and powerful search engines:

Google	http://www.google.com/
Lycos	http://www.lycos.com/
Overture	http://overture.com/
Yahoo	http://www.yahoo.com/
Yahoo Español	http://espanol.yahoo.com/

Sample Internet Activity—The Internet can be used for research and activities limited only by your imagination. One popular activity is a virtual city tour. Students use a search engine to find information on a city of their choice. They can locate maps of the city, identify sites of interest and look at pictures of those sites, learn about transportation in the city, research brief historical facts about the city, find airlines and/or trains serving the city, look for weather data and find out about typical cuisine.

Some Spanish-speaking cities have virtual tour Web sites that you may want to use.

Madrid, Spain
http://www.visualware.es/guiamad/index.htm
Mallorca, Spain
http://www.mallorcaservice.com/nueva/
Valencia, Spain
http://www.upv.es/cv/valbegin.html
Alicante, Spain
http://www.upv.es/cv/alibegin.html
Mar del Plata, Argentina
http://www.todomardelplata.com/360/
San Diego, California
http://www.sandiego360.com/
Ciudad de México
http://www.mexicocity.com.mx/
Cancún, México http://www.cancun.com/
select Mexico cities
http://www.mexconnect.com/
MEX/mxc/tour.index.html
multi-city sites http://www.virtualtourist.com
http://www.lonelyplanet.com

Alternatives for this activity include the following:

- Place students in small groups. Each small group "visits" a different section of the city. They determine which sites to visit during a 48-hour period on a given budget. For example, one group may visit several museums; another may travel to a park to see sculptures and attend a cultural event.
- Each group visits a different city in the same country. After groups have processed the information on the cities, they give a class presentation to highlight the attractions of the various cities.
- In small groups, students design a travel brochure about their city.

Cultural/Historical Studies and Presentations

Students work in small groups to become "experts" on a country where Spanish is spoken. The objectives of the activity are to help students get acquainted with the history, geography, economics, climate, attractions and current events of the target country and culture. Working in groups, students search for information pertaining to a country that is assigned or chosen. Once the search is completed, the groups summarize the information and present it to the class.

The search starts by selecting the name of the country and browsing through the results. Once a site with relevant information is found, it may be possible to do searches within that site. The information found may differ from country to country and from site to site, but suggest to students information that should be included in their presentation. Such content may include:

- geography
- maps
- history
- climate/weather
- major cities and tourist attractions
- popular events
- airlines serving the country
- economic activity and exchange rate
- major newspapers (include a copy of recent headlines)

In addition to sharing their findings with the class, students should submit to you the following:

1. A printed copy of the material found and used for the presentation.
2. A copy of the final presentation.
3. A reading/listening comprehension quiz prepared by the group and based on the presentation. The quiz should also include a key with the correct responses. To complete the quiz, the class does either a listening comprehension exercise while the presentation is given or a reading comprehension exercise at the conclusion of the presentation when printed copies of the presentation are made available to the class.

Virtual Museums and Works of Art

When teaching colors, emotions, description and even history, works of art may be downloaded to teach, illustrate and reinforce a variety of concepts. For example, students may be assigned to search for works of given artists to illustrate the concepts and/or vocabulary studied in class. Students also may be assigned to give a presentation on a given artist that includes the following:

- country of origin
- biographical information about the artist
- period of time in history when the artist lived
- style of work
- colors and shapes used by the artist
- feelings and aspects of life represented by his/her work
- examples of his/her work

Radio Broadcasts

The Internet offers access to radio broadcasts. Students can improve their listening comprehension skills and awareness of culture by listening to music originating from Spanish-speaking parts of the world and talk shows that are broadcast in Spanish.

Weather Reports

Weather reports, including satellite and infrared maps, are available on the Internet. When teaching about weather and weather conditions, have students access weather reports from Spanish-speaking countries and regions of the United States. The students then use this information to give weather reports or forecasts to the class. If used throughout the year, such information can be included in different units of the curriculum to link weather conditions with seasons, clothing, sports, outdoor activities and other topics.

As with other projects, the ability level of the students will be a factor in assigning specific tasks and content. For example, beginning students may give simple weather reports, including temperatures and precipitation, whereas advanced students may explore the relationship between weather conditions and lifestyle, tourism and the economy.

Newspapers and Magazines

The many newspapers and magazines on the World Wide Web are another outstanding resource for students and teachers in the language classroom. One possible activity involves these steps:

1. Locate appropriate newspapers and magazines from countries where Spanish is spoken.
2. Familiarize yourself with their format and content.

3. Divide the class into small groups.
4. Assign a content area to each member of the group or allow the students to choose an area of interest. Possible areas include international news, national news, politics, entertainment, weather and sports.
5. According to the number of groups in class, the level and the time allotted, develop a schedule that allows each group to present news from its newspaper or magazine on a regular basis. For example, a different group can do this at the beginning of class every day, or you may want to identify a day of the week for several group presentations. However done, the activity should not take more than five to ten minutes per group. It is helpful to give specific instructions about the content, length and depth you expect of the presentations and to post a calendar of presentation dates in the classroom.

A variation of this activity is to divide students into small groups and have them summarize the school newspaper in Spanish. Once done, the newspaper and/or summary are sent via e-mail to a collaborating class with which you have contact. Such an exchange of news can be an activity done throughout the year.

ASSESSING INTERNET PROJECTS

The following guidelines may be helpful when developing and assessing e-mail and Web projects:

1. Give specific instructions in writing about the project.
2. Post a calendar or time line corresponding to the project.
3. Remember that some flexibility may be necessary if students encounter difficulties (for example, with access or printing).
4. Develop clear criteria for grading and evaluation. Being specific about how student work will be evaluated will make it easier to assign a grade at the end of the project. Depending on the project, factors to consider may include:
   - whether students meet guidelines for content, length, etc.
   - whether the project is completed on time
   - the quality of the presentation and/or written assignment(s)
   - participation

TEACHER RESOURCES ON THE WORLD WIDE WEB

(**Note:** These addresses may change at any time. Visit sites to verify they are active before using them in class.)

Travel and tourism
http://www.embassyworld.com/
http://www.embassy.org
http://www.virtualtourist.com/
http://www.towd.com/
http://cityguide.lycos.com/
http://www.lonelyplanet.com
http://travel.discovery.com/destinations/main.html
http://www.lycos.com/travel/

Radio and television broadcasting
http://news.bbc.co.uk/hi/Spanish/news/
http://www.voanews.com/Spanish/
http://www.radio-locator.com/
http://www.univision.com/

Suggested sites for e-mail projects
http://www.epals.com/
http://www.linguistic-funland.com/penpalpostings.html/
http://www.worldwide.edu/index.html

Weather
http://cnnespanol.com/tiempo/
http://cnn.com/weather/
http://www.espanol.weather.com/
http://www.intellicast.com/

Newspapers and magazines
http://www.editorandpublisher.com/editorandpublisher/index.jsp
http://libraries.mit.edu/guides/types/flnews/spanish.html
http://yahoo.com/news/
http://cnnespanol.com/

Culture
http://www.lanic.utexas.edu/las.html
http://www.recetario.com/

Acceptable Use Policy

The major school rules provide the basic structure for the Acceptable Use Policy. All users must be honest and respectful of others. Their work must meet the schoolwide guidelines for appropriate language and subject matter; it must not violate the school's harassment policy.

All use of the computers must be within the law. Copyright laws must be observed. Only software licensed to the school may be put in school computers. Copyrighted files cannot be sent from or received by school computers without permission of the copyright owner.

Users may access only their own files and programs or those intended for their use. Access to another's account or files without authorization is forbidden. Students must not attempt to access administrative files.

Those using the school's computing resources for classroom use and school-related projects have priority for use of the lab and/or equipment. School facilities may not be used for commercial purposes. Individuals are expected to use the resources thoughtfully. Use that unnecessarily slows access to the network, wastes storage or wastes other resources is forbidden.

Students who violate these policies will be subject to the school's disciplinary process.

Students will be asked to read and sign a list of additional guidelines before being given access to the school's computers. These guidelines will give students additional information about safe and respectful use of the school's computing resources.

http://www.mcu.es/agenda/index.html

http://www.lacultura.com.ar/lacultura/
index.shtml

Education and teaching ideas

http://www.worldwide.edu/index.html

http://web66.coled.umn.edu/schools.html

http://www.lanic.utexas.edu/las.html

http://www.clta.net/lessons/topspanish.html

http://www.actfl.org

Language Professionals

The Foreign Language Teaching Forum is an integrated service for language teachers. The organization includes an Internet site (FLTEACH.com), e-mail (FLTEACH@listserv.buffalo.edu) LISTSERV Academic Discussion List, archives and the FLNEWS server at the State University of New York College at Cortland. The sites facilitate networking and dialog among language professionals. Topics include language teaching methods, school/college articulation, training of student teachers, classroom activities, curriculum and syllabus design. To subscribe to the list, send the following message: SUBSCRIBE FLTEACH [first name] [last name] to: LISTSERV@UBVM.CC.BUFFALO.EDU.

POLICY AND GUIDELINES FOR COMPUTER USERS

It is essential to create an acceptable use policy before allowing student access to the Internet. The development of such a policy should include all interested parties, such as school administrators, faculty, students, parents and members of the school board. The following policy and guidelines are an example created by one school. They were presented as a "working document" to allow for revisions and additions.

Guidelines for Computer Users

Permission to use the school's computing facilities is granted to those who agree to use them thoughtfully and respectfully. The following guidelines should be followed:

All use of school's computers must be consistent with the school's Acceptable Use Policy. You are expected to be honest, respect others, follow the school's rules about harassment and do nothing illegal.

Access only those files for which you are authorized. You must not use or attempt to use any other person's files or programs without permission. Attempting to access administrative files, even for fun, will be viewed as a serious offense.

Do not use offensive language, which includes both vulgar or insulting language and derogatory language.

Do not monopolize the use of the equipment. Users working on class-related projects have priority for the use of the facilities.

Do not give your home address or phone number over the Net. If you need to give someone an address or phone number, use the school's. If in doubt, check with a teacher.

Be a positive member of the school's computer-using community. Be helpful to those less knowledgeable than you. Avoid activities that earn some computer users bad reputations: Do not "hack," "spam," "flame," introduce viruses and so on.

Keep the system running legally and efficiently. Get rid of unwanted programs, files, and e-mail that take up valuable storage. "Unsubscribe" from mail lists that no longer interest you. Do not use illegal software. Do not store your own personal software at school.

Student use of the Internet is limited to the computers in the student computer lab unless they are working under the supervision of a faculty member.

TEACHING SUGGESTIONS

Navegando is a flexible program that allows teachers to cover material in the textbooks and ancillaries to suit their individual needs. This allows you to cover the various sections of a lesson with the degree of thoroughness suggested by your students' needs, your time and personal teaching style and your school's resources. In general, try to vary your presentations by using as many different resources as possible. Recombine similar materials for your students' diverse learning styles. For example, the Listening Activities offer comprehension practice; the Video/DVD Program allows students to observe native speakers using Spanish in contexts that require skills your students are learning; the CD-ROM tutorials and games individualize and personalize instruction; overhead transparencies offer visual support of spoken Spanish and can serve both to practice rote material and to provide situational contexts for conversations; activities in the textbook and Workbook and the Communicative Activities Manual offer additional writing practice.

The Program Manager offers day-by-day suggestions on using components of the series. Depending on the needs and time limitations set by individual circumstances, some activities may be skipped. The reading section titled *Tú lees* is optional, thus offering you additional flexibility in matching content to the needs, interests and curriculum requirements of your own particular situation.

Opening vocabulary spreads, dialogs, other narrative material and many activities in the textbook have been recorded and thus offer you additional choices about how to present or review the chapter content. For example, you may choose to have students listen to a recorded activity before going to the textbook, or you may choose instead to use the audio CD as additional reinforcement after having completed the activity in the textbook. Recorded activities are indicated by icons in the margins of the ATE, according to the activity type.

In addition, many ancillaries already discussed in this ATE Introduction supplement the textbook. These program components provide an abundance of textbook-related activities and teaching formats that will enable you to customize your teaching to the many and varied learning styles and needs of your students.

Every teacher has his or her own approach to teaching. Suggestions for including activities from the accompanying ancillaries have been offered in the margins of the ATE and in the Program Manager to give you an idea of the possible variations the teaching program offers. You should try to include an assortment of different activities, choosing some from the textbook and others from the ancillaries (the Workbook, the ATE, etc.), according to your needs.

ADDITIONAL ACTIVITIES AND GAMES

ACTIVITIES

The following activities and games offer additional avenues through which to enrich and supplement the lessons in the textbook. The ideas support skill development, cooperative learning, critical thinking, multiple intelligences and Total Physical Response (TPR). Pick and choose from the wide variety of activities and games as needed.

Skill Development

Listening—Before a dialog or other listening passage, have students use cues from accompanying illustrations to make an educated guess about what they are about to hear. Students may be able to determine such things as how many people are speaking, whether the speakers are young or old, male or female. Have students try to determine if they are hearing questions or statements. Then play the audio CD as students listen with their books closed.

Encourage students to learn to become good listeners by asking follow-up questions to listening activities: What are the speakers talking about? How are they feeling? What are their plans? Play the audio

CD again with books open, having students read along silently. Have students repeat after you as you read the content in short phrases. You may choose to act out or paraphrase the meanings of words and expressions, avoiding word-for-word repetition.

Reading—Prepare students for the content of a reading by asking some general questions on the reading topic, such as the questions found in the section *Preparación.* You may choose to read the first paragraph yourself as students follow along in the book. Give students a moment to look over the paragraph silently on their own and then have them ask questions. Ask for a student to volunteer to read the paragraph aloud. Continue in this way for subsequent paragraphs. After the reading, discuss the principal ideas and themes, secondary ideas and themes, cultural practices, etc.

Research—Assign projects that allow small groups of students to research aspects of the fascinating cultures of the Spanish-speaking world. Possible topics can involve history, art, architecture, government, social customs and cultural traits, for example.

Dictionary—Show students the glossary in the back of the book. Then teach some important dictionary skills by having them find the meanings of two or three new words. This activity can be done in any lesson, as often as you like. As an alternative, have students identify several infinitives in a Spanish dictionary. (The textbook glossary can serve as the dictionary.)

Mapping—Teach mapping skills on a regular basis. For example, use the map transparencies to practice pronouncing the names of countries and capitals in the Spanish-speaking world. Ask students *¿Cómo se llama?* while pointing to one of the countries on a map transparency; students should answer with *Es* (name of the country).

Say the name of a country, have a student point to the country on a map transparency or on a wall map and then ask the student to write the country's name on the board. (You may choose to have various students direct the class to add variety.)

To integrate cultural information, use a wall map or an overhead transparency of the maps in the book. Have individual students go to the map (*Ve* or *Camina*

al mapa) and touch (*Toca*) or point to (*Señala*) the items you mention: *Toca un país donde se puede esquiar en julio; Toca un país que produce mucho café;* and so forth.

Cooperative Learning

When students finish school and enter the workforce, the knowledge they will have acquired will be complemented by the socialization skills they have learned. The following activities are designed to help students work cooperatively to solve problems in Spanish.

Concentric Circles—Students form two concentric circles. Students in the inner ring pair up with students in the outer ring, each student asking the other for information (for example, his or her name and how it is spelled). Students in the outer ring move one student to their right and begin the process again.

Information Exchange—1) Have students gather information about other students in class by pairing up or working in small groups, asking and answering questions about one another's lives. They should then share the information with the class. 2) Have students write a description of themselves in Spanish, including information about where they live and their interests. Then photograph each student with an item showing a hobby or interest. Number each of the photos and have the class try to match the descriptions to the photo. As an extension of the activity, mail the descriptions and photos to a partner school for them to read and match. If the schools are connected by Internet, follow-up communication could include the correct matchup and any additional questions and information to establish long-term communication between the students of the different schools.

Critical Thinking

It is important for students to develop a variety of skills that go beyond the four basic skills of listening, speaking, reading and writing. As students move into the workplace, they will need to think critically and solve problems. Some possible activities for developing critical thinking skills include the following:

Analysis: Comparing and Contrasting—Have students pick out names that are unlike names they know in English: *Maite, Nuria* and so forth. Then have students select several names that are similar to names they know in English, while pointing out any spelling differences: *Susana—Susan.*

Analysis: Distinguishing—Have students identify the letters in the Spanish alphabet that are not in the English alphabet—*ñ, rr*—and differences in punctuation between English and Spanish.

Evaluation: Concluding, Comparing, Appraising—Discuss student conclusions about Hispanic cultures based upon the cultural information they learn in *Navegando* (gestures, physical contact when greeting others or saying farewell, etc.). Then have students tell how the culture they are learning about is similar to or different from their own culture. Finally, ask how students feel about the similarities and/or differences.

Multiple Intelligences

Educators have long agreed that not everyone learns in the same way, nor is everyone intelligent in the same way. For example, one person might have verbal or mathematical ability, whereas another may demonstrate musical ability. These different intelligences must be developed so that students can achieve their full potential. Activities that address the multiple intelligences include the following.

Logical-Mathematical Intelligence—After students have studied the days and months, ask the class some questions that require students to do some calculations with the days and months of the year. Call on a student to answer each question. Then, to keep everyone involved, call on another student to confirm whether the answer given was correct and to give the correct answer if it was not. Begin with some of the following questions: *¿Cuántos minutos hay en un cuarto de hora?; ¿Cuántos días hay en una semana?; ¿En tres semanas?; ¿Cuántos minutos hay en seis horas y media?; ¿Cuántos segundos hay en doce minutos?; ¿Cuántos meses hay en cinco años?; ¿Cuántos meses hay en tres siglos?; ¿Cuántos meses hay en cinco siglos?* This activity involves critical thinking and will develop your students' logical-mathematical intelligence.

Spatial Intelligence—Have students prepare maps of the Spanish-speaking world in Spanish, adding any details they wish to borrow from the color maps at the beginning of the textbook or from an atlas.

Total Physical Response (TPR)

Plural Commands—Practice recognition of the *Uds.* form of commands by having the entire class perform certain actions or gestures as you say them aloud in Spanish. The commands should be presented in logical thematic groups *(lean, escriban, borren; escuchen, hablen, repitan).* Practice the action or gesture two or three times with students, then repeat the pair of commands one or two times with no actions or gestures.

Singular Informal Commands—After students are adequately familiar with the *Uds.* commands, you may want to use the *tú* form of a few verbs for TPR activities. Ideally, the *Uds.* and the *tú* forms should be presented on separate days. Before proceeding to the familiar commands, briefly review the *Uds.* form of the verbs you plan to use by having students perform several actions. Examples include: *Abran Uds. los libros; Cierren Uds. los libros; Toquen Uds. los libros.* Then select several students to react to the informal commands of the corresponding verbs: *Abre el libro; Cierra el libro; Toca el libro.* Vary the commands slightly to further check for comprehension: (student's name), *abre el libro;* (student's name), *abre el cuaderno.* Perform the action or use gestures only if a student does not respond.

Colors—Combine the teaching of colors with teaching or reinforcing common commands. For example, say *Toca algo azul (rojo, verde,* etc.) and observe to see that students respond appropriately. Then broaden the activity to include clothing (or other objects). You may choose to bring in a bag of old clothing, especially clothing that is out of style, awful colors, unusual sizes and so forth as a humorous way to allow students to find and point out colors and items of clothing that you name or describe.

GAMES

The following games can be modified to suit the needs of your students or to support your particular approach to teaching.

Concentration—This game can be used for practicing numbers or for reviewing or practicing verbs. The same rhythm is maintained: students tap the tops of their desks twice, clap their hands twice and snap their fingers twice—words may be called out only during the snapping of fingers. For verb practice, for example, the first student in each row gives an infinitive *(hablar)* on the first snapping of fingers, the next student gives a subject pronoun *(tú)* on the second, and the third student must respond with the appropriate answer *(tú hablas)* on the third snapping of fingers. Students who make an error move to the end of the row and the other students move up. Try to have an uneven number of students in each row so that every student will have an opportunity to match the subject pronoun and verb ending. All the students in each row monitor each other for errors. You also may have the entire class participate rather than play the game by rows. In this case, you may want to point to students for a verb infinitive, subject pronoun and response.

El detective—This game may be played with a number of different objectives: to help students get to know one another, to practice specific vocabulary, to practice different verb tenses, and so on. Make a number of lists with five to ten different items on each list. If the object is for students to get to know each other, include items such as *le gusta el fútbol, el béisbol,* etc. (a different sport on each list); *come pollo, ensalada, hamburguesas,* etc. (a different food on each list); *mañana va a la playa, al concierto, al cine,* etc. (a different place on each list); and so on. Include an unusual category to make the activity more interesting. Copy the lists to equal the number of students you have, so that each member of a group (of five, for example) has the same list and different groups have different lists. *El detective* must fill in his or her list by asking fellow students if certain categories apply to them, and if so, they sign the list by the appropriate category. Students will practice the *tú* form while asking classmates questions *(¿Juegas al fútbol?),* and may practice the third-person singular by reporting the findings to the class after all students have completed the activity.

Dibujos—This game is designed to review vocabulary while allowing students to use their artistic abilities.

The class is split up into teams. Give one member of each group a word or phrase. The team member with the word or phrase then draws clues for his or her team members. Each team has one minute to guess the word or phrase from the drawn clues. Award points to the fastest team and continue with different vocabulary and artists until a team reaches a point total determined in advance.

¿Dónde está?—(directional vocabulary and commands)—Choose a small object such as a piece of chalk, show it to the students and ask them to hide it somewhere in the room. Go out of the room for a few minutes while they hide the item. When you return, they will help you find it by giving you directional commands or indicating direction *(Doble a la derecha, está cerca, mire en el suelo,* etc.*)*. Next, divide the class into groups of four or five, choose one person from each group to leave the room and then repeat the game, this time with familiar commands.

Hot Potato—This simple game will help beginning students gain confidence in speaking because it occupies students with a physical activity while they are conversing in Spanish, thus reducing their inhibitions about making an error. Hot Potato is played as follows: Students stand in a circle in the classroom. One student, who is holding a soft rubber ball, asks a question of another student in the circle and then calls the student by name. The first student then carefully tosses the ball to the second student, who must answer the question. Allow students ten to fifteen seconds to answer each question. The student who catches the ball and answers a question then asks a question and passes the ball to another student and so on. The game continues until all students have had at least two chances to answer a question. Questions can be based on chapter vocabulary and grammar, cultural topics or a textbook story. The teacher serves as the moderator.

Vary the game by restricting the amount of time a student can hold the ball. For example, tell students they cannot hold the ball for more than twenty seconds before beginning to ask or answer a question, or they will have to sit down. The last person standing wins the game.

The game eliminates a student's natural inclination to think in English before saying something in Spanish so that thinking in Spanish becomes a natural reflex. An added benefit is that all students actively participate in the activity since they are not just responding to the teacher's questions while passively sitting at their seats.

I Spy—Have students work in pairs to play guessing games. Students take turns describing an object they see (being certain to describe the colors, the size, what it is made of), mentioning one clue at a time while the partner guesses what the object is.

Jeopardy—This game is especially good as a general review before an exam, but it can be used at almost any time in many different ways. Similar to the television game show, it involves writing a series of categories horizontally on the board. Write the numbers ten through fifty by tens under each category. Prepare questions in advance. Unlike the television game show, students need not respond with a question. Questions may be completions, synonyms or antonyms, translations, direct questions, matching, and so forth. Divide the class into three or four teams and tell students that each person on the team must make a buzzer sound to indicate they are able to answer. (You may wish to locate an actual buzzer.)

To determine which team will go first, ask a question that may be answered by any student. The first student who sounds the buzzer gets a chance to answer. The team that correctly answers the opening question has the opportunity to choose a category and a dollar amount. Read the question, allowing that team to respond within a time limit (ten or fifteen seconds). If not answered within the specified time limit, the question is open to the entire class, but buzzers must be used; that is, students should not randomly blurt out answers.

Prepare several *Daily Double* questions, as well. Use these when enthusiasm for the game wanes. Whatever the dollar amount in the chosen category is at that moment, double it. These questions may be answered by any team, not just the team that chose the category.

When a question is answered correctly, write the answer in the space left by the erased dollar amount as you keep score. This will provide students with visual reinforcement of the material. When the entire board is filled with answers, total the scores. You may wish to offer prizes as an incentive.

El mensaje—This enjoyable activity is useful for reviewing vocabulary and reinforces listening, writing, reading and speaking skills. In advance, provide students with a list of the names of all the students in class. The list can be in alphabetical or in random order. As you hand out the list of names, inform students that they will be leaving phone messages with one another in Spanish and should hold on to this phone list to know whom to call with messages. Then, on a day when you would like to review vocabulary (or just to vary the routine), start several phone calls by whispering to several students a word or expression in Spanish that they must write down and then whisper to the next student on the list. Give students a set time when you will be collecting all phone messages (five minutes, for example). Compare what the final person wrote down to the "phone message" you whispered to the first person for each vocabulary word or expression.

Stop the Clock (vocabulary review)—Make up a series of small cards with pictures on one side and their Spanish definitions on the other, and distribute them to the class. Divide the class into two groups and choose one person to be "it" for each group (you will have two games going at once). The rest of the students sit on their desks (or stand in front of them) in a circle, holding their cards with the picture facing out. The person who is "it" stands in the center.

To begin the game, pick one student in each group. Each of those students must say the name in Spanish of the object pictured on the card he or she is holding and the name of the picture on another student's card. (It makes it harder on the person who is "it" to not be looking at the person whose card is named. Thus, you may wish to advise students to name a second card that is to the side of or behind the person who is "it.") The person in the center of the circle must find the second person and point at the corresponding picture, thus "stopping the clock," before the second student can name both his or her picture and another person's picture. Make sure the person in the center is accurately pointing at, or preferably touching, the picture. If someone's clock is stopped, that person is then "it."

Streetcar (vocabulary review)—Prepare file cards with the words you want to practice in Spanish on one side (it may be helpful to indicate infinitives with an asterisk and include articles with nouns) and in English on the reverse side. You may extend this game by using synonyms and antonyms. Your list could be based on the active vocabulary words listed at the end of each lesson. Decide whether you want the students to produce the English or the Spanish. Students should study the vocabulary before playing Streetcar. The object of this game is to get all the way back to one's seat. Every time a student answers correctly, he or she moves forward one seat. The teacher may direct the game or have a student do it.

Begin on the left side of class with the first row. The first student stands up next to the second, who remains seated. Show a card to these students while saying the word. The first student to respond correctly moves on to compete with the third student. Whoever answers correctly stands next to the third student. So if the second student wins the round, he or she moves on to the third student and the first student sits down in the second student's seat. If neither of the first two students can answer after five seconds, the third student is given an opportunity to respond. If there is still no answer, use the card as a free review, ask the class to define the problem word and choose a new card. This should be a relatively fast-paced game. By saying the target word as you show it, students practice assigning sound to visual cues as well.

Teatro—Students prepare a short list of action verbs, which they must act out in front of the class. Classmates then try to guess which Spanish verbs are being dramatized. Limit the time to encourage presenters to act out the list as quickly as possible.

CLASSROOM EXPRESSIONS

Use Spanish in the classroom beginning on the first day of class, and increase its use throughout the year. Although this may seem difficult at first, margin notes and activities and the model lesson plan included in the ATE Introduction offer suggestions, activities and tips for teaching that make using Spanish on a daily basis not only possible, but quite simple.

Be sure to let students know what your expectations are in advance. Although Spanish should serve as the primary means of communication, explain to students that you will paraphrase, use gestures or act out expressions to convey meaning and that you will avoid overusing English. Setting this tone will make your students aware of your expectations that they use the target language. You may choose, however, to note that important information about homework assignments, structures and other topics will be given or repeated in English as necessary.

Encourage students to respond to directions and give answers in Spanish. Initially, they may feel frustrated by their limited Spanish skills, so you may need to explain that people often use one-word answers and incomplete phrases to communicate in their native language. (Give some examples in English for comparison purposes.) Point out that the more students use Spanish, the more natural it will become as a means of communication. In addition, you may wish to introduce the following frequently used classroom expressions early in the year so that students have a communicative foundation on which to build:

Abre (Abran Uds.) el libro/cuaderno en la página....	Open your book/notebook to page....
Apunta/Señala (Apunten Uds./Señalen Uds.)....	Point at....
Borra (Borren Uds.) la pizarra.	Erase the board.
Cierra (Cierren Uds.) el libro/cuaderno.	Close your book/notebook.
Contesta/Responde (Contesten Uds./Responden Uds.).	Answer.
Continúa/Sigue (Continúen Uds./Sigan Uds.).	Continue.
Copia (Copien Uds.)....	Copy....
Cuenta (Cuenten Uds.)....	Count....
Da (Den Uds.) la vuelta.	Turn around.

Spanish	English
Dibuja (Dibujen Uds.)....	Draw....
Dime (Díganme Uds.)....	Tell me....
Empieza (Empiecen Uds.) ahora.	Begin now.
Escoge (Escojan Uds.)....	Choose....
Entrégame (Entréguenme Uds.) la tarea.	Hand in your homework to me.
Escribe (Escriban Uds.)....	Write....
Escribe (Escriban Uds.) a máquina....	Type....
Escucha (Escuchen Uds.).	Listen.
Estudia (Estudien Uds.)....	Study....
Formen Uds. grupos de....	Form groups of....
Habla (Hablen Uds.) en español.	Speak in Spanish.
Inserta (Inserten Uds.) el diskette en la computadora.	Insert the diskette into the computer.
Levanta (Levanten Uds.) la mano (para contestar).	Raise your hand (to answer).
Lee (Lean Uds.)...en voz alta.	Read...out loud.
Levántate (Levántense Uds.).	Stand up.
Llévate (Llévense Uds.)....	Take...with you.
Mira (Miren Uds.)....	Look....
Oye (Oigan Uds.).	Listen.
Para (Paren Uds.).	Stop.
Pasa (Pasen Uds.) a la pizarra.	Go to the board.
Piensa (Piensen Uds.).	Think.
Pon (Pongan Uds.)....	Put/Place....
Presta (Presten Uds.) atención a....	Pay attention to....
Pronuncia (Pronuncien Uds.)....	Pronounce....
Recoge (Recojan Uds.)....	Pick up....
Recuerda (Recuerden Uds.)....	Remember....
Repite (Repitan Uds.).	Repeat.
Revisa (Revisen Uds.)....	Review....
Quita (Quiten Uds.) todo de encima de sus pupitres.	Take everything off the top of your desks.
Saca (Saquen Uds.) una hoja de papel/un bolígrafo/ un lápiz.	Take out a sheet of paper/a pen/a pencil.
Siéntate (Siéntense Uds.).	Sit down.
Toca (Toquen Uds.)....	Touch....
Trabajen Uds. en parejas en....	Work in pairs on....
Trae (Traigan Uds.)....	Bring....
Trata (Traten Uds.).	Try.
Ve (Vayan Uds.) a....	Go to....
Ven (Vengan Uds.) aquí.	Come here.
Muy bien.	Very good.
Excelente.	Excellent.
Para mañana....	For tomorrow....
Más alto/bajo.	Louder/Softer.
Silencio.	Quiet.
Otra vez.	Once more.
Vamos a tener una prueba/un examen.	We're going to have a quiz/a test.
¿Quién sabe (la respuesta)?	Who knows (the answer)?
¿Alguien?	Anyone?
Todos juntos.	All together.

¿Hay preguntas?	Are there any questions?
¿Cómo se dice...(en español)?	How do you say...(in Spanish)?
¿Cómo se escribe...?	How do you write...?
¿Qué quiere decir...?	What does...mean?
No sé.	I don't know.
No comprendo/entiendo.	I don't understand.
No recuerdo.	I don't remember.
Tengo una pregunta.	I have a question.
Bueno (Pues, Este)....	Okay (Well, Um)....
Yo creo/pienso que....	I believe/think that....

TRANSCRIPT FOR TEXTBOOK LISTENING ACTIVITIES

Listening Comprehension Activities in *Navegando* are indicated by the icon 🔊. These activities are recorded and are available in the Audio CD Program. For teacher convenience, reproducible answer sheets have been provided for these activities and can be found at the end of the Audio CD Program Manual. The following section contains a transcript of the recorded activities for teachers who wish to read the activities aloud instead of using the recorded version in the Audio CD Program.

CAPÍTULO 1 (LECCIÓN A)

1. ¿Cómo se escribe? Escribe los nombres que oyes.

MODELO Me llamo Carlos. Carlos se escribe con c mayúscula, a, ere, ele, o, ese.

1. Me llamo Ana. Ana se escribe con a mayúscula, ene, a.
2. Me llamo José. José se escribe con jota mayúscula, o, ese, e con acento.
3. Me llamo María. María se escribe con eme mayúscula, a, ere, i con acento, a.
4. Me llamo Paz. Paz se escribe con pe mayúscula, a, zeta.
5. Me llamo Raúl. Raúl se escribe con ere mayúscula, a, u con acento, ele.
6. Me llamo Verónica. Verónica se escribe con ve mayúscula, e, ere, o con acento, ene, i, ce, a.

7. ¿Cuál es la respuesta correcta? Escoge una respuesta correcta a lo que oyes.

1. ¿Cómo se escribe Hugo? ¿Con hache?
2. Yo me llamo Hugo. ¿Y tú?
3. Me llamo Carmen.
4. Hasta luego.

12. Los países. Practice saying the names of the Spanish-speaking countries you hear.

1. Argentina
2. Bolivia
3. Colombia
4. Costa Rica
5. Chile
6. Cuba
7. Ecuador
8. El Salvador
9. España
10. Guatemala
11. Guinea Ecuatorial
12. Honduras
13. México
14. Nicaragua
15. Panamá
16. Paraguay
17. Perú
18. República Dominicana
19. Uruguay
20. Venezuela

18. **¿Cuántos años tienes? Escribe los números que oyes.**

MODELO Soy de Bogotá, la capital de Colombia. Tengo dieciséis años.

1. Soy de Santiago, la capital de Chile. Tengo veinte años.
2. Soy de la Ciudad de México, la capital de México. Tengo quince años.
3. Soy de La Paz, la capital de Bolivia. Tengo diez años.
4. Soy de Washington, la capital de Estados Unidos. Tengo ocho años.

CAPÍTULO 1 (LECCIÓN B)

1. **¿Saludo o despedida? Di si lo que oyes es: un saludo; una despedida; un saludo y una despedida.**

1. Hasta mañana.
2. Buenos días.
3. Hola.
4. Buenas tardes.
5. Buenas noches.

6. **¿Cuál es una respuesta correcta? Escoge una respuesta correcta a lo que oyes.**

1. Hola.
2. ¿Qué tal?
3. Adiós.

13. **Los números hasta cien. Escribe los números que oyes.**

MODELO Me llamo Raúl Varese. Tengo treinta años.

1. Me llamo Gabriela Cervantes. Tengo veintiséis años.
2. Soy el señor Carlos Eduardo Ramírez. Tengo setenta y nueve años.
3. Soy Amalia de la Torre. Tengo treinta y cuatro años.
4. Me llamo Ángela Torres. Tengo quince años.
5. Me llamo Dolores López Cruz. Tengo cien años.

17. **¿Qué hora es? Escribe la hora que oyes.**

MODELO Son las nueve y veinticinco.

1. Son las seis.
2. Es la una y media.
3. Son las tres y diez.

4. Son las cuatro y veinte.
5. Son las cinco y cuarto.
6. Es la una menos veinte.

CAPÍTULO 2 (LECCIÓN A)

1. **¿Quién? Selecciona la foto de la(s) persona(s) apropiada(s).**

1. Ellas son de Minnesota.
2. Ellos son de Texas.
3. Ella es de Colorado.
4. Él es de Nueva York.

5. **¡No es lógico! Escucha la información y corrige lo que no es lógico.**

1. Ella se llama Raúl.
2. Ellos son Laura y Diana.
3. Él es de Los Ángeles.

16. **¿Qué es? Identifica los objetos que oyes.**

1. la regla
2. el bolígrafo
3. el libro
4. el cesto de papeles
5. el cuaderno
6. el lápiz

20. **¿Sí o no? ¿Son lógicos los diálogos?**

1. ¿Quién es la chica con la mochila?
   Ella es la estudiante nueva de Los Ángeles.
2. ¿Qué quiere decir la palabra *mochila*?
   Quiere decir *chair*.
3. ¿Cómo se llama la chica nueva?
   Se llama Raúl y es mi amiga.
4. ¿Cómo se dice *clock* en español?
   Se dice *reloj*.

CAPÍTULO 2 (LECCIÓN B)

1. **¿Qué día es mañana? Contesta la pregunta *¿Qué día es mañana?* según lo que oyes.**

MODELO *You hear:* Es lunes. ¿Qué día es mañana?
You write: martes

1. Es jueves. ¿Qué día es mañana?
2. Es viernes. ¿Qué día es mañana?
3. Es martes. ¿Qué día es mañana?

4. Es domingo. ¿Qué día es mañana?
5. Es sábado. ¿Qué día es mañana?
6. Es miércoles. ¿Qué día es mañana?

6. ¿Qué clase es? Escribe la letra que identifica cada clase que oyes.
1. Hay una clase de arte el jueves a las ocho y cuarto.
2. La clase de español es a la una y cuarto de la tarde.
3. La clase de historia termina a las tres menos cinco.
4. La señora Valdés es la profesora de matemáticas.
5. Hay un estudiante nuevo en mi clase de inglés.

26. ¿Qué necesitan? Write the names Pilar and Julio. Next, listen and list under each of their names what Julio and Pilar need before they leave for college. Then circle any items on the lists that they both need.
1. Necesito una computadora nueva.
2. Necesito unos diskettes.
3. Necesito un ratón nuevo.
4. Necesito la dirección de correo electrónico de Julio.
5. Necesito unos CDs.
6. Necesito una impresora láser.
7. Necesito unos diskettes.
8. Necesito un teclado nuevo.
9. Necesito el número de celular de Pilar.
10. Necesito unos CDs.

35. Conexión con otras disciplinas: geografía. Say where each of these cities is located.
MODELO Malabo
      Malabo está en Guinea Ecuatorial.
1. San Antonio y Santa Fe
2. Sevilla y Madrid
3. Santiago
4. Managua
5. Maracaibo
6. Montevideo
7. Potosí
8. La Plata
9. Cali
10. Concepción

CAPÍTULO 3 (LECCIÓN A)

1. La ciudad. Selecciona la foto que corresponde con lo que oyes.
1. Rosa está en el dentista.
2. Los Ortega están en el hotel.
3. Belia y Jeff están en el parque.
4. Tomás está en la biblioteca.
5. La señora Elvira está en el médico.
6. Los chicos están en el restaurante.

5. Presentaciones. Indica la letra de la foto que corresponde con lo que oyes.
1. Sra. Gómez, le presento a Diana.
2. Mauricio y Armando, les presento a Carmen.
3. Alicia, te presento a Gonzalo.
4. Gloria, te presento al Sr. Iglesias.

21. ¿Qué medio de transporte es? Selecciona la foto que corresponde con lo que oyes.
1. Voy a México en avión.
2. Van a la oficina en autobús.
3. ¡Vamos al parque en bicicleta!
4. ¿Tomamos el tren a Guadalajara?
5. Es el caballo de mi amiga Inés.
6. ¿Por qué no vamos a la biblioteca en taxi?
7. Ellos van a pie.
8. ¡El lunes vamos en barco a Puerto Rico!

26. ¿Qué toman para ir? Selecciona la foto que corresponde con lo que oyes.
1. Tomás toma el carro para ir a la fiesta.
2. Yo tomo un taxi para ir al centro.
3. Los muchachos toman el autobús para ir a la escuela.
4. Mi profesora de inglés toma un barco para ir a Dominica y Barbados.
5. Mi profesor de biología toma el avión para ir a Cancún.

CAPÍTULO 3 (LECCIÓN B)

1. En el centro. Selecciona la ilustración del lugar apropiado, según lo que oyes.

1. Es un museo.
2. Es un teatro.
3. Es un edificio.
4. Es una ciudad.
5. Es una plaza.
6. Es una calle.
7. Es una tienda.
8. Es un cine.

6. ¿Qué vas a hacer hoy? Indica la letra de la ilustración que corresponde con lo que oyes.

1. Qué vas a hacer hoy?
   Voy a ir con Juana al nuevo restaurante El Charro.
2. ¿Dónde está?
   Está en la Avenida de la Independencia.
3. ¿No van a ir Uds. al Museo de Arte Moderno también?
   Sí. Vamos a la exhibición de Picasso.
4. ¿Qué van a hacer Uds. el sábado?
   Vamos a ir al concierto de Luis Miguel en el Teatro Arlequín.

13. ¿Dónde está? Di si lo que oyes está en un restaurante o en un colegio.

1. La chica con la tiza y el borrador se llama Marta.
2. Aquí está el menú.
3. El mesero está allí con las ensaladas y las bebidas.
4. Hay un cuaderno blanco allí en el pupitre.
5. La profesora de matemáticas está en la pizarra.
6. No veo pollo en mole en el menú.

18. ¿Cuál es la respuesta correcta? Escoge la letra de la respuesta correcta.

1. ¿Dónde está el restaurante?
2. ¿Qué vas a comer?
3. Siempre comes pollo en mole, ¿no?
4. ¿Qué vas a tomar?

CAPÍTULO 4 (LECCIÓN A)

1. ¿Cierto o falso? Di si lo que oyes es cierto o falso, según la información en el Vocabulario I. Si es falso, di lo que es cierto.

1. Los padres de Pepe se llaman Rodrigo y Mónica.
2. Rosa es una tía de Pepe.
3. Enrique, Nancy y Carmen son los primos de Pepe.
4. Las abuelas de Pepe se llaman Gloria y Pedro.
5. Álvaro es el tío de Pepe.
6. Mónica es el hermano de Pepe.

5. ¿Quién es? Escucha la información y, luego, escoge la letra de la respuesta correcta.

1. Es el hijo de mi abuelo y el esposo de mi madre.
2. Es el padre de mi madre.
3. Es la madre de mi prima.
4. Es la hija de mi tía.

19. ¿Cómo están? Selecciona la letra de la ilustración que corresponde con lo que oyes.

1. Está apurado.
2. Está nerviosa.
3. Está cansado.
4. Está triste.

23. ¿Cómo están todos? Listen as several people talk about how they are feeling. Then match the names with the description that fits each person.

1. Hoy voy a hacer mucho. Salgo para el colegio a las siete. Estoy en el colegio hasta las tres. Luego, voy al museo de arte en Ponce con unos amigos.
2. No estoy bien. Estoy mal, muy mal. Me duele el estómago.
3. El avión que voy a tomar sale pronto y yo estoy en casa.
4. Voy a un concierto con todos mis amigos. ¡Qué divertido!
5. Mi tío favorito va a estar en casa mañana pero yo voy a estar en clases.
6. Voy al dentista pero no quiero.

CAPÍTULO 4 (LECCIÓN B)

1. ¿Quién es? Selecciona la foto apropiada a lo que oyes.
1. Me gusta nadar.
2. Me gusta patinar sobre ruedas.
3. Quiero tocar el piano.
4. Voy a ir a un partido de fútbol.
5. Me gusta jugar al tenis.
6. Quiero ver la televisión.

5. ¿Qué les gusta? Write the names Natalia and Andrés. Next, listen and list under each person's name what he or she likes to do. Then circle any item on the lists that they both like to do.
1. Me gusta ir de compras con mis amigas.
2. También me gusta ir a la playa.
3. Me gusta mucho bailar.
4. Me gusta tocar el piano.
5. Me gusta jugar al tenis.
6. Me gusta jugar al béisbol.
7. Me gusta ir a la playa.
8. Me gusta bailar.
9. También me gusta patinar sobre ruedas.
10. Me gusta nadar.

18. ¿Cómo es? Mira las fotos y contesta las preguntas con *sí* o *no*, según lo que oyes.
1. ¿Es morena?
2. ¿Es calvo?
3. ¿Es bajo?
4. ¿Es delgado?
5. ¿Son guapas?
6. ¿Es fácil?
7. ¿Es pelirroja?
8. ¿Son canosos?

22. ¿Cuál es el opuesto? You will hear some descriptions of people and objects. Give the opposite of each adjective you hear.
MODELO Guillermo y Margarita son delgados. ¿Cuál es el opuesto de **delgados**?
1. Mi hermana, Teresita, siempre es buena. ¿Cuál es el opuesto de **buena**?
2. Yolanda es baja. ¿Cuál es el opuesto de **baja**?
3. Ellas están muy contentas. ¿Cuál es el opuesto de **contentas**?

4. Mi carro es rápido. ¿Cuál es el opuesto de **rápido**?
5. La clase de español es difícil. ¿Cuál es el opuesto de **difícil**?
6. Mis primos son inteligentes. ¿Cuál es el opuesto de **inteligentes**?
7. Su esposo es feo. ¿Cuál es el opuesto de **feo**?
8. Es un programa aburrido. ¿Cuál es el opuesto de **aburrido**?

CAPÍTULO 5 (LECCIÓN A)

1. ¿Qué buscan? Selecciona la ilustración que corresponde con lo que oyes.
1. Buscamos un casete de música rock.
2. Busco una grabadora de casetes.
3. Busco un disco compacto con música de piano.
4. Buscamos un reproductor de CDs.
5. Busco un equipo de sonido.
6. Buscamos un reproductor de MP3.

5. ¿Lo tienen? Write the names Marta and Sofía. Next, listen and list under their names what they are looking for at an electronics store. Then circle any items on the lists that are the same.
1. Busco unos DVDs.
2. Busco unos CDs.
3. Busco un reproductor de CDs.
4. Busco un quemador de CDs.
5. Busco una computadora.
6. Busco un equipo de sonido.
7. Busco un reproductor de MP3.
8. Busco unos DVDs.
9. Busco unos CDs.
10. Busco una impresora láser.

16. Las actividades de Javier la semana que viene. Selecciona la letra de la foto que corresponde con lo que oyes.
1. El lunes tengo práctica de tenis.
2. El martes voy a llevar al perro a caminar al parque.
3. El miércoles tengo que estudiar para un examen de historia.

4. El jueves voy a llamar a mis abuelos.

5. El viernes voy a montar en bicicleta.

6. El sábado voy a hacer la maleta para mi viaje a Puntarenas.

21. ¿Cuándo? Marta dice lo que tiene que hacer. Indica el día en que va a hacerlo, según el diálogo.

1. Tengo práctica de fútbol.

2. Voy a hacer un viaje.

3. Voy a estudiar para el examen de biología.

4. Voy a la librería.

5. Tengo práctica de tenis.

22. Las actividades de Tomás. Escribe en una hoja de papel lo que vas a escuchar.

El lunes voy a la tienda a buscar un disco compacto. Busco el CD de Alejandro Sanz. El martes voy a clase de piano en un edificio en el centro. El miércoles voy a montar en bicicleta con un compañero en el parque. El fin de semana que viene voy de viaje.

CAPÍTULO 5 (LECCIÓN B)

1. ¿Qué día es? Escoge una respuesta correcta a cada pregunta que escuchas.

1. Hoy es el primero de enero. ¿Qué día es hoy?

2. Hoy es miércoles y pasado mañana voy de compras. ¿Qué día voy de compras?

3. Hoy es lunes y mi cumpleaños fue anteayer. ¿Cuándo fue mi cumpleaños?

4. Ayer fue viernes y mañana es el cumpleaños de mi tía. ¿Qué día es su cumpleaños?

5. Hoy es mi día favorito. Es Navidad. ¿Cuál es la fecha?

6. ¿Cuál es la respuesta? Escoge una respuesta correcta a lo que escuchas.

1. Yo tengo dieciséis años. Mi hermano Javier tiene doce. ¿Qué es Javier?

2. Mi cumpleaños es pasado mañana y hoy es martes. ¿Qué día es mi cumpleaños?

3. Mi hermano mayor viene el día de Noche Vieja. ¿En qué fecha viene?

4. Mi hermano tiene veinticinco años. Yo tengo diecisiete. ¿Qué soy yo?

5. Hoy jueves es mi cumpleaños, pero voy a celebrar mañana. ¿Cuándo voy a celebrar?

6. Hoy es el veinticinco de diciembre. ¿Qué día es hoy?

14. ¿Cuándo cumplen años? Selecciona la letra de la fecha que corresponde con lo que escuchas.

1. Mi cumpleaños es el doce de noviembre.

2. El dos de marzo es mi cumpleaños.

3. Mario y yo cumplimos años el veintitrés de enero.

4. Cumplo años el veinte de mayo.

5. Mi cumpleaños fue el dieciséis de junio.

6. Nuestro cumpleaños es el treinta de agosto.

19. ¡Feliz cumpleaños, Sergio! Di si lo que oyes es cierto o falso, según el Diálogo II. Si es falso, corrige la información.

1. Hoy es el veinticinco de octubre.

2. ¡Hoy es el cumpleaños de Sergio!

3. Sergio es viejo.

4. Sergio cumple veintisiete años.

5. En dos meses llega la Navidad.

6. A Darío no le gusta la idea de la Navidad ni un poquito.

CAPÍTULO 6 (LECCIÓN A)

1. ¿Qué tenemos que hacer en la cocina? Selecciona la ilustración que corresponde con lo que oyes.

1. ¿Por qué no enciendes el lavaplatos?

2. Debes cerrar la puerta del refrigerador.

3. ¿Por qué no enciendes la lámpara del comedor?

4. Debes poner la mesa del comedor con aquellos platos.

5. ¿Por qué no enciendes la estufa?

6. Debes poner la mesa con aquellas servilletas.

5. ¿Qué hacen para ayudar? Mira las palabras de la lista. Di la que corresponde con lo que oyes.

1. Tu cuarto tiene buena luz.
2. Tu comida está fría aquí.
3. Tu comida está caliente aquí.
4. Tus platos están limpios aquí.
5. Tu plato con comida está aquí.
6. Tu refresco está aquí.

15. ¿Qué necesitas?

Di lo que necesitas para hacer lo que oyes.

MODELO Para tomar sopa.

1. Para poner mantequilla en el pan.
2. Para tomar agua.
3. Para comer el postre.
4. Para tomar café o té.
5. Para comer la ensalada.
6. Para tomar jugo.

21. Yo necesito…. Selecciona la letra de la frase que completa lógicamente cada oración que oyes.

1. Para comer pescado y una ensalada, voy a necesitar un….
2. Para la sopa, necesito….
3. No quiero café, gracias. Prefiero un vaso….
4. Por favor, pásame las….
5. Voy a poner los platos en….
6. Voy a poner un poco de mantequilla….
7. Necesito la pimienta y la….
8. Para la mesa voy a necesitar un….

CAPÍTULO 6 (LECCIÓN B)

1. Dictado. Escucha la información y escribe lo que oyes.

Hola papás,

¿Qué tal? Escribo desde Cartagena. Cartagena es una ciudad muy bonita e interesante. Cada día le gusta más a Daniela la idea de vivir aquí, pero también le gustaría vivir con Uds. en Caracas.

La casa del primo Julián es muy cómoda. Aquí va el dibujo de la casa donde vive él. Entramos en la casa por una puerta en el patio. El cuarto de Daniela está al lado de la cocina.

Tiene unas ventanas pequeñas. Yo estoy en el cuarto de Julián. Cuando yo estoy aburrido, voy a la sala a ver televisión. Por las noches siempre comemos en el patio.

El tío dice que en dos semanas vamos a ir a Barranquilla. Vamos a pasar siete u ocho días allí en la casa de su tía Isabel. Allá vamos a aprender a montar a caballo. Tenemos muchas ganas de ir.

A Daniela no le gusta escribir cartas. Entonces, ella los va a llamar por teléfono en estos días.
Un abrazo,
Santiago

7. ¿Está en la casa, en el colegio o en el parque? Di dónde están las siguientes personas según lo que oyes.

1. Veo televisión en la sala con mis padres.
2. Rodrigo habla con su profesora de historia, en la planta baja.
3. Mi profesor de español lee un libro en el cuarto de su hija.
4. Allí patina sobre ruedas Esperanza con sus amigas todos los sábados.
5. La Sra. Durán prepara la comida en la cocina al lado del garaje.
6. Pedrito juega con su perro en el patio que está al lado de la piscina.
7. Natalia toma un refresco en la cafetería del primer piso.
8. Rafael limpia el baño del cuarto de sus padres.

18. ¿Cierto o falso? Di si lo que oyes es cierto o falso, según la información en el *Vocabulario II*. Si es falso, di lo que es cierto.

1. Nicolás no tiene sueño.
2. Mateo tiene ganas de correr.
3. El abuelo dice que tiene calor.
4. Los tíos dicen que tienen frío.
5. Verónica tiene mucha hambre.
6. Cristina tiene prisa.

22. ¿Qué tienen? Selecciona la ilustración apropiada que corresponde con lo que oyes.

1. Ellas tienen frío.
2. Tienen hambre.

3. Ella tiene calor.

4. Él tiene ganas de correr.

5. Tengo sed.

6. ¿Tienes sueño?

HUGO: ¿Cuánto tiempo hace que no ves una película?

LUZ: ¡Uy! Hace mucho tiempo. Casi dos meses.

HUGO: ¡Entonces no vas a ver las mismas películas!

CAPÍTULO 7 (LECCIÓN A)

1. ¿Qué actividad es? Identifica la actividad que oyes.

1. Vamos a jugar al básquetbol.

2. Vamos a jugar al fútbol americano.

3. Vamos a jugar al ajedrez.

4. Vamos a jugar al béisbol.

5. Vamos a jugar a las cartas.

6. Vamos a jugar al voleibol.

5. ¿Qué comprendiste? Di si lo que oyes es cierto o falso, según el diálogo *¿No quieres jugar al ajedrez?*

1. Luz quiere jugar al tenis.

2. Hugo mira una telenovela en la televisión.

3. Hugo no quiere jugar al ajedrez.

4. Luz no recuerda cómo jugar al ajedrez.

5. Los chicos juegan a videojuegos.

13. El tiempo libre. Selecciona la ilustración que corresponde con lo que oyes.

1. Es tarde.

2. Está durmiendo.

3. Hace una hora que está viendo televisión.

4. Quiere alquilar una película nueva.

17. Dictado
Escucha la información y escribe lo que oyes.

HUGO: ¿Estás durmiendo?

LUZ: No. Estoy viendo televisión. ¿Por qué?

HUGO: Porque quiero ir a alquilar una película.

LUZ: ¿Ahora mismo?

HUGO: Sí, quiero ir antes de comer. ¿Quieres ir?

LUZ: Un segundo.... Ya voy.

LUZ: No quiero ver las mismas películas otra vez.

CAPÍTULO 7 (LECCIÓN B)

1. Las estaciones. Escoge la estación correcta, según lo que oyes.

1. Hace frío y puedes patinar sobre hielo.

2. Hay flores por todos lados y llueve mucho.

3. Hace sol y mucho calor.

4. No hace mucho calor.

5. ¿Qué actividades puedes hacer? Escucha la información y di qué actividad o actividades puedes hacer.

MODELO Es el otoño y hace sol.

1. Es invierno y hace mucho frío.

2. Es verano y hace mucho calor.

3. Es primavera y llueve.

4. Es otoño y no hace calor.

5. Es primavera y hace sol.

16. ¿Quién es? Selecciona la foto de la persona apropiada.

1. Soy tenista.

2. Soy futbolista.

3. Soy esquiadora.

4. Soy patinador.

5. Soy corredora.

6. Soy jugadora de fútbol.

21. ¿Qué tiempo hace? Selecciona la ilustración que corresponde con lo que oyes.

1. Hace calor.

2. Está nublado.

3. Hace viento.

4. Llueve mucho.

5. Hay neblina.

6. Nieva ahora.

CAPÍTULO 8 (LECCIÓN A)

1. ¿Qué tienen que hacer? Write the names Julia and Enrique. Next, listen and list under each of their names what chores each of them has to do. Then circle any items on the lists that they both have to do. The first one has been done for you.

1. Tengo que adornar la sala para la fiesta de cumpleaños de mi tía.
2. Tengo que cocinar el pollo.
3. Tengo que trabajar en el jardín.
4. Tengo que hacer mi cama.
5. Tengo que limpiar la cocina.
6. Tengo que adornar la sala para la fiesta de cumpleaños de mi tía.
7. Tengo que preparar la ensalada.
8. Tengo que doblar la ropa.
9. Tengo que hacer mi cama.
10. Tengo que limpiar la cocina.

6. ¿Me ayudas?
Mira las tres fotos que van con el diálogo y di si lo que oyes va con la primera, la segunda o la tercera foto.
MODELO La Sra. Zea está hablando con Inés y Víctor.

1. Inés le dice a la Sra. Zea que la cocina está limpia.
2. Víctor dice que está haciendo unos quehaceres.
3. Inés está colgando su abrigo.
4. La cocina ya está limpia.
5. Víctor le dice a Inés que tiene que terminar de limpiar la casa.

19. Los quehaceres. Selecciona la foto de la persona que corresponda con lo que oyes.

1. Pasa la aspiradora.
2. Arregla el cuarto.
3. Barre.
4. Lava las ollas.

23. ¿Vais a hacer un quehacer o un deporte? Las siguientes personas van a hablar de sus actividades de hoy. Di si lo que oyes es *un quehacer* o *un deporte*.

1. Hola. Me llamo Tomás. Voy a jugar al fútbol hoy.
2. Soy Ramón. Tengo que pasar la aspiradora por la sala hoy.
3. Me llamo Roberto. Voy a lavar las ollas esta noche para ayudar a mis padres.
4. Hola. Yo soy Verónica. Voy con unos amigos a esquiar.
5. Me llamo Margarita. Voy a buscar leche y pan en la tienda hoy.

CAPÍTULO 8 (LECCIÓN B)

1. En el supermercado. Selecciona la ilustración que corresponde con lo que oyes.

1. Los aguacates parecen muy maduros.
2. Los tomates están frescos.
3. Aquellos son los mejores pimientos.
4. Necesitamos el ingrediente más importante, el ajo.
5. Éstos son los peores guisantes.
6. Voy a llevar un kilo de pescado.

5. ¿Qué les hace falta? Di la letra de la ilustración que identifica lo que les hace falta comprar a las siguientes personas, según lo que oyes.

1. Ayer compré el pollo. Me hace falta comprar un kilo de arroz.
2. A nosotros nos hace falta comprar unas cebollas.
3. Yo necesito comprar una lechuga para la ensalada.
4. A mi madre le hace falta comprar unos pimientos y una lata de tomates.
5. Yo tengo todas las verduras, sólo me hace falta comprar un pollo.

20. En el mercado. Selecciona la ilustración que corresponde con lo que oyes.

1. Les di las mejores manzanas.
2. ¿A qué precio tiene las habichuelas?
3. Ayer estuve en el mercado y compré fresas.
4. Las zanahorias están a un euro el kilo.
5. Éstas son las mejores naranjas.
6. Este maíz es tan bueno como aquel maíz.

25. ¿Qué comprendiste?
Escucha lo que dicen las personas del diálogo *Comprando chorizo* y di si lo que oyes es cierto o falso. Corrige lo que no es cierto.

1. Ayer estuve con Víctor en el supermercado.
2. Compramos los ingredientes para hacer una ensalada.
3. Quiero comprar queso.
4. El chorizo del supermercado no me gusta.
5. Este es el peor supermercado de la ciudad.
6. El chorizo está a € 4,00 el kilo.

CAPÍTULO 9 (LECCIÓN A)

1. Comprando ropa. Selecciona la ilustración que corresponde con lo que oyes.

1. Quiero una blusa de seda rosada.
2. Busco una corbata morada.
3. Necesito unas botas marrones.
4. Busco un traje de baño anaranjado.
5. Quiero un pijama de algodón azul.
6. Necesito un vestido verde.

6. ¿Cuál prefieres? Selecciona la letra de la ilustración que corresponde con lo que las siguientes personas prefieren.

1. Prefiero el traje negro.
2. El negro no me gusta. Prefiero el marrón.
3. Prefiero los zapatos bajos.
4. Prefiero la camisa morada.
5. La morada no me gusta ni un poquito. Prefiero la anaranjada.
6. Yo prefiero los zapatos de tacón.
7. Prefiero el vestido rosado.
8. Prefiero las medias azules.

20. ¿Qué es? Escribe el artículo de ropa que oyes.

> **MODELO** Me gustó el sombrero rojo.

1. Preferí los guantes negros.
2. Quiero comprar un abrigo de lana.
3. Voy a buscar una chaqueta nueva.
4. Necesitas un impermeable porque va a llover.
5. ¿Llevas tu suéter de algodón?
6. Escogí el pantalón verde.

25. ¿Cuándo? Listen carefully to statements made by several people. Indicate whether each sentence you hear is in the past (*pretérito*) or in the present (*presente*).

1. ¿Te conté que ayer fui a una tienda por departamentos?
2. Puedes comprar ese abrigo nuevo, si quieres.
3. No me queda ninguno de lana.
4. Te prometí llevarte al centro comercial ayer, ¿verdad?
5. Te compré algo nuevo.
6. No quiero ni la chaqueta ni el impermeable.
7. Es un suéter para tus vacaciones.

CAPÍTULO 9 (LECCIÓN B)

1. ¿Qué les gustaría recibir de regalo? Selecciona la letra de la ilustración que corresponde con lo que oyes.

1. A mí me gustaría recibir una billetera.
2. A mí me gustaría recibir una pulsera de oro.
3. De regalo, a mí me gustaría recibir un paraguas.
4. Yo quiero recibir de regalo unos aretes de plata.
5. Yo quiero recibir un cinturón de cuero.
6. A mí me gustaría recibir un anillo de oro.

6. Bueno, bonito y barato. Selecciona la letra de la ilustración que corresponde con lo que buscan las siguientes personas.

1. Busco un bolsito de material sintético barato.
2. Busco una bufanda larga para usar todos los días.

3. Busco un paraguas bueno, bonito y barato.
4. Buscamos unos pañuelos de seda.
5. Busco un collar y unos aretes de perlas.
6. Buscamos una chaqueta de cuero corta.

18. ¿Cuál es la respuesta correcta? Escoge la letra de la respuesta correcta a lo que oyes.
1. ¿Cómo va a pagar?
2. ¿Quieres venir conmigo a la tienda?
3. ¿Qué necesito para cambiar este paraguas?
4. ¿Cuánto es mi cambio?
5. ¿Te gusta la calidad de la blusa?
6. ¿Es caro el collar?

22. ¿Sí o no? ¿Son lógicos los diálogos? Corrige lo que no es lógico.
1. ¿Cuánto cuesta el perfume?
   Cuesta veinte dólares.
2. ¿Está en oferta el perfume?
   Sí, es muy caro.
3. ¿Cómo va a pagar?
   Voy a pagar con recibos.
4. Aquí tiene su recibo y dos dólares de cambio.
   No, no lo voy a cambiar.
5. ¿Cómo puedo ahorrar dinero?
   Puedes ahorrar dinero si compras lo barato.

CAPÍTULO 10 (LECCIÓN A)

3. ¡Fue un año divertido! Di si lo que oyes es cierto o falso, según el Diálogo I. Si es falso, corrige la información.
1. Silvia dijo que el año fue muy aburrido.
2. Mario dijo que le gusta la historia.
3. Silvia dijo que le gusta la geografía.
4. Mario dijo que no le gusta la biología.

CAPÍTULO 10 (LECCIÓN B)

3. ¿Quién dijo qué? ¿Quién dijo lo siguiente, Inés o Luis?
1. Tuve que ayudar a mis padres.
2. Vamos a ir a las ruinas de Tikal.
3. Fui a Tikal el año pasado.
4. Me gustaría ir a California.
5. Pienso que debes ir a California.

Navegando 1

Authors

James F. Funston

Alejandro Vargas Bonilla

Contributing Writers

Belia Jiménez Lorente

Karin Fajardo

Rolando Castellanos

Consultants

Paul J. Hoff
University of Wisconsin—Eau Claire
Eau Claire, Wisconsin

Anne Marie Quihuis
Paradise Valley High School
Phoenix, Arizona

Heidi Oshima
Parsippany High School
Parsippany, New Jersey

Ana Selvás Watson
Henrico High School
Richmond, Virginia

Marne Patana
Middle Creek High School
Apex, North Carolina

Nancy Wrobel
Champlin Park High School
Champlin Park, Minnesota

EMCParadigm Publishing, Saint Paul, Minnesota

CREDITS

Editorial Consultants
Judy Cohen
Lori Coleman
Sharon O'Donnell
David Thorstad
Sarah Vaillancourt

Readers
Pat Cotton
Mónica Domínguez
Barbara Forney
Daniela Guzmán
Charisse Littiken
Barbara Peterson
Roy Sweezy
Beth Verdin

Proofreaders
Susana Petit
Mercedes Roffé
Gilberto Vázquez

Illustrators
Kristen Copham
Len Ebert
Tune Insisiengmay

Susan Jaekel
Nedo Kojic
Paul Mirocha
Hetty Mitchel
D.J. Simison

Photo Research
Jennifer Anderson

Design
Interior Design: Tina Widzbor,
Monotype Composition
Cover Design: Suzanne Montazer and
Ken Croghan, Monotype Composition

Cover Photo
Mónica Béjar Latonda

Production
Precision Graphics
Matthias Frasch, scan technician

We have attempted to locate owners of
copyright materials used in this book.
If an error or omission has occurred,
EMC/Paradigm Publishing will acknowledge
the contribution in subsequent printings.

ISBN 0-8219-2798-1

© 2005 EMC Corporation

Published by EMC/Paradigm Publishing
875 Montreal Way
St. Paul, Minnesota 55102
800-328-1452
www.emcp.com
Email: educate@emcp.com

Printed in the United States of America
2 3 4 5 6 7 8 9 10 X X X 08 07 06 05 04

¡Saludos!

You are about to embark on a journey that will take you to many countries and that will open doors you may never have imagined. Whether you are drawn to Spanish because of your interest in travel or your desire to learn how to communicate with others, this year offers you rewarding possibilities as you navigate your way through the Spanish-speaking world. This sense of real-life adventure and travel is reflected in the covers of the *Navegando* series.

Learning a language has always meant more than merely memorizing words and grammar rules and then putting them together, hoping to actually be able to communicate. Just as language is inseparable from culture, so is it inseparable from the authentic communication of thoughts and emotions. The culture of the Spanish-speaking world varies from one country to another. In *Navegando,* you will navigate your way, learning about others while at the same time learning how to share your ideas and feelings. These real-life learning experiences will introduce you to and expand your knowledge of language, geography, history and the arts. In *Navegando* you will learn not only fascinating information, but also problem-solving, survival and employment skills so that when you leave the classroom you can step right into the real world.

Are you ready to learn to use Spanish in the real world? Experience the authentic: *Navegando.*

Contents

MAPA
La lengua españ

VO GLACIAL ÁRTICO

LANDIA

26
27
28
BIELORRUSIA

UCRANIA
29
UMANIA
BULGARIA
9
ECIA
TURQUÍA
30 32
31
CHIPRE 21
SIRIA
ISRAEL IRAK
Jerusalem 22
EGIPTO
ARABIA
SAUDITA
25
QATAR
EMIRATOS
ÁRABES UNIDOS
OMÁN
YEMEN
ERITREA
SUDÁN
36
REP.
NTRO-
CANA
ETIOPÍA
SOMALIA
ÚBLICA
UGANDA
CRÁTICA
KENYA
37
38
CONGO
TANZANIA
MALAWI
ZAMBIA
ZIMBABWE
GWANA
MOZAMBIQUE
MADAGASCAR
24
23
CANA

RUSIA

KAZAJSTÁN
UZBEKISTÁN 33
TURKMENISTAN 34
AFGANISTÁN
IRÁN
PAKISTÁN
NEPAL
BHUTAN
BANGLA-
DESH
INDIA
BIRMANIA
VIETNAM
LAOS
THAILANDIA
CAMBOYA
BRUNEI
MALASIA
SINGAPUR
SRI LANKA
MALDIVAS

MONGOLIA

COREA
DEL NORTE
REP. POP. CHINA
COREA
DEL SUR

JAPÓN

TAIWÁN

Manila
FILIPINAS
REP. DE PALAOS

INDONESIA

PAPÚA
NUEVA GUINEA
SALOMÓN

SEYCHELLES
COMORES
MAURICIO

OCÉANO
ÍNDICO

Trópico de Capricornio

Alaska
(EE.UU.)

OCÉANO

PACÍFICO

40°

AUSTRALIA

NUEVA

ZELANDA
40°

Línea internacional
de cambio de hora

UNDI
la en el mundo

AL ANTÁRTICO

ÁRTIDA

	Países donde el español es la lengua oficial o co-oficial	**Madrid**	Ciudad de más de 1 millón de hab.
		Panamá	Ciudad de 100.000 a 1 millón de hab.
		Malabo	Ciudad de menos de 100.000 hab.
	Zonas donde el español es hablado por una parte de la población		Límite de Estado
		▪	Capital de Estado
		●	Otras ciudades

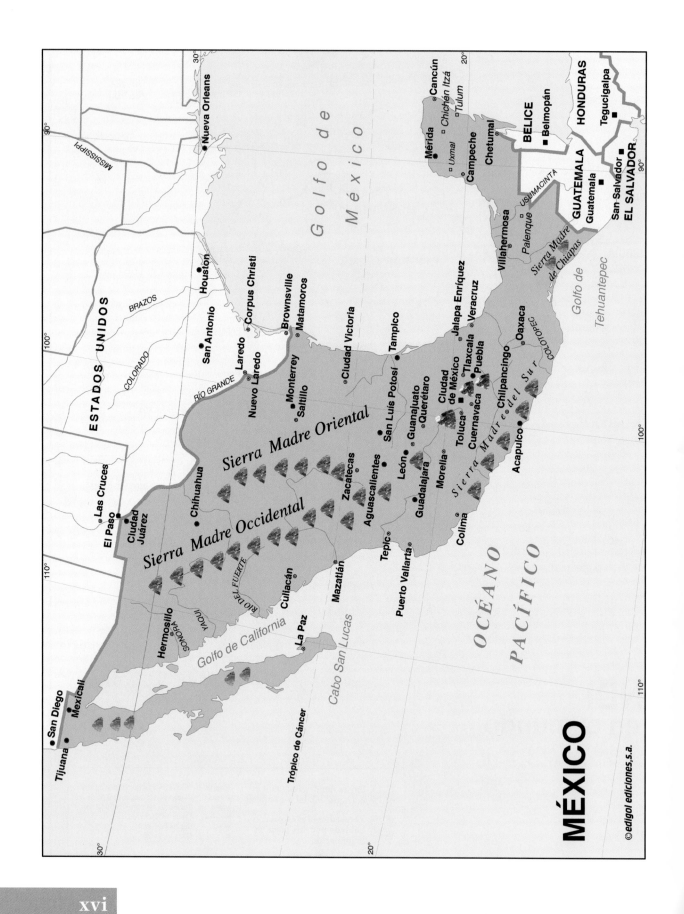

MÉXICO

© edigol ediciones, s.a.

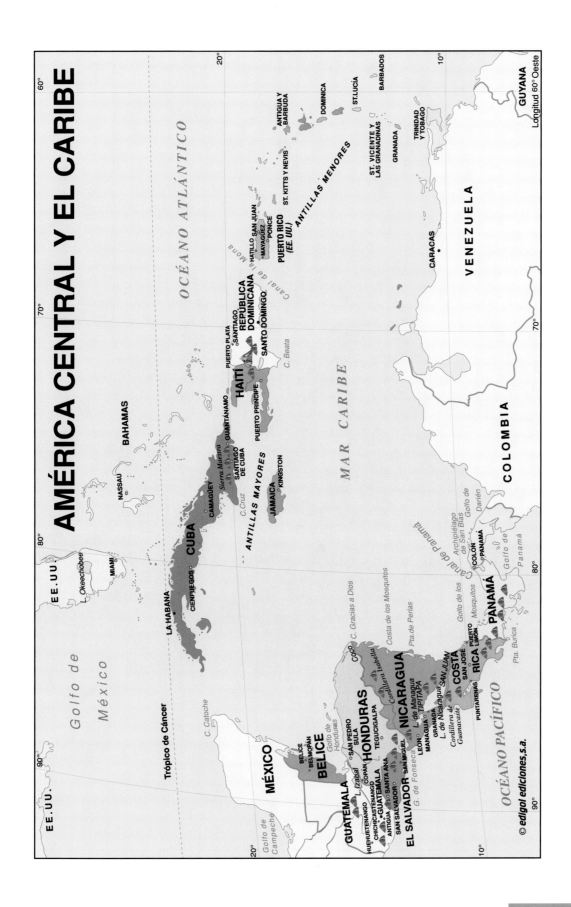

AMÉRICA CENTRAL Y EL CARIBE

© edigol ediciones, s.a.

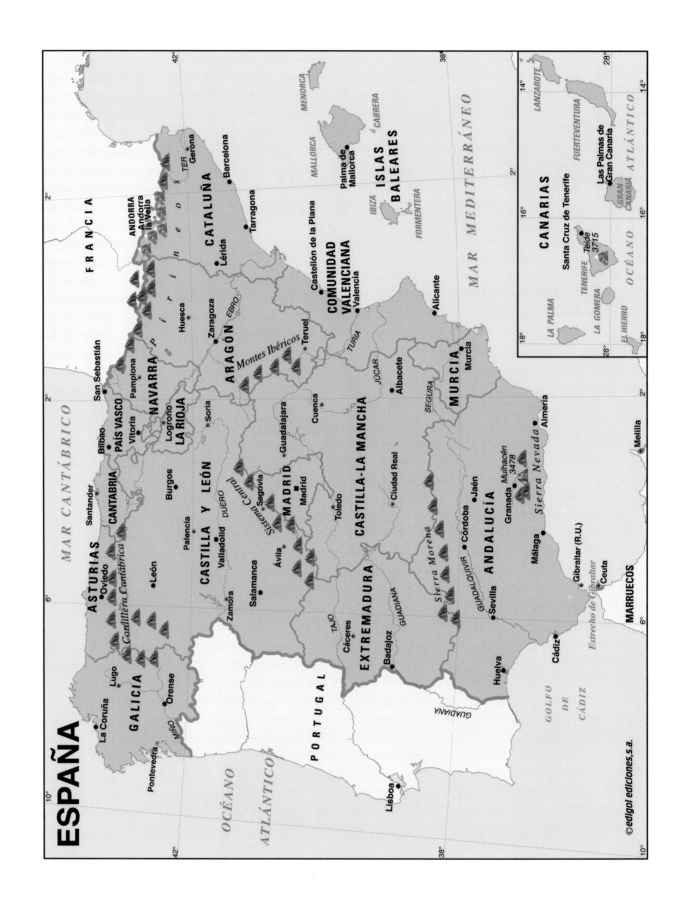

ESPAÑA

FRANCIA

MAR CANTÁBRICO

OCÉANO ATLÁNTICO

GALICIA
La Coruña
Lugo
Pontevedra
Orense
MIÑO

ASTURIAS
Oviedo
Cordillera Cantábrica

CANTABRIA
Santander

PAÍS VASCO
Bilbao
San Sebastián
Vitoria

NAVARRA
Pamplona

LA RIOJA
Logroño
Soria

CASTILLA Y LEÓN
León
Palencia
Burgos
Zamora
Valladolid
DUERO
Salamanca
Ávila
Segovia

MADRID
Madrid
Sistema Central

ARAGÓN
Huesca
Zaragoza
EBRO
Teruel
Montes Ibéricos

CATALUÑA
Gerona
Barcelona
TER
Lérida
Tarragona

ANDORRA
Andorra
la Vella

P i r i n e o s

COMUNIDAD VALENCIANA
Castellón de la Plana
Valencia
Alicante
TURIA
JÚCAR

CASTILLA-LA MANCHA
Guadalajara
Cuenca
Toledo
Ciudad Real
Albacete

TAJO

EXTREMADURA
Cáceres
Badajoz
GUADIANA

PORTUGAL
Lisboa

MURCIA
Murcia
SEGURA

ANDALUCÍA
Córdoba
Jaén
Sevilla
GUADALQUIVIR
Sierra Morena
Granada
Mulhacén 3478
Sierra Nevada
Almería
Málaga
Huelva
Cádiz
Gibraltar (R.U.)
Ceuta
Estrecho de Gibraltar
GUADIANA

GOLFO DE CÁDIZ

MARRUECOS
Melilla

MAR MEDITERRÁNEO

MENORCA
MALLORCA
Palma de Mallorca
IBIZA
CABRERA
FORMENTERA
ISLAS BALEARES

OCÉANO ATLÁNTICO

CANARIAS
LANZAROTE
FUERTEVENTURA
Las Palmas de Gran Canaria
GRAN CANARIA
Santa Cruz de Tenerife
Teide 3715
TENERIFE
LA GOMERA
LA PALMA
EL HIERRO
OCÉANO ATLÁNTICO

10° 6° 2° 38° 42° 28° 16° 14° 18°

© edigol ediciones, s.a.

AMÉRICA DEL SUR

80°

MAR CARIBE
G. de Venezuela
BARRANQUILLA
MARACAIBO   CARACAS
CARTAGENA
L. de
Maracaibo
Delta del
Orinoco
MÉRIDA
VENEZUELA
GEORGETOWN
BUCARAMANGA
ARAUCA
ORINOCO
PARAMARIBO
GUYANA
MEDELLÍN
SURINAM
CAYENA
BOGOTÁ, D.C.
CALI
VILLAVICENCIO
GUAYANA
FRANCESA
(Fra.)
MAGDALENA
PASTO
COLOMBIA
QUITO
Estuario del
Amazonas
ECUADOR
Cotopaxi
5896
Ecuador
GUAYAQUIL
Chimborazo
6267
CAQUETÁ
AMAZONAS
Golfo de
Guayaquil
CUENCA
IQUITOS
AMAZONAS
Pta. Negra
PERÚ
B R A S I L
FORTALEZA
CHICLAYO
Los Andes
TRUJILLO
RECIFE
CALLAO
Machu Picchu
SAN FRANCISCO
LIMA
CUZCO
ICA
JULIACA
L. Titicaca
SALVADOR
LA PAZ   BOLIVIA
COCHABAMBA
BRASILIA
ARICA
L. de Poopó
SUCRE
POTOSÍ
PARAGUAY
BELO HORIZONTE
0°
O C É A N O
Gran Chaco
PARAGUAY
PARANÁ
Trópico de Capricornio   ANTOFAGASTA
CONCEPCIÓN
PILCOMAYO
Itaipú
SÃO PAULO
PACÍFICO
Los Andes
ASUNCIÓN
Cataratas
del Iguazú
RÍO DE JANEIRO
20
SAN MIGUEL
DE TUCUMÁN
PARAGUAY
RESISTENCIA
URUGUAY
CORRIENTES
C H I L E
ARGENTINA
Aconcagua
6959
CÓRDOBA
URUGUAY
SAN JUAN
PARANÁ
SALTO
IS. JUAN FERNÁNDEZ
(Chile)
MENDOZA
PARANÁ
URUGUAY
VIÑA DEL MAR
VALPARAÍSO
SALADO
ROSARIO
BUENOS
AIRES
URUGUAY
O C É A N O
SANTIAGO
DE CHILE
Pampas
LA PLATA
MONTEVIDEO
TALCA
RÍO DE LA PLATA
A T L Á N T I C O
CONCEPCIÓN
COLORADO
Pta. Norte
BAHÍA BLANCA
NEUQUÉN
NEGRO
MAR DEL PLATA
VALDIVIA
Los Andes
SAN CARLOS DE
BARILOCHE
PUERTO
MONTT
Patagonia
C. Tres Puntas
Golfo de Penas
Bahía
Grande
ISLAS MALVINAS (R.U.)
Estr. de Magallanes
PUERTO STANLEY
TIERRA DEL
FUEGO
GEORGIA DEL SUR (R.U.)
PUNTA ARENAS
USHUAIA
Cabo de Hornos
Estr. de Drake

OCÉANO
ATLÁNTICO

60°

40°

©edigol ediciones,s.a.

Gente

Un día de fiesta en Oaxaca, México.

Susana es de Chile.

Bailan el tango.

¡Vamos a esquiar!

Unos amigos en un café.

Un gaucho argentino.

Carlos vive en Bogotá, Colombia.

Puertorriqueños en Nueva York.

Ellos van en bicicleta.

¡Jugamos al fútbol!

¡Somos del Perú!

Hernán es de España.

Somos de Bolivia.

Una fiesta en Quito, Ecuador.

Unos chicos en San Juan, Puerto Rico.

Soy de Cuba.

Lugares

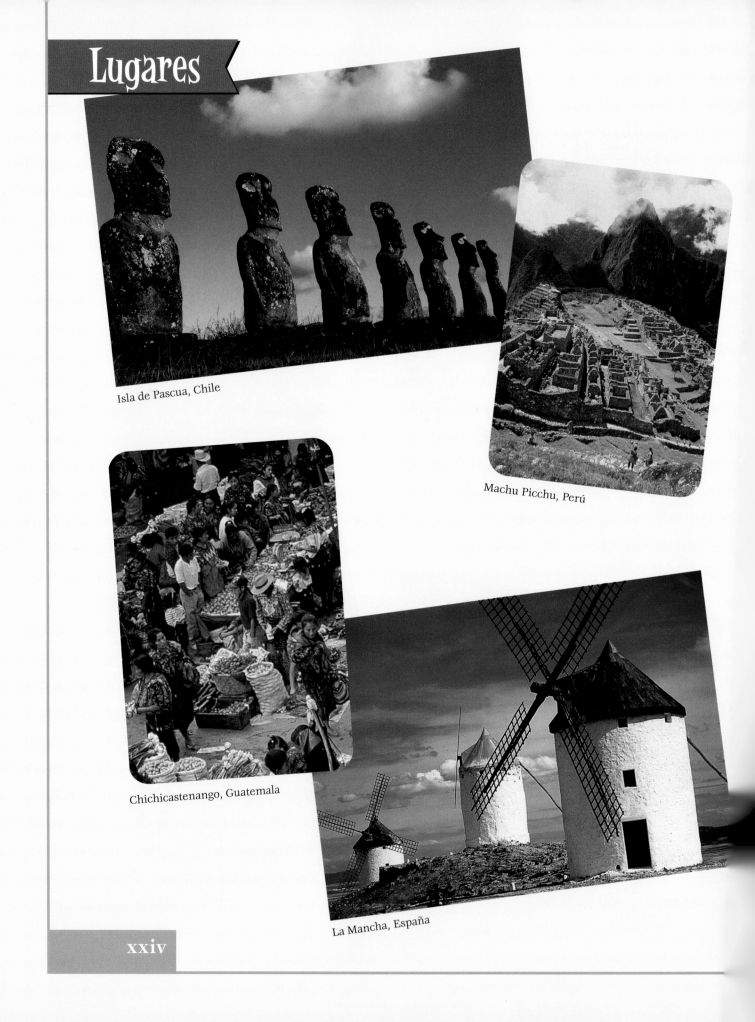

Isla de Pascua, Chile

Machu Picchu, Perú

Chichicastenango, Guatemala

La Mancha, España

Ciudad de Panamá, Panamá

La Paz, Bolivia

PROVINCIA DE
TIERRA DEL FUEGO
ANTARTIDA E ISLAS
DEL ATLANTICO SUR

USHUAIA

Tierra del Fuego,
Argentina

Parque Nacional los Glaciares, Argentina

Amazonas, Colombia

Isla de Roatán, Honduras

Festival de teatro en Bogotá, Colombia

Buenos Aires, Argentina

Ciudad de México

Catedral de la Sagrada Familia, Barcelona, España

El Castillo de San Felipe del Morro, Puerto Rico

Volcán Arenal, Costa Rica

onnections with Parents

Encouraging parents/guardians to become involved in what their children are learning in Spanish class will help to improve chances for student success. The margins of the Annotated Teacher's Edition (ATE) provide suggestions and reminders for establishing and maintaining good parental/guardian support. For example, during the first few days of class, you might wish to send a letter home explaining objectives and expectations for the course.

Activities

Critical Thinking

The photographs that appear on the opening pages of a chapter depict the functions, cultural setting and themes to be explored. These authentic materials serve to further student awareness of how Spanish is used outside the classroom. Try to employ these supportive visuals on a regular basis. Ask students about any similarities and differences they observe and what conclusions they can draw from the information.

Capítulo 1

¿Cómo te llamas?

Objetivos

❖ ask for and give names

❖ ask or tell where someone is from

❖ ask for and state age

❖ greet people and say good-bye

❖ ask and tell how someone is feeling

❖ express courtesy

❖ ask for and state the time

Visit the web-based activities at www.emcp.com

Notes Icons in the side margins of the ATE indicate components with additional activities to reinforce and expand upon the content taught in *Navegando*. These icons are explained in the ATE Introduction.

Functional and communicative objectives are provided at the start of each chapter to prepare students for the chapter they are about to begin. A list of these functions appears at the end of each chapter so students can evaluate their progress.

Contexto cultural

El mundo hispano
Spanish is the official language of Spain, eighteen Latin American countries, Ecuatorial Guinea and Puerto Rico. Although many more use Spanish daily for both business and pleasure, more than 450 million people throughout the world consider Spanish as their official language.

uno 1

Notes Students acquire new material in a variety of ways and at different speeds. Numerous activities in the left and right margins of this ATE have been provided to address students' multiple intelligences and to help meet the needs of individuals who require additional help in order to reach their maximum potential. Related activities can be found in the *Navegando* ancillaries.

The city shown in the small photograph is La Paz. The large photograph shows several girls in traditional dress in Oaxaca, Mexico.

¿Cómo te llamas?
El alfabeto

 Activity 1

 Activity 11

 Activities 1–2

 Activities 1–2

 Activity 1

Activities

Critical Thinking
Have students point out the letters that are not in the English alphabet: *ñ* and *rr*.

Pronunciation *(el alfabeto)*
Point out that words that begin with the letters *k* and *w* are foreign. Examples of *k* words include *kiosko* and *kilómetro*.

TPR
Use this TPR (Total Physical Response) activity to practice the alphabet: Tell students that you are going to call out letters and that if the letter you call appears in their first or last name, they should stand up as quickly as possible. The first student to stand when a letter from his or her name is called gets a point.

Lección A

El mundo hispanohablante

Vocabulario I
¿Cómo te llamas?

Hasta luego, Susana.

Adiós, Marcos.

Me llamo Raúl.

¡Hola! ¿Cómo te llamas?

Me llamo Juan. ¿Y tú?

¡Mucho gusto!

Yo me llamo Ana.

¿Cómo se escribe Hernán? ¿Con hache?

Sí, con hache mayúscula, e, ere, ene, a con acento, ene.

El alfabeto

a	a	ñ	eñe
b	be	o	o
c	ce	p	pe
d	de	q	cu
e	e	r	ere
f	efe	rr	erre
g	ge	s	ese
h	hache	t	te
i	i	u	u
j	jota	v	ve
k	ka	w	doble ve
l	ele	x	equis
m	eme	y	i griega
n	ene	z	zeta

H → mayúscula
h → minúscula

Notes Another word for *alfabeto* is *abecedario*. Several letters have different names in different parts of the Spanish-speaking world. For example, the letter *w* may become *doble v, v doble, doble u* or *uve doble*.

It is interesting to note that the Association of Spanish Language Academies met in Madrid for its annual conference in April of 1994 and voted to eliminate the letters *ch* and *ll* from the Spanish alphabet.

Inform students that a letter may be *mayúscula (A)* or *minúscula (a)*. In addition to teaching a letter *con acento (á)*, you may wish to teach *con tilde (ñ)*.

1 ¿Cómo se escribe?

 Escribe los nombres que oyes.

MODELO Carlos

muchachos

Alberto	Ernesto	José	Ramón
Alejandro	Esteban	Juan	Raúl
Andrés	Felipe	Julio	Ricardo
Ángel	Francisco	Lorenzo	Roberto
Antonio	Gerardo	Luis	Rodrigo
Benjamín	Guillermo	Marcos	Rogelio
Carlos	Héctor	Martín	Santiago
Daniel	Hernán	Miguel	Timoteo
David	Hugo	Nicolás	Tomás
Diego	Jaime	Pablo	Víctor
Eduardo	Jesús	Pedro	
Enrique	Jorge	Rafael	

muchachas

Alicia	Dolores	Laura	Pilar
Ana	Elena	Luisa	Raquel
Ángela	Elisa	Luz	Rosa
Bárbara	Esperanza	Margarita	Sandra
Blanca	Eva	María	Sara
Carlota	Gabriela	Marta	Susana
Carmen	Gloria	Mercedes	Teresa
Carolina	Inés	Mónica	Verónica
Catalina	Isabel	Natalia	Virginia
Claudia	Josefina	Patricia	Yolanda
Cristina	Juana	Paula	
Diana	Julia	Paz	

¡Extra!

Los apodos

Nicknames (*apodos*) are common in Spanish. Examples include **Isa** (for *Isabel*), **Fina** or **Pepa** (for *Josefina*), **Lola** (for *Dolores*), **Lupe** (for *Guadalupe*), **Paco** or **Pancho** (for *Francisco*), **Pepe** (for *José*) and **Quique** (for *Enrique*). Personal characteristics are also used for nicknames in Spanish: **Flaco** (Slim).

2 Me llamo....

Write the words *muchacho* and *muchacha* on a piece of paper. In the appropriate column, list any names from activity 1 of people you know. Then, list up to five names of your friends or family and write the name that you think is the Spanish equivalent. Can you find your own name or one that is similar to yours?

3 ¡Mucho gusto!

Contesta las siguientes preguntas. *(Answer the following questions.)*

1. How would you greet someone in Spanish?
2. What would you say to find out a person's name?
3. What would you answer if someone asked *¿Cómo te llamas?*
4. How might you politely tell someone you are pleased to meet him/her?
5. How do you say **Good-bye** in Spanish? And **See you later**?

4 ¿Cómo se escribe?

 With a classmate, read aloud at least five male and five female names from activity 1 as your partner writes the names in Spanish. Next, take turns asking one another how to spell the names on the lists.

MODELO A: ¿Cómo se escribe *(name from list)*?
B: Se escribe con *(spell name)*.
A: ¿*(Spell name)*?
B: Sí.

Capítulo 1   *tres* 3

Teacher Resources

 Los nombres
Activity 1

 Activity 3

 Activities 2–3

Answers

1
1. Ana
2. José
3. María
4. Paz
5. Raúl
6. Verónica

2 Creative self-expression.

3
1. Hola.
2. ¿Cómo te llamas?
3. Me llamo....
4. Mucho gusto.
5. Adiós. Hasta luego.

4 Answers will vary.

Activities

Spanish for Spanish Speakers
For different letters of the alphabet, ask students to think of other Spanish names. Write them on the blackboard under the headings *Muchachas/Muchachos*.

Notes The script for all *Navegando 1* recorded content is provided in the Audio CD Program Manual.

For teacher convenience, student answer sheets have been provided for the activities indicated in the student textbook by the audio speaker icon  (the first activity after *Vocabularios I* and *II* and the third activity after *Diálogos I* and *II*). These reproducible answer sheets can be found at the end of the Audio CD Program Manual.

The section *¡Extra!* offers additional vocabulary, notes, and suggestions to students. It is not required content.

3

Diálogo I

¡Hola!

CARMEN: ¡Hola! ¿Cómo te llamas?
HUGO: Yo me llamo Hugo. ¿Y tú?
CARMEN: Me llamo Carmen.

HUGO: ¡Mucho gusto, Carmen!
CARMEN: ¿Cómo se escribe Hugo?
HUGO: Se escribe con hache mayúscula, u, ge, o.

HUGO: Hasta luego.
CARMEN: Adiós.

5 ¿Qué recuerdas?

Completa las frases de la izquierda con una de las frases de la derecha, según el diálogo *¡Hola!* (*Complete the sentences on the left with the appropriate sentence on the right, according to the dialog ¡Hola!*)

1. ¡Hola! ¿Cómo...   A. ...gusto, Carmen!
2. Yo me...   B. ...te llamas?
3. Me llamo...   C. ...escribe Hugo?
4. ¡Mucho...   D. ...llamo Hugo. ¿Y tú?
5. ¿Cómo se...   E. ...hache mayúscula, u, ge, o.
6. Se escribe con...   F. ...Carmen.

6 Algo personal

1. ¿Cómo te llamas?
2. ¿Cómo se escribe *(your name)*?

7 ¿Cuál es la respuesta correcta?

 Escoge una respuesta correcta a lo que oyes. (*Choose a correct response to what you hear.*)

Adiós.   Me llamo Carmen.

¡Mucho gusto, Carmen!   Sí, con hache.

Notes *Navegando* stresses the use of authentic Spanish. Therefore, vocabulary is introduced in context, along with appropriate cultural notes.

The *Diálogos I* and *II* are intended to apply the vocabulary presented in the *Vocabularios I* and *II*. Students thus have the opportunity to see new words and expressions applied immediately in a functional context with follow-up factual and personal questions for practice.

Dialogs have been recorded by native speakers. The recordings are included in the *Navegando* Audio CD Program.

Cultura viva

Saludos y despedidas

Learning how to speak
Spanish involves more than
just learning vocabulary and
grammar. Gestures *(los gestos)*
go hand in hand with
speaking, which makes
conversation in Spanish seem
much more animated than in
English. Spanish-speaking
people commonly greet one
another with a quick, relaxed handshake,
which may be followed by a hug *(un abrazo)*
as they pat each other on the back. Often
women and young girls greet each other with
a light kiss on the cheek. In some countries,
men and women who know each other well
also greet one another with a kiss on the
cheek (or on both cheeks in Spain). These
same gestures are often repeated when
saying good-bye. The next time you see
people speaking Spanish, watch how they use
their hands, eyes and bodies to communicate.

¡Mucho gusto!

¡Hola!

8 Comparando

In two columns (labeled *Similar* and *Diferente*)
compare how you think the gestures and body
language of a native Spanish speaker are similar to or
different from yours when greeting someone or saying
good-bye.

MODELO

Similar	Diferente
1. We shake hands sometimes.	1. We do not kiss on the cheeks.
2.	2.

Me llamo Juan.

Teacher Resources

 Estrategia

 Activity 5

Activity 3

Answers

9 **A:** ¡Hola!
   B: ¡Hola! ... llamas?
   A: ... ¿Y tú?
   B: *No punctuation is missing.*
   A: ¡Mucho ...!
   B: ¿Con ...?
   A: ... ese.
   B: ..., Inés!

Activities

Cooperative Learning
After practicing the expressions in *Estrategia,* ask students to use the expressions with one another in pairs or in small groups. Select several pairs of students to demonstrate their use at the front of the class.

TPR
Practice the expressions in *Estrategia.* Say several expressions and call on students to respond to your instructions. Observe to see that students respond appropriately.

6

Estructura

Punctuation

¡Mucho gusto!

Have you noticed any punctuation marks in Spanish that are not used in English? Written Spanish requires two question marks and two exclamation points, one at the beginning and the other at the end of the sentence. The first is written upside down and tells you that a question or an exclamation will follow. No other punctuation (e.g., period, comma) follows this pattern.

¡Hola!

Práctica

¿Y tú?

¿Cómo te llamas?

9 Puntuación

Señala la puntuación que falta en el siguiente diálogo. *(Point out the missing punctuation marks in the following dialog.)*

A: Hola!
B: ¡Hola ¿Cómo te llamas
A: Me llamo Inés. Y tú?
B: Yo me llamo Andrés.
A: Mucho gusto, Andrés!
B: Mucho gusto. ¿Cómo se escribe Inés? Con i?
A: Sí, con i mayúscula, ene, e con acento, ese
B: ¡Adiós, Inés

> **Estrategia**
>
> **Learning tip: Recognizing classroom expressions**
> You will see and hear many of the following common expressions. You do not have to memorize them, but learning to recognize them will help you understand instructions and complete activities in class during this school year. Look through the textbook to find examples of these expressions. Do they help you understand instructions?
>
> | | |
> |---|---|
> | *Abre/Abran (el libro).* | Open (your book). |
> | *Busca/Busquen… en la página….* | Look for… on page…. |
> | *Cierra/Cierren (el libro).* | Close (your book). |
> | *Contesta/Contesten….* | Answer…. |
> | *Da/Den….* | Give…. |
> | *Di/Digan….* | Say (or tell)…. |
> | *Escoge/Escojan….* | Choose…. |
> | *Escribe/Escriban….* | Write…. |
> | *Escucha/Escuchen.* | Listen. |
> | *Habla/Hablen en español.* | Speak in Spanish. |
> | *Haz/Hagan….* | Make (or do)…. |
> | *Lee/Lean….* | Read…. |
> | *Levanta/Levanten (la mano).* | Raise (your hand). |
> | *Mira/Miren.* | Look. |
> | *Pasa/Pasen a (la pizarra).* | Go to (the board). |
> | *Responde/Respondan….* | Respond…. |
> | *Saca/Saquen (una hoja de papel).* | Take out (a sheet of paper). |
> | *Señala/Señalen (el mapa).* | Point at (the map). |
> | *Siéntate/Siéntense.* | Sit down. |

Notes Point out to students that learning common classroom expressions will help them function and succeed in Spanish class. In order to demonstrate this, give examples of the expressions listed in *Estrategia.* The word *señala* is used in activity 9, and *haz* is used in activity 10. Ask if students can understand instructions after learning these expressions.

Explain that this list offers two forms of some common expressions. The first form (the singular form before the slash) is used informally for talking with one person who is the students' age or younger, or a close friend or family member, whereas the second form (the plural form after the slash) is used when talking to more than one person.

10 ¿En qué orden?

Haz oraciones lógicas usando las siguientes pistas. *(Make complete sentences using the following cues.)*

MODELO llamo / Me / Alejandro / .
Me llamo Alejandro.

1. ¡ / ! / Hola
2. llamas / ? / te / ¿ / Cómo
3. Carlota / . / llamo / Me / ¿ / tú? / Y
4. Yo / Carlota / Jaime / . / me / gusto, / ! / llamo / ¡Mucho
5. se / ¡Mucho / ¿ / Cómo / Jaime? / gusto / ! / escribe
6. escribe / Se / jota / i, / con / eme, / mayúscula, / a, / e / .

✦ Comunicación

11 A escribir

Imagine you are a scriptwriter for a video that is being produced in Spanish. Write a scene in which two Spanish-speaking teenagers meet. They should: 1) greet one another; 2) ask each other's name and how to spell it; 3) say good-bye. Be sure to add director's notes, where appropriate, suggesting gestures and body language the actors should use.

SCENE ONE: THEY MEET

Boy: Hola. ¿Cómo te llamas?
Girl: Me llamo Claudia.
Boy: Yo me llamo Daniel.
       (They shake hands.)
       Mucho gusto.

Answers

10 1. ¡Hola!
2. ¿Cómo te llamas?
3. Me llamo Carlota. ¿Y tú?
4. Yo me llamo Jaime. ¡Mucho gusto, Carlota!
5. ¡Mucho gusto! ¿Cómo se escribe Jaime?
6. Se escribe con jota mayúscula, a, i, eme, e.

11 Creative writing practice.

Activities

Language through Action
Pair students up and have them play the role of one of the people in the video they wrote for activity 11. Inform students that if they are uncomfortable, they can pretend they are kissing one another on the cheek instead of actually touching one another.

Notes Some of the more common classroom expressions are taught in this lesson. For a complete list of classroom expressions, refer to the ATE Introduction.

Other useful classroom expressions: *¿Cómo se dice...en español?* (How do you say...in Spanish?); *¿Qué quiere decir...?* (What does...mean?); *No sé.* (I don't know.); *No comprendo.* (I don't understand.); *Tengo una pregunta.* (I have a question.)

Teacher Resources

 ¿De dónde eres?
Los números del 0 al 20

 Activities 2–4

 Activity 12

 Activities 6–10

 Activities 4–5

 Activities 4–8

Activities

Critical Thinking

Provide students with blank map outlines of the Spanish-speaking parts of the world (or have students prepare the maps) on which they can write the names of the countries and capitals they know. Extend the activity by having students add the names of non-Spanish-speaking countries and their capitals.

Multiple Intelligences (logical-mathematical)

Help students with conversion rates for different currencies to American dollars.

8 *ocho* **Lección A**

Notes The numbers 21–100 are presented with time on pages 24–25. For students asking for a comprehensive reference list of the numbers, and for teachers wishing to teach all the numbers at once, turn to the Appendices at the back of the book.

Use transparencies or a wall map to show students where Spanish is spoken in the world.

12 Los países

 Practice saying the names of the Spanish-speaking countries you hear. Write the name of each country after it is repeated.

 13 Los números

 In pairs, begin counting with *cero* and continue by twos to *veinte*. Start over, beginning with *uno*, and count by twos to *diecinueve*.

Soy de Honduras.

 14 Del cero al veinte

 Create your own pattern of at least four numbers from zero to twenty. Then with a classmate, read the numbers aloud as your partner writes them down. Next, have your partner spell aloud the numbers from the list while you write them. Compare the lists and make any needed corrections. Switch roles.

> **MODELO** **A:** cinco, diez, quince, veinte
> **B:** *(Write cinco.)*
> **B:** ce, i, ene, ce, o
> **A:** *(Write cinco.)*
> *(Compare the numbers you have written.)*

 15 Una encuesta

 Survey classmates to find out the range of ages in your Spanish class. Begin by preparing a chart. Then ask ten classmates how old they are in Spanish, filling in the blank space with their age and adding a mark in the column underneath for each person who is the same age. Summarize your findings for the class.

Encuesta				
14	15			
\\	\\\			

¿Cuántos años tienes?

Notes *Standards for Foreign Language Learning in the 21st Century* discusses philosophical issues, implications and strategies for maximizing proficiency and for empowering all students to become successful learners and users of world languages. *Navegando* is designed to support and advance the vision described by the authors of the national standards, blending the five Cs of communication, culture, connections, comparisons and communities with pedagogically sound content, fun activities and an ongoing discussion of the wealth of opportunities that learning a world language opens up for students.

Teacher Resources

 Activities 12–13

Answers

12 Check for correct pronunciation.
13 Check pronunciation and make sure students are saying the numbers in the correct order.
14 Numbers will vary. Check for correct pronunciation and spelling.
15 Creative self-expression.

Activities

Connections
Ask students to draw a map of the world without using any reference materials. They should then share their maps with others and discuss the following: What did they draw first? What parts of the world are they most/least familiar with? Where did they put the United States? Is a certain area too large or too small? Which Spanish-speaking areas/countries are included?

Cooperative Learning
Working in groups of three or four, students can practice counting aloud in Spanish from zero to ten, one number at a time. They must continue until everyone has said each number at least once. Have them practice the numbers through twenty in the same way.

Diálogo II

¿De dónde eres, Hugo?

CARMEN: ¿De dónde eres, Hugo?
HUGO: Soy de Bogotá, la capital de Colombia.

HUGO: ¿Y tú? ¿Eres de aquí?
CARMEN: No. Yo soy de México.

CARMEN: ¿Cuántos años tienes, Hugo?
HUGO: Tengo dieciséis años. ¿Y tú?
CARMEN: Yo tengo quince años.

16 ¿Qué recuerdas?

Completa las frases de la izquierda con una de las frases de la derecha, según el diálogo *¿De dónde eres, Hugo?*

1. ¿De dónde...   A. ...de aquí?
2. Soy de Bogotá,... B. ...tienes, Hugo?
3. ¿Y tú? ¿Eres...   C. ...la capital de Colombia.
4. No. Yo soy...   D. ...dieciséis años.
5. ¿Cuántos años...   E. ...eres, Hugo?
6. Tengo...   F. ...de México.

17 Algo personal

1. ¿De dónde eres?
2. ¿Cuántos años tienes?

18 ¿Cuántos años tienes?

Escribe los números que oyes.

MODELO

dieciséis

1

3

2

4

19 Conexión con otras disciplinas: geografía

Using the map at the front of the textbook, identify the capitals of the Spanish-speaking countries.

Notes Dialogs in *Navegando* provide exposure to authentic spoken Spanish in specific contexts. Explain to students that they will hear audio recordings of Spanish speakers. They are not expected to understand everything they hear. However, students should listen carefully to the sounds, tone and rhythm of the language while determining what topics are being discussed.

Note for students, before assigning activity 19, that Bolivia has the rare distinction of having two capitals: *Sucre* is the constitutional capital, but *La Paz* is the actual governmental center.

Los chambelanes en mi cumpleaños.

Los cumpleaños

Birthdays (los cumpleaños) are important events throughout the Spanish-speaking world. Carmen's fifteenth birthday (la quinceañera) was a big occasion since the event often symbolizes that a girl is ready to date. Traditionally, this coming-of-age celebration begins with a religious ceremony followed by a fancy reception at home or in a local banquet hall. The festivities include food, music and, often, a choreographed dance performed by the birthday girl and her

court, which is composed of male escorts (chambelanes) and maids of honor (damas). It takes a lot of time, money and effort to plan a fiesta de quinceañera. Today, instead of the traditional party, a growing number of fifteen-year-old girls (quinceañeras) prefer to receive a special gift. Spanish-speaking males, on the other hand, celebrate their fifteenth birthday (el quinceañero) like any other cumpleaños with a small party, an informal dance, a trip to the beach or a special dinner with their family.

Tengo quince años.

Soy quinceañera.

20 Comparando

Is the way Latin American teenagers celebrate their birthdays different from what you and your friends do? If you were a quinceañero or quinceañera in Mexico, how would you choose to celebrate your coming of age? Explain.

Notes The section Cultura viva contains interesting and useful cultural information that will help students understand how life in the many Spanish-speaking parts of the world may be similar to or different from what they are used to in their community.

Students are invited to broaden their learning to include subject matter that reaches beyond just the language skills they are learning in Spanish class.

Navegando provides cross-curricular connections to mathematics, history, geography, science and other disciplines, as seen in activity 19.

Teacher Resources

 Activity 6

Answers

20 Answers will vary.

Activities

Communities
Discuss the Cultura viva and activity 20 on page 11 with students. Ask if students know anyone who has celebrated a quinceañera. Ask them to describe what it was like. Then have students share with the class any celebrations they have in their home that may seem out of the ordinary to others.

Idioma

Estructura

Definite articles and countries

Some Spanish speakers use the definite articles *(artículos definidos)* *el, la* and *los* with these country names, whereas others prefer to omit the articles. Their use is optional.

la	**Argentina**	→	**Argentina**
el	**Ecuador**	→	**Ecuador**
los	**Estados Unidos**	→	**Estados Unidos**
el	**Paraguay**	→	**Paraguay**
el	**Perú**	→	**Perú**
la	**República Dominicana**	→	**República Dominicana**
el	**Uruguay**	→	**Uruguay**

 ## Práctica

21 Los países hispanohablantes

Working in pairs, list as many Spanish-speaking countries as you can in three minutes. Check your work by looking at the map in the book. How many are there?

22 Soy de la capital

Selecciona la respuesta más apropiada. *(Select the most appropriate response.)*

1. ¿Eres de Venezuela?
2. ¿Eres de la Argentina?
3. ¿Eres de España?
4. ¿Eres de Ecuador?
5. ¿Eres de El Salvador?

A. Sí, soy de la capital, San Salvador.
B. Sí, soy de la capital, Quito.
C. Sí, soy de la capital, Madrid.
D. Sí, soy de la capital, Caracas.
E. Sí, soy de la capital, Buenos Aires.

23 ¿Qué países quieres visitar?

What countries in the Spanish-speaking world would you like to visit? Why?

Notes Inform students they will learn more about the use of articles in *Capítulo 2.*

The icon indicates activities that students perform orally with one or more classmates. You may want to have students prepare the content in advance or follow up by writing a summary of their oral work.

Comunicación

24 **¿De dónde eres?**

 With a classmate, take turns asking for one another's names and where each of you is from. In your answer, choose a city and country from one of the Spanish-speaking countries you have studied.

Estructura

Cognates

Words in Spanish often resemble English words you already know (e.g., *acento* looks similar to the English word **accent**). Words that resemble one another and that have the same meaning in two languages are called **cognates** *(cognados)*. Do you recognize these cognates?

Argentina   *capital*   *diálogo*   *persona*   *teléfono*   *vocabulario*

When words look similar but have entirely different meanings in Spanish and English, they are called **false cognates.** Here are a few examples: *colegio* (school), *éxito* (success), *lectura* (reading), *sin* (without).

Buenos Aires, la capital de Argentina.

Capítulo 1

trece **13**

Teacher Resources

 Activity 5

 Activity 14

Answers

24 Role-playing activity.

Activities

Critical Thinking
It is always exciting for students to see how their vocabulary seems to grow after they learn about cognates. As a simple demonstration, ask students to name the Spanish-speaking countries that are cognates. Then have students classify the countries according to the following categories: 1) countries that appear exactly the same; 2) countries that are the same except for an accent mark; 3) countries that have a spelling change. Finally, ask if students can name a country that is not a cognate: *los Estados Unidos.* Other examples that students have not yet learned include Germany *(Alemania)* and England *(Inglaterra).*

Notes Encourage students to refer to the maps at the beginning of the book to see where the places mentioned in the textbook are located.

Whereas the *Práctica* activities offer basic mechanical and/or meaningful practice on structures, the *Comunicación* activities provide open-ended opportunities for self-expression.

Activity 25

Activity 15

Answers

25 Pronounce the words in the list for students or play the audio CD for students. Point out that although these cognates are similar in both languages, they are pronounced differently. Check pronunciation and correct words that students are mispronouncing.

26 1. C
2. B
3. A
4. D

Activities

Communities
Invite a professional who uses Spanish in his or her work to talk to the class.

Critical Thinking
Ask students how they think the people mentioned in activity 26 might use Spanish in their daily lives.

Technology
Have students who have access to a computer do an Internet search of occupations that require bilingual employees.

 Práctica

25 Los cognados

Practice pronouncing these cognates. Try to guess the meaning of the words as you say them.

1. favorito
2. estudiar
3. el chocolate
4. formal
5. México
6. el actor
7. la persona
8. la capital
9. el animal
10. la televisión
11. el restaurante
12. el teléfono
13. la posibilidad
14. el diálogo
15. el vocabulario

¡Oportunidades!

¿Por qué estudiar español?
Knowing Spanish offers you opportunities to communicate with people throughout the Spanish-speaking world. In addition, learning Spanish will…

- help you understand other cultures.
- offer you insights into and a better understanding of your own culture.
- improve your English skills.
- increase employment opportunities.

26 ¡Varias profesiones son cognados!

Indica la letra de la foto que corresponde con la profesión de las siguientes personas.

A   **B**   **C**   **D**

1. Es veterinario.
2. Es actor de televisión.
3. Es profesora.
4. Es policía.

Notes Have students compare English and Spanish using cognates introduced in this lesson.

Companies are requiring more from their workforce than mere rote knowledge of facts. The pages of *Navegando* reflect these changing requirements by preparing students for the many opportunities and challenges they will face in the ever-expanding international market.

If students have trouble with photograph B in activity 26, explain that the person shown is Wilmer Valderrama, from Venezuela, one of the stars of the television program *That Seventies Show*.

Comunicación

27 A conversar

 Working with a classmate, read and discuss this article. Do not use a dictionary to look up words. Then, prepare a list of the cognates. Finally, write a short summary of what you understood.

 www

www.mrshowbiz.go.com/celebrities/people

Si deseas ver la historia, la biografía, las fotos más recientes y las anécdotas de tus artistas favoritos, entra en esta página Web. Aquí encuentras toda la información sobre las estrellas; noticias y novedades de los famosos de Hollywood, así como enlaces que te llevan a los sitios personales de numerosos personajes.

Penélope Cruz

28 ¡Mucho gusto!

 Working with a partner, create a dialog in which you ask for one another's names and ages, and where each of you is from. Each person should prepare at least four lines. Practice the dialog and then present it in class. Remember to shake hands when appropriate.

¿De dónde eres tú?

Capítulo 1

quince **15**

Notes As part of your classroom management, consider setting a time limit for each pair or group activity. You can hold students accountable by selecting pairs or groups to perform the task they are practicing or by having students select one person from each group to give a summary of the activity to the class.

The word *actriz* is used by many people as the feminine for *actor.*

15

Answers

29 1. El desierto más árido del planeta está en Chile.
2. La capital más alta del planeta es La Paz, Bolivia.
3. La universidad más antigua de América está en la República Dominicana.
4. Ojos del Salado es el volcán activo más alto del planeta.
5. La pirámide más grande del planeta está en México.

30 Answers will vary.

Activities

Critical Thinking

Using a map for visual reinforcement, discuss what students know about the Spanish-speaking world. Ask both general and specific questions about geography, history, current events, etc. Name and point out the location of each site you mention. Then compare how each place is similar to or different from the United States.

Lectura cultural

La Catedral de Sevilla, España.

¡Visita las diez maravillas del mundo hispanohablante!

Si estás buscando[1] un destino diferente para tus próximas[2] vacaciones, te invitamos[3] a visitar los sitios de nuestro[4] "tour de los récords del mundo hispanohablante[5]". El tour incluye[6] diez maravillas fascinantes en diferentes lugares[7] del mundo: España, la república africana de Guinea Ecuatorial, América del Sur, América Central, México y el Caribe.

Diez maravillas para visitar:

1. La **Catedral** en Sevilla, España, el edificio[8] gótico[9] más grande[10] de Europa.
2. **Guinea Ecuatorial,** uno de los países más húmedos del planeta.
3. **Ojos del Salado,** Argentina, el volcán activo más alto[11] del planeta.
4. El **Desierto de Atacama,** Chile, el desierto más árido del planeta.
5. **La Paz,** Bolivia, la capital más alta del planeta.
6. **Cuzco,** Perú, la ciudad más antigua[12] habitada de forma continua[13] del continente.
7. El **Salto del Ángel,** Venezuela, la catarata[14] más alta del planeta.
8. **Granada,** Nicaragua, la ciudad colonial más antigua de América Central.
9. La **pirámide Quetzalcóatl** en Cholula, México, la pirámide más grande del planeta.
10. La **Universidad Autónoma de Santo Domingo,** la República Dominicana, la universidad más antigua de América.

[1]If you are looking for   [2]for your next   [3]we invite you   [4]our   [5]Spanish-speaking world   [6]includes   [7]places   [8]building   [9]Gothic (style of architecture)   [10]biggest   [11]highest   [12]oldest city   [13]continuously inhabited   [14]waterfall

29 ¿Qué recuerdas?

Corrige las siguientes oraciones. *(Correct the following sentences.)*

1. El desierto más árido del planeta está en Guinea Ecuatorial.
2. La capital más alta del planeta es Cuzco, Perú.
3. La universidad más antigua de América está en México.
4. El Salto del Ángel es el volcán activo más alto del planeta.
5. La pirámide más grande del planeta está en Egipto.

30 Algo personal

1. Name three facts that you learned in this reading. What is the most surprising one? Which world records, if any, did you already know about?
2. If you took this trip around the Spanish-speaking world, which of the ten places would you like to visit the longest? Explain why.

El Salto del Ángel, Venezuela.

Notes The section *¿Qué aprendí?* that appears at the end of lessons (pp. 17, 31, etc.) enables students to check their own progress. The section provides a self-test *(Autoevaluación)* they can use to measure their progress in learning the main elements of the lesson when preparing for the lesson test. It also has a thematic vocabulary list students can use to evaluate which words they recognize and which words they should review.

The *Lectura cultural* offers students the opportunity to use newly acquired skills in Spanish to learn about the culture of the Spanish-speaking world.

¿Qué aprendí?

Autoevaluación
As a review and self-check, respond to the following:

Visit the web-based activities at www.emcp.com

1. Answer the question *¿Cómo te llamas?*
2. Say hi to someone in Spanish.
3. How can you ask where someone is from?
4. What do you say to find out how old someone is? How would you answer that question?
5. How can you tell someone in Spanish that you are pleased to meet them?
6. How will learning Spanish be beneficial to you in the future?

Palabras y expresiones

Despedidas
Adiós.
Hasta luego.

Números
cero
uno
dos
tres
cuatro
cinco
seis
siete
ocho
nueve
diez
once
doce
trece
catorce
quince
dieciséis
diecisiete
dieciocho
diecinueve
veinte

Países
la Argentina
Bolivia
Chile
Colombia
Costa Rica

Cuba
el Ecuador
El Salvador
España
los Estados Unidos
Guatemala
Guinea Ecuatorial
Honduras
México
Nicaragua
Panamá
el Paraguay
el Perú
Puerto Rico
la República
   Dominicana
el Uruguay
Venezuela

Palabras interrogativas
¿cómo?
¿(de) dónde?

Personas
tú
yo

Saludos
Hola.
Mucho gusto.

Verbos
eres
me llamo
se escribe

soy
te llamas
tengo
tienes

Otras expresiones
el acento
aquí
la capital
¿Cómo te llamas?
con
¿Cuántos años tienes?

de
¿Eres (tú) de...?
la mayúscula
la minúscula
el muchacho,
   la muchacha
no
el país
sí
Tengo *(number)* años.
y

¡Extra!

¡Ojo!

The section *Palabras y expresiones* lists vocabulary that you are responsible for knowing how to use. Words and expressions that are for recognition only are not included here. Refer to the *Vocabulario* at the end of *Capítulo 1* for a reference list of definitions or learn to use the Spanish/English dictionary at the back of this book to look up any words and expressions you cannot figure out.

Teacher Resources

Activity 16

Activity 9

Information Gap Activities
Postcard Activities
Funciones de Comunicación

Answers

Autoevaluación
Possible answers:
1. Me llamo....
2. ¡Hola!
3. ¿De dónde eres?
4. ¿Cuántos años tienes?/Tengo...años.
5. ¡Mucho gusto!
6. Answers will vary.

Activities

Spanish for Spanish Speakers
Tell students to imagine being the minister of tourism for their country of origin or for that of their relatives. They have to produce a brochure to encourage tourists from the United States to visit their country. What information and photos would they include in their brochure?

Notes Begin a discussion about student answers for *Autoevaluación* activity 6 by pointing out that the international marketplace demands that employees demonstrate a wide range of competencies and knowledge. Today's student must develop the ability to adapt quickly to new workplace requirements to compete and excel. Encourage students to explore what opportunities learning Spanish will provide them in the areas of work, travel, college, personal fulfillment, etc.

Students can obtain answers to the *Autoevaluación* activities by visiting the **EMC**Paradigm Web site at emcp.com.

Teacher Resources

 Saludos y despedidas

 Activities 1–2

 Activity 13

 Activities 1–4

 Activity 1

 Activities 1–2

Content reviewed in *Lección B*
- greeting people and saying good-bye
- Spanish-speaking countries
- numbers 1–20

Connections with Parents

Success during the first couple of weeks can lead to positive results throughout the rest of the year. If you have not yet done so, send a letter home with the students explaining your grading policy and your classroom management expectations.

---

18   *dieciocho*   **Lección B**

Notes The script for all *Navegando 1* recorded content is provided in the Audio CD Program Manual. This includes the *Vocabulario I* on page 18 and activity 1 on page 19. In addition, student answer sheets have been provided for the activities indicated in the student textbook by the audio speaker icon 🔊))), such as activity 1, for teachers who wish to use them. These reproducible answer sheets can be found at the end of the Audio CD Program Manual.

1 ¿Saludo o despedida?

 Di si lo que oyes es: *un saludo; una despedida; un saludo y una despedida.* (*Say if what you hear is:* a greeting, a farewell or a greeting and a farewell.)

Es un saludo.

ES UN SALUDO Y UNA DESPEDIDA.

Es una despedida.

2 ¡Hola!

Completa los siguientes diálogos de una manera lógica. (*Complete the following dialogs logically.*)

A: ¡Hola! ¿Qué (1)?
B: Estoy (2).

A: Buenos días, Sra. Fernández. ¿Cómo (3) Ud.?
B: Estoy bien, (4).

A: ¿(5) tal?
B: (6), muy (7).

A: ¿(8) estás, Julia?
B: Estoy (9) mal, Pedro.

> ### ¡Extra!
> **Las abreviaturas**
>
> Just as **Mr.** is a shortened form of the word **mister** in English, *Sr.* is an abbreviation *(abreviatura)* for *señor* in Spanish. Other abbreviations: *Srta. (señorita), Sra. (señora), Ud. (usted), Uds. (ustedes), Dr. (doctor)* and *Dra. (doctora)*.

3 ¿Adiós?

Escoge la despedida apropiada para las siguientes situaciones.

Hasta luego.   Buenas noches.
Adiós.
Hasta pronto.   Hasta mañana.

1. A friend's family is moving away to live in Madrid.
2. It is Monday morning and you are leaving home to go to school.
3. You are leaving friends at the end of the school day.
4. It is Saturday night and you are leaving your friends to go home after a basketball game.

Capítulo 1   *diecinueve*

Notes Clarify that the expression *mal* is seldom used to say how you are feeling unless the speaker wants to convey an illness or a personal catastrophe, such as the death of a close friend or family member.

Inform students that another way to express *regular* (okay or average) is *así así*.

Answers

4 1. C
　2. A
　3. F
　4. B
　5. E
　6. D
5 Creative self-expression.
6 1. Buenos días.
　2. Bien, gracias.
　3. Adiós, no. Hasta pronto.

Activities

Critical Thinking
In groups of four, have one student act out how he or she is feeling, while the others guess what that feeling is. Make sure all students have an opportunity to act out their feelings.

Language through Action
Have students write their own dialog and present it to the class, incorporating appropriate gestures.

Prereading Strategy
Instruct students to cover up the dialog with one hand and look at the photographs. Ask them to imagine where the conversation takes place and what the people are saying to one another.

Diálogo I
Buenos días

ALICIA: Buenos días, Quique. ¿Cómo estás?
QUIQUE: Estoy muy bien.

QUIQUE: ¿Y tú? ¿Qué tal?
ALICIA: Bien, gracias.

ALICIA: Adiós, Quique.
QUIQUE: Adiós, no. Hasta pronto.

4 ¿Qué recuerdas?

Completa las frases de la izquierda con una de las frases de la derecha, según el diálogo *Buenos días*.

1. ¿Cómo...　　　　A. ...muy bien.
2. Estoy...　　　　B. ...gracias.
3. ¿Y tú? ¿Qué...　C. ...estás?
4. Bien,...　　　　D. ...pronto.
5. Adiós,...　　　　E. ...Quique.
6. Hasta...　　　　F. ...tal?

5 Algo personal

Greet four or five students in class and ask how each one is. Your classmates then answer and ask how you are.

MODELO **A:** Buenos días/Buenas tardes, *(name of student* **B***)*. ¿Qué tal?
　　　　B: Mal. ¿Y tú?
　　　　A: Muy bien, gracias.

¡Extra!

¡Estoy muy mal!

¿Por qué?	*Why?*
Me duele la cabeza.	*I have a headache./ My head hurts.*
Me duele el estómago.	*My stomach hurts.*
Me duele la garganta.	*I have a sore throat.*
Tengo catarro.	*I have a cold.*

6 ¿Cuál es una respuesta correcta?

 Escoge una respuesta correcta a lo que oyes.

> Bien, gracias.
>
> BUENOS DÍAS.
>
> Adiós, no. Hasta pronto.

Notes Point out for students that the expression *¿Qué tal?* is provided as an equivalent for *¿Cómo estás?*. Both *¿Cómo estás?* and *¿Qué tal?* are commonly used in informal conversation.

While teaching the expression *Me duele...* teach students some additional body parts in Spanish: *el brazo* (arm), *la mano* (hand), *la boca* (mouth), *el ojo* (eye), *la oreja* (ear), *la pierna* (leg), *el pie* (foot), *la cara* (face).

Cultura viva

Más sobre los saludos

Spanish is the official language in Spain, in eighteen Latin American countries, in the African nation of Equatorial Guinea and in the Commonwealth of Puerto Rico. Spanish is also used extensively in the United States, in Europe and elsewhere for both business and pleasure. Because so many people speak Spanish in so many places around the world, you can well imagine that the words and expressions people use vary a great deal. For example, the most

Buenos días.

common Spanish greetings are the informal *hola* and the more formal *buenos días* (which is used until around noon), *buenas tardes* (which is used until around dusk) and *buenas noches* (which can be used as an evening greeting or as another way to take leave of someone). However, *buenas* is sometimes used by itself as a short form of either *buenas tardes* or *buenas noches.* The word *muy* can then be added to these expressions for emphasis, as in *muy buenos días* or *muy buenas.*

Buenas tardes.

7 Los saludos en el mundo hispano

¿Sí o no? Corrige lo que no es lógico.

1. *Hola* and *Buenos días* are both formal ways to say good-bye.
2. *Buenas tardes* is used to greet someone in the morning.
3. *Buenas noches* is used to greet someone in the evening.
4. You may hear *Buenas* or *Muy buenas* when someone is greeting you in the afternoon or in the evening.

8 Saludos y despedidas

Haz una lista en español de saludos y una lista de despedidas.

Saludos	Despedidas
Muy buenas.	Hasta pronto.

Answers

7 1. No. Both are greetings. *Hola* is used casually; *Buenos días* is more formal.
2. No. *Buenas tardes* is used to greet someone in the afternoon.
3. Sí.
4. Sí.

8 Answers will vary.

Activities

Critical Thinking

Call on three students to go to the board (or ask for volunteers). One student writes the word *Saludo,* another writes the word *Despedida* and the third student writes *Saludo y despedida.* Say several greetings and farewells aloud: *hasta luego, hola, adiós, buenas tardes, hasta mañana, buenas noches, hasta pronto,* etc. Students must write the word under the appropriate column. When a student answers by spelling the word correctly and placing it into the correct column, he or she gets to call on a classmate to come to the board and continue the game.

21

Answers

9 1. tú; 2. tú; 3. Ud.; 4. Uds.;
5. Ud.; 6. Uds.; 7. vosotras;
8. vosotros

Activities

Critical Thinking

After students complete activity 9, ask them to come up with a list of other people in their lives. Call on students to share their lists with the class as a volunteer writes the list on the board. Then call on individuals to say whether they would use *tú, usted, ustedes, vosotros* or *vosotras* with the people on the list.

Idioma

Estructura

Formal/Informal

Spanish has several words for **you.** Use the informal *tú* when talking to someone you refer to by a first name. Use the more formal *usted* (abbreviated *Ud.*) when talking to someone you would address using a title (*señor Torres, señorita Jiménez*).

Although throughout the Spanish-speaking world the plural **you** is *ustedes* (abbreviated *Uds.*), in Spain you have two choices for **you** when speaking to more than one person: 1) use the informal *vosotros* (for males or a combination of males and females) or *vosotras* (for females) with two or more friends, family members or younger people; 2) use the more polite and formal *ustedes* (or *Uds.*) when talking with two or more people you address using a title.

	singular	**plural**
informal	tú	ustedes (*Uds.*)
		vosotros (*masculine*)/vosotras (*feminine*)
formal	usted (*Ud.*)	ustedes (*Uds.*)

  Práctica

9 A saludar

How would you address these people? Choose either *tú, Ud., Uds., vosotros* or *vosotras.*

1. a friend at school
2. your sister
3. your teacher
4. an elderly couple you have just met
5. the principal at your school
6. two close friends (Latin America)
7. two close female friends (Spain)
8. two close male friends (Spain)

Estrategia

Learning from mistakes
Do not be afraid to make mistakes when you use Spanish. They are a natural part of learning a language. By using Spanish every day and by completing assignments, gradually you will notice that you are able to say and understand more and more as the year continues. Of course, there will be challenges throughout the year, but one result of your effort will be a profound sense of accomplishment as your skills and knowledge improve.

Notes Inform students that *vosotros/vosotras* is used in Spain. Although the subject pronouns *vosotros* and *vosotras* are introduced here, you should decide what role these words will have in your class. In *Navegando,* verb paradigms include the *vosotros/vosotras* verb forms for recognition. However,

activities do not require students to practice the *vosotros/vosotras* verb forms.

Point out that in some Latin American countries, such as Argentina, *vos* is used instead of *tú.*

10 ¿Tú, usted, ustedes, vosotros o vosotras?

Would you use *tú*, *usted*, *ustedes*, *vosotros* or *vosotras* when talking to these people?

1. María y Lupe (México) **2.** Amalia y José (España) **3.** la Sra. Sánchez (República Dominicana)

4. Paz, Mercedes y Marta (España) **5.** Pepe (Ecuador) **6.** el Sr. Fernández y el Sr. García (España)

11 ¿Cómo están?

Greet these people in Spanish and ask how they are feeling.

MODELO Paula
Hola, Paula. ¿Cómo estás?/¿Qué tal?

1. Sr. y Sra. Uribe **2.** Antonio **3.** Jaime y Marta **4.** Srta. Sosa **5.** Teresa y Raquel

✶ Comunicación

12 Estoy....

 You have just walked up to some friends. In groups of three, talk about how you are feeling. Be sure everyone in the group practices each of the roles shown (*A*, *B* and *C*).

MODELO **A:** *(Greet two classmates and ask how they feel.)*
B: *(Say how you feel.)*
C: *(Say how you feel and ask how student **A** feels.)*
A: *(Say how you feel.)*

¿Qué hora es?

 Activities 4–5

 Activities 14–15

 Activities 7–10

 Activity 3

 Activities 4–6

Activities

Connections

For additional practice on the numbers, have students count backwards in Spanish, one number at a time, by twos, by threes, etc.

Expansion

Try holding up a card with a number on it while saying a number and have your students say out loud the words *sí* or *no* to indicate if you are holding up the number you have said. As a variation, call on students to identify the number orally in Spanish or have a student go to the board and write the numeral you are holding.

Notes Review the numbers 1–20 before presenting 21–100. The numbers 101 to 999,999 are taught in *Capítulo 5*.

Explain that the numbers beginning with *treinta y uno* may require the combination of three words, even though the numbers *cero* through *treinta* are written as one word. Likewise, your students may find it useful if you point out the spelling change that occurs in the combination of three words in the numbers *dieciséis (diez y seis)* through *veintinueve (veinte y nueve)*.

Los números del 21 al 100

21	veintiuno	31	treinta y uno
22	veintidós	32	treinta y dos
23	veintitrés	40	cuarenta
24	veinticuatro	50	cincuenta
25	veinticinco	60	sesenta
26	veintiséis	70	setenta
27	veintisiete	80	ochenta
28	veintiocho	90	noventa
29	veintinueve	100	cien
30	treinta		

Answers

13 1. veintiséis; 2. setenta y nueve;
3. treinta y cuatro; 4. quince
5. cien

14 1. quince, veinte, veinticinco, treinta, treinta y cinco, cuarenta, cuarenta y cinco, cincuenta, cincuenta y cinco, sesenta, sesenta y cinco, setenta, setenta y cinco, ochenta, ochenta y cinco, noventa, noventa y cinco, cien

2. veintiuno, veintiocho, treinta y cinco, cuarenta y dos, cuarenta y nueve, cincuenta y seis, sesenta y tres, setenta, setenta y siete, ochenta y cuatro, noventa y uno, noventa y ocho

3. treinta y tres, cuarenta y cuatro, cincuenta y cinco, sesenta y seis, setenta y siete, ochenta y ocho, noventa y nueve

4. cincuenta y dos, sesenta y cinco, setenta y ocho, noventa y uno

---

 13 **Los números hasta cien**

🔊 **Escribe los números que oyes.**

MODELO treinta

14 **Conexión con otras disciplinas:** matemáticas

Completa de forma lógica las siguientes series de números hasta 100.

1. cero, cinco, diez...
2. cero, siete, catorce...
3. cero, once, veintidós...
4. cero, trece, veintiséis, treinta y nueve...

Nueve por nueve, ochenta y uno.

Notes Ask students to identify the many ways they use numbers on a daily basis. Then they should identify numbers that are especially important to them (phone numbers, ages, etc.).

The Appendices at the back of the book provide all the numbers in one place if you choose to teach them all at the same time or if students ask about the numbers after 100.

Activities with the title *Conexión con otras disciplinas* are intended specifically to offer cross-curricular learning opportunities.

Diálogo II
¿Cómo te llamas?

QUIQUE: Por favor, ¿qué hora es?
PALOMA: Son las tres y diez.
QUIQUE: Muchas gracias.

QUIQUE: Perdón, ¿cómo te llamas?
PALOMA: Me llamo Paloma.
QUIQUE: Mucho gusto. Me llamo Quique.

PALOMA: Con permiso.
QUIQUE: Sí, lo siento.

15 ¿Qué recuerdas?

1. ¿Qué hora es en el diálogo?
2. ¿Qué dice el muchacho antes de preguntar el nombre a la muchacha? *(What does the boy say before asking the girl's name?)*
3. ¿Cómo se llama la muchacha?
4. ¿Cómo se llama el muchacho?
5. ¿Qué dice la muchacha antes de bajar del autobús? *(What does the girl say before getting off the bus?)*

16 Algo personal

1. ¿Qué hora es?
2. ¿Cómo te llamas?

17 ¿Qué hora es?

 Escribe la hora que oyes. *(Write the time you hear.)*

MODELO 9:25

```
3:10              6:00    4:20
      1:30
9:25        12:40   5:15
```

26 *veintiséis*   Lección B

Cultura viva

Con cortesía

The expressions *Perdón* and *Con permiso* are equivalent to "Excuse me." However, these expressions are used in different situations. Use *Perdón* to interrupt a conversation, to get someone's attention, to indicate you do not understand what someone said or to excuse yourself if you bump into someone. *Con permiso,* on the other hand, is used more specifically to ask someone to let you pass by or to politely let someone know you are about to leave.

Perdón, ¿dónde está... ?

18 Lo cortés no quita lo valiente

Selecciona la respuesta más apropiada para cada *(each)* situación en la ilustración.

- De nada.
- Muchas gracias.
- Perdón, ¿qué hora es?
- Con permiso.
- Cuatro, por favor.
- Perdón.
- Con mucho gusto.
- Perdón. Lo siento.

19 ¿Qué dices?

Indicate which of these expressions you would use in the following situations.

Con permiso.   Perdón.   Dos, por favor.
De nada.   Con mucho gusto.   No, gracias.
Muchas gracias.   Perdón. Lo siento.   Perdón, ¿qué hora es?

1. You want to politely refuse an offer to do something.
2. A friend asks you for help.
3. Someone thanks you for doing something.
4. You step on someone's foot.
5. You are on an elevator standing behind other people and you want to exit.
6. You politely ask for two movie tickets.
7. Someone speaks to you so quickly in Spanish that you cannot understand what the person is saying.

Teacher Resources

 Activity 4

Answers

18 1. Con mucho gusto.
2. Cuatro, por favor.
3. Perdón. Lo siento.
4. Muchas gracias.
5. De nada.
6. Con permiso./Perdón.
7. Perdón, ¿qué hora es?
19 1. No, gracias.
2. Con mucho gusto.
3. De nada.
4. Perdón. Lo siento.
5. Con permiso.
6. Dos, por favor.
7. Perdón.

Activities

Language through Action
Have students walk around the room and practice the courtesy expressions they have learned in short conversations. For example, they may interrupt someone to ask for the time, thank someone for information provided, say they are sorry to hear someone doesn't feel well, etc.

Notes Point out that when they travel, students may meet people who seem overly polite and more formal. Explain that their familiarity with the expressions in activity 19 will come in handy when talking with others in Spanish.

Activity 6

 Activities 11–13

 Activity 5

 Activity 7

Answers

20 1. Es la una menos diez.
2. Son las once y veinticinco.
3. Son las dos menos cuarto (menos quince).
4. Son las tres y media (y treinta).
5. Son las seis y cinco.
6. Es la una y cuarto (y quince).
7. Son las doce./ Es mediodía./ Es medianoche.
8. Son las siete menos veinte.

Activities

Connections

In many countries where Spanish is spoken, people use the twenty-four-hour clock to tell time. For example, tell students they are visiting Spain during their summer vacation. Have them convert the following times to A.M. and P.M.: 1. 18:00 (6:00 P.M.); 2. 23:00 (11:00 P.M.); 3. 13:00 (1:00 P.M.); 4. 19:00 (7:00 P.M.); 5. 21:00 (9:00 P.M.).

Idioma

Estructura

Time

You can find out what time it is by asking *¿Qué hora es?* When giving the time in Spanish, use *Es la una* to refer to one o'clock and *Son las* (+ number) to indicate any other hour.

  1:00 *Es la una.*   2:00 *Son las dos.*

Use *y* (+ number of minutes through *veintinueve*) to add minutes after the hour or *menos* (+ number of minutes through *veintinueve*) to indicate time before the hour.

  2:29 *Son las dos y veintinueve.*   2:31 *Son las tres menos veintinueve.*

Add *y cuarto* for a quarter past the hour, *y media* for half past the hour and *menos cuarto* for a quarter to the hour.

  4:15 *Son las cuatro y cuarto.*   4:30 *Son las cuatro y media.*
  4:45 *Son las cinco menos cuarto.*

In Spanish, the expression A.M. is equivalent to *de la mañana* (in the morning). Morning goes from midnight to noon. P.M. is equivalent to *de la tarde* (in the afternoon) or to *de la noche* (at night). Afternoon is from noon to around 6:00 P.M., and night extends from 6:00 P.M. to midnight.

Two additional useful expressions: *Es mediodía* (It is noon) and *Es medianoche* (It is midnight).

Práctica

20 La hora

Indica qué hora es.

MODELO

Son las cinco.

1

2

3

4

5

6

7

8

28 *veintiocho*   **Lección B**

Notes Tell your students that **o'clock** can be conveyed in Spanish as *en punto* when you want to emphasize the exact hour on the hour (e.g., It's three o'clock. *Son las tres en punto.*).

Es mediodía and *Es medianoche* can also be expressed by *Son las doce.*

21 La entrevista

Completa el siguiente diálogo de una manera lógica.

LORENZO: Buenos (1), Sra. Vargas.
SRA. VARGAS: ¡Hola, Lorenzo! ¿Cómo (2)?
LORENZO: Estoy bien, (3). ¿Y (4)?
SRA. VARGAS: (5) muy bien.
LORENZO: (6), ¿(7) hora es?
SRA. VARGAS: (8) las diez y media de la (9).
LORENZO: ¿No son (10) nueve y media?
SRA. VARGAS: No.
LORENZO: ¡Uy! Tengo clase de español. Hasta (11).
SRA. VARGAS: Adiós, hasta (12).

¡Extra!

Los gestos

Gestures and other non-spoken language are important when talking with people in Spanish about how they feel: In several countries, turning your thumb up indicates you feel well, whereas turning your thumb down signals you do not feel well.

bien   mal

Comunicación

22 Por favor, ¿qué hora es?

 Imagine you have stopped someone on the street to politely ask what time it is. Take turns asking for and stating the indicated time.

MODELO

A: Por favor, ¿qué hora es?
B: Son las siete y cuarto (y quince) de la mañana.
A: Muchas gracias.

1

2

3

4

5

6

7

8

Notes Point out that *Es mediodía* and *Es medianoche* are not modified by a number of minutes or by the expressions *y cuarto, menos cuarto* or *y media.*

Mention that *quince* may be used instead of *cuarto.*

Answers

23 1. D
2. C
3. E
4. A
5. F
6. B

24 Answers will vary.

Cantantes y grupos musicales

Dirección http://www.emcp.com/músico/ola/index.htm ▲ Archivo   Edición   Ver   Favoritos   Herramientas   Ayuda

página principal   miembros   e-diario

Grupo musical **La OLA**

Faltan ocho días para la Gira Mundial

❶ Yo me llamo Manuel. Tengo diecinueve años. Soy de Panamá.

❷ Hola. Me llamo Xavier. Tengo dieciocho años y soy mexicoamericano, de Chicago.

❸ ¡Hola! Me llamo Yadira. Tengo quince años y soy de México.

❹ Hola, me llamo Chantal. Soy de la República Dominicana y tengo dieciséis años.

❺ Hola. Me llamo Carlos. Soy de Chile. Tengo diecisiete años.

❻ ¡Hola! Yo me llamo Ceci. Tengo dieciocho años y soy de Uruguay.

23 ¿Qué recuerdas?

Match the person on the right with the information on the left.

1. 19 años   A. Yadira
2. Uruguay   B. Xavier
3. 17 años   C. Ceci
4. México   D. Manuel
5. 16 años   E. Carlos
6. Chicago   F. Chantal

24 Algo personal

1. What kind of music do you think the band La Ola plays? Do you listen to music in Spanish? If so, what is the name of the band or singer?

2. You have now seen pictures of people who are from various Spanish-speaking countries. Do you think you can tell what language someone speaks just by looking at the person?

Notes *La Ola* is the name for the singing group depicted in the *Lectura personal* that concludes each even-numbered lesson. Explain that the word *ola* means **wave**. Students will enjoy band members' personal viewpoints as they reflect on the many cultures of the Spanish-speaking world during their travels.

The accompanying audio CD concludes with the song *Es sólo una cuestión de actitud*, which was written by Rodolfo "Fito" Páez. You may wish to play the audio CD recording of the song so students can hear the kind of music the band performs. Students will see the lyrics and hear the entire song again in *Capítulo 10*.

¿Qué aprendí?

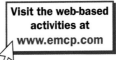**Visit the web-based activities at www.emcp.com**

Autoevaluación

As a review and self-check, respond to the following:

1. How would you greet your teacher in the morning in Spanish?
2. What might you ask to find out how a friend feels? Two classmates?
3. Ask for the time in Spanish.
4. Say it is 8:45 at night.
5. What should you say to ask for something politely in Spanish?
6. What do you say to thank someone in Spanish?

Palabras y expresiones

Cortesía
con mucho gusto
con permiso
de nada
(muchas) gracias
lo siento
perdón
por favor

Gente
el señor (Sr.)
la señora (Sra.)
la señorita (Srta.)
usted (Ud.)
ustedes (Uds.)
vosotros,-as

La hora
de la mañana
de la noche
de la tarde
Es la…. / Son las….
Es medianoche.

Es mediodía.
la hora
la mañana
menos
la noche
¿Qué hora es?
la tarde
y cuarto
y media

Números
veintiuno
veintidós
veintitrés
veinticuatro
veinticinco
veintiséis
veintisiete
veintiocho
veintinueve
treinta (y uno, etc.)

cuarenta
cincuenta
sesenta
setenta
ochenta
noventa
cien

Saludos y despedidas
Buenas noches.
Buenas tardes.
Buenos días.
Hasta mañana.
Hasta pronto.

Verbos
es
está (él, ella)
está (Ud.)

están (Uds.)
estás (tú)
estoy
son

Otras expresiones
bien
mal
muy
pronto
¿Qué tal?
regular

¡Con permiso!

Teacher Resources

📝 **Activity 14**

💬 **Information Gap Activities**
Postcard Activities
Funciones de Comunicación

Answers

Autoevaluación
Possible answers:
1. Buenos días, Sr./Sra./Srta. ¿Cómo está Ud.?
2. ¿Cómo estás? (¿Qué tal?)/¿Cómo están Uds.?
3. ¿Qué hora es?
4. Son las nueve menos cuarto de la noche.
5. Por favor.
6. Gracias.

Activities

Expansion
Add additional activities or questions to the *Autoevaluación* as you see fit: How would students greet a best friend? How would they say good-bye to several friends as they leave school Monday or Tuesday afternoon? What can students say to thank someone in Spanish? Can students identify a popular Hispanic musician/singer? Can they say what kind of music they perform?

Notes The *Autoevaluación* provides several self-check activities students can use for evaluating their own progress. Assign them as time and your own judgment allow.

Have students check their own understanding of the vocabulary by reviewing the list of *Palabras y expresiones*. Then have them find the words they do not recognize where they are first presented in the lesson.

Answers

Preparación

1. Answers will vary.
2. Possible answers: *oficial, República*, names of countries, *capital, person, famosa*, etc.

Activities

Expansion

In groups of three or four, have students pass around a piece of paper while each group member adds the name of a famous person who speaks Spanish. After two minutes, add up the number of names each group has listed.

Multiple Intelligences (bodily-kinesthetic)

Have students create an autobiographical poster/collage that includes some of the following information in Spanish: name, place of origin, age, a favorite greeting, a Spanish-speaking place of interest and three cognates that describe him/her.

Tú lees

Estrategia

Using cognates to understand Spanish
Spanish will be more enjoyable to read if you learn some techniques that will help you recognize cognates. For example, many words that end in *-ión* have English counterparts that end in **-tion,** such as *información* (information). Look at the endings in these words: *adicional, biología.* Can you guess what they mean? What would be the endings of their English equivalents?

Preparación

Contesta a las siguientes preguntas como preparación para la lectura:

1. Give five examples of cognates you have seen in *Capítulo 1.*
2. Find at least five cognates in the country information that follows.

El mundo hispanohablante

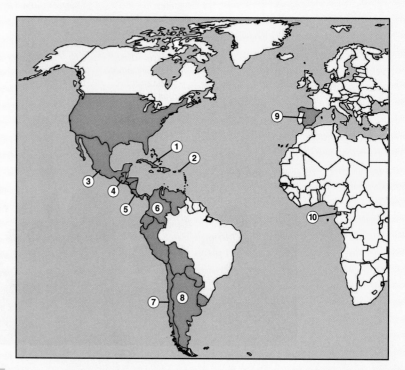

Notes Chapters in *Navegando* conclude with *¡Viento en popa!* (Full speed ahead!), a selection of activities that combine the themes and content of the lesson.

The *Tú lees* provides a formal opportunity for students to improve their ability to read in Spanish. Note for students that it is not essential to understand every word in order to read in Spanish. Equivalents for most of the unfamiliar words have been provided to help students enjoy reading without having to look up important but passive vocabulary. Be sure to go over *Estrategia* and *Preparación* prior to beginning the *Tú lees* reading.

① **Nombre oficial:** República de Cuba
Capital: La Habana
Poblacion aproximada: 11,2 millones
Moneda: el peso
Persona famosa: José Martí (escritor, revolucionario)

② **Nombre oficial:** Puerto Rico
Capital: San Juan
Población aproximada: 3,9 millones
Moneda: el dólar (EE.UU.)
Persona famosa: Ricky Martin (cantante)

③ **Nombre oficial:** Estados Unidos Mexicanos
Capital: México, D.F.
Población aproximada: 101 millones
Moneda: el peso
Persona famosa: Octavio Paz (escritor, premio Nobel de Literatura)

④ **Nombre oficial:** República de El Salvador
Capital: San Salvador
Poblacion aproximada: 6,3 millones
Moneda: el colón
Persona famosa: Francisco Gavidia (dramaturgo)

⑤ **Nombre oficial:** República de Costa Rica
Capital: San José
Población aproximada: 3,9 millones
Moneda: el colón
Persona famosa: Óscar Arias Sánchez (ex-presidente, premio Nobel de la Paz)

⑥ **Nombre oficial:** Colombia
Capital: Bogotá
Población aproximada: 43 millones
Moneda: el peso
Persona famosa: Gabriel García Márquez (escritor, premio Nobel de Literatura)

⑦ **Nombre oficial:** República de Chile
Capital: Santiago de Chile
Población aproximada: 15 millones
Moneda: el peso
Persona famosa: Isabel Allende (escritora)

⑧ **Nombre oficial:** República Argentina
Capital: Buenos Aires
Población aproximada: 37 millones
Moneda: el peso
Persona famosa: Jorge Luis Borges (escritor, poeta)

⑨ **Nombre oficial:** España
Capital: Madrid
Población aproximada: 40 millones
Moneda: el euro
Persona famosa: Pablo Picasso (pintor)

⑩ **Nombre oficial:** Guinea Ecuatorial
Capital: Malabo
Población aproximada: 500.000
Moneda: el franco XFA
Persona famosa: Teodoro Obiang (presidente)

A ¿Qué recuerdas?

Match the famous person named in column A with the country he or she is from under column B.

Column A	Column B
1. Jorge Luis Borges	A. México
2. Isabel Allende	B. Costa Rica
3. Pablo Picasso	C. Chile
4. Octavio Paz	D. Guinea Ecuatorial
5. Teodoro Obiang	E. Argentina
6. Óscar Arias	F. España
7. José Martí	G. El Salvador
8. Francisco Gavidia	H. Cuba

B Algo personal

1. Can you name any famous Hispanic people? Who? Name four or five people, if you can, and say why they are well known.
2. If you could have a conversation with one of the famous people mentioned above, who would it be? Why?

Answers

A 1. E
2. C
3. F
4. A
5. D
6. B
7. H
8. G
B Answers will vary.

Notes Other countries:
Nombre oficial: República de Honduras
Capital: Tegucigalpa
Población aproximada: 6,4 millones
Moneda: el lempira
Persona famosa: José Antonio Velázquez (pintor)

Nombre oficial: Bolivia
Capitales: La Paz, Sucre
Población aproximada: 8,5 millones
Moneda: el boliviano
Persona famosa: Nataniel Aguirre (dramaturgo)

Tú escribes

Estrategia

Using the dictionary

In addition to checking how words are spelled, you can use a dictionary to get a clearer and more accurate understanding of what words mean and to avoid misunderstandings. For example, you have already learned the difference between cognates and false cognates. A good way to make sure that a word is not a false cognate is to look it up in a dictionary.

A How many of these words can you recognize?

Look them up in the dictionary and decide which are cognates *(cognados)* and which are false cognates *(cognados falsos)*.

pariente parque practicar

dinero

sopa

CHOCOLATE *ropa*

pasaporte

largo programa

lectura

estudiante

vaso

B Make a list of some cognates you have learned.

Use what you know about word endings to think of words that might have cognates in Spanish. Then check your guesses in the dictionary. Find at least three new cognates.

Proyectos adicionales

A Comunidades

You have already learned where Spanish is spoken in the world. Working in groups of three or four, prepare a list of several famous people *(las personas famosas)* who speak Spanish and say where they are from.

Estrategia

Recognizing community connections

As you learn Spanish this year, you will also learn about the culture of the people who speak Spanish. Who are they? Where do they live? What is their history? What contributions have they made to the world? Read newspapers, watch television, search the Internet and try to find out more about the influence Spanish has on the world today.

B Conexión con la tecnología

Research one of the countries where Spanish is the official language. You might surf the Web to try to find a home page that provides information on festivals, holidays, restaurants, maps and so forth. Then create your own travel brochure that features that country.

C Conexión con otras disciplinas: geografía

Draw your own map of the Spanish-speaking world. Include the names of the Spanish-speaking countries, their capital cities, major bodies of water, large mountain chains, etc. Make the finished map attractive by adding color and any other details you wish. Present the map to the class.

Visita Honduras

Answers

A Answers will vary.
B Creative self-expression.
C Creative self-expression.

Activities

Communities

Suggest to students that they talk to their parents or guardians about ways they may use the Spanish skills they are developing by volunteering in the community. For example, students may wish to volunteer at the local library and use Spanish to work with Spanish-speaking customers. Brainstorm with the class other ways in which students might participate in community service.

Technology

To help students in their search for information about Spanish-speaking countries, suggest these Web sites as a starting point: **The Electronic Embassy** offers addresses, telephone numbers and additional links (http://www.embassy.org); the **Consulate General of Mexico in New York** (http://consulmexny.org); the **Tourism Office of Spain** (http://www.okspain.org). Additional Web sites can be found by using a search engine and entering a keyword such as the name of a city, country or region.

Notes Many activities in *Navegando* provide an opportunity for students to learn about where Spanish is spoken and to begin to make comparisons between the student's knowledge and the reality of what life is like in the Spanish-speaking world. Other activities provide an opportunity for students to establish connections with their communities that will encourage them to become lifelong learners.

The National Standards are practiced throughout the chapter. The projects that appear at the end of every chapter offer additional standards practice you may or may not choose to use, depending on student needs.

Activities

Multiple Intelligences (linguistic)

You may choose to have students begin to create a Writer's Journal consisting of student writing activities. The Writer's Journal offers appropriate portfolio activities for addressing student writing skills and is an ideal opportunity for an ongoing dialog with students about their writing progress. How to create a Writer's Journal is addressed more thoroughly in the *Tú escribes* at the end of *Capítulo 2*.

Repaso

Now that I have completed this chapter, I can ...	Go to these pages for help:
ask for and give names.	2
ask or tell where someone is from.	8
ask for and state age.	8
greet people and say good-bye.	18
ask and tell how someone is feeling.	18
express courtesy.	24
ask for and state the time.	24

I can also ...	
spell words in Spanish.	2
use appropriate gestures to greet people.	5
identify where Spanish is spoken.	8
state why learning Spanish may be beneficial in one's life.	14
recognize the difference between informal and formal in Spanish.	22
read a simple narrative in Spanish.	30

Trabalenguas

Tres tristes tigres tragaban trigo
en tres tristes trastos sentados tras un trigal.

Notes Through the *Repaso*, students can measure their own progress in learning the main elements of the chapter.

Review the functions and other objectives in the *Repaso* and assign the activities. Answer questions so students can prepare for the chapter test. Follow up by reviewing the activities as a class.

Loose translation of the *Trabalenguas*: Three sad tigers swallowed wheat out of three sad bowls, sitting behind a wheat field.

Vocabulario

el **acento** accent *1A*
Adiós. Good-bye. *1A*
aquí here *1A*
la **Argentina** Argentina *1A*
bien well *1B*
Bolivia Bolivia *1A*
Buenas noches. Good night *1B*;
  Buenas tardes. Good afternoon *1B*
Buenos días. Good morning *1B*
la **capital** capital *1A*
catorce fourteen *1A*
cero zero *1A*
Chile Chile *1A*
cien one hundred *1B*
cinco five *1A*
cincuenta fifty *1B*
Colombia Colombia *1A*
¿cómo? how?, what? *1A*; *¿Cómo te llamas?* What is your name? *1A*
con with *1A*; *con mucho gusto* I would be very glad to *1B*; *con permiso* excuse me, may I *1B*
Costa Rica Costa Rica *1A*
¿Cuántos años tienes? How old are you? *1A*
cuarenta forty *1B*
cuatro four *1A*
Cuba Cuba *1A*
de from *1A*; *(¿de) dónde?* (from) where? *1A*; *de la mañana* in the morning, A.M. *1B*; *de la noche* at night, P.M. *1B*; *de la tarde* in the afternoon, P.M. *1B*; *de nada* you are welcome *1B*
diecinueve nineteen *1A*
dieciocho eighteen *1A*
dieciséis sixteen *1A*
diecisiete seventeen *1A*
diez ten *1A*
doce twelve *1A*
dos two *1A*
el **Ecuador** Ecuador *1A*
El Salvador El Salvador *1A*
eres you (informal) are *1A*; *¿Eres (tú) de...?* Are you from...? *1A*
es you (formal) are, he/she/it is *1B*; *Es la una.* It is one o'clock. *1B*; *Es medianoche.* It is midnight. *1B*; *Es mediodía.* It is noon. *1B*
España Spain *1A*
está (él, ella) you are *1B*; *está (Ud.)* you (formal) are *1B*
los **Estados Unidos** United States *1A*
están (Uds.) you are (pl.) *1B*
estás (tú) you (informal) are *1B*
estoy I am *1B*
Guatemala Guatemala *1A*

Guinea Ecuatorial Equatorial Guinea *1A*
Hasta luego. See you later. *1A*; *Hasta mañana.* See you tomorrow. *1B*; *Hasta pronto.* See you soon. *1B*
Hola. Hello. *1A*
Honduras Honduras *1A*
hora hour *1B*
lo siento I am sorry *1B*
mal badly *1B*
mañana tomorrow *1B*
la **mañana** morning *1B*
la **mayúscula** capital letter *1A*
me llamo my name is *1A*
menos (cinco, cuarto, etc.) minus, to, until, before (to express time) *1B*
México Mexico *1A*
la **minúscula** lowercase *1A*
la **muchacha** girl, young woman *1A*
el **muchacho** boy, guy *1A*
(muchas) gracias thank you (very much) *1A*
¡Mucho gusto! Glad to meet you! *1A*
muy very *1B*
Nicaragua Nicaragua *1A*
no no *1A*
la **noche** night *1B*
noventa ninety *1B*
nueve nine *1A*
ochenta eighty *1B*
ocho eight *1A*
once eleven *1A*
el **país hispano** Hispanic country *1A*
Panamá Panama *1A*
el **Paraguay** Paraguay *1A*
perdón excuse me, pardon me *1B*
el **Perú** Peru *1A*
por favor please *1B*
pronto soon, quickly *1B*
Puerto Rico Puerto Rico *1A*
¿Qué hora es? What time is it? *1B*
¿Qué tal? How are you? *1B*
quince fifteen *1A*
regular average, so-so, regular *1B*
la **República Dominicana** Dominican Republic *1A*
se escribe it is written *1A*
seis six *1A*
el **señor (Sr.)** gentleman, sir, Mr. *1B*
la **señora (Sra.)** lady, madame, Mrs. *1B*

la **señorita (Srta.)** young lady, Miss *1B*
sesenta sixty *1B*
setenta seventy *1B*
sí yes *1A*
siete seven *1A*
son they are *1B*; *Son las* (+ number). It is (+ number) o'clock. *1B*
soy I am *1A*
la **tarde** afternoon *1B*
te llamas your name is *1A*
tengo I have *1A*; *Tengo (number) años.* I am (number) years old. *1A*
tienes you have *1A*
trece thirteen *1A*
treinta (y uno, etc.) thirty (one, etc.) *1B*
tres three *1A*
tú you (informal) *1A*
uno one *1A*
el **Uruguay** Uruguay *1A*
usted (Ud.) you (s.) *1B*
ustedes (Uds.) you (pl.) *1B*
veinte twenty *1A*
veinticinco twenty five *1B*
veinticuatro twenty four *1B*
veintidós twenty two *1B*
veintinueve twenty nine *1B*
veintiocho twenty eight *1B*
veintiséis twenty six *1B*
veintisiete twenty seven *1B*
veintitrés twenty three *1B*
veintiuno twenty one *1B*
Venezuela Venezuela *1A*
vosotros,-as you (Spain, pl.) *1B*
y and *1A*; *y cuarto* quarter past, quarter after *1B*; *y media* half past *1B*
yo I *1A*

Activities

Expansion
Model each word or expression and have students repeat. Then call on students to use the word or expression in a sentence. This activity would be appropriate for all lists of vocabulary found in *Navegando*.

Students with Special Needs
Help students practice the numbers by having them count around the class, each person saying one number. Go front to back, back to front or across the rows. When students are comfortable with numbers, use the same technique to have them count by 5s, 3s, 2s. You may also wish to have students count off in order numbers containing a 3 (for example, 3, 13, 23).

Estrategia ◆◆◆◆◆◆

Learning vocabulary
Try to learn new vocabulary in a context (illustration, dialog, word groupings, etc.), since that will help you to use Spanish without having to translate word for word. Look at the words and expressions in the *Vocabulario* to see how many you remember. Say them aloud. If you have forgotten a word, return to where it was first introduced in order to check its meaning.

◆◆◆◆◆◆

Notes This *Vocabulario* provides a reference list of new words and expressions that students are required to know for the chapter test and for future chapters.

Connections with Parents

Although somewhat time consuming, this activity will help establish parental support for what you are trying to accomplish with students in the classroom: Look for and note something good that each student has done in Spanish class and then call the individual's parents/guardians to explain what their child did that merited a call home. The call does not have to be long, but doing so will break the mold of calling only when there is a problem. You will find that both parents/guardians and students will better understand and accept future calls that involve a problem because you will have already established that you do not just call with bad news. As an alternative, send a note containing similar information home with students.

Capítulo **2**

En mi colegio

Objetivos

❖ **identify people and classroom objects**

❖ **ask for and give names**

❖ **ask or tell where someone is from**

❖ **discuss school schedules and daily activities**

❖ **describe classroom objects and clothing**

❖ **say some things people do**

❖ **state location**

❖ **talk about how someone feels**

Visit the web-based activities at www.emcp.com

38 *treinta y ocho*

Notes Communicative objectives are provided at the start of each chapter to prepare students for the chapter they are about to begin. A list of the functions appears again at the end of chapter 2 so that students can do a self-check to evaluate their progress.

More than thirty million people in the United States use Spanish every day. In fact, in some parts of the United States—such as Florida, California, New Mexico and Texas—knowing Spanish proves very advantageous because Spanish is spoken by so many people for both pleasure and business.

Activities

Critical Thinking
The visuals that appear on the opening two pages of the chapter depict the functions, cultural setting and themes of the chapter. These authentic materials further student awareness of and connections to how Spanish is used outside the controlled environment of the classroom. Ask students what words they are able to understand, what conclusions they can draw from the information, and so forth. For example, ask students the following: 1) In what country or part of the world does the chapter take place?; 2) What are students in the photographs doing?; 3) What is a *colegio?*

treinta y nueve **39**

Notes Take some time reviewing the contents of these two pages. First, point out and call on students to read the objectives shown on page 38. Then ask questions about what students see in the photographs. For example, ask if students can figure out the country where the small photograph on page 38 was taken (United States). Ask what students think the people in the large photograph are doing (an assignment for school).

Teacher Resources

 ¿Quién es?

 Activities 1–2

 Activity 16

 Activities 1–2

 Activity 1

Content reviewed in *Lección A*
- asking for and giving names
- talking about where someone is from
- Spanish-speaking countries

Lección A

Estados Unidos

Vocabulario I
¿Quién es?

Notes Names for states and cities often reflect the rich Hispanic heritage in the United States. Ask students to name several such locations and identify them on a map. Point out how the pronunciation of the names changes when students say them in Spanish (e.g., *California, Texas*).

An alternative spelling for *Texas* is *Tejas*.

1 ¿Quién?

 Selecciona la foto de la(s) persona(s) apropiada(s).

A   B   C   D

2 Minidiálogos

Completa los minidiálogos con las palabras apropiadas. *(Complete the mini-dialogs with appropriate words.)*

A

eres   **quién**   **él**

dónde

te llamas   *ella*

B

SOY   *es*   **me**

se llama

A: ¿Quién <u>es</u> él?
B: <u>Él</u> es José.

A: ¿Cómo se llama <u>(1)</u>?
B: <u>(2)</u> Alejandro.

A: ¿<u>(3)</u> es?
B: ¿Ella?
A: No, <u>(4)</u> no. ¿Quién es él?

A: ¿De <u>(5)</u> es Daniel?
B: <u>(6)</u> de Miami.

A: Y, ¿cómo <u>(7)</u> tú?
B: Yo <u>(8)</u> llamo Marta.

A: ¿De dónde <u>(9)</u> tú?
B: <u>(10)</u> de El Paso.

Él es José.

Notes Reproducible answer sheets have been provided for the activities indicated in the student textbook by the audio speaker icon . These reproducible answer sheets can be found at the end of the Audio CD Program Manual.

Teacher Resources

Activity 1

Answers

1 1. C
     2. A
     3. D
     4. B
2 1. él
     2. Se llama
     3. Quién
     4. ella
     5. dónde
     6. Es
     7. te llamas
     8. me
     9. eres
     10. Soy

Diálogo I

¿Cómo se llama ella?

RAÚL: Laura, ¿quién es?
LAURA: ¿Él?
RAÚL: No, ella.

RAÚL: ¿Cómo se llama ella?
LAURA: Se llama Diana.
RAÚL: ¿Es de aquí?
LAURA: No, ella es de Los Ángeles.

DIANA: ¿Quién eres tú?
RAÚL: Perdón. Me llamo Raúl.
DIANA: Mucho gusto, Raúl.
RAÚL: Mucho gusto, Diana.

3 ¿Qué recuerdas?

1. ¿Quién es el muchacho?
2. ¿Es Laura un muchacho?
3. ¿Cómo se llama la muchacha de Los Ángeles?

4 Algo personal

1. ¿Eres tú de California? ¿De dónde eres?
2. ¿Cómo se llama la capital de los Estados Unidos?

5 ¡No es lógico!

 Escucha la información y, luego, corrige lo que no es lógico en las oraciones que siguen. *(Listen to the information and correct what is not logical in the sentences that follow.)*

1. Ella se llama Raúl.
2. Ellos son Laura y Diana.
3. Él es de Los Ángeles.

Los Ángeles, California.

Notes The *Diálogos I* and *II* contextualize the new words and expressions that are introduced in the *Vocabularios I* and *II,* allowing students to practice the new vocabulary in complete-sentence answers to activities.

The activities that follow the dialog are recorded in *Lección 2A* of the Audio CD Program. Student answer sheets for activity 5 can be found in the back of the Audio CD Program Manual.

Comparisons. Point out how the pronunciation of the city and state names in the dialog and in activity 6 changes when students say them in Spanish.

Cultura viva

La influencia hispana en los Estados Unidos

Have you been to a Mexican or Spanish restaurant? Do you recognize the names Sammy Sosa or Shakira? Perhaps you have studied art by famous Latino/Hispanic artists. Examples of how the Hispanic culture has influenced daily life in the United States abound. Words that have Spanish origins are one example that you experience every day of the strong influence that Spanish cultures have probably had in your community. Have you ever

Adobe en Santa Fe, Nuevo México.

sat outside on a **patio** or taken a **siesta** in your free time? If so, then you have enjoyed some of the rich Hispanic heritage that exists in the United States today. Here are other words that have been borrowed from Spanish:

adobe   rodeo   plaza   mosquito   chile

The Spaniards explored and settled parts of America years before the arrival of the pilgrims on the *Mayflower*. Thanks to these early settlers, communities throughout the United States today reflect their rich Spanish colonial architecture, delicious foods, interesting geographical names and much more.

6 Conexión con otras disciplinas: geografía

Using a dictionary, encyclopedia or the Internet, research these geographical names that have come to the English language from the Spanish language. Give the English equivalent for each word. Then find each place on a map.

1. Los Ángeles
2. Las Vegas
3. Amarillo
4. Boca Ratón
5. Florida
6. Río Grande
7. Colorado
8. Alcatraz
9. Nevada

7 Conexión con la comunidad

Tell where Spanish is used in your community or state. Are you aware of any other Hispanic influences in your community?

Teacher Resources

Activities 3–4

Answers

6 1. the angels
2. the fertile lowlands
3. yellow
4. mouth of the mouse
5. full of flowers
6. big river
7. red-colored
8. pelican
9. snow-covered

7 Answers will vary.

Activities

Cooperative Learning
Have students work in groups to identify ten cities/states in the United States with Spanish names. Each group should share its list with the class. As an extension, research a location of interest on the Internet to learn more about its Hispanic heritage.

Expansion
Bring to class some newspapers or magazines published in Spanish. Ask students to look at the advertisements to identify cognates. Next ask students to identify three Hispanics mentioned in the newspapers or magazines. Who are they? Where are they from? Why are they in the news?

Students with Special Needs
Have students correctly pronounce several cities in the United States that have Spanish names: *Los Ángeles, California; Las Vegas, Nevada; Amarillo, Texas; Boca Ratón, Florida.*

Notes **Cultures.** In Santa Fe, New Mexico (shown in the photograph on the left side of the *Cultura viva),* some descendants of the Spaniards who founded the city in 1610 still speak Spanish today.

Some additional words that have come to the English language from the Spanish language include: lasso, from *lazo* (slipknot); maize, from *maíz* (corn); poncho, from *poncho* (blanket-like cloak); and bronco, from *bronco* (rough, wild).

Teacher Resources

 Activity 3

 Activities 5–8

 Activity 2

 Activities 1–3

Activities

Cooperative Learning

Have your students pretend to be from one of the Spanish-speaking countries (other than the United States). Then have students ask three other students near them in Spanish for their name (*¿Cómo te llamas?*) and where they are from (*¿De dónde eres?*). Finally, test how much information the students obtained by asking them to report to the class what they learned (*Se llama...y es de...*).

Idioma

Estructura

Subject pronouns and the verb *ser*

You will often use subject pronouns (*pronombres personales*) when discussing people in Spanish. You have already used subject pronouns with the following forms of the verb *ser* (to be) to identify people and to say where someone is from.

ser					
yo	**soy**	*I am*	nosotros nosotras	**somos**	*we are*
tú	**eres**	*you are*	vosotros vosotras	**sois**	*you are*
Ud. él ella	es	*you are* *he (it) is* *she (it) is*	Uds. ellos ellas	**son**	*you are* *they are* *they are*

Make a sentence negative in Spanish by placing *no* before the verb.

> *Alicia es de Arizona.*　　　→　　　*Alicia **no** es de Arizona.*

Subject pronouns may be used with or without a verb. They may not be needed if the subject is already known or if the verb form itself identifies the subject.

*¿De dónde eres **(tú)**?*	Where are **you** from?
(Yo) *Soy de Indiana. ¿Y **él**?*	**I** am from Indiana. And **he**?
(Él) *Es de Virginia.*	**He** is from Virginia.

The plural forms *nosotras, vosotras* and *ellas* refer only to females, while the subject pronouns *nosotros, vosotros* and *ellos* are used to refer either to males only or to a mixed group of both males and females.

***Ellos** son de Miami.*	**They (the boys)** are from Miami.
***Ellas** son de Charleston.*	**They (the girls)** are from Charleston.

but:

***Ellos** son de los Estados Unidos.*	**They (the boys and girls)** are from the United States.

Notes Point out that in Spanish the subject pronouns are often unnecessary unless the speaker wishes to add emphasis or clarity to a sentence.

Explain that *tú* is the singular familiar form of **you** and is used with family, friends, children and others with whom you have informal relationships.

Point out for students that the subject pronoun *ellos* may refer to more than one boy, to a boy and a girl or to a group of boys and girls.

Práctica

8 En tu colegio

Complete this conversation with your teacher as you review a list of people who speak Spanish. Use the appropriate subject pronoun.

MODELO A: ¿Felipe?
   B: No, él no.

1. A: ¿Yo?
   B: Sí, __ sí.
2. A: ¿La Srta. Barnés?
   B: No, __ no.
3. A: ¿Paul y Luisa?
   B: Sí, __ sí.
4. A: ¿David y Ud.?
   B: Sí, __ sí.
5. A: ¿La profesora de música?
   B: No, __ no.

6. A: ¿Uds.?
   B: Sí, __ sí.
7. A: ¿Teresa, Daniel y yo?
   B: Sí, __ sí.
8. A: ¿Miguel y Jaime?
   B: Sí, __ sí.
9. A: ¿Tú y yo?
   B: Sí, __ sí.

9 Los estudiantes de mi colegio

Completa las oraciones de una manera lógica con la forma correcta del verbo *ser*. (*Complete the sentences logically with the correct form of the verb* ser.)

1. ¿Tú __ de South Bend, Indiana?
2. Él __ de Seattle, Washington.
3. Ellas __ de San Antonio, Texas.
4. Ella __ de Denver, Colorado.
5. Ellos __ de San Diego, California.
6. Yo __ de (*name of your city and state*).
7. Nosotros __ de (los)....

¡Extra!

Ser

Ser is irregular, which means its six different forms do not follow the same predictable pattern that regular verbs do. Also, although the subject pronouns *Ud., él* and *ella* are different in meaning, they share the same verb form, as do *Uds., ellos* and *ellas*.

10 ¡No!

Show that you disagree with these statements by making them negative.

MODELO Teresa y Daniel son de España.
   Teresa y Daniel no son de España.

1. Soy de París.
2. Diana es de Nueva York.
3. Ella es de aquí.
4. Me llamo Hernán.
5. Se llama Luz.
6. Nosotros somos de la Argentina.

Teresa y Daniel no son de España.

Teacher Resources

 Activity 10

Answers

8 1. tú/Ud.
2. ella
3. ellos
4. nosotros
5. ella
6. nosotros,-as
7. Uds./vosotros
8. ellos
9. nosotros,-as

9 1. eres
2. es
3. son
4. es
5. son
6. soy
7. somos

10 1. No soy de París.
2. Diana no es de Nueva York.
3. Ella no es de aquí.
4. No me llamo Hernán.
5. No se llama Luz.
6. Nosotros no somos de la Argentina.

Notes With the exception of activity 8, the *vosotros/vosotras* verb forms are included in *Navegando* for passive recognition only. However, you may choose to require students to learn and use the *vosotros* and *vosotras* pronouns and verb forms.

Clarify for students that questions like ¿*Cómo se llama?* can be the English equivalent of "What is your/his/her name?" Eliminate confusion by adding *Ud., él* or *ella* to the end of the question. In the same way they can clarify a statement such as *Se llama...* by placing *Ud., él* or *ella* at the beginning of the sentence.

11 La influencia hispana

 Your class is studying Hispanic influence in the United States. With a classmate, take turns asking and answering where some well-known people are from.

MODELO Shakira / Colombia
A: ¿De dónde es Shakira?
B: Ella es de Colombia.

1. Penélope Cruz y Antonio Banderas / España
2. Jimmy Smits y Christina Aguilera / Estados Unidos
3. Don Francisco / Chile
4. Pedro Martínez y Sammy Sosa / la República Dominicana
5. Juan Pablo Montoya y Carlos Vives / Colombia
6. Rubén Blades / Panamá
7. Daisy Fuentes y Gloria Estefan / Cuba
8. Salma Hayek / México

Shakira es de Colombia.

12 ¿Por qué son famosos?

You are going to do a report about famous Spanish-speaking people. Find out who these people are and say what field of expertise they have in common.

MODELO Jorge Luis Borges, Isabel Allende, José Martí
Ellos son escritores.

> cantantes *(singers)*
> atletas *(athletes)*
> actores *(actors)*
> pintores *(painters)* escritores *(writers)*

1. Jimmy Smits, Penélope Cruz, Salma Hayek
2. Shakira, Enrique Iglesias, Ricky Martin
3. Sergio García, Sammy Sosa, Juan Pablo Montoya
4. Fernando Botero, Pablo Picasso, Diego Rivera

Comunicación

13 ¡Son de muchos países!

 With a classmate, talk about where the famous people mentioned in activity 12 are from. Then look up a few other Spanish-speaking celebrities, indicating their profession and/or where they are from.

MODELO Jorge Luis Borges
A: ¿De dónde es Jorge Luis Borges?
B: Es de Argentina.

Notes **Cultures.** Suggest that students use one of many available Internet search engines to do research about the famous Spanish-speaking individuals mentioned in activity 11:

Google	http://www.google.com
All the Web	http://www.alltheweb.com
Lycos	http://www.lycos.com
Yahoo	http://www.yahoo.com
Ask Jeeves	http://www.askjeeves.com
Hot Bot	http://www.hotbot.com

14 Es de...

With a partner, discuss where the following people are from, according to the illustration.

MODELO Alicia
   A: ¿De dónde es Alicia?
   B: Es de (los) Estados Unidos.

¡Extra!

EE.UU.

Can you guess the abbreviation *(abreviatura)* in Spanish for *Estados Unidos?* It is *EE.UU.* As in English, some proper nouns are abbreviated in Spanish. Although most abbreviations use only one letter, this Spanish abbreviation uses double letters because *Estados Unidos* is a plural noun.

1. Pablo
2. Luis
3. tú
4. Jorge y Luisa
5. Daniel, tú y yo
6. la Srta. Muñoz
7. yo
8. el Sr. y la Sra. Vargas

15 Juego: ¿De dónde es?

Write the names of three famous Hispanics who are well known in the United States, adding where they are from. Next, in groups of three, take turns asking where someone on your list is from. Others in the group must try to guess where each celebrity is from until one person guesses the correct country.

MODELO **A:** ¿De dónde es Jennifer López?
   B: Es de Ecuador.
   A: No, no es de Ecuador.
   C: Es de Estados Unidos.
   A: Sí, es de Estados Unidos.

Capítulo 2

cuarenta y siete **47**

¿Qué hay en la clase?

 Activities 4–5

 Activities 17–18

 Activities 9–11

 Activity 3

 Activity 4

Activities

Critical Thinking

Have students name classroom items that also are found in their homes.

Pronunciation

Have students practice pronouncing in Spanish the names of the objects that are in the illustration of a classroom. Check for correct pronunciation.

Vocabulario II
¿Qué hay en la clase?

la pared · el reloj · el mapa · la profesora · la pizarra · la tiza · la chica · el chico · el cesto de papeles · la puerta · el periódico

Teresa es mi amiga y es la chica nueva de México.

el cuaderno · el pupitre · la estudiante · la mochila · el estudiante · el reloj · el libro · la página · el lápiz · la silla · el bolígrafo · el papel

Notes Explain to students that synonyms exist in Spanish just as they are common in English. Then ask if students can remember the synonyms for *chico* and *chica* that they saw in *Capítulo 1: muchacho, muchacha.* Point out that students now know two terms for **boy** and **girl:** *chico* is an alternate form of *muchacho; chica* is an alternate form of *muchacha.*

16 ¿Qué es?

 Identifica los objetos que oyes. *(Identify the objects you hear.)*

A   **B**   **C**

D   **E**   **F**

17 No comprendo una palabra

With a classmate, take turns pretending you do not know the word in Spanish to identify various objects in your classroom. Ask one another *¿Cómo se dice (plus a word in English)?* as you point to an object. Your partner must then tell you how to say the word in Spanish using *Se dice (plus the word in Spanish).*

MODELO   **A:** ¿Cómo se dice *wall?*
             B: Se dice *pared.*

No comprendo una palabra. ¿Qué quiere decir la palabra *tiza?*

¿Cómo se dice *chair?*

la ventana

Se dice *la silla.*

Quiere decir *chalk.*

el sacapuntas

la regla

el profesor

el borrador   la revista

el escritorio

Capítulo 2

Teacher Resources

Activity 16

Answers

16 1. D
        2. A
        3. B
        4. F
        5. C
        6. E
17 Role-playing activity.

Activities

TPR
Use TPR in order to reinforce classroom vocabulary: *señala el mapa,* etc.

Notes The following are additional classroom vocabulary terms you may wish to introduce: *el resaltador* (highlighter), *el gancho/la grapa* (clip), *la calculadora* (calculator), *el calendario* (calendar), *el cartel* (poster), *la computadora/ el computador/el ordenador* (computer), *la impresora* (printer), *el mapa* (map).

49

Diálogo II

La nueva estudiante de Los Ángeles

CARLOS: ¿Quién es la chica con la mochila?
RAÚL: ¿Qué quiere decir la palabra *mochila*?
CARLOS: Quiere decir *backpack*.

RAÚL: Ella es la estudiante nueva de Los Ángeles.
CARLOS: ¿Cómo se llama?
RAÚL: Se llama Diana y es mi amiga.

DIANA: Perdón, chicos. ¿Cómo se dice *clock* en español?
CARLOS: Se dice *reloj*.
DIANA: Muchas gracias.

18 ¿Qué recuerdas?

1. ¿Qué quiere decir la palabra *mochila*?
2. ¿De dónde es la chica con la mochila?
3. ¿Quién es la estudiante nueva?
4. ¿Es la estudiante nueva amiga de Carlos?
5. ¿Cómo se dice *clock* en español?
6. ¿Hay un reloj en la clase?

¡Extra!

En otras palabras

As in English, Spanish words and expressions can vary according to where the speaker has lived. Look at these examples:

el bolígrafo	*el boli, la pluma, el lapicero, el estilo*
el borrador	*la goma*
el cesto de papeles	*la papelera, la caneca, el basurero*
el escritorio	*el buró*
el estudiante	*el alumno, el compañero (de clase)*
la estudiante	*la alumna, la compañera (de clase)*
la mochila	*la bolsa, el bulto*
el sacapuntas	*el afilalápices, el cortalápices*

19 Algo personal

1. ¿Tienes una mochila?
2. ¿Tienes un reloj? ¿Qué hora es?

20 ¿Sí o no?

 ¿Son lógicos los diálogos? Corrige lo que no es lógico.

21 Tu propio diálogo

 With a partner, use the previous dialog as a model to create your own dialog. Use your own names, change the italicized words and make any other changes you feel are appropriate.

Notes If students ask about *nuevo/nueva*, explain that *nuevo* is used with masculine nouns much as *el* accompanies masculine nouns, and *nueva* is used with feminine nouns much as *la* accompanies feminine nouns. Adjective/noun agreement will be taught in *Lección 2B*.

Point out the accent mark on *Los Ángeles* in *Diálogo II*. Then have students practice pronouncing the Spanish equivalent of several cities in the United States: *San Antonio, Miami, Chicago, Santa Cruz.*

El español en los Estados Unidos

In the United States, over thirty million people use Spanish daily for business or pleasure. Many American cities are becoming bilingual because of their large Spanish-speaking communities. In fact, Spanish is the second language of the United States. Los Angeles, Miami, San Antonio, New York and numerous other cities across the United States have Spanish television and radio stations, Spanish newspapers and magazines and bilingual signs in most public places. The Hispanic presence is increasing rapidly in the United States and influencing many aspects of the American culture and economy. Look around, you may find you can experience more Spanish than you ever realized!

Teacher Resources

 Activity 6

 Activity 4

Answers

22 1. One year; two years; three years.
2. Call 312-100-7799. Send curriculum vitae (résumé) to the addresses listed.
3. Chicago.
4. A bank.
5. The bilingual secretary job.
6. The teaching job. Answers will vary.

Activities

Spanish for Spanish Speakers
Have students write a short composition in Spanish listing three or four benefits available to them because they know Spanish.

---

22 Oportunidades de trabajo

Answer the questions below based on the following classified advertisements.

> **Compañía multinacional ubicada en Chicago**
> busca
> **Secretario/a bilingüe Español-inglés**
> Responsabilidades: mantener archivos, contestar teléfonos y escribir cartas para los clientes hispanohablantes.
> Experiencia mínima: 1 año
> Salario: $30.000 anuales
> Para mayor información llame al (312) 100-7799.

> **BANCO CAMINO REAL**
> necesita
> **Director(a) de Servicio al Cliente**
> Se prefiere persona bilingüe (español e inglés), con fluidez y excelentes habilidades de escritura en ambas lenguas, buen manejo de las relaciones personales e impecable presentación. Se requiere experiencia mínima de 3 años. Interesados por favor enviar curriculum vitae a: Banco Camino Real, 201 SW Black Rd., Austin, TX 78701-6384.

> **Se requieren profesores para Español y Literatura**
> Prestigiosa escuela privada busca profesores de español y literatura para la primavera. Los interesados deben tener un Masters en educación y tener licencia para enseñar en el estado de New Mexico. Se requiere un mínimo de dos años de experiencia. Candidatos favor enviar su CV con carta de presentación a P.O Box 75634, Albuquerque, NM 87106.

1. How much experience is needed for the job as a bilingual secretary? For the position as a teacher? For the position as the director of customer service at the bank?
2. How do you find out about the *secretario/a bilingüe* job? About the other two jobs?
3. Where is the company located that is looking for a bilingual secretary?
4. What type of business do you think *Banco Camino Real* is?
5. Which job includes keeping archives, answering phones and writing letters?
6. Which job requires a college degree? Why do you think a degree is important for this job?

> **¡Oportunidades!**
>
> **Las ventajas de ser bilingüe**
> Many American companies today are searching for bilingual employees who can expand their market and increase sales to the growing population of Spanish speakers in the United States. Being bilingual may be the advantage you need to compete in the job market.

Notes Communities. The choices for obtaining information in Spanish about the Spanish-speaking world (and news and entertainment in general) are growing greater every year. Television stations that broadcast in Spanish across the world include cable stations such as *Univision, CBS Telenoticias* and *CNN en Español*.

Cultures. Job listings in activity 22 are for cities in the United States with large Hispanic populations.

The section *¡Oportunidades!* gives students an opportunity to see how learning Spanish is beneficial now and in the future.

Idioma

Estructura

Using definite articles with nouns

Nouns refer to people, places, things or concepts. All nouns in Spanish have a gender: They are either masculine or feminine. Nouns that end in *-o* are generally masculine and are often used with the definite article *el* (the), whereas nouns that end in *-a, -ción, -sión* or *-dad* are usually feminine and are often used with the definite article *la* (the).

> *masculino:* **el** *chico*
> *femenino:* **la** *chica*   **la** *pronunciación*   **la** *misión*   **la** *posibilidad*

Some nouns do not follow these patterns.

> *masculino:* **el** *día*   *femenino:*   *la noche*

Also, some nouns that refer to people have only one form and the gender of the person being referred to is indicated by the definite article.

> *masculino:* **el** *estudiante*   *femenino:* **la** *estudiante*

Make most nouns in Spanish plural by adding *-s*. The accompanying plural of the definite articles are *los* (masculine) or *las* (feminine).

> *masculino:* *el amigo* → **los** *amigos*   *el libro* → **los** *libros*
> *femenino:* *la amiga* → **las** *amigas*   *la revista* → **las** *revistas*

Make nouns that end with a consonant plural by adding *-es*.

> *el papel* → **los** *papeles*   *la actividad* → **las** *actividades*
> *el reloj* → **los** *relojes*   *la pared* → **las** *paredes*

Nouns that end in *-z* change the *-z* to *-c* in the plural.

> *el lápiz* → *los lápices*

It may be necessary to add or remove an accent mark when making a noun plural.

> *el examen* → **los** *exámenes*   *la lección* → **las** *lecciones*

¡Extra!

¿Masculino o femenino?
Remember ... use the masculine form of the noun when you refer to males and females as a group or to masculine and feminine objects simultaneously.

> *los chicos*   the boys
>   the boys and the girls

Notes You may wish to tell students that the gender of nouns has nothing to do with the nature of an object. Gender has grammatical significance because it determines the form of articles and adjectives that accompany the noun.

Práctica

23 Objetos en la clase

Da cada sustantivo con su artículo definido. Sigue el modelo. *(Give each noun with its definite article. Follow the model.)*

MODELO pupitre
el pupitre

1. puerta
2. cuaderno
3. ventana
4. borrador
5. ESCRITORIO
6. lápiz
7. lección
8. página
9. mapa
10. actividad

24 Más de uno

Da la forma plural de cada palabra de la actividad anterior. *(Give the plural of each word in the preceding activity.)*

MODELO el pupitre
los pupitres

25 Periódicos en la clase de español

Identify the nouns in these magazine and newspaper headlines and ads and tell which ones are masculine *(masculino)* and which are feminine *(femenino).*

1. CULTURA
Exposición
Por la puerta grande

2. ¡Es la hora de comer bien!

3. ═══ OPINIÓN ═
Contra la pared
Por Felipe López

4. Bento
El reloj que marca la hora

5. Los lápices PRISMACOLOR
Dan color a tu clase

6. Todo está en las Páginas Amarillas

7. El papel reciclado está de moda

Notes Before beginning activity 24, note for students that there are certain exceptions to the rules for making nouns plural. For example, many words ending in *-es* and *-is* do not change in the plural, such as the days of the week *(el lunes, los lunes); la crisis, las crisis.*

Have students look at the clippings that appear in activity 25. Then ask if they recognize any of the words. Are they able to understand any of these advertisements?

Answers

23 1. la puerta; 2. el cuaderno;
3. la ventana; 4. el borrador;
5. el escritorio; 6. el lápiz;
7. la lección; 8. la página;
9. el mapa; 10. la actividad

24 1. las puertas
2. los cuadernos
3. las ventanas
4. los borradores
5. los escritorios
6. los lápices
7. las lecciones
8. las páginas
9. los mapas
10. las actividades

25 Students should not be expected to find all nouns.

Probable common answers:
1. la puerta (femenino)
2. la hora (femenino)
3. la pared (femenino)
4. el reloj (masculino), la hora (femenino)
5. los lápices (masculino)
6. las páginas (femenino)
7. el papel (masculino)

Other nouns include the following: *cultura (femenino), exposición (femenino), opinión (femenino), color (masculino), clase (femenino), moda (femenino).*

Activities

Critical Thinking
For activity 23, have students explain how they know which nouns are *masculino* and which are *femenino.*

26 Answers will vary.

27 Possible answers:

1. ¿Quién es el chico con los libros?/Se llama Felipe y es mi amigo.

2. ¿Quién es la chica con el periódico?/Se llama Rosa y es mi amiga.

3. ¿Quién es la chica con la tiza y el borrador?/Se llama Doris y es mi amiga.

4. ¿Quién es el chico con los cuadernos?/Se llama Luis y es mi amigo.

5. ¿Quién es la chica con el profesor?/Se llama Sandra y es mi amiga.

6. ¿Quién es el chico con los bolígrafos, la regla y el cuaderno?/Se llama Daniel y es mi amigo.

Activities

Critical Thinking

Have students return to previous dialogs and practice identifying masculine and feminine words. Inform students that the ending *-ción* is the equivalent of **-tion** at the end of many English words and the *-dad* ending on many Spanish words appears as **-ty** in English. Then ask if students can guess the meaning of *presentación, pronunciación, actividad, posibilidad* and *realidad*.

Spanish for Spanish Speakers

Give students a few paragraphs from a newspaper or magazine article written in Spanish and have them find all the nouns.

26 Juego

Working in pairs, take two minutes to list in Spanish everything you can see in your classroom.

MODELO

```
el papel
la tiza
```

✦ Comunicación

27 Unos amigos

Pretend you are looking at pictures of friends with a classmate. Working in pairs, take turns asking and answering questions about the people shown. For each question, mention what the person is holding or whom the person is with. Answer by giving the person's name and then say he or she is your friend.

MODELO Adriana

A: ¿Quién es la chica con la profesora?

B: Se llama Adriana y es mi amiga.

¡Extra!

En la clase

la computadora	*computer*
el disco compacto (el CD)	*compact disc (CD)*
el disco DVD (el DVD)	*digital video disc (DVD)*
la pantalla	*computer screen*
el proyector	*overhead projector*
el reproductor de discos compactos	*CD player*
el reproductor de DVDs	*DVD player*
la videocasetera	*VCR*

1. Felipe   **2.** Rosa   **3.** Doris

4. Luis   **5.** Sandra   **6.** Daniel

Notes Words ending in *-ista* are invariable and the same form is used for both masculine and feminine. The distinction is made with the appropriate definite article: *el violinista/la violinista, el dentista/la dentista.*

Inform students that many Spanish nouns ending in *-ma, -pa* and *-ta* are derived from Greek and are usually masculine: *el problema, el poema, el drama, el mapa, el telegrama, el planeta.*

28 Objetos en la clase

Working in pairs, take turns telling one another to point at an object in the classroom. Use the phrase *Señala...* and add any of the classroom objects you have learned. Check to be sure your partner has pointed at the correct object before continuing.

MODELO Señala la puerta.

 29 En la clase

Identify and talk about the people and objects in your classroom with another student. You may wish to use some of the words shown and add some of your own as needed.

MODELOS A: ¿Quién es el chico con la *mochila*?
B: Es Pablo.

A: ¿Cómo se dice *pencil sharpener*?
B: Se dice sacapuntas.

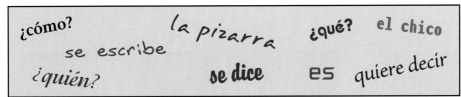

¿cómo? se escribe la pizarra ¿qué? el chico
¿quién? se dice es quiere decir

Estructura

Using indefinite articles with nouns

Whereas the definite articles *el, la, los* and *las* (the) are used to designate a specific person or thing, indefinite articles refer to nonspecific people or things (e.g., **a, an, some** or **a few**). The singular forms of the indefinite articles are *un* (masculine) and *una* (feminine).

el lápiz	→	**un** lápiz	la página →	**una** página
(the pencil)		(**a** pencil)	(the page)	(**a** page)

The plural forms of the indefinite articles are *unos* (masculine) and *unas* (feminine).

los lápices	→	**unos** lápices	las páginas →	**unas** páginas
(the pencils)		(**a few/some** pencils)	(the pages)	(**a few/some** pages)

> **¡Extra!**
>
> **Las palabras *un, una* y *uno***
> The words *un* and *una* can also mean **one** when used before a singular noun. *Uno* (the number **one**) is never used before a noun.
>
> *dos cuadernos y* **un** *libro*   *tres chicos y* **una** *chica*

Capítulo 2

Notes Several nouns in Spanish at first glance may appear to be masculine or feminine by their endings but are in fact just the opposite: *el día, la mano, el programa.*

 Activity 8

 Activities 14–16

 Activity 7

 Activity 8

Answers

28 Answers will vary.
29 Answers will vary.

Activities

Cooperative Learning
Working in pairs, students should name aloud a classroom object they have learned in Spanish. Each student's partner then spells the word. Have pairs check their spelling and then switch roles. This will reinforce vocabulary to be used with indefinite articles.

Critical Thinking
Say aloud several nouns and ask students to provide the appropriate indefinite article and repeat the noun that you give. Then give students several words with definite articles *(el chico, la amiga)* and ask them to give the corresponding indefinite article with the same noun *(un chico, una amiga).*

Multiple Intelligences (linguistic)
Have students make a copy of a news article in Spanish and bring it to class. Working in pairs, students should identify and circle the definite and indefinite articles.

55

Práctica

30 ¿Qué ves?

Di lo que ves en las ilustraciones. *(Say what you see in the illustrations.)*

MODELOS Es un escritorio.   Son unos estudiantes.

1   **2**   **3**   **4**

5   **6**   **7**   **8**

31 En la clase hay...

Completa el párrafo con *un, una, unos* o *unas* para indicar qué hay en la clase. *(Complete the paragraph with **a, an** or **some/a few** to indicate what is in the classroom.)*

La clase tiene cuatro paredes y dos ventanas. La profesora es la Sra. Martínez. En la clase hay (1) escritorio, (2) cesto de papeles, (3) sillas y (4) pupitres con (5) libros, (6) lápices y (7) bolígrafos. En las paredes hay (8) reloj, (9) sacapuntas y (10) pizarra.

En la clase hay unas ventanas y un mapa.

Notes This may be a good time to use transparencies 17 and 18 for *Navegando 1*, if you have not already done so, to teach or reinforce the new vocabulary for *Vocabulario II*. As an alternative, try using transparency 17 (without labeled words) and quiz students on the classroom vocabulary. Have students answer your questions orally or have them write their answers and turn them in for a grade.

32 Conexión con otras disciplinas: matemáticas

Create a shopping list of some school supplies you would like to buy. Write the prices offered at *Papelería Nueva Era* next to the items on your list. Then, add up the total cost of your purchases and write a complete sentence stating the total in dollars *(dólares)* and cents *(centavos)*. You only have $40.00, so be careful not to spend more than you have!

una mochila "Mochil-In"	$25,00
unos bolígrafos "Bolimétrico"	$ 2,22
un lápiz "Trazo"	$ 0,10
Total	$27,32

PAPELERÍA NUEVA ERA

Mini Pizarra con tizas de colores
$4,95

3 colores
$1,65

Libro de mapas de Planeta Editores
$12,95

Papel de cuaderno
$0,79

Reglas de plástico 3 colores
$0,79

Precio fantástico!

Mochil-in $25,00

Bolimétrico 6/$2,22

$0,99
Lápices Trazo

sacapuntas eléctrico de Puntafina $11,99

$0,10

◈ Comunicación

33 Es.../Son...

In pairs, take turns identifying people or objects in class using the expressions *¿Qué es?/¿Quién es?* and adding any new words from this lesson. Point out where each person or object is located.

> **MODELOS** **A:** *(Point to a chair.)* ¿Qué es?
> **B:** *Es una silla.*
>
> **A:** *(Point to a student.)* ¿Quién es?
> **B:** *Es mi amigo Rafael.*

34 ¿Qué hay en la clase de español?

In pairs, talk about what is or is not in the Spanish class. Make sure to ask about the meaning of words you do not remember.

> **MODELOS** **A:** ¿Hay una ventana en la clase?
> **B:** *¿Qué quiere decir ventana?*
>
> **A:** Quiere decir *window*.
> **B:** No, no hay una ventana en la clase.

Notes Before beginning activity 32, check student comprehension of the advertisement on page 57 for *Nueva Era* stationary store by giving a price and asking students to identify the corresponding items in Spanish using indirect object pronouns. You say: *Cuesta cuatro dólares con noventa y cinco.* Student says: *Es una pizarra.*

La Ola de gira
Activity 35

Answers

35 1. no
2. sí
3. sí
4. no
5. sí

36 Answers will vary.

Activities

Expansion
Conduct a discussion about singers and musicians who perform in Spanish: Ask students which singers and groups are popular; find out which individuals and groups they think will be popular in the future; ask students if they can name anyone who won a Latin Grammy Award the last time the show aired.

Prereading Strategy
Have students look quickly through the *Lectura cultural* to find cognates and other words they recognize.

Spanish for Spanish Speakers
Have students do a report about one of their favorite singers or musical groups. Then ask them to bring in examples of the person's best work to share with the class.

Lectura cultural

La Ola de gira

La gira[1] mundial[2] de La Ola arranca[3] con un concierto en Los Ángeles

La Ola, el nuevo grupo juvenil de rock en español, lanza[4] su CD con una serie de conciertos en todo el continente y España. Sus fans pueden ver[5] el primer concierto en el Greek Theatre en Los Ángeles, California a las ocho de la noche del 20 de septiembre. ¿Por qué[6] La Ola empieza[7] su gira en Los Ángeles? ¿Qué quiere decir esto? ¿Es Los Ángeles la capital de la música latina en los Estados Unidos? Muchos opinan que sí. Después de todo[8], los Premios Grammy de la música latina se celebran en Los Ángeles. Con cinco millones de latinos, Los Ángeles es la ciudad con la mayor[9] concentración de latinos en los Estados Unidos. Es la segunda ciudad con mayor población mexicana después[10] de la Ciudad de México. Tiene una población salvadoreña mayor que[11] la población en San Salvador, la capital de El Salvador.

[1]tour [2]world [3]starts off [4]launches [5]can see [6]Why [7]starts [8]After all
[9]the highest [10]after [11]larger than

35 ¿Qué recuerdas?

¿Sí o no?

1. El primer concierto del grupo La Ola es en España.
2. Los Premios Grammy de la música latina se celebran en Los Ángeles.
3. La mayor concentración de latinos en los Estados Unidos está en Los Ángeles.
4. Hay un millón de mexicanos en Los Ángeles.
5. Hay una mayor población salvadoreña en Los Ángeles que en San Salvador.

36 Algo personal

1. Have you ever seen the Latin Grammy Awards on television? What did you like about it? Why do you think the Latin Grammy Awards are celebrated in Los Angeles?
2. You can see Hispanic influences all over the United States, not only in large cities like Los Angeles. Discuss the Hispanic influence in your own community.

58 *cincuenta y ocho*   **Lección A**

Notes The choice of which words to define or leave for students to discern the meaning of is a subjective one. Words that your students are unable to recognize are glossed at the end of the reading or can be found in the glossary that appears at the end of the book.

Communities. Due to its significant Hispanic population, Los Angeles is one of the largest Spanish-speaking cities in the world.

Connections. Activities 35 and 36 make the cross-curricular connection to geography.

¿Qué aprendí?

Visit the web-based activities at www.emcp.com

Autoevaluación
As a review and self-check, respond to the following:

① How might you ask who your classmates are and where they are from during the first day of school?

② Name two Spanish-speaking celebrities and tell where they are from.

③ Identify objects in your classroom in Spanish.

④ Ask someone how to say "computer" in Spanish.

⑤ What are the benefits of learning Spanish?

Palabras y expresiones

La clase
el bolígrafo
el borrador
el cesto de papeles
el cuaderno
el escritorio
el lápiz
el libro
el mapa
la mochila
la página
el papel
la pared
el periódico
la pizarra
la puerta
el pupitre
la regla

el reloj
la revista
el sacapuntas
la silla
la tiza
la ventana

Gente
el amigo, la amiga
el chico, la chica
él
ella
ellas
ellos
el estudiante, la
   estudiante
nosotros,-as
el profesor, la
   profesora

Palabras interrogativas
¿qué?
¿quién?

Verbos
comprendo
   (comprender)
hay
se dice
sé
ser

Otras expresiones
hay
¿Cómo se dice...?
¿Cómo se llama
   (Ud./él/ella)?
el, la
en la clase
la palabra

los, las
mi
nuevo,-a
¿Qué quiere decir...?
quiere decir
(Ud./Él/Ella) se
   llama...
un, una
unos, unas

Unas estudiantes.

Unos estudiantes.

Teacher Resources

📄 **Activity 17**

💬 **Information Gap Activities**
Postcard Activities
Funciones de Comunicación

Answers

Autoevaluación
Possible answers:
1. ¿Quién es? ¿Cómo se llama el/la estudiante nuevo/a? ¿De dónde es?
2. Daisy Fuentes (Cuba), Juan Luis Guerra (República Dominicana), Antonio Banderas (España), Salma Hayek (México), Jimmy Smits (Estados Unidos), Isabel Allende (Chile), Edgar Rentería (Colombia), Rubén Blades (Panamá), Gloria Estefan (Cuba)
3. Hay un escritorio, unos libros, unos bolígrafos, un cesto de papeles, unas chicas, unos chicos y una pizarra.
4. ¿Cómo se dice *computer*?
5. Answers will vary.

Activities

Multiple Intelligences (musical)
Ask for volunteers to play a popular musical selection for the class using a guitar or other instrument. As a simpler alternative, ask for volunteers to bring in CDs of popular musicians who perform in Spanish. Then conduct a class discussion about what they do or do not like about the music.

Notes Have students check their own understanding of the *Palabras y expresiones*. Point out that the active vocabulary on this page is vocabulary that will be used throughout the book and that it will appear on the chapter test. Words appear again with English equivalents in the end-of-chapter *Vocabulario* and in the vocabulary glossary at the end of *Navegando 1.*

Teacher Resources

 Las clases

 Activity 1

 Activity 19

 Activities 1–3

 Activity 1

 Activities 1–5

> **Content reviewed in *Lección B***
> * classroom objects
> * asking for and stating the time
> * numbers 0–100
> * expressing courtesy
> * noun recognition and plural of nouns

Activities

Cooperative Learning
While introducing the topic of school schedules, ask small groups of students to brainstorm an ideal schedule by noting favorite classes and times of day. They should use their imagination, and their ideas should then be shared with the class. You may wish to teach basic expressions of approval and disapproval so that students can react to the ideas presented.

Lección B

Estados Unidos

Vocabulario I
Las clases

HORA	LUNES	MARTES	MIÉRCOLES	JUEVES	VIERNES	SÁBADO	DOMINGO
7:55	español	español	español	español	español	N	C
8:50	historia	historia	historia	historia	historia	O	L
9:45	biología	biología	biología	biología	biología		A
10:40	biología	inglés	inglés	inglés	inglés	H	S
11:35	matemáticas	matemáticas	matemáticas	matemáticas	matemáticas	A	E
12:30	A L M U E R Z O					Y	S
1:00	computación	computación	computación	computación	computación		
1:55	música	arte	música	música	arte		

Highland High School Horario de Clases

gris

negro

amarillo

blanco

rojo   verde

azul

> Daniel y Teresa son amigos de Ernesto y Rosa.
> Daniel y Teresa estudian mucho.
> Daniel y Teresa no hablan en clase.
> Teresa necesita un lápiz nuevo.
> Daniel lleva una camiseta roja.

Notes Explain to students that school schedules vary greatly throughout the Spanish-speaking world. For example, classes in some countries begin at 8:00 in the morning and end at 2:00. Elsewhere, students may go home for lunch and then return to continue classes until 4:30 or 5:30. Many schools in South America and in Mexico have begun to move to a system consisting of *horario de la mañana* (7:00 to 12:00) and *horario de la tarde* (12:00 to 5:00) to deal with traffic, rush-hour congestion and overcrowding.

1 ¿Qué día es mañana?

🔊 **Contesta la pregunta** *¿Qué día es mañana?* **según lo que oyes.** *(Answer the question ¿Qué día es mañana? according to what you hear.)*

MODELO *You hear:* Es lunes. ¿Qué día es mañana?
You write: martes

2 A corregir

Corrige la información incorrecta, según el Vocabulario I. *(Correct the incorrect information, using Vocabulary I.)*

MODELO La clase de español es <u>a las doce menos cinco.</u>
La clase de español es <u>a las ocho menos cinco.</u>

1. <u>La clase de inglés</u> es lunes, martes, miércoles, jueves y viernes a las diez menos cuarto de la mañana.
2. La clase de computación es <u>a la una y cinco de la mañana.</u>
3. Hay clases de música <u>martes y viernes</u> a las dos menos cinco de la tarde.
4. <u>La clase de historia</u> es a las doce y media.
5. No hay clases <u>los jueves y los viernes.</u>
6. Daniel y Teresa <u>son amigos de Eduardo y Amalia.</u>

¡Extra!

La palabra *de*

The word *de* (of, from) has several different uses in Spanish. For example, *de* can be used to talk about where someone is from (*¿De dónde eres?/Soy de...*) or to describe someone or something (*la clase de español*). Several expressions use *de* (*de nada, de la mañana*). In addition, *de* takes the place of the English apostrophe and the letter *s* (*'s*) to indicate possession or relationships.

*Es la mochila **de** Marta.* It is Marta**'s** backpack.
*Son los amigos **de** Sara y **de** Rodrigo.* They are Sara and Rodrigo**'s** friends.

3 ¿Qué llevan?

Name five people in class and say what each is wearing.

MODELO La profesora lleva una falda azul.

Notes Encourage students to use *¿Cómo?, ¿Perdón?* or a similar expression of your choosing when they do not understand what has been said, as Ernesto does at the top of this page.

Activity 1 is recorded and is part of the Audio CD Program. Reproducible answer sheets have been provided at the end of the Audio CD Program Manual.

Teacher Resources

🔅 **Activity 1**

Answers

1 1. viernes
2. sábado
3. miércoles
4. lunes
5. domingo
6. jueves
2 1. La clase de biología
2. a la una de la tarde
3. lunes, miércoles y jueves
4. El almuerzo
5. los sábados y los domingos
6. son amigos de Ernesto y Rosa
3 Answers will vary.

Activities

Critical Thinking
Have students identify which of the listed classes they have in their schedule. Then give an English equivalent for one of the classes shown on the schedule and have students give the Spanish for each class you say.

Expansion
Give the time for a class listed on the schedule. Call on students to state what class is at the time stated.

Teacher Resources

 El horario de clases
Activities 4–6

Answers

4 1. No, no es nuevo el pantalón. Los zapatos son nuevos.
2. No, no hay.
3. Sí, sí hay.
4. Es el viernes.
5. Necesita unos lápices rojos y verdes.
6. Es a las once y cinco.

5 Answers will vary.

6 1. A
2. D
3. E
4. G
5. F

Activities

Critical Listening

Play the audio CD version of the dialog. Remember to instruct students to cover up the words with one hand since you want them to develop good listening skills. Tell students to look at the photographs while they listen. Then ask several individuals to state what they believe the main theme of the conversation is.

Prereading Strategy

Instruct students to cover up the dialog with one hand and look at the photographs. Ask them to imagine where the conversation takes place and what the people are saying to one another. Finally, have students look through the dialog quickly to find cognates and other words they recognize.

Diálogo I

El horario de clases

RAÚL: Laura, ¿es nuevo tu pantalón?
LAURA: No, pero los zapatos son nuevos.

LAURA: Oye, Raúl, ¿hay clase de música mañana martes?
RAÚL: No, mañana no hay clase de música, mañana hay clase de arte. La clase de música es el viernes.
LAURA: ¡Ah, sí! Mañana hay clase de arte y necesito unos lápices rojos y verdes.

RAÚL: ¿Qué hora es?
LAURA: Son las once. ¿A qué hora es la clase de historia?
RAÚL: Es a las once y cinco.
LAURA: Bueno, es la hora de la clase.

4 ¿Qué recuerdas?

1. ¿Es nuevo el pantalón de Laura?
2. ¿Hay clase de música el martes?
3. ¿Hay clase de arte el martes?
4. ¿Cuándo es la clase de música?
5. ¿De qué colores necesita unos lápices Laura?
6. ¿A qué hora es la clase de historia?

5 Algo personal

1. ¿De qué color es tu ropa?
2. ¿Qué clases hay en tu colegio?
3. ¿Cuántas clases hay en tu horario en un día?
4. ¿Hay clase de arte en tu horario?
5. ¿Tienes lápices de colores? ¿De qué colores son?
6. ¿A qué hora es tu clase de español?
7. ¿A qué hora terminan tus clases?

¡Extra!

Las clases: un poco más

el álgebra	*algebra*
las asignaturas	*subjects*
las ciencias naturales	*earth sciences*
la educación física	*physical education*
la geografía	*geography*
la geometría	*geometry*
la literatura	*literature*

6 ¿Qué clase es?

 Escribe la letra que identifica cada clase que oyes.

A. arte
B. biología
C. computación
D. español
E. historia
F. inglés
G. matemáticas
H. música

Notes When talking about daily schedules, remind students they may wish to use the following expressions to indicate time of day: *de la mañana, de la tarde* and *de la noche.*

The activities that follow the dialog are recorded and can be found in the Audio CD Program. Student answer sheets for activity 6 are located in the back of the Audio CD Program Manual.

Cultura viva

Los colegios en el mundo hispano

What do you think schools are like in Spanish-speaking countries? The options include either public schools or somewhat expensive but numerous private schools. In addition, some teenagers attend technical institutes instead of traditional high schools. Secondary schools in Spanish-speaking countries are often very rigorous. Schools do not offer many extracurricular activities, such as clubs or sports, nor do they have a wide selection of elective courses to choose from. Instead, all students follow the same demanding curriculum consisting of courses such as calculus, chemistry, physics and philosophy.

The classroom atmosphere is different, too. In Spain, for example, students do not actively participate in class as much as in the United States since courses are usually taught through lectures. Students have few tests, must complete several projects and take a comprehensive exam at the end of the year to determine whether they will pass or fail. In many South American countries, however, quizzes and exams are more common, and a student's grade is determined by participation and achievements over the course of the entire grading period.

7 Los colegios en el mundo hispano

¿Sí o no?

1. Students in Spanish-speaking countries may choose from many extracurricular school activities.
2. Students in schools in many Spanish-speaking countries often follow the same demanding curriculum.
3. In Spain, courses are usually taught through lectures and students do not participate in class as much as in the United States.
4. In South America, quizzes and exams are not common, and a student's grade is based upon classroom participation and achievements during an entire grading period.

¡Extra!

En otras palabras
There are several words in Spanish that mean **school.** You have already learned *el colegio,* but here are a few additional words you might hear Spanish speakers use to talk about school: *la escuela, la preparatoria, la academia, el instituto, el liceo, la secundaria, el plantel.*

8 Comparando

Compare the schools in your community with what you know about schools elsewhere in Spanish-speaking countries of the world. What do you consider to be the advantages and disadvantages of the school system you attend? What would you change?

Notes **Comparisons.** Ask students to investigate school life in one of the Spanish-speaking countries they have studied. Then ask them to compare some aspect of school in that country with their school. Topics may include the calendar year, vacation schedule, school activities, classes offered, etc. Suggest that students obtain information on the Internet, at the library, or from Spanish-speaking members of the community.

Use a Venn diagram to complete activity 8.

 Activity 4

Teacher Resources

Answers

7 1. no
   2. sí
   3. sí
   4. no
8 Creative problem solving.

Activities

Spanish for Spanish Speakers
Have students make a detailed report of the educational system of a Spanish-speaking country of their choice. Then have students present their findings to the class and contrast them to the school system in the United States.

Answers

9 1. masculino, el colegio, los colegios
2. masculino, el día, los días
3. femenino, la falda, las faldas
4. masculino, el lápiz, los lápices
5. femenino, la camiseta, las camisetas
6. masculino, el papel, los papeles
7. masculino, el mapa, los mapas
8. masculino, el zapato, los zapatos
9. masculino, el calcetín, los calcetines

Activities

Cooperative Learning
Have students describe several common objects (a pen, newspaper, the door, paper, etc.). Then ask them to pair up and take turns reading their descriptions to see if their partner can guess the object. After completing all their sentences, have students discuss how they might improve each description.

 # Idioma

Repaso rápido: nouns

Nouns in Spanish are either masculine or feminine. Many masculine nouns end in *-o* and many feminine nouns in *-a*. Make most nouns plural by adding *-s*.

	masculino	**femenino**
singular	*un bolígrafo*	*una silla*
plural	*unos bolígrafos*	*unas sillas*

Remember that some nouns may require you to add or remove an accent mark in their plural form.

*el exa*men → ***los** exámenes*   *el calcetín* → ***los** calcetines*

9 ¿Qué sabes sobre los sustantivos?

Say if the following nouns are masculine (*masculino*) or feminine (*femenino*) by giving the corresponding definite article. Then, give the plural form of each.

MODELO clase
femenino, la clase, las clases

1. colegio
2. día
3. falda
4. lápiz
5. camiseta
6. papel
7. mapa
8. zapato
9. calcetín

Hay unos cuadernos rojos.

Estructura

Using adjectives to describe

Adjectives (*adjetivos*) describe (or modify) nouns. In Spanish, they must match the gender (masculine or feminine) and number (singular or plural) of the nouns they describe. Singular masculine adjectives often end in *-o* (*rojo*), singular feminine adjectives often end in *-a* (*roja*) and either form can be made plural by adding *-s* (*rojos, rojas*).

Hay un cuaderno amarillo.	There is one yellow notebook.
Hay una regla amarilla.	There is one yellow ruler.
Hay dos cuadernos amarillos.	There are two yellow notebooks.
Hay dos reglas amarillas.	There are two yellow rulers.

64 *sesenta y cuatro*   **Lección B**

Notes The section *Repaso rápido* provides a review of previously learned grammar and is intended to help prepare students for a related grammar point, in this case adjective-noun agreement.

Have students name several objects in the classroom and then tell whether each is masculine or feminine.

Adjectives that end in -e generally have only one singular form, which can be made plural by adding -s.

singular	plural
Hay un bolígraf**o** verd**e**.	Hay dos bolígraf**os** verd**es**.
Hay una puert**a** verd**e**.	Hay dos puert**as** verd**es**.

Adjectives that end with a consonant usually have only one singular form, which can be made plural by adding -es.

singular	plural
Hay un cuadern**o** azul.	Hay dos cuadern**os** azul**es**.
Hay una puert**a** azul.	Hay dos puert**as** azul**es**.

Although Spanish adjectives generally follow the nouns they modify, adjectives of quantity such as numbers *(dos, tres)* and question-asking words are exceptions. They precede their nouns.

*Tengo **dos** cuadernos verdes.*　　I have two green notebooks.
*¿**Cuántas** sillas hay?*　　How many chairs are there?

 Práctica

10 **¡No estoy de acuerdo!**

Correct these descriptions by replacing the underlined words with the words in parentheses. Remember to make all the nouns and adjectives agree and to change the verb forms when necessary.

MODELOS　Es una camisa <u>azul</u>. (verde)
　　　　No, es una camisa verde.

　　　　<u>Julia</u> es la estudiante nueva. (Armando y Juan)
　　　　No, Armando y Juan son los estudiantes nuevos.

1. <u>El chico</u> nuevo se llama Julián Fernández. (el profesor)
2. Marta lleva <u>la camiseta</u> gris. (el pantalón)
3. Hay <u>dos zapatos</u> nuevos en el pupitre. (una revista)
4. Hay <u>un cuaderno</u> blanco en el escritorio. (una tiza)
5. Son unos calcetines <u>verdes</u>. (negro)
6. Belia lleva los zapatos <u>blancos</u>. (negro)

Julia es la estudiante nueva.

Notes Ask students to identify several adjectives in Spanish that are cognates: *moderno, natural, artificial, personal, ideal.*

When an adjective modifies two or more nouns, one of which is masculine, use the masculine form of the adjective.

Answers

11 Answers should match the colors of these items in your classroom. Check to be sure students use the correct forms of the adjectives.

12
1. El color negro quiere decir excelente. El color amarillo quiere decir regular. El color azul quiere decir horrible o fatal.
2. No, es un día superior para el romance.
3. El domingo es fatal para la energía física. El jueves y el viernes son superiores para la energía física.
4. El domingo es excelente en las categorías de familia y también de dinero.
5. La profesión es azul.
6. No, no tengo energía física el martes. Sí, tengo energía física el lunes.
7. *Possible answer:* El mejor día es el (viernes).

13 Conversations may include the questions *¿Qué es/son?*, *¿De qué color es?* or *¿De qué colores son?*, among others (to review the forms of *ser*). Possible descriptions (to review the definite and indefinite articles, forms of *ser*, colors, gender, etc.) include the following:
1. Es un libro de historia. Es gris.
2. Es una mochila. Es azul.
3. Es una puerta. Es amarilla.
4. Son una pizarra y un borrador. La pizarra es negra y el borrador es rojo.
5. Es un mapa. Es verde y azul.
6. Es un periódico. Es blanco y negro.
7. Son unas reglas. Son rojas.

11 ¿De qué color es?

Describe objects in your classroom by combining words from the two columns.

MODELO Los bolígrafos de Laura son verdes.

1. el escritorio
2. la puerta
3. la pizarra
4. los lápices
5. las sillas
6. los libros
7. las revistas
8. los bolígrafos

A. verde
B. negro
C. gris
D. amarillo
E. rojo
F. azul
G. blanco

12 Los colores de tu día

Imagine you are reading a newspaper in Spanish and you see this horoscope. How much can you understand? Pretend it pertains to your sign and answer the questions.

1. ¿Qué quiere decir el color negro? ¿El color amarillo? ¿El color azul?
2. ¿Es el jueves un día malo para el romance?
3. ¿Qué día es fatal para la energía física?
4. ¿Es el domingo un día excelente?
5. En general, ¿de qué color es la profesión?
6. ¿Tienes energía física el martes? ¿Y el lunes?
7. En tu opinión, ¿qué día es el mejor *(best)*?

Comunicación

13 Los objetos en la clase

 En parejas, hablen Uds. de los siguientes objetos en la clase. *(In pairs, talk about the following objects in the classroom.)*

MODELOS A: ¿Qué es?
B: Es una silla.

A: ¿De qué color es la silla?
B: Es amarilla.

1 2 3 4 5 6 7

Notes Point out that colors can act as nouns (*El azul es un color.*) or adjectives (*Es una camisa azul.*).

Remind students that colors are descriptive adjectives and that like other descriptive adjectives they usually follow the noun they describe.

Consider teaching students the following colors: *beige, café, rosado, morado, anaranjado.*

You may wish to introduce the following: *¿Cuál es tu color favorito?* (What is your favorite color?); *Mi color favorito es azul/amarillo/blanco.* (My favorite color is blue/yellow/white.).

14 Juego

Working in pairs, take turns describing three or four people and three or four objects in the classroom. See how quickly you can communicate to your partner what you are describing.

Estructura

Saying what someone does: present tense of -ar verbs

Verbs express actions (to do something) or states of being (to be). The form of the verbs found in Spanish dictionaries is called an **infinitive.** In English, an infinitive generally is used with the word **to** (to study, to eat, to live). Spanish infinitives end with -ar, -er or -ir.

Spanish verbs are considered regular if their various forms follow a predictable pattern. To form the present tense of a regular -ar verb, such as *hablar* (to speak), remove the -ar ending. Then attach the endings that correspond to each of the subject pronouns.

hablar			
yo	habl**o**	nosotros nosotras	habl**amos**
tú	habl**as**	vosotros vosotras	habl**áis**
Ud. él ella	habl**a**	Uds. ellos ellas	habl**an**

A present-tense Spanish verb may have several different equivalents in English.

Hablo español.
    I **speak** Spanish.
    I **do speak** Spanish.
    I **am speaking** Spanish.

Other useful -ar verbs that follow the same pattern are: *estudiar* (to study), *llevar* (to wear), *necesitar* (to need) and *terminar* (to end, to finish).

Capítulo 2   *sesenta y siete* **67**

Teacher Resources

 Activity 3

 Activities 6–8

 Activity 3

 Activities 9–10

Answers

14 Creative self-expression.

Activities

Critical Thinking
Have students identify several infinitives in a Spanish dictionary. (The glossary at the end of the textbook can serve as the dictionary.) Students prepare a written list of infinitives, or as an alternative, you may want to review their lists orally in class. As an extension to this, have students find additional infinitives in dialogs and reading passages.

Multiple Intelligences (spatial)
Ask students to look carefully at several well-known paintings by Spanish and Latin American artists. What colors can they identify? What other words can they use to describe what they see? Encourage interested students to learn more about the paintings and artists via the Internet.

TPR
Many -ar verbs are easily dramatized through total physical response. Use TPR to reinforce verbs, such as *hablar,* that appear in this chapter and to preview others that will be learned later.

Notes Model correct pronunciation several times to ensure that students accentuate the correct syllable of the verb forms.

You may wish to tell students that the present tense can also express an action intended or planned for the near future: *Hablamos mañana.*

67

Activity 16

Answers

15 The *-ar* infinitives: *pasar, terminar, descansar, quedar, regresar, entrar, estar, jugar, cantar, levantar, buscar, encontrar, comprar, disfrutar, quedar, aguantar.*

16
1. Sí, yo hablo español.
2. Sí, mis amigos hablan español.
3. Sí, mi amiga habla español.
4. Sí, mi amigo y yo hablamos español.
5. Sí, Uds. hablan español.
6. Sí, el estudiante nuevo habla español.

Activities

Spanish for Spanish Speakers
Have Spanish-speaking students pair up with nonbilingual students to talk about the poem that appears on page 68. As an alternative, ask for a Spanish-speaking student to teach the poem to the class.

 Práctica

15 Un poema sobre el colegio

Busca los infinitivos que terminan en *-ar* en este poema.

EL BUS VUELVE A PASAR

Ya las vacaciones van a terminar,
y bastante te has dedicado a descansar
pero si burro no te quieres quedar,
de nuevo a la escuela has de regresar.

Carlos, José, Cristina y Pilar,
ansiosos de entrar al colegio deben estar,
ellos para fútbol y canicas jugar,
y ellas para en la rueda volver a cantar.

Todos gruñendo se van a levantar,
el día en que el bus los vuelva a buscar,
pero todos felices van a estar,
por el sólo hecho de volverse a encontrar.

Nuevos útiles y ropa te van a comprar,
para que tus estudios puedas disfrutar,
y tan buen mozo e inteligente vas a quedar
que Cristina y Pilar no se van a aguantar.

16 ¿Hablan español?

Di que las siguientes personas hablan español.
(Say that the following people speak Spanish.)

MODELO ¿Tú?
Sí, tú hablas español.

1. ¿Yo?
2. ¿Mis amigos?
3. ¿Mi amiga?
4. ¿Mi amigo y yo?
5. ¿Uds.?
6. ¿El estudiante nuevo?

Estrategia

Scanning
Scanning is a quick way to get the main idea of what you are about to read. You can increase your understanding of this poem by first scanning the text for cognates (words with similar spelling and meaning in two languages). Also, by scanning headings, boldface words and lists, you are focusing on the important information that will help you get the main point of the text you are about to read.

Before doing activity 15, scan the poem *El bus vuelve a pasar* and jot down all the cognates you recognize. Can you understand the poem more easily now?

Hablamos español.

Lección B

Notes Have students find words they recognize in the poem *El bus vuelve a pasar*. Then have them apply the scanning strategy to try and discern the meaning of lines of the poem. Finally, discuss the poem so students have a general idea of what the poem is about.

Consider having students memorize the poem on page 68. You may want to give a grade for their work or offer extra credit.

17 Un día típico en el colegio

Di lo que ocurre en un día típico en el colegio, usando los verbos indicados.
(Say what happens on a typical day at school, using the indicated verbs.)

MODELO Carolina y Víctor <u>necesitan</u> papel en la clase de historia. (necesitar)

1. Yo __ español con mi profesor. (hablar)
2. La clase de historia __ a las ocho menos cinco. (terminar)
3. Paz y Ricardo __ computación. (estudiar)
4. Tú y yo __ español en la clase de español. (hablar)
5. Rosita __ un bolígrafo en la clase de matemáticas. (necesitar)
6. Tú __ con una amiga. (estudiar)
7. Uds. __ biología con unos amigos. (estudiar)
8. Las clases de mi colegio __ a las tres de la tarde. (terminar)
9. Nueve o diez estudiantes __ jeans. (llevar)
10. Un estudiante o una estudiante __ ropa nueva. (llevar)

18 En el colegio

Haz siete oraciones lógicas usando palabras de las tres columnas.

1. una estudiante	terminar	con el profesor de arte
2. mi amigo y yo	estudiar	unos cuadernos amarillos
3. unos estudiantes	necesitar	a las tres
4. la clase de español	hablar	unos jeans y zapatos negros
5. el estudiante nuevo	llevar	una mochila nueva
6. tú		arte y computación
7. yo		inglés y español

◇ Comunicación

19 Una encuesta

Working in groups of three, complete a survey of your classmates to find out what they are studying in school. Each person should select one subject (choosing from *arte, biología, computación, historia, matemáticas* or *música*). Then find out how many boys and how many girls in class study the subject you are investigating. Record the results under the headings *Chicos* and *Chicas*. Summarize your findings for the members of your group.

MODELO **A:** Mario, ¿estudias computación?
B: Sí, estudio computación.

Computación	
Chicos	Chicas
‖‖‖ ‖‖‖ ‖‖	‖‖‖ ‖‖‖ ‖‖

Sí, estudio computación.

Capítulo 2

Answers

17 1. hablo
2. termina
3. estudian
4. hablamos
5. necesita
6. estudias
7. estudian
8. terminan
9. llevan
10. lleva
18 Answers will vary.
19 Creative self-expression.

Activities

Students with Special Needs
As preparation or warm-up before assigning activity 17, do a quick verb conjugation "round-robin" activity with the class. Give students a subject pronoun and an *-ar* infinitive to be conjugated appropriately: *yo/necesitar (yo necesito), tú/hablar (tú hablas)* and so on.

Notes Have students create their own sentences about what happens during a typical day at school, similar to activity 17.

Explain to students that some of their sentences for activity 18 will use the same verb more than once.

20 Los resultados de la encuesta

While working with the same students as in activity 19, tabulate the results of the three surveys each of you completed in the previous exercise. One member of each group should then report the findings to the class. Compare what you learned from the survey results of other students in the class to determine if your survey is accurate.

MODELO Veinticuatro estudiantes estudian computación.
Son doce chicos y doce chicas.

 21 ¿Qué necesitan Uds.?

Pretend you are in a bookstore. Working in groups of four or five, take turns playing the roles of the clerk and customers. Find out which item(s) your customers need. If you would like, you may answer with *Aquí está* (Here it is) or *Aquí están* (Here they are).

Estructura

Talking about schedules: ¿A qué hora?

To ask when something is going to occur ask **¿A qué hora** (+ verb + event)? Answer with the following: **Verb + a la/las** (+ time) or simply with **A la/las** (+ time).

¿A qué hora es la clase de español? When (At what time) is Spanish class?

Es a la una.

It is at one o'clock.
At one o'clock.

Note: The twenty-four hour clock (i.e., military time) often appears in railroad, airline and bus timetables or in movie and theater advertising. When expressing time this way, the day begins at one minute after midnight. The numbers one to twelve refer to the time of day between midnight and noon. After noon, each hour is added to twelve: 13:00 hours would be the equivalent of 1:00 P.M. *(Es la una de la tarde.)*.

Práctica

22 Mi horario en el colegio

Contesta las siguientes preguntas.

1. ¿A qué hora es tu clase de español? ¿A qué hora termina?
2. ¿A qué hora es tu clase de inglés? ¿A qué hora termina?
3. ¿A qué hora es tu clase de historia? ¿A qué hora termina?
4. ¿A qué hora es tu clase de matemáticas? ¿A qué hora termina?

¿Qué hora es?

Notes When students discuss their own schedules, be sure they use *mi/tu clase* rather than *la clase* in their questions and answers.

Select one or two groups to present their skits from activity 21. As an alternative, have all groups present their skits over several days and assign grades.

23 En la televisión

Contesta las siguientes preguntas, según el horario de Telemundo.

1. ¿A qué hora es *De Mañanita*?
2. ¿A qué hora termina *Cotorreando*?
3. ¿Qué hay a las cinco de la tarde?
4. ¿A qué hora es *La Corte de Familia*?
5. ¿*Laura* termina a las siete de la noche?
6. ¿Es *Pobre Pablo* una telenovela (soap opera)?

HORARIO	PROGRAMA	GÉNERO
6:00	Noticiero Telemundo	Noticias
6:30	Noticiero Telemundo	Noticias
7:00	De Mañanita	Noticias
10:00	Pobre Pablo	Novela
10:30		
11:00	¿Sabía usted?	Variedad
11:30	¡Ay Caramba!	Comedia
12:00	Maritere	Talk Show
12:30		
13:00	Cotorreando	Variedad
13:30		
14:00	Sala de Parejas	Variedad
14:30		
15:00	La Corte de Familia	Variedad
15:30	La Corte del Pueblo	Variedad
16:00	Laura	Talk Show
16:30		
17:00	Al Rojo Vivo con María Celeste	Noticias
17:30		
18:00	La Corte del Pueblo	Variedad
18:30	Noticiero Telemundo	Noticias

◈ Comunicación

24 ¿A qué hora?

Ask several classmates about their school schedules. Discuss what they are studying and when each class is.

25 El horario de clases de Mónica

Mónica just e-mailed you a copy of her new class schedule. Working in pairs, look at her schedule and talk about what she is studying, when the classes are and when they end.

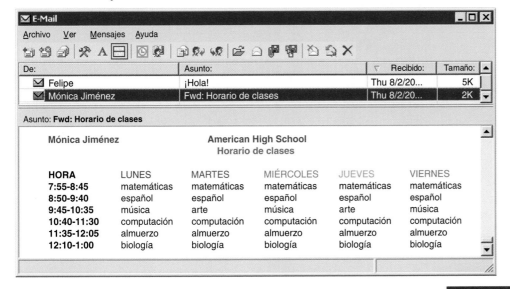

E-Mail
Archivo Ver Mensajes Ayuda

De:	Asunto:	Recibido:	Tamaño:
Felipe	¡Hola!	Thu 8/2/20...	5K
Mónica Jiménez	Fwd: Horario de clases	Thu 8/2/20...	2K

Asunto: **Fwd: Horario de clases**

Mónica Jiménez   **American High School**
Horario de clases

HORA	LUNES	MARTES	MIÉRCOLES	JUEVES	VIERNES
7:55-8:45	matemáticas	matemáticas	matemáticas	matemáticas	matemáticas
8:50-9:40	español	español	español	español	español
9:45-10:35	música	arte	música	arte	música
10:40-11:30	computación	computación	computación	computación	computación
11:35-12:05	almuerzo	almuerzo	almuerzo	almuerzo	almuerzo
12:10-1:00	biología	biología	biología	biología	biología

Capítulo 2   *setenta y uno* **71**

Answers

23 1. Es a las siete de la mañana.
   2. Termina a las dos de la tarde.
   3. Hay Al Rojo Vivo con María Celeste.
   4. Es a las tres de la tarde.
   5. No, Laura termina a las cinco de la tarde.
   6. Sí.
24 Creative self-expression.
25 Creative self-expression.

Activities

Cooperative Learning
Have students work in pairs, writing their actual schedules (help them with Spanish words for subjects they take). They should exchange schedules and ask *¿A qué hora es tu clase de...?*. (Because A has B's schedule, A can verify if B answers correctly.)

Spanish for Spanish Speakers
Have students write a short composition about their favorite class. Ask them to explain why they like it. Students should also discuss their least favorite class.

Technology
If you have located a class with which to do e-mail projects in a Spanish-speaking country or in another city in the United States, have students exchange and compare their schedules. You may wish to try the following sources before assigning the activity to students: Intercultural E-mail Exchanges and Intercultural E-mail Connections. Also, the State Department is a good source for American schools abroad.

Notes **Comparisons.** After completing activity 23, ask similar questions in relation to television shows popular with your students.

Just as **TV** is a common abbreviation in English, *televisión* is often shortened to *tele* in informal conversations in Spanish.

Teacher Resources

 ¿Dónde está?

 Activities 5–6

 Activity 20

 Activities 10–11

 Activity 4

 Activities 12–13

Activities

Critical Listening
Say aloud several telephone or fax numbers. Have students write the number they hear. Then call on a student to write the number on the chalkboard.

Multiple Intelligences (bodily-kinesthetic/linguistic)
Have students draw and label the parts of a computer with all peripherals (mouse, mouse pad, etc.). Display the drawings around the room or use them to review vocabulary.

Students with Special Needs
Create labels (or have students create labels) for classroom objects, and attach the labels to the objects with string or tape. This can be a good opportunity to enrich student vocabulary by adding words that are not yet active in *Navegando*, for example: *la bandera, el calendario, el diccionario* and so forth.

Notes Point out the article *el* is needed in a complete-sentence response to *¿Cuál es tu número de teléfono?*.

Tell students that the plural form of *la impresora láser* is *las impresoras láser*.

Help students with the meanings of some of the new words and expressions.

In Spain, the term *móvil* is used instead of *celular*.

los diskettes

¿Hay un examen de biología mañana?

la impresora láser

la pantalla

los discos compactos (CDs)

el ratón

el teclado

Sí, mañana hay un examen.

26 ¿Qué necesitan?

 Write the names Pilar and Julio. Next, listen and list under each of their names what Julio and Pilar need before they leave for college. Then circle any items on the lists that they both need.

27 Información personal

In groups of four, take turns asking for your classmates' phone numbers, fax numbers and e-mail addresses. (You may invent any of the information you wish.)

28 La computadora

Mira la ilustración y contesta las siguientes preguntas en español.

1. ¿De qué color es la pantalla?
2. ¿Hay dos teclados?
3. ¿Dónde está la computadora?
4. ¿Dónde está el papel?
5. ¿Hay un ratón?
6. ¿Cuántos diskettes hay en el escritorio?

¡Extra!

El plural de algunas palabras

Note that the word *ratón* changes when it is plural. The accent on the *o* disappears *(ratones)*. Words ending in *-ón, -ión, -és* and *-án* lose the accent when the plural ending *-es* is attached: *ratón → ratones; dirección → direcciones.*

Notes You may wish to have students use a Venn diagram to do activity 26.

Activity 26 is intended to practice listening comprehension. Play the audio CD of the activity that is part of the Audio CD Program.

Instead of having students list the names Pilar and Julio, you may wish to use the student answer sheet for activity 26, which can be found at the end of the Audio CD Program Manual.

Teacher Resources

 ¿Cuál es tu dirección de correo electrónico?
Activities 29–30

Answers

29 1. Carlos habla con Diana.
2. En clase de computación.
3. No, no está en la mochila. No, no está sobre el pupitre tampoco.
4. Está sobre el escritorio del profesor.
5. Es dianavelez, arroba, latinored, punto, com.

30 Answers will vary.

31 Role-playing activity.

Activities

Prereading Strategy
Before students open their books, have them brainstorm in Spanish different objects that can be found in a classroom. Then instruct students to cover up the dialog with one hand and look at the photographs. Ask them to imagine where the conversation takes place and what the people are saying to one another. Finally, have students look through the dialog quickly to find cognates and others words they already know.

Diálogo II
¿Cuál es tu dirección de correo electrónico?

CARLOS: Diana, necesito una nota de ocho en computación. ¿Estudiamos?
DIANA: Sí, Carlos.
CARLOS: Muy bien... ¿Cuál es tu dirección de correo electrónico?
DIANA: Es dianavelez@....
CARLOS: ¡Ay, perdón!

CARLOS: ¿Dónde está mi bolígrafo?
DIANA: No sé. ¿No está en tu mochila?
CARLOS: No, no está y tampoco está sobre mi pupitre.

DIANA: ¡Mira! Allí hay un bolígrafo sobre el escritorio del profesor. ¿Es tu bolígrafo?
CARLOS: ¡Ay, sí! Muchas gracias. ¿Cuál es tu correo electrónico?
DIANA: Es dianavelez, arroba, latinored, punto, com.

 29 ¿Qué recuerdas?

1. ¿Con quién habla Carlos?
2. ¿En qué clase necesita Carlos una nota de ocho?
3. ¿Está el bolígrafo de Carlos en la mochila? ¿Sobre el pupitre?
4. ¿Dónde está el bolígrafo de Carlos?
5. ¿Cuál es la dirección de correo electrónico de Diana?

¡Extra!
Más sobre la tecnología

la almohadilla	*mouse pad*
el archivo	*file*
el disco duro	*hard drive*
la Internet/la Red	*Internet*
el micrófono	*microphone*
navegar por Internet/la Red	*to surf the Web*
los parlantes	*speakers*
la unidad CD-ROM	*CD-ROM drive*
el software	*software*
la Web/la Red	*World Wide Web*

30 Algo personal

1. ¿Qué tienes en tu mochila?
2. ¿Cuál es tu dirección de correo electrónico?
3. ¿Cuál es tu dirección de Internet favorita?

31 En la clase

Trabajando en parejas, haz el papel de una de las personas del diálogo anterior. *(Working in pairs, play the part of one of the people in the preceding dialog.)*

¿Qué tienes en tu mochila?

Notes If students ask about *¡Mira!* in the dialog, remind them they have already seen the expression in *Capítulo 1* and need only to recognize how to use this command naturally in conversation. Commands are addressed in the Appendices at the back of this book.

In addition to their own e-mail addresses, students can give others that they know because of frequent correspondence.

Activity 31 is a pair activity. As such, it has not been recorded as part of the Audio CD Program for listening comprehension practice.

Cultura viva

¡Qué notas!

Escala:

10	Superior (S)
9	Excelente (EX)
8	Muy Bueno/Muy Buena (MB)
7-6	Bueno/Buena (B)
5	Necesita Mejorar (NM)
4-0	Deficiente (D)

Las notas

Schools in many Spanish-speaking countries often base report card grades *(las notas)* on a numerical scale such as 1-10 instead of using the letter grades *A-F*. Descriptive categories sometimes accompany the number grade to further clarify the numerical values. In general, *cinco* or *seis* is the minimum passing grade, while *un/una estudiante de diez* (an *A* student) is a very difficult distinction to achieve.

If you were a student in Mexico or the Dominican Republic and your report card contained the grades *EX* and *MB,* would you be pleased? Would the parents of a student from Chile or Honduras be happy with a *B*? Look at this grading scale found at the bottom of a report card and determine what grades they would be equivalent to at your school.

¿Soy una estudiante excelente?

32 ¿Qué nota?

Using the scale from the *Cultura viva* reading, what grade would you assign the following students based upon the comments about their work?

MODELO Paquito does okay in biology, but he does not study enough.
Cinco. Necesita mejorar en biología.

1. Sara is a computer genius. She aces every assignment!
2. Jaime scores 100 on every English test.
3. Luisa is an average student in history.
4. Julio didn't turn in three math assignments.
5. Teresa is a good singer and enjoys music class.
6. The average of Daniel's quizzes in Spanish is 84.
7. Laura likes to draw. Her artwork is good, but she does not pay attention to the instructor.

Teacher Resources

 Activity 12

 Activity 5

Answers

32 Answers will vary. Students should give a reasonable grade. Possible answers:
1. ¡Diez! Es superior en computación.
2. ¡Diez! Es superior en inglés.
3. Siete. Es buena en historia.
4. Cinco. Necesita mejorar en matemáticas.
5. ¡Nueve! Es excelente en música.
6. Ocho. Es muy bueno en español.
7. Seis. Es buena en arte.

Notes Students have already seen the words *bueno* (*buenos días*) and *buena* (*buenas tardes*). Ask if the students know the meaning of these terms as they refer to grades.

Another way of referring to grades is: *Sobresaliente* (9/10); *Notable* (7/8); *Bien* (6); *Suficiente* (5); *Insuficiente* (3/4); *Deficiente* (0/2).

Teacher Resources

 Activity 7

 Activities 13–14

 Activity 6

 Activities 14–15

Activities

Expansion

Ask students to identify several people at your school and explain where they are at a given time *(La Sra. Codina está en la clase de inglés.).*

Multiple Intelligences (bodily-kinesthetic/linguistic)

Have students draw a map of the United States that includes seven cities with Spanish names. Then they must explain where each city is located *(San Antonio está en Texas.).*

Idioma

Estructura

Talking about location or how someone feels: *estar*

The verb *estar* (to be) is irregular in the present tense. You already have seen several forms of this verb.

estar					
yo	**estoy**	*I am*	nosotros nosotras	**estamos**	*we are*
tú	**estás**	*you are*	vosotros vosotras	**estáis**	*you are*
Ud. él ella	**está**	*you are* *he (it) is* *she (it) is*	Uds. ellos ellas	**están**	*they are*

Estar indicates location or a state of being or a condition at a given moment.

location:	*¿Dónde **está** el profesor?*	Where is the teacher?
	***Está** en clase.*	He is in class.
state of being or condition:	*¿Cómo **estás**?*	How are you?
	***Estoy** bien, gracias.*	I am well, thanks.

¿Cómo estás?

¿Dónde está el Alamo?

Notes Explain that although both *es* and *está* can mean **is** in English, their usage is quite different. For example, *está* has been used to express health and is also used here to indicate location, whereas *es* conveys existence. Forms of the verb *ser* are used to describe more permanent, basic characteristics of a person, place or thing, whereas forms of *estar* are used to describe more changeable aspects of a person, place or thing. Some examples of changeable aspects include emotions, feelings, locations and temporary conditions.

Práctica

33 Un mensaje para Felipe

Complete María's e-mail message to Felipe with the appropriate words before she sends him the message.

termina   estamos

estás

necesito   estoy

☒ E-Mail	_ ☐ ✕

Archivo Ver Mensajes ?

🖆🖆🖆 ✕ A ⊟ ⊠📷 ⋮⋮⋮ ⋮⋮⋮ ✕

A...	Felipe
Cc...	
Asunto:	¡Hola!

¡Hola!
Unos amigos y yo (1) en la clase de español. ¿Cómo (2) tú? Yo (3) muy bien.
La clase (4) en cinco minutos y yo (5) hablar con la profesora.
Hasta pronto.

María

Estoy bien, gracias.

Capítulo 2

setenta y siete 77

Notes **Comparisons.** Have students compare English and Spanish: Explain that words such as *yo* and *tú* are often omitted when the subject of the sentence is understood. Similarly, the English subject **it** seldom requires a Spanish equivalent: *¿Dónde está el lápiz?* (Where is the pencil?); *Está aquí.* (**It is** here.).

Answers

34 1. Felipe está en Los Ángeles.
2. Pedro y Francisco están en Denver.
3. Amalia y Virginia están en Atlanta.
4. Josefina, Kathy y yo (Nosotras) estamos en Santa Fe.
5. Mi tía Sandra está en Miami.
6. Yo estoy en (*name of city*).

35 1. San Antonio y Santa Fe están en Estados Unidos.
2. Sevilla y Madrid están en España.
3. Santiago está en Chile.
4. Managua está en Nicaragua.
5. Maracaibo está en Venezuela.
6. Montevideo está en Uruguay.
7. Potosí está en Bolivia.
8. La Plata está en Argentina.
9. Cali está en Colombia.
10. Concepción está en Paraguay.

---

34 En EE.UU.

María is sending e-mail messages to family and friends across the United States. Tell where she and her acquaintances are located according to the illustration.

MODELO María está en Dallas.

1. Felipe
2. Pedro y Francisco
3. Amalia y Virginia
4. Josefina, Kathy y yo
5. mi tía *(aunt)* Sandra
6. ¿Y tú? ¿Dónde estás?

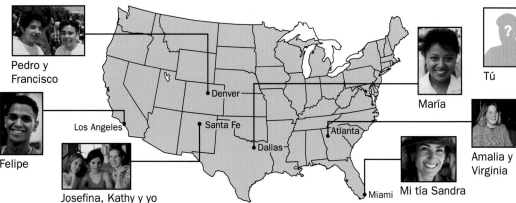

35 Conexión con otras disciplinas: geografía

Amalia is studying for a geography quiz. Can you tell her where each of the following Spanish-speaking cities is located?

MODELO Malabo
Malabo está en Guinea Ecuatorial.

1. San Antonio y Santa Fe
2. Sevilla y Madrid
3. Santiago
4. Managua
5. Maracaibo
6. Montevideo
7. Potosí
8. La Plata
9. Cali
10. Concepción

Malabo está en Guinea Ecuatorial.

Notes **Connections.** The verbs *ser* and *estar* can serve to reinforce the geography of the Spanish-speaking world that was emphasized in *Capítulo 1*. Remind students that *ser* is used for origin, whereas *estar* is used for location.

Communities. Just as many young people in the United States study Spanish, many students in Spain and Latin America study English. Encourage students to consider ways they may learn more about people throughout the Spanish-speaking world (e-mail, partnerships, study abroad, exchanges), make friends and practice what they are learning in Spanish class.

36 En la clase del Sr. Ardila

Mira la ilustración y contesta las preguntas en español.

Sarita Ortíz

el profesor Ardila

MODELO ¿Dónde está el profesor Ardila?
Está en clase.

1. ¿Dónde está el reloj?
2. ¿Dónde está Sarita Ortíz?
3. ¿Dónde están los libros verdes?
4. ¿Dónde está el mapa de México?
5. ¿Dónde está la revista *Shock*?
6. ¿Dónde están las sillas?
7. ¿Dónde está el periódico?
8. ¿Dónde están los libros de biología?
9. ¿Dónde está el colegio Highland High School?
10. ¿Dónde está Mazatlán?

Comunicación

37 Después de las clases

Pretend you are looking for someone or something. Working with a classmate, take turns asking about where several people and objects are. Be sure to be polite and say "please" and thank the other person for information about each person or object you are trying to find.

38 Mi colegio

Create your ideal schedule for next year. Include six classes and a lunch. Then, in pairs, create a telephone conversation in which you discuss your schedules. Find out who has math, times for classes, if you have the same lunch period, how many books each of you will need and so forth.

Capítulo 2

setenta y nueve **79**

Notes Have students work together in small groups and take turns asking and answering where several objects or people in activity 36 are located.

Remind students before assigning activity 38 that the questions containing the possessive adjective *tu (tu clase)* have answers that contain the word *mi*.

As part of your classroom management, set a time limit for activity 38.

You may wish to obtain several play or real telephones for students to use as they present the conversation for activity 38 in front of the class.

36 Possible answers:
1. Está en la pared.
2. Está en la clase (en la silla azul).
3. Están en el escritorio.
4. Está en la pared.
5. Está en la mochila.
6. Están en la clase.
7. Está en el cesto de papeles.
8. Están sobre la computadora.
9. Está en Dallas, Texas.
10. Está en México.
37 Creative self-expression.
38 Creative self-expression.

Activities

Cooperative Learning
Have students work in pairs, asking and answering questions about their school for activity 38. They should say where the school is, when classes are, what their schedule is like and who their teachers are.

Expansion
Conduct a class discussion about students' classes. Start with Spanish class: when the class starts and ends, who the teacher is, who is in the class, what objects are in the class, etc. Then continue on to include other classes and other topics.

Language through Action
Have students describe what they see in the illustration that accompanies activity 36. Then they should find and identify similar items or people in the classroom as they point to each and describe it.

Teacher Resources

Lectura personal
Activity 39

Answers

39 1. Se llama Preparatoria
Benito Juárez.
2. Son de las 2:00 P.M.
a las 8:00 P.M.
3. Es inglés.
4. Hay cuarenta estudiantes.
5. Estudia con un profesor
particular.
40 Answers will vary.

Activities

Cooperative Learning
Have students work in pairs to
create a dialog, using the Spanish
they have learned in this lesson.
Each student should prepare four
to eight lines. Ask them to be as
creative as possible! Then ask for
volunteers to present their dialog
in class. All students should
speak Spanish and work
cooperatively to prepare for this
activity. Students who have
completed the lesson successfully
will be able to do what is
requested and should
demonstrate creative
self-expression.

Prereading Strategy
Have students look quickly
through the *Lectura cultural* about
the musical group La Ola to find
cognates and other words they
recognize.

Lectura personal

Cantantes y grupos musicales

Dirección http://www.emcp.com/música/ola/e.diario-1.htm ▲ Archivo Edición Ver Favoritos Herramientas Ayuda

página principal   miembros   e-diario

Grupo musical La OLA

Nombre: **Yadira Ortega**
Edad: **15 años**
Nacionalidad: **mexicana**
Color favorito: **rojo**
Clase favorita: **inglés**

Mañana viernes tengo que decir[1] adiós a mi colegio. Se llama Preparatoria Benito Juárez. Tiene dos horarios: el horario de la mañana y el horario de la tarde. Yo tengo[2] el horario de la tarde, de las 2:00 P.M. a las 8:00 P.M. En mi clase hay cuarenta estudiantes. Los estudiantes y los profesores son buena onda[3]. ¡Los echaré de menos![4] Durante[5] la gira, estudio con un profesor particular[6]. No sé cómo se llama. Tampoco sé de dónde es. ¡Ojalá sea[7] buena onda[8]! Bueno, amigos, ¡hasta pronto!

[1]I have to say   [2]have   [3]nice   [4]I'll miss them   [5]During   [6]private   [7]I hope he will be   [8]lucky

39 ¿Qué recuerdas?

1. ¿Cómo se llama el colegio de Yadira?
2. ¿De qué hora a qué hora son sus clases?
3. ¿Cuál es su clase favorita?
4. ¿Cuántos estudiantes hay en su clase?
5. ¿Con quién estudia en la gira?

40 Algo personal

1. How many schedules does Yadira's school have? Why do you suppose many Latin American schools have more than one schedule? Which schedule would you choose? Explain why.
2. What are the advantages and disadvantages of studying with a private tutor? Do you think Yadira will like being tutored or will she miss being in a classroom with forty students?

80 *ochenta*

Lección B

Notes Play the recorded version of the reading on page 80 that is part of the Audio CD Program.

Help students with the reading: Apply some of the strategies they have been learning such as scanning.

Use the questions for the *Algo personal* as the basis for a discussion with students about school life.

80

¿Qué aprendí?

Autoevaluación

As a review and self-check, respond to the following:

 Visit the web-based activities at www.emcp.com

1. Ask when Spanish class is.
2. How would you tell a friend that English ends at 2:15 P.M.?
3. Say you study art on Saturdays.
4. Identify differences between your high school and a high school in one of the Spanish-speaking countries.
5. Describe several objects around you by telling what color they are.
6. How would you ask a friend where the compact discs (CDs) are?
7. What might the person on the other end say to you in Spanish if you have dialed the wrong telephone number?

Palabras y expresiones

Clases
el arte
la biología
el colegio
la computación
el español
la historia
el horario
el inglés
las matemáticas
la música

Colores
amarillo,-a
azul
blanco,-a
gris
negro,-a
rojo,-a
verde

Días
el domingo
el jueves
el lunes
el martes
el miércoles
el sábado
el viernes

Por teléfono
aló
¿cuál?
la dirección (de correo electrónico)
el número de teléfono/de fax/de teléfono celular/equivocado
el teléfono

Ropa
la blusa
el calcetín
la camisa
la camiseta
la falda
los jeans
el pantalón
el zapato

Tecnología
la arroba
la computadora
el disco compacto (CD)
el diskette
la impresora (láser)
la pantalla
el punto
el ratón *(pl. los ratones)*
el teclado

Verbos
estar
estudiar
hablar
llevar
necesitar
terminar

Otras expresiones
a
allí
el almuerzo
¿a qué hora?
el color
¿Cómo?
¿cuánto,-a?
el día
el examen
¡mira!
o
sobre
tampoco
tu

La clase de computación.

Mi número de teléfono es...

Notes Assign the *Autoevaluación* to provide students with an opportunity to measure their own progress learning the main elements of the lesson and as preparation for the end-of-chapter test.

Have students work together in groups of three to create a dialog using the expressions and new vocabulary from the lesson. Remind students to be creative.

Teacher Resources

 Activity 15

Information Gap Activities
Postcard Activities
Funciones de Comunicación

Answers

Autoevaluación
Possible answers:
1. ¿A qué hora es la clase de español?
2. La clase de inglés termina a las dos y cuarto de la tarde.
3. Estudio arte los sábados.
4. Hispanic high schools can be rigorous; there are not many extracurricular activities; there are not many elective courses; private schools are common; grades are often based upon a numerical scale.
5. Objects will vary. Be sure students match number and gender.
6. ¿Dónde están los discos compactos (CDs)?
7. Tienes el número equivocado.

Activities

Expansion
Model new words and expressions from the *Palabras y expresiones* and have students repeat after you. Then call on students to use the words or expressions in sentences.

81

Answers

Preparación

1. Chicano literature is taught in states close to the Mexico-United States border in California, Texas, New Mexico and Arizona, but may also be offered elsewhere across the United States.
2. Possible answers: They would not be able to speak English, get a job, borrow money for a car or have a place to live.
3. Key vocabulary might include: *fronteras*/borders, *dividen*/divide, *puente*/bridge, *dos Californias*/two Californias, *pases*/you can cross, *sur*/south, *norte*/north.

Activities

Multiple Intelligences (bodily-kinesthetic/linguistic)

Have students write a four- or five-line poem in Spanish with an English equivalent about a theme of their choosing. They should try to choose from vocabulary and structures they have learned, but you may wish to help particularly ambitious and gifted students who may want to use a dictionary and create a more complex poem.

Technology

Many universities in the United States offer courses in Chicano literature. Students can surf the Web and find Chicano literature courses that can be taken via the Internet.

Tú lees

Conexión con otras disciplinas: literatura

Estrategia

Activating background knowledge

Applying what you already know about a topic when you read will prepare you for the type of information and vocabulary that will likely appear in the reading. For example, in this chapter, you have become more aware of how the Hispanic culture has influenced the United States. Do you know Hispanic culture also enriches American literature? The themes of Chicano literature reflect the difficulties faced by Hispanics as they adjust to life in the United States. In her bilingual book of Chicano poetry, *Puentes y fronteras/Bridges and Borders,* Gina Valdés patterns her poems after one of the oldest styles of Spanish poetry, called a *copla*. The *coplas* were popular in medieval Spain (13th century) because they were composed of short lines of poetry that were easily memorized. Minstrels often sang *coplas* to villagers they encountered in their travels. This established an oral tradition that passed stories and information from one person to another for centuries.

Preparación

Contesta las siguientes preguntas como preparación para la lectura.

1. Where do you think courses on Chicano literature might be offered?
2. What difficulties might Hispanic immigrants face when they move to the United States?
3. What key words in the following poems do you think most likely reflect some of the issues found in Chicano literature?

Cruzando la frontera *(crossing the border)*.

Notes Ask students to identify factors that may influence immigration from Spanish-speaking nations to the United States. Then assign the strategy on activating background knowledge on this page. Next, ask the questions that appear in the *Preparación*.

Puentes y fronteras/*Bridges and Borders* (selecciones)
por Gina Valdés

Hay tantísimas fronteras
que dividen a la gente,
pero por cada frontera
existe también un puente.

* * *

Entre las dos Californias
quiero construir un puente,
para que cuando tú quieras
te pases del sur al norte,
caminando libremente
no como liebre del monte.

There are so many borders
that divide people,
but for every border
there is also a bridge.

* * *

Between the two Californias
I want to build a bridge,
so whenever you wish
you can cross from south to
    north,
walking freely
not like a wild rabbit.

A ¿Qué recuerdas?

1. What are the "two Californias" the poet talks about?
2. Whom is the author referring to that would cross the border "like a wild rabbit" *(como liebre del monte)*?
3. Which words rhyme in the two poems?

B Algo personal

1. Why do you think the author uses the old style of *coplas* to express her modern poetry?
2. Besides the physical border, in what other ways are the Mexican and American cultures divided?
3. Themes found in poetry are based upon human experiences. What themes are depicted in these poems?

 Puentes y fronteras

Answers

A 1. The two Californias refer to the state of California (United States) and Baja California (Mexico). They could also symbolize the Anglo California and the Hispanic California that coexist in the United States.
   2. The author is referring to the illegal immigrants that cross the border between Mexico and California.
   3. Possible answers include: *gente* and *puente*, *Californias* and *quieras*, *puente* and *libremente*, *norte* and *monte*.

B Answers will vary.

Activities

Expansion
Additional questions *(Algo personal)*: *¿Qué divide a la gente?*; *¿Qué existe por cada frontera?*; *¿Para qué quiere la poeta construir un puente?*; *¿Tienes algún amigo de un país de habla hispana?*; *¿Eres de algún país de habla hispana?*

Notes The two *coplas* presented here are individual poems from the same book of poetry.

Have students read these selections by Gina Valdés. Finally, discuss *Puentes y fronteras* (Bridges and Borders) using the questions in the activities *¿Qué recuerdas?* and *Algo personal.*

83

Creative writing pratice.

Critical Thinking

As an alternative writing activity, have students write a five- or six-sentence paragraph in Spanish telling about themselves. Ask them to include such things as their name, where they are from, telephone number, family or friends' names and where they go to school. Have them add a visual element about themselves to decorate it. Display the final products on a bulletin board for parents to see when they visit the classroom.

Tú escribes

Writing a dialog journal

Whether you write in a spiral notebook, a composition book or a loose-leaf binder, writing your thoughts in a journal offers a written means of recording your experiences, wishes and dreams. In addition, keeping a journal offers a way for you as a student writer to respond personally to what you are reading or learning in class. You may even choose to create an electronic journal using a computer. Regardless of the format you choose, writing down your thoughts regularly and expressing yourself freely in a dialog journal can increase your motivation to write as you look back and reflect upon where you have been and as you consider where you are going. Communicating your thoughts and feelings through journal writing allows you and your teacher to get to know each other more rapidly on a deeper, more personal level.

Choose one of the topics below and write at least a paragraph to your teacher to express how you feel about it.

1. How will learning Spanish benefit you personally?
2. If you were attending school in a Hispanic country, what do you think you would like? What would you dislike?
3. How is the Hispanic culture evident in your community? What aspects of this culture would you like to learn more about?
4. What famous Spanish-speaking person would you like to interview? Why?
5. Imagine you are an immigrant who has just entered the United States to live. What is going through your mind?

El activista César Chávez.

La escritora Isabel Allende.

Notes The journal entries should pertain to the chapter content and should serve to provide feedback on the topic, to promote communication between you and your students and to give students grammar and vocabulary practice. Your purpose is not to correct the entry, but rather to comment on students' ideas and answer students' questions. You can model correct spelling and grammar in your return entry. The most important thing is to get to know one another and to motivate your students to keep writing.

Consider having students write journal entries every lesson.

Proyectos adicionales

A Comparaciones

Imagine you are attending high school in a Spanish-speaking country and you are writing to a key pal in your Spanish class back home describing the experience. Compare what you know about school life in a Spanish-speaking country with school life in the United States. Create your class schedule based on what you have learned about the different systems of education and describe your daily routine. Use color and computer-generated artwork or designs to make the schedule appear interesting. Be prepared to discuss your schedule in class, naming similarities and differences between the different systems.

> **MODELO** El colegio se llama....
> Tengo la clase de... a las dos y media.

B Conexión con la tecnología

Search the Internet for additional information about one of the famous Spanish speakers mentioned in *Capítulo 2*. Prepare a short report about the person and share the information with your classmates.

El artista Pablo Picasso.

C Comunidades

Do you know any people in your community who speak Spanish? Are there any restaurants, radio stations, grocery stores, etc. that are owned or run by a Spanish-speaking individual? Name some people and places in your community that have a connection to Spanish and the cultures of the Spanish-speaking world. If you can, interview someone on the list and find out more about that connection to Spanish (where the person is from, difficulties the person experienced coming to the United States, etc.).

Teacher Resources

 Trabalenguas

Activities

Communities
Have students investigate businesses in your community that require Spanish-speaking employees. Then discuss the results. As an alternative, have one or two students share their findings with the class.

Critical Listening
Say several nouns aloud in Spanish and ask students to provide the appropriate definite article and repeat the noun that you give. First give words that students have seen. Then give words that are unknown to students, including some ending in *-o, -a, -ción, -dad*. If necessary, point out to students that they should be able to give the appropriate definite article even if the word is unknown by generalizing about the information provided on noun gender.

Repaso

Now that I have completed this chapter, I can...	Go to these pages for help:
identify people and classroom objects.	40, 48
ask for and give names.	40
ask or tell where someone is from.	40
discuss school schedules and daily activities.	60
describe classroom objects and clothing.	60
say some things people do.	67
state location.	76
talk about how someone feels.	76

I can also...	
identify Hispanic influences in the United States.	43
identify some well-known people who speak Spanish.	43
name places in the United States where Spanish is spoken.	51
name some ways learning Spanish can enhance career opportunities.	51
scan an article in Spanish for cognates.	68
talk about technology.	72
compare Hispanic and American school systems and grading scales.	75
read a poem in Spanish.	83
write in Spanish.	84

Trabalenguas

Teresa trajo tizas hechas trizas.

Notes Talk with students about why it is important to know about the culture and other background information of a person with whom someone is establishing business relations. Explain that foreign businesspeople are much more willing to do business with people who respect their culture as well as their language. When doing business with someone in Spanish, they should remember the expression *la cortesía mucho vale y poco cuesta* (courtesy is worth a lot and costs little).

Loose translation of the *Trabalenguas:* Teresa brought broken-up chalk.

Vocabulario

a to, at, in *2B*
¿a qué hora? at what time? *2B*
allí there *2B*
el **almuerzo** lunch *2B*
aló hello (telephone greeting) *2B*
amarillo,-a yellow *2B*
el **amigo,** la **amiga** friend *2A*
la **arroba** at (the symbol @ used for e-mail addresses) *2B*
el **arte** art *2B*
¡ay! oh! *2A*
azul blue *2B*
la **biología** biology *2B*
blanco,-a white *2B*
la **blusa** blouse *2B*
el **bolígrafo** pen *2A*
el **borrador** eraser *2A*
el **calcetín** sock *2B*
la **camisa** shirt *2B*
la **camiseta** jersey, polo, t-shirt *2B*
el **cesto de papeles** wastebasket *2A*
el **chico,** la **chica** boy, girl *2A*
la **clase** class *2A*
el **colegio** school *2B*
el **color** color *2B*
¿Cómo se dice...? How do you say...? *2A*
¿Cómo se llama (Ud./él/ella)? What is (his/her) name? *2A*
¿Cómo? How? *2B*
comprendo (comprender) I understand (to understand) *2A*
la **computación** computer science *2B*
la **computadora** computer *2B*
el **cuaderno** notebook *2A*
¿cuál(es)? which one(s)? *2B*
¿cuánto,-a? how many? *2B*
el **día** day *2B*
la **dirección** (*de correo electrónico*) address (e-mail) *2B*
el **disco compacto (CD)** compact disc *2B*
el **diskette** diskette *2B*
el **domingo** Sunday *2B*

él he *2A*
el, la the *2A*
ella she *2A*
ellas they (f.) *2A*
ellos they (m.) *2A*
en in, on, at *2A*
el **escritorio** desk *2A*
el **español** Spanish *2B*
estar to be *2A*
el **estudiante,** la **estudiante** student *2A*
estudiar to study *2B*
el **examen** exam, test *2B*
la **falda** skirt *2B*
gris grey *2B*
hablar to speak *2B*
hay there is, there are *2A*
la **historia** history *2B*
el **horario** schedule *2B*
la **impresora (láser)** (laser) printer *2B*
el **inglés** English *2B*
los **jeans** jeans, blue jeans *2B*
el **jueves** Thursday *2B*
el **lápiz** pencil *2A*
el **libro** book *2A*
llevar to wear *2B*
los, las the (m.pl.), the (f.pl.) *2A*
el **lunes** Monday *2B*
el **mapa** map *2A*
el **martes** Tuesday *2B*
las **matemáticas** mathematics *2B*
mi my *2A*
el **miércoles** Wednesday *2B*
¡mira! look! *2B*
la **mochila** backpack *2A*
la **música** music *2B*
necesitar to need *2B*
negro,-a black *2B*
nosotros,-as we *2A*
nuevo,-a new *2A*
el **número de teléfono/de fax/de teléfono celular** phone number/fax number/cell phone number *2B*
la **página** page *2A*
la **palabra** word *2A*

la **pantalla** screen *2B*
el **pantalón** pants *2B*
el **papel** paper *2A*
la **pared** wall *2A*
el **periódico** newspaper *2A*
la **pizarra** blackboard *2A*
el **profesor,** la **profesora** teacher *2A*
la **puerta** door *2A*
el **punto** dot (term used in Internet address) *2B*
el **pupitre** desk *2A*
¿Qué quiere decir...? What does ... mean? *2A*
¿qué? what? *2A*
¿quién? who? *2A*
quiere decir it means *2A*
el **ratón** mouse *2B*
la **regla** ruler *2A*
el **reloj** clock, watch *2A*
la **revista** magazine *2A*
rojo,-a red *2B*
la **ropa** clothing *2A*
el **sábado** Saturday *2B*
el **sacapuntas** pencil sharpener *2A*
sé I know *2A*
se dice it is called *2A*
ser to be *2A*
la **silla** chair *2A*
sobre on, over, on top of *2B*
tampoco neither *2B*
el **teclado** keyboard *2B*
el **teléfono** telephone *2B*
terminar to finish *2B*
la **tiza** chalk *2A*
tu your *2B*
(Ud./Él/Ella) se llama... (you/his/her) name is ... *2A*
un, una a, an, one *2A*
unos, unas some, any, a few *2A*
la **ventana** window *2A*
verde green *2B*
el **viernes** Friday *2B*
el **zapato** shoe *2B*

Teacher Resources

Introducción

Episode 2

Testing/ Assessment
Test Booklet
Portfolio Assessment

Activities

Critical Listening
Say several nouns aloud in Spanish and ask students to provide the appropriate definite article and repeat the noun that you give. First give words that students have seen, such as those on this page. Then give words that are unknown to students, including some ending in *-o, -a, -dad*. If necessary, point out to students that they should be able to give the appropriate definite article even if the word is unknown by generalizing about the information provided on noun gender.

Expansion
Model the words and expressions and have students repeat. Then call on students to make statements using the vocabulary from the chapter.

Notes The words and expressions on this page are provided as a handy reference list with English equivalents of all active vocabulary. Encourage students to return to either *Lección 2A* or *Lección 2B* (as indicated after each English equivalent) to review words and expressions they do not recognize.

Quizzes have been formatted to allow teachers to evaluate how well students are learning key content. Teachers may opt to combine these quizzes at the end of a lesson as a comprehensive test over the contents of the entire lesson.

Communities

Encourage students to use their newly acquired skills as service volunteers assisting Spanish-speaking families in your community. For example, the library, the local park system and the school system are all organizations that often can use help from volunteers with the ability to speak Spanish.

Critical Thinking

Photographs, maps and artwork appear throughout the book and encourage students to connect with the countries and people they are studying. The photographs and other selected visuals depict the functions, cultural setting and themes of the chapter and further student connections to how Spanish is used outside the controlled environment of the classroom. Try to employ these supportive visuals on a regular basis. Ask about any similarities and differences students observe, what words students are able to understand, what conclusions students can draw from the information, etc.

Capítulo **3**

¡Vamos a la ciudad!

Objetivos

❖ **talk about places in a city**

❖ **make introductions and express courtesy**

❖ **ask and answer questions**

❖ **discuss how to go somewhere**

❖ **say some things people do**

❖ **say where someone is going**

❖ **talk about the future**

❖ **order food and beverages**

Visit the web-based activities at www.emcp.com

Notes Communicative objectives are provided at the start of each chapter to prepare students for the chapter they are about to begin. A list of such functions appears at the end of chapters so students can do a self-check to evaluate their progress.

México
Nombre oficial: **Estados Unidos Mexicanos**
Población: **101.880.000**
Capital: **México, D.F.**
Ciudades importantes: **Monterrey, Guadalajara**
Unidad monetaria: **el peso**
Fiesta nacional: **16 de septiembre, Día de la Independencia**
Gente famosa: **Luis Miguel (cantante); Frida Kahlo y Diego Rivera (artistas); Octavio Paz y Carlos Fuentes (escritores); Emiliano Zapata (líder popular)**

Activities

Connections
Have students name some cities in Mexico. Then ask what students know about Mexico. Conduct a class discussion about places students or their family or friends have visited in Mexico.

ochenta y nueve **89**

Notes **Culture.** Ask students what country they think they will be studying in the chapter. Inform them the photographs on this page are of Mexico City: The large photograph is of the Cathedral on the *Zócalo* (main square); the small one depicts a typical downtown street scene. Then discuss what students know about the country (e.g., Spanish is Mexico's official language; the capital is Mexico City; the country is a favorite vacation spot for many North Americans). Point out that Mexico is the United States' nearest neighbor to the south. It is a country with a rich and varied history.

Activities

Language through Action
Have students perform charades to illustrate city places using vocabulary from this lesson.

Prereading Strategy
Have students look at *Vocabulario I* and identify cognates and other words they recognize. Then ask students to guess what the people along the bottom of pages 90 and 91 are saying to one another.

TPR
Using overhead transparencies 21 and 22, ask students to come up and point to the different places you name in Spanish.

Notes Use transparencies 21 and 22 to introduce the new words and expressions in *Vocabulario I*. Begin by showing students transparency 21 and point to one of the buildings and identify it in Spanish. Students should repeat after you. Continue on to the next building and repeat the process. As a second step, show students transparency 22. Once again identify the buildings in Spanish, allowing students to see how each word is spelled.

1 La ciudad

 Selecciona la foto que corresponde con lo que oyes. *(Select the photo that matches what you hear.)*

A

B

C

D   **E**   **F**

2 Juego

Haz una lista de tantos lugares en una ciudad como puedas en un minuto.
(Make a list of as many places in a city as you can in one minute.)

El gusto es mío.

Encantado, Laura.

Laura, te presento a Gabriel y a Jaime.

Tanto gusto.

caminar

Notes Explain that the expression *El gusto es mío* is often used as a response to someone saying *Mucho gusto*, *Tanto gusto* or *Encantado/encantada*.

Activity 1 is intended for listening comprehension practice. Play the audio CD of the activity that is part of the Audio CD Program or use the transcript that appears in the ATE Introduction if you prefer to read the activity yourself.

Teacher Resources

 Activity 1

Activity 2

Answers

1 1. D
 2. E
 3. F
 4. A
 5. B
 6. C

2 Discuss the lists. Find out how many places students came up with in the time allotted and announce who has the longest list.

Activities

Pronunciation *(la letra e)*
Review the sound of *e* by practicing the following words: *problema, fiesta, también, en, nueve, es, noche, número, teléfono, ella, tres, seis, siete*. Point out that the sound of *e* in Spanish has two basic variations. In syllables that combine *e* with *d* (except a final *e* after a *d*), *m*, *n* and *s*, for example, the sound of *e* is similar to the sound of *e* in the English word **bet**: *cuaderno* (note the difference after a final *d*: *dónde*), *número, Inés, ser*. In syllables that combine *e* with any other consonant or diphthong, the sound is a little more open than the vowel sound in the English word **date**: *cero, colegio, bien, pues*.

Answers

3 1. Están en (la Ciudad de)
México.
2. Hay una fiesta en la ciudad,
en el Zócalo.
3. Olga es simpática.
4. ¡Claro! Tomás va al Zócalo.
5. Quiere ir al parque.
4 Answers will vary.
5 1. A; 2. D; 3. B; 4. C

Activities

Critical Listening
Play the audio CD version of the
dialog. Remember to instruct
students to cover up the words
with one hand, as you want them
to develop good listening skills.
Tell students to look at the
photographs while they imagine
what the people are saying to one
another. Have several individuals
state what they believe the main
theme of the conversation is.

Prereading Strategy
Ask students to recall different
ways to greet people in Spanish.
Then instruct students to open
their books and to cover up the
dialog with one hand and look at
the photographs. Ask them to
imagine where the conversation
takes place and what the people
are saying to one another.
Finally, have students look
through the dialog quickly to find
cognates.

Diálogo I

En la Ciudad de México

MARISOL: ¡Hay una fiesta
fantástica en la ciudad!
TOMÁS: ¿Cuándo es la fiesta?
PILAR: Es mañana en el Zócalo.
¿Por qué no vamos?
TOMÁS: ¡Claro! ¡Vamos!

TOMÁS: Y... Olga va también,
¿no? Es muy simpática.
PILAR: Sí, ella va.
TOMÁS: ¡Ah, muy bien!

PILAR: Allí está mi amiga. ¡Hola,
Ana! Te presento a Tomás.
TOMÁS: Tanto gusto.
ANA: Encantada. ¿Por qué no
caminamos al parque?
TOMÁS: Sí, quiero caminar.

 3 ¿Qué recuerdas?

1. ¿Dónde están los muchachos?
2. ¿Dónde hay una fiesta?
3. ¿Cómo es Olga?
4. ¿Va Tomás al Zócalo?
5. ¿Adónde quiere ir Ana?

4 Algo personal

1. ¿Eres tú simpático/a? ¿Y tus amigos/as?
2. ¿Hay un parque en tu ciudad? ¿Cómo se llama?
3. ¿Caminas a la escuela?

5 Presentaciones

 Indica la letra de la foto que corresponde con lo que oyes.

A   **B**   **C**   **D**

Notes Point out for students that the
Zócalo (referred to in the dialog) is the
nickname for the *Plaza de la Constitución*
in Mexico City. The *Zócalo* is an open
quadrangle built on the earlier central
square of the Aztec capital. Here you can
visit the largest cathedral in North
America, see Diego Rivera's murals in the
National Palace and view the excavation of
a sacred Aztec temple *(templo mayor)*.

Play the audio CD version of activity 5 for
listening comprehension practice.

Point out that the people are shaking hands
in activity 5 as they meet one another.

Cultura viva

El Parque de Chapultepec, México, D.F.

De visita en la Ciudad de México

When you are in Mexico, you may hear the terms *México, La República* or *los Estados Unidos Mexicanos,* all of which are used interchangeably to refer to the country. Similarly, when you are planning to travel to the capital, you may say you are going to visit Mexico City. However, according to Mexicans, you will be in *el D.F. (Distrito Federal), la Ciudad de México* or just in *México.* Once there, start your sightseeing in the center of the city—the *Zócalo*—or main plaza. Mexico was once the center of the ancient Aztec capital *Tenochtitlán.* Today the site offers visitors a view of the excavated ruins of the *templo mayor* (main temple). Walk a short distance and you will find the wide and elegant *Paseo de la Reforma.* This street was built by the emperor Maximilian to join his palace at Chapultepec with his office in the National Palace (where works by one of Mexico's most famous artists, Diego Rivera, are on display) in the *Zócalo.* Chapultepec today is a large park where you can enjoy *el zoológico* (zoo), *las atracciones* (amusement park rides) or *el Castillo* (castle). Transportation inside the park is limited to walking and biking, so many people come just to enjoy the outdoors. The park also includes the world-famous *Museo Nacional de Antropología,* which contains three miles of exhibits of art, architecture and culture of the ancient civilizations that existed in Mexico before Spanish colonization.

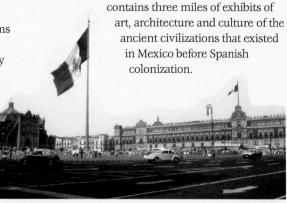

El Zócalo.

6 De visita en la Ciudad de México

¿Sí o no?

1. Los mexicanos llaman a la capital La República.
2. *D.F.* quiere decir *Distrito Federal.*
3. El Zócalo es una biblioteca.
4. El Paseo de la Reforma es una avenida elegante.
5. En el Parque de Chapultepec hay un zoológico, atracciones y un castillo.
6. En el Museo Nacional de Antropología hay exhibiciones de arquitectura y cultura.

7 En el D.F.

Make a list of four places mentioned in *Cultura viva* that you might visit on a trip to Mexico City. Search the Internet or go to the library and describe what you would see or do at one of the places you listed.

Capítulo 3   *noventa y tres* **93**

Teacher Resources

 Activity 6

 Activity 2

 Activity 3

Answers

6 1. No.; 2. Sí.; 3. No.; 4. Sí.;
5. Sí.; 6. Sí.
7 Possible answers:
el Zócalo, el templo mayor,
el Paseo de la Reforma,
el parque de Chapultepec,
el Castillo del emperador
Maximiliano, el Museo
Nacional de Antropología.

Activities

Communities
Ask if students can name any well-known Mexicans or celebrities of Mexican descent. Then find out how many of the following Mexican and Mexican-American figures students can identify: Frida Kahlo (painter); Octavio Paz (writer, winner of the Nobel Prize in literature); Selena Quintanilla (Grammy Award-winning singer); Emiliano Zapata (leader of the Mexican Revolution); Diego Rivera (muralist).

Technology
Have students search the Internet to research some well-known Mexicans or American celebrities of Mexican descent. Students should prepare a list of facts (or summarize what they found in a couple paragraphs) and then share their findings with the class.

Notes The official name for Chapultepec Park is *el Bosque de Chapultepec,* which includes several major attractions in addition to the park, such as the castle, museums, botanical gardens, amusement park and a lake. In Mexico, the word *bosque* is a synonym for *parque* since it refers loosely to an unpopulated outdoor or sanctuary area in an urban environment. Chapultepec Park is popular throughout the week, but it is especially popular on weekends, when individuals, couples, families and groups congregate in the park to take advantage of the many sites and activities offered.

Answers

8 1. te, al; 2. les, al, del; 3. les, al;
4. le, a; 5. les, a; 6. les, a la, de;
7. te, a, a

Activities

Expansion
Have students introduce themselves to the teacher and each other in small groups.

Pronunciation (la letra a)
Write several sentences on the board. Break the sentences into individual words and sounds and then have students use the words you have practiced in meaningful sentences. For example, it would be appropriate to review the sound of *a* at this point with the following words, which appeared in *Diálogo I: Tomás, a, amiga, Ana, caminamos* and *encantada.* Point out that the sound of *a* in Spanish is similar to the *a* of the English word **father,** but a little more open. (As an alternative, you may wish to provide your own list of words or have students find appropriate words.) After practicing the *a* sound, have students use the words by acting out the dialog or by creating their own dialogs.

94

Idioma

Estructura

Making introductions: *te, le, les*

Follow these guidelines when you wish to introduce people:

te	(to one person, informal)	Laura, **te presento a** Gabriel.
le	(to one person, formal)	Sra. Durán, **le presento a** María.
les	(to two or more people, informal and formal)	Luis y José, **les presento** a Margarita y *a* Pablo.

Note: When the definite article *el* (the) follows *a* or *de,* the two words combine to form *al* or *del.*

a + el = al	de + el = del

*Tomás y Pilar, les presento **al** señor Rojas.*
*Te presento **al** amigo **del** estudiante nuevo.*

You have several responses to choose from when meeting someone, among them: ***Mucho gusto, Tanto gusto*** or ***El gusto es mío.*** In addition, males can say ***Encantado,*** while females may wish to say ***Encantada.***

Práctica

8 Presentaciones

Completa las siguientes oraciones con palabras de la lista.

de	te	a la	al
les	le	del	a

MODELO ¡Ay, Rosario! <u>Te</u> presento a mi amigo Iván.

1. Jorge, __ presento __ señor Francisco Ortiz.
2. Rodolfo y Ana, __ presento __ amigo __ Sr. Rodríguez.
3. Paco y Antonio, __ presento __ señor Pedraza.
4. Profesor Vallejo, __ presento __ doña Marina.
5. Rodrigo y Pablo, __ presento __ Diana y a Catalina.
6. Sr. y Sra. Gaviria, __ presento __ profesora __ historia.
7. Rosario, __ presento __ don Carlos y __ Ernesto.

Encantada.

Notes **Comparisons.** The titles *don* and *doña* do not have English equivalents. They are used to show respect and closeness when addressing or speaking of a person with whom *señor* or *señora* would be too formal or with adults of the same age but of a higher social status or business rank. *Don* can be used when addressing or referring to any male, single or married; however, *doña* usually is reserved for older, married or widowed women. One exception is royalty, in which case *doña* can be used with the name of an unmarried woman such as *la princesa doña Isabel.* The abbreviations for *don (Dn.* or *D.)* and *doña (Dña.* or *D.ª)* are always capitalized.

9 En la fiesta del Zócalo

Completa los diálogos.

Roberto:	Sr. y Sra. Ortega, (1) presento (2) mi amiga Estefanía.
Sr. Ortega:	Tanto (3), Estefanía.
Sra. Ortega:	Encantada, Estefanía.
Sra. Tovar:	Sra. Santos, (4) presento a Felipe, mi amigo de Acapulco.
Sra. Santos:	(5), Felipe.
Felipe:	El (6) es mío, Sra. Santos.
Sofía:	Marcos, te (7) a Pilar y a Daniel. Marcos es el estudiante nuevo de Veracruz.
Marcos:	¡(8) gusto! Me llamo Marcos Castilla.
Pilar:	(9).
Iván:	¿(10) estás?
Daniel:	Bien, gracias.

¡Mucho gusto!

10 En la Ciudad de México

You and two classmates are greeting some friends and family who have decided to visit Mexico City. Introduce everyone using the words shown.

MODELO Hernando / presento a / el profesor de música, el señor Villamil
      Hernando, te presento al profesor de música, el señor Villamil.

1. Maribel / presento a / mi amigo, Jorge Contreras
2. Carmen y Gabriel / presento a / Edgar
3. Sra. Giraldo / presento a / la señora Suárez
4. Sr. y Sra. Ruiz / presento a / el profesor de historia de / el colegio, el señor Botero
5. Enrique y Sonia / presento a / el amigo de / el profesor Osorio, el señor Jaramillo
6. Sr. y Sra. Reyes / presento a / la amiga de Silvia, Juliana
7. Isabel / presento a / el amigo de / el señor Rueda, don Carlos

✦ Comunicación

11 En el Zócalo

You are with some friends and classmates at the Zócalo while on a study abroad program in Mexico City. In small groups, act out these introductions. Take turns playing the part of each person.

1. Your friend Miguel meets your friend Margarita for the first time.
2. Your classmate Pedro sees one of his neighbors *la señora Carvajal* whom you do not know.
3. Two other students you know from the exchange program pass by while you are with your other friends.
4. The mother of one of your friends, *la señora García,* is crossing the Zócalo and runs into you and your friends.

Activities

Cooperative Learning

Have students pretend they are at a meeting where there are many people who do not know one another. They must walk around the room, asking for the names of other people at the meeting. They then must take turns introducing one another to other people nearby, using the expressions they have learned (*¿Cómo te llamas?; Me llamo...; ¡Mucho gusto!; Encantado/a; Perdón; Te/le/les presento a...*). Remind students to shake hands as they meet one another. You may wish to have students introduce their new acquaintances to you, too.

Students with Special Needs

Have students pair up to create questions for activity 13. Then review the questions students created as part of a class discussion about how students have learned to form questions and as part of your introduction to the *Estructura* on page 97.

---

 12 En una fiesta de bienvenida

In groups of three or four, pretend you are guests at a *quinceañera* party at the home of the study abroad program director. Practice introducing one another in Spanish and then start conversations with the other guests: ask where they are from, how they are, if they speak Spanish and English and so on. Exchange phone numbers with at least one other person. Remember to use appropriate greetings, gestures and responses in your conversations.

Repaso rápido: question-asking words

You are already familiar with several words used for asking information questions:

*¿**Cómo** estás?*	**How** are you?
*¿**Cuál** es tu cuaderno?*	**Which (one)** is your notebook?
*¿**Cuáles** son?*	**Which (ones)** are they?
*¿**Cuándo** es la clase de español?*	**When** is the Spanish class?
*¿**Cuánto** es?*	**How much** is it?
*¿**Cuántos** hay?*	**How many** are there?
*¿**Dónde** están ellos?*	**Where** are they?
*¿**Por qué** está ella allí?*	**Why** is she there?
*¿**Qué** es?*	**What** is it?
*¿**Quién** es de Cancún?*	**Who** is from Cancún?
*¿**Quiénes** son ellos?*	**Who** are they?

Note: Unlike *qué*, *cuál* (or *cuáles*) may never be followed by a noun: *¿Qué autobús tomas?* (What bus are you taking?); *¿Cuál de los autobuses tomas?* (Which of the buses are you taking?).

13 Unas preguntas

Escribe preguntas usando cada una de las palabras interrogativas del Repaso rápido. *(Write questions using each of the question-asking words in the Repaso rápido.)*

¿Dónde está el Museo Nacional de Antropología?

Notes Have students role-play the *quinceañera* party in activity 12. Have a few students create signs with the word *Ud.* that they wear to play the part of adults so participants practice both *tú* and *Ud.* Next, have everyone prepare cards with questions they wish to ask others at the party. After asking a question on the card and receiving an answer, students should ask the person to sign the card.

Comparisons. Inform students that *¿Cómo?* used alone is a way of asking for clarification when one doesn't understand something that was said.

Estructura

Asking questions

One way to ask a question is by making your voice rise at the end of the sentence.

Hay un museo en Chapultepec. → *¿Hay un museo en Chapultepec?*

Another way to ask a question in Spanish is to place the subject after the verb.

Tomás está en el museo. → *¿Está Tomás* en el museo?
  1   2   2   1

You can also create a question by adding a tag word such as *¿no?* or *¿verdad?* to the end of a sentence, much as you might add **isn't she?** or **right?,** etc. in English.

Eva va al restaurante, ¿no?   Eva is going to the restaurant, **isn't she?**
Uds. van al Zócalo, ¿verdad?   All of you are going to the Zócalo, **right?**

When forming information questions with interrogative words (*¿cómo?*, *¿cuál?*, *¿cuáles?*, and so forth), the verb precedes the subject, just as in English (*¿Cuándo es la fiesta?*). Some interrogative words may be used alone or in combination with various prepositions (*¿De dónde eres tú? ¿A qué hora termina?*).

Práctica

14 En forma de pregunta

Cambia las siguientes oraciones a preguntas.

MODELO La amiga de Pilar es simpática.
           ¿Es la amiga de Pilar simpática?

1. Ana es la amiga de Pilar.
2. Ana y Tomás estudian música en la Ciudad de México con la señora Alvarado.
3. La señora y el señor Alvarado son de Puebla.
4. Los dos chicos caminan en el Parque de Chapultepec.
5. Ellos hablan con la señora Alvarado en el Museo de Antropología.
6. La señora Alvarado toma el camión a Puebla.

La amiga de Pilar es simpática.

15 A contestar

Working in pairs, take turns reading and answering the questions you created for the previous activity. Remember to answer each question with *Sí* or *No,* followed by a complete sentence.

MODELO **A:** ¿Es la amiga de Pilar simpática?
          B: Sí, la amiga de Pilar es simpática./ No, la amiga de Pilar no es simpática.

Notes Explain that learning to ask questions is an essential skill. For example, when they visit Mexico or another country, students will need to inquire about transportation, locations, lodging, schedules and more.

16 Possible answers:
1. Cuándo/Dónde; 2. Quién;
3. qué; 4. Por qué; 5. dónde;
6. qué; 7. Cuál; 8. Cómo

17 Possible answers:
1. ¿Qué necesita doña Cecilia?/¿Quién necesita el horario de camiones?
2. ¿Quién camina en el parque de Chapultepec?/¿Dónde está el señor Galindo?
3. ¿Qué está en el D.F.?/¿Dónde está el Paseo de la Reforma?
4. ¿Quiénes estudian en Mazatlán?/¿Qué hay en Mazatlán?/¿Dónde estudian Cesar, Ignacio y Pedro?

18 Creative self-expression.

Critical Thinking

With only the interrogative as a prompt, students should be able to predict the type of information they are going to be asked. (This critical thinking activity will help students learn to anticipate forthcoming information.) Write the following question words and responses in random order on the board or on an overhead transparency. Have students match questions to responses: *¿Cómo...?/Muy bien; ¿Cuál...?/ 7-24-38-56; ¿Cuáles...?/Las chicas de Acapulco; ¿Cuándo...?/Por la mañana; ¿Cuánto...?/$79.40; ¿Cuántos...?/29 estudiantes; ¿Dónde...?/En la clase; ¿De dónde...?/De México; ¿Quién...?/ Cristina, la chica nueva.*

16 Palabras interrogativas

Completa las siguientes oraciones de una manera lógica.

1. ¿__ hay una fiesta fantástica?
2. ¿__ va a la fiesta?
3. ¿A __ hora es la fiesta?
4. ¿__ no vamos al parque?
5. ¿De __ es ella?
6. ¿De __ ciudad son?
7. ¿__ es tu número de teléfono?
8. ¿__ es ella? ¿Simpática?

17 Unas preguntas

Make as many different questions as you can for each of the following statements.

 MODELO Mañana hay una fiesta fantástica en el Zócalo.
¿Qué hay mañana en el Zócalo?/¿Dónde hay una fiesta mañana?/ ¿Cuándo es la fiesta?

1. Doña Cecilia necesita el horario de camiones.
2. El señor Galindo camina en el Parque de Chapultepec.
3. El Paseo de la Reforma está en el D.F.
4. César, Ignacio y Pedro estudian en una escuela en Mazatlán.

Comunicación

18 México

 Referring to *Cultura viva,* create five questions in Spanish about Mexico. Then, with a classmate, take turns asking and answering the questions.

¿Están en el Parque de Chapultepec?

Notes Clarify that when a speaker is trying to determine which item or items are being discussed, he or she should use the word *cuál* if the next word is a verb and *qué* if the next word is a noun. Examples: *¿Cuál es tu cuaderno? ¿Qué cuaderno es?* Also, explain to the students that the word *porque* means **because** and *por qué* means **why?**

Asking questions. Note for students that question words require a written accent mark whether they are used in questions or in statements where a question is implied: *No sé dónde está* (in which the implied question is **Where is it?**).

19 Una entrevista

Write five or six questions you would like to ask a classmate. Then pair up with another student and take turns interviewing one another using the questions you prepared. Take notes during the interview and report your findings to the class. Be creative.

¿De qué ciudad es Ud.?

20 En el teléfono

Working in pairs, create a telephone conversation in which you discuss details about some future activity you are going to do together. Tell when, where and at what time the activity takes place.

¿Aló?

MODELO

A: ¿Aló?

B: Hola, Pedro. ¿Vamos a la fiesta de Juan?

A: ¿Cuándo es?

B: Es el sábado.

A: ¿A qué hora es?

B: Es a las ocho.

¿Vamos a caminar en el D.F.?

Answers

19 Creative self-expression.
20 Creative self-expression.

Activities

Cooperative Learning
Have students work in pairs asking and answering questions about illustrations, photographs and realia found in this chapter.

Expansion
Show students several magazine or newspaper clippings and have them ask questions about each article.

Multiple Intelligences (spatial)
Creative visual learners will enjoy creating a pop-up version of a city. Have them label the buildings and any geographical features in Spanish.

Notes Note for students that *bueno* is a common telephone greeting in Mexico. The greeting *aló* is used in activity 20 because it is more universal. Tell students which greeting you prefer they use.

Remind students to use correct Spanish punctuation (*¿ ?*) when writing questions.

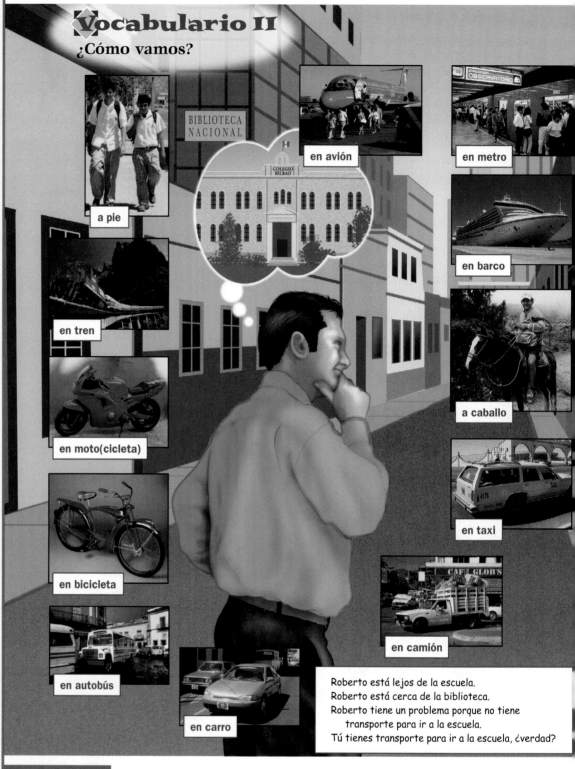

Vocabulario II
¿Cómo vamos?

a pie

en tren

en moto(cicleta)

en bicicleta

en autobús

en carro

en avión

en metro

en barco

a caballo

en taxi

en camión

BIBLIOTECA NACIONAL

COLEGIO BILBAO

Roberto está lejos de la escuela.
Roberto está cerca de la biblioteca.
Roberto tiene un problema porque no tiene transporte para ir a la escuela.
Tú tienes transporte para ir a la escuela, ¿verdad?

Notes Remind students that these words will change as they travel from one part of the Spanish-speaking world to another, just as expressions in English change from country to country and from one region to another.

The word *moto* is feminine because it is short for *la motocicleta*.

Mexicana and *Aeroméxico* are two airlines that fly to and from Mexico and the United States.

21 ¿Qué medio de transporte es?

 Selecciona la foto que corresponde con lo que oyes.

A

B

C

D

E

F

G

H

22 ¿Cómo vamos?

 Cut photographs of various means of transportation from magazines. On the back of each cutout, identify what it is in Spanish. Working in pairs, take turns asking and answering what each item is.

23 ¿Cómo vas?

Say which means of transportation you would use to go to the following places.

MODELO la oficina de tu padre
en autobús

1. la escuela
2. la biblioteca
3. el parque
4. México, D.F.
5. el dentista
6. el cine
7. tu restaurante favorito
8. el médico

¡Extra!

En otras palabras

el autobús	*el bus, la buseta, el camión, el colectivo, la flota, la guagua, el micro, el ómnibus*
el barco	*el buque, la nave*
la bicicleta	*la bici*
el carro	*el automóvil, el auto, el coche*
el metro	*el subterráneo (el subte)*

Capítulo 3

ciento uno **101**

Notes The universally recognized word for truck is *camión*, although in Mexico, this word is widely used for **bus.** Whereas in Mexico the word for **bus** is *camión*, in other countries there are various words that refer to **bus**: *bus, colectivo, guagua, micro* and *ómnibus* to name a few. Decide if you want students to know *camión* as a term for **bus** or whether you want them to recognize *camión* only as **truck.** The more universally recognized word *autobús* will be taught later in this lesson.

Teacher Resources

 Activity 21

Answers

21 1. B
2. A
3. F
4. C
5. E
6. D
7. H
8. G

22 Tell students how many words they must find and identify in Spanish. Then, as students work in pairs, walk around the room to be sure they stay on task and are using good pronunciation.

23 Answers will vary.

101

Teacher Resources

 ¿Qué?
Activities 24–26

Answers

24 1. Tomás está lejos.
2. Habla con Olga.
3. Porque no tiene transporte.
4. Porque Tomás tiene carro.
25 Answers will vary.
26 1. B
2. A
3. C
4. D
5. E

Activities

Critical Listening
Play the audio CD version of the dialog. Instruct students to cover up the words with one hand to develop good listening skills. Tell students to look at the photographs while they imagine what the people are saying to one another. Have several individuals state what they believe is the main theme.

Expansion
Additional questions *(Algo personal):* ¿Vas a una fiesta mañana?; ¿Cuándo vas a una fiesta?

Prereading Strategy
Instruct students to cover up the dialog with one hand and look at the photographs. Ask them to imagine where the conversation takes place and what the people are saying. Finally, have students look through the dialog quickly to find cognates.

102

Diálogo II
¿Qué?

TOMÁS: Hola, Olga, tú vas mañana a la fiesta, ¿verdad?
OLGA: ¿Cómo? Estás muy lejos.
TOMÁS: Lo siento.

TOMÁS: ¿Vas tú mañana a la fiesta en el Zócalo?
OLGA: Estás muy cerca, Tomás.
TOMÁS: Perdón.

OLGA: No, no voy porque no tengo transporte.
TOMÁS: Bueno, no hay problema.
OLGA: ¿Por qué no hay problema?
TOMÁS: Porque yo tengo carro para ir a la fiesta.

24 ¿Qué recuerdas?

1. ¿Quién está lejos?
2. ¿Con quién habla Tomás?
3. ¿Por qué no va Olga a la fiesta?
4. ¿Por qué no hay problema?

25 Algo personal

1. ¿Qué transporte tomas para ir a la escuela?
2. ¿Qué tomas para ir al parque? ¿Está lejos o cerca?
3. ¿Vas a fiestas con amigos? Explica.

26 ¿Qué toman para ir?

 Selecciona la foto que corresponde con lo que oyes.

A　　　**B**　　　**C**　　　**D**　　　**E**

102 *ciento dos* 　　　**Lección A**

Notes Activities 24, 25 and 26 have been recorded by professional native speakers and are recorded as part of the Audio CD Program.

Activity 26 is intended for listening comprehension practice. You may either use the audio CD of the activity or you may find a transcript for the recorded portion of the activity in the Introduction to the ATE if you choose to read it yourself.

Cultura viva

Nosotros viajamos en metro.

¿Cómo viajamos en el D.F.?

Transportation options in Mexico are varied and abundant. One option, owning a car and driving in Mexico, can present challenges. Cars are expensive to purchase and maintain since taxes are steep. In addition, finding parking can be difficult and is expensive when available. Most people prefer to use the excellent public transportation that is available.

Taxis are numerous and usually relatively inexpensive compared to the United States. In Mexico City, governmental regulations require taxi drivers to be licensed and that each taxi operate with a working meter and a driver's picture identification placed in a visible location inside the cab.

The buses in Mexico are clean and reasonably priced. The best public transportation bargain in Mexico City is undoubtedly its subway system (*el metro*), which allows a rider to travel from one area of the city to another with a single ticket. For this reason, the *metro* can be a little overcrowded during rush hours.

¡Hay mucho tráfico en el D.F.!

27 Comparando

Compara el transporte en México con el transporte en tu ciudad.

México	Mi ciudad
1. owning a car presents challenges	1. driving a car also presents challenges
2.	2.
3.	3.

Teacher Resources

 Activity 6

Answers

27 Answers will vary.

Activities

Connections
Tell students that in many ways the history of Mexico is closely connected to that of the United States. Have students choose one of the following topics and write a brief report (two to three paragraphs) to share with the class. They may use reference materials from the library or they may search the Internet to gather information for their reports. Some possible topics: Treaty of Guadalupe Hidalgo, Constitution of 1917, North American Free Trade Agreement (NAFTA), Battle of the Alamo.

Expansion
Have students identify various modes of transportation and say where they would go in each if they could.

Notes Due to the smog in Mexico City, private cars can drive only during certain days of the week, according to the number on the license plate.

Have students create a Venn diagram for activity 27.

Consider conducting a follow-up discussion about driving in the United States and in Mexico, using information from the *Cultura viva* and activity 27 as a starting point.

103

Answers

28 1. va
2. vamos
3. van
4. van
5. vamos
6. vas
7. voy

Activities

Critical Thinking

Say the various conjugated forms of the verb *ir* as students write the corresponding subject pronoun. Then say the subject pronouns and have the students write the corresponding verb forms.

Expansion

Review vocabulary for places people go and the means of transportation they use. Then ask questions using *ir a* followed by a place or a means of transportation: *¿Vas a un restaurante mañana? ¿Cómo vas a ir?; ¿Quién va a ir a la biblioteca? ¿Cómo vas a ir?*

Idioma

Estructura

Saying where someone is going: *ir*

The verb *ir* (to go) is irregular in the present tense.

ir			
yo	**voy**	nosotros nosotras	**vamos**
tú	**vas**	vosotros vosotras	**vais**
Ud. él ella	**va**	Uds. ellos ellas	**van**

The verb *ir* is usually followed by the preposition *a* (or the contraction *al*) and a destination.

| *¿Por qué no vamos **a** la biblioteca?* | Why don't we go to the library? |
| *Voy **al** cine.* | I am going to the movies. |

Note: When you want to suggest going somewhere or doing something ("Let's go somewhere/do something!"), use ***Vamos a* (+ a place or an infinitive).**

| *¡Vamos a la ciudad hoy!* | Let's go into town today! |
| *¡Vamos a tomar el autobús!* | Let's take the bus! |

 ## Práctica

28 ¿Adónde van mañana?

Completa las siguientes oraciones con la forma apropiada de *ir*.

MODELO Nuria y Rosario <u>van</u> al Museo Nacional de Antropología.

1. Tomás __ a la fiesta en el Zócalo, ¿no?
2. Nosotros __ a la fiesta con él, ¿verdad?
3. El señor y la señora Morales __ en avión a Veracruz.
4. Andrea y tú __ en metro a un restaurante en el D.F., ¿verdad?
5. ¡Claro! Andrea y yo __ con Mauricio al Paseo de la Reforma.
6. Tú __ a la Ciudad de México con ellos.
7. Yo __ a *(give a location)*.

Notes **Comparisons.** Point out for students that in Spanish the subject can be omitted because the verb form implies who is doing the action. For example, the subject of *vamos* is understood to be *nosotros* or *nosotras*; the subject of *voy* is understood to be *yo*. Finally, explain that the word *a* is a necessary part of this expression in Spanish, but that it is not used in the English equivalent.

The preposition *a* used with the verb *ir* also contracts with the article *el: Voy al centro.*

29 ¿Adónde van en la ciudad?

With a classmate, take turns asking and answering questions about where these people are going in the city. You may answer either affirmatively or negatively.

MODELO Gloria / al banco

> **A:** ¿Adónde va Gloria? Al banco, ¿verdad?
> **B:** Sí, va al banco. / No, no va al banco.

1. don Francisco / la médica
2. los muchachos / el restaurante
3. nosotros / el dentista
4. el Sr. López / la oficina
5. tú / el parque
6. Uds. / la escuela

¡Extra!

En la ciudad

la cafetería	*cafeteria, coffee shop*
el hospital	*hospital*
la iglesia	*church*
la oficina de correos	*post office*
el supermercado	*supermarket*

30 Todos vamos a lugares diferentes

Indica adónde van las siguientes personas.

MODELO

Héctor

Héctor va a la oficina.

1. yo

2. tú

3. la señora Sabogal

4. las muchachas

5. Nicolás

6. Ud.

Capítulo 3

ciento cinco **105**

Answers

31 1. ...van al parque a caballo.
2. ...vamos a la oficina en tren.
3. ...van al restaurante en bicicleta.
4. ...va al banco en moto(cicleta).
5. ...vas al Zócalo en metro.
6. ...voy a Isla Mujeres en barco.

32 Answers will vary.

Activities

Cooperative Learning
Have students bring in several magazine pictures of places they go (el cine, el banco). Encourage them also to bring pictures of places they would like to go (beach, island, lake, mountains). Students should learn the words for these places before class. They should then use the pictures to discuss where various people are going (imaginary trips are fine): *Voy a la playa.; ¿Vas a la playa también?; ¿Tus amigos van a las montañas?*. As a follow-up discussion, ask individual students where they are going. They should show the picture to the class as they respond.

31 ¿Cómo van?

Say how these people are going to arrive at the places indicated.

MODELO

Ángela y Carlota / cine
Ángela y Carlota van al cine en autobús.

1. Uds. / parque   **2.** nosotros / oficina   **3.** Uds. / restaurante

4. Jaime / banco   **5.** tú / Zócalo   **6.** yo / Isla Mujeres

 Comunicación

 32 ¿Cómo vamos?

Working in pairs, alternate mentioning places in the city and suggesting how you might go to each one.

MODELO

A: el banco
B: ¡Vamos al banco en bicicleta!

¡Vamos al banco en bicicleta!

106 *ciento seis*   **Lección A**

Notes Before beginning activity 31, remind students that the bus shown in the model is commonly referred to as *el camión* in Mexico, although elsewhere in the Spanish-speaking world *camión* is the term used to refer to a truck.

For number 6, tell students that Isla Mujeres is an island north of Cancun just off the coast of Mexico.

Tell students that in Spanish, the contractions *al* and *del* are obligatory whenever *a* or *de* is followed by *el*, unlike in English, where it is a matter of choice whether to contract words (e.g., **can't** for **cannot**).

33 ¡Vamos al Hotel San Gabriel!

This information card was left in your room at the Hotel San Gabriel in Mexico City. With a partner, answer the questions that follow. When you finish, ask each other two original questions.

1. ¿Dónde está el Hotel San Gabriel?
2. Necesitas transporte. ¿Cuál es el número de teléfono?
3. ¿Cómo se llama el cine? ¿Y el banco?
4. ¿Dónde está la Oficina de Turismo?
5. ¿Cuántos restaurantes hay cerca del hotel?
6. ¿La Cafetería Don Chang está cerca o lejos del hotel?
7. La Azteca es un restaurante fantástico. ¿Vas tú allí?
8. ¿Adónde van Uds. mañana?

San Gabriel HOTEL
Avenida de la Defensa, 23 • México, DF • 294 87 86/294 87 42

DIRECCIONES Y TELÉFONOS DE URGENCIA Y DE INTERÉS

Urgencia	Teléfono
Policía	091
Médico	297 33 33

Interés	
Recepcionista	97
Autobús	256 29 39
Taxi	299 43 01
Restaurante La Azteca Calle Ponce, 75	357 55 02
Cafetería Don Chang Avenida de la Defensa, 99	291 77 86
Banco Nacional Calle Once, 50	356 19 61
Oficina de Turismo Avenida de la Defensa, 98	354 00 01
Cine Máximo Calle 23 y Calle Ponce	459 78 03
Metro—Información y horario	290 10 16

PARA MÁS INFORMACIÓN, FAVOR LLAMAR
AL/A LA RECEPCIONISTA AL 97.

34 Planeando un viaje a México

Plan a trip to Mexico with a classmate using the advertisements. Decide on places to visit, transportation options, schedules and other necessary details for the trip.

MODELO A: El lunes vamos de Tampico a Guanajuato en camión. ¿A qué hora vamos?
B: Vamos a las ocho de la mañana.
A: No, vamos a las once menos diez de la mañana.

CAMIONES TRANSMEX
Reservaciones, 965 99 88   Información, 965 43 21
HORARIO: LUNES A VIERNES

de: a:	DF	Guadalajara	Guanajuato	Morelia	Tampico	Veracruz
DF		6:40, 9:25	7:05, 11:20	7:35, 10:00	8:00, 11:00	8:15
Guadalajara	7:20, 10:05		7:55, 12:00	8:20, 11:05	8:35, 10:40	9:25
Guanajuato	7:05, 9:15	7:35, 11:25		8:25, 11:50	8:00	No hay servicio.
Morelia	8:20, 10:00	6:40, 8:00	6:30, 7:55		7:50, 11:10	9:00, 12:00
Tampico	7:35	7:05, 9:15	8:00, 10:50	8:35, 11:25		7:20, 10:00
Veracruz	7:55, 9:00	8:20, 10:00	No hay servicio.	7:35, 10:20	7:05, 11:40	

¡TAXI YA!
Con servicio a toda la ciudad de México
• Conveniente   • Cómodo
• Rápido   • Y listo... ¡YA!
Llamar 24 horas . . . 577 36 79

Aerolínea Yucatecas   *Tu amigo en el aire*
Con servicio entre 12 ciudades mexicanas

• Acapulco   • Distrito Federal (México) • León   • Morelia
• Chihuahua   • Guadalajara   • Mérida   • Tampico
• Cuernavaca   • Guanajuato   • Monterrey • Veracruz

los lunes - los viernes • 8 vuelos los sábados y domingos • entre Acapulco, DF, Mérida y Veracruz
Para reservaciones e información llamar al **480 12 17/482 08 19**

---

33 1. Está en México en la Avenida de la Defensa, 23.
2. Es el dos, noventa y nueve, cuarenta y tres, cero, uno./Es el dos, cincuenta y seis, veintinueve, treinta y nueve.
3. El cine se llama Cine Máximo. El banco se llama Banco Nacional.
4. Está en la Avenida de la Defensa, 98.
5. Hay dos restaurantes.
6. Está muy cerca del hotel.
7. Sí, (No, no) voy allí.
8. Answers will vary.
34 Creative self-expression.

Activities

Expansion
Possible questions for activity 34:
Uds. están en Guanajuato y necesitan ir a Veracruz. Van en los camiones de Transmex, ¿verdad?; ¿A qué hora vamos de Guadalajara a Veracruz en camión (autobús)? Uds. están en la capital y necesitan ir a Tampico el viernes. ¿Cómo van Uds. a Tampico?; La señora Pérez necesita tomar un taxi. ¿Hay servicio de taxi en el D.F.? ¿Cómo se llama la compañía de taxis? ¿Sabes el número de teléfono?; Yo quiero ir de Monterrey a Nuevo Laredo en avión con la Aerolínea Yucatecas. ¿Hay un problema? ¿Cuál es?; ¿Cómo es el servicio de ¡Taxi Ya!?; El señor Pérez necesita ir de Veracruz al D.F. el viernes. ¿A qué hora va?; ¿Adónde vas en autobús (camión)? ¿en avión?

Notes Point out for students that daily hours for businesses and other services (such as bus and airline schedules in activity 34) may be very different from schedules students are used to in the United States.

Have students find on a map the sites mentioned in the realia on page 107.

Teacher Resources

 El metro de la Ciudad de México es fantástico
Activities 35–36

Answers

35 1. El metro de la Ciudad de México es moderno, limpio, barato, seguro y eficiente.
2. Identifican las estaciones del metro con símbolos y colores.
3. Hay una pirámide azteca.
4. Hay restos de un mamut.
5. Cinco millones de personas toman el metro todos los días.

36 Answers will vary.

Activities

Prereading Strategy
Have students look over the realia on page 108 and pick out cognates and other words they recognize before assigning activities 35 and 36.

Spanish for Spanish Speakers
Ask your native Spanish speakers to contribute any information they may know about Mexico, such as recent news stories, articles about celebrities and famous people and so on.

Lectura cultural

MAPA DE BOLSILLO
Ciudad de México

El metro de la Ciudad de México es fantástico

La pirámide azteca en la estación de Pino Suárez.

¿Vas de vacaciones a la Ciudad de México y no sabes qué hacer? ¿Por qué no pasas[1] un día fantástico usando[2] el metro? Toma la línea 2 a Chapultepec y camina por el parque. O toma la línea 3 a la estación de Pino Suárez y mira la pirámide azteca descubierta[3] en 1968 durante la construcción del metro. O toma la línea 4 a la estación de Talismán y mira los restos de un mamut[4] que tiene 13.000 años. Todos los días[5], cinco millones de personas toman el metro para ir al trabajo[6] o la escuela. Tú y tus amigos pueden[7] tomar el metro para divertirse[8]. El metro es un transporte moderno, limpio[9], seguro[10] y eficiente. ¡Vamos en metro!

Datos interesantes del metro de México, D.F.:
• Es el primer sistema que usa símbolos y colores para identificar las estaciones.
• Es el metro más barato[11] del planeta porque sólo cuesta[12] US $0,20.
• La estación Pantitlán es la estación de transbordo[13] más grande del planeta.

[1]spend [2]using [3]discovered [4]mammoth
[5]Every day [6]work [7]can [8]have fun [9]clean
[10]safe [11]cheapest [12]costs [13]transfer

35 ¿Qué recuerdas?

1. ¿Cómo es el metro de la Ciudad de México?
2. ¿Cómo identifican las estaciones del metro?
3. ¿Qué hay en la estación de metro Pino Suárez?
4. ¿Qué hay en la estación de metro Talismán?
5. ¿Cuántas personas toman el metro todos los días?

36 Algo personal

1. ¿Hay un sistema de metro en tu ciudad?
2. ¿Cuánto cuesta el transporte público en tu ciudad?
3. ¿Cómo son las estaciones (de metro o de bus) en tu ciudad?

• Have you ever taken the subway? Describe your experience. How did it compare with the Mexican subway described in the article?

• Why do you think they built stations around the Aztec pyramid and the remains of the mammoth instead of transferring these discoveries to a museum? Is that a good idea?

108 *ciento ocho*

Lección A

Notes **Connections.** Note the cross-curricular connections to history in this reading about Mexico City.

Encourage students to visit the Web site for the Mexico City subway system:

http://www.iwm.com.mx/mexinter/dfmetro2.html

In Mexico the first two or three cars of *metro* trains are often reserved for senior citizens and mothers traveling with children. It is also interesting to note that indigenous ruins have been found when digging for the *metro*.

108

¿Qué aprendí?

Autoevaluación
As a review and self-check, respond to the following:

 Visit the web-based activities at www.emcp.com

1. In Spanish, identify five places in a city.

2. There is going to be a party in a nearby restaurant. Ask what time the party is.

3. A new girl who speaks Spanish has moved into your neighborhood. Tell her if the following places are near or far and what means of transportation you use to go to each place: *la escuela, el parque, el cine.*

4. What would you say in Spanish when introducing these people to your teacher: a friend named Diana? don Diego? two friends?

5. Give an example of a courteous response in Spanish when you are introduced.

6. How would you confirm that your friends are going to the movie theater near the library?

7. You are about to travel to Mexico. What would you like to see and do?

Palabras y expresiones

La ciudad
el banco
la biblioteca
el cine
el dentista, la dentista
la escuela
el hotel
el médico, la médica
la oficina
el parque
el restaurante

Palabras interrogativas
¿adónde?
¿cuándo?
¿por qué?
¿quiénes?

Transporte
a caballo
a pie
el autobús
el avión
el barco
la bicicleta
el caballo
el camión
el carro
en carro
en *(means of transportation)*
el metro
la moto(cicleta)

el taxi
el transporte
el tren

Verbos
caminar
ir
presento
quiero
sabes
tomar
¡vamos!

Otras expresiones
al
cerca (de)
¡claro!

del
El gusto es mío.
encantado,-a
fantástico,-a
la fiesta
lejos (de)
le/les/te presento a
porque
el problema
simpático,-a
también
Tanto gusto.
¿verdad?

Teacher Resources

📝 **Activity 16**

🗨 **Information Gap Activities**
Postcard Activities
Funciones de Comunicación

Answers

Autoevaluación
Possible answers:
1. La biblioteca, el cine, el restaurante, el parque, la escuela, etc.
2. ¿A qué hora es la fiesta?
3. La escuela está cerca de aquí. Yo voy a la escuela a pie. El parque está cerca de aquí. Yo voy al parque en bicicleta. El cine está lejos. Yo voy al cine en metro.
4. Diana, te presento al profesor (a la profesora) de español. Don Diego, le presento al profesor (a la profesora) de español. *(Names of two friends),* les presento al profesor (a la profesora) de español.
5. Mucho gusto./Encantado (Encantada).
6. Van al cine cerca de la biblioteca, ¿verdad?/... ¿no?
7. Answers will vary.

Activities

Expansion
Model the words and expressions on page 109 and have students repeat. Then call on students to use the words or expressions in sentences.

Notes Extend number 7 of the *Autoevaluación* by having students locate additional information that will help them plan a trip, such as maps, restaurant names and locations, currency rates, etc.

If you have not yet done so, explain that various forms of physical contact may accompany greetings or introductions.

Depending on the participants, a handshake, hug or kiss(es) may be appropriate.

En el centro

 Activity 1

 Activity 25

 Activities 1–2

 Activity 1

 Activities 1–2

Content reviewed in *Lección B*
- city destinations
- seeking and providing personal information
- transportation
- discussing schedules

Activities

Critical Thinking

Ask students if the city is important in their lives. Is it a popular place to live? Does it offer important cultural events that they attend? Are there important places of interest they enjoy visiting? Discuss city life with the class and have students compare their city's downtown with what they are learning about life in Spanish-speaking cities of the world.

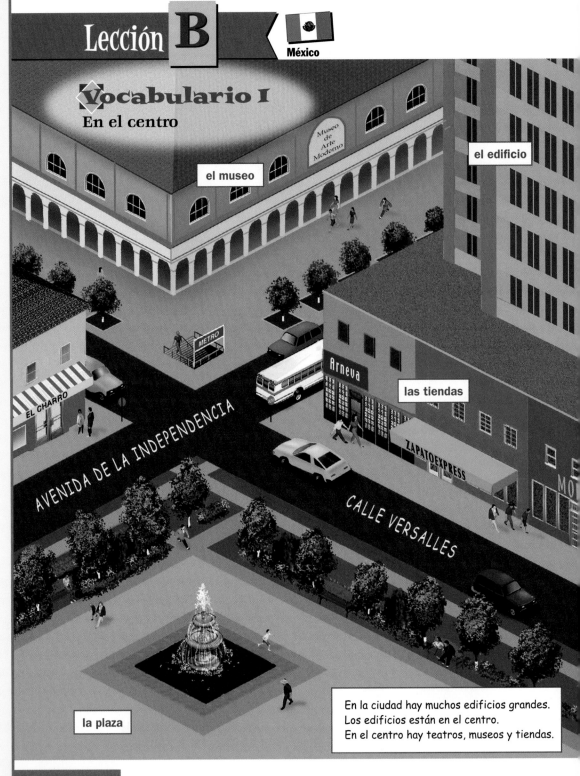

Lección B

México

Vocabulario I
En el centro

el museo

el edificio

las tiendas

la plaza

En la ciudad hay muchos edificios grandes.
Los edificios están en el centro.
En el centro hay teatros, museos y tiendas.

Notes **Comparisons.** In Spanish-speaking parts of the world, a city's downtown is often a popular place to live (in addition to offering cultural events and places of interest). Conduct a class discussion about how this compares with cities in the United States.

Note that a main square *(plaza)* is often at the heart of a city or neighborhood in the Spanish-speaking world.

1 En el centro

🔊 Selecciona la ilustración del lugar apropiado, según lo que oyes.

A

B

C

D

E

F

G

H

2 La ciudad

Completa las oraciones de acuerdo con las ilustraciones del Vocabulario I.

1. El autobús va por la __.
2. Gabriela y Ana van al __ de arte.
3. Luis Miguel va a estar mañana en el __ Arlequín.
4. El Museo de Arte Moderno está en la __ de la Independencia.
5. Moda In y Zapato Express son __ en la Calle Versalles.
6. Hay ocho personas en la __ .
7. En el __ hay muchas oficinas.
8. ¿Vamos al __ El Charro?

3 ¿Adónde vas?

Haz una lista de los lugares adónde vas.

Capítulo 3   *ciento once* **111**

Teacher Resources

🔘 Activity 1

Answers

1
1. H
2. A
3. G
4. E
5. B
6. D
7. C
8. F

2
1. calle
2. museo
3. Teatro
4. Avenida
5. tiendas
6. plaza
7. edificio
8. restaurante

3 Answers will vary.

Activities

Critical Thinking
Ask students how the city shown on pages 110–111 is similar to or different from cities in the United States.

Multiple Intelligences (linguistic)
Play a CD of some of Luis Miguel's songs and have students identify and write down words they recognize.

Answers

4 1. Va al centro con Pilar.
   2. No. Ella va al museo.
   3. Es un edificio grande.
   4. El restaurante está en la Avenida de la Independencia.
5 Answers will vary.
6 1. B
   2. C
   3. D
   4. A

Activities

Critical Listening
Play the audio CD version of the dialog. Instruct students to cover up the words with one hand since you want them to develop good listening skills. Tell students to look at the photographs while they imagine what the people are saying to one another. Have several individuals state what they believe the main theme of the conversation is.

Prereading Strategy
Instruct students to cover up the dialog with one hand and look at the photographs. Ask them to imagine where the conversation takes place and what the people are saying to one another. Finally, have students look through the dialog quickly to find cognates.

Diálogo I
Vamos al museo

TOMÁS: Olga, ¿qué vas a hacer el sábado?
OLGA: Voy a ir al centro con Pilar.

TOMÁS: ¿Van a las tiendas?
OLGA: No. Vamos al museo de arte.
TOMÁS: El museo está en un edificio grande.

OLGA: Sí, luego, vamos al restaurante El Charro. ¿Vas?
TOMÁS: ¡Claro! ¿Está el restaurante en la calle Versalles?
OLGA: No, está en la Avenida de la Independencia.

4 ¿Qué recuerdas?

1. ¿Qué va a hacer Olga el sábado?
2. ¿Va ella a las tiendas?
3. ¿Cómo es el edificio del museo?
4. ¿Dónde está el restaurante?

5 Algo personal

1. ¿Qué vas a hacer el sábado?
2. ¿Hay muchos edificios grandes en el centro de tu ciudad?
3. ¿En qué calle está tu colegio?

6 ¿Qué vas a hacer hoy?

Indica la letra de la ilustración que corresponde con lo que oyes.

A   **B**   **C**   **D**

Notes Native Spanish speakers tend to stand closer to one another than most people might in the United States. It is not unusual to see mothers and their teenage sons or daughters walking arm in arm as they tour ruins and museums in Mexico and throughout Europe. Also, two girls who are good friends may be walking around arm in arm in the parks or other public sites of interest. In addition, explain to students that because personal space is more limited in many Spanish-speaking countries, they should not find it particularly surprising when they are jostled a bit in lines where they are making a purchase such as admittance tickets to a museum.

Cultura viva

El Distrito Federal (el D.F.)

Mexico City is not only the capital of the country, the *Distrito Federal* is also the center of Mexico's government, economy, culture and educational system. Internationally known sites you may want to visit include *El Palacio Nacional, el Museo de Antropología* and one of the largest universities in the world, *la Universidad Autónoma de México (UNAM)*, among others. Downtown, virtually every street offers an array of interesting sites and experiences, including Aztec ruins *(la Plaza de las Tres Culturas)*, beautiful parks *(Alameda)*, museums and art galleries *(el Palacio de Bellas Artes)*, as well as many interesting colonial buildings.

Mexico City also faces challenges. Like most large U.S. cities, downtown streets are

Contaminación del aire (*air pollution*) en el D.F.

crowded, noisy, polluted and frequently congested with traffic jams. In addition, early Spanish colonists constructed the city on top of the original Aztec capital, Tenochtitlán, which had been built on an island in the middle of Lake Texcoco. Consequently, parts of the city are now sinking because of this soft land, and this creates problems providing fresh drinking water to millions of residents.

When you travel to *el D.F.*, you will experience a cosmopolitan atmosphere that is both similar to and yet very different from other cities in the world. While there, you see why Mexicans take great pride in their heritage. Now they are focused on an even brighter future.

El Palacio de Bellas Artes.

7 Un viaje a México

Plan an itinerary for a trip to Mexico. First, decide what you want to see and do and indicate why each site or activity interests you (e.g., *el Palacio Nacional* – to see Diego Rivera's artwork in person). Next, list hotels (with addresses and rates) where you want to stay. Include in your travel plans flight schedules to and from the destinations you want to visit, including Mexico City. Finally, map out your daily schedule from beginning to end.

¡Extra!

Está en la internet

You can find all of the information needed to complete a travel itinerary by searching the Internet. Alternative sources of information include travel agents, airlines and the library.

Answers

8 1. Uds. van a ir al museo de arte, ¿verdad?
2. Manolo va a ir a la fiesta en la plaza, ¿verdad?
3. Fabiola y Gerardo van a ir al teatro, ¿verdad?
4. Nosotros vamos a ir a las tiendas, ¿verdad?
5. Doris va a ir a la oficina, ¿verdad?
6. Ud. va a ir al banco, ¿verdad?
7. Tú vas a ir a la biblioteca, ¿verdad?
8. Doña Ester va a ir al médico, ¿verdad?

9 Answers will vary.

Activities

Expansion
After reviewing activity 9 with the class, ask students how people are going to go to the places named: *¿Cómo van los Martínez al centro el lunes?*

Students with Special Needs
Review the present tense of the verb *ir* before presenting the future with *ir + a +* infinitive.

114

Estructura

Talking about the future: *ir a* + infinitive

Say what you are going to do or what is going to happen by using the present tense of *ir*, followed by *a* and an infinitive *(infinitivo)*.

ir + *a* + infinitive

*Laura **va a ser** médica.*   Laura is going to be a doctor.
*Uds. **van a estar** en México, ¿verdad?*   You are going to be in Mexico, right?

 Práctica

8 Van a ir a diferentes lugares

Ask where these people are going tomorrow in downtown Guadalajara, using tag questions.

MODELO Juán / restaurante El Amanecer
Juán va a ir al restaurante El Amanecer, ¿verdad?

1. Uds. / museo de arte
2. Manolo / fiesta en la plaza
3. Fabiola y Gerardo / teatro
4. nosotros / tiendas
5. Doris / oficina
6. Ud. / banco
7. tú / biblioteca
8. doña Ester / médico

¿Adónde van Uds.?

9 ¿Adónde van a ir en Cuernavaca?

Haz oraciones lógicas usando palabras y expresiones de cada columna.

MODELO Los Martínez van a ir al cine a las seis.

los Martínez	centro	el lunes
la Sra. Sandoval	concierto	en la tarde
nosotros	restaurante	a las seis
yo	tienda	a las 10:30 P.M.
doña Angelina	edificio nuevo	el domingo
Ariel Tovar	museo	al mediodía
tú	plaza	en la mañana
Mónica y Jairo Ruíz	teatro	
	cine	

Notes **Comparisons.** You may wish to tell students that in addition to being used to indicate a future action, *vamos a +* infinitive may also be used to express a suggestion similar to **let's** or **shall we?** in English.

Comunicación

 10 En el Distrito Federal

As part of a summer study program, you have the opportunity to take classes at *la UNAM* and a classmate has prepared a list to help you find your way around the city. Answer the questions about places to go in the city.

1. ¿Cómo vas a ir a los museos de Chapultepec?
2. ¿Qué museo de arte está en Chapultepec?
3. ¿A qué museos vas a ir?
4. Tomas un taxi a la Calle 16 de Septiembre. ¿De qué plaza vas a estar cerca?
5. ¿Dónde está el restaurante con "mole fantástico"?
6. ¿Dónde está el Palacio de Bellas Artes? ¿Cómo vas a ir allí?
7. Quiero ir al Museo de Arte Moderno. ¿Sabes el número de teléfono del museo?

> **Adónde ir en el D.F.**
>
> Parque de Chapultepec (ir en metro):
> · Museo Nacional de Antropología
> · Museo Nacional de Historia (en el Castillo)
> · Casa del Lago (parque de atracciones)
> · Museo Tecnológico
> · Museo de Arte Moderno (en Av. Reforma): 776-83-41
> · Museo de Historia Natural
>
> Otros lugares interesantes:
> · Palacio de Bellas Artes (museo y teatro en el Centro Histórico)
> — Está en la Alameda Central y la Avenida Juárez.
>   (camiones Nº 16 ó 52) Información: 683-48-05
>
> · El Zócalo (plaza central)
> — Calle 16 de Septiembre (cerca de la Calle Seminario)
>
> Restaurantes:
> · La Bodega (¡Mole fantástico!)
> Popocatépetl 25, Colonia Hipódromo Condesa, Zona Centro
> Teléfono: 525-84-73
>
> · SpaceNet Café
> Calz. del Hueso 160 local 3-B Fuentes Plaza Ex Hacienda Coapa,
> Zona Sur
> Teléfono: 567-35-52

 11 Sus propios planes

Working in pairs, use the list from the previous activity to make your own plans for what you are going to do while in Mexico City.

MODELO A: ¿Vamos a ir al Museo de Antropología?
B: Sí. Vamos a ir allí en taxi.

 12 ¿Qué van a hacer mañana?

Talk with two classmates about going downtown tomorrow. Start by asking each other what you are going to do. Then ask where you are going to go, how you are going to get there, etc. Use a variety of expressions and as many new words as you can.

MODELO A: ¿Qué van a hacer mañana?
B: Voy a ir al centro.
C: ¿Cómo vas a ir?
B: Voy a ir en metro.

¡Oportunidades!

Se habla español en México y en tu ciudad
It is not always necessary to travel to Mexico or to go a great distance in order to use Spanish. In the United States, nearly every community offers opportunities to apply language skills you are learning this year. Many American cities have large Spanish-speaking populations, so you may find yourself using your new language skills in a restaurant, at a museum, in a store or while you are simply strolling along a city street. Knowing Spanish opens doors and offers opportunities you might otherwise never experience!

Capítulo 3 *ciento quince* **115**

Vocabulario II
En el restaurante

¡Comida mexicana!

No veo pollo en mole en el menú.

¿Qué van a comer?

Pues, ¿por qué no le preguntas al mesero?

De acuerdo.

Yo quiero comer una ensalada.

¡Cómo no!

el mesero

la mesera

Un momento, por favor. Oye, Natalia, ¿qué vas a comer?

Él toma jugo de naranja.

el menú

Bueno, siempre como pollo, pero hoy voy a comer pescado.

Natalia y Lucía van a comer ahora.
Las chicas leen el menú.
El mesero hace una pregunta a las chicas.

para comer hay

el pescado

el pollo

la ensalada

los frijoles

Para tomar hay

FRESA

el refresco

AGUA

el agua mineral

el jugo de naranja

las comidas

las bebidas

13 ¿Dónde está?

 Di si lo que oyes está en un restaurante o en un colegio.

Está en un restaurante.

Está en un colegio.

14 ¿Qué sabes?

Haz una lista de tres comidas y tres bebidas.

15 En el restaurante

Completa las siguientes oraciones en forma lógica.

1. Las chicas leen en el __ lo que hay para comer y para tomar.
2. El __ pregunta a las chicas "¿Qué van a comer?".
3. Natalia y Lucía toman __ mineral.
4. La __ que toma el señor de camisa azul es un jugo de naranja.
5. La señora quiere pollo en mole de __ pero no está en el menú.
6. Lucía quiere pescado para __ .

¡Extra!

Más bebidas y comidas

Para tomar:

el café	coffee
el chocolate	hot chocolate
la gaseosa, el refresco	soft drink
la leche	milk
el té	tea

Para comer:

la carne	meat
la ensalada	salad
la hamburguesa	hamburger
el pan	bread
las papas fritas	french fries
el postre	dessert

Capítulo 3 *ciento diecisiete* **117**

Teacher Resources

 Activity 13

 Activity 6

Answers

13
1. Está en un colegio.
2. Está en un restaurante.
3. Está en un restaurante.
4. Está en un colegio.
5. Está en un colegio.
6. Está en un restaurante.

14 Discuss the lists. Find out if students can name other foods.

15
1. menú
2. mesero
3. agua
4. bebida
5. comida
6. comer

Activities

Multiple Intelligences (bodily-kinesthetic)
Give students a simple Mexican recipe. Then have students prepare the food and share it with the class. (You may want to make arrangements with a Family and Consumer Sciences instructor in the building to prepare the food during school hours.)

Diálogo II

¿Qué van a comer?

TOMÁS: Perdón, ¿sabe dónde está el restaurante El Charro?
SEÑORA: ¡Sí! Está allí, cerca de la biblioteca, en la Avenida de la Independencia.
TOMÁS: Muchas gracias.

TOMÁS: Hola, Olga. Hola, Pilar.
OLGA: ¡Hola, Tomás! Oye, ¿qué vas a comer?
TOMÁS: Yo siempre como pollo en mole.

MESERA: ¿Qué van a comer, señoritas?
OLGA: Este... quiero el pescado y un refresco.
PILAR: Yo voy a comer unos frijoles y a tomar un jugo de naranja.
MESERA: De acuerdo.

16 ¿Qué recuerdas?

1. ¿Dónde está el restaurante El Charro?
2. ¿Qué come Tomás siempre?
3. ¿Qué va a comer Olga?
4. ¿Va Pilar a comer una ensalada?

17 Algo personal

1. ¿Dónde está tu restaurante favorito?
2. ¿Qué comida vas a comer allí?
3. ¿Tomas agua mineral, jugo de naranja o refresco?

18 ¿Cuál es la respuesta correcta?

 Escoge la letra de la respuesta correcta.

> A. Sí, pero hoy no quiero pollo en mole.
> B. Está allí, cerca de la biblioteca.
> C. Pues, un momento, por favor... Voy a comer pescado hoy.
> D. Quiero tomar agua mineral, por favor.

¡Extra!

Para ser natural

Do you ever use a word while you are talking just to fill in the conversation while you are thinking, such as **well, um** or **hey**? Adding some of these pause words to conversations will make your speech sound more natural:

a ver	*let's see*
bueno	*okay, well*
este	*well, so*
mira	*look, hey*
oye	*hey, listen*
pues	*thus, well, so, then*
es que...	*well, it's just that...*

118 *ciento dieciocho* **Lección B**

Cultura viva

Unos tamales deliciosos.

Salir a comer en México

Mexican cuisine consists of much more than *enchiladas, tacos, tamales, quesadillas* and *burritos*. Each region of Mexico has its own particular type of food. In Mexico City, restaurants and cafés are everywhere. To eat well at reasonable prices, imitate the Mexicans and make your main meal *(la comida principal)* a large, late lunch *(el almuerzo)*.

Tacos en la taquería.

Mole is one of the most popular dishes, consisting of a thick, spicy, dark brown sauce of various chiles, sesame seeds, chocolate, herbs and spices. Served over chicken *(pollo)* or turkey *(pavo)*, it is called *mole poblano.* You can also eat crispy chicken in a *rosticería*, order standard Mexican cuisine such as *tacos* or *enchiladas* at a *taquería*, or try fruit shakes, sodas, ice cream or fruit salads at a juice *(jugo)* shop. Other eating choices range from inexpensive coffeehouses and pastry shops to international Chinese, Japanese, French and Middle Eastern restaurants. Beverage choices are varied, too, and consist of popular fruit drinks *(jugos)*, milk, bottled mineral waters *(aguas minerales)*, soft drinks with or without ice *(hielo)* and much more.

TIPOS DE PLATOS

Entrada
Es el primer plato de una comida. Usualmente es una sopa, una crema, un coctel de mariscos o de frutas, o un antipasto.

Ensalada
Puede servir de acompañamiento al plato fuerte, o como plato único cuando es con pollo o mariscos.

Plato fuerte
El pollo, las carnes y pescados son generalmente la base de esta parte de la comida.

Postre
Es el tercer o cuarto plato en una comida. Debe ser dulce y los cubiertos que se usan para comerlo son una cuchara pequeña y un tenedor, también pequeño.

19 Salir a comer en México

Contesta las siguientes preguntas.

1. ¿Hay muchos restaurantes en el Distrito Federal?
2. ¿Qué comida es muy popular en México?
3. ¿Adónde vas a ir para comer pollo rostizado en México?
4. ¿Adónde vas a ir para comer tacos y enchiladas en México?
5. ¿Qué hay para tomar en México?
6. ¿Cuántos tipos de platos *(courses)* hay?

Capítulo 3

ciento diecinueve **119**

Teacher Resources

 Activity 19

 Activity 4

 Activity 4

Answers

19 1. Sí, hay muchos restaurantes en el Distrito Federal.
2. El mole (poblano) es muy popular.
3. Voy a ir a la rosticería.
4. Voy a ir a la taquería.
5. Hay jugos, leche, aguas minerales, refrescos, etc. (Students may decide to add other nonactive vocabulary from the *¡Extra!*.)
6. Hay cuatro tipos.

Activities

Communities
Arrange a field trip to a local Mexican restaurant so students have an opportunity to try some of the foods they are learning about. While on the trip, require that everyone use Spanish to reinforce the value of the trip for both cultural and linguistic benefits.

Expansion
Have students create a list of all the foods they have learned in Spanish. Then have them use a dictionary and find five other words they would like to know.

Notes Explain that shopping for food also entails cultural traditions. Most Mexican families buy fresh food daily, often at a local market *(mercado)* that features a great variety of produce and specialty items.

Corn tortillas are an important staple in nearly all Mexican meals. They can be eaten alone or with other ingredients in tacos, enchiladas, burritos and quesadillas.

Idioma

Estructura

Saying what someone does: present tense of *-er* verbs

Form the present tense of regular *-er* verbs, such as *comer* (to eat), *comprender* (to understand) and *leer* (to read), by first removing the *-er* ending and then attaching endings that correspond to each of the subject pronouns shown in this chart.

comer			
yo	com**o**	nosotros nosotras	com**emos**
tú	com**es**	vosotros vosotras	com**éis**
Ud. él ella	com**e**	Uds. ellos ellas	com**en**

Three additional verbs that end in *-er, hacer* (to do, to make), *saber* (to know information) and *ver* (to see), are regular except for the *yo* forms.

> *hacer* yo **hago**   *saber* yo **sé**   *ver* yo **veo**

In addition, the *vosotros* form of *ver* does not require an accent mark: *vosotros* **veis**.

> **Veo** la calle Versalles.
> ¿**Veis** vosotros la Avenida Suárez en el mapa?

 # Práctica

 20 ¿Qué comes?

Working in pairs, take turns asking questions about whether each of you does or does not eat the items listed.

MODELO tacos
> **A:** ¿Comes tacos?
> **B:** Sí, (No, no) como tacos.

1. ensalada
2. frijoles
3. pescado
4. pollo

Notes This might be a good time to practice the conjugation of the verb *beber*.

Point out the similarities in forming regular *-ar* and *-er* verbs. Show students how to remove the infinitive ending and add endings that correspond with the subject pronouns, as indicated in the paradigm.

21 Tenemos mucho en común

Read the following statements and say who else does the same thing, according to the cue in parentheses. Add an expression such as *pues* or *bueno* before each sentence.

> **MODELO** Leo periódicos en español y comprendo muy bien. (Elena)
> Pues, Elena lee periódicos en español y comprende muy bien también.

Leo periódicos en español.

1. Josefina lee una revista y toma jugo de naranja. (yo)
2. El señor y la señora Correa leen libros en español. (nosotros)
3. El profesor comprende inglés y español. (José y Ana)
4. Comemos pescado y ensalada en el centro hoy. (los Peña)
5. Roberto come tacos en el restaurante Los Rancheros. (tú)

22 ¿Comprenden y hablan inglés y español?

Say that the following people all understand and speak English and Spanish.

> **MODELO** Alejandro
> Alejandro comprende y habla inglés y español.

1. yo
2. tú
3. mi amiga y yo
4. el profesor
5. los estudiantes en la clase de español
6. la chica nueva

23 En el restaurante El Charro

Complete the following paragraph with the present tense of the verbs in parentheses.

Los viernes, mi amiga Pilar y yo siempre *(1. comer)* en el restaurante El Charro. Hoy muchos chicos del colegio *(2. comer)* aquí. En la mesa número uno, Paco y María *(3. leer)* el menú. Paco no *(4. saber)* qué comer. María siempre *(5. comer)* pescado. En la mesa dos, el mesero pregunta a Jorge, Daniel y Patricia qué van a comer. Ellos *(6. hacer)* una pregunta al mesero: "Nosotros no *(7. ver)* tacos en el menú. ¿Hay tacos aquí?" "Sí, ¡cómo no!" responde el mesero. En la mesa tres estamos Graciela y yo. Graciela *(8. leer)* el menú. Yo siempre *(9. comer)* ensalada, pero no *(10. saber)* qué tomar hoy. Graciela dice "Un momento, por favor". Yo *(11. ver)* que ella no *(12. comprender)* una palabra del menú. Luego, ella dice "¡Ahora *(13. comprender)*! Yo quiero el pollo en mole y un refresco por favor". "De acuerdo".

Teacher Resources

 Activity 22

Answers

21 Possible answers:
1. Pues, yo leo una revista y tomo jugo de naranja también.
2. Bueno, nosotros leemos libros en español también.
3. Oye, José y Ana comprenden inglés y español también.
4. Bueno, los Peña comen pescado y ensalada en el centro hoy también.
5. Pues, tú comes tacos en el restaurante Los Rancheros también.

22
1. Yo comprendo y hablo inglés y español.
2. Tú comprendes y hablas inglés y español.
3. Mi amiga y yo comprendemos y hablamos inglés y español.
4. El profesor comprende y habla inglés y español.
5. Los estudiantes en la clase de español comprenden y hablan inglés y español.
6. La chica nueva comprende y habla inglés y español.

23 1. comemos; 2. comen; 3. leen; 4. sabe; 5. come; 6. hacen; 7. vemos; 8. lee; 9. como; 10. sé; 11. veo; 12. comprende; 13. comprendo

Notes Because the *vosotros/vosotras* verb forms are included in *Navegando* for passive recognition only, you are free to determine whether students must learn the corresponding verb forms. If your students are going to learn to conjugate verbs with *vosotros* and *vosotras,* you may modify one of the existing sentences for activities such as 22 or simply add a sentence or two to each activity and have students use *vosotros* and *vosotras* when conjugating the corresponding verbs.

24 Unas personas en mi comunidad

Using the verbs *comer, comprender* and *leer,* tell what these people are doing.

MODELO · la mesera
La mesera come pollo.

1. Graciela

2. Camilo

3. los muchachos

4. Laura y Elena

5. Edgar y Vivian

6. Don Pedro

25 ¿Qué hacen?

Working with a partner, read the following statements about Alfredo and his friends. Tell your partner that you do the same things as Alfredo, and then ask what your partner does.

MODELO · **A:** Alfredo va a un colegio grande en el centro.
B: Pues, yo también voy a un colegio grande en el centro. ¿Y tú?
A: Yo (no) voy a un colegio grande en el centro.

1. Alfredo sabe historia.
2. Alfredo siempre lee muchas revistas y periódicos.
3. Los sábados Alfredo y Rebeca hacen pollo en mole.
4. Alfredo y Tomás hacen muchas preguntas en la clase de biología.
5. Alfredo comprende español.
6. Alfredo, Rebeca y Tomás comen pescado y pollo.

Alfredo va a un colegio grande en el centro.

Notes · The Appendices contain a grammar review and a reference section on verb conjugations. Refer to the chart anytime you would like additional help explaining verb conjugation to students. The reference provides a concise and comprehensive review of both regular and irregular verb forms.

26 ¿Qué ves?

Say what these people do, see or know, according to what you see in each illustration.

1. Gabriel y María

El número de teléfono de Juan es el 6-65-45-20.

2. ellos

3. Mónica

4. Diego

5. los Montoya

¿El cine? Sí, calle León, número 10.

6. la Sra. Ruiz

✦ Comunicación

27 En El Charro

In groups of four, two students play the role of friends who are considering going to a popular restaurant in town, El Charro. The other two students should pretend they often go to eat at El Charro. Then, four of you meet on the street and discuss the restaurant (the restaurant's name, if it is new, where it is, etc.). Be sure to ask your friends what they eat when they go to El Charro. Then say what you are going to eat when you go there. Switch roles.

28 ¿Qué leen los estudiantes en la clase?

Survey your classmates to find out how many are reading a book right now. Next, find out the names of the books and how many students are reading each one. Finally, summarize your findings in a short paragraph.

Hay seis estudiantes que leen libros. Uno lee Marianela. Dos leen

Estrategia

The importance of reviewing
Whenever you do an activity that requires you to be creative, look at previous activities, dialogs, readings, etc. for words, grammar and cultural information you have already learned that may be useful in the new activity (e.g., the word *nuevo* in activities 9 and 22, asking for or giving names in activities 27 and 28, the question-asking words for activities 27 and 28). This recombining of old and new content will help you remember what you learned. It will also help you express yourself naturally in ever more complex situations.

Capítulo 3

ciento veintitrés **123**

Teacher Resources

Lectura personal
Activities 29–30

Answers

29 1. Está en un restaurante de donde ve el Zócalo.
2. Imagina el Zócalo en diferentes épocas de la historia.
3. La Ciudad de México era una isla desierta en 1325.
4. El nombre de la Ciudad de México era Tenochtitlán.
5. Hernán Cortés conquistó a los aztecas en 1525.

30 Answers will vary.

Activities

Multiple Intelligences (musical)
Working with a music teacher, ask if students are interested in learning a musical piece by a Mexican singer or composer. After allowing time to practice, have a student perform the piece in class. As an extension, have students work in pairs: One student performs the musical piece and the partner writes an article about the Mexican singer/composer and the musical piece that the other student performs.

Technology
Have students search the Internet to find out more about one of the points mentioned in the *Lectura personal* (Mexican museums, history of Mexico). They should then write a short summary about what they learned.

Lectura personal

Cantantes y grupos musicales

Dirección http://www.emcp.com/músico/ola/e.diario-2.htm ▲ Archivo Edición Ver Favoritos Herramientas Ayuda

[página principal] [miembros] [e-diario]

Grupo musical La OLA

Nombre: **Xavier Rodríguez Guerra**
Edad: **18 años**
Ciudad natal: **Chicago**
Comida favorita: **pollo en mole**
Cantante favorito: **Alejandro Sanz**

¡Fantástico concierto en Ciudad de México! Gracias, amigos. Nunca[1] voy a olvidar[2] esta ciudad de más de veinte millones de personas, edificios impresionantes y museos famosos. ¡Es una ciudad extraordinaria! Ahora estoy en un restaurante y veo el Zócalo. Imagino esta plaza en diferentes épocas de la historia... En 1325 era[3] una isla desierta en el lago[4] Texcoco donde los mexicas se establecieron[5].

En 1519 Tenochtitlán (hoy Ciudad de México) era la capital del imperio azteca, una ciudad grande, importante, magnífica. Los palacios y las casas estaban[6] en chinampas[7] y las personas se desplazaban[8] por canales. En 1525, cuando Hernán Cortés conquistó[9] a los aztecas, la ciudad era ruinas y destrucción. Hoy el Zócalo es la plaza más grande del mundo[10].

[1]Never [2]to forget [3]it was [4]lake [5]settled down [6]were [7]pieces of land floating on a lake
[8]traveled [9]conquered [10]world

29 ¿Qué recuerdas?

1. ¿Dónde está Xavier cuando escribe el e-diario?
2. ¿Qué imagina Xavier?
3. ¿Qué era la Ciudad de México en 1325?
4. ¿Cuál era el nombre de la Ciudad de México en 1519?
5. ¿Cuándo conquistó Hernán Cortés a los aztecas?

30 Algo personal

1. ¿Cuántos años tiene la Ciudad de México? ¿Cuántos años tiene tu ciudad?
2. ¿Qué grupo indígena habitó en la región donde tú vives?
3. ¿Hay una plaza en tu ciudad? Compara tu *town square* con el Zócalo en la Ciudad de México.

- How has Mexico City changed over time? How long has it been a capital city?
- What's the name of Mexico City's main plaza? How does it compare with your town's main square?

124 *ciento veinticuatro* **Lección B**

Notes The Aztec capital Tenochtitlán was characterized by its canals. Mexico City's soft land base is one reason the city is susceptible to earthquakes.

Comparisons. Explain to students that *el D.F.* is a federal district and is comparable to the District of Columbia, or Washington, D.C.

Mexico City is growing by 50,000 people per month. Population experts predict that by 2010 Mexico City will reach a population of 35 million people.

Mexico City is located in the southern portion of the Valley of Mexico at an altitude of 7,349 feet.

¿Qué aprendí?

Autoevaluación

As a review and self-check, respond to the following:

1. Ask a friend what he or she is going to do today.

2. If you were in Mexico City, name some things you might see.

3. Tell a friend what you are going to do this week (go to school at 8:00 A.M. on Monday, study in the library on Tuesday, etc.).

4. What opportunities does knowing Spanish offer you?

5. Name four or five things you can order from a menu in Spanish.

6. Imagine you are driving around town. Name in Spanish two or three buildings you see.

Visit the web-based activities at www.emcp.com

Palabras y expresiones

En la ciudad
la avenida
la calle
el centro
el edificio
el museo
la plaza
el teatro
la tienda

En un restaurante
el agua (mineral)
la bebida
la comida

la ensalada
los frijoles
el jugo
el menú
el mesero, la mesera
la naranja
el pescado
el pollo
el refresco

Otras expresiones
ahora
bueno
el cantante, la cantante

¡cómo no!
el concierto
de acuerdo
favorito,-a
grande
hacer una pregunta
hoy
el momento
mucho,-a
oye
pero
pues
siempre

Verbos
comer
hacer
ir a *(+ infinitive)*
leer
preguntar
saber
tomar
¡vamos a *(+ infinitive)*!
ver

Museo de Antropología.

¡Comida mexicana!

Capítulo 3

ciento veinticinco **125**

Teacher Resources

Answers

Autoevaluación
Possible answers:

1. ¿Qué vas a hacer hoy?

2. El teatro, la tienda, los edificios grandes, el restaurante, la plaza, el museo, el Palacio de Bellas Artes, el Zócalo, el parque de Chapultepec, etc.

3. Voy a ir al colegio a las ocho de la mañana el lunes. Voy a estudiar en la biblioteca el martes. Voy a ir al cine el miércoles. Voy a comer en mi restaurante favorito el jueves. Voy a ir al centro el viernes. Voy a caminar en el parque el sábado. Voy a ir al museo el domingo.

4. Answers will vary. Whether traveling or staying in the United States, students may be able to communicate with someone in Spanish when ordering from a menu, when shopping in a store or strolling through their own hometown.

5. Ensalada, pollo, pescado, frijoles, un refresco, jugo de naranja, agua mineral, etc.

6. Veo un cine, un teatro, un restaurante, etc.

Notes **Comparisons.** Have students compare large cities in the United States and Mexico City.

Cultures. Two popular gathering places in Mexico City are the *Zona Rosa* and *Polanco*. Both offer an incredible variety of shops, sidewalk cafés and elegant restaurants. Another favorite weekend spot is the floating gardens called Xochimilco—a series of canals left over from the former Aztec capital.

Frida Kahlo, una artista universal

Answers

Preparación
1. B
2. D
3. C
4. E
5. A

Activities

Critical Thinking

Have the students guess the meaning of *pintora,* pointing out the relationship to *pintar.* Then ask if students can guess what words ending in *-ora* mean (the word ending *-ora* signifies a person who does the activity indicated by the stem of the word).

Multiple Intelligences

Using visual examples, talk with students about Frida Kahlo's art. Ask questions about themes in her art, techniques and anything else that you or your students wish to discuss.

¡Viento en popa!

Tú lees

Conexión con otras disciplinas: arte

Estrategia

Anticipating special vocabulary
It will be easier for you to read and understand specialized subject matter if you try anticipating some of the words and expressions you may encounter. Identifying specialized vocabulary beforehand will help you zero in on what a writer is saying since your mind will already be thinking about the topic. For example, in this reading you will learn about the famous Mexican artist Frida Kahlo. What words would you anticipate might appear in the reading?

Preparación

Selecciona las palabras de la columna I que van con las palabras en inglés de la columna II.

I	II
1. un estilo	A a painting
2. un autorretrato	B a style
3. una pintora	C a painter, artist
4. un tema	D a self-portrait
5. un cuadro/ una pintura	E a theme

Frida Kahlo, una artista universal

Frida Kahlo es una de las pintoras más importantes de México. Como[1] su esposo[2], Diego Rivera, ella comprendió[3] el impacto social de combinar el arte y la política, pero sus temas son más universales. Por ejemplo[4], ella trató[5] los aspectos negativos de la industrialización como la contaminación del aire y de la naturaleza[6]. Otros temas que trató son los problemas de la vida[7]. Frida siempre tuvo[8] problemas físicos. De muchacha, ella tuvo polio. A los dieciocho años, tuvo un accidente terrible de tráfico en la Ciudad de México. Después[9] del accidente, sufrió mucho dolor[10] porque tuvo muchas operaciones. Frida muestra[11] su dolor en muchas de sus pinturas.

La pintora Frida Kahlo en 1931.

Notes Words presented in the *Preparación* are not glossed in this reading on Frida Kahlo in an effort to encourage students to apply new passive vocabulary.

The use of cognates in the readings requires students to use skills developed in reading strategies that have already been presented. This careful use of cognates enables students to read authentic Spanish without having to look up a large number of words.

Un tema que Frida y Diego tienen en común es el orgullo[12] de la cultura indígena[13] de México. Frida tenía raíces[14] indígenas y adoptó el estilo de la ropa y del pelo[15] de una india para expresar su orgullo indígena. Además[16], sus autorretratos representan la cultura indígena mediante el uso de[17] plantas, animales y colores de la naturaleza.

[1]As, Like [2]her husband [3]understood
[4]For example [5]dealt with [6]nature [7]life [8]had
[9]After [10]pain [11]shows [12]pride [13]native [14]roots
[15]hair [16]In addition [17]by means of

A ¿Qué recuerdas?

1. ¿Qué comprendió Frida Kahlo?
2. ¿Cuáles son los temas de los cuadros de Frida?
3. ¿Por qué sufrió Frida mucho dolor?
4. ¿Qué representa Frida en su autorretrato?

B Algo personal

1. ¿Es importante el arte de Frida Kahlo? ¿Por qué?
2. ¿Cuál te gusta más, la foto de Frida Kahlo o su autorretrato? ¿Por qué?

Autorretrato con mono (Self-Portrait with Monkey), Frida Kahlo, 1938. Albright-Knox Art Gallery, Buffalo, N.Y.

Raíces (Roots), Frida Kahlo, 1943. Private collection.

Capítulo 3   *ciento veintisiete* **127**

Teacher Resources

  Activities A–B

Answers

A 1. Comprendió el impacto de combinar el arte y la política.
  2. Los temas son los aspectos negativos de la industrialización, los problemas de la vida y el orgullo de la cultura indígena.
  3. Ella tuvo polio y tuvo un accidente de tráfico.
  4. La cultura indígena.
B Answers will vary.

Activities

Connections
Have students do some research on some aspect of Frida Kahlo or her art. Then have them summarize what they found out and present the information to the class.

Expansion
Additional questions *(Algo personal):* *¿Qué tipo de arte te gusta?; ¿Crees que la industrialización tiene aspectos negativos?; ¿Te gustan los autorretratos?; ¿Te gusta ir a exposiciones de arte?*

Notes Students may learn more about Frida Kahlo via the following Web site:

Frida Kahlo Museum
http://www.mexconnect.com/mex_/travel/grandall/grfridamuseo.html

Tú escribes

Estrategia

Combining images to build word pictures

Poems make pictures out of your words that can be seen by the mind's eye. They can be about any theme and can appear in any form. For example, a stair poem permits you to build up ideas one on another following a stair pattern. Just as the Aztecs built their pyramids layer upon layer, you can construct a poem in the shape of stairs using your knowledge of Spanish, following these steps:

Step 1: State the main idea (usually composed of just one word).

Step 2: List two or three words that describe the topic. (Use adjectives or nouns.)

Step 3: Name a place or time connected with the topic.

Step 4: Summarize the main idea with a phrase that expresses your feelings about the topic.

Write a stair poem about any topic you choose, such as school, a class, a city, a person, etc. Follow the "steps" to build your poem. When you finish constructing your stair poem, add artwork or graphics to make it visually appealing.

Pues, ¡vamos a la Ciudad de México!

la capital

museos parques

el D. F.

Proyectos adicionales

A Conexión con otras disciplinas: historia

Prepare a tourist guide for Mexico City. Include information about history, the main tourist attractions, museums, places to shop, places to eat and transportation in the city. Be sure to use photos or illustrations to illustrate your guide.

B Conexión con la tecnología

In pairs or in small groups, search the Internet and complete one of the following activities:

1. Find a restaurant in Mexico City. Then, write down the name, say where the restaurant is, describe the menu selection and prices, etc.
2. Research Mexican food and then describe a dish that sounds good to you. Try to name the ingredients, say what the food looks like, discuss how it is prepared and tell what state/region of Mexico the dish is from.
3. Find a map of Mexico City and locate major landmarks *(el Zócalo, el Palacio Nacional, la Catedral, el Palacio de Bellas Artes, la Zona Rosa, el parque de Chapultepec, etc.).* Say what each site offers that makes it special.

C Conexión con otras disciplinas: matemáticas

You are going out to dine at the *Restaurante Danubio* in Mexico City. Choose what you would like to eat. Then calculate the total price of the food items you ordered, add 7 percent in taxes, 10 percent in tips and convert the total amount from pesos into U.S. dollars. Obtain the current exchange rate from the Internet or from a newspaper.

Restaurante Danubio
Cocina Internacional

Ensaladas

Ensalada mixta	44 pesos
Ensalada especial Danubio	61 pesos

Para comer

Mojarra	95 pesos
Calamares	99 pesos
Ostras	92 pesos
Filete con champiñones	98 pesos
Filete a la parrilla	92 pesos
Pollo frito	44 pesos
Pollo a la cacerola	53 pesos

Bebidas

Refrescos	16 pesos
Jugo de naranja	13 pesos
Limonada	12 pesos

Teacher Resources

 Situation Cards

 Capítulo 3

Answers

A Creative self-expression.
B Creative self-expression.
C Answers will vary.

Activities

Connections

Have students imagine they were just elected mayor *(el alcalde/la alcaldesa)* of a city in Mexico. Their first duty is to create a plan for a new park and business district to be located in the heart of the city. As good mayors, they want the new area to have a balance of business, culture and green space. How would students design one of the new neighborhoods? What would they name the streets and avenues? the buildings? What sort of transportation would service the area? Students should draw a proposed plan of their project and then write a brief paragraph giving an overview of what they included in their model.

Notes Follow up the activities with a fiesta, allowing students to try some of the recipes they created in activity B.

Activities

Communities
See if students can name any well-known Mexicans or celebrities of Mexican descent. Then find out how many of the following Mexican and Mexican-American figures students can identify: Frida Kahlo (painter); Diego Rivera (muralist); Octavio Paz (writer, winner of the Nobel Prize in literature); Selena Quintanilla (Grammy Award-winning singer); Emiliano Zapata (leader of the Mexican Revolution); Luis Miguel (popular singer).

Cooperative Learning
For additional group practice of introductions, have students work in groups of four and play these roles: a fifty-five-year-old executive from a Spanish-speaking country who is in the United States looking for a possible employee; the executive's thirty-year-old assistant; and two eighteen-year-old graduates who are looking for employment. Students should create a dialog that uses expressions they have learned to make the appropriate introductions. Ask group members to switch roles so everyone plays each part one time.

Repaso

Now that I have completed this chapter, I can...

	Go to these pages for help:
talk about places in a city.	90
make introductions and express courtesy.	90
ask and answer questions.	90
discuss how to go somewhere.	90
say some things people do.	100
say where someone is going.	110
talk about the future.	110
order food and beverages.	116

I can also...

identify some things to do in Mexico.	93
state personal benefits to learning Spanish.	115
use pause words in conversation.	116
talk about food and drink in Mexico.	119
recognize the importance of review.	123
read in Spanish about Mexican artists.	126
write a simple poem in Spanish.	128

Trabalenguas

Erre con erre pizarra, erre con erre barril.
Rápido corren los carros, los carros del ferrocarril.

Notes Loose translation of the *Trabalenguas:* R with R in blackboard, R with R in barrel. Quickly the cars are running, the cars of the train.

Explain to students that the edible part of the popular food *tamales* is baked inside corn husks. For this reason, when people eat a tamale, they must peel back the layers of corn husks and just eat the filling in the center. *Tamales* come in two major varieties—cornmeal and meat filling or a sweetened cornmeal filling.

Vocabulario

a caballo on horseback *3A*
a pie on foot *3A*
¿adónde? (to) where? *3A*
el **agua (mineral)** (mineral) water *3B*
ahora now *3B*
al to the *3A*
el **autobús** bus *3A*
la **avenida** avenue *3B*
el **avión** airplane *3A*
el **banco** bank *3A*
el **barco** boat, ship *3A*
la **bebida** drink *3B*
la **biblioteca** library *3A*
la **bicicleta** bicycle *3A*
bueno well, okay *3A*
el **caballo** horse *3A*
la **cafetería** cafeteria *3A*
la **calle** street *3B*
caminar to walk *3A*
el **camión** truck *3A*
el **cantante, la cantante** singer *3B*
el **carro** car *3A*
el **centro** downtown, center *3B*
cerca (de) near *3A*
el **cine** movie theater *3A*
la **ciudad** city *3A*
¡claro! of course! *3A*
comer to eat *3B*
la **comida** food *3B*
¡cómo no! of course! *3B*
el **concierto** concert *3B*
¿cuándo? when? *3A*
de acuerdo agreed, okay *3B*
del of the, from the *3A*
el **dentista, la dentista** dentist *3A*
el **edificio** building *3B*

El gusto es mío. The pleasure is mine. *3A*
en *(means of transportation)* by *3A*
en carro by car *3A*
encantado,-a delighted, the pleasure is mine *3A*
la **ensalada** salad *3B*
la **escuela** school *3A*
fantástico,-a fantastic, great *3A*
favorito,-a favorite *3B*
la **fiesta** party *3A*
los **frijoles** beans *3B*
grande big *3B*
hacer to do, to make *3B*
hacer una pregunta to ask a question *3B*
el **hotel** hotel *3A*
hoy today *3B*
ir to go *3A*
ir a *(+ infinitive)* to be going to (do something) *3B*
el **jugo** juice *3B*
le/les/te presento a let me introduce you to *3A*
leer to read *3B*
lejos (de) far (from) *3A*
el **médico, la médica** doctor *3A*
el **menú** menu *3B*
el **mesero, la mesera** food server *3B*
el **metro** subway *3A*
el **momento** moment *3B*
la **moto(cicleta)** motorcycle *3A*
el **museo** museum *3B*
la **naranja** orange *3B*
la **oficina** office *3A*

oye hey, listen *3B*
el **parque** park *3A*
para for, to, in order to *3A*
pero but *3B*
el **pescado** fish *3B*
la **plaza** plaza, public square *3B*
el **pollo** chicken *3B*
¿por qué? why? *3A*
porque because *3A*
preguntar to ask *3B*
el **problema** problem *3A*
pues thus, well, so, then (pause in speech) *3B*
¿quiénes? who? (pl.) *3A*
quiero I want, I love *3A*
el **refresco** soft drink, refreshment *3B*
el **restaurante** restaurant *3A*
saber to know *3B*
sabes you know *3A*
siempre always *3B*
simpático,-a nice, pleasant *3A*
también also, too *3A*
Tanto gusto. So glad to meet you. *3A*
el **taxi** taxi *3A*
el **teatro** theater *3B*
la **tienda** store *3B*
tomar to take; to drink; to have *3B*
el **transporte** transportation *3A*
el **tren** train *3A*
¡vamos a *(+ infinitive)*! let's *(+ infinitive)* *3B*
¡vamos! let's go! *3A*
ver to see; to watch *3B*
¿verdad? right? *3A*

Cómo viajar por México gastando menos

Secretaría de Turismo

Module 1

Episode 3

Testing/Assessment
Test Booklet
Portfolio Assessment

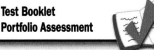

Activities

Multiple Intelligences (bodily-kinesthetic)
Have students draw and label places and objects from the chapter (e.g., places, foods). Display the drawings around the room or use them to review vocabulary.

Students with Special Needs
Review some places where students could go in the downtown area of a city. Then, using transparency 25, have students create sentences saying they are going to the place named and asking other students if they are going to go to the named place also.

Notes Tell students that some food names vary, according to the country. In Mexico, *el maíz* is *el elote; los tomates* would be *los jitomates.* Remind students that even in the United States there can be different names for food items. A submarine sandwich, for example, is called a sub, hoagie, dagwood, hero, poor boy or torpedo, depending on where in the United States it is served.

Connections with Parents

Because this chapter deals with relationships with family and friends, take a moment and encourage your students to spend some time interacting with their families. For example, suggest that students teach a parent or guardian some of the expressions they are learning in class. To clarify the assignment, send a brief note home with each student explaining the homework activity, leaving blank lines for parents/guardians to sign, date and indicate how much time he/she/they spent with the student practicing the expressions.

Activities

Connections
Show students where Puerto Rico and the Dominican Republic are located, using the maps in the front of the book or the transparencies that are part of this program.

Capítulo 4

Mi familia y mis amigos

Objetivos

❖ **talk about family and relationships**

❖ **seek and provide personal information**

❖ **express possession**

❖ **say some things people do**

❖ **express an opinion**

❖ **state likes and dislikes**

❖ **describe people and things**

Visit the web-based
activities at
www.emcp.com

Notes **Service Learning.** As you begin this chapter about family, friends and relationships, remind students they have talents and skills they can use in the community to help others. Students may wish to inquire how they may volunteer (e.g., with the bookmobile, in a senior citizen center, etc.).

The communicative objectives are provided on page 132 to help prepare students for the chapter they are about to begin. A list of such functions appears on page 178 along with other objectives so students can do a self-check to evaluate their progress.

Puerto Rico

Nombre oficial: Estado Libre Asociado de Puerto Rico

Población: 3.937.000

Capital: San Juan

Ciudades importantes: Ponce, Mayagüez, Bayamón

Unidad monetaria: el dólar (EE.UU.)

Gente famosa: Raúl Julia (actor); Miguel Pou (pintor); Roberto Clemente (beisbolista); Ricky Martin (cantante)

República Dominicana

Nombre oficial: República Dominicana

Población: 8.581.000

Capital: Santo Domingo

Ciudades importantes: Santiago de los Caballeros, Puerto Plata

Unidad monetaria: el peso dominicano (RD$)

Fiesta nacional: 27 de febrero, Día de la Independencia

Gente famosa: Juan Luis Guerra (cantante); Sammy Sosa (beisbolista); Óscar de la Renta (diseñador de ropa)

Activities

TPR

Using overhead transparencies 1–10 (maps of the Spanish-speaking world), ask students to come forward and point to places in the Caribbean as you name them in Spanish (e.g., *Puerto Rico, República Dominicana, San Juan, Santo Domingo*).

ciento treinta y tres 133

Notes Review the contents of these opening pages with the class. Can students guess the theme of the chapter? Ask students what part of the world they think they will be studying in the chapter.

Mi familia

 Activities 1–2

 Activities 27–28

 Activities 1–2

 Activity 1

 Activities 1–4

Content reviewed in *Lección A*
- gender and number of adjectives
- seeking and providing personal information
- stating the time
- saying how someone is feeling

Lección A
Puerto Rico

Vocabulario I
Mi familia

abuela Gloria — abuelo Pedro — abuela Carlota — abuelo Guillermo

hijos — hijos

esposos — hermanos

Rosa (mi tía) — Álvaro (mi tío) — Rodrigo (mi padre) — Carmen (mi madre) — Juan — Clara

hija única — hijos — hijos

sobrino

Julia (mi prima) — Soy yo, José. — Mónica (mi hermana) — Nancy — Enrique

Diego

mis primos

nietos

Notes Be sure students understand that Pepe is the nickname that the family uses for José García Rojas.

Ask students what they know about Puerto Rico. Find out if they have heard recent news stories or read articles about Puerto Rican famous people, notable events, etc.

Ask for student volunteers to create a bulletin board or travel brochure about this Spanish-speaking commonwealth of the United States.

134

Me llamo José García Rojas, pero para mi familia soy Pepe. Estoy todo el verano en Puerto Rico con unos parientes, en la casa de mi abuelo. ¡Soy su nieto favorito! Mis padres y yo vivimos en Nueva York.

la casa

Aquí está mi padre. Quiero mucho a mi padre. Él nunca está mucho tiempo en casa.

Mónica está en la playa con Enrique y Diego, ¡los primos más divertidos! Ella es muy guapa y popular.

Ésta es Julia, la hija única de mi tío Álvaro. Ella es bonita y amable. Siempre sale con sus amigos.

Esta foto es de mi abuelo, mi tío Álvaro y su esposa.

1 ¿Cierto o falso?

Di si lo que oyes es cierto o falso, según la información en el Vocabulario I. Si es falso, di lo que es cierto.

2 Pepe y su familia

Completa el párrafo sobre Pepe y su familia.

Soy José García Rojas. Mi (1) se llama Mónica. Ella es muy popular. Mi (2), Julia, es la (3) de mi (4) Álvaro y mi (5) Rosa. Ellos son divertidos. El (6) Juan es el (7) de mi (8), Carmen. Mi (9) es Rodrigo. Quiero mucho a mi padre. También quiero mucho a mi (10) Pedro. ¡Soy el (11) favorito de él!

¡Extra!

Los papás o los padres

Some people prefer to use the terms *mamá y papá* (mom and dad) instead of *madre y padre* (mother and father). Regardless of which terms you use, when referring to both parents simultaneously, use the masculine plural form: *padres* or *papás* (parents).

el padre + la madre = los padres
el papá + la mamá = los papás

Capítulo 4   *ciento treinta y cinco* **135**

135

Activities

Critical Listening
Play the audio CD version of the dialog as students cover the words and listen to develop good listening skills. Ask several individuals to state what they believe is the main theme of the dialog.

Critical Thinking
Have students look at the photographs as they imagine what the speaker is saying. Then ask if students know where the dialog takes place and what the main theme of the dialog is.

Language through Action
Ask for volunteers to come to the front of the class to act out the dialog *En la fiesta del abuelo*.

Diálogo I
En la fiesta del abuelo

JOSÉ: Hola, Javier. Te presento a mi prima, Julia.
JULIA: Mucho gusto.
JAVIER: Encantado, Julia.
JOSÉ: Ella es la nieta favorita de mi abuelo Pedro.

JAVIER: Tu abuelo es muy amable.
JULIA: Sí, y muy cariñoso. Vivimos con él en Puerto Rico todo el verano.
JOSÉ: ¡Mira, allí está el abuelo!

JAVIER: ¡Ay, sí! ¡Allí está! ¿Quiénes están con él?
JULIA: La señora de rojo es la esposa de mi tío Juan, y la chica de azul es su hija.
JAVIER: ¡Es muy guapa!

3 ¿Qué recuerdas?

1. ¿Cómo se llama la nieta favorita de Pedro?
2. ¿Quién es amable y cariñoso?
3. ¿Quién es la señora de rojo?
4. ¿Quién es la chica de azul?

4 Algo personal

1. ¿Dónde está tu casa? ¿Estás en casa mucho?
2. En tu familia, ¿quién es amable? ¿Divertido/a? ¿Popular?
3. ¿Tienes muchos parientes? ¿Quiénes son?
4. ¿Cómo se llaman tus abuelos? ¿Y tus tíos?
5. ¿Tienes sobrinos? ¿Cómo se llama(n)?
6. ¿Cuántos primos tienes?
7. ¿Quién es tu pariente favorito? ¿Por qué?

5 ¿Quién es?

 Escucha la información y, luego, escoge la letra de la respuesta correcta.

A. Es mi abuelo.   **B.** Es mi tía.   **C.** Es mi prima.   **D.** Es mi padre.

Notes **Comparisons.** Etiquette related to social gatherings offers an interesting cultural comparison. In the Spanish-speaking world, it is common to arrive later than the time stated on an invitation to a party, and a written invitation does not indicate an ending time, as sometimes occurs in the United States.

Mention to students that many Hispanics celebrate both a birthday and a saint's day. For example, a person named Juan might celebrate his birthday on October 8 and his saint's day on June 24 (*el día de San Juan*).

Cultura viva

Puerto Rico

What do you know about the enchanting Caribbean island of Puerto Rico? Did you know, for example, that English and Spanish are official languages and are required courses in school? Why? The answer lies hidden in Puerto Rico's history. After landing on a small tropical island that inhabitants called *Borinquén* (originally *Boriquén*) in 1493, Christopher Columbus (*Cristóbal Colón*) claimed the land for Spain. Spain then ceded the island to the United States in 1898 as a result of the Spanish-American War, beginning Puerto Rico's continuous affiliation with the United States. In 1952, the island became a Commonwealth (*Estado Libre Asociado*) of the United States, which means residents are United States citizens but the main governmental functions remain independent.

Unas casas en el Viejo San Juan.

What might you see and do on a visit to Puerto Rico? You can experience city life in the capital, San Juan; stroll along beautiful beaches (e.g., *la playa de Luquillo*); visit quaint ports like Fajardo; or travel to the mountains, all within a matter of hours. Do you like fine dining? Puerto Rico offers some of the finest cuisine in the Caribbean. Does music talk to your soul? Listen and dance to the beat of Caribbean music (*salsa* is popular in Puerto Rico). Interested in history? Be swept back in time as you admire colonial architecture in old San Juan (*el Viejo San Juan*), such as *El Castillo de San Felipe del Morro,* a fort that was constructed in 1591 to protect the island. Does art move you? The fascinating *Museo de Arte* in Ponce will inspire you! Are you active outdoors? You can hike through the only tropical rain forest (*el Yunque*) found in the U.S. National Forest System or surf along Puerto Rico's Atlantic coast.

El Castillo de San Felipe del Morro, Puerto Rico.

6 En Puerto Rico

Imagine you are going on vacation to Puerto Rico. Describe some things you might like to see and do while you are there. List five bits of information you learned that would be helpful to know before touring the country.

7 Conexiones con otras disciplinas: historia

Complete the statements about Puerto Rico logically, using the answers shown in the column on the right.

1. Puerto Rico es...
2. Las lenguas oficiales de Puerto Rico son...
3. Cristóbal Colón llegó a la isla en...
4. San Juan es...

A. el inglés y el español.
B. 1493.
C. un Estado Libre Asociado.
D. la capital.

 Activity 3

 Activity 3

Answers

6 Creative problem solving.
7 1. C
    2. A
    3. B
    4. D

Activities

Communities
Conduct a class discussion about Puerto Rico's status as a commonwealth. (Have your native Spanish-speaking students conducting research about the topic assist by providing information and insights.) Finally, conduct a poll about whether students think Puerto Rico should remain a commonwealth or become a state or an independent nation.

Spanish for Spanish Speakers
Have students write a short composition in Spanish summarizing what they know about Puerto Rico. Expand the activity by having students seek out additional information about Puerto Rico at the library.

Technology
Have students use the Internet to research and then compare and contrast food and eating in Puerto Rico and Mexico.

Notes Inform interested students that more than 100 billion gallons of rain fall in *el Yunque* each year! Also, surfers claim the best season for surfing in Puerto Rico is October through April.

Because U.S. minimum-wage laws apply, Puerto Rico has one of the most dynamic economies in the Caribbean. Many American firms have invested heavily in Puerto Rico. However, tourism remains one of the island's leading industries.

The names of certain cities and countries in Latin America reflect the Spanish exploration and colonization of the region that began with Columbus. *Puerto Rico* literally means **rich port.**

Activities

Cooperative Learning

To illustrate the use of last names in the Spanish-speaking world, divide students into groups. Each group should become a family with its corresponding members and first and last names. Students must prepare a short presentation for the class including information such as names, family roles, ages and professions. Encourage creativity.

Idioma

Repaso rápido: adjectives

You will recall that adjectives (e.g., colors) may be masculine or feminine and singular or plural since they must match the gender and number of the noun they are describing. To make a singular adjective plural, add *-s* if the adjective ends in a vowel or *-es* if the adjective ends in a consonant. Although most adjectives usually follow the nouns they modify, adjectives of quantity, such as *cinco, mucho (mucha), otro (otra), todo (toda),* and question-asking words precede their nouns.

8 Mis parientes puertorriqueños

Completa las oraciones con la forma apropiada de las palabras en paréntesis.

MODELO Tengo __ parientes en Puerto Rico. (mucho)
Tengo <u>muchos</u> parientes en Puerto Rico.

1. Mi tío __, Diego, es de San Juan. (favorito)
2. ¡Qué __ es mi tío Diego! (amable)
3. También tengo dos primas __ en San Juan, Alicia y Ana. (divertido)
4. Pero no __ mi familia está en San Juan. (todo)
5. Mi __ prima, Marta, está con mi tía, Eva, en Ponce. (otro)
6. ¡Qué __ son Marta y la tía Eva! (simpático)
7. La tía Eva es __. (cariñoso)
8. Ella es muy __ también. (bonito)
9. Alicia, Ana y Marta son todas __. (popular)
10. ¡Tengo unos parientes __. (fantástico)

¡Extra!

Exclamaciones

The word *qué* may be followed by an adjective (or other descriptive phrase) as in the second and sixth sentences of activity 8 to express strong feelings, much as you might use **How...!** in English: *¡Qué amable!* (How nice!).

Tengo muchos parientes en Puerto Rico.

Notes For several years, Puerto Rico has been considering whether to become a U.S. state or an independent nation or remain a commonwealth.

Explain to students that Puerto Ricans are U.S. citizens, with most of the same rights and obligations. One difference is that they cannot vote in presidential elections unless they reside in one of the fifty states.

Remind students that Spanish punctuation has certain unique features, including the inverted exclamation point at the beginning of expressions such as *¡Qué interesante!*

Estructura

Expressing possession: possessive adjectives

Possessive adjectives *(adjetivos posesivos)* express possession or describe relationships between people. In Spanish, possessive adjectives precede the noun they modify and must agree in number and in gender with that noun.

mi(s)	hermano(s) hermana(s)	*my*	brother(s) sister(s)
tu(s)	tío(s) tía(s)	*your (informal)*	uncle(s) aunt(s)
su(s)	sobrino(s) sobrina(s)	*your (formal)*	nephew(s) niece(s)
su(s)	sobrino(s) sobrina(s)	*his*	nephew(s) niece(s)
su(s)	sobrino(s) sobrina(s)	*her*	nephew(s) niece(s)
nuestro(s) **nuestra(s)**	hermano(s) hermana(s)	*our*	brother(s) sister(s)
vuestro(s) **vuestra(s)**	tío(s) tía(s)	*your (informal)*	uncle(s) aunt(s)
su(s)	sobrino(s) sobrina(s)	*your (formal)*	nephew(s) niece(s)
su(s)	sobrino(s) sobrina(s)	*their*	nephew(s) niece(s)

Possessive adjectives have both singular and plural forms. Although the masculine and feminine forms for *mi, mis, tu, tus, su* and *sus* are the same (i.e., *su abuelo* and *su abuela*), notice that *nuestro/nuestra, nuestros/nuestras* and *vuestro/vuestra, vuestros/vuestras* have recognizably different masculine and feminine forms.

*Pepe es **nuestro** primo.*	Pepe is **our** cousin.
*Teresa es **nuestra** hermana.*	Teresa is **our** sister.

You can clarify the meaning of *su* and *sus*, and you can add emphasis to what you are saying, by replacing the possessive adjective with *de* plus a pronoun or a person's name.

*Es **su** tía.* → *Es la tía **de ella.** (Es la tía **de Teresa.**)*

Teacher Resources

 Activity 4

 Activities 4–6

 Activity 2

 Activity 6

Activities

Language through Action
Tell the class you are going to borrow certain items for a class activity. Collect objects such as a book, notebook, watch, pen and pencil. For each item ask several students the question *¿Es tu (name the object)?"* or *¿Son tus (name the objects)?"* Then ask *¿De quién es/son (name the objects)?* so that the owner identifies himself/herself. When an item has been returned to its original owner, ask *¿De quién es/son (name the object or objects)?* once more to show possession with an object plus *de* plus the owner or with the possessive adjective *su(s)*.

Students with Special Needs
Tell students to write each subject pronoun and each possessive adjective on separate slips of paper or on small index cards (including the words that follow in parentheses). Then have them mix up each set and try to match the appropriate cards. You may choose to have them work individually, in pairs or in small groups.

Notes Inform students that the subject pronoun *tú* has a written accent mark, whereas the possessive adjective *tu* does not.

You may wish to tell students that possessive adjectives are not used with body parts as they are in English: *Me lavo la cara.*

Nuestro and *vuestro* are the only possessive adjectives that have four forms.

Remind students that *vuestro* is the plural of *tu* and that it is used only in Spain.

139

Práctica

9 **¿Quiénes son?**

 En parejas, alternen en preguntar y confirmar quiénes son las siguientes personas. *(In pairs, take turns asking and confirming who the following people are.)*

MODELO Verónica / hermana
    A: ¿Es Verónica tu hermana?
    B: Sí, es mi hermana.

1. Pablo / hermano
2. Rodrigo y José / primos
3. doña Amalia y don Rogelio / abuelos
4. ellas / tías
5. María / sobrina
6. él / tío

10 **Nuestra familia**

Marta and her cousins, Elena and Diego, are discussing the digital photos Marta took with her new camera. Complete their conversation with the possessive adjectives indicated by the cues in parentheses.

Elena: Aquí hay una foto de <u>nuestros</u> abuelos en la playa. (nosotros)
Diego: Están con (1) madre en la playa de Luquillo. (nosotros)
Marta: ¿Hay dos fotos de (2) tía? (yo)
Elena: Sí. Una con doña Carmen y don Enrique, y otra es con (3) padres. (tú)
Diego: Aquí están doña Carmen y don Enrique en (4) casa nueva. (ellos)
Elena: ¿Están todos (5) nietos en la foto con ellos? (ellos)
Marta: No, yo no estoy en la foto y soy (6) prima favorita. (Uds.)
Diego: Pues, mi foto favorita está aquí con (7) hermano, Kathy, la *au pair,* y yo en El Yunque. ¡Qué día tan divertido! (tú)

¡Oportunidades!

¿Quieres ser *au pair*?
Are you interested in experiencing life with a Spanish-speaking family and getting to really know their lifestyle and culture? If so, you might be interested in becoming an au pair.

There are many reliable agencies in the United States that place young people with Spanish families for periods of up to a year. Au pairs live with the family and take care of the children. You would learn how the family lives day to day and you could also attend educational courses, make new friends, travel and improve your Spanish. Find out through local agencies how you might become part of a real *familia.*

11 **¿Quién va a venir a nuestra fiesta?**

Use an appropriate possessive adjective to complete this guest list for a cookout at your home.

1. Julia y_____ amigas, Amy y Paula
2. la Sra. y el Sr. García y_____ tres hijos
3. los Ganzález y_____ sobrino, Enrique
4. Juana Ruiz y_____ dos hermanas
5. Amalia y Rogelio de la Torre y_____ madre
6. el doctor Diego Fernández y_____ familia

Comunicación

12 Mis parientes

 Create your own family tree. Next, in small groups, take turns naming the people and asking and answering questions about how members of your family are related. Finally, describe the people you name and add any additional information you wish.

MODELO Soy Juana. Mateo es mi tío. Es muy amable.

Estructura

Saying what someone does: present tense of *-ir* verbs

Form the present tense of a regular *-ir* verb, such as *vivir* (to live), by removing the *-ir* ending and attaching the endings shown. Note that except for *-imos* and *-ís,* the endings are the same as those of *-er* verbs.

vivir			
yo	viv**o**	nosotros nosotras	viv**imos**
tú	viv**es**	vosotros vosotras	viv**ís**
Ud. él ella	viv**e**	Uds. ellos ellas	viv**en**

Another verb that ends in *-ir, salir* (to go out, to leave), is regular in all forms except the first-person singular: *yo* **salgo.**

Yo **salgo** a las dos.　　　　　I leave at two.
Nosotros **salimos** a las cuatro.　　We leave at four.

Notes Sometimes students are hesitant to provide personal information when doing activities. Before assigning activity 12, inform the class that it is okay to make up information for their family tree.

Point out the similarities in forming regular *-ar, -er* and *-ir* verbs: Remove the infinitive ending and add endings that match the subject pronouns, as indicated in the paradigm.

Teacher Resources

 Activity 5

 Activities 7–8

 Activity 3

 Activities 7–8

Answers

12 Creative self-expression.

Activities

Expansion
As a variation for activity 12, suggest that students create an imaginary family including several well-known Spanish-speaking people.

Multiple Intelligences (linguistic)
Have students write an original composition about their family as a follow-up to activity 12.

Prereading Strategy
Review Pepe's family tree first as an introduction to activity 12. Have students look at the family tree and identify the members of Pepe's family. Then ask students to read about his family and look at the pictures from the family photo album.

Teacher Resources

Activities 14–15

Answers

13 1. vivimos; 2. viven; 3. viven;
4. vive; 5. viven; 6. vive;
7. viven; 8. vives

14 Possible answers:
1. ¿... vive...?/Vive en....
2. ¿... viven...?/Viven en....
3. ¿... vive...?/Vive en....
4. ¿... vive...?/Vive en....
5. ¿... viven...?/Viven en....
6. ¿... vives... ?/Vivo en....

15 1. ¿A qué hora salen...?/
Ellos salen a las once.
2. ¿A qué hora salimos...?/
Nosotros salimos a las tres
y cuarto.
3. ¿A qué hora sale...?/Ella
sale a las once y cuarto.
4. ¿A qué hora salen...?/Ellas
salen a las dos menos
cuarto.
5. ¿A qué hora sales...?/Yo
salgo a las tres.

Activities

Critical Thinking
Have students find examples of
several infinitives that end in *-ir* in
the Spanish/English glossary at
the end of *Navegando 1*. Students
can prepare a written list of
infinitives to turn in or, as an
alternative, you may want to
review their lists orally in class. As
an extension to this, have students
find additional infinitives in
magazine or newspaper articles.

142

 Práctica

13 **Viven en....**

Pepe's cousin, Julia, is contacting family and friends to invite them to her
mother's birthday party. Complete this paragraph with the appropriate forms
of the verb *vivir*.

Nosotros (1) aquí en San Juan. Los tíos (2) cerca de nosotros aquí en la
capital, pero los abuelos (3) lejos de nosotros en Ponce. La hermana de mi
madre, la tía Rosa, también (4) en San Juan. Clara y Rafael (5) en Arecibo,
pero van a estar en Miami. Yoli (6) en Orlando pero va a estar en casa de sus
primos, Mona y Jorge. Ellos (7) en Bayamón. Y tú, ¿dónde (8)? ¿Vienes tú a
nuestra fiesta?

14 **¿Dónde viven?**

 With a classmate, take turns asking and answering questions about where
various people live. Answer using the words in parentheses.

MODELO tu hermano (San Juan)
A: ¿Dónde vive tu hermano?
B: Vive en San Juan.

1. el hijo único de tu tío Alfonso (Ponce)   4. mi tía (París)
2. ellos (una casa grande y nueva)   5. tu madre y tu padre (San Juan)
3. Hernán (la casa de su tío)   6. tú (?)

15 **¿A qué hora salen?**

 Working in pairs, take turns asking and telling when the following people are
leaving their houses to arrive on time for the birthday party.

MODELO ¿Los tíos?   PM 5:00

A: ¿A qué hora salen los tíos?
B: Ellos salen a las cinco.

1. ¿Los abuelos?   AM 11:00

2. ¿Nosotros? PM 3:15

3. ¿La madre de una amiga?   AM 11:15

4. ¿La tía Rosa y Julia? PM 1:45

5. ¿Tú?   PM 3:00

Los tíos salen a las cinco.

Notes Students may find it interesting
to learn how names associated with Puerto
Rico's geography changed over time.
Shortly after his arrival, Columbus
renamed the island of Borinquén *San Juan
Bautista* (Saint John the Baptist). In 1508,
Juan Ponce de León founded the first
Spanish village on the island, Villa de
Caparra, which the king of Spain renamed

San Juan de Puerto Rico. A year later,
Ponce de León was named the first
governor and the city of Ponce was named
after him. The island eventually became
known as Puerto Rico, and its capital was
called San Juan.

Review how to ask for and tell time before
assigning activity 15.

✦ Comunicación

16 Tu familia y la familia de Julia

Imagine you attend school in Puerto Rico. With a classmate, pretend you are discussing your family and Julia's family with another student. Use words from each column to get started. Make up any information you would like to create logical sentences.

> **MODELO** **A:** ¿Dónde viven los abuelos de Julia?
> **B:** Los abuelos de Julia viven en Arecibo. Van a vivir en Ponce no lejos del Museo de Arte.

el primo	salir	de	Bayamón
los abuelos	vivir	aquí en	Mayagüez
yo		allí en	Arecibo
nosotros		en	San Juan
Uds.		lejos de	el Yunque
las hermanas		cerca de	el Morro
tú			Ponce
la madre y el padre			la Playa de Luquillo

17 Mi familia

With a classmate, take turns asking and answering questions about your relatives (where they live, what they are like, etc.). You may wish to include in your questions and answers some of the adjectives you have learned, such as *divertido, fantástico, favorito, guapo* and *simpático*.

> **MODELO** **A:** ¿Cómo se llama tu prima?
> **B:** Se llama Diana. Es profesora y vive en Chicago. Es amable.

¡Extra!

Otros miembros de la familia

el hermanastro, la hermanastra	stepbrother, stepsister
el hijastro, la hijastra	stepson, stepdaughter
el medio hermano, la media hermana	half brother, half sister
el padrastro, la madrastra	stepfather, stepmother

18 ¿Dónde viven?

Working in small groups, talk about your families and/or friends. Discuss such things as the names of various family and/or friends, their ages and where they live, adding any other interesting information you wish.

> **MODELO** **A:** ¿Dónde viven tus abuelos?
> **B:** Viven en Chicago.
> **A:** ¿Tienes familia o amigos en otro país?
> **B:** Mis abuelos viven en Puerto Rico.
> **C:** Mi amigo Rafael vive en Puerto Rico también, pero no es un país. Es un Estado Libre Asociado de los Estados Unidos.

Notes Activities 17 and 18 are similar. However, because activity 17 is for pairs and 18 is for groups, 17 may be used to prepare students for 18.

Answers

16 Creative self-expression.
17 Creative self-expression.
18 Creative self-expression.

Activities

Pronunciation (*la letra* h)
Review the pronunciation of the letter *h* by practicing the following: *Humberto, Hernández, Hatillo, Héctor* and *Hilda*. Point out that the consonant *h* is always silent in Spanish. You may wish to add that words beginning with *h* in Spanish are usually linked in pronunciation to the preceding word. Have students practice the following sentence: *Humberto Hernández y su hermana Hilda están en un hotel en La Habana.*

Students with Special Needs
As preparation for the *Comunicación* activities, practice verb conjugation using choral response to each form of the verbs *vivir* and *salir*. Start with the *yo* form of each verb (remind students that *salir* has an irregular *yo* form). Then ask for the *tú* form of each verb, and so on, until students have had a chance to practice all forms of each verb.

Teacher Resources

 ¿Cómo está?

 Activity 6

 Activity 29

 Activities 9–10

 Activity 4

Activities

Prereading Strategy

Have students look at *Vocabulario II* and identify cognates and other words they recognize. Then ask students to guess what the people on pages 144 and 145 are feeling.

Students with Special Needs

After reviewing the present-tense forms of *estar*, have students practice creating sentences using *estoy*, *estás*, *está*, *estamos*, *estáis* and *están* with the adjectives on pages 144–145.

Vocabulario II
¿Cómo está?

Está abierta.

Está apurado.

Está cansado.

Está loco.

Está nerviosa.

Está triste.

Está contenta.

Está limpio.

Está sucio.

Está frío.

Notes Explain to the class the difference between *estar cansado* (to be tired) and *tener sueño* (to be sleepy).

Review how to conjugate the verb *estar* in the present tense.

Quickly check student comprehension of the descriptions that accompany the illustrations on these two pages.

Está cerrada.

Está ocupada.

Está libre.

Está enferma.

Está caliente.

19 ¿Cómo están?

Selecciona la letra de la ilustración que corresponde con lo que oyes.

A **B** **C** **D**

20 A corregir

Corrige la información incorrecta, según el Vocabulario II.

MODELO Mi hermana está <u>triste</u>.
Mi hermana está <u>contenta</u>.

1. El teléfono está <u>ocupado</u>.
2. Mi tía está <u>muy bien</u>.
3. El refresco está <u>caliente</u>.
4. La comida está <u>fría</u>.
5. La ventana está <u>cerrada</u>.

Estamos contentos.

Notes Activity 19 has been recorded as part of the Audio CD Program. A reproducible answer sheet for activity 19 can be found at the end of the Audio CD Program Manual.

Note for students that masculine adjectives are used with forms of *estar* when describing males and feminine adjectives are used with females.

Diálogo II
¿Por qué estás triste?

JAVIER: Julia, ¿por qué estás triste?
JULIA: Mi abuelo está enfermo.
JAVIER: ¿Don Pedro García Montoya?

JULIA: Sí, y estoy muy nerviosa.
JAVIER: Él va a estar bien.
JULIA: Gracias. Eres muy amable.

JAVIER: Bueno, adiós. Estoy apurado.
JULIA: ¿Adónde vas?
JAVIER: Voy a casa, estoy muy cansado.

21 ¿Qué recuerdas?

1. ¿Quién está triste?
2. ¿Por qué está triste?
3. ¿Cómo se llama el abuelo?
4. ¿Quién está nervioso?
5. ¿Dónde va Javier?

22 Algo personal

1. ¿Estás triste o contento/a? Explica.
2. ¿Estás enfermo/a?

23 ¿Cómo están todos?

 Listen as several people talk about how they are feeling. Then match the names with the description that fits each person.

1. Ángel
2. Esperanza
3. Benjamín
4. Natalia
5. Josefina
6. Verónica

A. Está contenta.
B. Está muy ocupado.
C. Está nerviosa.
D. Está apurado.
E. Está triste.
F. Está enferma.

Está nerviosa.

Notes Explain that it is common for Spanish-speaking people to have two last names. The first last name is the father's and the second is the mother's, as seen in this dialog, although only the father's name is used in most conversation.

Activity 23 has been recorded as part of the Audio CD Program. A reproducible answer sheet for the activity has been included at the end of the Audio CD Program Manual for your convenience.

Cultura viva

El autor, Gabriel García Márquez.

¿Cómo se llama?

Most people in Spanish-speaking countries have not one, but two last names. They use their father's family name followed by their mother's. For example, to find the phone number of a friend named José García Rodriguez, look in the phone directory under *G* for *García Rodríguez*, not *R* for *Rodríguez*. To find books by the famous author Gabriel García Márquez, look under *G* for *García Márquez*.

Traditionally, when a woman married, she would add the name of her husband, preceded by *de*, meaning "of" or "belonging to". For example, if Jennifer López married Gabriel García Márquez, she would become Jennifer López *de García*. Today, however, many women are opting to keep the same name they had before marriage.

24 ¿Cuál es su nombre completo?

Look at some information about students' families. Write down each person's complete name, according to what you learned in the *Cultura viva* titled *¿Cómo se llama?*

MODELO Margarita es la hija de Pablo Cruz y Josefina Miranda.
Se llama Margarita Cruz Miranda.

1. Alicia es la hija de Marta Fuentes de Bazán y Ernesto Bazán Rojas.
2. La madre de Bárbara es Carmen Prado Correa y su padre es Martín Sosa Tovar.
3. Paz es la hija de Ricardo Olmedos Acosta y Natalia Bravo de Olmedos.
4. Los padres de Jorge son Virginia Triana Gómez y Enrique Sandoval Gaviria.
5. Andrés es el hijo de Antonio Cervantes Díaz y Luisa Carrillo de Cervantes.
6. Los padres de Mercedes son Ernesto Lorente Soto y Gabriela Medina Gálvez.

Capítulo 4   *ciento cuarenta y siete* **147**

Teacher Resources

 Activity 24

 Activity 7

 Activity 11

 Activity 5

Answers

24 1. ... Alicia Bazán Fuentes.
2. ... Bárbara Sosa Prado.
3. ... Paz Olmedos Bravo.
4. ... Jorge Sandoval Triana.
5. ... Andrés Cervantes Carrillo.
6. ... Mercedes Lorente Medina.

Activities

Cooperative Learning
Have students ask one another *¿Cuál es tu apellido paterno?* (for the paternal name) and *¿Cuál es tu apellido materno?* (for the maternal name) to get a feel for this cultural point.

Notes Explain to the class that last names are made plural in Spanish by putting the plural definite article in front of the name: *los López, los Marín,* etc.

Comparisons. Have students compose their last names using the system described in the *Cultura viva* on page 147.

147

Idioma

Estructura

Describing people and things with *estar*

You have already learned to use the verb *estar* to indicate location. *Estar* can also be used with adjectives to describe conditions that are likely to change *(caliente, cansado, frío)* or to express how someone or something is at a given moment *(bonito, nervioso, sucio)*.

*El agua está **caliente**.*	The water is hot.
*¿Está ella **cansada**?*	Is she tired?
*Ellos están **nerviosos**.*	They are nervous.
*¡Estás muy **bonita** hoy!*	You are (look) very pretty today!
*El carro está **sucio**.*	The car is dirty.

Note, however, that some adjectives that describe appearance or personality can be used with either *ser* or *estar*, but with a difference in meaning.

*Eduardo **está guapo** hoy.*	Eduardo is (looks) handsome today.
*Eva **es** una muchacha **guapa**.*	Eva is a beautiful girl.

Práctica

25 ¿Cómo están?

Can you describe what you see in these photos? Complete the following sentences with the correct form of *estar* and an appropriate adjective.

1. Andrés y Miguel __.

2. Clara __.

3. Los refrescos __.

4. La comida __.

5. La playa __.

6. El profesor Fernández __.

26 Una barbacoa con los parientes

Pretend your family is having a cookout at one of your grandparents' house and one of your friends came with you. Take turns asking one another questions about some of the things you see there, using the words provided. Answer each question using the cues in parentheses.

MODELO estar abierto / la puerta de la casa de tus abuelos (ventanas)

    A: ¿Está abierta la puerta de la casa de tus abuelos?

    B: No, no está abierta, pero las ventanas están abiertas.

1. estar sucio / el carro de tu padre (el carro de mi tía)
2. estar apurado por ir a la playa / tus tíos de Fajardo (mis primos)
3. estar muy enfermo / tu tía (mi hermana)
4. estar cansado / tus abuelas (mi abuelo)
5. estar nervioso / tus padres (mis abuelos)
6. estar libre para ir al Yunque mañana / tú (mis primas)
7. estar triste / tus tías (la nueva esposa de mi primo)
8. estar ocupado / tus padres (tú y yo)

27 Hoy mi familia está...

Make a list of your family members (include yourself) and tell how each person is doing today. Then give a reason why the person is feeling that way. You may wish to use some of the following words in your descriptions: *apurado, contento, enfermo, loco, nervioso, triste.*

MODELO Mi hermano está contento hoy porque va a estar con sus amigos.

Mi hermana está contenta.

¿Está la puerta abierta o cerrada? La puerta está cerrada.
¿Cómo está la abuela? La abuela está muy cansada.
¿Cómo están los refrescos? Los refrescos están fríos.
¿Cómo está Félix/el gato? Félix está nervioso.
¿Cómo está María? María está enferma.
¿Cómo está Lucas/el perro? Lucas está loco.
¿Cómo está Andrea? Andrea está ocupada.
¿Cómo está Jaime? Jaime está apurado.

29 Creative self-expression.

Activities

Cooperative Learning
Working in pairs, have students describe the classroom and the people in it, as an extension and reinforcement of activity 28. For example, they might talk about how many boys and how many girls there are in the class (*¿Cuántos muchachos hay en la clase?*). Then they might comment on how others in the class are feeling today (*¿Cómo está el professor/la profesora hoy?*). Circulate around the room to be sure students are using the correct form of *estar* and the new adjectives from this lesson in their conversation.

◈ Comunicación

 28 ¿Cómo está todo hoy?

With a classmate, discuss what you see in this illustration. Talk about who the people are and say how they feel (including the pets). You also may ask and answer questions about anything else you see.

> **MODELO** **A:** ¿Cuántas personas hay en la casa hoy?
> **B:** Hay cinco personas y dos animales.
> **A:** ¿Cómo está Humberto?
> **B:** Está ocupado.

 29 ¡Hola! ¿Cómo estás?

Working in groups, form two circles with six to eight students. Half of the students should be in an inside circle facing the students in an outside circle. Students who are facing one another should pretend they meet and begin a conversation about their families' health or emotional condition. Next, students in the outer circle move one to the right and begin a similar conversation with a new partner. Be sure to have a conversation with everyone in the opposing circle.

> **MODELO** **A:** Hola, Jaime. ¿Qué tal?
> **B:** Estoy bien, pero apurado. Y tú, ¿cómo estás?
> **A:** Yo estoy bien, gracias. ¿Cómo están tus padres?
> **B:** Están nerviosos porque van a Vieques en avión.

Notes As a follow-up to activity 28, conduct a class discussion about the contents of the illustration on page 150.

Ask students to find Vieques on a map. Point out that Vieques and Culebra are two islands that are part of Puerto Rico. Vieques is a small community; Culebra offers some of the world's most beautiful and secluded beaches for swimming. Students may want to find out more about what each island offers.

30 ¡Tengo una familia famosa!

Create an imaginary family using photos of famous people cut from a magazine and indicate how they are related to you. Then, working in small groups, tell your classmates who the people are and what each one is like, using some of the adjectives you have learned in this lesson.

> **MODELO** Es mi hermana y es muy bonita. *(Show a photo of a famous female such as Salma Hayek.)*

31 Te presento a mi familia

In small groups, pretend you are all members of the same family (decide who will play each role). Then, form concentric circles with another group so that members of your family in the circle face another group's family. Opposing family members should then alternate telling one another the names and relationships of family members in the circle, adding any relevant descriptions. When each opposing pair of students completes all introductions, the family in the inner circle rotates one person to the left and begins the activity again.

> **MODELO** Aquí está mi primo. Es divertido.
> Allí está mi abuela favorita, Ana María.

¿Es Salma Hayek tu hermana?

familia 1   familia 2

Aquí están mi mamá y mis dos hermanas.

¡Te presento a mi tío favorito!

Capítulo 4   *ciento cincuenta y uno* 151

Notes Set a time limit for activities 30–31. Then, while students are completing the activity, walk around the classroom and listen to some of the descriptions. Stop to offer help as needed and check to be sure students remain on task. While facilitating the conversations, extend the activity by selecting a few of the better descriptions for students to share with the class.

Answers

32 1. No.
2. No.
3. No.
4. Sí.
5. Sí.

33 Answers will vary.

Activities

Communities

Conduct a class discussion about family life in your community. Use the cultural reading *¿Qué es la familia?* and the questions in *Algo personal* as your starting point. Ask students how families seem similar or different in Puerto Rico.

Lectura cultural

¿Qué es la familia?

¿Cómo es una familia típica de Puerto Rico? Según el censo más reciente[1], aproximadamente 3,5 personas viven en una casa y las familias tienen aproximadamente 1,9 hijos. Tres o más generaciones viven juntas[2] en solamente 7,36% de las casas.

Una familia hispana.

El censo dice que las familias puertorriqueñas son pequeñas[3], pero los números no lo dicen todo. El término *familia* — en Puerto Rico y en muchos países hispanos — no solamente incluye a los padres y a los hijos sino también a los abuelos, tíos, primos y a los parientes políticos[4]. Tal vez[5] en una casa no vivan muchas personas, pero la familia sigue siendo[6] extensa y es una red de apoyo[7] importante. En toda celebración (o hasta[8] para una despedida en el aeropuerto) la familia extendida se junta[9].

Aunque[10] los censos muestran[11] que la familia hispana se vuelve[12] más pequeña (en México, por ejemplo, una madre tiene ahora 3 hijos, a diferencia de 6,5 hijos en 1973), la familia sigue siendo muy importante. De niños, los hispanos aprenden a ser leales[13] a su familia, a estar unidos y a ayudarse[14] siempre. La familia hispana enseña a los niños respeto, honor y cortesía. Es el grupo social más importante en la cultura hispana.

El cumpleaños de la abuela.

[1]most recent census [2]together [3]small [4]in-laws [5]Perhaps [6]continues to be [7]support system [8]even [9]gets together [10]Even though [11]show [12]is becoming [13]loyal [14]to help each other

32 ¿Qué recuerdas?

¿Sí o no?

1. Las familias en Puerto Rico tienen muchos hijos.
2. En Puerto Rico, los abuelos típicamente viven con sus hijos y sus nietos.
3. Por lo general, para el hispano la palabra *familia* se refiere *(refers)* solamente a los parientes que viven en su casa.
4. Muchas familias hispanas enseñan a los niños respeto, honor y cortesía.
5. En la cultura hispana, la familia es el grupo social más importante.

33 Algo personal

1. Al describir tu familia, ¿a quiénes incluyes? ¿Es tu definición de "familia" igual *(the same)* o diferente que la definición hispana? Explica.
2. ¿Es la familia importante para ti? Explica.
3. Compara una familia típica en Puerto Rico con una familia típica en los Estados Unidos.

- After reading the article, what generalization can you make about the size of Puerto Rican families? The importance of the family unit?

Notes You may wish to introduce additional family vocabulary: *cuñado* (brother-in-law), *cuñada* (sister-in-law), *suegro* (father-in-law), *suegra* (mother-in-law), and so on.

The family is the focal point of life in the Hispanic world. Almost all activities—parties, outings, etc.—include the family.

Communities. Tell students that because of Puerto Rico's political affiliation with the United States, its people are U.S. citizens and can travel freely between the island and the mainland. For this reason, there are very large Puerto Rican populations in the United States, especially in the northeast.

¿Qué aprendí?

Autoevaluación

As a review and self-check, respond to the following:

Visit the web-based activities at www.emcp.com

1. Give the names of five members of your family and say how each is related to you.

2. Describe two or three members of your family.

3. Imagine you are looking at a picture of your best friend's family. Name the people in the picture and their relationship to your friend.

4. Name three or four friends or relatives who do not live in your state and say where they live.

5. What might you ask someone in Spanish who looks happy? Sad?

6. What do you know about family life in the Spanish-speaking world?

Palabras y expresiones

Para describir
abierto,-a
amable
apurado,-a
bonito,-a
caliente
cansado,-a
cariñoso,-a
cerrado,-a
contento,-a
divertido,-a
enfermo,-a
frío,-a
guapo,-a
libre
limpio,-a
loco,-a
más
mis
nervioso,-a
nuestro,-a
ocupado,-a
otro,-a
popular
su, sus
sucio,-a
todo,-a
triste
tus
único,-a

Familia
el abuelo, la abuela
el esposo, la esposa
la familia
el hermano, la hermana
el hijo, la hija
la madre
el nieto, la nieta
el padre

los padres
el pariente, la pariente
el primo, la prima
el sobrino, la sobrina
el tío, la tía

Otras expresiones
la casa
la foto(grafía)
mucho
nunca

la playa
por
¡qué (+ *description*)!
el tiempo
el verano

Verbos
quiero
salir
vivir

¡Qué playa más bonita! (Crash Boat Beach, Puerto Rico.)

Capítulo 4   *ciento cincuenta y tres*   153

Teacher Resources

Activity 13

Information Gap Activities
Postcard Activities
Funciones de Comunicación

Answers

Autoevaluación
Possible answers:
1. *(Name)* es mi hermano.
2. Mis padres son amables.
3. Ella es su madre. Tomás y Mario son sus hermanos.
4. Mis primos viven en *(name of city, state or country)*.
5. ¿Estás contento/contenta? ¿Estás triste?
6. Answers will vary.

Activities

Cooperative Learning
Have students play the parts of various members of two families, *la familia Chávez* and *la familia Galván,* who meet for the first time while attending an event in the Grand Ballroom of the *Hotel San Juan.* Working in groups of five or six, members of each family should take turns introducing one another and offering any details they can about their families. Try to include brothers, sisters, parents, grandparents, etc.: *Tengo dos tías. Ellas son de Ponce.*

Notes **Communities.** There are many famous people of Puerto Rican descent born in the United States, such as actors Rosie Pérez and Jimmy Smits.

Comparisons. Cultural differences will vary. However, you may want to point out that in Hispanic families there generally are fewer conflicts between adults and children than in many families in the United States. On the other hand, family structure in the United States produces a more self-sufficient adult who is less emotionally and financially dependent on his or her family.

Activities

Expansion
With books closed, call on one or more students to act out a word or expression for the class. The person doing the pantomime then calls on a classmate to say the new expression in Spanish.

Spanish for Spanish Speakers
Have students model words and expressions in *Vocabulario I* for the class and then call on classmates to try pronouncing the new vocabulary.

Lección B

República Dominicana

Vocabulario I
A mí me gusta...

nadar

patinar (sobre ruedas)

jugar al béisbol

Tigres vs. Osos

jugar al tenis

ir a un partido de fútbol

bailar

cantar

¿Dónde vives?

Vivo en la República Dominicana.

ir de compras

preguntar y contestar

comprar

Notes Use a variety of *Navegando 1* support materials to teach and reinforce the vocabulary presented on pages 154–155. For example, the Audio CD Program Manual, the Listening Activities Manual, Overhead Transparencies, Workbook and Grammar and Vocabulary Exercises Manual. Quizzes support the teaching and evaluation of the content on these pages.

Consider playing the audio CD of *Vocabulario I* and have students practice their pronunciation before looking at the new words and expressions. Use any of the other ancillaries to tailor the content to match your teaching style.

mirar fotos

tocar el piano

hacer la tarea

oír (la) radio

ver (la) televisión

Answers

1 1. F
   2. A
   3. C
   4. B
   5. D
   6. E
2 Answers will vary.

Activities

Expansion
Play the audio CD version of the vocabulary and have students practice repeating the expressions in Spanish before opening their books and seeing how the new words and expressions are written.

Language through Action
Use TPR and overhead transparencies 31–32 to teach and reinforce the vocabulary shown in *Vocabulario I*.

1 ¿Qué es?

 Selecciona la foto apropiada a lo que oyes.

A   **B**   **C**

D   **E**   **F**

2 Me gusta...

Write sentences saying five things you like to do and with whom you like to do each activity.

MODELO   Me gusta ver la televisión con mi familia.

Capítulo 4   *ciento cincuenta y cinco* **155**

Notes Inform students that in Spanish, *televisión* is the signal we watch; a *televisor* is the apparatus that receives a picture and audio signal. Likewise, *la radio* (short for *radiotransmisión*) is the signal; *el radio* is the apparatus that receives an audio signal.

Explain that both *mirar* (to look at) and *ver* (to see) are used to say that someone watches television.

Teacher Resources

Me gusta mucho
Activities 3–5

Answers

3 1. A Andrés le gusta mucho la playa.
2. Natalia y otros amigos.
3. Hay un partido de fútbol.
4. Le gusta nadar.
5. Van al partido y a la playa.

4 Answers will vary.

5 **Natalia**
1. ir de compras
②. ir a la playa
③. bailar
4. tocar el piano
5. jugar al tenis

Andrés
6. jugar al béisbol
⑦. ir a la playa
⑧. bailar
9. patinar sobre ruedas
10. nadar

Activities

Critical Listening

Have students read the *Estrategia* on page 156. Then play the audio CD version of the dialog as students listen carefully and look for clues in the photographs about what the boys are saying to one another. Call on several individuals to state what they believe is the main theme of the conversation.

Expansion

Additional questions *(Algo personal): ¿Cómo se llama tu playa favorita?; ¿Dónde está?; ¿Con quién vas a la playa?; ¿Te gusta nadar?*

Diálogo I
Me gusta mucho

ANDRÉS: Felipe, ¡vamos a la playa!
FELIPE: ¿A la playa? ¿Te gusta la playa?
ANDRÉS: Sí, me gusta mucho.

ANDRÉS: Natalia y otros amigos van a ir allí.
FELIPE: Bueno, yo quiero ir al partido de fútbol.
ANDRÉS: Ah, sí... pero me gusta más nadar.

FELIPE: A ti no te gusta nadar. A ti te gusta Natalia.
ANDRÉS: ¿Por qué no vamos al partido y, luego, a la playa?
FELIPE: Está bien, chico. ¡Vamos!

3 ¿Qué recuerdas?

1. ¿A quién le gusta mucho la playa?
2. ¿Quiénes van a ir a la playa?
3. ¿De qué hay un partido?
4. ¿Qué le gusta a Andrés hacer en la playa?
5. ¿Adónde van los muchachos hoy?

4 Algo personal

1. ¿Te gusta ir a la playa?
2. ¿Te gusta ir a los partidos de fútbol?
3. ¿Qué te gusta hacer?

5 ¿Qué les gusta?

¿Qué les gusta?

Estrategia

Using contextual cues
The context in which a word is used often determines its meaning. One example of this is *chico,* which can mean **boy** or **small.** In the dialog, however, Felipe uses *chico* as a term of friendship that Andrés does not take literally, much as you might use the words **buddy** or **pal.** Additional terms that are used include *hombre, compa* (from *compadre*), *chica, niña* and *guapa* (used among female friends). Other contextual cues include facial expressions and gestures. Looking at the context often indicates the intended meaning of words.

Write the names Natalia and Andrés. Next, listen and list under each person's name what he or she likes to do. Then circle any item on the lists that they both like to do.

Notes Play activities 3, 4 and 5 from the Audio CD Program or use the transcript that appears in the ATE Introduction if you prefer to read the activities yourself.

A reproducible answer sheet for activity 5 can be found at the end of the Audio CD Program Manual.

You may wish to have students use a Venn diagram to do activity 5.

Cultura viva

La República Dominicana

Actividades

Do you like baseball? More foreign-born U.S. professional baseball players originate from the Dominican Republic than from any other country. Do you enjoy sun-filled days on beautiful beaches, snorkeling, scuba diving or other water sports? Visitors may choose to explore beautiful beaches, such as *Boca Chica* and *El Dorado.* Does lively music make you want to get up and dance? Dominican music, particularly the *merengue,* a unique, fast-paced Caribbean music style, is popular throughout Latin America. If any of these activities appeal to you, you may want to visit *la República Dominicana.*

Unos amigos en la playa.

Geografía

The Caribbean island of Hispaniola *(La Española)* is shared by the Dominican Republic, which occupies the eastern three-fourths of this tropical island, and Haiti, which is located on the remaining western portion of the island. Christopher Columbus *(Cristóbal Colón)* claimed the Caribbean island for Spain in December 1492.

Historia

Santo Domingo, the capital of the Dominican Republic and the first capital in the Americas, was founded by Christopher Columbus' brother Bartholomew *(Bartolomé)* in 1496. You may recognize the names of other explorers who visited the Dominican Republic such as Ponce de León, Hernán Cortés, Diego de Velázquez and Vasco Núñez de Balboa.

Una estátua de Cristóbal Colón en la capital, Santo Domingo.

6 Conexiones con otras disciplinas: historia y geografía

Use an encyclopedia or search the Internet for information about the Dominican Republic and list four or five interesting details about some aspect of the country's history (explorers, development as a country, native populations, important dates, etc.). Then create a map of Hispaniola, indicating the border between the two countries that make up the island and identify major cities, rivers, etc.

Capítulo 4   *ciento cincuenta y siete* **157**

Notes Conduct an information-gathering class discussion to find out what students know about the Dominican Republic. For example, ask if anyone knows of any recent news about the country, if they have read any articles about celebrities or famous people, etc. Then ask for student volunteers to gather information and create a bulletin board or travel brochure about the country.

There is controversy today about where Christopher Columbus is buried: in Santo Domingo or in Sevilla, Spain. Groups from both countries have argued about this claim for centuries.

Answers

6 Creative self-expression.

Activities

Expansion

Ask questions about the *Cultura viva: ¿Cuándo llegó Cristóbal Colón a La Española?; ¿Cómo se llama el hermano de Cristóbal Colón?; ¿Dónde está la tumba de Colón?; ¿Hay playas bonitas en la República Dominicana?; ¿Cómo se llaman?*

Multiple Intelligences (spatial/linguistic)

Using the resources of the Internet and the library, have students prepare a report about Dominican designer Óscar de la Renta. Have students illustrate their report with magazine photos, illustrations or computer graphics.

Spanish for Spanish Speakers

Have students read *In the Time of the Butterflies* by Dominican writer Julia Álvarez. Then they write a paper in which they discuss how Rafael Leónidas Trujillo's dictatorship is depicted in the book.

Activity 7

 Activity 3

 Activity 4

 Activity 2

 Activities 3–6

Answers

7 1. Sí, (No, no) me gusta....
2. Sí, (No, no) me gusta....
3. Sí, (No, no) me gusta....
4. Sí, (No, no) me gustan....
5. Sí, (No, no) me gustan....

Activities

Language through Action
Use magazine pictures of items and activities found in *Vocabulario I*, glued or taped to stiff paper or cardboard. Place them individually along the chalk tray and write a number above each. Then use several commands to ask students to point out objects they like or dislike: (name), *ve (camina) a la pizarra; Toca el número...; ¿Te gusta (item or activity pictured)?* Listen for an appropriate response. Have each student touch two or three pictures, each time asking whether or not the student likes the item or activity he or she is touching.

Idioma

Estructura

Using *gustar* to state likes and dislikes

When talking about what they like or dislike, Spanish-speaking people use the verb *gustar*. Use the words *me, te, le, nos, os* or *les* before the singular *gusta* to say what someone likes when referring to an infinitive or a singular noun. Use the same *me, te, le, nos, os* or *les* before *gustan* when referring to a plural noun.

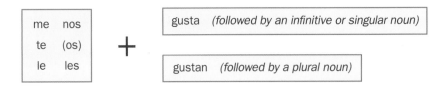

singular noun:	***¿Te gusta** el libro?*
plural noun:	***Me gustan** todos los libros.*
infinitive:	***Me gusta** mucho leer.*

Do you like the book?
I like all books.
I like to read a lot.

Note: Earlier in this lesson, you learned to consider the context when determining the meaning of words like *chico* (in the dialog between Andrés and Felipe). You may need to apply this same skill when determining the meaning of *le* and *les*. For instance, in the following example, it would be necessary to hear the entire conversation or to see the people involved in order to determine the meaning of the sentence.

*¿**Le** gusta jugar al béisbol?*

Do **you** (*Ud.*) like to play baseball?
Does **he** like to play baseball?
Does **she** like to play baseball?

Make a sentence negative by placing *no* before *me, te, le, nos, os* or *les gusta/gustan.*

*___**No** me gusta hacer la tarea._
*¿**No** te gustan las fotos de tu amiga?*
*___**No** nos gusta ir de compras._

I do not like to do homework.
Don't you like your friend's pictures?
We do not like to go shopping.

Práctica

7 ¿Te gusta(n)...?

Contesta las siguientes preguntas.

1. ¿Te gusta el colegio?
2. ¿Te gusta la clase de español?
3. ¿Te gusta hacer la tarea?

4. ¿Te gustan los sábados?
5. ¿Te gustan los partidos de fútbol en la televisión?

Notes Activity 7 is appropriate for individuals or may be assigned to pairs or small groups of students, according to your individual preference and class needs.

You may wish to introduce other verbs, such as *encantar* and *molestar*, that follow a pattern similar to that of *gustar*.

8 Me gusta(n)...

En parejas, alternen en preguntar y contestar si lo que *(what)* ven en la ilustración les gusta(n) o no.

MODELO **A:** ¿Te gustan los partidos de béisbol?
  B: Sí, (No, no) me gustan los partidos de béisbol.

1

2

3

4

5

6

✿ Comunicación

9 Encuesta

Working in small groups, create a survey to determine what activities your classmates enjoy. (The survey should consist of the same number of activities as there are members in your group.) Each person in your group selects one activity from the list and must then ask other students in class if they like that activity. Finally, one person from each group should give a summary *(resumen)* of the results of the survey to the class.

MODELO **A:** ¿Te gusta mirar fotos?
  B: Sí, me gusta./No, no me gusta.
  Resumen: A tres estudiantes les gusta mirar fotos y a un estudiante no le gusta mirar fotos.

ENCUESTA

¿Te gusta...?	Sí	No
1. mirar fotos	☑	☐
2. cantar	☐	☑
3. tocar el piano	☑	☐
4. jugar al fútbol	☑	☐

¡Extra!

¿Qué más te gusta hacer?

Me gusta jugar...	Me gusta tocar...
al básquetbol	el clarinete
a los bolos	la flauta
al fútbol americano	la guitarra
al golf	el saxofón
al hockey	el tambor

Capítulo 4 *ciento cincuenta y nueve* **159**

Answers

8 Possible answers:
 1. ¿Te gusta escuchar la radio?
   Sí, (No, no) me gusta escuchar la radio.
 2. ¿Te gustan las naranjas?
   Sí, (No, no) me gustan las naranjas.
 3. ¿Te gusta patinar sobre ruedas?
   Sí, (No, no) me gusta patinar sobre ruedas.
 4. ¿Te gustan las motocicletas?
   Sí, (No, no) me gustan las motocicletas.
 5. ¿Te gusta nadar?
   Sí, (No, no) me gusta nadar.
 6. ¿Te gustan los refrescos?
   Sí, (No, no) me gustan los refrescos.

9 Creative self-expression.

Activities

Cooperative Learning
Have students create their own surveys about pastime activities similar to the ones in activity 9. You may wish to have students work in pairs and exchange surveys. Then ask volunteers to give a summary of their partner's answers.

Language through Action
Play a game of charades in which students dramatize different sports and musical performances.

Notes Remind students as they do activities 8 and 9 that an infinitive can follow *gusta* but not *gustan*.

Make sure students keep moving around the classroom as they complete activity 9. Circulate among them, monitoring their use of Spanish. If you wish, participate in the survey by answering their questions.

Estructura

Using *a* to clarify or emphasize what you are saying

You can add *a* plus someone's name, a noun or a pronoun to clarify an otherwise confusing sentence or to emphasize what you are saying. Look at the following:

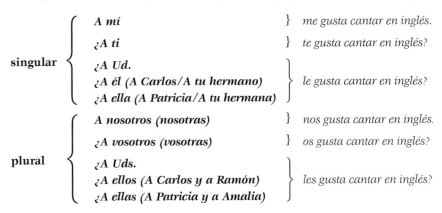

singular	*A mí*	}	*me gusta cantar en inglés.*
	¿A ti	}	*te gusta cantar en inglés?*
	¿A Ud. / *¿A él (A Carlos/A tu hermano)* / *¿A ella (A Patricia/A tu hermana)*	}	*le gusta cantar en inglés?*
plural	*A nosotros (nosotras)*	}	*nos gusta cantar en inglés.*
	¿A vosotros (vosotras)	}	*os gusta cantar en inglés?*
	¿A Uds. / *¿A ellos (A Carlos y a Ramón)* / *¿A ellas (A Patricia y a Amalia)*	}	*les gusta cantar en inglés?*

 ## Práctica

10 ¿Qué nos gusta hacer en casa?

Completa el siguiente párrafo con una palabra apropiada de cada columna.

me	
te	gusta
le	gustan
nos	
les	

En mi casa a todos nosotros (1) mucho escuchar la radio y ver la televisión. A mi abuelo (2) todos los deportes en la televisión, como el fútbol, el béisbol y el básquetbol. A mi abuela (3) un programa de música española en la radio. A mis hermanos (4) los conciertos de rock y de música pop en la televisión pero también (5) escuchar música en la radio. A mamá y a mis hermanas siempre (6) un programa por cable donde hablan de la construcción, de la remodelación y de la decoración de las casas. ¡Es su programa favorito! Personalmente, a mí (7) los programas que le permiten a uno comprar por teléfono productos fantásticos. Y a ti, ¿qué (8) escuchar en la radio o ver en la televisión?

Notes Discuss activity 10 with students. Ask them to explain how the addition of *a* and a name, a noun or a pronoun helped them choose the correct form of *gustar* to clarify an otherwise confusing sentence.

11 ¿Está claro?

Working in pairs, take turns reading these unclear sentences and clarify them by adding the given cues and making any other changes necessary. Follow the model.

> MODELO
> **A:** Le gusta escuchar la radio y bailar. (Diana)
> **B:** ¿A quién?
> **A:** A Diana le gusta escuchar la radio y bailar.
>
> **B:** Les gusta bailar merengue. (mis hermanas)
> **A:** ¿A quiénes?
> **B:** A mis hermanas les gusta bailar merengue.

1. Les gustan mucho los conciertos de música dominicana. (los Suárez)
2. Les gusta ir de compras. (mis primas)
3. Le gustan los partidos de béisbol. (Eduardo)
4. Le gusta patinar sobre ruedas. (ella)
5. Les gusta jugar al tenis. (Sara y Alberto)
6. Les gustan mucho las ciudades de Santo Domingo y Puerto Plata en la República Dominicana. (la Sra. y el Sr. García)

12 ¿Qué les gusta?

The following people all have strong opinions about what they like and what they do not like. In pairs, take turns asking and answering questions using the cues below, clarifying each person's preference.

> MODELO ella / nadar / jugar al tenis
> **A:** ¿A ella le gusta nadar?
> **B:** ¡No! ¡A ella no le gusta nadar! Le gusta jugar al tenis.

1. tú / ver televisión / ir al cine
2. Uds. / jugar al fútbol / jugar al béisbol
3. él / tocar el piano / bailar
4. ellas / ir de compras / escuchar música en la radio y cantar
5. los Fernández / las playas de Puerto Rico / las playas de la República Dominicana
6. los estudiantes / contestar en inglés / contestar en español

Me gustan las playas en la República Dominicana. (Las Terrenas Beach, R.D.).

Answers

11
1. ¿A quiénes?/A los Suárez les gustan mucho los conciertos de música dominicana.
2. ¿A quiénes?/A mis primas les gusta ir de compras.
3. ¿A quién?/A Eduardo le gustan los partidos de béisbol.
4. ¿A quién?/A ella le gusta patinar sobre ruedas.
5. ¿A quiénes?/A Sara y Alberto les gusta jugar al tenis.
6. ¿A quiénes?/A la Sra. y al Sr. García les gustan mucho las ciudades de Santo Domingo y Puerto Plata en la República Dominicana.

12
1. ¿A ti te gusta...?/¡No! ¡A mí no me gusta...! Me gusta....
2. ¿A Uds. les gusta...?/¡No! ¡A nosotros no nos gusta...! Nos gusta....
3. ¿A él le gusta...?/¡No! ¡A él no le gusta...! Le gusta....
4. ¿A ellas les gusta...?/¡No! ¡A ellas no les gusta...! Les gusta....
5. ¿A los Fernández les gustan...?/¡No! ¡A ellos no les gustan...! Les gustan....
6. ¿A los estudiantes les gusta...?/¡No! ¡A ellos no les gusta...! Les gusta....

Notes Point out that the prepositional phrases for emphasis or clarity shown on page 160 do not change to match verb phrases. For example: *A mí me gusta la playa. A mí me gustan las playas de la República Dominicana. A ellos les gusta la ciudad. A ellos les gustan las ciudades grandes.*

Activities

Critical Thinking
Ask students to express their preferences in relation to the following options: *¿Te gusta más la música rock o la música clásica? ¿Te gusta más el fútbol (americano) o el béisbol? ¿Te gusta más el golf o el tenis? ¿Te gusta más la comida mexicana o la comida italiana? ¿Te gusta más la televisión o el cine? ¿Te gusta más leer o ver la televisión? ¿Te gustan más los coches o las motos?* Have students explain each preference by posing the question *¿Por qué?*

---

 13 ¿Les gusta a todos en tu familia?

 Working with a classmate, take turns asking and answering questions about what everyone in your family likes to do. If there is someone who does not like an activity that follows, say who that person is.

MODELO bailar

> **A:** ¿Les gusta bailar a todos en tu familia?
> **B:** Sí, nos gusta bailar a todos./No, no nos gusta bailar a todos porque a mi padre no le gusta bailar.

1. ir a restaurantes
2. leer libros
3. pasear en el parque
4. vivir en los Estados Unidos
5. visitar a la familia
6. salir de casa los sábados
7. ir a conciertos de rock

Nos gusta bailar.

 14 A mi familia y a mis amigos...

Name at least six people who are important in your life and say how you know each person (they are either family or friends). Then say something each person likes and at least one thing the person does not like.

MODELO A mi amigo Miguel le gustan las playas.
A Miguel no le gusta nadar.

✤ Comunicación

15 Nos gusta(n)...

With a classmate, find out four things that both of you like. Write down your findings, using *Nos gusta(n)*.

MODELO
> **A:** ¿Te gusta tocar el piano?
> **B:** No, no me gusta. ¿A ti te gusta cantar?
> **A:** ¡Sí, claro! Me gusta mucho.
> **A y B:** (*Write* Nos gusta cantar.)

A Ricky Martin le gusta cantar.

16 Sus actividades favoritas

In small groups, discuss the activities you like most and least. Each member of the group must then compile a list of two things others in the group like and do not like to do. Finally, choose one member of your group to report the information to the class.

> **MODELO** **A:** A mí me gusta nadar. ¿Qué les gusta hacer a Uds.?
>   **B:** A mí me gusta ir de compras.
>   **C:** A mí me gusta escuchar música en la radio.
>   **B:** A *(name of student A)* le gusta nadar, a *(name of student C)* le gusta escuchar la radio y a mí me gusta ir de compras.

17 ¿Les gusta(n)?

Make a list of seven activities or items that are common in your daily life. Then ask your classmates if they like the activity or item. When you find someone who likes what you named, have the person sign his or her name *(Firma aquí, por favor.)* next to the appropriate activity or item. You have ten minutes to locate one person for each activity or item on your list. Next, summarize your findings in several short sentences. Finally, report the results to the class.

> **MODELO** ver televisión
>   **A:** Ana, ¿te gusta ver la televisión?
>   **ANA:** Sí, me gusta ver la televisión.
>   **A:** Firma aquí, por favor.
>   **A:** *(Writes and says:* A Ana le gusta ver la televisión.*)*

A ellos les gusta leer el periódico.

¿Le gusta/Le gustan?	Sí	No	Firma
1. los partidos de tenis	X		María A.
2. jugar al béisbol			
3. ...			

Teacher Resources

 ¿Cómo son?

 Activity 5

 Activities 32–33

 Activities 7–8

 Activity 4

 Activities 10–11

Activities

Expansion

Model the pronunciation of the words for student repetition. Then model sentences that include the new vocabulary as you act out adjectives from pages 164–165.

Vocabulario II

¿Cómo son?

guapa · feo · lenta · rápido · cómica · alto · bajo · difícil · inteligente · fácil · importante · malo · bueno · divertido · ideal · aburrido · gordo · interesante · fantástico · delgado · horrible

$$\int f(x)\,dx = g(b) - g(a)$$

2 + 2 = 4

Notes Explain that *aburrido/aburrida* means **boring** when it is used with *ser*, but the meaning changes to **bored** when this adjective is used with *estar*: *El programa es aburrido.* (The program is boring.); *Mi hermana está aburrida.* (My sister is bored.).

Additional adjectives for describing people: *tímido* (timid), *valiente* (valiant), *estudioso* (studious), *serio* (serious) and *activo* (active).

rubia
moreno
tonta
pelirrojo
calvo
egoísta
generosa

18 ¿Cómo es?

🔊 Mira las fotos y contesta las preguntas con *sí* o *no*, según lo que oyes.

1

2

3

4

5

6

7

8

19 ¿Quién y cómo?

Create a list of six friends or relatives and indicate their relationship to you. Under each name write words that describe the person, categorizing the words according to whether they refer to physical traits (*características físicas*) or personality characteristics (*características de personalidad*).

MODELO Patti Funston (hermana)

características físicas	características de personalidad
guapa y delgada	inteligente y divertida

Capítulo 4   *ciento sesenta y cinco*   **165**

Notes Activity 18 is intended to offer listening comprehension practice on the adjectives on pages 164 and 165. A reproducible answer sheet for the activity is located at the end of the Audio CD Program Manual.

Note for students that *moreno/morena* is used to refer to skin or hair color.

Answers

20 1. Es morena y es muy inteligente.
2. Es de Santo Domingo.
3. A las muchachas de Santo Domingo les gusta bailar.
4. Con una chica pelirroja.

21 Answers will vary.

22 1. mala
2. alta
3. tristes
4. lento
5. fácil
6. tontos
7. guapo/bonito
8. divertido/interesante

Activities

Pronunciation
Explain to students that if it sometimes seems that native speakers of Spanish are speaking very quickly it is because they link words together. For example, native speakers pronounce similar sounds at the end of one word and at the beginning of another as if they were connected (*¿dónde está?/doctor Rivera*); link dissimilar vowel sounds that occur in sequence (*a ella*); link a consonant sound that ends a word to a vowel sound that occurs at the beginning of the following word (*el esposo*). Practice this point by having students either act out the dialog from the book or create their own dialogs to be presented orally in class.

Diálogo II

¿Cómo es ella?

FELIPE: ¿Cómo es tu amiga Natalia?
ANDRÉS: Es morena y es muy inteligente.
FELIPE: ¡Qué bien!

ANDRÉS: Sí, y también es muy guapa.
FELIPE: ¿De dónde es ella?
ANDRÉS: Ella es de Santo Domingo.

FELIPE: ¡A las muchachas de Santo Domingo les gusta bailar!
ANDRÉS: Sí, ella baila muy bien el merengue. ¡Mira, allí está!
FELIPE: ¡Ah, sí!, con la chica pelirroja.

20 ¿Qué recuerdas?

1. ¿Cómo es Natalia?
2. ¿De dónde es Natalia?
3. ¿A quiénes les gusta bailar?
4. ¿Con quién está Natalia?

21 Algo personal

1. ¿Cómo eres tú?
2. ¿Cómo es tu amigo/a favorito/a?
3. ¿Dónde estás ahora?

22 ¿Cuál es el opuesto?

 You will hear some descriptions of people and objects. Give the opposite (*el opuesto*) of each adjective you hear.

MODELO gordos

Mis amigos son inteligentes.

Notes *Diálogo II* contextualizes the new words and expressions that are introduced in *Vocabulario II,* allowing students to practice the new vocabulary in complete-sentence answers to activities.

Diálogo II and the activities that follow have been recorded by native Spanish speakers and can be found in the Audio CD Program. Student answer sheets for activity 22 can be found in the back of the Audio CD Program Manual.

Have students match the gender and number of the antonyms they give for activity 22.

Cultura Viva

El merengue

What do you associate with the Dominican Republic? Along with baseball, this Spanish-speaking Caribbean country is known for its music and dance. One example is the folkloric dance and musical style known as the *merengue*. Although *merengue* music is varied in tempo, the dance is recognizable because the dancing couples hold one another in a waltz-like position as they move about the floor dragging one foot with each step they take. *Merengue* has existed for over one hundred years. Although no one can be certain exactly how *merengue* evolved, most probably it has African and European roots. One interesting theory

Ellos bailan merengue.

Juan Luis Guerra.

suggests the music consists of a mix of African slave songs and the sophisticated French minuet of the late eighteenth century. Regardless of how it originated, *merengue* remains the national dance of the Dominican Republic and is extremely popular throughout the Caribbean and South America as well. When you visit the country, you will more than likely see people dancing *merengue* and you will most certainly hear *merengue* music performed by a number of popular musicians such as Juan Luis Guerra.

23 Conexión con otras disciplinas: música

Using an encyclopedia or the Internet, research some aspect of Dominican music that interests you (e.g., *merengue*, Juan Luis Guerra, Wilfrido Vargas). Prepare a short report on your findings. If possible, demonstrate what you found out (dance the *merengue*, play a CD with Dominican music, etc.).

24 Comparando

Compare music in the Dominican Republic with popular music you usually listen to in the United States. What seems similar? What is different? What do you like about both kinds of music?

Capítulo 4   *ciento sesenta y siete*   **167**

Answers

25 1. C; 2. A; 3. F; 4. C; 5. D; 6. B

Activities

Critical Listening

Tell the class that they will hear several statements about two sisters who are named Clara and Ana. After each statement they must say whether *ser* or *estar* was used and briefly explain why: *Clara y Ana son hermanas; Clara y Ana están en el colegio; Ana está cansada; Clara es cómica y simpática; A Ana le gusta jugar al tennis. Su partido es en el colegio; Los padres de Clara y Ana son profesores; Su madre es de España y su padre es de los EE.UU.*

Critical Thinking

Write several phrases on the board that are preceded by *ser (de Puerto Rico, inteligente, las 8:00)* and several that are preceded by *estar (bien, regular, en Santo Domingo, en la clase).* Point to a word or phrase and ask: "*¿Ser o estar?*"; after students respond, ask "*¿Por qué?*" and call on one student to support the answer. (The response may be in English unless you prefer to give students the Spanish words: *origen, característica, condición* and *lugar.*)

Idioma

Ser vs. *estar*

Both *ser* and *estar* are equivalent to the English verb **to be.** However, the two verbs are used in very different situations.

- *Ser* may be used to express origin.

  Soy de la República Dominicana.   I am from the Dominican Republic.

- *Ser* is also used to indicate characteristics that distinguish people or objects from one another.

  Jaime es alto.   Jaime is tall.

- *Estar* is used to express a temporary condition.

  ¡Qué bonita está hoy!   How pretty she is (looks) today!

- *Estar* may also refer to where someone or something is located.

  ¿Dónde está tu casa?   Where is your house?

Note: Although *estar* is generally used to express location, *ser* is used to refer to the location of an event, in which case it means **to take place.**

  ¿Dónde es el concierto?   Where is the concert (taking place)?

Práctica

25 ¿De dónde son?

Selecciona la letra de la forma apropiada de *ser* para completar las oraciones.

1. Juan Luis Guerra __ de la República Dominicana.
2. Yo __ de los Estados Unidos.
3. Shakira y Juan Pablo Montoya __ de Colombia.
4. ¿__ Ricky Martin de Puerto Rico?
5. ¿Pues, __ tú y yo de la misma ciudad?
6. ¿De dónde __ tú?

A. soy
B. eres
C. es
D. somos
E. sois
F. son

¿De dónde es Juan Pablo Montoya?

Notes Review the present-tense forms of *ser* and *estar* with students before explaining their differences in usage.

Many Dominican baseball players in the United States originate from San Pedro de Macorís.

26 ¿Cómo son?

Describe your relatives, your friends and yourself, using the appropriate form of *ser* and one or two adjectives. You may make up any of the information you wish.

MODELO el profesor/la profesora de inglés
El profesor de inglés es calvo y muy divertido.

1. yo
2. mi madre
3. mis abuelos
4. mi dentista
5. mi amiga favorita
6. los otros estudiantes de la clase de español y yo

27 ¿Cómo están allí?

Completa las oraciones con la forma apropiada de *estar.*

1. Yo __ en mi clase favorita ahora.
2. Mi amiga favorita no __ en la clase.
3. Tres estudiantes __ enfermos hoy.
4. La profesora es simpática y hoy __ muy bonita.
5. Nosotros __ muy cansados pero contentos porque mañana es sábado.
6. ¿Cómo __ tú hoy?

28 ¿*Ser* o *estar*?

Usa la forma correcta de *ser* o *estar* para completar las siguientes oraciones.

1. Óscar de la Renta __ de la República Dominicana.
2. Su casa __ en Santo Domingo.
3. Eduardo __ el tío de Mónica.
4. No __ cansado... ¡Estoy apurado!
5. El carro __ de Hernán y Gloria.
6. El Yunque __ en Puerto Rico.
7. ¡Qué simpática __ tú!
8. Nosotros __ contentos de estar en San Pedro de Macorís.
9. ¿Tienes calor o __ bien?
10. ¿Dónde __ el concierto de merengue?

El Yunque está en Puerto Rico.

Notes In activity 28 have students give a reason for their choices of *ser* or *estar,* such as origin, location, condition, characteristic.

Point out the sign in the photograph and ask students if they recall where El Yunque is located.

29 **¿Cuál es tu opinión?**

En parejas, describan a las personas en las fotos.

1   **2**   **3**

30 **Biografía**

Bring to class magazine cutouts of a famous person (e.g., singer, athlete, television/film star). Next, working in small groups, decide who will be the "biographer" and write down what others say about and how they describe each person (everyone in the group should be the biographer one time). Finally, one student holds up a picture, while the others add a sentence to describe the person shown (and the biographer writes down what everyone in the group says).

MODELO   **A:** ¿Cómo es Jennifer López?
          B: Es guapa.
          C: Es una cantante popular.
             (The biographer writes *Jennifer López es guapa y es una cantante popular.*)

Jennifer López es guapa y es una cantante popular.

◈ Comunicación

31 **¿Quién es?**

Write five or six sentences about a celebrity, including where the person is from, what the person is like, why the person is famous, etc. Do not name the celebrity. Then, working with a partner, describe the celebrity as your classmate draws the person's picture. The activity ends when your partner guesses the name of the person. Switch roles.

Notes As a follow-up to activity 30, ask for volunteers to read the biographers' summaries in front of the class as an assistant holds up the pictures.

After completing activity 31, play a guessing game with the class to see if students know who is being described:

1) Call on a student to read the first sentence from one of the descriptions he or she discussed with another student for activity 31; 2) ask *¿Quién es?* and see if anyone recognizes the person; 3) continue one sentence at a time, either until someone guesses who the person is or until there are no more sentences to read.

32 Juego

 In groups of three, two of you choose a classmate you all know well. Then those two members of the group talk about the person without naming him/her, while the third member of the group listens. Discuss what the person likes or dislikes, talk about his/her personality and give a physical description of the classmate. Keep the descriptions positive! The third person in the group must then try to guess whom you were talking about. Switch roles.

Hacemos preguntas.

33 Entrevista

Write six questions you would like to ask someone in class. Include questions about how the person feels today, what the person likes and dislikes, favorite pastimes, personality, what the person's family is like, and so forth. Next, interview a classmate you do not know well and take notes. Then switch roles. Finally, write a summary describing how you are alike and different, making positive statements only. Present the results to the class.

¿Te gusta nadar?

¿Cómo es tu familia?

¿Te gusta escuchar música?

Capítulo 4   *ciento setenta y uno*   **171**

Answers

32 Creative self-expression.
33 Creative self-expression.

Activities

Students with Special Needs
Provide the following for students who require a model of what to do for activity 33:

A: *¿Cómo te llamas?*
B: *Me llamo* (name of B).
A: *¿Qué te gusta hacer?*
B: *Me gusta....*
A: *¿Qué más te gusta?*
B: *Me gusta....*
A: *¿Qué no te gusta?*
B: *Pues, no me gusta....*

Resumen: Mi nuevo/nueva amigo/amiga se llama (name of B). *Le gusta...y.... A mí me gusta más.... A* (name of B) *no le gusta...y a mí no me gusta...tampoco.* (Name of B) *es generoso/generosa, alto/alta.*

Notes Have students prepare the interview questions as homework. Pair students of varying language ability levels so that less accomplished students can work with more advanced students. Also, if you pair them up, your students will become accustomed to working with different peers instead of always choosing their friends.

Answers

34 1. Sammy Sosa nació en la
República Dominicana en
San Pedro de Macorís.
2. Tiene seis hermanos.
3. Manuel admira a Sammy
Sosa porque juega muy
bien al béisbol y es una
persona generosa y
amable.
4. Anotó un nuevo récord de
jonrones en 1998.
5. Va a ver la casa en donde
vivió Sammy Sosa.

35 Answers will vary.

Activities

Technology

Have students do an Internet
search using the words **Sammy
Sosa** to find out more about this
Dominican baseball player.

Lectura personal

Cantantes y grupos musicales

Dirección http://www.emcp.com/músico/ola/e.diario-3.htm ▲ Archivo Edición Ver Favoritos Herramientas Ayuda

página principal miembros e-diario

Grupo musical La OLA

Nombre: **Manuel Andrade Blanco**
Edad: **17 años**
País natal: **Panamá**
Deporte favorito: **el béisbol**
La muchacha ideal: **alta, morena, generosa, inteligente**

Estamos ahora en la bonita isla de la República
Dominicana, el país natal de mi héroe: el beisbolista
Sammy Sosa. A mí me gusta mucho el béisbol y
admiro mucho a Sammy Sosa. Sé todo sobre él.
Samuel Peralta Sosa nació[1] el doce de noviembre
de 1968. Su familia era pobre[2] y por lo tanto[3]
Sammy jugaba[4] al béisbol (o a la pelota como dicen
los dominicanos) con un palo[5] y un calcetín[6].
Empezó[7] a jugar profesionalmente a los dieciséis
años con los Texas Rangers. En 1998, anotó[8] 64
jonrones, un nuevo récord. En mi opinión, Sammy

Sosa es uno de los grandes jugadores de la historia
y también es una persona generosa y amable. Él ha
donado[9] millones de dólares a su país. Estoy muy,
muy contento porque esta tarde voy a ir a San
Pedro de Macorís para ver la casa donde vivió[10]
Sammy Sosa con su madre y sus seis hermanos. Es
una casa pequeña y rosada[11]. Claro, ¡voy a sacar
muchas fotos!

[1]was born [2]poor [3]therefore [4]played [5]stick [6]sock [7]He began [8]he hit [9]has donated [10]lived [11]small and pink

34 ¿Qué recuerdas?

1. ¿Dónde nació Sammy Sosa?
2. ¿Cuántos hermanos tiene?
3. ¿Por qué admira Manuel a
Sammy Sosa?
4. ¿En qué año anotó Sammy Sosa un
nuevo récord de jonrones?
5. ¿Qué va a ver Manuel en San Pedro
de Macorís?

35 Algo personal

1. ¿Te gusta el béisbol? ¿Cuántos jugadores de la República
Dominicana puedes nombrar?
2. ¿Quién es tu héroe? ¿Por qué admiras a esa persona?
3. ¿Piensas *(Do you think)* que los jugadores famosos deben
ayudar *(should help)* a sus países? Explica.

• How does your hero's
childhood compare
with Sammy Sosa's
childhood?

172 *ciento setenta y dos*

Lección B

Notes Sammy Sosa is one of the most
famous baseball players from the
Dominican Republic. He received
international attention in 1998 due to his
race against Mark McGwire to break the
single-season home-run record.

Students interested in baseball may wish
to visit the following Internet site:
Dominican Republic Baseball
http://dominicanrepinfo.com/
Baseball.htm

¿Qué aprendí?

Visit the web-based activities at www.emcp.com

Autoevaluación

As a review and self-check, respond to the following:

1. Name two activities you enjoy.
2. Ask if your friend likes something. How would you ask your teacher the same question?
3. Your cousin tells you he likes to study. How would you respond, emphasizing that you like to play tennis?
4. Describe your best friend in Spanish.
5. How would you say in Spanish that something is interesting? Sad?
6. How would you say Marta is a good student, but she is bored today?
7. What do you know about the Dominican Republic?

Palabras y expresiones

Para describir

aburrido,-a
alto,-a
bajo,-a
bueno,-a
calvo,-a
canoso,-a
cómico,-a
delgado,-a
difícil
egoísta
fácil
feo,-a
generoso,-a

gordo,-a
horrible
ideal
importante
inteligente
interesante
lento,-a
malo,-a
moreno,-a
pelirrojo,-a
rápido,-a
rubio,-a
tonto,-a

Otras expresiones

el béisbol
la compra
el fútbol
me
mí
nos
el partido
el piano
la radio
la tarea
la televisión
el tenis
ti

Verbos

bailar
cantar
comprar
contestar
escuchar
gustar
ir de compras
jugar (ue)
jugar a *(+ sport/game)*
mirar
nadar
patinar (sobre ruedas)
tocar

En la vida hay buenos y malos.

Capítulo 4　　　　　　　　　*ciento setenta y tres*　**173**

Teacher Resources

📝 **Activity 13**

💬 **Information Gap Activities**
Postcard Activities
Funciones de Comunicación

◄ Answers

Autoevaluación
Possible answers:
1. Me gusta....
2. ¿Te gusta...?/¿Le gusta...?
3. A mí me gusta jugar al tenis.
4. Mi amigo/amiga es.... Le gusta....
5. Es interesante. Es triste.
6. Marta es una estudiante buena, pero está aburrida hoy.
7. Answers will vary.

◄ Activities

Cooperative Learning
Have students work in pairs, asking one another to describe people and objects in their lives. Students should use *¿Cómo es...?* and *¿Cómo son...?* and the provided nouns. The student answering should respond with the correct form of an appropriate adjective. Have students switch roles so each has an opportunity to use all the nouns. (Nouns: *tu profesor/ profesora favorito/favorita; tu amigo favorito; tu hermana; tus padres; tu casa; tu carro; tus fiestas.* Adjectives: *amable, popular, cariñoso, divertido, favorito, simpático, nuevo, fantástico.*)

Notes Although 80 percent of the island is mountainous, the Dominican Republic's valleys have lush vegetation and fertile farmland. Agriculture is the country's leading industry and provides its most important trading partner, the United States, with sugar, coffee, bananas and cocoa. Tourism is also important to the economy. In fact, the Dominican Republic is the second most visited Caribbean destination.

Model words from the list of *Palabras y expresiones* and have students repeat after you. Then call on individuals to simultaneously practice and evaluate pronunciation.

Answers

Preparación

1 El béisbol es muy popular en los países hispanos y muchos beisbolistas profesionales son hispanos. La familia Martínez tiene tres hijos que son lanzadores profesionales en los EE.UU.

2
1. D
2. J
3. B
4. H
5. C
6. G
7. A
8. E
9. F
10. I

Activities

Prereading Strategy

Note for students that it is not essential to understand every word to read in Spanish. As with most readings in *Navegando*, equivalents for some unknown words have been provided and others may be understood through context and background knowledge.

¡Viento en popa!

Tú lees

Estrategia

Skimming

Before beginning to read an article, quickly look over the contents. Skimming through the reading will give you an idea what the article is about and will tell you whether the content interests you or not. To skim the article that follows, read the title and first line or two of each paragraph, note highlighted words and look for supportive visuals such as photographs or illustrations.

Preparación

Contesta las siguientes preguntas como preparación para la lectura.

1. ¿Cuál es la idea principal de la lectura?
2. Selecciona los equipos de la columna de la derecha que van con las ciudades de la columna de la izquierda.

1. Cleveland	A. los Rancheros
2. Cincinnati	B. los Atléticos
3. Oakland	C. los Bravos
4. Boston	D. los Indios
5. Atlanta	E. los Dodgers
6. Filadelfia	F. los Gigantes
7. Texas	G. los Filis
8. Los Ángeles	H. los Medias Rojas
9. San Francisco	I. los Piratas
10. Pittsburgh	J. los Rojos

El béisbol y la familia Martínez

El béisbol no sólo es un deporte[1] muy popular en los Estados Unidos, también es muy popular en muchos de los países hispanos. A muchas personas de Puerto Rico, Cuba y la República Dominicana les gusta mucho jugar al béisbol y muchos beisbolistas profesionales son hispanos.

La familia Martínez de la República Dominicana, por ejemplo, tiene tres hijos que han sido[2] beisbolistas en las ligas profesionales de los Estados Unidos. Su hijo mayor[3], Ramón Martínez, fue[4] un lanzador[5] para los Dodgers de Los Ángeles. Pedro Martínez, que es el hermano menor[6], es un lanzador para los Medias Rojas

Pedro Martínez.

Notes Be sure to review the contents of the *Estrategia* on skimming before assigning this reading about Pedro Martínez.

Additional information about the Dominican Republic can be located on the Internet:

Dominican Republic News and Travel Information http://www.dr1.com
Electronic Embassy
http://www.embassy.org
Organization of American States
http://www.oas.org
general travel information
http://www.expedia.com

Ramón Martínez.

de Boston. Además, Jesús Martínez, el hijo menor de la familia, fue un lanzador en las ligas menores de los Dodgers.

Ramón es el ídolo de sus hermanos menores, pero Pedro es el más[7] famoso de los tres porque es el primer[8] dominicano que ha ganado[9] tres veces el premio[10] Cy Young. Los tres hermanos no juegan al béisbol todo el tiempo. También les gusta nadar, escuchar música y pasar tiempo con sus padres en la República Dominicana. Los Martínez—una familia unida por el béisbol.

[1]sport [2]have been [3]older [4]was [5]pitcher
[6]younger [7]the most [8]first [9]has won
[10]award

A ¿Qué recuerdas?

1. ¿Dónde es popular el béisbol?
2. ¿A qué personas les gusta jugar mucho al béisbol?
3. ¿Cuántos hijos de la familia Martínez han sido beisbolistas?
4. ¿En qué posición juega Pedro Martínez?
5. ¿Para qué equipo juega Pedro?
6. ¿Por qué es muy famoso Pedro?
7. ¿Qué hacen los hermanos Martínez además de jugar al béisbol?

B Algo personal

1. ¿Te gusta jugar al béisbol? ¿Qué deporte te gusta jugar?
2. ¿Cuál es tu equipo de béisbol profesional favorito?
3. ¿Quién es tu beisbolista favorito?
4. ¿Ves por televisión o vas a los partidos profesionales? ¿A cuáles?
5. ¿Cuál es el deporte más popular donde vives?

Los hermanos Ramón y Pedro Martínez.

Notes The reading *El béisbol y la familia Martínez* and the activities that follow have been recorded by native speakers and are available on the *Navegando 1* Audio CD Program.

Tú escribes

A Make a list of everyone who is in your family, leaving space under each name to write comments. Then write related ideas in the space, creating an outline consisting of everyone's ages, their interests and your opinion about each person.

B Summarize the ideas from your outline in a complete paragraph in Spanish that describes your family. Do not forget to give your paragraph a title. Finally, add a family photograph or add original artwork and graphics to make your paragraph more attractive.

Mi familia.

Proyectos adicionales

A Conexión con la tecnología

Research your family's history using the resources available on the Internet. If you prefer, make up an identity or pretend to be someone famous (preferably someone Hispanic). Do you have any Spanish-speaking ancestors? Where did your ancestors come from? Investigate the life of one relative who was born and lived in another country. Find out the name of the country (and city) where the person was born, where the country (and city) is located on a map and details about the country (population, principal attractions, capital, holidays, etc.). Share your research with the class.

B Conexión con otras disciplinas: geografía/cultura

In small groups, create a travel brochure on Puerto Rico or the Dominican Republic. Include information such as: geographical location, capital city, population, main cities, major tourist attractions, events and anything else you find interesting or fun. Use the Internet or the library for your research. Present your group's travel brochure to the rest of the class as if you were a travel agent or a representative of the country's Tourist Bureau.

C Comparaciones

Give the Spanish equivalents for the baseball terms shown. You can find them on the Internet or in a dictionary. Next, draw a baseball field and identify in Spanish as many of the people and other elements as you can (e.g., infield, baseball, umpire, pitcher, etc.). Label the drawing *el campo de béisbol*. Then, compare your drawing with a classmate's to see what is similar and what is different.

los jugadores *(players)*
1. the batter
2. the catcher
3. the first baseman
4. the outfielder
5. the pitcher
6. the player
7. the second baseman
8. the shortstop
9. the third baseman
10. the umpire

el juego *(game)*
11. first/second/third base
12. out
13. strikeout
14. ball
15. bat
16. baseball glove
17. home run
18. infield
19. inning
20. outfield
21. run
22. strike

Teacher Resources

 Situation Cards

 Capítulo 4

Answers

A Creative self-expression.
B Creative self-expression.
C Possible answers:
1. the batter = *el bateador*
2. the catcher = *el receptor*
3. the first baseman = *el inicialista, el primer base*
4. the outfielder = *el jardinero, el guardabosque*
5. the pitcher = *el lanzador, el serpintero, el abridor*
6. the player = *el pelotero*
7. the second baseman = *el intermedista, el segunda base, el camarero*
8. the shortstop = *el jardinero corto*
9. the third baseman = *el antesalista, el tercera base*
10. the umpire = *el árbitro*
11. first/second/third base = *la primera/segunda/terecera base*
12. out = *out, fuera el hombre*
13. strikeout = *ponche, ponchado, ponchete*
14. ball = *la bola, la pelota*
15. bat = *el bate*
16. baseball glove = *el guante*
17. home run = *el cuadrangular, el jonrón*
18. infield = *el campo interior*
19. inning = *el inning, la entrada, el episodio*
20. outfield = *el campo exterior*
21. run = *la carrera*
22. strike = *el strike, el estrike*

Notes The National Standards are practiced throughout the chapter. These end-of-chapter culminating projects are optional. They offer additional standards practice, opportunities for applying technology to problem-solving activities and cross-curricular learning opportunities. Pick and choose the activities that suit your style and that help you accomplish your teaching goals and curriculum requirements.

Teacher Resources

 Trabalenguas

Activities

Connections
As a connection with both science and art, have students prepare posters that depict some of the plants and animals found in El Yunque National Park in Puerto Rico and then share them with the class.

Multiple Intelligences (spatial)
This is an appropriate time for a right-brain activity to accommodate visual learners. Divide the class into groups of three or four. Give each group one piece of paper and some colored markers. Have them make a drawing on half of the paper to depict the concept of using *ser* for basic characteristics and traits and on the other half depict the concept of *estar* for temporary condition and location. Label each side. Have one student from each group explain the visuals. You may wish to make a bulletin board of the best examples.

Spanish for Spanish Speakers
Have students give a complete answer to the following question, listing the pros and cons of each alternative: *¿Debe Puerto Rico convertirse en un estado de los Estados Unidos, en una nación independiente o permanecer como estado libre asociado?*

Repaso

Now that I have completed this chapter, I can...

	Go to these pages for help:
talk about family and relationships.	134
seek and provide personal information.	134
express possession.	134
say some things people do.	154
express an opinion.	154
state likes and dislikes.	158
describe people and things.	164

I can also...

identify members of my family in Spanish.	134
talk about life in Puerto Rico and the Dominican Republic.	137, 157
talk about *merengue* dance.	167
read in Spanish about baseball in Spanish-speaking countries.	174
read and use Spanish words in context.	174
write a paragraph in Spanish.	176

Trabalenguas

Papá, pon para Pepín pan.

Notes Additional information about Puerto Rico can be located in many sites on the Internet:

Escape to Puerto Rico
http://escape.topuertorico.com
Welcome to Puerto Rico
http://welcome.topuertorico.org

Organization of American States
http://www.oas.org
general travel information
http://www.expedia.com

Loose translation of the *Trabalenguas:*
Daddy, get some bread to Pepín.

Vocabulario

abierto,-a open *4A*
el abuelo, la abuela grandfather, grandmother *4A*
aburrido,-a bored, boring *4B*
alto,-a tall, high *4B*
amable kind, nice *4A*
apurado,-a in a hurry *4A*
bailar to dance *4B*
bajo,-a short (not tall), low *4B*
el béisbol baseball *4B*
bonito,-a pretty, good-looking, attractive *4A*
bueno,-a good *4A*
caliente hot *4B*
calvo,-a bald *4B*
canoso,-a white-haired *4B*
cansado,-a tired *4A*
cantar to sing *4B*
cariñoso,-a affectionate *4A*
la casa house *4A*
cerrado,-a closed *4A*
cómico,-a comical, funny *4B*
la compra purchase *4B*
comprar to buy *4B*
contento,-a happy, glad *4A*
contestar to answer *4B*
delgado,-a thin *4B*
difícil difficult, hard *4B*
divertido,-a fun *4A*
egoísta selfish *4B*
enfermo,-a sick *4A*
escuchar to listen to *4B*
el esposo, la esposa husband, wife, spouse *4A*
fácil easy *4B*
la familia family *4A*
feo,-a ugly *4B*
la foto(grafía) photo *4A*
frío,-a cold *4A*
el fútbol soccer *4B*
generoso,-a generous *4B*
gordo,-a fat *4B*
guapo,-a good-looking, attractive, handsome, pretty *4A*
gustar to like, to be pleasing to *4B*
el hermano, la hermana brother, sister *4A*
el hijo, la hija son, daughter *4A*
horrible horrible *4B*
ideal ideal *4B*
importante important *4B*

inteligente intelligent *4B*
interesante interesting *4B*
ir de compras to go shopping *4B*
jugar (ue) to play *4B*
jugar a (+ *sport/game*) to play *4B*
lento,-a slow *4B*
libre free *4A*
limpio,-a clean *4A*
loco,-a crazy *4A*
la madre mother *4A*
malo,-a bad *4A*
más more, else *4A*
me (to, for) me *4B*
mí me (after a preposition) *4B*
mirar to look (at) *4B*
mis my (*pl.*) *4A*
moreno,-a brunette, dark-haired, dark-skinned *4B*
mucho,-a much, a lot, very, very much *4B*
nadar to swim *4B*
nervioso,-a nervous *4A*
el nieto, la nieta grandson, granddaughter *4A*
nos (to, for) us *4B*
nuestro,-a our *4A*
nunca never *4A*
ocupado,-a busy, occupied *4A*
otro,-a other, another *4A*
el padre father *4A*
los padres parents, fathers *4A*
para for, to, in order to *4A*
el pariente, la pariente relative *4A*

el partido game, match *4B*
patinar (sobre ruedas) to in-line skate *4B*
pelirrojo,-a red-haired *4B*
el piano piano *4B*
la playa beach *4A*
popular popular *4A*
por for *4A*
el primo, la prima cousin *4A*
¡qué (+ *description*)! how (+ *description*)! *4A*
quiero I love, I want *4A*
la radio radio (broadcast) *4B*
rápido,-a rapid, fast *4B*
rubio,-a blond *4B*
salir to go out *4A*
el sobrino, la sobrina nephew, niece *4A*
su, sus his, her, its, your (*Ud./Uds.*), their *4A*
sucio,-a dirty *4A*
la tarea homework *4B*
la televisión television *4B*
el tenis tennis *4B*
ti you (*after a preposition*) *4B*
el tiempo time *4A*
el tío, la tía uncle, aunt *4A*
tocar to play *4B*
todo,-a all, every, whole, entire *4A*
tonto,-a silly *4B*
triste sad *4A*
tus your (*pl.*) *4A*
único,-a only, unique *4A*
el verano summer *4A*
vivir to live *4A*

Mira la foto de mis padres y yo.

Teacher Resources

 Module 1

 Episode 4

Testing/ Assessment
Test Booklet
Portfolio Assessment

Activities

Cooperative Learning
Have students pair up for this fun activity called *¿Cómo es tu novio/novia ideal?* Students should pretend they are on a reality televisión show where they get to pick their mate *(pareja)*. Working in pairs, have students discuss physical and behavioral traits for their ideal boyfriend *(novio)* or girlfriend *(novia)*. They must then explain how important those qualities are in a relationship.
Modelo

    A: ¿Es tu novia ideal guapa?
    B: No, no es importante. ¿Es tu novio ideal generoso?
    A: ¡Claro! Es importante.

Expansion
Model new words and expressions and have students repeat them after you to improve their pronunciation. Then call on individuals to use the new words and expressions in sentences.

Notes Point out and explain why the verb *jugar* is listed in the *Vocabulario* for the chapter with the letters *ue* in parentheses: *jugar (ue)*. Explain that the letters following the infinitive indicate the verb has a spelling change in its conjugated forms. The conjugation of verbs with the *u → ue* changes is taught later in *Lección 7A*.

Quizzes have been formatted to allow you to evaluate how well students are learning key content. If you did not use all quizzes where indicted in the margins of the ATE, you may choose to use those quizzes at the end of a lesson as a comprehensive test over the contents of the entire lesson.

⊂onnections with Parents

There are numerous benefits to increasing the involvement of parents and guardians in their children's school lives. Teachers can do many things to encourage parents and guardians to have a larger role in their children's classroom education. Some examples include parent/teacher organizations, letters, school visitations, open houses, conferences, volunteer opportunities and assignments that involve interaction between the students and their parents or guardians.

Activities

Critical Thinking

Use the visuals that appear on pages 180–181 to elicit student interest in the functions, cultural setting and themes of the chapter ahead. For example, ask students if they can guess why the girls on these two pages are dressed as they are. Then ask what students think they will be learning in the chapter.

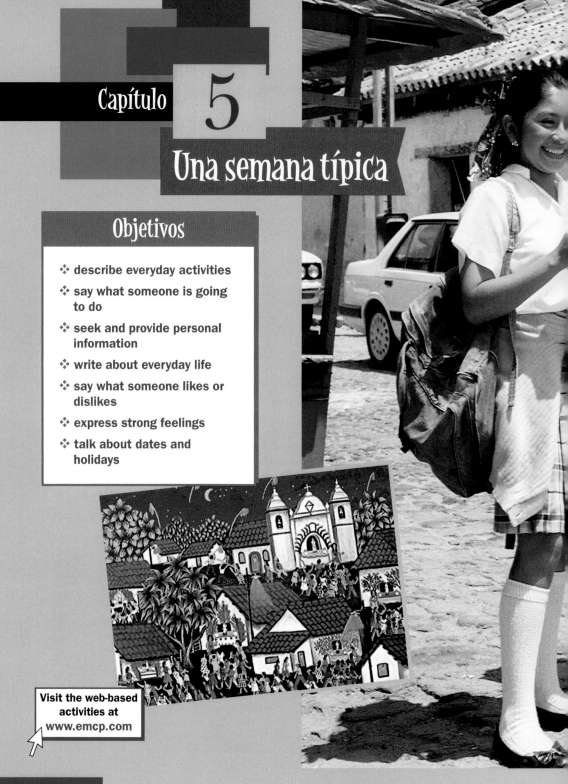

Capítulo **5**

Una semana típica

Objetivos

❖ describe everyday activities

❖ say what someone is going to do

❖ seek and provide personal information

❖ write about everyday life

❖ say what someone likes or dislikes

❖ express strong feelings

❖ talk about dates and holidays

Visit the web-based activities at www.emcp.com

180 *ciento ochenta*

Notes Talk with students about the contents of these pages. Explain that the small picture is an artistic rendition of *La Gritería*, a festival that is described in the *Lectura personal* on page 216. The large photograph depicts four girls in uniform in Costa Rica on a typical school day.

Communicative objectives are provided on page 180 to prepare students for the chapter they are about to study. A list of such functions appears on page 222 so students can do a self-check to evaluate their progress.

Costa Rica
Nombre oficial: **República de Costa Rica**
Población: **3.936.000**
Capital: **San José**
Ciudades importantes: **Alajuela, Cartago, Puerto Limón**
Unidad monetaria: **el colón**
Fiesta nacional: **15 de septiembre, Día de la Independencia**
Gente famosa: **Óscar Arias Sánchez (ex-presidente); Ana Brown-Hernández (escritora)**

Nicaragua
Nombre oficial: **República de Nicaragua**
Población: **4.918.000**
Capital: **Managua**
Ciudades importantes: **Granada, León**
Unidad monetaria: **el córdoba**
Fiesta nacional: **15 de septiembre, Día de la Independencia**
Gente famosa: **Violeta Barrios de Chamorro (ex-presidente); Rubén Darío (escritor)**

Activities

Connections
Have students name some cities in Nicaragua and Costa Rica. Then ask if anyone in class has visited or knows someone who has visited either country. Ask what students know about these countries.

ciento ochenta y uno **181**

Notes The cultural focus of this chapter combines the Central American countries of Costa Rica and Nicaragua. The Costa Rican currency is *el colón,* which is named after Christopher Columbus *(Cristóbal Colón),* who first explored the country on his fourth voyage to the Americas in 1502.

The monetary unit of Nicaragua, *el córdoba,* is also named after an explorer; in this case, Francisco Fernández de Córdoba, who founded the major Nicaraguan cities of Granada and León.

Un sábado en la tienda de artículos electrónicos

 Activity 1

 Activities 34–35

 Activity 1

 Activity 1

 Activity 1

Content reviewed in *Lección A*
- schedules and daily activities
- expressing likes and dislikes
- days of the week
- family
- telling time
- making a sentence negative

Activities

Prereading Activity

Play the audio CD recording of the new vocabulary. Instruct students to close their books or cover the words as they listen to and repeat the new words and expressions. Call on one or two students to see if they can name the setting.

Lección A — Costa Rica

Vocabulario I
Un sábado en la tienda de artículos electrónicos

la grabadora

¡Qué lástima! Ahora no tenemos el CD con las canciones de la película *¡Loco por ti!*

el reproductor de DVDs

el equipo de sonido

Buscamos el CD con la canción *Loco amor*, que es de la película *¡Loco por ti!*

¿No tienen el CD? ¡Caramba! ¡Qué sorpresa!

el quemador de CDs

el dinero

La chica entra a la tienda.

el casete

Los chicos pasan tiempo cada semana en la tienda de artículos electrónicos.

el DVD

el reproductor de MP3

el reproductor de CDs

el disco compacto (CD)

Notes Use the ancillaries listed under Teacher Resources above to introduce the new vocabulary and to begin to teach elements of the lesson. The audio CDs can be used to practice pronunciation of new words; overhead transparencies offer a visual introduction to the new vocabulary as well as spelling reinforcement; written practice is available using Listening Activity 1. Evaluate student comprehension of the new vocabulary using Quiz 1. Pick and choose materials that suit your goals.

1 ¿Qué buscan?

 Selecciona la ilustración que corresponde con lo que oyes.

A

B

En la tienda de artículos electrónicos

C

D

E

F

2 Lógico

Completa en forma lógica las frases de la izquierda con una de las frases de la derecha.

1. Buscamos el DVD...
2. Los chicos pasan...
3. ¡Qué lástima! No tenemos...
4. La chica entra...
5. ¡Caramba, no tenemos dinero...

A. ...para comprar el CD.
B. ...a la tienda de artículos electrónicos.
C. ...el CD con la canción *Loco amor*.
D. ...tiempo cada semana en la tienda de artículos electrónicos.
E. ...de la película *¡Loco por ti!*

Busco un equipo de sonido.

Me gustan las tiendas
Activities 3–5

3 1. Van a ver si tienen el CD de Alejandro Sanz.
2. No, no tienen CDs de Alejandro Sanz.
3. A Marta le gustan las tiendas.
4. Answers will vary.

4 Answers will vary.

5 **Soy Marta**
 ①unos DVDs
 ②unos CDs
 3. un reproductor de CDs
 4. un quemador de CDs
 5. una computadora

Soy Sofía
 6. un equipo de sonido
 7. un reproductor de MP3
 ⑧unos DVDs
 ⑨unos CDs
 10. una impresora láser

Activities

Prereading Strategy
Ask students to tell what they might find in a store where they sell CDs and audio equipment. Then instruct students to open their books and to cover up the dialog with one hand and look at the photographs. Ask them to imagine where the conversation takes place and what the people are saying to one another. Finally, have students look through the dialog quickly to find cognates and words they recognize.

Diálogo I
Me gustan las tiendas

MARTA: Vamos a ver si tienen el CD de Alejandro Sanz en la tienda.
SOFÍA: ¿Otra tienda? No tenemos más dinero.
MARTA: Sólo quiero mirar si tienen el disco compacto.

MARTA: Buenas. Buscamos el CD de Alejandro Sanz.
SEÑOR: No, no tenemos CDs de Alejandro Sanz.
MARTA: ¡Qué lástima! Bueno, gracias.

SOFÍA: ¡Ahora sí! ¡Vamos a casa!
MARTA: No. ¿Por qué no vamos a otra tienda?
SOFÍA: ¡Caramba! ¡Qué sorpresa!

3 ¿Qué recuerdas?

1. ¿Qué van a ver Marta y Sofía si tienen en la tienda de artículos electrónicos?
2. ¿Tienen el CD de Alejandro Sanz en la tienda de artículos electrónicos?
3. ¿A quién le gustan las tiendas?
4. ¿Van a casa las chicas?

4 Algo personal

1. ¿Cuál es tu disco compacto favorito?
2. ¿Qué canción te gusta? ¿Por qué?
3. ¿Te gustan las tiendas de artículos electrónicos? Explica.
4. ¿Qué artículos electrónicos tienes en casa?

5 ¿Lo tienen?

 Write the names Marta and Sofía. Next, listen and list under their names what they are looking for at an electronics store. Then circle any items on the lists that are the same.

Marta　　　Sofía

Notes Several musical instruments were introduced earlier in *Navegando 1*. You may wish to share additional vocabulary with students interested in musical performance: *la guitarra, el bajo, el arpa, el violín, la viola, el violoncelo, el contrabajo (instrumentos de cuerda); la flauta, el clarinete, el oboe, la trompeta, el trombón, la tuba (instrumentos de viento); el* *piano, el tambor, los címbalos, el triángulo, el xilófono, el timbal (instrumentos de percusión).*

Play the audio CD version of activity 5 for listening comprehension practice. A reproducible student answer sheet for the activity is provided for your convenience at the end of the Audio CD Program Manual.

Cultura viva

Costa Rica

El volcán Arenal y una orquídea (orchid) en Costa Rica.

Christopher Columbus visited Cariari (now the city of *Puerto Limón*) in 1502. He named the land Costa Rica (rich coast) because he thought the area offered a wealth of gold and silver. Today, this small, Spanish-speaking country has a population of about three million people, most of whom live in the capital and industrial city of San José. Situated at the center of the American continent, Costa Rica features a diverse landscape of beaches, mountains, volcanos (like the *Irazú*) and rain forests (*selvas tropicales* or *bosques lluviosos*). In fact, Costa Rica is famous throughout the world for its ecological tourism and has dedicated over twenty-five percent of its land as protected areas, national parks and reserves, which are the seasonal home for 10 percent of the world's birds, over 9,000 species of plants and 1,200 species of orchids. The country has a long democratic tradition, spends more money on education than many of its Latin American neighbors and has had no army for more than fifty years. It is noteworthy in this peace-loving nation that one of Costa Rica's former presidents, Óscar Arias, was awarded the Nobel Peace Prize.

Una selva tropical en Monteverde, Costa Rica.

6 Conexiones con otras disciplinas: geografía y ciencias

Use an encyclopedia or search the Internet for information about Costa Rica and plan a vacation there. Find out about places to visit, things to do, what you will see or eat and so forth. Summarize your findings, adding visuals (e.g., photographs, maps), and share your plans with the class.

MODELO Voy a visitar el volcán Irazú en Cártago.

¡Oportunidades!

¿Trabajar en Costa Rica?
How would you like to be paid for traveling and having a good time? Travel-related companies throughout the world require bilingual employees and since tourism is one of the top industries in countries like Costa Rica, the job prospects are nearly limitless. Companies that offer eco-touring, hotels, cruise lines, travel agencies and airlines all need employees who can speak both Spanish and English. If you are hired by a company in a country you would like to visit for pleasure, the rewards are double. For example, during your free time in Costa Rica you might enjoy river rafting, camping on the side of a volcano (*Poás* or *Irazú*) or spending a week in a wildlife sanctuary or government-protected rain forest.

Teacher Resources

 Activity 2

 Activity 2

Answers

6 Creative self-expression.

Activities

Connections
Offer an opportunity to connect with language arts by having students write a journal page about an imaginary trip to Costa Rica. They should include what they saw and did.

Multiple Intelligences (visual)
Have students create a brochure or travel poster in Spanish on Costa Rica using information gathered from the Internet, the library, travel agents, etc. Encourage them to include photographs, magazine clippings or illustrations to make the brochure or travel poster more colorful.

Students with Special Needs
Read the culture section aloud to the student(s) having difficulties, or prepare a tape recording for the student(s) to listen to, allowing time to stop and repeat if needed. Pair a student requiring additional help with another student with strong reading skills and allow them to work on the *Cultura viva* reading together.

Notes Encourage students to contribute any information they may have about Costa Rica, such as recent news stories, articles on the environment, etc.

Activity 6 is a cross-curricular activity that addresses Spanish as well as geography and science.

Have students use a dictionary to find words they do not know as they complete activity 6. Decide what you would like students to do with the completed work. They might present their work to the entire class; you may want them to discuss their project in small groups; or you may choose to have students submit their work as a written assignment.

Answers

7 1. tiene
2. tiene
3. Tienen
4. tenemos
5. tenemos
6. tenemos
7. tengo
8. tengo
9. tienes
10. tengo

Activities

Cooperative Learning

After students complete the dialog for activity 7 in writing, have them form groups of three to practice the dialog orally. Inform the class you will be selecting two or three groups to perform the dialog in front of the class. Encourage groups to be creative and expressive. For example, they can insert the name of a current movie and song, ask for another item at the store, etc.

Students with Special Needs

Practice the verb *tener* by combining it with vocabulary students have already studied: *¿Cuántos hermanos tienes?*; *¿Cuántos tíos tienes?*; *¿Cuántas clases tienes?*; *¿Cuántos años tiene el profesor/la profesora de español?*

Idioma

Estructura

Saying what someone has: *tener*

The verb *tener* (to have) is an irregular verb.

tener			
yo	**tengo**	nosotros nosotras	**tenemos**
tú	**tienes**	vosotros vosotras	**tenéis**
Ud. él ella	**tiene**	Uds. ellos ellas	**tienen**

Tengo un equipo de sonido nuevo. **I have** a new sound system.
Marisol tiene veinte CDs. Marisol **has** twenty CDs.

Note: *Tener* is sometimes used in Spanish expressions where the verb **to be** is used in English. One such expression is *tener (+ number) años*, which you have already used to talk about someone's age.

¿Cuántos años tienes? How old **are you**?
Tengo dieciséis años. **I am** sixteen (years old).

Práctica

7 Un CD para Susana

Completa el diálogo con las formas apropiadas de *tener*.

Jorge: Quiero ver si la tienda de artículos electrónicos (1) un CD para Susana.
Pilar: ¿Qué CD buscas?
Jorge: Ella no (2) el nuevo disco compacto del grupo Presuntos Implicados.
Pilar: Bueno, vamos a preguntar.
Jorge: Hola, señor. ¿(3) Uds. el nuevo disco compacto de Presuntos Implicados?
Señor: Nosotros (4) muchos CDs, pero no (5) CDs de Presuntos Implicados.
Jorge: ¡Caramba! ¡Qué lástima! Muchas gracias.
Pilar: Son las siete, nosotros (6) una hora. ¿Vamos a otra tienda?
Jorge: Está bien, pero sabes, yo (7) un problema. No (8) dinero. ¿Cuánto (9) tú?
Pilar: Pues, Jorge, yo tampoco (10) dinero.

Notes As with all verb paradigms in *Navegando 1*, the *vosotros/vosotras* verb endings have been provided for passive reference. If you have decided to make these forms active, adapt the provided activities as necessary.

Frequently used expressions that include *tener* will be taught in *Capítulo 6*.

The indefinite article is often omitted after the verb *tener*, except when it is used with a modified noun: *Tengo una amiga de Limón, Costa Rica.*

8 Todos tienen algo

Working in pairs, take turns asking one another questions about what various people have. Answer according to what you see in the illustrations, adding any details you wish.

MODELO

don Carlos
A: ¿Qué tiene don Carlos?
B: Tiene un reproductor de MP3 fantástico

1. tú

2. Silvia y su hermano

3. yo

4. Ud.

5. Elvira y Alejandra

6. nosotros

9 Conexión con otras disciplinas: matemáticas

Di cuántos años tienen las siguientes personas de acuerdo al año en que nacieron *(were born)*.

1. Kathy / 1961
2. Doña Marta / 1927
3. Daniel y Estefanía / 2002
4. Keeley / 1989
5. Rafael y Gustavo / 1976
6. el Sr. Cortés / 1956
7. yo / 1953
8. tú / ?

Comunicación

10 Tengo muchos CDs

Working in pairs, talk about your interests in entertainment. For example, find out what kind of music and films you like. You might also discuss such things as how many CDs you have of different types of music, whether or not you have DVDs, which CDs or DVDs you have and what equipment you use to play the CDs and DVDs. Try to determine what interests you have in common *(en común)* and how your interests are different. Be creative!

¡Extra!

Tipos de música

clásica	mariachi	rock
cumbia	merengue	romántica
disco	popular	salsa
flamenco	ranchera	tejana (Tex-Mex)
jazz	rap	vallenato

MODELO
A: ¿Te gusta la música rock?
B: Sí, me gusta mucho. Tengo veinte CDs y tres son de JLo.

Capítulo 5   *ciento ochenta y siete* **187**

Answers

11 Creative self-expression.
12 Possible answers:
1. ¡Qué divertido!
2. ¡Qué frío!
3. ¡Qué sucio!
4. ¡Qué triste!
5. ¡Qué fantástico!

Activities

Critical Listening
Tell the class that you are going to read aloud several recent news headlines. For each headline, the students should provide several logical exclamations by using ¡Qué...! with a noun or with an adjective (e.g., ¡Qué música!; ¡Qué divertido!).

---

 11 ¿Qué tenemos en casa?

Working in small groups, take turns talking about your families' entertainment preferences. First, find out who is in each person's family. Then discuss family members' favorite music, television and radio programs *(programas de televisión y radio)* and movies. Next, find out what kind of electronics your classmates' families have for listening to music or watching movies at home.

MODELO A: Tengo dos hermanos y una hermana. A mis hermanos les gusta ver partidos de fútbol en la televisión. A mi hermana le gusta escuchar música en su reproductor de MP3.
B: Yo tengo un hermano. Le gusta la música merengue y le gusta ver películas en DVD.
C: Yo no tengo hermanos, pero tengo muchos tíos. A ellos les gustan los CDs de música clásica.

Estructura

Expressing strong feelings with *¡Qué* (+ adjective/noun)*!*

There are times when you may wish to express strong feelings — both positive and negative — about something or someone. In Spanish, use *qué* followed by an adjective as the equivalent of **How...!** Similarly, when *qué* is followed by a person, place or thing, it is equivalent to **What a...!**

¡Qué (+ adjective)*!*	*¡Qué* (+ noun)*!*
¡Qué fantástico! How fantastic!	*¡Qué CD!* What a CD!
¡Qué aburrido! How boring!	*¡Qué lástima!* What a shame!

 ### Práctica

12 ¿Cómo reaccionas?

Using *qué* and an adjective, react to the following circumstances.

MODELO *A good friend buys you your favorite CD.*
¡Qué amable!

1. *You are watching a very funny DVD.*
2. *It is very cold outside.*
3. *You just dropped a brand new MP3 player in the mud.*
4. *Your parents tell you some really sad news.*
5. *You have just learned to use your new CD burner.*

¡Qué amable!

Notes Activity 11 reviews family vocabulary and the numbers while offering students an open-ended opportunity to discuss their daily life at home, their family's interests and their entertainment preferences.

Model the examples in the *Estructura* for students with varying tone and intonation to show how *qué* (+ noun) can convey delight *(¡Qué película!)*, fear *(¡Qué perro!)* or sadness/disappointment *(¡Qué lástima!)*.

13 Expresando tu opinión

Write captions for the following photos, using *qué* plus a noun.

MODELO ¡Qué equipo de sonido!

1   **2**   **3**

4   **5**   **6**

 14 Me gusta lo que tienen

The following people have just purchased some electronic equipment. Say what they have and express how much you like each item.

MODELO   Belia / una computadora rápida
Belia tiene una computadora rápida. ¡Qué computadora!

1. mis primos / equipo de sonido nuevo
2. Clara / reproductor de CDs para diez CDs
3. Sonia / dos DVDs fantásticos
4. los López / carro BMW nuevo
5. tú / CD nuevo de Alejandro Sanz

 Comunicación

15 ¡Qué tienda tan estupenda!

Imagine that you and a friend are window-shopping at a fantastic home audio and video store that carries computers, DVD and CD players, CD burners, etc. With your partner, create a dialog in which you talk about some of the things you see, expressing how you feel about each one. Discuss who you know has each item you are looking at and add any other details you wish. Be creative!

MODELO   **A:** Oye, Carlos. ¡Mira! ¡Qué equipo de sonido!
        B: Sí, muy bonito. Rogelio tiene uno.

Capítulo 5   *ciento ochenta y nueve*   **189**

Notes   You may want to teach the students that when they are exclaiming about something bad, the **Oh!** they might say in English is the equivalent of ¡*Ay!* before the exclamation: ¡*Ay, qué lástima!;* ¡*Ay, qué terrible!*

Point out to students that they should use the verb *tocar* (to play) when referring to electronic equipment such as CD and DVD players.

Answers

13 Possible answers:
   1. ¡Qué música!
   2. ¡Qué caballo!
   3. ¡Qué piano!
   4. ¡Qué sorpresa!
   5. ¡Qué casa!
   6. ¡Qué CD!

14 1. Mis primos tienen un equipo de sonido nuevo. ¡Qué equipo de sonido!
   2. Clara tiene un reproductor de CDs para diez CDs. ¡Qué reproductor de CDs!
   3. Sonia tiene dos DVDs fantásticos. ¡Qué DVDs!
   4. Los López tienen un carro BMW nuevo. ¡Qué carro!
   5. Tú tienes un CD nuevo de Alejandro Sanz. ¡Qué CD!

15 Creative self-expression.

Activities

Critical Thinking
As a follow-up to activity 13, show students several visuals featuring interesting people, places and things. For each visual the students should provide several logical exclamations by using ¡*Qué...!* with a noun or with an adjective.

Multiple Intelligences (interpersonal)
Have students say an exclamation in reaction to pictures that other students in class cannot see. Then have the class guess the content of the picture based on their interpretation of the student's facial expression, etc.

Teacher Resources

 Las actividades de Virginia la semana que viene

 Activities 5–6

 Activity 36

 Activity 7

 Activity 4

 Activities 6–7

Activities

Cooperative Learning
Ask students to imagine that they are going to take a one-week trip to Costa Rica. In small groups they should write their itineraries for the week, including the activities planned for each day. They may wish to include information on Costa Rica found in the lesson or additional information by accessing the Internet, doing library research, etc.

Critical Thinking
Have students scan Virginia's schedule for cognates and other words they recognize. Ask if they can guess what month *febrero* is.

Students with Special Needs
Have students identify the days of the week that appear in Virginia's schedule. Then have students read what Virginia has planned for each day.

◆Vocabulario II
Las actividades de Virginia
la semana que viene

Librería Nacional

Febrero

Lunes   Estudiar en la biblioteca para el examen de historia
        Ir a la práctica de fútbol
Martes Comprar el libro nuevo en la librería
        Montar en bicicleta con unas compañeras

Miércoles Ir a la práctica de tenis

Jueves   Llamar a mi tía Pepa primero y, luego, llamar a mi amiga Sara
         Ir a la práctica de béisbol
Viernes Comprar el nuevo CD de Shakira (la tienda abre a las 10:00)
         Fin de semana
Sábado   Hacer la maleta para ir de viaje a la casa de mis abuelos
         Llevar el perro y el gato a la casa de mis primos
Domingo Salir para la casa de mis abuelos

Examen de historia

Prodiscos

Abrimos de
10:00 A.M.
a
8:00 P.M.

Virginia siempre está tan ocupada.
Ella escucha música todos los días.
Ella hace muchos deportes y hace actividades.
Está un poco cansada.

Notes Give students the phrases *salir de viaje* (to leave on a trip), *hacer un viaje* (to take a trip) and *estar de viaje* (to be on a trip), all of which recycle active verb forms.

Refer to the Teacher Resources at the top of the page for ancillaries that offer activities for expanding or reinforcing the content of the pages of the pupil's edition of the textbook.

The word for the month of February *(febrero)* appears here for passive recognition. The months will be taught in *Lección 5B* (page 208).

16 Las actividades de Javier la semana que viene

🔊 Selecciona la letra de la ilustración que corresponde con lo que oyes.

A   B   C

D   E   F

17 El horario de Josefina

Unscramble the following sentences to find out about a typical week in Josefina's life.

MODELO   el lunes / de fútbol / práctica / tiene
El lunes tiene práctica de fútbol.

1. en bicicleta / monta / el martes / con unas compañeras
2. tiene / el miércoles / un partido de fútbol
3. el jueves / con una amiga / de compras / va / a la librería
4. un examen de historia / el viernes / tiene
5. hace / el sábado / para / la maleta / ir de viaje / a Limón
6. de la película / compra / nuevo / el DVD / el domingo / de Penélope Cruz

18 Una semana típica

Make a list of the activities you would normally do on each day of a typical week.

MODELO   El lunes voy a la librería.
El martes tengo clase de piano.

¡Extra!

¿Cómo son los días de la semana?

In most Spanish-speaking countries, the first day of the week is *lunes* and days of the week are not capitalized. Only *sábado* and *domingo* have different plural forms *(sábados, domingos)*. In addition, you must use *el* or *los* with the days of the week when telling when activities or events take place. Spanish does not use *en* as English uses **on**: *Josefina tiene práctica de fútbol el lunes* (Josefina has soccer practice on Monday).

Answers

16 1. D
2. B
3. F
4. E
5. C
6. A
17 Possible answers:
1. El martes monta en bicicleta con unas compañeras.
2. El miércoles tiene un partido de fútbol.
3. El jueves va de compras a la librería con una amiga.
4. El viernes tiene un examen de historia.
5. El sábado hace la maleta para ir de viaje a Limón.
6. El domingo compra el DVD nuevo de la película de Penélope Cruz.
18 Creative self-expression.

Activities

Students with Special Needs
To help students master the days of the week in Spanish, have them practice discussing daily schedules. Give them a day of the week and a time of day. Students then must say something they will do or something that will occur on that day at the time indicated. For example, say *"sábado, a las cuatro."* A possible response might be *"El sábado a las cuatro voy al parque con mis amigos."*

Notes Activity 16 has been recorded as part of the Audio CD Program. A reproducible answer sheet for the activity has been included at the end of the Audio CD Program Manual for your convenience.

Whereas Friday the 13th is considered bad luck in the United States, *martes 13* symbolizes bad luck in many Spanish-speaking countries.

Answers

19 1. Marta está muy ocupada.
2. Primero tiene que estudiar para el examen de biología.
3. Tomás está un poco cansado.
4. A Marta le gustan el tenis y el fútbol.
5. Tiene que ir de viaje a Puntarenas.
20 Answers will vary.
21 1. B; 2. F; 3. A; 4. C; 5. B
22 Check for correct spelling.

Activities

Critical Thinking
Have students look at the photographs as they imagine what the speaker is saying. Then ask if students know where the dialog takes place and what the main theme of the dialog is.

Expansion
Additional questions (*¿Qué recuerdas?*): *¿Cuándo va a estudiar Marta? ¿Por qué?; ¿Cuándo va Marta a la librería?; ¿A quién llama Marta?*

Additional questions (*Algo personal*): *¿Te gusta el tenis?; Los sábados, ¿te gusta jugar al fútbol o te gusta estudiar?; ¿Estás muy ocupado/ocupada? Explica.*

Language through Action
Ask for volunteers to come to the front of the class to act out the dialog ¡Qué semana!

Diálogo II
¡Qué semana!

MARTA: ¡Caramba, tico! Estoy tan ocupada la semana que viene.
TOMÁS: ¿Por qué? ¿Qué vas a hacer?
MARTA: El lunes voy a estudiar para el examen de biología.

TOMÁS: Yo también, pero estoy un poco cansado.
MARTA: El martes tengo práctica de tenis y, luego, de fútbol.
TOMÁS: ¡Pues, Marta, te gusta hacer muchos deportes!

MARTA: El miércoles voy a la librería y el sábado voy a hacer un viaje.
TOMÁS: ¿Adónde vas?
MARTA: A casa de mi tía en Puntarenas. ¡Ay! La voy a llamar. Adiós.
TOMÁS: ¡Adiós! ¡Qué semana!

19 ¿Qué recuerdas?

1. ¿Quién está muy ocupada la semana que viene?
2. ¿Qué va a hacer Marta primero?
3. ¿Quién está un poco cansado?
4. ¿Qué deportes le gusta hacer a Marta?
5. ¿Adónde tiene que ir de viaje Marta?

20 Algo personal

1. ¿Estás un poco cansado/a hoy? Explica.
2. ¿Te gustan los deportes? ¿Cuáles?
3. ¿Qué haces primero los fines de semana? ¿Y luego?

21 ¿Cuándo?

 Marta dice lo que tiene que hacer. Indica el día en que va a hacerlo, según el diálogo.

A. lunes   D. jueves
B. martes   E. viernes
C. miércoles   F. sábado

22 Las actividades de Tomás

 Escribe en una hoja de papel lo que vas a escuchar.

192 *ciento noventa y dos*   **Lección A**

¿Te gustan los deportes?

Notes Point out Marta's use of the *tico* the first time she talks. The term is explained in the *Cultura viva* on page 193.

Activities 19–22 have been recorded for listening comprehension practice. They are included in the Audio CD Program. In addition, reproducible student answer sheets for activities 21–22 are provided for your convenience at the end of the Audio CD Program Manual.

Using a wall map or the *Navegando 1* transparencies, point out where Puntarenas is.

Cultura viva

¡Pura vida!

Costa Ricans have their own regional words and expressions that give their Spanish its own special flavor. For example, they refer to themselves as *ticos* or *ticas,* which is a typical ending they add to everyday words *(chico—chiquitico). Ticos* and *Ticas* are courteous and respectful and do not use *tú* as freely as people from other Spanish-speaking countries. When you are visiting the country, you may hear the phrase *pura vida* (pure life), which is very popular as a positive response or reaction to almost any situation. Other popular expressions in Costa Rica include the following:

expresión	equivalente
¡Buena nota!	Okay!
el chunche	thing (or whatchamacallit)
macho, macha	refers to anyone with blond hair
maje	buddy, pal (among friends)

La Buena Nota
Beachwear and Gifts
• Info Center • Souvenirs
• New and Used Books
• International Newspapers and Magazines
• Vacation Rentals
Tel: 777-1002 Fax : 777-1946
Manuel Antonio between Karahé & Piscis

Una tica macha.

23 ¡Dilo en Tico!

Answer the questions on the left with the most appropriate response on the right.

1. ¿Cómo estás, tico?
2. ¿Vamos a comer?
3. Oye, ¿quién es la macha?
4. Maje, ¿vamos a la práctica de tenis?
5. ¿Qué es ese chunche?

A. La rubia es la tica nueva.
B. Es un reproductor de CDs.
C. No, amigo, hoy estoy un poco cansado.
D. Pura vida.
E. ¡Buena nota!

Capítulo 5

ciento noventa y tres **193**

Activities

Expansion
Provide further basic practice with direct object pronouns by asking students simple questions about various classroom objects. They may make up their answers: *¿Tienes la regla? (Sí, la tengo./No, no la tengo.)*

Idioma

Estructura

Direct object pronouns

A direct object is the person or thing in a sentence that receives the action of the verb directly and answers the question **what?** or **whom?** Add the word *a* (called the *a personal*) before any direct object that refers to a person. Note, however, that you should not use the *a personal* with the verb *tener*.

Veo el reproductor de DVDs.	(I see **what?**)	I see the DVD player.
*Veo **a** la profesora y **a** Sandra.*	(I see **whom?**)	I see the teacher and Sandra.
*Tomás **tiene** dos hermanas en San José.*	(He has **what?**)	Tomás has two sisters in San José.

Sometimes the following direct object pronouns (*pronombres de complemento directo*) replace a direct object.

los pronombres de complemento directo			
me	*me*	**nos**	*us*
te	*you* (tú)	**os**	*you* (vosotros,-as)
lo	*him, it, you* (Ud.)	**los**	*them, you* (Uds.)
la	*her, it, you* (Ud.)	**las**	*them, you* (Uds.)

Notice in the following examples that direct object pronouns usually precede the conjugated form of the verb and any negative expressions (such as *no* or *nunca*) are placed before the object pronouns. In addition, the direct object pronouns *lo, la, los* and *las* can refer to either people or objects.

*No **la** veo.*	I do not see **her** *(Blanca).*
	I do not see **it** *(la biblioteca).*
*Nunca **lo** veo.*	I never see **him** *(Rubén).*
	I never see **it** *(el libro).*

Sometimes the direct object pronoun *lo* is used to refer to a nonspecific direct object or a direct object that is expressed as an idea or a phrase (instead of a person or object).

¿Sabes dónde está el gato?	Do you know where the cat is?
*Sí, **lo** sé.*	Yes, I do (know it).

Note: Some people place an *a* in front of a direct object that refers to a pet they consider part of the family: *Veo **al** perro* (I see the dog).

Notes Extend the explanation if students ask about the use and meaning of the direct object pronoun *la* in a sentence *(No la veo)* by pointing out that English words sometimes appear alike but have different meanings when they are used in different contexts.

Remind students that they have already learned to recognize *la* as the definite article that accompanies a feminine singular noun *(la regla, the ruler).* Now they are learning that *la* may also be a direct object pronoun that replaces a feminine singular noun or pronoun *(No la veo;* I do not see **her**).

Práctica

24 La *a* personal

Completa las siguientes oraciones con la *a personal* cuando sea necesario.

1. El sábado voy a ver __ una película en mi nuevo reproductor de DVD.
2. Veo __ mis abuelos cada semana.
3. Sí, quiero __ mi mamá.
4. Busco __ un quemador de CDs.
5. ¿Te gusta escuchar __ música en un reproductor de MP3?
6. ¿Tienes __ tres hermanos?
7. Voy a llamar __ mi primo el lunes.
8. Llevo __ mi gato a casa de mis padres.

25 Unas preguntas

 Alterna con un(a) compañero/a de clase en hacer y contestar las siguientes preguntas.

1. ¿A quién ves ahora?
2. ¿Buscas a tus amigos los fines de semana para escuchar CDs?
3. ¿A quién llamas hoy por teléfono?
4. ¿A quién escribes un correo electrónico hoy?
5. ¿Comprendes a tu profesor(a) de español?
6. ¿Ves a tus amigos todos los días?

Veo a mi perro.

¿Ves a tus amigos todos los días?

Notes Tell students that the personal *a* has no equivalent in English. Stress how essential its use is in Spanish.

Explain to students that *no lo veo* should be used when they do not see an object named by a masculine noun; *no la veo* is used when they do not see an object named by a feminine noun.

Teacher Resources

 Activity 25

Answers

24 The sentences 2, 3, 7 and perhaps 8 require the *a personal*.

25 Answers will vary.

Activities

Pronunciation *(las letras* r y rr*)*
Explain that the sound of (intervocalic) *r* usually is soft, consisting of a single vibration that is produced when the tip of the tongue briefly touches the roof of the mouth just behind the teeth. The sound is similar to the *dd* in the English word **ladder**. The sound is modified slightly when *r* ends a word. When the letter *r* begins a word, when *r* follows the consonants *l, n* or *s*, and for *rr,* the tongue flaps softly against the palate two, three or even four times. (This can vary from word to word and from one person to another.) Then review and contrast the sound of *r* and *rr* by practicing the following words: *comer, entrar, comprar, ahora, estar, entran, caramba, sorpresa, amor, popular, otros, gracias, dinero* (these words all involve a single tap on the alveolar ridge); *Ricardo, República Dominicana, Costa Rica, rápido, rápidamente, carro, guitarra, pizarra* (these words are trilled).

Spanish for Spanish Speakers
Pair bilingual and nonbilingual students for activity 25.

196

---

26 ¡Lo veo!

With a classmate, take turns asking and answering whether or not you can see the following from where you are sitting.

MODELO **A:** ¿Ves la puerta?
B: Sí, (No, no) la veo.
A: ¿Ves el reproductor de CDs?
B: Sí, (No, no) lo veo.

1. ¿Ves la pizarra?
2. ¿Ves el pupitre?
3. ¿Ves los discos compactos?
4. ¿Ves la computadora?
5. ¿Ves el libro de español?
6. ¿Ves el reloj?
7. ¿Ves los casetes?
8. ¿Me ves?

Estrategia

Avoiding interference with English
Try to avoid letting English interfere with new structures and vocabulary that you are learning in Spanish. For example, the pronouns *lo* and *la* are the Spanish equivalents of the English pronoun **it** only when **it** functions as a direct object of the verb. When **it** is the subject of a sentence, the Spanish subject pronoun is omitted.

*¿**Lo** ves?*	Do you see **it**?
*No, no **lo** veo.*	No, I do not see **it**.
but:	
No está aquí.	**It** is not here.
Es bonito.	**It** is pretty.

27 Un fin de semana con mis abuelos

Completa el párrafo, escogiendo de las siguientes palabras.

me	nos	la
las	lo	los

Este fin de semana voy a ir a Puntarenas para estar con mis abuelos. No (1) veo mucho porque mi familia y yo vivimos en San José. Pero ellos (2) ven en el verano porque les gusta ir a la capital. A mí me gusta pasar tiempo en Puntarenas porque mi abuelo Raúl (3) comprende. A él le gusta mucho la música y (4) toca también en el piano. Las canciones de amor son sus canciones favoritas. Siempre (5) canta. También compra muchos CDs y (6) escucha todos los días. Mi abuelo Raúl es muy cariñoso. ¡(7) quiero mucho!

28 ¿Qué haces todos los días?

 Trabajando con un compañero o una compañera, contesta las siguientes preguntas. Usa *lo, los, la* o *las* para las respuestas.

MODELO **A:** ¿Practicas tenis todos los días?
B: Sí, (No, no) lo practico.

1. ¿Llevas a tu perro a caminar todos los días?
2. ¿Montas en bicicleta todos los días?
3. ¿Lees revistas en español todos los días?
4. ¿Escuchas discos compactos de tu cantante favorito/a todos los días?
5. ¿Llamas a tus parientes todos los días?
6. ¿Cantas canciones de amor todos los días?
7. ¿Ves películas en DVD todos los días?

Practico tenis todos los días.

196 *ciento noventa y seis*

Lección A

Notes After reading the *Estrategia,* write additional examples on the board of object pronouns that cause interference with English. Discuss the sentences with the class.

Have students write answers to activities 26 and 28 in addition to completing the activities orally with a classmate in order to reinforce basic writing skills.

29 Visita Puntarenas

Pretend you and a classmate are members of a tour that is going to visit Puntarenas, Costa Rica. Ask your partner questions using the cues given to find out if members of the group have the indicated items. Your partner should answer each question affirmatively or negatively, using a direct object pronoun.

MODELO   la Sra. Ordóñez / tener / mapa de Puntarenas
   A: ¿Tiene la Sra. Ordóñez el mapa de Puntarenas?
   B: Sí, (No, no) lo tiene.

1. nosotros / tener / maletas
2. tú / tener / discos compactos para el viaje
3. yo / tener / reproductor de CDs
4. Gabriel / tener / reproductor de MP3 para el viaje
5. tú / tener / número de la oficina de turismo de Puntarenas
6. Néstor y Lina / tener / dinero para el viaje

Comunicación

La Playa Coco en Costa Rica.

30 Adivina, adivinador

Try this guessing game *(juego de adivinanzas)* with a classmate. First, one partner writes on a piece of paper the name of another classmate. Then the other partner asks questions about people in class until he or she can guess the person's name. It may be helpful to use the verbs *ver, mirar* and *buscar* as you play the game. Switch roles.

MODELO   **A:** ¿A quién ves?
   B: Veo a un muchacho moreno y delgado.
   A: ¿Ves a Raúl?
   B: Sí. Veo a Raúl.

31 Un viaje a Costa Rica

Imagine that you and a friend are planning to go to Costa Rica. Discuss what you are going to do to prepare for the trip. Then ask and answer questions about when and how you are going to do each activity.

MODELO   **A:** ¿Cuándo compramos el libro sobre Costa Rica en la librería?
   B: Lo compramos el martes. ¿Cuándo vas a hacer las maletas?
   A: Las hago mañana, hoy estoy un poco cansado. ¿Vas a llevar tus CDs de Presuntos Implicados?
   B: Sí, los llevo.

Capítulo 5   *ciento noventa y siete*   **197**

Answers

29 1. ¿Tenemos las maletas?/Sí, (No, no) las tenemos.
2. ¿Tienes discos compactos para el viaje?/Sí, (No, no) los tengo.
3. ¿Tengo el reproductor de CDs?/Sí, (No, no) lo tienes.
4. ¿Tiene Gabriel el reproductor de MP3 para el viaje?/Sí, (No, no) lo tiene.
5. ¿Tienes el número de la oficina de turismo de Puntarenas?/Sí, (No, no) lo tengo.
6. ¿Tienen Néstor y Lina el dinero para el viaje?/Sí, (No, no) lo tienen.

30 Creative self-expression.
31 Creative self-expression.

Activities

Students with Special Needs
Write on the board these examples of how to find a direct object and explain them for the class: They see **the library.** (They see **what?**); Rúben sees **Blanca.** (Rúben sees **whom?**). Extend the activity with additional sentences as needed.

Notes If you have not already done so, you may wish to tell students about the places of interest in and around San José: *el Museo Nacional, la Catedral de San José* and *el Tren Histórico,* which takes passengers on a guided excursion through the rain forest. Also of interest are the day trips to visit *el Parque Nacional del Volcán Irazú.*

Sarchí, a small town near San José, is famous for its handicrafts, especially for the traditional multicolored ox carts for which Costa Rica is known.

Extend activity 31 by having students develop an itinerary for their trip to Costa Rica.

Answers

32 1. Susana va a la escuela a las 8:00 A.M.
2. Va a la casa de una amiga o habla por teléfono.
3. Van a un parque, a la casa de una amiga, al estadio, al cine o a bailar en un club para jóvenes. Regresan a casa a las 11:00 P.M.
4. Escuchan rock en español, rave, pop, vallenato. Les gusta ver el fútbol.
5. No, no trabajan cuando hay escuela.

33 Answers will vary.

Activities

Critical Thinking

Have students create a Venn diagram depicting similarities and differences between teenagers in Costa Rica and teenagers in the United States.

Spanish for Spanish Speakers

Have students write a short composition in Spanish summarizing what they know about Costa Rica. Expand the activity by having students seek out additional information about Costa Rica at the library. As an alternative, have students write a report about Costa Rica's ecological reserves.

Lectura cultural

Los chicos ticos

¿Cómo es la vida diaria[1] de los chicos costarricenses[2]? La revista SOMOS entrevistó[3] a Susana Paniagua Vargas, de dieciséis años, que vive en San Rafael de Heredia, Costa Rica, con esa misma[4] pregunta.

Somos: ¿Cómo es un día típico?

Susana: Voy a la escuela de las 8:00 a.m. hasta las 2:20 p.m. Luego, llego[5] a mi casa y tomo un refresco. Cuando no puedo[6] ir a casa de alguna amiga, por lo general, paso toda la tarde en el teléfono.

Somos: ¿Qué hacen tú y tus amigos los fines de semana?

Susana: Nos reunimos[7] en un parque o en casa de una amiga. Cuando hay partidos de fútbol vamos al estadio. O, vamos al cine y después pasamos a algún[8] club de jóvenes[9] a bailar.

Somos: ¿Qué tipo de música escuchan?

Susana: Rock en español, rave, pop, vallenato[10].

Somos: ¿A qué hora tienen que regresar[11] a casa?

Susana: Entre semana[12] a las 9:00 p.m. pero los fines de semana a las 11:00 p.m.

Somos: Cuando salen, ¿qué medio[13] de transporte usan?

Susana: Generalmente[14] el bus, pero prefiero el taxi. (Para manejar[15] carro se necesita tener 18 años.)

Somos: ¿Algunos trabajan medio tiempo?

Susana: No es común que los jóvenes de mi edad trabajen en Costa Rica cuando hay clases; sin embargo[16], cuando hay vacaciones muchos trabajan en tiendas de ropa.

[1]daily life [2]Costa Rican [3]interviewed [4]same [5]I arrive [6]not able to [7]We get together [8]any [9]youth [10]a combination of African, European and Colombian folkloric sounds [11]return [12]Weekdays [13]means [14]Generally [15]drive [16]however

32 ¿Qué recuerdas?

1. ¿A qué hora va Susana a la escuela?
2. ¿Qué hace por las tardes?
3. ¿Adónde van Susana y sus amigos los fines de semana? ¿A qué hora regresan a casa?
4. ¿Qué música escuchan los jóvenes en Costa Rica? ¿Qué deporte les gusta ver?
5. ¿Trabajan los estudiantes en Costa Rica cuando hay escuela?

33 Algo personal

1. ¿A qué hora vas tú a la escuela? ¿Qué haces después? ¿Tienes un trabajo?
2. ¿Adónde van tú y tus amigos los fines de semana? ¿En qué van?
3. ¿Qué música escuchan tus amigos? ¿Qué deporte ven tus amigos?
4. ¿A qué hora tienes que estar en casa entre semana? ¿Y los fines de semana?

> • How are teenagers in Costa Rica similar to teenagers in the U.S.? What are some differences?

Notes Costa Rica was one of the first countries in the world to be concerned with ecological issues. People in Costa Rica and in the United States are working together to try to find ways to preserve the rain forests and their rich animal life, such as buying some of the land away from developers. Encourage students to learn more about this beautiful country and this issue that is so critical to the health of the entire planet.

¿Qué aprendí?

Visit the web-based activities at www.emcp.com

Autoevaluación
As a review and self-check, respond to the following:

1. Name one item you have in your house from an electronics store. Then name one thing you want to buy there.

2. Name an activity you usually do at least once a week and say what day you do the activity.

3. What activity are you going take part in during the coming weekend?

4. What might you say in Spanish as a reaction in the following situations: you are watching a funny DVD; you heard some bad news about a family member.

5. Ask if a friend sees the following: the new compact discs, the teacher.

6. How would you answer the questions you asked in number 5?

7. What is your schedule for this week? Name two of your activities for next week.

8. Say two things you have learned about Costa Rica.

Palabras y expresiones

Artículos electrónicos
el casete
el DVD
el equipo de sonido
la grabadora
el quemador de CDs
el reproductor de CDs/DVDs/MP3

Actividades
la actividad
el deporte
la librería
la película
la práctica
el viaje

Pronombres
la
las
lo
los
me
nos
te

Otras expresiones
el amor
cada
la canción
¡caramba!
el compañero, la compañera

el dinero
el fin (de semana)
el gato, la gata
la lástima
la maleta
el perro, la perra
un poco
primero
que
¡qué (+ noun)!
que viene
la semana

si
la sorpresa
tan
tener (+ *number*) años
todos los días
hacer un viaje

Verbos
abrir
buscar
entrar
llamar
montar
pasar
tener

¿El dinero? Yo lo tengo.

Capítulo 5

Notes The Costa Rican government provides small plots of land for the citizens of San José so they can plant flowers and vegetables.

Many Central and South American countries are known for their production of coffee. Some coffee connoisseurs consider Costa Rican coffee to be among the best in the world.

The front and back of a bill for 500 *colones* (the currency of Costa Rica) appears at the bottom of the page.

Teacher Resources

Activity 14

Information Gap Activities
Postcard Activities
Funciones de Comunicación

Answers

Autoevaluación
Possible answers:
1. Tengo un reproductor de CDs. Quiero comprar un DVD.
2. Miro una película en DVD los sábados.
3. Voy a buscar una computadora en la tienda de artículos electrónicos.
4. ¡Qué divertido!; ¡Qué lástima!
5. ¿Ves los CDs nuevos? ¿Ves al/a la profesor(a)?
6. Sí, (No, no) los veo. Sí, (No, no) lo/la veo.
7. Answers will vary.
8. Answers will vary.

Activities

Cooperative Learning
Have students work in pairs by asking and answering questions using *tener* and possessive adjectives. Provide some models on the board: *¿Tienes tu cuaderno?; ¿Tiene él/ella su libro?*

Multiple Intelligences (logical-mathematical)
Have students find out the value in dollars for the *colón* (Costa Rican currency) and for the *córdoba* (Nicaraguan currency). Sources for currency exchange rates include newspapers (e.g., the *Wall Street Journal*) and the Internet.

199

La fecha

 Activity 1

 Activity 37

 Activities 1–2

 Activity 1

 Activities 1–2

Content reviewed in *Lección 5B*

- days of the week
- asking for and stating age
- present tense to indicate future
- transportation

Activities

Critical Thinking

Have students scan Virginia's schedule for cognates and other words they recognize. Ask if they can guess what month *febrero* is. Ask if they remember having seen any other months in Spanish. (They saw *febrero* in the schedule on page 190.)

200

Lección B

Nicaragua

Vocabulario I
La fecha

DICIEMBRE

Ayer, dos de diciembre, fue mi cumpleaños. Me gusta mucho celebrar mi cumpleaños.

Aquí estoy con mi hermana menor, mi hermano mayor y mi tía. Mi tía siempre viene para mi cumpleaños.

Mi tía y yo vamos mañana temprano a hacer compras.

El cumpleaños de mi tía es el primero de enero, el Día de Año Nuevo.

Voy a escribir en el periódico de mi colegio sobre mi fiesta de cumpleaños.

Notes The preterite tense form *fue* appears here as a lexical item so students can refer to the past as well as the present and the future when talking about days. All forms of the preterite tense of *ser* appear in the *¡Extra!* on page 201 should you decide to expand the presentation and explain the conjugation of this past tense, which is practiced in activity 3.

The end-of-book Appendices provide a comprehensive overview of the preterite forms that you can use for expanding the presentation to other commonly used verbs.

1 ¿Qué día es?

 Escoge una respuesta correcta a cada pregunta que escuchas.

1. **A.** Navidad **B.** Año Nuevo **C.** mi cumpleaños
2. **A.** sábado **B.** lunes **C.** viernes
3. **A.** sábado **B.** martes **C.** jueves
4. **A.** miércoles **B.** sábado **C.** domingo
5. **A.** 24 de diciembre **B.** 25 de diciembre **C.** 31 de diciembre

2 Un e-mail

Gonzalo escribe un e-mail a su amiga Rosario. Completa el e-mail de una manera lógica.

¡Extra!

El pretérito de *ser*

You already have learned how to form and use the present tense of some verbs in Spanish. Here are the past-tense (preterite) forms of the verb *ser*. Other past-tense verbs can be found in the Appendices at the back of this textbook.

ser

yo	**fui**	nosotros nosotras	**fuimos**
tú	**fuiste**	vosotros vosotras	**fuisteis**
Ud. él ella	**fue**	Uds. ellos ellas	**fueron**

E-Mail

Archivo Ver Mensajes ?

A... Rosario
Cc...
Asunto: Mi cumpleaños

(1), Rosario. ¿Cómo estás? Yo estoy muy (2). Ayer viernes fue mi cumpleaños. ¡17 años!
Fue un día (3). Ahora estoy en Managua con mis tías y mis dos hermanos. Mañana, (4),
voy de compras muy (5) con mi tía y mi hermano (6) de 12 años, Jorge. A mi hermano (7),
Ernesto, no le gusta ir de compras. El martes voy a un partido de fútbol.
Y tú, ¿cuándo vienes? ¿En (8), para Navidad?
Ahora no voy a (9) más porque mi tía necesita la computadora.
Adiós,
Gonzalo

3 Las fechas

Contesta las siguientes preguntas.

1. Si hoy es jueves, ¿qué día es mañana?
2. Si hoy es jueves, ¿qué día es pasado mañana?
3. Si hoy es jueves, ¿qué día fue ayer?
4. Si hoy es jueves, ¿qué día fue anteayer?
5. Si ayer fue domingo, ¿qué día es hoy?
6. Si mañana es martes, ¿qué día fue ayer?
7. Si hoy es miércoles, ¿qué día es mañana?
8. ¿Qué día es hoy?
9. ¿Cuál es la fecha?
10. ¿En qué mes estamos?

Capítulo 5 *doscientos uno* **201**

Teacher Resources

 Activities 1 and 3

Answers

1
1. B
2. C
3. A
4. C
5. B

2 Possible answers:
1. Hola
2. bien
3. fantástico
4. domingo
5. temprano
6. menor
7. mayor
8. diciembre
9. escribir

3
1. Mañana es viernes.
2. Pasado mañana es sábado.
3. Ayer fue miércoles.
4. Anteayer fue martes.
5. Hoy es lunes.
6. Ayer fue domingo.
7. Mañana es jueves.
8. Hoy es....
9. Hoy es el (*today's day, month and year*).
10. Estamos en....

Activities

Prereading Strategy
Have students look at *Vocabulario I* and identify cognates and other words they recognize. Then ask students to summarize what each box on page 200 says.

Pronunciation
Model the pronunciation of several words and phrases from *Vocabulario I* for students to repeat.

Notes Explain to the class that the verb forms that appear in the *¡Extra!* are preterite, or past-tense, forms (referred to as the *pretérito* in Spanish) of the verb *ser*. The chart has been provided for reference purposes only in this *¡Extra!*

The preterite tense will be presented and applied beginning in *Capítulo 8*.

You may decide to mention that the past-tense (*pretérito*) forms of the verbs *ser* and *ir* are identical. Context will make clear which verb is being used.

201

4 1. Es pasado mañana.
2. Va a tener una fiesta.
3. Su hermano mayor viene de Arizona.
4. Viene mañana temprano.
5. Está en la Florida.

5 Answers will vary.

6 1. B
2. A
3. B
4. B
5. A
6. A

Activities

Critical Listening
Play the audio CD version of the dialog. Tell students to listen for the main ideas and two specific events of importance.

Expansion
Additional questions *(Algo personal)*: *¿Tienes una fiesta de cumpleaños?*; *¿Tienes fiestas de cumpleaños con los amigos? ¿con la familia?*; *¿Te gusta la Navidad?*

Prereading Strategy
Ask students how they like to celebrate their birthday. Also ask them what special things other family members do for them on their birthday. Finally, have students look through the dialog quickly to find cognates and words they recognize.

Diálogo I
¿Cuándo es tu cumpleaños?

ISABEL: Oye, Sergio, ¿cuándo es tu cumpleaños?
SERGIO: ¡Chica! ¡Mi cumpleaños es pasado mañana!
ISABEL: ¡Ay, sí!

DARÍO: Y, ¿cómo lo vas a celebrar?
SERGIO: Voy a tener una fiesta. Mi hermano mayor viene de Arizona. Mis primos van a estar aquí también.
ISABEL: ¡Fantástico!

DARÍO: ¿Y cuándo viene tu hermano Jaime?
SERGIO: Viene mañana temprano.
ISABEL: ¿Y tu hermana menor?
SERGIO: Ella está en la Florida, pero viene para la Navidad.

4 ¿Qué recuerdas?

1. ¿Cuándo es el cumpleaños de Sergio?
2. ¿Cómo va a celebrar su cumpleaños?
3. ¿Quién viene de Arizona?
4. ¿Cuándo viene Jaime?
5. ¿Dónde está la hermana menor de Sergio?

5 Algo personal

1. ¿Cuándo es tu cumpleaños?
2. ¿Celebras los cumpleaños con tu familia?
3. ¿Tienes un(a) hermano/a mayor? ¿Menor? ¿Cómo se llama?

6 ¿Cuál es la respuesta?

 Escoge una respuesta correcta a lo que escuchas.

1. A. mi hermano mayor	B. mi hermano menor
2. A. el jueves	B. el domingo
3. A. el 25 de diciembre	B. el 31 de diciembre
4. A. su hermano mayor	B. su hermano menor
5. A. el viernes	B. el sábado
6. A. el día de la Navidad	B. el Día de Año Nuevo

para ti en tu cumpleaños

Notes Point out to students that many Spanish speakers celebrate their birthday and also their saint's day. For example, the saint's day for someone named Juan is June 24 *(el Día de San Juan).*

For students who may celebrate a holiday other than Christmas, offer the following alternatives: *el Janucá* (Hanukkah), *el Kwanzaa* (Kwanzaa).

Cultura viva

Managua, Nicaragua.

El Lago Nicaragua es muy grande.

Nicaragua

Costa Rica's Spanish-speaking neighbor to the north is the largest country of Central America, Nicaragua. This beautiful country of lakes, mountains, volcanoes, forests and friendly people suffered through a long civil war, and a U.S. trade embargo during the 1980s hurt the economy. Many roads are damaged or unpaved and communication systems do not extend to the rural areas. However, improvements are being made and the capital,

Granada, Nicaragua.

Managua, is a large and growing commercial center with a population of one million. It is located on the shores of Lake Managua and is connected by the river Tipitapa to Lake Nicaragua, which was once an ocean bay and today is one of the largest lakes in the world. In fact, it is the only freshwater lake in the world to have swordfish and sharks *(tiburones)*.

7 Nicaragua

¿Cierto o falso?

1. Costa Rica está muy lejos de Nicaragua.
2. La capital de Nicaragua es Managua.
3. Un millón de personas viven en la capital.
4. Managua no está cerca del Lago Managua.
5. El Lago Nicaragua tiene tiburones.

8 Conexión con otras disciplinas: geografía

Find out more about Nicaragua on the Internet or at the library. Then create a map in Spanish showing major cities, lakes, rivers, mountains, surrounding countries and oceans.

Idioma

Estructura

Telling where someone is coming from: *venir*

The present tense of *venir* (to come) is very similar to that of the irregular verb *tener.*

venir			
yo	**vengo**	nosotros nosotras	**venimos**
tú	**vienes**	vosotros vosotras	**venís**
Ud. él ella	**viene**	Uds. ellos ellas	**vienen**

¿*Vienes* tú para la Navidad?
No, pero **vengo** para el Año Nuevo.

Are you coming for Christmas?
No, but **I am coming** for New Year's Day.

¿Viene Ud. para la Navidad?

Práctica

9 El cumpleaños de la abuela

Completa el párrafo que sigue con las formas apropiadas de *venir*.

Pasado mañana es el cumpleaños de la abuela. Va a cumplir ochenta años y hay una fiesta grande en un hotel de Managua. Pero, ¿cómo (1) todos a la fiesta? Pues, mis tíos y mis primos (2) en carro de León. ¡Mi tío siempre (3) a celebrar el cumpleaños de la abuela! Claro, yo (4) a pie porque el hotel está cerca de mi casa. Francisca, la nieta favorita de la abuela, (5) en avión de Costa Rica. Doris y Leonardo (6) de Granada el día de la fiesta. El tío Ricardo (7) en bicicleta porque también vive muy, muy cerca. Y tú, ¿cómo (8)?

Notes The *vosotros/vosotras* verb endings are included for passive recognition. If you have decided to make these forms active, adapt the provided activities as necessary.

You can teach other verbs in the present tense anytime you would like using the Appendices, a handy reference at the end of *Navegando 1.*

10 La fiesta de Año Nuevo

Sergio's parents are having a New Year's party. Working in pairs, take turns asking and answering how each of the guests will arrive. Include an appropriate means of transportation (a pie, en autobús, bicicleta, carro, metro, taxi) in your answers.

MODELO **A:** ¿Cómo vienen tus abuelos a la fiesta?
B: Mis abuelos vienen en taxi.

1. los tíos
2. Isabel y tu hermana
3. Darío
4. el primo de Sergio
5. los padres de Sergio
6. mis abuelos
7. yo
8. tú

Los abuelos vienen en taxi.

Repaso rápido: Present tense to indicate the future

You have learned to use the present tense of a verb to say what people are doing now or what they do frequently. The present tense of a verb can also be used to refer to the not-too-distant future as long as a future time expression is used.

*Ella **viene** a mi casa el fin de semana.*   She **is coming** to my house on the weekend.
*Mañana **celebro** mi cumpleaños.*   Tomorrow I **will celebrate** my birthday.
*¿Uds. **están** en casa el domingo?*   **Will you be** home on Sunday?
*Laura **va** a la fiesta el sábado.*   Laura **is going** to the party on Saturday.

Mañana celebro mi cumpleaños.

Notes As you review the contents of the *Repaso rápido,* remind students that a definite article followed by a day (or days) of the week can convey the message that something happens on that/those given day(s): *Los martes tengo que trabajar; No voy a la fiesta el sábado.* Unlike in English, in Spanish there is no need for a preposition.

Teacher Resources

Activity 10

GV Activity 6

Answers

10 Answers will vary.

Activities

Expansion
To practice the use of the present tense in expressing the not-too-distant future, ask students to explain their plans for later today and tomorrow. Summarize their activities on an overhead transparency or the chalkboard and then review the future by asking students to restate their plans with *ir a* (followed by an infinitive).

11 El concierto de Navidad

Pretend that you and your partner are in charge of the invitations for the Christmas holiday concert at your school. Using this incomplete invitation list, take turns asking and answering questions about who is attending on Saturday night and who is attending on Sunday night.

MODELO **A:** ¿Mis padres?
　　　　 B: Vienen el domingo.

Lista de invitaciones

sábado	domingo
Marta y su prima	Srta. López y su hermano
Gabriel	Sr. Robles
yo	mi padres
tú	yo
la madre de Fernando Peña	tú

1. ¿El Sr. Robles?
2. ¿Gabriel?
3. ¿La Srta. López y su hermano?
4. ¿Marta y su prima?
5. ¿Tú?
6. ¿La madre de Fernando Peña?
7. ¿Yo?
8. ¿Tú y yo?

INVITACIÓN
Colegio los Pinos

Gran Concierto
de
NAVIDAD

12 Los planes del mes

Pretend today is *el miércoles 8* and you are talking with a friend about activities that happened or will happen this month. Among the activities that will happen, include a birthday celebration that you are having for someone you know and say who is coming to the celebration. Use the calendar as a guide.

MODELO **A:** ¿Cuándo es la fiesta para celebrar el cumpleaños de Julia?
B: La fiesta es pasado mañana, el viernes diez.
A: ¿Y quién viene a la fiesta?
B: Vienen muchos amigos.

L	M	M	J	V	S	D
		1	2	3	4	5
6	7	⑧	9	10	11	12
13	14	15	16	17	18	19

13 Año nuevo, vida nueva

Imagine today is December 26th and you are writing an e-mail to your best friend to tell him/her about the New Year's party your family is having for your relatives and special friends. Tell them who is invited and how and when each person is coming. Include as many details as you can.

¡Feliz Año Nuevo!

Capítulo 5

doscientos siete **207**

Answers

12 Creative self-expression.
13 Creative written expression.

Activities

Cooperative Learning
Ask students to bring in magazine pictures of a site they have learned to name in Spanish (beach, city, school, etc.). Then ask them to talk about where they are now and if they are coming back, using the cutouts. For example: *Estamos en la playa ahora. Vengo a la playa mañana también. ¿Vienes a la playa mañana?*

Notes Offer these helpful expressions for completing activities 12 and 13: *¿Qué día es hoy?* (What day is today?); *Hoy es lunes.* (Today is Monday.); *Ayer fue domingo.* (Yesterday was Sunday.); *Mañana es martes.* (Tomorrow is Tuesday.); *Los sábados no tengo clases.* (I don't have classes on Saturday.); *Voy el viernes que viene.* (I am going next/this coming Friday.).

Stress the use of cardinal numbers when expressing the date, noting *el primero* as the only exception.

Teacher Resources

 Los meses

 Activity 4

 Activities 38–39

 Activity 7

 Activity 3

 Activities 7–9

Activities

Expansion

Use overhead transparencies 38 and 39 to introduce the new words and expressions in *Vocabulario II*. Begin by showing students transparency 38 and say the months one at a time in Spanish. Students should repeat after you. Continue with overhead transparency 39 and practice the numbers in Spanish, allowing students to see how the word is spelled.

Students with Special Needs

Say a month of the year and have students tell you the months that follow in order. Repeat this activity several times starting with a different month.

Vocabulario II
Los meses

marzo, abril, mayo

junio, julio, agosto

diciembre, enero, febrero

septiembre, octubre, noviembre

Notes In relation to the twelve months, you may wish to introduce the four seasons of the year at this time: *la primavera, el verano, el otoño, el invierno.*

Activity 14 is intended for listening comprehension practice. Play the audio CD of the activity that is part of the Audio CD Program or use the transcript that appears in the ATE introduction if you prefer to read the activity yourself.

**Los números
del 101 al 999.999**

101	ciento uno
122	ciento veintidós
200	doscientos, -as
201	doscientos uno
300	trescientos, -as
400	cuatrocientos, -as
500	quinientos, -as
600	seiscientos, -as
700	setecientos, -as
800	ochocientos, -as
900	novecientos, -as
1.000	mil
1.001	mil uno
1.999	mil novecientos noventa y nueve
2.000	dos mil
100.000	cien mil

14 ¿Cuándo cumplen años?

 Selecciona la letra de la fecha que corresponde con lo que escuchas.

A. 16.06 C. 20.05 E. 12.11
B. 02.03 D. 30.08 F. 23.01

15 ¡Me gusta!

Say how much you like or dislike the following situations, using *gustar* and any expressions you have learned.

MODELO El mes que viene es diciembre. ¡Es Navidad!
¡Qué bueno! Me gusta mucho./No me gusta ni un poquito.

1. Las horas de clase no pasan rápidamente.
2. Mi cumpleaños es en enero.
3. Un día vamos a ser viejos.
4. Soy muy joven.
5. Hoy es el día de mi cumpleaños.
6. Tengo una fiesta y vienen todos mis amigos.
7. A veces celebro mi cumpleaños con mis abuelos.
8. No tengo CDs ni reproductor de CDs.

16 Conexión con otras disciplinas: matemáticas

Continue the pattern up to the number shown in parentheses.

1. ciento cincuenta, trescientos, cuatrocientos cincuenta... (1.050)
2. cuatrocientos, seiscientos, ochocientos... (2.000)
3. nueve mil, ocho mil, siete mil... (1.000)
4. treinta y cinco mil seiscientos, treinta mil quinientos, veinticinco mil cuatrocientos... (5.000)
5. cien mil, noventa mil, ochenta mil... (10.000)

Capítulo 5 *doscientos nueve* **209**

Notes Before beginning activity 14, point out to students that the day precedes the month. The day and the month are often separated by a period. *(8.10 would be el ocho de octubre.)* Given that this order differs from what they are used to in English, remind students to pay special attention when completing any form in Spanish that requires birthdates or other dates of importance.

Answers

17 1. Es el veinticinco de octubre.
2. Cumple diecisiete años.
3. Los años pasan rápidamente.
4. No le gusta la idea ni un poquito.
18 Answers will vary.
19 1. Cierto.
2. Cierto.
3. Falso. / ...es joven.
4. Falso. / ...diecisiete años.
5. Cierto.
6. Cierto.

Activities

Prereading Strategy
Instruct students to cover up the dialog with one hand and look at the photographs. Ask them to imagine where the conversation takes place and what the people are saying to one another. Finally, have students look through the dialog quickly to find cognates and words they recognize.

Diálogo II
¡Feliz cumpleaños!

ISABEL: ¿Cuál es la fecha de hoy?
DARÍO: Hoy es el veinticinco de octubre.
ISABEL: ¡Hoy es el cumpleaños de Sergio!
DARÍO: ¡Pues vamos a su casa!

ISABEL: ¡Feliz cumpleaños, Sergio!
DARÍO: ¿Cuántos años cumples? ¿Veinticinco? ¿Treinta?
SERGIO: ¡Oye, no! Yo soy joven. Cumplo diecisiete años.
DARÍO: Ja, ja. Pero los años pasan rápidamente.

SERGIO: ¡Los años y el tiempo pasan rápidamente!
ISABEL: Sí, en dos meses estamos en Navidad.
SERGIO: ¡Qué bueno!
DARÍO: ¿Bueno? No me gusta la idea ni un poquito.

17 ¿Qué recuerdas?

1. ¿Cuándo es el cumpleaños de Sergio?
2. ¿Cuántos años cumple Sergio?
3. ¿Qué pasan rápidamente?
4. ¿Le gusta la idea de la Navidad a Darío?

18 Algo personal

1. ¿Cuándo es la fecha de tu cumpleaños?
2. ¿Cuántos años vas a cumplir?
3. En tu opinión, ¿pasan los años rápidamente?

¿Te gusta la Navidad?

19 ¡Feliz cumpleaños, Sergio!

 Di si lo que oyes es cierto o falso, según el Diálogo II. Si es falso, corrige la información.

OCTUBRE 25

Notes Activities 17–19 have been recorded for listening comprehension practice. They are included in the Audio CD Program. A reproducible student answer sheet for activity 19 is provided for your convenience at the end of the Audio CD Program Manual.

Cultura viva

Celebramos el Día de los Reyes Magos.

Los días de fiesta

Family life in Nicaragua, Costa Rica and throughout the Spanish-speaking world reflects Catholic traditions such as baptisms, communions and weddings. Holidays honoring local patron saints, as well as other Catholic holidays, are important events throughout the country. In addition, the Nicaraguan people are very sociable and on *días especiales* they enjoy being with their family and friends and perhaps listening to music, dancing and sharing good food. Here are some important holidays (*días especiales*) celebrated throughout the Spanish-speaking world:

1. el Día de Año Nuevo (*New Year's Day*) el primero de enero

La Nochebuena es el 24 de diciembre.

2. el Día de los Reyes Magos (*Epiphany*) el 6 de enero
3. el Día de San Valentín (*Valentine's Day*) el 14 de febrero
4. la Semana Santa (*Holy Week*) variable date, usually April
5. el Domingo de Ramos (*Palm Sunday*) variable date, usually April
6. el Viernes Santo (*Good Friday*) variable date, usually April
7. el Domingo de Resurrección (*Easter Sunday*) variable date, usually April
8. el Día del Trabajo (*Labor Day*) el primero de mayo
9. el Día de la Raza/de la Hispanidad (*Columbus Day*) el 12 de octubre
10. el Día de Todos los Santos (*All Saints' Day*) el primero de noviembre
11. la Nochebuena (*Christmas Eve*) el 24 de diciembre
12. la Navidad (*Christmas*) el 25 de diciembre
13. el Día de los Santos Inocentes (*Fools' Day*) el 28 de diciembre
14. la Noche Vieja (*New Year's Eve*) el 31 de diciembre

 20 Los días de fiesta

Create a list of at least ten holidays or events in Spanish. Then, working with a partner, take turns asking and answering in what month the holidays or events take place.

MODELO el Día de San Valentín

A: ¿En qué mes es el Día de San Valentín?
B: Es en febrero.

21 Comparando

Compare the holidays in the *Cultura viva* with holidays where you live. For example, say which holidays you celebrate that are not listed and which holidays are celebrated on the same date or different dates.

Capítulo 5   *doscientos once* **211**

Notes Let students know that November 1st (*el primero de noviembre*) can be also referred to as *Día de los muertos* or *Día de los difuntos*.

Another way to say **holidays** in Spanish is *días festivos*.

El Día de la Raza is referred to as *el Día de la Hispanidad* in some countries, such as Costa Rica. Similarly, some people use *el Día de los Enamorados* instead of *el Día de San Valentín*.

Teacher Resources

 Los días de fiesta

 Activity 5

 Activity 10

 Activity 4

Answers

20 Answers will vary.
21 Creative self-expression.

Activities

Expansion
Ask students to find the name of a holiday that is not listed in *Cultura viva* and that is celebrated by Spanish-speaking people where you live. Have students investigate and report on the significance of the holiday in your state.

Multiple Intelligences (intrapersonal)
As a follow-up to *Los días de fiesta*, ask students which of the days listed they celebrate with family or friends. For each day listed they should briefly describe their typical activities.

Spanish for Spanish Speakers
Ask students to write a dialog between two friends who are in charge of preparations for a party to celebrate any of *Los días de fiesta* listed on page 211. You may also instruct them to perform the completed dialog with another student in front of the class.

211

Idioma

Estructura

Using the numbers 101 – 999,999

You have already learned to use *cien* (100) before a noun. Use *ciento* in place of *cien* for the numbers 101 to 199: *Tengo **cien** casetes y **ciento** veinte discos compactos.* The numbers from 200 to 999 have masculine and feminine forms that agree with the noun they describe: *Hay quinient**os** ochenta chic**os** y seiscient**as** cincuenta chic**as** en el colegio.* Mil (1,000) has only one form. Numbers beginning with *mil* are written with a period in Spanish instead of a comma: *1.000.*

4.000	=	cuatro mil
105.800	=	ciento cinco mil ochocientos
999.999	=	novecientos noventa y nueve mil, novecientos noventa y nueve

When the year is written in Spanish, it has no period. When it is spoken, it is read like any other four-digit number, **not** grouped two numbers at a time, as is done in English.

1562	=	mil quinientos sesenta y dos

Práctica

22 Un regalo de cumpleaños

Imagine you are shopping for a birthday gift while visiting friends in Managua and you see the items that follow. Make a list of each article along with the price written out as you would write out numbers on a check. Remember that the prices are given in *córdobas nicaragüenses (NIO)*.

MODELO

 El reproductor de CDs

NIO 4.256

1. NIO 582

2. NIO 291

3. NIO 11.640

4. NIO 7.275

5. NIO 2.910

6. NIO 873

212 *doscientos doce* **Lección B**

Notes Explain to the class that in countries where the period is used in place of the comma, the comma is used to separate the decimal figures from the number. In other words, the period and comma are switched around: *NIO 1.459,75* (to refer to *córdobas*).

Be sure students understand the abbreviation *NIO* in activities 22 and 24: *córdobas nicaragüenses*.

23 Conexión con otras disciplinas: matemáticas

Imagine that Nicaragua is hosting a world youth meeting *(reunión juvenil mundial)* and you are in charge of recording how many boys and girls are attending the event and where they are from. Write out how many people are coming from each of the following countries.

MODELO 2.800 / Ecuador
Vienen dos mil ochocientos muchachos de Ecuador.

1. 153 / El Salvador
2. 721 / Bolivia
3. 2.199 / Argentina
4. 362 / Venezuela
5. 586 / Colombia
6. 3.537 / México
7. 3.738 / Chile
8. ¿Cuántos muchachos vienen en total?

¿Cuántos muchachos vienen del Ecuador?

24 ¿Cuánto dinero tienen?

Trabajando en parejas, alternen en preguntar y contestar cuánto dinero tienen las personas indicadas y qué van a comprar.

MODELO tú / NIO 200

A: ¿Cuánto dinero tienes tú?
B: Tengo doscientos córdobas.
A: ¿Qué vas a comprar?
B: Voy a comprar unos calcetines.

1. tus padres / NIO 4.500
2. Gloria / NIO 950
3. Antonio / NIO 5.700

4. los hermanos Ruiz / NIO 18.000
5. la profesora / NIO 820
6. yo / NIO 250

Capítulo 5   *doscientos trece* **213**

Notes Activity 23 makes the cross-curricular connection to mathematics.

Using maps at the front of *Navegando 1,* overhead transparencies or a wall map, show students where the countries mentioned in activity 23 are located.

Comunicación

 25 La fiesta de fin de año

Imagine you and a friend are in charge of organizing a party for 200 people to celebrate the end of the year at your school. The school has allocated a budget of $5,000 *(dólares)* for the party. Working in pairs, prepare a list of the things you would need for the party and discuss how much money you would need to allocate for each item. Be creative!

MODELO **A:** Bueno, necesitamos mil quinientos dólares para comida.
B: Mil quinientos es mucho. Para comida necesitamos setecientos.
A: Está bien. ¿Y para refrescos?
B: Para los refrescos necesitamos trescientos cincuenta dólares.

> Fiesta de fin de año
> • comida
> • refrescos
> • música

Estructura

Asking for and giving the date

Use *¿Cuál es la fecha de hoy?* to ask for the date in Spanish. The answer follows this pattern:

> form of *ser* + *el* + number for day of month (or *primero*) + *de* + month + *de/del* + year

Note: The word *primero* (abbreviated *1º*) is used for the first day of a month instead of *uno*.

Es el ocho de marzo.	It is March eighth.
Es el primero de enero.	It is January first.

In written form the date may appear as follows:

8 de marzo de 2006   or   *8.3.04 (or 8/3/06)*

The following expressions may be helpful when talking about days and dates:

¿Qué día es hoy?	*Hoy es viernes.*
¿En qué mes estamos?	*Estamos en mayo.*
¿En qué año?	*En 2006.*

When you want to express **on** in Spanish, use the definite article *el* or *los*.

*No voy **el sábado**.*   I am not going **on Saturday.**

Práctica

26 Fechas memorables

Give the following dates, first in numbers and then in words.

1. *(day, month and year you were born)*
2. *(date you obtained or plan to obtain your driver's license)*
3. *(year you plan to buy a car)*
4. *(year you will be able to vote)*
5. *(year of your high school graduation)*
6. *(date of some other important future event in your life)*

¿Cuál es la fecha
de tu graduación?

27 Conexión con otras disciplinas: historia

In pairs, take turns asking and answering questions about several important dates in Nicaragua's history. Follow the model.

MODELO Nicaragua / tener / su fiesta nacional de independencia: septiembre
A: ¿En qué mes tiene Nicaragua su fiesta nacional de independencia?
B: Nicaragua tiene su fiesta nacional de independencia en septiembre.

1. los nicaragüenses / celebrar / 200 años de independencia: 2021
2. en Nicaragua / el Día del Trabajo / ser: 1º mayo
3. los nicaragüenses / celebrar / el Día de la Liberación: 19 de julio
4. Nicaragua / declarar / la independencia de España: 1821

Comunicación

28 Días especiales

With another student, talk about events or special occasions you celebrate during the year. Discuss when these special days occur (name the day of the week, if possible), say what you do to make the day(s) special and mention what you do or do not like about each occasion. If possible, bring a photo that depicts how you celebrate or observe the special event.

MODELO ¿Qué celebras en mayo?
Celebro el Día del Trabajo.

Notes Because students do not know how to form the past tense yet, allow them to use the historical present tense for activity 27.

Activity 27 makes the cross-curricular connection to history.

Answers

29 1. Nicaragua es el único país que celebra La Gritería.
2. Es el siete de diciembre.
3. Empieza a las 6:00 P.M.
4. Hay cohetes y grupos de personas que van de casa en casa. Cantan canciones a la Virgen María y, luego, comen frutas y dulces.
5. Esta celebración es en honor a la Virgen María.

30 Answers will vary.

Activities

Spanish for Spanish Speakers
Have students write a short composition in Spanish summarizing what they know about Nicaragua. Expand the activity by having students seek out additional information about Nicaragua at the library.

Lectura personal

Cantantes y grupos musicales

Dirección http://www.emcp.com/músico/ola/e.diario-4.htm ▲ Archivo Edición Ver Favoritos Herramientas Ayuda

página principal   miembros   e-diario

Grupo musical La OLA

Nombre: **Ceci Eugenia Madrigal**
Edad: **18 años**
Cumpleaños: **28 de febrero**
País natal: **Uruguay**
Actividad favorita: **bailar**

Les da dulces a la gente en la Gritería.

Queridos amigos, estamos ahora en Nicaragua. Ayer fue el concierto en Managua... ¡Fue fantástico! Me gustan mucho los nicaragüenses porque son muy alegres. Esta noche estamos en casa de un pariente de Manuel que vive en Managua. Es el siete de diciembre y ¡qué noche! Desde las 6:00 P.M. se escuchan cohetes[1]. Hay grupos de niños y adultos que van de casa en casa gritando[2], "¿Quién causa tanta alegría? ¡La concepción de María!"[3] Luego, cantan canciones especiales a la Virgen María y las personas de las casas les dan[4] frutas y dulces[5]. ¡Novecientas personas han venido[6] a esta casa! ¿Qué celebración es? Se llama La Gritería, una fiesta católica muy popular que solamente se celebra en Nicaragua. Interesante, ¿verdad?

[1]firecrackers [2]shouting [3]Who causes so much joy? The Conception of the Virgin Mary! [4]they give them [5]candy [6]have come

29 ¿Qué recuerdas?

1. ¿Cuál es el único país que celebra La Gritería?
2. ¿En qué fecha es la fiesta de La Gritería?
3. ¿A qué hora empieza la fiesta?
4. ¿Cómo celebran La Gritería en Nicaragua?
5. ¿En honor a quién es esta celebración?

• **What holiday does La Gritería remind you of? Compare and contrast the two holidays.**

30 Algo personal

1. ¿Cuál es una fiesta popular en tu comunidad? ¿Es una fiesta religiosa o no?
2. ¿Qué fiestas religiosas conoces? ¿En qué fecha se celebran?
3. ¿Hay una fiesta que solamente se celebra en los Estados Unidos? ¿Cuál(es)?

216 *doscientos dieciséis*   **Lección B**

Notes Be sure students understand that *La Gritería* is unusual because, as Ceci points out, although it is a Catholic celebration, it is celebrated only in Nicaragua.

Encourage students to find out more about Nicaragua by going to the following Web sites:

Nicaraguan Institute of Tourism
http://www.intur.gob.ni/
Electronic Embassy
http://www.embassy.org
Organization of American States
http://www.oas.org
general travel information
http://www.expedia.com

¿Qué aprendí?

Autoevaluación

As a review and self-check, respond to the following:

Visit the web-based activities at www.emcp.com

1. How would you say in Spanish that your birthday was yesterday?

2. Imagine your birthday is today. In Spanish, say who is coming to the party.

3. What do you say to wish someone a happy birthday in Spanish? How would you ask how old the person is?

4. Write an e-mail to a friend describing your plans for next week.

5. What day is today? What was yesterday?

6. What is today's date?

7. Name two common holidays/celebrations in Spanish-speaking countries.

8. Say two things you have learned about Nicaragua.

Palabras y expresiones

Para describir
feliz
joven
mayor
menor
pasado,-a
poquito
primero,-a
rápidamente
viejo,-a

Números
ciento
doscientos,-as
trescientos,-as
cuatrocientos,-as

quinientos,-as
seiscientos,-as
setecientos,-as
ochocientos,-as
novecientos,-as
mil

Fechas
abril
agosto
el año
el Año Nuevo
anteayer
ayer
el cumpleaños
diciembre

enero
febrero
la fecha
julio
junio
marzo
mayo
el mes
la Navidad
noviembre
octubre
pasado mañana
septiembre

Verbos
celebrar
cumplir (años)
fue
venir

Otras expresiones
a veces
¿de veras?
¡Feliz cumpleaños!
la idea
ni
temprano
la vez (pl. veces)

Teacher Resources

📝 **Activity 13**

🗣 **Information Gap Activities**
Postcard Activities
Funciones de Comunicación

Answers

Autoevaluación
Possible answers:
1. Mi cumpleaños fue ayer.
2. Mi amiga viene. Vienen mis primos.
3. ¡Feliz cumpleaños! ¿Cuántos años cumples?
4. The e-mails should include the phrase *El fin de semana que viene voy a...*
5. Answers will vary.
6. Answers will vary.
7. Answers will vary.
8. Answers will vary.

Activities

Critical Listening
To practice recognition of larger numbers, divide students into groups of ten and tape a number (zero through nine) on the back of each student. In turn, as you state different numbers, the groups compete by seeing who can line up first in the appropriate order. (**Note:** If the class does not divide evenly into groups of ten, certain digits may be repeated in a group or the remaining students may serve as number readers and judges.)

Notes Nicaragua shares the same date for the *fiesta nacional* as Costa Rica.

Note that in many Spanish-speaking homes throughout the world, gifts are traditionally given on January 6, *el Día de los Reyes Magos.* Children look forward to the arrival of the three Wise Men, who often arrive the afternoon or evening the night before.

In the hot climate of Nicaragua and Costa Rica, Hispanic men often wear an embroidered dress shirt, called a *guayabera,* instead of a coat and tie. It fits loosely, is open at the neck, and is cut straight across the bottom so it can be worn outside the trousers.

Teacher Resources

 Viaje por Costa Rica

Activities

Critical Listening
Play the audio CD version of the reading. Tell students to listen for the main ideas the speaker is addressing. Finally, have several individuals state what they believe the main theme of the reading is.

Expansion
Ask if students can identify other popular ecotourism destinations.

Prereading Strategy
Tell students they do not need to understand every word in order to read in Spanish. Equivalents for most unknown words have been provided to help students enjoy the contents of the readings without having to look up important but passive vocabulary. Be sure to cover the *Preparación* and *Estrategia* prior to beginning *Tú lees*.

Tú lees

Estrategia

Scanning for details before reading
Quickly look over what you are about to read and search for specific details. For example, imagine you want to buy something and are hoping to find a sale in the newspaper. You would not read every advertisement you find. Instead, you would look very quickly for the item and prices. The same holds true when you scan any article you are about to read: Instead of trying to understand every word, just look for specific details that stand out and that help you understand the main idea of a reading.

Preparación
Busca estos detalles como preparación para la lectura.

1. ¿En qué país hace viajes Safaris Corobicí?
2. En los viajes, ¿qué observan los turistas?

Viaje por Costa Rica

Safaris Corobicí
Viajes en bote por Costa Rica

- Especializado en tours escénicos en el Río[1] Corobicí para naturalistas y observadores de aves[2]

- Viajes en bote diarios–desde las 7 A.M. hasta las 4 P.M.

- Viajes desde 2 horas hasta medio día de duración

Los viajes pueden ser arreglados para su comodidad[3]–familias con niños[4] o personas con requerimientos especiales. Organizamos viajes para grupos grandes (21 hasta 100 personas) o grupos pequeños (1 hasta 20 personas). Nuestros guías reman[5] el bote y Uds. sólo disfrutan[6] del río. Excepto por algunas[7] pequeñas partes, este río no tiene aguas turbulentas. En el Río Corobicí, hay varias zonas para nadar. Este es un paraíso donde los turistas pueden observar muchas aves tropicales, monos con caras blancas[8], tres especies de iguanas y cocodrilos en las orillas[9] del Río Corobicí. Uds. sólo necesitan traer un traje de baño[10], un sombrero[11], una cámara, unos binoculares y loción de protección solar.[12]

[1]river [2]birds [3]comfort [4]children [5]row [6]enjoy [7]some [8]white faced monkeys [9]riverbank
[10]bathing suit [11]hat [12]sun-protection lotion

Notes Costa Rica has evolved into a popular destination for ecotourism, a style of tourism focused on environmental issues and evaluation of the individual's own connections to nature.

José Figueres Ferrer was president of Costa Rica from 1953 to 1958 and again from 1970 to 1974. He led a rebellion in 1948 to abolish the army and devote the military budget to education. Today Costa Rica has one of the highest literacy rates in Latin America.

Escapes Ecológicos

Turismo Colón

Información General

A ¿Qué recuerdas?

1. ¿Para cuántas personas son los viajes?
2. ¿Por cuánto tiempo es el viaje más corto?
3. ¿A qué hora son los viajes?
4. ¿De cuántas personas es un grupo grande?
5. ¿Qué necesitan traer los turistas?

B Algo personal

1. ¿Te gusta hacer viajes en bote? ¿Dónde?
2. ¿Te gusta observar animales? ¿Cuáles?
3. ¿Qué te gusta de los safaris Corobicí?

Vamos a hacer un viaje por Costa Rica.

El tucán es un ave tropical que vive en Costa Rica.

Unos monos con caras blancas.

Answers

A
1. Son para grupos grandes y para grupos pequeños también.
2. Es por dos horas.
3. Son desde las siete de la mañana hasta las cuatro de la tarde.
4. De 21 hasta 100 personas.
5. Necesitan traer un traje de baño, un sombrero, una cámara, unos binoculares y loción de protección solar.

B Answers will vary.

Activities

Expansion

Additional questions (*¿Qué recuerdas?*): *¿De cuántas personas es un grupo pequeño?*; *¿Quiénes disfrutan del río?*; *¿Tiene el río aguas turbulentas?*; *¿Puedes nadar en el río Corobici?*

Additional questions (*Algo personal*): *¿Te gusta la naturaleza?*; *Te gusta nadar?*; *¿Dónde te gusta nadar más, en un río, en un lago o en una piscina?*

Technology

Ask students to search the Internet for ecotours in Costa Rica. Have them summarize their findings in a written report. Then ask for one or two volunteers to share their findings about dates, prices, locations, etc. with the rest of the class as the basis for a class discussion.

Capítulo 5

doscientos diecinueve **219**

Notes Encourage students to find out more about Costa Rica by going to the following Web sites:

Costa Rica Tourism Board
http://www.tourism-costarica.com
Electronic Embassy
http://www.embassy.org

Organization of American States
http://www.oas.org
general travel information
http://www.expedia.com

Tú escribes

Estrategia

Brainstorming

Brainstorming consists of setting your mind free to think about everything that relates to a certain topic. Concentrating on one or two of the main ideas and jotting down what comes to mind will provide information you need to organize and express your ideas about a topic.

A Brainstorm about your favorite and least favorite holidays of the year. Think about as many ideas as you can relate to both of them—where you are, people you are with, activities and so on. Finally, list what you like or do not like about each holiday.

B Write at least two short paragraphs in Spanish that contrast the two holidays you have chosen. In one paragraph write about the holiday that you like and in the other write about the one you do not like. Develop each contrasting theme of your paper with information such as when the holiday occurs, whom you are with, what activities go on, where you are, how you feel about the holiday and anything else you wish to include. Finally, add graphics or artwork to make the composition attractive and interesting.

¿Te gusta el Día de los Reyes Magos?

Proyectos adicionales

A Conexión con la tecnología

Imagine you are about to take a vacation to Costa Rica. Locate information from the Internet or at the library to help you plan your trip (e.g., cities you wish to visit, weather, food, things to do, important events, geography, means of transportation, where you can stay and cost). Finally, create an itinerary for every day of the trip and present it to the class.

B Comparaciones

Choose a Spanish-speaking country and find out how the people there celebrate a special holiday of your choosing. You can do your research at the library, on the Internet or, if you prefer, you can use e-mail and write to a key pal who lives in the selected country. Find out about traditions that make the holiday special, if there are certain foods that people eat and any other information you might consider interesting. Then compare how the holiday is similar or different in that country and where you live.

C Conexión con otras disciplinas: música

Working in pairs, complete a survey *(encuesta)* identifying what kind of music your peers enjoy. Ask if they are familiar with Latin American music *(vallenato, merengue, salsa,* etc.) or Spanish music *(flamenco).* Then find out if someone watches musical performances in Spanish on television and, if so, when. Share your findings with the class.

Bailamos el merengue todos los fines de semana.

MODELO A cinco estudiantes les gusta la música rock. A mí me gusta la música popular y a diez estudiantes les gusta el rap. Tres estudiantes ven cantantes famosos que cantan en español los sábados en Univisión.

Nombre	Tipo de música	Música latina o española que conocen	Ven cantantes que cantan en español
yo	popular	flamenco	no
Carlos	rock	salsa	no
Stephanie	rap	no	sí, sábados en Univisión
David	rap	merengue	no

Teacher Resources

 Situation Cards

P *Capítulo 5*

Answers

A Creative self-expression.
B Creative self-expression.
C Answers will vary.

Activities

Connections
Have students do a report about Lake Nicaragua. They may want to search the Internet and/or write to the Nicaraguan embassy.

Multiple Intelligences (artistic)
Have students design their own birthday card in Spanish like the one on page 202.

Technology
Have each student choose a Spanish-speaking country that he or she would like to visit. Each student may search the Internet for a list of its holidays, or *días festivos*. Students can then compare the number and type of the country's holidays with those in U.S. culture.

Notes Activity C offers cross-curricular connections to music.

You may wish to have students create a Venn diagram to help them visualize the similarities and differences when doing activity B of the *Proyectos adicionales*.

Display the more interesting projects around the room or arrange to display the better projects in a public place in the school if one is available. (You may want to ask students first if they would mind having their work displayed for others to see.)

Teacher Resources

 Trabalenguas

Activities

Expansion

Ask students to use the Internet or library resources to obtain the populations of the following cities: León, Granada, Matagalpa, Bluefields (Nicaragua); Limón, Cartago, Puntarenas (Costa Rica). As an alternative, provide the populations on a visual. Ask students to correctly state the numbers in Spanish.

Multiple Intelligences (musical)

Call on students to say what kind of music they like. Play excerpts of various types of the music listed in the *¡Extra!* Section on page 187. Have students try to identify the type of music being played. Then have students look for examples of music from Spanish-speaking countries and bring them to class. They may find newspaper or magazine articles, concert advertisements, television shows, movies, library records, etc. As an extension, have students play a piece of music or a song and describe what they like or do not like about it. As an alternative to this activity, borrow from the school band (or have students bring in) some percussion instruments that are used in Latin American music (bongos, tambourines, maracas, etc.). Students should take turns playing the instruments to accompany examples of Latin American music that you select and play for the class.

Repaso

Now that I have completed this chapter, I can...

	Go to these pages for help:
describe everyday activities.	182
say what someone is going to do.	190
seek and provide personal information.	200
write about everyday life.	200
say what someone likes or dislikes.	209
express strong feelings.	209
talk about dates and holidays.	209

I can also...

identify some objects in an electronics store.	182
describe music you like.	182
identify opportunities to use Spanish for work or leisure travel.	185
talk about life in Costa Rica and Nicaragua.	185, 203
talk about the days of the week.	190
recognize how my English can interfere with learning Spanish.	196
read in Spanish about things to do in Costa Rica.	198
talk about the months.	200
state when something happened or will happen.	200
use the numbers 101– 999,999.	209
use some weather expressions.	209
identify and discuss special days.	211
write in Spanish about special times of the year.	211

Trabalenguas

Hoy ya es ayer y ayer ya es hoy,
ya llegó el día y hoy es hoy.

¡Viento en popa!

Notes Loose translation of the *Trabalenguas:* Today is already yesterday and yesterday is today, the day has arrived and today is today.

Note for your students that some holidays may have more than one name. *El Domingo de Pascua* is also called *el Domingo de Resurrección* and *la Víspera del Día de Todos los Santos* is also called *la Noche de Brujas.* Additionally, *el Día del Trabajo* can be *el Día de los Trabajadores; el Día de los Muertos* sometimes is *el Día de los Fieles Difuntos; el Día de Fin de Año* can be *la Noche Vieja. El Día del Padre* could be *el Día de los Padres* and *el Día del Año Nuevo* could be *el Año Nuevo,* depending upon the country.

Vocabulario

a veces sometimes, at times *5B*
abril April *5B*
abrir to open *5A*
la **actividad** activity, exercise *5A*
agosto August *5B*
el **amor** love *5A*
anteayer the day before yesterday *5B*
el **año** year *5B*
el **Año Nuevo** New Year's Day *5B*
el **artículo** article, item *5A*
ayer yesterday *5B*
buscar to look for *5A*
cada each, every *5A*
la **canción** song *5A*
¡caramba! wow! *5A*
el **casete** cassette *5A*
celebrar to celebrate *5B*
ciento one hundred *5B*
el **compañero**, la **compañera** classmate, partner *5A*
cuatrocientos,-as four hundred *5B*
el **cumpleaños** birthday *5B*
cumplir (+ *años*) to become (+ *number of years*), to reach *5B*
¿de veras? really? *5B*
el **deporte** sport *5A*
diciembre December *5B*
el **dinero** money *5A*
doscientos,-as two hundred *5B*
el **DVD** DVD, digital videodisc *5A*
electrónico,-a electronic *5A*
enero January *5B*
entrar to go in, to come in *5A*
el **equipo de sonido** sound system *5A*
febrero February *5B*
la **fecha** date *5B*

feliz happy *5B*
¡Feliz cumpleaños! Happy Birthday! *5B*
el **fin (de semana)** weekend *5A*
el **gato**, la **gata** the cat *5A*
la **grabadora** tape recorder *5A*
hacer un viaje to take a trip *5A*
la **idea** idea *5B*
joven young *5B*
julio July *5B*
junio June *5B*
la the (*f., s.*) *5A*
las the (*f., pl.*) *5A*
la **lástima** shame *5A*
la **librería** bookstore *5A*
llamar to call, to telephone *5A*
lo him, it, you (*d.o.*) *5A*
los them, you (*d.o.*) *5A*
la **maleta** suitcase *5A*
marzo March *5B*
mayo May *5B*
mayor older, oldest *5B*
me me (*d.o.*) *5A*
menor younger, youngest *5B*
el **mes** month *5B*
mil thousand *5B*
montar to ride *5A*
la **Navidad** Christmas *5B*
ni not even *5B*
nos us (*d.o.*) *5A*
novecientos,-as nine hundred *5B*
noviembre November *5B*
ochocientos,-as eight hundred *5B*
octubre October *5B*
pasado,-a past *5B*
pasado mañana the day after tomorrow *5B*
pasar to pass, to spend (*time*) *5A*
la **película** movie, film *5A*
el **perro**, la **perra** dog *5A*
poquito a very little (*bit*) *5B*
la **práctica** practice *5A*
primero first (*adverb*) *5A*
primero,-a first *5B*

¡qué (+ *noun*)! what a (+ *noun*)! *5A*
que that, which *5A*
el **quemador de CDs** CD burner *5A*
que viene upcoming, next *5A*
quinientos,-as five hundred *5B*
rápidamente rapidly *5B*
el **reproductor de CDs/DVDs/MP3** CD/DVD/MP3 player *5A*
seiscientos,-as six hundred *5B*
la **semana** week *5A*
septiembre September *5B*
setecientos,-as seven hundred *5B*
si if *5A*
la **sorpresa** surprise *5A*
tan so *5A*
te you (*d.o.*) *5A*
temprano early *5B*
tener (+ *number*) **años** to be (+ *number*) years old *5A*
tener to have *5A*
todos los días every day *5A*
trescientos,-as three hundred *5B*
un poco a little (bit) *5A*
venir to come *5B*
la **vez** (*pl.* veces) time *5B*
el **viaje** trip *5A*
viejo,-a old *5B*

Tengo una maleta vieja.

¿Es el cumpleaños del perro?

Teacher Resources

 La familia Miranda

 Module 2

 Episode 5

Testing/Assessment
Test Booklet
Portfolio Assessment

Activities

Communities
Ask students to listen to a local radio station or visit a music store to find out the names of some of the top-rated Spanish-speaking singing groups and/or songs. Students should bring a sample of the music to share with the class.

Expansion
Bring in (or have students bring in) samples of music styles and discuss the following: *Salsa* is an Afro-Latin musical rhythm that originated in New York City among Caribbean immigrants. *Flamenco (música flamenca)* is music from southern Spain that is usually played on the guitar and that is characterized by a syncopated and varied rhythm. *Merengue* is a fast tropical rhythm from the Dominican Republic. *Mariachi* is a very popular type of music from Jalisco, Mexico, that is played by a small group of musicians who use a large guitar (*guitarrón*), smaller guitars, trumpets and violins.

Notes Remind students that the words and expressions listed on page 223 are provided as a handy reference list of vocabulary they are required to know from *Capítulo 5*. Students should review and test themselves on the content of the *Vocabulario* in preparation for the chapter test and for future chapters in *Navegando 1*.

Model words from the list by having students repeat after you. Then call on individuals to repeat words to simultaneously practice and evaluate pronunciation.

TPRS *Capítulo 6*

Capítulo 6

Connections with Parents

Involve more parents and guardians in their children's school lives. Ask for volunteers to assist in class; assign activities that require students and their parents or guardians to interact; have the parents or guardians sign homework. The benefits of increased parental and guardian involvement in student learning are undeniable.

Capítulo **6**

En casa

Objetivos

❖ **identify items in the kitchen and at the dinner table**

❖ **express obligations, wishes and preferences**

❖ **talk about everyday activities**

❖ **state an opinion**

❖ **discuss food and table items**

❖ **point out people and things**

❖ **describe a household**

❖ **tell what someone says**

❖ **say how someone is doing**

Visit the web-based
activities at
www.emcp.com

224 *doscientos veinticuatro*

Notes Be sure to review the communicative objectives that are provided on page 224 in order to give students an idea what they will be able to do after completing the chapter. A list of the functions appears at the end of the chapter on page 266 so students can do a self-check to evaluate their progress.

Contexto cultural

Venezuela
Nombre oficial: **República de Venezuela**
Población: **23.917.000**
Capital: **Caracas**
Ciudades importantes: **Maracaibo, Valencia, Barquisimeto**
Unidad monetaria: **el bolívar**
Fiesta nacional: **5 de julio, Día de la Independencia**
Gente famosa: **Simón Bolívar ("El Libertador"); Rómulo Gallegos (escritor)**

Colombia
Nombre oficial: **República de Colombia**
Población: **43.071.000**
Capital: **Bogotá**
Ciudades importantes: **Medellín, Cali, Cartagena**
Unidad monetaria: **el peso**
Fiesta nacional: **20 de julio, Día de la Independencia**
Gente famosa: **Fernando Botero (pintor); Gabriel García Márquez (escritor)**

Activities

Connections
Ask students to name some cities in Venezuela and Colombia. Then ask if anyone in class has visited or knows someone who has visited either country. Ask if students can tell the class any interesting information about these countries.

doscientos veinticinco **225**

Notes The cultural focus of this chapter combines the South American countries of Venezuela and Colombia. The two countries have had many connections over the years. They remain connected today due in part to the disputes about oil reserves located between the two countries.

Students will find it interesting that Venezuela is named after Venice due to its extensive waterways; Colombia is named for Christopher Columbus.

The small photograph on page 224 is of a house in Colombia. The large photograph depicts a typical family in their home.

> **Content reviewed in *Lección A***
> • family
> • express courtesy
> • discuss food
> • the verb *tener*

Activities

Expansion

Use overhead transparencies 40 and 41 to introduce the new words and expressions in *Vocabulario I*. Begin by showing students transparency 40. Point to one of the objects in the kitchen and identify it in Spanish. Students should repeat after you. Continue on to the next item and repeat the process. As a second step, show students transparency 41. Once again identify the objects in Spanish, allowing students to see how each word is spelled.

Prereading Strategy

Play the audio CD recording of the vocabulary and have students repeat the words while showing them overhead transparency 40.

Lección A

Venezuela

Vocabulario I
¿Qué tenemos que hacer en la cocina?

¿Qué cosas tenemos que hacer?

el horno microondas

la estufa

Él enciende las luces.

el refrigerador

¿La pongo con los platos de todos los días?

¡Ah, sí! ¡Ya los veo!

el plato

Para empezar, Santiago, debes cerrar la puerta del refrigerador.

Después, pienso que tienes que hacer más arepas. Y, Daniela, tú debes poner la mesa.

No. Prefiero los platos especiales.

el lavaplatos

el fregadero

los cubiertos

Los chicos quieren ayudar en la cocina. Mañana ellos viajan otra vez a Colombia.

226

Notes The verb *poner* is presented here as new vocabulary in the expression *poner la mesa*. Students will not learn all forms of *poner* until *Lección 7B*. For the time being, however, they are able to use all present-tense forms of this new verb except for the first-person singular form *pongo*. Page 424 of the Appendices contains a chart with the present-tense forms.

Tell students that *poner* is also used with appliances to mean **to turn on**: *poner la televisión*.

la luz (las luces)

el comedor

la lámpara

la mesa

las servilletas

el vaso

1 ¿Qué tenemos que hacer en la cocina?

Selecciona la ilustración que corresponde con lo que oyes.

A   B   C   D   E   F

2 ¿Adónde llamo?

Imagine you live in Caracas, Venezuela, and several appliances in your home are broken. Decide whom you would call to come and have them fixed.

ELÉCTRICOS GALAXIA

¡Los mejores técnicos en reparación de electrodomésticos en Caracas!

Todas las marcas: estufas, lavaplatos, fregaderos y triturador de desperdicios, lavadoras, secadoras, aspiradoras, planchas. Garantía total, domicilios, Av. Junín, llámenos hoy: 614-22-64.

A

CENTRALES

Somos especialistas en la reparación de microondas, refrigeradores, lavaplatos, licuadoras, tostadoras, procesadores de comida. Servicio a domicilio. Venta de repuestos. 40 años sirviendo a Caracas. Servicio las 24 horas del día. Línea directa: 215-58-78.

B

1   2   3   4   5

Teacher Resources

Activity 1

Activities 1–2

Activity 1

Answers

1 1. E
2. F
3. B
4. A
5. D
6. C

2 1. A
2. B
3. A, B
4. B
5. A

Activities

Prereading Strategy
Have students look at *Vocabulario I* and identify cognates and other words they recognize. Then ask students to summarize what each box on page 226 says.

Pronunciation
Model the pronunciation of several words and phrases from *Vocabulario I* for students to repeat.

Students with Special Needs
Help students with the two advertisements on page 227. Then give a model for activity 2.

Notes Select ancillaries listed under Teacher Resources at the top of pages 226 or 227 for introducing and reinforcing the new content on these pages. For example, you may wish to introduce vocabulary using overhead transparencies 40 and 41 or you may prefer to use the audio CD. Written activities for practicing the new vocabulary are available in the Workbook and in the Grammar and Vocabulary Exercises Manual. Choose support items that help you accomplish your goals.

Diálogo I

¿Me vas a ayudar?

JULIO: ¿Qué haces, mamá?
MAMÁ: Hago la comida. ¿Me vas a ayudar?
JULIO: ¿Qué debo hacer?

MAMÁ: ¿Por qué no enciendes el lavaplatos?
JULIO: ¿Qué más?
MAMÁ: ¿Por qué no limpias el refrigerador?

JULIO: No, ¡el refrigerador no! Prefiero otra cosa mamá.
MAMÁ: Bueno, ¿por qué no pones la mesa?
JULIO: ¡Sí, cómo no!

3 ¿Qué recuerdas?

1. ¿Qué hace la mamá de Julio?
2. ¿Va a ayudar Julio a su mamá?
3. ¿Qué hace Julio primero?
4. ¿Julio va a limpiar el refrigerador o prefiere hacer otra cosa?

4 Algo personal

1. ¿Ayudas en la cocina en tu casa?
2. ¿Qué cosas haces para ayudar en la cocina?
3. ¿Qué cosas hay en la cocina de tu casa?

5 ¿Qué hacen para ayudar?

 Mira las palabras de la lista. Di la que corresponde con lo que oyes.

el refrigerador	la lámpara	la estufa
el vaso	la mesa	el fregadero

Cultura viva

Explorando Venezuela

When European explorers came to the shores of Lake Maracaibo, they named the area Venezuela (meaning "Little Venice") because the homes that were located along the shores of the lake reminded them of Venice, Italy. Venezuela is a land of varied geography, with wonderful beaches *(Playa Medina, Playa Colorada)*, mountains

Caracas, Venezuela.

(Andes), plains and deserts *(Médanos de Coro)*. One of the most sensational natural attractions found in the country is Angel Falls *(el Salto del Ángel)*, the highest waterfall in the world. Venezuela also has big industrialized cities, such as Caracas, the capital and economic and political center of the nation. Other large cities include Maracaibo, known for its petroleum production, Mérida, a cultural and intellectual center, and Puerto Cruz, a very popular destination for tourists from all over the world.

At one time Venezuela had one of the highest standards of living in South America due to its many natural resources, especially the vast abundance of oil *(el petróleo)* found near Lake Maracaibo. The country is one of the world's principal producers of oil and an important member of OPEC (in Spanish, *OPEP,* or *Organización de Países Exportadores de Petróleo)*. Venezuela is also known for its pearl industry. In addition to exporting big quantities of oil and pearls *(las perlas)*, the country is one of the world's largest exporters of cocoa beans *(el cacao)*, the basic ingredient for chocolate.

When Venezuelans gather, they enjoy talking, laughing and sharing good food, such as *arepas, ropa vieja* and *cachapas.* Investigate this fascinating South American country. You may be surprised by what you find!

Venezuela exporta petróleo, perlas y cacao.

6 Explorando Venezuela

Completa las siguientes oraciones sobre Venezuela.

1. *Venezuela* quiere decir...
2. Dos playas famosas en Venezuela son...
3. Una de las atracciones más importantes de Venezuela es...
4. La capital de Venezuela es...
5. Tres productos de exportación de Venezuela son...
6. Tres comidas famosas de Venezuela son ropa vieja, cachapas y...

Notes *Ropa vieja*, literally **old clothes,** is a hearty stew-like dish of shredded meat and vegetables that is served over rice or in a warm flour tortilla. *Cachapas* are similar to corn cakes. They can be eaten with cheese, whipped cream or butter.

The acronym OPEC stands for the Organization of Petroleum Exporting Countries.

New words that students may not recognize include the following: *exportadores* (exporters); *petróleo* (oil).

Teacher Resources

 Activity 2

 Activity 3

Answers

6 1. Little Venice.
   2. Playa Medina y Playa Colorada.
   3. el Salto del Ángel.
   4. Caracas.
   5. petróleo, perlas y cacao.
   6. arepas.

Activities

Expansion
Ask students to use the Internet and/or library to learn more about a topic they find interesting in the *Cultura viva.* They should then list in Spanish three or four interesting facts they found and share the information with the class.

Technology
Have students search the Internet for Web pages advertising trips to Venezuela. Are any of the sites written in Spanish? Students should print information from a Spanish-language site, skim it for phrases that they recognize and then share it with the class.

229

Answers

7 Possible answers:
1. Debo
2. Tengo que
3. Debo
4. debo
5. Tengo que
6. Tengo que

8 1. Ellos deben ayudar a su madre
2. Mi hermana debe llamar....
3. Tengo que poner....
4. Debes cerrar siempre....

Activities

Cooperative Learning
Have students write three sentences stating they have to do something when they should be doing something else. Then have students work in small groups correcting one another's sentences and making appropriate changes. Inform students that groups have five minutes to make any necessary corrections, after which time you will select students from each group to read aloud their sentences. Example: *Sé que debo ayudar en la cocina, pero tengo que tocar el piano.*

Idioma

Estructura

Expressing obligations with *tener que* and *deber*

Use the expressions *tener que* (+ infinitive) and *deber* (+ infinitive) when you wish to express what someone is obligated to do. Whereas *tener que* (+ infinitive) indicates what someone has to do, *deber* (+ infinitive) implies more of a moral obligation or what someone should do.

Tengo que poner la mesa.	**I have to** set the table.
Debo ayudar a mi madre.	**I should (ought to)** help my mother.

Práctica

7 *¿Debo o tengo que?*

Complete the following sentences with the correct form of *deber* or *tener que* as appropriate.

1. Mi padre tiene mucho que hacer en la cocina. __ ayudarlo.
2. __ comer todos los días para vivir.
3. Los refrescos están calientes y me gustan fríos. __ ponerlos en el refrigerador.
4. Para comer la comida caliente rápidamente __ usar el horno microondas y no la estufa.
5. Mañana hay un examen de historia. __ estudiar mucho hoy.
6. El fin de semana viajo a Colombia. __ tener un pasaporte.

8 *¿Deben hacerlo o tienen que hacerlo?*

Create sentences using the following cues and adding the appropriate form of either *deber* or *tener que*, according to what fits logically.

MODELOS lavar los platos mañana (Pedro)
Pedro tiene que lavar los platos mañana.

estudiar primero y hacer deportes después (los estudiantes)
Los estudiantes deben estudiar primero y hacer deportes después.

1. ayudar a su madre (ellos)
2. llamar a nuestra abuela (mi hermana)
3. poner los platos sucios en el lavaplatos (yo)
4. cerrar siempre la puerta del refrigerador (tú)

Los estudiantes deben estudiar.

Notes Point out that *deber* is a regular *-er* verb.

Students have already learned the various forms of *tener* in *Capítulo 5*. Do a quick review of the forms of *tener* at this time. Explain that the verbs *tener* and *venir* have this same stem change *e → ie*, except for the *yo* irregular forms of these two verbs (*tener: tengo; venir: vengo*).

Remind students that when two verbs appear together (e.g., *tener que* + verb), the first is conjugated and the second must remain an infinitive.

Comunicación

 9 Nuestras obligaciones

First, create a list of at least two things you must do and two things you should do this week. Then, in small groups, talk about your schedules and obligations.

MODELO **A:** El jueves tengo que ir de compras.
B: Por las tardes yo debo estudiar.

Estructura

Stem-changing verbs: e → ie

The verb *pensar* (to think) requires the spelling change *e → ie* in all forms of the present-tense stem except for *nosotros* and *vosotros*. Note, however, that this stem change does not affect the regular verb endings (*o, as, a, amos, áis, an*).

pensar (ie)	
p**ie**nso	pensamos
p**ie**nsas	pensáis
p**ie**nsa	p**ie**nsan

When combined with other words, *pensar* has several different uses:

- When followed immediately by an infinitive, *pensar* indicates what someone plans or intends to do.

  ***Pienso ir** a Venezuela.*   I plan to go to Venezuela.
  *¿Cuándo **piensas ir?***   When do you intend to go?

- When combined with *de*, *pensar* is used to ask for an opinion. Use *pensar* followed by *que* to express your opinion or thoughts.

  *¿Qué **piensas de** los platos nuevos?*   What do you think of the new plates?
  ***Pienso que** son bonitos.*   I think they are pretty.

- *Pensar* may be combined with *en* to indicate whom or what someone is thinking about.

  *¿**En** qué **piensas?***   What are you thinking about?
  ***Pienso en** mi tarea de español.*   I am thinking about my spanish homework.

Pensar (ie) is just one of many *e → ie* stem-changing verbs. (The letters in parentheses after the infinitive are to help you identify these verbs and to indicate the change that occurs in the stem.) Others include the following: *cerrar (ie), empezar (ie), encender (ie), preferir (ie), querer (ie)* and *sentir (ie)*.

Note: The verb *empezar* is used with *a* when an infinitive follows, as in *Empiezo a estudiar* (I am beginning to study).

Answers

9 Creative self-expression.

Activities

Expansion
After completing activity 9, have a member of each group summarize the information for the class as a way of practicing the plural forms. *Dos personas en nuestro grupo tienen que hacer....; Todos nosotros debemos estudiar,* etc.

Students with Special Needs
Review the conjugation of *-ar* verbs before introducing the stem change *e → ie*.

Notes Explain to students that the letters *ie* shown in parentheses after infinitives listed in *Navegando* serve as a help for students to remember how these verbs are formed: *cerrar (ie).*

Note for students that the verbs *tener* and *venir* have this same stem change *e → ie* except for the *yo* irregular forms.

Comparisons. Note the distinction between *pensar* (to think) and *creer* (to believe). Tell students that the equivalent in Spanish for **I think so** is *Creo que sí* (I believe so). Likewise, to say **I don't think so**, they should use *Creo que no* (I don't believe so).

Práctica

10 ¿Qué piensan hacer?

Tell what these people are planning to do, using words from each column and
the appropriate form of *pensar*. Verb forms may be repeated.

A	B	C
Juan y Raúl	pienso	hacer un almuerzo especial
unos amigos y yo	piensas	hacer arepas
yo	piensa	comer en el comedor
una amiga	pensamos	buscar los platos de todos los días
Ana y Eva	piensan	poner la mesa
tú		ayudar en la cocina

11 Un almuerzo especial

Completa el siguiente párrafo con la forma correcta de los verbos indicados
entre paréntesis.

Paco y Aurora *1. (pensar)* hacer un almuerzo especial para su amiga María. Ella
va a estudiar a Colombia por un año. Aurora *2. (pensar)* hacer unas arepas y Paco
3. (querer) hacer un pollo con mole y una ensalada. Ellos *4. (empezar)* a hacer la
comida muy temprano. Otros amigos *5. (pensar)* venir al almuerzo. Rafael
6. (venir) y Carmen y José *7. (pensar)* venir también. Graciela lo *8. (sentir)*
mucho, pero no *9. (venir)* al almuerzo porque tiene que estudiar. Pedro *10. (deber)*
ayudar a sus padres en la casa y *11. (preferir)* venir después del almuerzo. Él *12.*
(querer) decirle "adiós" a María. Y tú, ¿qué *13. (pensar)*? ¿*14. (venir)* al almuerzo?

12 ¡Somos diferentes!

Use the cues that follow to create sentences that
compare and contrast how different Sara and Julio are
from their parents.

> **MODELO** empezar a escuchar música / empezar a leer
>   Si nosotros empezamos a escuchar música, ellos
>   empiezan a leer.

1. querer nadar en la playa / querer caminar en la playa
2. pensar ir al parque / pensar ir a un museo
3. encender el reproductor de CDs / encender el
   televisor
4. tener que hacer la tarea / tener que lavar los platos
5. querer comer en un restaurante / querer hacer arepas
   y comer en casa otra vez
6. cerrar la puerta / abrir las ventanas
7. preferir ir al cine / preferir ver un DVD en casa
8. empezar a mirar la televisión / empezar a escuchar la
   radio

¿Prefieres nadar o caminar en la
playa? (Los Roques, Venezuela.)

Notes Although students have already
seen the expression *lo siento,* in this
chapter they are learning how to
conjugate the entire present-tense
conjugation of *sentir* and other stem-
changing verbs.

Remind students that when a verb like
pensar is followed by another verb, the
second verb must be an infinitive.

13 Una fiesta

 In pairs, take turns asking and answering questions about what your family and friends are thinking about, according to the illustrations, as you all prepare for a holiday dinner.

MODELO tu madre

    A: ¿En qué piensa tu madre?

    B: Mi madre piensa en la comida.

1. yo

2. Gloria

3. tus hermanos

4. Andrés y Camila

5. nosotros

6. tú

❖ Comunicación

14 Pensamos hacer mucho

In small groups, talk about some things you are planning to do next summer or at some time during your life. Be creative. You might also discuss what you think of each person's aspirations. Then decide what your remarks have in common. One student should report the results of your discussion to the class.

MODELO
    A: Pienso viajar a otro país. Quiero ir a Venezuela el verano que viene.
    B: En el verano yo pienso ayudar a mis padres en casa y leer cien libros.
    C: Pienso cantar con JLo en un concierto.

¡Oportunidades!

¿Piensas viajar a otro país?
Do you enjoy travel? Have you ever wondered what it might be like to live in another country? What if you were transferred to Venezuela to work? Do you think you would enjoy the experience? Do any members of your family live in another country? Would you like to visit them if they did? Can you think of any benefits your language skills might afford you while traveling?

Teacher Resources

 En la mesa

 Activity 5

 Activities 42–43

 Activities 9–11

 Activity 4

 Activities 10–12

Activities

Expansion
Use overhead transparencies 42 and 43 to introduce the new words and expressions in *Vocabulario II*. First, using transparency 42, point to the objects on the table and identify them in Spanish one at a time. Ask students to repeat after you. Then, using transparency 43, identify each vocabulary item in Spanish, allowing students to see how each object is spelled. As an alternative, use an actual table setting to introduce the new dinner-table vocabulary *(el plato, la taza, el tenedor, etc.)*.

Vocabulario II
En la mesa

el postre

Mamá, pásame esa cuchara que está allá.

Quiero poner un poco de sal en la sopa.

el cuchillo

la sopa

el tenedor

la cucharita

la taza

el azúcar

la mantequilla

la sal   la pimienta

Esta arepa está muy buena.

el aceite

la cuchara

el pan

el mantel

Notes Introduce the new vocabulary and reinforce the content of pages 234 and 235 by using overhead transparencies 42 and 43, the audio CD recording of *En la mesa* and other ancillaries listed under Teacher Resources at the top of these two pages. You can evaluate student progress using Quiz 4.

234

15 ¿Qué necesitas?

 Di lo que necesitas para hacer lo que oyes. *(Say what you need in order to do what you hear.)*

MODELO Necesito una cuchara.

16 A la hora de comer

Completa las siguientes oraciones, según las ilustraciones.

MODELO Pásame un <u>tenedor</u>, por favor.

1. El __ es de nuestra abuela.

2. Pásame la __, por favor.

3. Necesito la __.

4. Pásame el __, por favor.

5. Me gusta la __ bien caliente.

6. Quiero más __ para la ensalada.

7. Necesitan unas __ para el postre.

8. Son las __ de los días especiales.

9. Quiero un __ de agua fría.

10. Los __ son muy bonitos.

17 ¿Qué vemos en el comedor?

 Working in pairs, take turns asking what your partner needs while you point to an item shown in the illustration *En la mesa.* Your partner then must ask you to pass the item to him or her.

MODELO A: ¿Qué necesitas? ¿Qué quieres?
B: Pásame el pan, por favor.

18 ¿Qué buscamos?

Create a drawing similar to the one in the illustration *En la mesa,* but with three items missing. Then, in pairs, take turns asking each other questions about which objects are missing (or not) from your illustration. List in Spanish the objects missing from your partner's illustration. Check to see if you guessed which objects were missing.

Capítulo 6   *doscientos treinta y cinco*   **235**

Notes Point out that *azúcar* is feminine although it requires the masculine definite article for pronunciation reasons similar to the word *agua,* which students have already learned.

For additional listening comprehension practice, play the recorded version of the activity that is available in the Audio CD Program or read the activity using the transcript that appears in the ATE Introduction. A reproducible student answer sheet for the activity can be found at the end of the Audio CD Program Manual if you choose to use it.

235

¿Te gusta la sopa?
Activities 19–21

Activities

Expansion
Additional questions (*¿Qué recuerdas?*): *¿Dónde están Julio, Sara y sus padres?; ¿Quién es Sara?*

Additional questions (*Algo personal*): *¿Come tu familia mucho en el comedor?; Si no comen en el comedor, ¿dónde comen Uds.?*

Prereading Strategy
Ask students to list things typically found in a kitchen and at the dinner table. Then instruct them to cover up the dialog with one hand and look at the photographs. Ask them to imagine where the conversation takes place and what the people are saying to one another. Finally, have students look through the dialog quickly to find cognates.

Diálogo II
¿Te gusta la sopa?

JULIO: Mamá, pásame esa cucharita, por favor.
MAMÁ: ¿Cuál? ¿Esta cucharita?
JULIO: Sí, esa cucharita, mamá.

PAPÁ: Sara, ¿cómo está la sopa?
SARA: Me gusta, pero necesita un poco más de sal.
JULIO: Mira, aquí está la sal.

MAMÁ: ¿Y tú, amor? ¿Te gusta la sopa?
PAPÁ: No sé. No tengo cuchara.
MAMÁ: Lo siento. Aquí está.
PAPÁ: Esta arepa está buena.

19 ¿Qué recuerdas?

1. ¿Qué quiere Julio?
2. ¿Le gusta a Sara la sopa?
3. ¿Qué necesita un poco más de sal?
4. ¿Qué no tiene el papá?
5. ¿Qué le gusta al papá?

20 Algo personal

1. ¿Tiene comedor tu casa?
2. ¿Cómo es la mesa del comedor de tu casa?
3. ¿Qué sopa te gusta? Explica.

21 Yo necesito...

Selecciona la letra de la frase que completa lógicamente cada oración que oyes. *(Select the letter of the phrase that logically completes each sentence you hear.)*

A. de agua mineral   E. arepas
B. sal   F. sobre el pan caliente
C. tenedor   G. una cuchara y un plato
D. el lavaplatos   H. mantel

Mi casa tiene un comedor elegante.

¿Te gustan estos platos?

Notes Point out to students the lack of article in Spanish when using negative phrases: *No tengo cuchara.; No quiero postre.; Nunca como pan.*

Provide some of the following expressions as students discuss quantities at the table: *más* (more), *menos* (less), *mucho* (a lot), *poco* (a little), *un poco de sal* (a little salt), *un poquito* (very little), *un poco más/menos* (a little more/less).

Whereas *uno, mucho* and *poco* have masculine, feminine, singular and plural forms, *más, menos, un poco (de)* and *(ni) un poquito* require no additional changes in their forms.

Cultura viva

Las arepas venezolanas

Arepas are perhaps the most common food in Venezuela. Originally they were made from corn that was ground to make corn meal. As with many everyday foods in the United States, however, *arepas* today are usually prepared using packaged, precooked white corn flour, salt and water. The resulting easy-to-make buns can be eaten alone or as a kind of bread to accompany a meal. *Arepas* can also be stuffed with meat, cheese, scrambled eggs or other fillings, much like *tortillas* or *empanadas*. Another very popular Venezuelan dish is *hallaca*, which is served in nearly every Venezuelan home at Christmas. This typical food consists of a corn-flour pie filled with pork, chicken, vegetables and spices. It is cooked in plantain leaves from a variety of bananas called *plátano*.

Las arepas son populares en Venezuela.

Preparando arepas.

De la cocina de _____

Las arepas
2 tazas de harina de maíz
2 cucharitas de sal
2 tazas de agua caliente

Preparación
Para empezar, poner la harina de maíz[1] en una taza grande y poco a poco poner el agua con sal. Luego, mezclar[2] el agua con la harina hasta que se convierta en masa. Después, dejar[3] la masa en reposo[4] por cinco minutos. Hacer con la masa unos rollos[5] de tres pulgadas[6] de diámetro y de una pulgada a dos pulgadas de ancho[7]. En una sartén[8] con un poco de aceite, freír[9] las arepas hasta ver los rollos dorados[10]. Después, poner las arepas en el horno a 350 grados para cocinar por aproximadamente treinta minutos, hasta tener arepas crujientes[11].

[1]corn flour [2]mix [3]leave [4]rest [5]rolls [6]inches [7]thick [8]frying pan [9]fry [10]golden [11]crunchy

22 Conexión con otras disciplinas: habilidades para la vida diaria

You can easily prepare the recipe at home for a taste of this typical Venezuelan bread. Look at the recipe for *arepas* and answer these questions.

1. ¿Cuáles son los ingredientes para hacer arepas?
2. ¿Qué debes hacer para empezar?
3. ¿Qué diámetro deben tener los rollos?
4. Después de hacer rollos con la masa, ¿qué debes hacer?
5. ¿A qué temperatura tiene que estar el horno?
6. ¿Cuánto tiempo deben estar las arepas en el horno?

Capítulo 6 *doscientos treinta y siete* 237

Teacher Resources

 Las arepas venezolanas
Activity 22

 Activity 5

Answers

22 1. Los ingredientes son sal, harina de maíz y agua.
2. Para empezar, debo poner la harina de maíz en una taza grande y poco a poco poner el agua con sal.
3. Los rollos deben tener tres pulgadas de diámetro.
4. Debo poner un poco de aceite en una sartén para cocinar las arepas hasta ver los rollos dorados.
5. El horno tiene que estar a 350 grados.
6. Deben estar en el horno aproximadamente treinta minutos.

Activities

Multiple Intelligences (bodily-kinesthetic)
Have students prepare *arepas* using the recipe found in *Cultura viva*. Then they may share the *arepas* with the rest of the class.

Spanish for Spanish Speakers
Ask students to explain to the class (in Spanish) how to prepare their favorite dish. Make sure they give a detailed explanation.

Notes The special flour made from ground corn is not cornmeal and is not available everywhere. Suggest students look for ground corn in a specialty foods store or a store that specializes in Hispanic foods.

Tell students the meaning of *habilidades para la vida diaria* (life skills).

Before students attempt to make *arepas* at home, point out that the shapes should not look like pancakes. The *arepas* should look more like small hamburger buns.

Activity 22 is a cross-curricular activity that addresses Spanish as well as cooking.

237

Activities

Critical Thinking
You can practice both demonstrative and possessive adjectives by providing several models and then cuing students with words to which they may respond: *Este libro es mi libro. Ese libro es tu libro. Aquel libro es su libro* (pointing to another student). Cue students with a variety of nouns that are masculine, feminine, singular and plural.

Idioma

Estructura

Pointing out someone or something: demonstrative adjectives

Use a demonstrative adjective *(adjetivo demostrativo)* before a noun to point out or draw attention to where someone or something is located in relation to yourself ("this house," "that car," etc.).

aquel refrigerador

ese refrigerador

este refrigerador

Los adjetivos demostrativos

singular		plural	
masculino	**femenino**	**masculino**	**femenino**
este vaso *(this glass)*	esta taza *(this cup)*	estos vasos *(these glasses)*	estas tazas *(these cups)*
ese vaso *(that glass)*	esa taza *(that cup)*	esos vasos *(those glasses)*	esas tazas *(those cups)*
aquel vaso *(that glass over there)*	aquella taza *(that cup over there)*	aquellos vasos *(those glasses over there)*	aquellas tazas *(those cups over there)*

When pointing out people or objects that are nearby, use *este, esta, estos* or *estas* (this/these). Use *ese, esa, esos* or *esas* (that/those) to draw attention to people or objects that are farther away. Call attention to people or objects that are even farther away ("over there") by using *aquel, aquella, aquellos* or *aquellas* (that/those over there).

near speaker *(aquí)*	Me gusta **este** refrigerador.	I like **this** refrigerator.
away from speaker *(allí)*	¿Te gustan **esos** refrigeradores?	Do you like **those** refrigerators?
far away from speaker *(allá)*	Prefiero **aquel** refrigerador.	I prefer **that** refrigerator **(over there)**.

Notes Emphasize that *este, esta, estas* and *estos* in English mean **this/these**. *Ese, esa, esos* and *esas* mean **that/those** and *aquel, aquella, aquellos* and *aquellas* mean **that/those over there.**

The demonstrative pronouns will be taught in the *Navegando 2* textbook.

Tell students that demonstrative adjectives always precede the noun they modify.

Práctica

23 ¡Otra cocina!

Completa las oraciones con la forma apropiada de *este*.

Quiero otra cocina para mi casa porque (1) cocina es muy fea. (2) paredes tienen un color muy triste. La puerta de (3) horno microondas no cierra. (4) fregadero es muy pequeño, necesito un fregadero doble. (5) refrigerador está muy viejo y (6) lavaplatos es muy malo. (7) luces no encienden y (8) lámpara es muy fea. No me gusta (9) mesa y (10) sillas son horribles.

24 ¿Qué vamos a poner en la mesa?

With a classmate, pretend you are discussing whether or not you need the following items as you are preparing the table for dinner. Answer each question negatively as shown in the model.

MODELO las servilletas verdes
  A: ¿Quieres estas servilletas verdes?
  B: No, no quiero esas servilletas verdes.

1. los cubiertos
2. el mantel
3. la mantequilla
4. el aceite
5. los platos de sopa
6. las tazas
7. el cuchillo
8. los vasos nuevos
9. la silla

25 ¿Qué prefieres?

Imagine you are in a department store buying kitchenware for your new house. Use the appropriate form of *este, ese* or *aquel* to say what items you prefer, based upon the cues shown in the illustration.

MODELO ¿Qué platos prefieres?
Prefiero esos platos.

1. ¿Qué mantel prefieres?
2. ¿Qué cubiertos prefieres?
3. ¿Qué servilletas prefieres?

4. ¿Qué lámpara prefieres?
5. ¿Qué taza prefieres?
6. ¿Qué vasos prefieres?

Capítulo 6 *doscientos treinta y nueve* **239**

Notes Point out that the distinction among the demonstratives that many Spanish speakers make is to use forms of *este* for items near the speaker, forms of *ese* for items near the person spoken to and forms of *aquel* for items that are far from both.

Comunicación

 26 Para la nueva casa de mi familia

 Imagine you are with a friend in the store shown in the illustration. With a classmate, discuss which items you are thinking about buying. Express your preferences, ask each other's opinion and try to decide which things you want to, have to or ought to buy.

MODELO   **A:** ¿Qué piensas de estos cubiertos?
         B: Prefiero aquellos cubiertos porque son más bonitos.

 27 En un restaurante en Caracas

During lunch with a friend in Caracas, you discuss your plans for the week. Talk about some things you want to do, ought to do, have to do or prefer to do each day this week. Make the conversation realistic by politely interrupting one another, asking for things to be passed to you and commenting on things and people you see.

MODELO   **A:** El lunes tengo que ir con mi mamá a la tienda a mirar unas estufas nuevas.
         B: ¿Unas estufas?... ¡Ay, qué aburrido! Por favor, pásame esa cucharita.
         A: Sí, cómo no.

240   *doscientos cuarenta*   **Lección A**

Notes For simple activities, have students write out the answers before assigning students to work with a partner; for more difficult activities, pair students requiring additional help with stronger students. Follow up some oral activities (e.g., activity 27) by assigning a variation of the exercise as written homework.

Comparisons. You may wish to explain to students that demonstrative adjectives are also used to indicate time in relation to the present moment: *esta tarde* (**this** afternoon); *esa tarde* (**that** afternoon); *aquella tarde* (**that** afternoon **farther off in the past**).

28 En el comedor

Working in small groups, pretend you are having dinner together in your dining room in Venezuela. Each member of the group should make at least four questions or statements including some of the following: requests for items at the table, questions about what your friends think and need, comments about the food, questions about what your friends are going to do during the week, and so on. Be polite (use *por favor* and *gracias*).

 A: Pásame ese cuchillo y la mantequilla, por favor.
B: Aquí tienes. ¿Qué piensan de las arepas?
C: Están muy buenas, pero la ensalada necesita un poco de aceite.

¡Extra!

Más comida

el flan	*caramel custard*
el panecillo	*bread roll*
la papa	*potato*
el pastel (la torta)	*cake*
las verduras	*vegetables*

La comida está muy buena.

El plato.

El aceite.

Capítulo 6   *doscientos cuarenta y uno*   241

Answers

28 Creative self-expression.

Activities

Cooperative Learning
Ask small groups of students to prepare a dinner menu featuring items from several Spanish-speaking countries. Possible sources of information include *Navegando*, personal experiences, ethnic cookbooks and foreign exchange students in your school. Each group should share its menu with the class. As a follow-up activity, you may wish to identify a day or event when the students prepare and then bring sample menu items for tasting.

Notes Ask for volunteers or select several groups to present their dining-room conversations for the entire class. Consider bringing utensils and table items to class that students can use for role-playing.

If you or your students prepared *arepas* using the recipe in the *Cultura viva* on page 237, this would be a good time to share the recipe with the class.

Answers

29 1. la hallaca.
   2. un plato indígena llamado Hayaco Iritari.
   3. tamal grande.
   4. elaborada.
   5. Amigos y parientes
30 Answers will vary.

Lectura cultural

Una deliciosa tradición

Es diciembre y, por toda Venezuela, muchas familias hacen las tradicionales hallacas. Es una vieja tradición y es el plato representativo de la Navidad venezolana. El origen de las hallacas viene de un plato de los indígenas llamado[1] Hayaco Iritari. La hallaca es similar a un tamal grande envuelto[2] en una hoja de plátano[3].

La mayoría de las familias hacen una fiesta de la preparación de las hallacas. En las cocinas, se reúnen[4] parientes y amigos para participar en este animado proceso. Mientras que[5] escuchan la gaita — ritmo típico venezolano — todos en la cocina ayudan en la labor, desde lavar[6] las hojas donde se pone la masa[7] hasta amarrar[8] las hallacas.

El proceso es laborioso[9] porque la preparación es elaborada y porque se preparan muchas para almacenar[10] en el refrigerador y comer durante todo el mes de diciembre.

Cuando los venezolanos piensan en la Navidad, piensan en hallacas.

Cuando comes hallaca, tienes que abrir la hoja de plátano. Comes la masa con un tenedor. No debes comer la hoja. Muchas personas prefieren comer las hallacas con pan.

[1]called   [2]wrapped   [3]plantain/banana leaf   [4]get together   [5]While   [6]from washing
[7]dough   [8]tie   [9]tedious   [10]to store

29 ¿Qué recuerdas?

Completa las siguientes oraciones.

1. En Venezuela, el plato típico de la Navidad es...
2. El nombre *hallaca* viene de...
3. La hallaca es como un...
4. La preparación de hallacas es...
5. ... se reúnen en la cocina para ayudar a hacer hallacas.

- How do Venezuelans make the preparation of *hallacas* fun? Describe something your family or your acquaintances do that is also hard work yet fun.

30 Algo personal

1. ¿Cuál es un plato representativo de la Navidad en los Estados Unidos? Compara ese plato con las hallacas de Venezuela.
2. ¿Se reúnen tu familia o tus amigos en la cocina? ¿Qué hacen?
3. ¿Preparan en tu casa un plato que tiene un proceso laborioso? ¿Cómo dividen la labor?

Notes Encourage students to find out more about Venezuela by going to the following Web sites:

The Venezuela Online Tour
http://www.ve.net/travel/
Electronic Embassy
http://www.embassy.org

Organization of American States
http://www.oas.org
general travel information
http://www.expedia.com

¿Qué aprendí?

Autoevaluación
As a review and self-check, respond to the following:

1. Name three items you might see on the table while having dinner with a Venezuelan family in Caracas.

2. You are in charge of preparing dinner. Tell the people helping you three things they have to do or should do to help you.

3. What might you say to ask a friend what he or she is thinking about?

4. Ask two friends what they are thinking about doing this Saturday.

5. Say that you like *arepas* but that you prefer bread with butter.

6. Imagine you are seated at the dining-room table and the glass and silverware you need are far away from you, near your friend. How can you ask your friend politely to pass you that glass and that silverware?

7. Name two typical Venezuelan dishes.

Visit the web-based activities at www.emcp.com

Palabras y expresiones

En la cocina
el aceite
el azúcar
la cocina
los cubiertos
la cuchara
la cucharita
el cuchillo
la estufa
el fregadero
el horno microondas
el lavaplatos
la luz
el mantel
la mantequilla
la mesa
el pan

la pimienta
el plato
el postre
el refrigerador
la sal
la servilleta
la sopa
la taza
el tenedor
el vaso

Otras expresiones
allá
aquel, aquella
   (aquellos, aquellas)
el comedor
la cosa

de todos los días
después
entonces
ese, esa (esos, esas)
especial
este, esta (estos, estas)
la lámpara
otra vez
pensar de/en/que
un poco de
poner la mesa
ya

Verbos
ayudar
cerrar (ie)
deber
empezar (ie)
encender (ie)
pásame
pensar (ie)
poner
preferir (ie)
querer (ie)
sentir (ie)
tener que
viajar

Una taza.

Los cubiertos.

Teacher Resources

Activity 16

Information Gap Activities
Postcard Activities
Funciones de Comunicación

Answers

Autoevaluación
Possible answers:
1. Hay un mantel, unas servilletas y unos vasos.
2. Deben encender las luces. Tienen que poner la mesa. Tienen que ayudar con la comida.
3. ¿En qué piensas?
4. ¿Qué piensan hacer este sábado?
5. Me gustan las arepas, pero prefiero el pan con mantequilla.
6. Pásame ese vaso y esos cubiertos, por favor.
7. arepas, hallacas, ropa vieja, cachapas

Activities

Communities
Ask small groups of students to identify interesting professions involving Spanish. In turn, they should discuss the requirements and obligations of this job by using the expressions *tener que* (+ infinitive) and *deber* (+ infinitive). Have students share their conclusions with the class.

Notes Talk with the class about Venezuela's national hero, Simón Bolívar (1783–1830). This diplomat and military leader was born in Caracas. He was a Pan-American and helped liberate Bolivia, Ecuador, Colombia, Peru and Venezuela from Spain. Bolivia was named after him.

The monetary unit of Venezuela, *el bolívar*, is named after the national hero Simón Bolívar.

La casa de Julián

 Activity 1

 Activities 44–45

 Activities 1–3

 Activity 1

 Activities 1–4

Content reviewed in *Lección B*
- noun/adjective agreement
- present tense of regular verbs
- the verbs *deber* and *querer*
- family

Activities

Critical Listening

Play the audio CD of the letter. Tell students to listen for the main ideas the speaker is addressing. Finally, have several individuals state what they believe is the main theme of the reading.

Expansion

You may want to ask some of the following questions about the letter: *¿Cuál es la fecha de la carta?; ¿Dónde está Cartagena?; ¿De dónde son Daniela y Santiago?; ¿Qué no le gusta a Daniela?; ¿Adónde van a viajar Daniela y Santiago con su tío?; ¿Cuándo va a llamar Daniela a sus padres?; ¿Qué escribe Jorge para terminar la carta?*

Lección B
Colombia

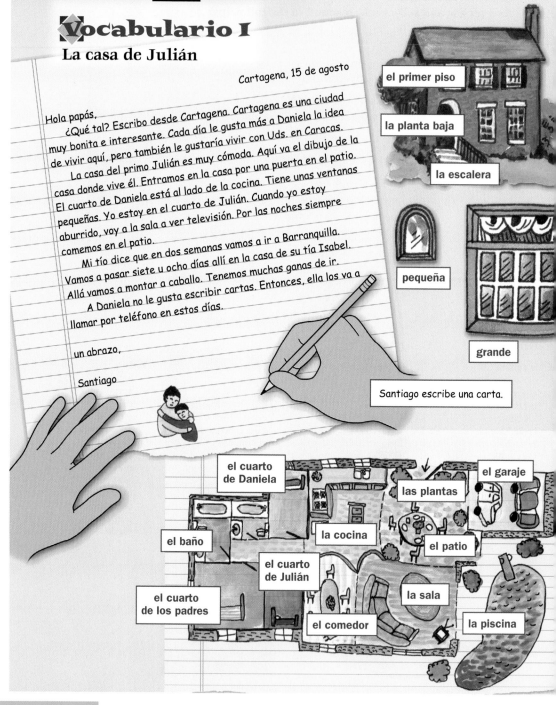

Vocabulario I
La casa de Julián

Cartagena, 15 de agosto

Hola papás,

¿Qué tal? Escribo desde Cartagena. Cartagena es una ciudad muy bonita e interesante. Cada día le gusta más a Daniela la idea de vivir aquí, pero también le gustaría vivir con Uds. en Caracas.

La casa del primo Julián es muy cómoda. Aquí va el dibujo de la casa donde vive él. Entramos en la casa por una puerta en el patio. El cuarto de Daniela está al lado de la cocina. Tiene unas ventanas pequeñas. Yo estoy en el cuarto de Julián. Cuando yo estoy aburrido, voy a la sala a ver televisión. Por las noches siempre comemos en el patio.

Mi tío dice que en dos semanas vamos a ir a Barranquilla. Vamos a pasar siete u ocho días allí en la casa de su tía Isabel. Allá vamos a montar a caballo. Tenemos muchas ganas de ir.

A Daniela no le gusta escribir cartas. Entonces, ella los va a llamar por teléfono en estos días.

un abrazo,

Santiago

el primer piso

la planta baja

la escalera

pequeña

grande

Santiago escribe una carta.

el cuarto de Daniela

el garaje

las plantas

el baño

la cocina

el patio

el cuarto de Julián

el cuarto de los padres

la sala

el comedor

la piscina

244 *doscientos cuarenta y cuatro*   **Lección B**

Notes Remind students that when two verbs are combined in one sentence, the first verb is conjugated and the second verb is usually an infinitive.

Cultures. Note that Daniela and Santiago are visiting a cousin in Colombia. In the Spanish-speaking world it is common to spend vacation time with extended family members.

Point out several characteristics of informal letter writing in Spanish. The month is not capitalized; the most popular salutation is *Querido(s)* or *Querida(s)* plus one or more names; common farewells include *un abrazo; un fuerte abrazo; besos.*

1 Dictado

 Escucha la información y escribe lo que oyes.

2 ¿Dónde están?

Look at these illustrations and tell what Santiago and Daniela's relatives are doing somewhere in their house in Cartagena.

MODELO su abuela
Su abuela come en el patio.

1. su prima pequeña
2. su abuelo
3. su primo Julián
4. su tío
5. su tía

3 ¿Adónde deben ir?

Read the statements and say where the people should go.

MODELO Quiero un vaso de agua.
Debes ir a la cocina.

1. Mi hermana quiere buscar una naranja y un refresco.
2. Mis padres necesitan usar el carro.
3. Yo tengo ganas de ver televisión.
4. Mis abuelos están aquí para comer con la familia.
5. Mi hermana viene de jugar al fútbol.
6. Voy a leer y escuchar CDs.

4 Conexión con otras disciplinas: dibujo

Create a blueprint (or make a pop-up) of the floor plan of your home and label the rooms in Spanish. Make up the information if you wish. Then write at least five sentences in Spanish that describe your blueprint. For example, state if the blueprint is of a house *(casa)* or an apartment *(apartamento)*, how large it is, the number and type of rooms, etc.

Capítulo 6   *doscientos cuarenta y cinco* 245

Teacher Resources

 Activities 1 and 3

Answers

1 Play a portion of the recorded letter and have students write what they hear. As an alternative, you may choose to read the selection yourself. Check the accuracy of student spelling.

2 Possible answers:
1. Su prima pequeña juega en el garaje.
2. Su abuelo lee el periódico en el comedor.
3. Su primo Julián juega en el cuarto con la computadora.
4. Su tío lee un libro en la sala.
5. Su tía ve televisión en la cocina.

3 Possible answers:
1. Debe ir a la cocina.
2. Deben ir al garaje.
3. Debes ir a la sala.
4. Deben ir al comedor.
5. Debe ir al baño.
6. Debes ir al patio/a tu cuarto.

4 Creative writing practice.

Activities

Critical Thinking
Ask students to think of typical activities in different parts of a house. Mention various rooms/areas and ask the students to explain what they do there.

Notes **Comparisons.** Note that the concept of *casa* may vary among cultures and even among Spanish speakers. For example, a home for a family in an urban area may be an apartment or a condominium in a multiresidence building. In other cases, a home may be a freestanding structure with a yard and a garage.

Additional words students might want to use when talking about their home: *el ático/el desván* (attic), *el apartamento* (apartment), *el jardín* (garden, yard), *el sótano* (basement), *el techo* (ceiling), *el tejado* (roof).

245

Diálogo I

La casa de Elisa

JAVIER: Juan dice que la casa de Elisa es muy grande.
ROSA: Sí, yo tengo ganas de ir a su casa.
JAVIER: A mí también me gustaría mucho verla.
ROSA: ¡Vamos mañana!

JAVIER: Mira, allí está Juan.
ROSA: Oye, Juan, ¿cómo es la casa de Elisa?
JUAN: Es una casa grande e interesante. Tiene tres pisos.

ROSA: ¡Qué grande!
JUAN: Sí, tiene siete u ocho cuartos, dos salas y una piscina.
JAVIER: ¡Es la casa ideal!
ROSA: ¿Ideal? No pienso eso, prefiero casas pequeñas.

5 ¿Qué recuerdas?

1. ¿Quién dice que la casa de Elisa es grande?
2. ¿Quién tiene ganas de ir a la casa de Elisa?
3. ¿A quién le gustaría mucho ver la casa de Elisa?
4. ¿Cómo es la casa de Elisa?
5. ¿Cuántos pisos tiene la casa de Elisa?
6. ¿Y cuántos cuartos tiene?

6 Algo personal

1. ¿Cómo es tu casa ideal?
2. ¿Te gustan las casas grandes o pequeñas? Explica.

¡Extra!

Las palabras *e* y *u*

Before words that begin with *i* or *hi*, the word *y* becomes *e*. Similarly, the word *o* changes to *u* before words that begin with *o* or *ho*.

*Marcos **e** Inés viven en Cartagena.*
*Dicen que van a montar a caballo mañana **u** otro día.*

7 ¿Está en la casa, en el colegio o en el parque?

Di dónde están las siguientes personas según lo que oyes.

Está en la casa.   Está en el parque.

Está en el colegio.

Notes Point out that *gustaría* is the conditional tense of the verb *gustar*. (The conditional tense will not be taught until level 2.) Tell students they can use this form of the verb with the indirect object pronouns *(me, te, le, nos, les)* to say what people would or would not like, as Javier does in the dialog.

Students have already learned to use the indirect object pronouns with *gusta* and *gustan*. Give them examples of indirect object pronouns used with *gustaría*: *¿Te gustaría ir a Venezuela?; A mi hermana le gustaría hacer un viaje.*

Cultura Viva

Colombia

Bogotá, Colombia.

The Spaniards founded *Cartagena de Indias* on the northwest coast of Colombia in 1533. Pirates frequently attacked the port seeking gold and other valuables, so a wall was constructed around the city as a means of defense. The wall *(la muralla)* remains today, one of the symbols of colonial times in Colombia. The capital, *Bogotá*, was founded in 1538. The city is vibrant and modern today, but you can catch a glimpse of the country's extensive history if you visit the exceptional *Museo del Oro* (Gold Museum), which holds over 30,000 pieces of pre-Columbian gold.

Colombia has a varied terrain, consisting of mountains, tropical jungles, plains, lowlands and a lengthy coastline that touches on two oceans. The country's climate does not change with the seasons but rather is determined by Colombia's elevations. Whereas the

Cartagena, Colombia.

lowlands and the coastal areas offer a tropical climate, such as you might experience when visiting the beautiful city of *Cartagena,* the temperature in the capital ranges between fifty and seventy degrees all year long.

Most people know that Colombia is famous for producing large quantities of excellent coffee, but not everyone knows it is a major exporter of emeralds. The country is also famous for its music, including the distinctive dance rhythms of *la cumbia, el porro, el merecumbé* and the accordion accompaniment of songs known as *vallenatos.* Visit Colombia sometime and experience this South American jewel!

Máscara de oro en el Museo del Oro, Bogotá.

8 ¿Qué sabes de Colombia?

Tell whether the statements are *cierto* or *falso*.

1. Colombia está en América Central.
2. Cartagena es una ciudad muy nueva.
3. El clima en Colombia es determinado por la elevación.
4. Cartagena es un símbolo del período colonial.
5. Cali es la capital del país.
6. Colombia es famosa por el café, las esmeraldas y la música.

9 Conexiones con otras disciplinas: geografía

Create a map of Colombia that shows major cities and rivers, mountains and surrounding countries.

Notes Explain that in Colombia, coffee is the primary agricultural export product. Point out that many people are employed in this important industry. Also note that Colombian exports include many other important products such as coal, minerals, flowers and 95 percent of the world's emeralds.

The majority of the people in Colombia live in large cities, such as *Santa Fe de Bogotá, Medellín, Cali, Barranquilla, Cartagena* and *Bucaramanga*. Other towns with interesting names are *Anapoima, Facatativá, Tocaima, Cúcuta, Armenia* and *Popayán*.

Teacher Resources

 Activity 10

 Activities 3–4

 Activities 5–7

 Activity 2

 Activity 5

Answers

10 Possible answers:
1. Yo digo "¡Lo siento!"
2. Nosotros decimos "¡Feliz cumpleaños!"
3. Uds. dicen "¡Qué problema!"
4. Tú dices "¡Qué bonitas!"
5. Ellas dicen "¡Qué bueno!"
6. Daniela dice "Sí, habla con ella".

Activities

Critical Listening

Tell the class that you are going to share with them several interesting news headlines and pieces of personal information. Some statements will be true and others will be false. The students should listen to each statement and then decide: *Dice la verdad* or *No dice la verdad/Dice una mentira.* As an extension, ask pairs of students to prepare a list of recent headlines to present to the class.

Idioma

Estructura

Telling what someone says: *decir*

The present tense of *decir* (to say, to tell) has an irregular *yo* form and requires a stem change for all forms except *nosotros/as* and *vosotros/as.* Use *decir* to tell what someone says.

decir	
digo	decimos
dices	decís
dice	dicen

When you are summarizing what someone says, use *que* between *decir* and the expression or phrase that follows:

¿Qué dice Javier?
*Dice **que** la casa de Elisa es muy grande.*

What does Javier say?
He says (**that**) Elisa's house is very big.

 Práctica

10 ¿Qué dicen?

What might the response be to what the following people say?

MODELO ¿Cómo te llamas? (Ramiro)
Ramiro dice "Me llamo Ramiro".

1. Estoy enfermo. (yo)
2. Hoy es mi cumpleaños. (nosotros)
3. No hay luz en mi casa. (Uds.)
4. ¿Te gustan mis plantas? (tú)
5. Voy a comprar una casa con una piscina muy grande. (ellas)
6. ¡Aló¡ ¿Puedo hablar con Daniela? (Daniela)

Me llamo Ramiro.

Notes Review the following verbs with students, which also can be used with *que* to connect two thoughts: *pensar, sentir, escribir, comprender, contestar, saber, leer, ver.* Example: *¿Qué escribe Ana en su carta? Escribe que a ella le gusta Colombia.*

Point out the difference between *decir* (to say, to tell) and *hablar* (to speak, to talk).

Check for correct conjugation of the verb *decir.*

11 Una encuesta

Results of a poll show who would like to spend the summer in Colombia as part of an exchange program with a high school in Cartagena. Summarize whether the indicated people say they would like to participate or not.

MODELO Julia
Julia dice que no.

1. Ud.
2. Raúl y la señorita García
3. el señor Gaviria y César
4. Sara
5. la señora Sosa y Eva
6. Ernesto y yo

Viaje de Intercambio

Sí	No	
☑	☐	Sara
☑	☐	yo
☑	☐	Ernesto
☑	☐	la señorita García
☑	☐	Raúl
☐	☑	Julia
☑	☐	Enrique
☐	☑	Eva
☐	☑	Ud.
☐	☑	el señor Gaviria
☐	☑	la señora Sosa
☐	☑	César

Comunicación

12 En tu casa

In groups, discuss your homes *(casa* or *apartamento)* and weekly activities. What is similar and what is different about the homes, your routines and your lives in general? You may wish to include some of the following activities in your discussion: *comer, escribir cartas, leer* and *ver televisión*. Make up any information you would like. Take notes as you talk and report what you discuss to the class.

MODELO A: ¿Dónde come tu familia?
B: Comemos en la cocina. ¿Y Uds.?
A: Nosotros comemos mucho en restaurantes. En casa comemos en la sala y vemos televisión.
C: En mi casa comemos en la sala, pero no los domingos. Los domingos comemos en el comedor.
A: B dice que su familia come en la cocina. C dice que en su casa comen en la sala, pero no los domingos. Mi familia come mucho en restaurantes, pero en casa comemos en la sala y vemos televisión.

Nosotros comemos en el comedor.

Answers

11 1. Ud. dice que no.
2. Raúl y la señorita García dicen que sí.
3. El señor Gaviria y César dicen que no.
4. Sara dice que sí.
5. La señora Sosa y Eva dicen que no.
6. Ernesto y yo decimos que sí.

12 Creative self-expression.

Activities

Critical Listening
Ask pairs of students to prepare a list in Spanish of recent headlines, quotes that are common knowledge or other bits of information someone has said. (The information should be public knowledge.) The students should also make up some headlines that are not true. In front of the class, one student reads the headline or statement aloud: *El presidente va a Colombia en dos semanas.* The partner says whether he or she thinks the statement is true or not (*...dice que....*) and then calls on a classmate to agree or disagree. The classmate must say whether the statement is true or not, and then responds with *Dice la verdad* or *No dice la verdad/Dice una mentira.*

Capítulo 6   *doscientos cuarenta y nueve*   **249**

Notes Students may choose to elect one person from their group to take notes for activity 12 or have one person from each group present to the class a summary of what members of the group discussed.

Comparisons. Although the Spanish word *que* must always be used when joining two phrases, the word **that** may be eliminated from an English sentence: They say **(that)** we are going to Colombia.

Answers

13 1. Yo quiero tener una piscina.
2. A ti te gustaría tener un cuarto en la planta baja.
3. Mi hermano quiere una cocina con un lavaplatos.
4. A mis padres les gustaría tener un garaje para dos carros.
5. A nosotros nos gustaría tener un comedor cómodo.
6. A mí me gustaría tener plantas en el patio.
7. Mis hermanas quieren tener cuartos en el primer piso.
14 Creative self-expression.

Activities

Cooperative Learning
Working in groups of three or four, have students discuss what they wrote for activity 14.

Multiple Intelligences (intrapersonal)
Ask several questions to further practice the expression of wishes: *¿Qué quieres ser/hacer en el futuro?; ¿Dónde te gustaría estudiar o trabajar?; ¿Dónde quieres vivir?; ¿Te gustaría ser famoso/famosa?; ¿Adónde te gustaría viajar?; ¿Qué países quieres visitar?*

Estructura

Expressing wishes with *querer* or *gustaría*

You have learned to express someone's wishes by using a form of *querer* and an infinitive. You can also express wishes by combining *me, te, le, nos, os* or *les* with the more polite but less emphatic *gustaría* and an infinitive.

Quiero viajar a Colombia.	**I want to travel** to Colombia.
Me gustaría viajar a Colombia.	**I would like to travel** to Colombia.
Quieren comprar una estufa nueva.	They **want to buy** a new stove.
Les gustaría comprar una estufa nueva.	They **would like to buy** a new stove.

 Práctica

13 Una casa nueva

Choose a word or expression from each column and create complete sentences telling what members of the Martínez family want when they buy a new house.

MODELO Nosotros queremos comprar una casa grande.

A	B
yo	quieren tener cuartos en el primer piso
a ti	te gustaría tener un cuarto en la planta baja
mi hermano	les gustaría tener un garaje para dos carros
a mis padres	queremos comprar una casa grande ✓
a nosotros	me gustaría tener plantas en el patio
a mí	quiero tener una piscina
mis hermanas	nos gustaría tener un comedor cómodo
nosotros ✓	quiere una cocina con un lavaplatos

14 ¿Qué te gustaría?

Completa las oraciones de una manera original.

MODELO Me gustaría tener...
Me gustaría tener una casa grande.

1. No me gustaría vivir....
2. Me gustaría viajar....
3. No me gustaría ir....
4. Me gustaría vivir....
5. Me gustaría comprar....
6. Me gustaría ir....

Me gustaría tener una casa grande.

Notes Remind students that they may need to add *a* (plus a person's name or a pronoun) or *a mí, a ti, a él, a ella, a Ud., a nosotros, a nosotras, a vosotros, a vosotras, a ellos, a ellas, a Uds.* to clarify the meaning of *gustaría: A mis padres les gustaría comprar un refrigerador nuevo.*

Encourage students to make up funny or out-of-the-ordinary sentences for activity 14.

15 Comparaciones

Write a paragraph of four or five sentences describing the wishes, intentions and obligations of people you know well, using *gustaría, pensar, preferir* and *querer*. Then exchange your paper with a partner and take turns asking and answering questions about what each of you wrote.

MODELO A: ¿Adónde les gustaría ir a tus padres?

B: A mis padres les gustaría ir a Bogotá para ver a mis abuelos.

> Mis padres quieren viajar a Colombia en julio. Les gustaría ver a mis abuelos en Bogotá. Un día pienso vivir en Bogotá, pero tengo que terminar las clases en el colegio.

Comunicación

16 Encuesta

Complete a survey about what rooms and furnishings your classmates would like to have in their ideal house (*casa ideal*). Talk with at least two other people and, then, compare the information you obtained with a partner. Finally, one of you should report your survey results to the class.

MODELO A: ¿Cómo es tu casa ideal?

B: Me gustaría tener una casa grande de dos pisos.

C: Yo prefiero una casa cómoda de un piso y también quiero tener una piscina.

A: **B** dice que le gustaría tener una casa grande con dos pisos, pero **C** dice que prefiere una casa cómoda de un piso y tener una piscina.

17 ¿Cómo es tu casa?

In Spanish, write several statements describing your home, what you or someone in your family would like to buy for the house and where you would like to live in the future (*el futuro*). Then, based on what you have written in small groups, talk about the homes. Try to use some of the alternative words suggested in the *Estrategia* during the discussion. You might talk about such things as the number of rooms, what you like or do not like, where the home is located and whether or not there is something you would like to buy for the house. Add details making up any of the information you wish.

MODELO A: ¿Cómo es tu casa?

B: Es muy grande. Tiene cinco piezas y cada pieza tiene un cuarto de baño. También tiene dos salas y un comedor grande. A mis padres les gustaría comprar una mesa grande para el comedor.

C: Pues, mi casa es pequeña. Tiene seis cuartos: dos alcobas, un baño, una sala, un comedor y una cocina.

Estrategia

Recognizing words in context
Words and expressions you read and hear in Spanish vary from speaker to speaker and from one country to another. You may hear *cuarto, habitación* and *pieza* are all used to refer to a **room**. For the word **bedroom** you may see the words *alcoba, dormitorio, habitación, pieza, recámara* and *cuarto de dormir* (literally, a **room for sleeping**), which is sometimes shortened to *cuarto*. However, you should not confuse this shortened form of *cuarto* for the expression *cuarto de baño* (bathroom), which is usually shortened to *baño*. Knowing that these differences exist will help you in your goal of becoming fluent in Spanish. Always keep in mind that your goal is communication.

Capítulo 6   *doscientos cincuenta y uno*   251

Notes Note that activity 15 has two parts. First students must write sentences that use *gustaría* or a form of *pensar, preferir* or *querer*; then they must have a conversation with a classmate about what they wrote.

Read and discuss the *Estrategia* with students before assigning activities 16 and 17. Encourage students to use context to determine meaning as they converse.

Un día en casa

 Activity 5

 Activity 46

 Activity 8

 Activity 4

 Activities 7–8

Activities

Prereading Strategy

Have students look at the illustration and determine what the people are doing. Inform them that what the people are saying matches their actions. Next, ask students to look at each speech bubble and look for cognates and other words they recognize. Finally, ask students to guess what each person is saying.

TPR

Write the expressions from the illustration *Un día en casa* on separate pieces of paper. Have students select one of the pieces of paper at random. Call on several students to act out the expressions while classmates guess what the expressions are.

252 *doscientos cincuenta y dos*   **Lección B**

Notes Review the forms of the verb *tener* prior to introducing the *tener* expressions.

Comparisons. Compare the expressions using *tener* (+ noun) and meaning **to be** (+ adjective) with English equivalents. Examples: *tengo hambre* = **I am hungry;** *tengo miedo* = **I am afraid.** Then remind students that in Spanish, some expressions use *estar* (+ adjective) whereas others may use *tener* (+ noun).

Use support materials indicated under Teacher Resources at the top of the page to introduce and practice words and expressions in *Vocabulario II*.

Tengo dieciséis años.

Yo tengo quince años.

Eso es mentira. Debes pedir perdón.

Sí, lo siento. Es una mentira. Tengo treinta años.

Clara dice la verdad.

Guillermo quiere decir que prefiere ser joven.

Lo siento. Eres muy pequeño.

"Lo siento. Eres muy pequeño."

El chico pide prestado el carro de su hermano.

La chica repite lo que dice su hermano.

  18 ¿Cierto o falso?

Di si lo que oyes es cierto o falso, según la información en el Vocabulario II. Si es falso, di lo que es cierto.

19 Un día en casa

 With a classmate, take turns asking and answering the following questions, according to the illustration.

MODELO **A:** ¿Qué tiene Cristina?
B: Cristina tiene prisa.

1. ¿Qué tiene Nicolás?
2. ¿Qué tiene Rogelio?
3. ¿Quién tiene mucha sed?
4. ¿Quién tiene frío?
5. ¿Qué tiene Mateo?
6. ¿Quién tiene mucha hambre?
7. ¿Quiénes tienen mucho calor?
8. ¿Qué tienes tú?

Marisela tiene hambre.

Notes Play the audio CD version of activity 18 for listening comprehension practice or read the activity using the transcript that appears in the ATE introduction.

Teacher Resources

Activities 18–19

Activities 9–10

Answers

18 Possible answers:
1. Falso. Nicolás tiene sueño.
2. Cierto.
3. Falso. El abuelo dice que tiene frío.
4. Falso. Los tíos tienen calor.
5. Cierto.
6. Cierto.

19
1. Nicolás tiene sueño.
2. Rogelio tiene poca hambre.
3. La abuela tiene mucha sed.
4. El abuelo tiene frío.
5. Mateo tiene ganas de correr.
6. Verónica tiene mucha hambre.
7. Los tíos tienen mucho calor.
8. Tengo....

Activities

Critical Thinking
See if students can use an appropriate *tener* expression to make a statement about the following situations: *1) Carlitos tiene nueve años. Está en casa solo y son las 11:00 de la noche. 2) Son las 2:30 de la mañana pero Juan no va a su cuarto. Tiene mucho trabajo y está cansado. 3) Don Pedro está en el desierto del Sahara y es el mediodía. 4) El señor Vega está en Alaska en febrero. 5) Marisol busca algo de comer pero no hay nada en la casa.*

Diálogo II
Tengo mucho calor

JAVIER: Tengo mucho calor.
ROSA: Ya estamos cerca de la casa de Elisa.
JAVIER: También tengo mucha sed.
ROSA: ¡Allí está la casa de Elisa!

ROSA: ¡Qué grande y bonita es tu casa!
ELISA: Muchas gracias. Es tu casa también.
JAVIER: A Rosa no le gusta tu casa.
ROSA: Mentira, Elisa. No es verdad.

JAVIER: Pero dices que te gustan las casas pequeñas.
ROSA: Lo que digo es que prefiero una casa pequeña.
ELISA: Está bien. Yo comprendo. ¡Vamos a la playa!
JAVIER: Buena idea. Tengo mucho calor.

20 ¿Qué recuerdas?

1. ¿Quién tiene mucho calor?
2. ¿Quién tiene mucha sed?
3. ¿De quién es la casa grande y bonita?
4. ¿Es verdad que a Rosa no le gusta la casa de Elisa?
5. ¿Adónde quiere ir Elisa?

21 Algo personal

1. ¿Tienes calor? ¿Y sed?
2. ¿Dices mentiras? Explica.
3. ¿Adónde vas cuando hace mucho calor?

22 ¿Qué tienen?

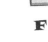 Selecciona la ilustración apropiada que corresponda con lo que oyes.

A   **B**   **C**   **D**   **E**   **F**

¡Hogar, dulce hogar!

Homes in Spanish-speaking parts of the world are like castles in sentiment, if not in actual size. They offer a private refuge from the outside world and vary in their styles to reflect individual tastes, customs and availability of construction materials. Homes in rural areas are often small and simple, whereas homes in large cities and suburbs can be large and impressive. Interestingly, many Hispanic families in metropolitan areas live in

Una casa grande en Cartagena.

front yard. These homes traditionally have a patio at the back or the center of the residence that offers privacy and a place to relax among plants, birds and, sometimes, even small trees and beautiful fountains. In addition, older homes often have a flat roof (*la azotea*), which may be accessible by stairs, usually from the patio or a room near the back of the home. The *azotea* is sometimes used for hanging the laundry to dry or growing flowers and herbs, and even some vegetables, in pots. Today, *chalets* (e.g., houses with yards that resemble homes in the United States) are becoming popular, especially on the outskirts of some cities in part because city apartments and condos are becoming prohibitively expensive for most middle class families.

Esta casa tiene un patio bonito.

apartment buildings or condos, which they may own instead of renting. These homes can have as many as four or five bedrooms, a balcony, two bathrooms, a kitchen and a living room. In some older Hispanic neighborhoods, homes often adjoin the sidewalk, leaving little or no room for a

Una casa en México.

23 ¡Hogar, dulce hogar!

Write five sentences stating what you know about homes in the Spanish-speaking world.

24 Nuestras casas

Compare housing in the United States with what you know about homes in the Spanish-speaking world.

Capítulo 6

doscientos cincuenta y cinco **255**

Teacher Resources

 Activity 5

Answers

23 Possible answers:
1. Home is a private place reserved for family and close friends.
2. Rural homes are often smaller and simpler than city homes.
3. Many Hispanic families in metropolitan areas live in apartment buildings or condos.
4. A patio offers a private place where families can relax amongst plants, birds and fountains.
5. Houses on the outskirts of town are becoming popular in part due to their lower cost.

24 Answers will vary.

Activities

Cooperative Learning
Working in pairs, have students take turns naming the rooms of a house as the partner makes a sketch of what he or she hears. Students may choose to describe the house more fully if they wish.

Notes Inform the class that houses in the Spanish-speaking world may be large or small, made from concrete, brick, wood or adobe, or have one or more floors. There is no one model that fits the variety of sizes and shapes.

Many homes in Spanish-speaking cities are apartments or condominiums and do not have a yard. These buildings are commonly made out of concrete and steel. The inhabitants probably park their vehicles in a parking garage tucked under the apartments or condominiums.

25 1. vivimos; 2. tenemos;
3. tiene; 4. prefiero;
5. quiere; 6. gustan;
7. estudio; 8. dice;
9. tenemos; 10. escribe;
11. escriben; 12. pienso;
13. Quiero

Activities

Cooperative Learning

Have students work in pairs to practice asking and answering questions using the *tú* and *yo* forms of several verbs (make sure they use the rising intonation of questions). Student A could ask *¿Comes ...?; ¿Corres ...?; ¿Comprendes ...?;* etc. Student B would then respond affirmatively to each question (*Sí, como ...*). After all verbs have been covered, Student A again asks the questions and Student B responds negatively (*No, no corro ...*). Then have students change roles.

Critical Thinking

For additional practice with *-ar, -er* and *-ir* verbs, have students prepare a list of seven or eight things they do during the week. They may use the following verbs and any other verbs they have learned: *caminar, cantar, comer, correr, estudiar, hablar, hacer, ir, leer, nadar* and *ver.* Then, working in pairs, have students talk about their lists of activities and take turns asking and answering when they do each activity listed.

Idioma

Repaso rápido: regular present-tense verbs

You are already familiar with how to conjugate regular verbs:

hablar		comer		vivir	
hablo	hablamos	como	comemos	vivo	vivimos
hablas	habláis	comes	coméis	vives	vivís
habla	hablan	come	comen	vive	viven

25 La familia de Elisa

Completa el siguiente párrafo con las formas apropiadas de los verbos entre paréntesis.

Me llamo Elisa y soy la amiga de Javier y Rosa. Mis padres y yo *1. (vivir)* en Cartagena, Colombia. Nosotros *2. (tener)* una casa muy grande. La casa *3. (tener)* cinco cuartos y cuatro baños. Yo *4. (preferir)* tener una casa más pequeña. Mi madre también *5. (querer)* una casa un poco más pequeña. Mi padre es de San José, California, y le *6. (gustar)* las casas grandes y cómodas. Ahora yo *7. (estudiar)* inglés en el colegio. Mi padre *8. (decir)* que yo hablo muy bien el inglés. Mis hermanos y yo *9. (tener)* ganas de ir a Estados Unidos. Mi papá tiene mucha familia en California—sus padres, seis hermanos, tres tíos y quince primos. Él les *10. (escribir)* muchos mensajes por correo electrónico a ellos, pero ellos *11. (escribir)* muy poco. Yo *12. (pensar)* que para Navidad vamos a California. *13. (Querer)* conocer a la familia de mi padre.

¿Tienes ganas de ir a Cartagena, Colombia?

Notes Skip the *Repaso rápido* and activity 25 if you feel students have a good grasp of the present tense.

Estructura

Stem-changing verbs: *e → i*

You have already learned to use verbs like *pensar (ie)* that require the spelling change *e → ie: yo pienso, nosotros pensamos.* The verb *pedir (i, i)* requires the spelling change *e → i* in all forms of their present-tense stem except for *nosotros* and *vosotros.*

pedir	
pido	pedimos
pides	pedís
pide	piden

Pedir is the English equivalent of "to ask for, to request, to order (in a restaurant)". Take care to avoid using *pedir* instead of *preguntar* or *hacer una pregunta,* which are both used for "to ask a question." Other expressions with *pedir:*

- **Pedir permiso (para)** is "to ask for permission (to do something)."
- **Pedir perdón** can be used to excuse yourself and to ask for forgiveness for having done something wrong.
- **Pedir prestado/a** is "to ask for a loan" or "to borrow something."

¡Extra!

Con permiso y Perdón

Although they may be used with the verb *pedir, Con permiso* and *Perdón* can also be used alone for "Excuse me" or "Pardon me."

The verbs *repetir* and *decir* follow the same pattern as *pedir,* with the exception of the irregular *yo* form or *decir: digo.*

Práctica

26 Mi amigo Javier

Completa este párrafo con la forma apropiada del verbo *pedir* o *repetir.*

Hola, soy Juan. Javier y yo somos amigos. Javier siempre (1) prestado muchas cosas. Un día (2) prestado unos cubiertos; otro día (3) azúcar. A veces tiene que (4) prestado dinero para comer más porque siempre tiene hambre. Cuando va a un restaurante, él y su hermana (5) muchas bebidas porque siempre tienen sed, y cuando están en el colegio siempre (6) ropa prestada a sus amigos porque siempre tienen frío. Yo nunca (7) prestado nada, y lo (8), nada. A mí no me gusta cuando los estudiantes (9) cosas prestadas. ¡Es muy malo! Yo siempre le debo (10) a Javier una y otra vez, "No debes pedir más cosas prestadas" pero él dice que yo soy egoísta. Mmm, ¿qué opinas si nosotros le (11) prestadas cosas a Javier todos los días? ¿Qué va a pensar?

Notes Explain that while the *e → ie* spelling change can occur in *-ar, -er* or *-ir* verbs, only *-ir* verbs make the *e → i* stem change. This change is indicated in *Navegando* by the first *i* shown in parentheses after listed infinitives.

You may wish to let students know that the second *i* in parentheses after the verbs

pedir (i, i) and *repetir (i, i)* will be explained in *Capítulo 7.*

The *vosotros/vosotras* verb endings are included for passive recognition. If you have decided to make these forms active, adapt the provided activities as needed.

Teacher Resources

 Activities 6–7

 Activities 11–14

 Activity 6

 Activities 10–12

Answers

26 1. pide
2. pide
3. pide
4. pedir
5. piden
6. piden
7. pido
8. repito
9. piden
10. repetir
11. pedimos

Activities

Expansion
Have a class discussion about how to use the expressions *pedir permiso (para), perdir perdón* and *pedir prestado/prestada.* Then call on students to use the *pedir* expressions in sentences as a volunteer writes each on the board.

Students with Special Needs
Review the *e → ie* stem-changing verbs before introducing the change *e → i.*

257

Activities

Critical Thinking

Check your students' ability to write what they hear, using the following dictation: *Julio pide la cucharita a su mamá. Sara piensa que la sopa necesita sal. Julio le pasa la sal a Sara. Papá necesita una cuchara también. Al papá de Julio y Sara le gustan las arepas. La mamá de Julio y Sara cocina todos los días. Todos pedimos permiso para salir.*

---

27 ¿Pedir o preguntar?

Completa las siguientes oraciones con la forma apropiada de *pedir* o *preguntar*.

1. ¿__ Ud. ayuda con su tarea a sus amigos?
2. Mi hermana y yo nos __ ¿cuándo vamos a vivir en una casa nueva?
3. A veces Rocío tiene que __ blusas prestadas a su mamá.
4. Javier siempre __ perdón cuando no comprende lo que dice la profesora.
5. Claudia siempre __ mucho en la clase de historia.
6. ¿__ siempre tú permiso para hablar por teléfono en tu casa?
7. Mis padres siempre me __ adónde voy.
8. Mi abuela siempre __ ayuda para subir la escalera.

Pido ayuda a la profesora.

28 ¿Qué haces o dices?

Match the circumstances in the column on the left with the most appropriate response in the column on the right.

1. Tienes que poner una mesa para diez amigos.
2. Necesitas con qué escribir.
3. Dices lo que no debes decir a tu madre.
4. Quieres salir del comedor.
5. No comprendes nada en clase de matemáticas.
6. Caminas en la calle y tienes prisa.
7. Dices una mentira a tu padre y él lo sabe.

A. Pido prestado un lápiz.
B. Digo "con permiso".
C. Hago preguntas al profesor.
D. Pido perdón.
E. Pido ayuda.

29 En familia

¿Qué dices o haces en estas situaciones? Sigue el modelo.

MODELO **Situación:** Tu madre te pide hacer muchos quehaceres antes de poder ver la televisión.
Pido ayuda a mis hermanos menores.

1. **Situación:** Estás en el comedor y tu madre dice que debes hablar poco y comer más.
2. **Situación:** Eres el primero/la primera en terminar de comer y quieres ir a tu cuarto porque tienes mucho sueño.
3. **Situación:** Quieres ir con tus amigos a una fiesta por la noche.
4. **Situación:** Tú dices que tienes mucha sed y tu madre te pasa un refresco.
5. **Situación:** Vas a salir para ir al colegio y ves que no tienes una camisa limpia.

Nuestra madre nos pide hacer muchos quehaceres.

Notes Note that *pedir* doesn't require the preposition **for** because it is already included in the verb.

Comunicación

 30 ¿Cuándo pides perdón?

 In large groups, choose one person to be the moderator. Then conduct a discussion about circumstances in which you must ask someone to forgive you for what you have done. Make up any of the information you wish.

> MODELO A: Margarita, ¿cuándo pides perdón?
> B: Pido perdón cuando digo lo que no debo decir.

31 Para su cumpleaños

In groups or three talk first about a relative, and then say what he or she always asks for his/her birthday but never gets.

Mi hermano pide un carro nuevo para su cumpleaños.

> MODELO A: Tienes un hermano, ¿verdad?
> B: Sí. Se llama Miguel. Tiene dieciocho años.
> C: ¿Qué pide siempre tu hermano para su cumpleaños?
> B: Mi hermano siempre pide un carro nuevo.

32 ¿Qué piden prestado?

 Working in pairs, each of you must create two columns on a piece of paper. In the first column, list five or six family members or friends you know very well. Leave the other column blank for your partner to fill in as you talk. Exchange lists and discuss what the people listed always ask to borrow (e.g., *un bolígrafo, dinero*). As your partner talks, list next to the person's name in the second column what your partner says each person borrows. See if the people on the lists seem to borrow some objects more than others.

> MODELO A: ¿Qué pide siempre prestado tu prima?
> B: Siempre pide prestado dinero.

```
mi prima          dinero
mi hermano        _____
mi amigo Julio    _____
Ana y Diego       _____
yo                _____
```

Answers

33 Possible answers:
1. Están en Pereira, en la región cafetera de Colombia.
2. Practican agroturismo.
3. Villa María es una finca cafetera. La casa tiene cinco cuartos, cuatro baños, una cocina y una sala.
4. Hay una piscina para nadar, caballos y senderos donde caminar.
5. Tiene ganas de continuar los conciertos.

34 Answers will vary.

Activities

Connections

As a connection to language arts, have students create the following scenario. They should imagine they are travel writers for a local newspaper. Have them write a one-page article about the Colombian city of their choice. They should include what to see and do, where to stay and where to find good, inexpensive restaurants.

Technology

Have students search the Internet for Web pages advertising trips to Colombia. They should skim the contents for phrases they recognize and then share the information with the class.

Lectura personal

Cantantes y grupos musicales

Dirección http://www.emcp.com/músico/ola/e.diario-5.htm ▲ Archivo Edición Ver Favoritos Herramientas Ayuda

página principal   miembros   e-diario

Grupo musical La Ola

Nombre: **Chantal Morales Rivera**
Edad: **16 años**
País natal: **República Dominicana**
Actividad favorita: **correr por la playa**

Una plantación de café en Colombia.

¡Otro gran concierto en Cali, Colombia! Ya son diez conciertos y la verdad es que estamos un poco cansados. Por eso[1] desde el viernes estamos en la región cafetera[2] de Colombia, disfrutando[3] de una forma de turismo relativamente nueva: el agroturismo. En los años noventa, los caficultores[4] decidieron que sus plantaciones de café no solamente servían[5] para exportar "*the richest coffee in the world*" sino también para importar turistas y generar ingresos[6] complementarios. Así fue como[7] cientos de fincas[8] han sido[9] adaptadas para invitar al turista. La finca en que estamos se llama Villa María y está a veinte minutos de Pereira. La casa tiene cinco cuartos, cuatro baños, una cocina y una sala. También hay piscina, caballos y muchos senderos[10]. De aquí me gustan mucho el olor[11] del café, el silencio del campo[12] y los diferentes verdes de las montañas. Ya comprendo por qué miles de personas se dedican al agroturismo en la tierra[13] del café. Ahora estoy descansada[14] y tengo ganas de continuar los conciertos. ¡Gracias, Colombia!

[1]That is why [2]coffee growing [3]enjoying [4]coffee growers [5]served [6]income [7]That is how [8]plantations
[9]have been [10]pathways [11]smell [12]countryside [13]land [14]rested

33 ¿Qué recuerdas?

1. ¿Dónde están los miembros del grupo musical La Ola?
2. ¿Qué tipo de turismo practican?
3. ¿Qué es Villa María? ¿Cómo es la casa?
4. ¿Qué hay para hacer en Villa María?
5. Al final, ¿qué tiene ganas de hacer Chantal?

- Make several comparisons between the coffee-growing region of Colombia and the region in the United States in which you live. Which one emphasizes rural life more?

34 Algo personal

1. ¿Adónde te gusta ir de vacaciones? ¿Qué haces allí?
2. Describe tu hotel ideal.
3. ¿Te gustaría hacer agroturismo? ¿Por qué sí o por qué no?

260 *doscientos sesenta*   **Lección B**

Notes Students may write to the Colombian embassy or the Organization of American States (OAS) in Washington, D.C., for information regarding tourism in Cali and other Colombian cities. They also may search the Internet, where they will find a number of different sites with information about travel in Colombia. (Give students the addresses listed in the ATE margin on page 261 or refer to the *Navegando 1* ATE Introduction for help with using the Internet.)

¿Qué aprendí?

Visit the web-based activities at www.emcp.com

Autoevaluación

As a review and self-check, respond to the following:

1. Describe your house.

2. Tell a friend what two different people say, including yourself.

3. Say where you would like to live.

4. Tell how you feel in these situations: it is hot and your mouth is dry, it is noon and you have not eaten, you stayed up too late and it is the next morning.

5. Imagine a classmate needs to borrow a pen and paper. How can you tell the person he or she should borrow the items from someone else because you do not have them?

6. What two things have you learned about Colombia?

Palabras y expresiones

La casa
el baño
el cuarto
la escalera
el garaje
el patio
la piscina
el piso
la planta
la planta baja
el primer piso
la sala

Para describir
al lado de
cómodo,-a
cuando

desde
donde
el lado
pequeño,-a
poco, -a
por
por la noche
primer

¿Cómo estás?
el calor
el frío
la gana
el hambre *(f.)*
el miedo
la prisa
¿Qué (+ tener)?

la sed
el sueño
tener (calor, frío, ganas
  de, hambre, miedo
  de, prisa, sed,
  sueño)

Otras expresiones
el abrazo
la carta
el dibujo
lo que
me/te/le/nos/les
  gustaría
la mentira
pedir (perdón, permiso,
  prestado,-a)

por teléfono
querer decir
querido,-a
la verdad

Verbos
aprender a
correr
decir (+ que)
escribir
gustaría
pedir (i, i)
repetir (i, i)

Nuestra casa tiene una piscina.

¿Te gusta mi cuarto?

Capítulo 6

doscientos sesenta y uno **261**

Teacher Resources

📝 **Activity 15**

💬 **Information Gap Activities**
Postcard Activities
Funciones de Comunicación

Answers

Autoevaluación
Possible answers:
1. Mi casa es azul. Tiene dos pisos. Mi cuarto está al lado del baño en el primer piso.
2. Mi mamá dice que debo estudiar más. Yo digo que Colombia es un país interesante.
3. Me gustaría vivir en Cartagena.
4. Tengo sed. Tengo hambre. Tengo sueño.
5. Debes pedir prestados un bolígrafo y papel de otro/otra estudiante porque yo no los tengo.
6. Answers will vary.

Activities

Spanish for Spanish Speakers
Have students write a short composition in Spanish summarizing what they know about Colombia. Expand the activity by having students seek additional information about Colombia at the library or via the Internet.

Notes Encourage students to find out more about Colombia by going to the following Web sites:

Lonely Planet World Guide
http://www.lonelyplanet.com/destinations/south_america/colombia/
Electronic Embassy
http://www.embassy.org

Organization of American States
http://www.oas.org
general travel information
http://www.expedia.com

Preparación
1. El dibujo es de una casa.
2. Hay tres cuartos.
3. Hay un piano.
4. Answers will vary.

Pronunciation *(las letras* g y j*)*
Review the sound of *g* with students by explaining that when *g* is followed by *a*, *o* or *u* or by a consonant, the sound is similar to the sound of *g* in the English word **goat**: *ganas, tengo, gustar.* In addition, be sure to point out that students should pronounce both vowels in the letter combinations *ua* and *uo (ambiguo, guapo),* whereas the letter combinations *ue* and *ui* should be pronounced as one sound *(Miguel, guitarra).* The letters *j* and *g* sound similar when the *g* is followed by *e* or *i.* The sound is similar to the sound of *wh* in the English word **who** *(baja, relojes, jirafa, dibujo, jueves, Cartagena, página).* **Note:** It may be necessary to explain the meaning of the two example words *ambiguo* (ambiguous) and *jirafa* (giraffe).

¡Viento en popa!

Tú lees

Preparación
Mira el dibujo para contestar las siguientes preguntas como preparación para la lectura.

1. ¿De qué es el dibujo?
2. ¿Cuántos cuartos hay en el dibujo?
3. ¿Qué hay en la sala?
4. ¿Qué piensas que vas a leer?

La casa de mis sueños

Me llamo Santiago y soy de Caracas. Aquí hay un dibujo de la casa de mis sueños[1]. Claro que[2] el dibujo no es perfecto. En la casa de mis sueños hay tres cuartos y todos son grandes. En la sala hay un piano para tocar música clásica y una biblioteca con todos los libros que me gustan. Al lado de la sala hay un cuarto para ver la televisión y películas en DVD. También hay una computadora con quemador de CDs y muchos videojuegos. Mi cuarto es grande, con una cama también grande, muchos pósters en la pared y un equipo de sonido. El cuarto de mis padres tiene una puerta que abre al patio y al jardín. El patio y el jardín son bonitos, con muchas flores. La flor favorita de mi mamá es el jazmín. Nuestro jardín está rodeado[3] de jazmines. En el jardín hay también una piscina olímpica con un trampolín donde puedo nadar todos los días.

Notes Complete the *Preparación* with the class. Ask what students think the reading is about.

The reading *La casa de mis sueños* is recorded and available in the Audio CD Program. You may wish to play the CD to allow students to hear Santiago's description of his dream home.

En la casa de mis sueños, el lugar favorito de mis papás es la cocina. En la cocina papá y mamá preparan comidas exquisitas para cenar. Mi comida favorita es el ajiaco, ¡esa sopa de Colombia tan rica de papas, pollo, maíz, aguacate y crema de leche[4]! Como la cocina es tan grande[5], ellos siempre tienen muchos invitados[6]. La casa tiene muchas ventanas y mucha luz. ¡Quiero algún día construir[7] la casa de mis sueños!

[1]dreams   [2]Of course   [3]surrounded by   [4]potatoes, chicken, corn, avocado and whipping cream   [5]so big
[6]guests   [7]some day build

A ¿Qué recuerdas?

1. ¿De quién es el dibujo de la casa?
2. ¿Cómo son los cuartos de la casa?
3. ¿Qué hay en la biblioteca?
4. ¿Dónde están la computadora y los videojuegos?
5. ¿Qué hay en el cuarto de Santiago?
6. ¿Cuál es el lugar favorito de los padres de Santiago?
7. ¿Qué hacen los padres en la cocina?
8. ¿Qué flores hay en el jardín?
9. ¿Qué es el ajiaco y de dónde es?

B Algo personal

1. ¿Cómo es la casa de tus sueños?
2. ¿En qué son diferentes la casa de los sueños de Santiago y tu casa de los sueños? ¿En qué son similares?
3. ¿Cómo es tu cuarto en la casa de tus sueños? ¿Qué hay en él?
4. ¿Cuál es tu lugar favorito en la casa de tus sueños?

¿Cómo es la casa de tus sueños?

Answers

A 1. Es de Santiago.
  2. Son grandes.
  3. Los libros que le gustan a Santiago.
  4. Están en un cuarto al lado de la sala.
  5. Hay una cama grande, muchos pósters en la pared y un equipo de sonido.
  6. Su lugar favorito es la cocina.
  7. Preparan comidas exquisitas.
  8. Hay muchos jazmines.
  9. Es una sopa de Colombia.
B Answers will vary.

Activities

Multiple Intelligences (spatial)
Ask for volunteers to create a pop-up version of the home and present it to the class.

Prereading Strategy
Remind students they should not feel they must understand every word to read in Spanish.

Technology
Search the Internet for free floor plans to get ideas for completing a project titled *La casa de mis sueños*.

Notes Whereas in Spanish-speaking countries a patio is an outdoor area that may have plants and a place where people might sit and chat, when talking about homes in the United States, the word *patio* in Spanish can mean **yard.**

Tú escribes

Estrategia

Connecting phrases
Your writing style may seem choppy in Spanish unless you connect your thoughts using transition words like *a causa de* (because of), *como* (since, like, as), *después* (later), *entonces* (then), *pero* (but), *por eso* (therefore), *sin embargo* (however), *también* (also), *y* (and). These words can act like adhesive to bind together the ideas in a paragraph as a connected unit.

First, write several sentences that describe your *casa de tus sueños*. Include information such as what the house looks like, where it is located, what rooms it has, how many windows and doors it has, where rooms are located and any other details you wish to include. Then add transition words to make your sentences flow more smoothly and put the sentences together, one after another in paragraph form, to create a composition. Finally, create a colorful drawing of the house, including details that match your description.

MODELO La casa de mis sueños está en una playa en América del Sur. Es muy grande. Tiene muchos cuartos y jardines....

La casa de mis sueños está en la playa.

Notes Review the contents of the *Estrategia* with the class. Then give several examples of sentences that contain connecting words before assigning the writing.

Consider having students pair up to review one another's sentences before having them finalize their compositions.

Ask individuals if it is all right to display their composition for others in the class to read.

Proyectos adicionales

A Conexión cultural

Imagine you are traveling with your family to Venezuela and Colombia on vacation and your parents have asked you to make suggestions about what to see and do. Use the library or the Internet to investigate cities you might visit. Then create a travel itinerary offering suggestions for the trip to both countries. Consider including the following in your list of recommendations: cities to visit, tourist attractions, your recommendation for the best time to visit South America and any other information you can find that may be of use during the trip.

B Conexión con la tecnología

Write a short e-mail in Spanish to someone you know about your home and family. Use Santiago's letter (see p. 244) as a model, if necessary.

Castillo de San Felipe, Cartagena.

C Comparando

Working in pairs, talk about what you know about housing and home life in the United States and in Spanish-speaking parts of the world such as Venezuela, Colombia, Puerto Rico and the Dominican Republic. Then make a side-by-side comparison listing at least five similarities or differences.

D ¡A escribir!

Help Santiago's parents write back to him (see p. 244). Include the following information: They are happy to hear from their dear son; they know that he is far from home in Caracas, but not far from his family; they want to see the photos of the trip to Cartagena. Include any other details you wish. Remember to include the city and the date and use appropriate greetings and farewells.

Answers

A Creative problem solving.
B Creative self-expression.
C Creative self-expression.
D Creative self-expression.

Activities

Critical Thinking
One of the many fascinating results of European exploration was the food exchange that brought new foods and animals to the Americas and took others to Europe. For example, the Spaniards brought cattle and spices to the Americas and returned with many foods new to Europe, such as tomatoes and potatoes. Ask students to research this food exchange and consider its impact on the diets of people around the world.

Multiple Intelligences (spatial)
Invite students to make a collage in which they profile a Spanish-speaking country of special interest. Good sources of information include sites on the Internet and materials provided by national tourism offices.

Notes **Cultures.** Note for students that in Latin America, many middle- and upper-class families traditionally employ a maid to assist with household chores.

Two well-known literary figures from Venezuela are Rómulo Gallegos, author of *Doña Bárbara* and former president of Venezuela, and Arturo Uslar Pietri, critic, short-story writer and novelist. Pietri's best-known work is *Las lanzas coloradas*. In 1990 he received the *Príncipe de Asturias* prize, one of the most important literary prizes in the Hispanic world.

One of Colombia's most famous citizens is Gabriel García Márquez, winner of the Nobel Prize in literature.

Teacher Resources

 Trabalenguas

Activities

Connections
In groups of four, have students research the life of Simón Bolívar. Then have them write a simple dialog, design a piece of art or prepare some other artistic reflection of an important period of his life and present it to the class.

Language through Action
Bring in table place settings and food items (or magazine pictures of these items). Then use the *tú* and *Uds.* commands of *pasar*, *comer*, *tomar* and other verbs, along with the food and table vocabulary from this lesson. Students should show comprehension by actually handing the items to the appropriate person: *pásame la sal, pásale el pan a* (name of student).

Spanish for Spanish Speakers
Have students research and write about Rómulo Gallegos, Arturo Uslar Pietri or Gabriel García Márquez.

Repaso

Now that I have completed this chapter, I can...	Go to these pages for help:
identify items in the kitchen and at the dinner table.	226
express obligations, wishes and preferences.	226
talk about everyday activities.	226
state an opinion.	231
discuss food and table items.	231
point out people and things.	238
describe a household.	244
tell what someone says.	252
say how someone is doing.	252

I can also...	
talk about products and foods from Venezuela and Colombia.	229, 247
discuss home life in Venezuela and Colombia.	237, 255
describe my home.	244
recognize words in context.	251
recognize when to use *pedir* or *preguntar*.	257
plan a trip to Venezuela or Colombia.	265

Trabalenguas

La casa está en la plaza, en la casa hay un cuarto, dentro del cuarto hay un piso, encima del piso hay una mesa, encima de la mesa hay una jaula, dentro de la jaula hay un loro que canta y dice: de loro en jaula, jaula en mesa, mesa en piso, piso en cuarto, cuarto en casa, casa en la plaza.

Notes Loose translation of the *Trabalenguas:* The house is on the square, in the house there is a room, in the room there is a floor, on the floor there is a table, on the table there is a bird cage, in the bird cage there is a parrot who sings and says: from parrot to bird cage, bird cage to table, table to floor, floor to room, room to house, house to the square.

Although large earthquakes *(terremotos)* are not common in Colombia, they do sometimes occur. In January of 1999, an earthquake that measured 6.0 on the Richter scale destroyed the cities of Pereira and Armenia and several villages in the coffee-producing region of Colombia. The earthquake killed nearly 1,000 people.

Vocabulario

el **abrazo** hug *6B*
el **aceite** oil *6A*
al lado de next to, beside *6B*
allá over there *6A*
aprender a *6B*
aquel, aquella (aquellos, aquellas) that, (those) *far away 6A*
ayudar to help *6A*
el **azúcar** sugar *6A*
el **baño** bathroom *6B*
el **calor** heat *6B*
la **carta** letter *6B*
cerrar (ie) to close *6A*
la **cocina** kitchen *6A*
el **comedor** dining room *6A*
cómodo,-a comfortable *6B*
correr to run *6B*
la **cosa** thing *6A*
cuando when *6B*
el **cuarto** room, bedroom *6B*
los **cubiertos** silverware *6A*
la **cuchara** spoon *6A*
la **cucharita** teaspoon *6A*
el **cuchillo** knife *6A*
de todos los días everyday *6A*
deber should, to have to, must, ought *6A*
decir (+ *que*) to tell, to say *6B*
desde since, from *6B*
después afterwards, later, then *6A*
el **dibujo** drawing, sketch *6B*
dónde where *6B*
e and *(used before a word beginning with* i *or* hi) *6B*
empezar *(ie)* to begin, to start *6A*
encender *(ie)* to light, to turn on *(a light)* *6A*
entonces then *6A*
la **escalera** stairway, stairs *6B*
escribir to write *6B*
ese, esa (esos, esas) that (those) *6A*

especial special *6A*
este, esta (estos, estas) this (these) *6A*
la **estufa** stove *6A*
el **fregadero** sink *6A*
el **frío** cold *6B*
la **gana** desire *6B*
el **garaje** garage *6B*
gustaría would like *6B*
el **hambre** *(f.)* hunger *6B*
el **horno microondas** microwave oven *6A*
el **lado** side *6B*
la **lámpara** lamp *6A*
el **lavaplatos** dishwasher *6A*
lo que what, that which *6B*
la **luz** light *6A*
el **mantel** tablecloth *6A*
la **mantequilla** butter *6A*
me/te/le/nos/les gustaría I/you/he/she/it/we/they would like *6B*
la **mentira** lie *6B*
la **mesa** table *6A*
el **miedo** fear *6B*
otra vez again, another time *6A*
el **pan** bread *6A*
pásame pass me *6A*
el **patio** courtyard, patio, yard *6B*
pedir (i, i) to ask for, to order, to request; *pedir perdón* to say you are sorry; *pedir permiso (para)* to ask for permission (to do something); *pedir prestado,-a* to borrow *6B*
pensar (ie) to think, to intend, to plan *6A*
pensar de/en/que to think about *6A*
pequeño,-a small *6B*
el **permiso** permission, permit *6B*
la **pimienta** pepper *(seasoning)* *6A*
la **piscina** swimming pool *6B*
el **piso** floor *6B*
la **planta** plant *6B*
la **planta baja** ground floor *6B*

el **plato** dish, plate *6A*
el **plato de sopa** soup bowl *6A*
poco, -a not very, little *6B*
poner to put, to place *6A*
poner la mesa to set the table *6A*
por through, by *6B*
por la noche at night *6B*
por teléfono by phone *6B*
el **postre** dessert *6A*
preferir (ie) to prefer *6A*
primer first *6B*
el **primer piso** first floor *6B*
la **prisa** rush, hurry, haste *6B*
¿Qué (+ *tener)?* What is wrong *(with someone)* *6B*
querer (ie) to love, to want, to like *6A*
querer decir to mean *6B*
querido,-a dear *6B*
el **refrigerador** refrigerator *6A*
repetir (i, i) to repeat *6B*
la **sal** salt *6A*
la **sala** living room *6B*
la **sed** thirst *6B*
sentir (ie) to be sorry, to feel sorry, to regret *6A*
la **servilleta** napkin *6A*
la **sopa** soup *6A*
el **sueño** sleep *6B*
la **taza** cup *6A*
el **tenedor** fork *6A*
tener (calor, frío, hambre, miedo de, prisa, sed, sueño) to be (hot, cold, hungry, afraid, in a hurry, thirsty, sleepy) *6B*
tener ganas de to feel like *6B*
tener que to have to *6A*
u or *(used before a word that starts with* o *or* ho) *6B*
un poco (de) a little (bit) *6A*
el **vaso** glass *6A*
la **verdad** truth *6B*
viajar to travel *6A*
ya already *6A*

Notes Other ways to say *la estufa* include *la hornilla* and *el fogón.* In some countries people refer to the **stove** as *la cocina.*

El refrigerador is also called *el frigorífico,* although some people prefer to use the term *la nevera,* which is equivalent to **icebox.**

Teacher Resources

 Module 2

 Episode 6

Testing/ Assessment
Test Booklet
Portfolio Assessment

Activities

Critical Listening
Pronounce the following carefully, having students say the sentence several times before writing what they hear: *Zoraida, Susana y yo vamos a hacer un mapa de Venezuela con la tiza en la pizarra.* Ask students if they understand the meaning of the sentence.

Pronunciation *(las letras c, s y z)*
Review the pronunciation of the letters *c, s* and *z* with students by explaining that the letter *c* (followed by *e* or *i*), the letter *s* and the letter *z* are pronounced like the *s* in the English word **Sally,** except in most of Spain, where *c* and *z* followed by *e* or *i* are pronounced like *th* in the English word **thin.** Your students may find it interesting to hear you model this difference in pronunciation.

Activities

Critical Thinking

The poster and large photograph that appear on pages 268–269 depict the chapter functions, cultural setting and themes for *Capítulo 7*. The visual support is intended to help further student awareness of and connections to how Spanish is used outside the controlled environment of the classroom as well as to help prepare them for learning about *el tiempo libre*. Ask students what conclusions they can draw from the two images. Ask if students can guess in what two countries or part of the world this chapter takes place.

Capítulo **7**

El tiempo libre

Objetivos

❖ talk about leisure time activities

❖ discuss sports

❖ say what someone can do

❖ discuss length of time

❖ describe what is happening

❖ talk about the seasons and weather

❖ indicate order

Visit the web-based activities at www.emcp.com

268 *doscientos sesenta y ocho*

Notes Discuss the contents of pages 268–269. Explain that the small photo is a poster of Carlos Gardel, who is considered to be the father of the tango. The *Cultura viva* on page 279 discusses the tango in greater detail. The large photograph depicts two skiers in Portillo, Chile. Chile is discussed in greater detail on page 293.

Communicative objectives are provided here to prepare students for the chapter they are about to begin. Discuss the objectives for *Capítulo 7* with students. A checkoff list of functions appears on page 314, along with additional objectives, so students can do a self-check to evaluate their progress.

Contexto cultural

Argentina
Nombre oficial: **República Argentina**
Población: **37.488.000**
Capital: **Buenos Aires**
Ciudades importantes: **Córdoba, Mendoza, San Juan**
Unidad monetaria: **el peso**
Fiesta nacional: **9 de julio, Proclamación de la Independencia**
Gente famosa: **Jorge Luis Borges (escritor); Evita Perón (líder popular)**

Chile
Nombre oficial: **República de Chile**
Población: **15.403.000**
Capital: **Santiago de Chile**
Ciudades importantes: **Valparaíso, Viña del Mar**
Unidad monetaria: **el peso**
Fiesta nacional: **18 de septiembre, Día de la Independencia**
Gente famosa: **Pablo Neruda, Isabel Allende, Gabriela Mistral (escritores)**

Activities

Expansion
Ask students what they know about Argentina and Chile. Ask for two volunteers to go to the board. One student should list what students know about Argentina and the other student should write down what classmates say about Chile. After five or six points are listed for each country, have students decide how the countries are similar and how they are different. (Start the list by stating that both are countries in South America.)

doscientos sesenta y nueve **269**

Notes The cultural focus of this chapter is on the South American countries of Argentina and Chile. Students will be learning to discuss what people do in their free time, in particular what people in Argentina and Chile do during their free time.

Lección A

Argentina

Vocabulario I
Los pasatiempos

Toda Una Vida

¿Cuándo vas a hacer las tareas?

¿No recuerdas que quiero ver mi programa favorito? Vuelvo en cinco minutos.

Todavía no. Esta noche, después del partido.

Sí, sí, está bien.

el televisor

El Equipo de Argentina

A Graciela le gusta ver la telenovela *Toda Una Vida* y ahora no puede. A Graciela le gustaría tener un televisor en su cuarto pero cuestan mucho. El papá de Graciela le va a dar un televisor para su cumpleaños.

Notes The word *dar* is presented in *Lección A* in its infinitive form only. The present tense of *dar* is taught in *Lección B*.

Explain to the class that the word *televisor* refers specifically to the television set. Thus, native Spanish speakers say *poner el televisor* but *ver televisión*.

Point out that students may hear *encender* or *prender* used as they travel in some countries instead of *poner* to mean **to turn on** a light or appliance.

Telenovelas are very popular in Hispanic countries.

jugar a los videojuegos
jugar al fútbol americano
jugar al básquetbol
jugar al voleibol
jugar a las damas
jugar al ajedrez
hacer aeróbicos
jugar a las cartas
dibujar

1 ¿Qué actividad es?

Identifica la actividad que oyes.

A   B   C

D   E   F

2 ¡Yo sé lo que vas a hacer!

Create a list of at least ten leisure activities. Then, working in small groups, take turns playing charades to act out activities on your list. The winner is the person who first says *¡Yo sé lo que vas a hacer!*

Teacher Resources

 Activity 1

 Activity 1

 Activities 47–48

 Activities 1–2

 Activity 1

GV Activities 2–3

Answers

1 1. C
2. A
3. B
4. D
5. E
6. F
2 Creative self-expression.

Activities

TPR
In advance, write on separate pieces of paper the Spanish terms for the pastimes shown on page 271. Then have students select one of the pieces of paper at random. Call on several students to act out the expressions while classmates guess what the expressions are in Spanish.

Notes Point out for students that the word **volleyball** has several variations in Spanish, the most common being *voleibol* and *volibol*.

Ask your students if they have ever seen a soap opera in Spanish. Spanish-language television channels in the United States present soap operas primarily from Mexico and Venezuela.

Teacher Resources

¿No quieres jugar al ajedrez?
Activities 3–5

Answers

3 1. Ella quiere jugar al ajedrez.
2. Ve su telenovela favorita.
3. Va a jugar el equipo de Argentina.
4. Va a ver fútbol.
5. Su vida ahora es ver televisión y jugar al fútbol.
4 Answers will vary.
5 1. Falso.; 2. Cierto.; 3. Cierto.; 4. Falso.; 5. Falso.

Activities

Expansion
Additional questions *(Algo personal)*: ¿Hay telenovelas en español en tu ciudad? ¿Cómo se llaman?; ¿Cómo se llama tu programa favorito? ¿A qué hora es el programa?; ¿Te gusta ver deportes en la televisión?

Prereading Strategy
Prepare students for the reading by having them cover up the dialog with one hand and look at the photographs. Then ask them to imagine where the conversation takes place and what the people are saying to one another. Finally, have students scan the dialog to find cognates and other words they recognize.

272

Diálogo 1
¿No quieres jugar al ajedrez?

LUZ: ¿No quieres jugar al ajedrez?
HUGO: Sí, pero después de este programa.
LUZ: ¿Qué programa es?
HUGO: Es mi telenovela favorita.

LUZ: ¿Ahora sí?
HUGO: ¿Por qué no vienes en dos horas?
LUZ: ¿Cómo? ¿No vamos a jugar al ajedrez?
HUGO: Es que el equipo de Argentina va a jugar ahora.

LUZ: ¡Veo que ya no sabes jugar al ajedrez!
HUGO: Sí, ya no recuerdo cómo jugar.
LUZ: ¡Claro! Tu vida ahora es ver televisión.
HUGO: No. ¡Mi vida ahora es ver televisión y jugar al fútbol!

3 ¿Qué recuerdas?

1. ¿A qué quiere jugar Luz?
2. ¿Qué programa ve Hugo?
3. ¿Qué equipo va a jugar?
4. ¿Qué va a ver Hugo?
5. ¿Cómo es ahora la vida de Hugo?

¡Extra!

La fiebre del gol

It is easy to understand why Hugo is distracted as he talks with Luz. For many people, soccer *(el fútbol)* is more than just a simple pastime in Argentina and throughout the Spanish-speaking world. During the World Cup *(la Copa Mundial)* fans of all ages follow the action and nearly everyone has *la fiebre del gol* (goal fever).

4 Algo personal

1. ¿Sabes jugar al fútbol?
2. ¿Te gusta jugar al ajedrez?
3. ¿Qué vas a hacer esta noche?
4. ¿Te gusta ver televisión?

5 ¿Qué comprendiste?

Di si los que oyes es cierto o falso, según el diálogo *¿No quieres jugar al ajedrez?*

¿Sabes jugar al ajedrez?

272 *doscientos setenta y dos* **Lección A**

Notes *La fiebre del gol* is at its peak during *la Copa Mundial de fútbol* (World Cup), which is held every four years. Ask if students are able to name recent World Cup winners or host countries.

The *Navegando 1* Video/DVD Program uses a soap opera format and was filmed on location by professional actors.

Episodes were written to reflect the content of corresponding chapters in the textbook. Students will enjoy meeting the characters and following them through the challenges they face in everyday life.

Cultura viva

Buenos Aires, Argentina.

Argentina

Whether you enjoy countryside landscapes, soaring mountains, beautiful beaches or the hustle and bustle of modern city life, Argentina has it all. As the largest Spanish-speaking country in the world, the southernmost tip of Argentina begins near the frigid South Pole and extends north to the tropics of central South America. The plains of Patagonia in the south are the heart of the sheep-raising industry. In the central plains *(las pampas),* cowboys known as *gauchos* tend herds of cattle on large ranches called *estancias.* (Argentina produces beef that is sold and shipped throughout the world.) In addition, world-class ski resorts, such as Bariloche, draw visitors from many countries. Argentina's capital, Buenos Aires, is a vibrant, modern city that combines skyscrapers *(rascacielos),* plazas and parks, outstanding food and interesting old buildings into what has been called the "Paris of the Spanish-speaking world."

Una gaucha.

While visiting Argentina, you may find yourself alone atop a mountain *(Aconcagua)* or in a crowded cafe. Argentina's population includes descendants from large numbers of people from Spain, Italy, Poland, Germany, Great Britain and Japan. Wondering what to do? Ski the famous slopes of the *Andes,* dance the tango in the colorful neighborhood called *La Boca,* participate in the national sport— *el fútbol* or sit back and gaze at the breathtaking *Iguazú* waterfalls. And before you leave, try grilled beef *(carne a la parrilla)* in one of the capital's many fine restaurants or have a seat and sip a wonderful tea-like hot drink called *mate.*

Las cascadas de Iguazú.

6 Argentina

¿Cierto o falso?

1. Hay playas bonitas en la Argentina.
2. El país más grande de habla hispana es Ecuador.
3. Los gauchos viven en grandes estancias de las pampas.
4. Bariloche es la capital de la Argentina.
5. Hay muchas personas en la Argentina de Italia y Polonia.
6. El baile más famoso de la Argentina es el tango.
7. *Mate* es una ciudad en la Argentina.
8. El deporte nacional de la Argentina es el fútbol.

Teacher Resources

 Activity 6

 Activity 2

 Activity 3

Answers

6 1. Cierto.
2. Falso.
3. Cierto.
4. Falso.
5. Cierto.
6. Cierto.
7. Falso.
8. Cierto.

Activities

Critical Listening
Explain to the class that the term *rascacielos* (skyscraper) comes from a combination of the words *rascar* and *cielos.* Other such combinations exist in both Spanish and English. Ask students to listen to the following words and try to identify their English equivalents: *telenovela, aeropuerto, paraguas, parabrisas, quitasol, quitanieves.*

Notes The gauchos of Argentina have a rich and colorful history and can be compared in many ways to the cowboys of the United States. Their main tool is the *bola,* a type of sling consisting of heavy weights tied to the ends of a leather cord. It is thrown to entangle the legs of cattle or game.

Argentina produces a lot of beef, much of which is exported.

Aconcagua is the highest mountain peak in the Western Hemisphere.

The tango is discussed in greater detail later in this lesson.

Idioma

Estructura

Stem-changing verbs: *o → ue* and *u → ue*

Some verbs require the change *o → ue (poder)* or *u → ue (jugar)* in all forms of their present-tense stem except for *nosotros* and *vosotros.* These stem changes do not interfere with regular verb endings.

poder	
puedo	podemos
puedes	podéis
puede	**pue**den

jugar	
juego	jugamos
juegas	jugáis
juega	**jue**gan

Other *o → ue* stem-changing verbs include *costar (ue), recordar (ue)* and *volver (ue).*

 Práctica

7 Todos quieren ayudar

If everyone works together they will be free to do what they want later in the day. Say what these people can do to help with lunch, according to the cues.

MODELO Marta (buscar los platos)
Marta puede buscar los platos.

1. papá (comprar leche y pan)
2. yo (buscar los cubiertos)
3. mi mamá (hacer el almuerzo)
4. tú (poner la mesa)
5. nosotros (preparar un postre)
6. mis hermanos (poner los platos sucios en el lavaplatos)

¿Quién puede buscar los platos?

8 El televisor

Completa el siguiente párrafo con la forma apropiada de uno de los siguientes verbos: *poder, costar, volver, jugar, recordar.*

Yo siempre (1) cuando (2) el equipo de Argentina. Mi papá y yo vemos el partido por televisión. A mi hermana no le gusta el fútbol pero ella (3) leer o salir con sus amigos. No (4) tener otro televisor porque (5) mucho y nuestra casa no es grande. Mi hermana (6) a las cuatro, ella (7) ver su telenovela y entonces yo (8) al fútbol con mis amigos en el parque.

Notes The verbs *poder* and *recordar* can be followed by an infinitive in double-verb constructions: *puedo ir con ella a la tienda; recuerda comprar un vestido azul.*

The preposition *a* typically follows the verb *jugar* and precedes the name of a sport or game: *jugar al fútbol* and *jugar a las cartas.*

9 Una invitación

In pairs, take turns inviting one another to do the indicated activities. Answer by either refusing or accepting the invitation, giving an excuse if you refuse or changing the suggested time if you accept.

MODELO jugar al básquetbol

> **A:** ¿Puedes jugar al básquetbol hoy?
> **B:** Lo siento, pero no puedo. Es muy tarde.

1. jugar a los videojuegos esta tarde
2. ver mis fotos de Chile ahora
3. ir al cine pasado mañana
4. jugar al fútbol americano el sábado
5. jugar al voleibol a las 6:30
6. hacer aeróbicos mañana

 10 ¿Cuándo vuelven?

 In pairs, talk about when these people will be returning from the places mentioned.

MODELO Eva / la casa de Gloria   `PM 7:00`

> **A:** ¿A qué hora vuelve Eva de la casa de Gloria?
> **B:** Eva vuelve de la casa de Gloria a las siete.

1. Ana y Luz / la piscina   `PM 6:40`
2. tú y yo / la tienda   `PM 1:25`
3. tú / el cine   `PM 1:50`
4. Esteban / el partido   `PM 9:30`

✥ Comunicación

 11 ¿A qué juegan?

With a classmate, talk about what these people are doing.

 1   2   3   4

 12 Los pasatiempos

In small groups, ask one another about your favorite pastimes (*pasatiempos*). Start with the activities shown in *Vocabulario I,* taking notes as you talk. Then choose one member of the group to report the information to the class.

MODELO **A:** ¿Juegas al fútbol?

> **B:** Sí, (No, no) juego al fútbol. Es mi pasatiempo favorito. ¿Y tú?

Capítulo 7   *doscientos setenta y cinco*   **275**

Notes Tell students that many Spanish-speaking natives drop the *al, a la, a las* and *a los* after *jugar* when naming a sport or game they play: *juego fútbol.* This practice is becoming common in speech.

Jugar is the only verb in Spanish that changes *u* to *ue* as part of a regular pattern.

Inform students whether you will be selecting the person to present the information to the class for activity 12 or whether students may choose their own group representative.

Teacher Resources

 Activity 9

Answers

9 Answers will vary.
10 1. ¿...vuelven ... de la piscina...?/...vuelven ... a las siete menos veinte.
2. ¿...volvemos ... de la tienda?/...volvemos ... a la una y veinticinco.
3. ¿...vuelves ... del colegio?/...vuelvo ... a las dos menos diez.
4. ¿...vuelve...?/...vuelve ... a las nueve y media.
11 Possible answers:
1. Los chicos juegan al fútbol americano.
2. Ellas juegan a las cartas.
3. Ella juega al básquetbol.
4. Ellos juegan al ajedrez.
12 Creative self-expression.

Activities

Expansion
Practice the stem-changing verbs by asking the following personalized questions: *¿Quién es tu atleta favorito/favorita y qué deporte juega?*; *¿Cuánto cuesta un televisor nuevo? ¿Lo puedes comprar?*; *¿Cuánto cuesta una bicicleta nueva? ¿La puedes comprar?*; *En un día normal, ¿a qué hora vuelves a casa (después del colegio)?*; *¿Cuándo vuelves tarde a casa?*

El tiempo libre

 Activity 4

 Activity 49

 Activities 8–9

 Activity 3

 Activities 7–8

Activities

Critical Thinking
Before playing the audio CD for *Vocabulario II,* ask students questions about the scene: Who are the people? What do students think the boy is doing? What is the man saying? What are the girls doing? What do they want to do in the afternoon?

Vocabulario II
El tiempo libre

276   *doscientos setenta y seis*   **Lección A**

Notes As you review *Vocabulario I,* explain that centuries are expressed with cardinal numbers in Spanish and that years cannot be abbreviated in spoken Spanish as they are in English. For example, **the 21st century** would be *el siglo veintiuno* and **2005** would be *dos mil cinco.*

Help students with the meaning of the sentences in the speech bubbles and in the boxes.

Note the pause word *Bueno* when the father talks. Ask students if they remember any other pause words he could have used.

13 El tiempo libre

 Selecciona la ilustración que corresponde con lo que oyes.

A

B

Tienda de video ABC

Nuevas películas:
· Historia de amor
· El hombre araña V
· El cuarto misterioso

C

PM 11:50

D

14 ¿Cuánto tiempo hay en...?

Contesta las siguientes preguntas.

1. ¿Cuántas semanas hay en un año?
2. ¿Cuántos años hay en un siglo?
3. ¿Cuántas horas hay en un día?
4. ¿Cuántos cuartos de hora hay en una hora?
5. ¿Cuántos segundos hay en un minuto?
6. ¿Cuántos minutos hay en una hora?
7. ¿Cuántos segundos hay en una hora?
8. ¿Cuántas horas hay en una semana?

¿Cuántos minutos hay en una hora?

Answers

13 1. D
2. A
3. B
4. C

14 1. Hay cincuenta y dos semanas en un año.
2. Hay cien años en un siglo.
3. Hay veinticuatro horas en un día.
4. Hay cuatro cuartos de hora en una hora.
5. Hay sesenta segundos en un minuto.
6. Hay sesenta minutos en una hora.
7. Hay 3.600 segundos en una hora.
8. Hay ciento sesenta y ocho horas en una semana.

Activities

Critical Thinking
Additional questions: *¿Cuántos minutos hay en un cuarto de hora?; ¿Cuántos días hay en una semana? ¿en tres semanas?; ¿Cuántos minutos hay en cuatro horas y media?; ¿Cuántos segundos hay en cuarenta y siete minutos?; ¿Cuántos meses hay en siete años?; ¿Cuántos meses hay en dos siglos?; ¿Cuántos meses hay en siete siglos?*

Notes Activity 13 is intended for listening comprehension practice. Play the audio CD of the activity or use the transcript that appears in the ATE Introduction if you prefer to read the activity yourself.

Before assigning activity 13, point out the symbols AM and PM in the two clocks.

You may want to have students complete activity 14 working in pairs.

Diálogo II

Quiero alquilar una película

HUGO: ¿Estás durmiendo?
LUZ: No. Estoy viendo televisión. ¿Por qué?
HUGO: Porque quiero ir a alquilar una película.

LUZ: ¿Ahora mismo?
HUGO: Sí, quiero ir antes de comer. ¿Quieres ir?
LUZ: Un segundo.... Ya voy.

LUZ: No quiero ver las mismas películas otra vez.
HUGO: ¿Cuánto tiempo hace que no ves una película?
LUZ: ¡Uy! Hace mucho tiempo. Casi dos meses.
HUGO: ¡Entonces no vas a ver las mismas películas!

15 ¿Qué recuerdas?

1. ¿Está Luz durmiendo?
2. ¿Qué quiere hacer Hugo?
3. ¿Cuándo quiere ir Hugo?
4. ¿Cuánto tiempo hace que Luz no ve una película?

16 Algo personal

1. ¿Cuánto tiempo hace que no alquilas una película?
2. ¿Haces una lista de películas antes de ir a alquilar una?
3. ¿Cuánto tiempo hace que no ves una película?
4. ¿Por cuánto tiempo ves televisión en una semana?
5. ¿Cuánto tiempo libre tienes en una semana? ¿Qué haces?

17 Dictado

 Escucha la información y escribe lo que oyes.

¿Cuánto tiempo hace que no alquilas una película?

Cultura viva

Che, bailá conmigo...

In the world of dance and music, *tango* is synonymous with Argentina, and especially Buenos Aires. This well-known song was born a century ago near the docks of the capital in the neighborhood known as *La Boca*. While there, if you look carefully, you will see a street sign with the name *Caminito* that denotes the short dead-end street *(callejuela).* This street's name has its

Bailamos el tango.

origins in one of Carlos Gardel's most famous tangos. Carlos Gardel is considered the father of the tango and he is revered in Argentina still today, decades after his death. From the docks in *La Boca,* the *tango* spread throughout the Americas to Europe and,

El Caminito, una callejuela en La Boca, Buenos Aires.

today, is popular in ballrooms throughout the world.

El tango es de la Argentina.

---

18 Conexiones con otras disciplinas: baile y música

Prepare a project on the tango, choosing from one of the following options or making up your own:

- Search the word *tango* on the Internet or by looking up the words *Argentina* and *tango* in an encyclopedia at the library and write a summary of your findings.
- Locate someone who teaches the tango and invite the person to speak or demonstrate the tango for the class.
- Attend tango classes at a local community center or at a local dance studio and demonstrate the dance for the class.
- Play a tango for the class, comparing it to another musical style.

Capítulo 7   *doscientos setenta y nueve*   **279**

Notes Remind students that language changes as people travel, as demonstrated in the title of this *Cultura viva*. For example, in Argentina, the word *che* is equivalent to **buddy** or **friend** and is used in informal conversations. Costa Ricans would probably use the term *maje* in the same circumstances. Similarly, *vos bailás* is used in Argentina to say **you dance,** whereas in most other Spanish-speaking countries people would probably say *tú bailas.*

    The title of this *Cultura viva* is derived from the combination of *che* (explained above) with the informal command *bailá* (formed by dropping *tú* and the final *-s*) and adding the word *conmigo* (meaning **with me**) to complete the invitation.

Answers

19 1. Hace más de un siglo que juegan al béisbol en los Estados Unidos.
2. Hace un año que jugamos al voleibol.
3. Hace quince años que vivo aquí.
4. Hace veinte minutos que Uds. juegan a los videojuegos.
5. Hace un cuarto de hora que mi sobrina dibuja una casa.
6. Hace treinta segundos que jugamos al ajedrez.

Activities

Students with Special Needs
Give a second model sentence for activity 19.

Idioma

Estructura

Expressions with *hace*

You can describe an action that began in the past and has continued into the present using **hace** + **a time expression** + **que** + **the present tense of a verb.**

Hace diez minutos que veo televisión.

I have been watching television for ten minutes. (Ten minutes ago I started watching television.)

Reverse the order of *hace* and the time expression if a form of *¿cuánto?* introduces the question.

¿Cuánto tiempo hace que ves televisión?

How long have you been watching television?

Práctica

19 ¿Cuánto tiempo hace?

Say how long the following activities have been taking place.

MODELO haces aeróbicos / una hora
Hace una hora que haces aeróbicos.

1. juegan al béisbol en los Estados Unidos / más de un siglo
2. jugamos al voleibol / un año
3. vivo aquí / quince años
4. Uds. juegan a los videojuegos / veinte minutos
5. mi sobrina dibuja una casa / un cuarto de hora
6. jugamos al ajedrez / treinta segundos

Hace una hora que hacen aeróbicos.

Notes Note for your students the difference between the use of *hace* as a form of the verb *hacer* and *hace* as it is used here to indicate an amount of time that has elapsed.

Point out to students the possible confusion between *¿Cuánto tiempo hace que...?* and *¿Qué tiempo hace?*

20 ¿Qué haces?

 In pairs, take turns asking and answering the following questions. Then summarize your partner's answers for each question.

> **MODELO** A: ¿Juegas a los videojuegos?
> B: Sí, juego a los videojuegos.
> A: *(Write: B juega a los videojuegos.)*

1. ¿Cuánto tiempo hace que no juegas al ajedrez? ¿Y a las damas?
2. ¿Sabes jugar al ajedrez o a las damas?
3. ¿Cuánto tiempo hace que no lees una revista?
4. ¿Qué revistas lees?
5. ¿Cuánto tiempo hace que dibujas?
6. ¿Sabes dibujar?
7. ¿Cuánto tiempo hace que no ves una telenovela?
8. ¿Te gusta ver televisión? ¿Te gustan las telenovelas?
9. ¿Cuánto tiempo hace que estudias español?
10. ¿Cuánto tiempo hace que no escribes una carta?

Juego a los videojuegos.

Comunicación

 21 Mis pasatiempos

Prepare a list of your pastimes. Include at least six or seven activities. Then, with a partner, ask and answer questions about your favorite pastimes.

¡Extra!

¿Damas en los baños?

The games *ajedrez* (chess) and *damas* (checkers) are two of the world's oldest pastimes. However, if you see the word *Damas* (Ladies) on the door of a public restroom not very far from another door labeled *Caballeros* (Gentlemen), do not assume you are going in to play checkers. Remember what you have learned: The meaning of any word may vary according to the context in which the word is used.

Nuestro pasatiempo favorito es el ajedrez.

¿Te gusta dibujar?

Capítulo 7

doscientos ochenta y uno **281**

Teacher Resources

 Activity 20

Answers

20 Answers will vary.
21 Creative self-expression.

Activities

Multiple Intelligences (interpersonal)
First, have students make a list in Spanish consisting of their relatives' and friends' favorite pastimes. For each person or activity identified, they should write a logical statement with *hace* (+ time + *que* + the present tense of a verb). For example, *Hace cinco años que mi amigo Marco juega al golf.* Then have students talk about their sentences with a partner or with the class.

Spanish for Spanish Speakers
Have students write a composition of at least 100 words describing their favorite *pasatiempos.*

Notes Vary the way you assign oral activities. For example, pair students requiring additional help with stronger students for activity 21. You might even consider asking several volunteers to share with the class some of the pastimes from their discussions in pairs.

In addition to *Damas* and *Caballeros*, students may see *Señoras* and *Señores* or *Mujeres* and *Hombres* to indicate women's and men's bathrooms.

Estructura

Saying what is happening: present progressive

You can say what is happening right now using the *presente progresivo*, which consists of the present tense of *estar* plus a present participle (*gerundio*).

*¿Qué **están haciendo** Uds.?*
*Marta **está dibujando**, Enrique **está** **comiendo** y yo **estoy saliendo.***

What **are** (all of) you **doing?**
Marta **is drawing**, Enrique **is** **eating** and I **am leaving.**

Form the present participle of most verbs by changing the infinitive endings (*-ar, -er, -ir*) to *-ando* for *-ar* verbs or to *-iendo* for *-er* and *-ir* verbs.

-ar	-er	-ir
alquil**ar** → alquil**ando**	hac**er** → hac**iendo**	permit**ir** → permit**iendo**

Some *-ir* verbs with a stem change in the present tense require a different stem change in the present participle. This second change is shown in parentheses after infinitives in this book. Three verbs that follow this pattern are *dormir (ue, **u**)*, *preferir (ie, **i**)* and *sentir (ie, **i**).*

verbo	presente	gerundio
dormir (**ue, u**)	d**ue**rmo	d**u**rmiendo
preferir (**ie, i**)	pref**ie**ren	pref**i**riendo
sentir (**ie, i**)	s**ie**nto	s**i**ntiendo

Some verbs have minor irregularities in their present participles. For example, the *i* in *-iendo* changes to *y* after most verb stems that end in a vowel and for the verb *ir*: *leer* (stem: *le*) → le**y**endo; *oír* (stem: *o*) → o**y**endo; *ir* → **y**endo. The present participle for the irregular verb *venir* requires a change in the stem from *e* to *i*: *venir* → v**i**niendo. Finally, the present participle for *poder* involves a stem change from *o* to *u*: p**u**diendo.

Práctica

22 **Todos están haciendo algo**

Using the *presente progresivo* and the provided cues, say what these people are doing right now.

 nosotros / leer el periódico
Nosotros estamos leyendo el periódico.

1. mi padre y mi madre / salir de casa
2. mi hermano / buscar el control remoto
3. Esteban / alquilar una película estupenda
4. tú / pensar en tus pasatiempos
5. Uds. / apagar la luz de la cocina
6. María / poner la mesa

Ellas están leyendo el periódico.

Notes **Comparisons.** It may help some students to know that the present participle (*gerundio*) is equivalent to **-ing** in English.

Review the forms of the verb *estar* with students.

23 ¿Qué estás haciendo?

In pairs, take turns asking and answering what you are doing right now, according to the illustrations.

> **MODELO** A: ¿Qué estás haciendo?
> B: Estoy alquilando una película.

1 **2** **3** **4** **5**

24 Tomando un mate

Pretend you are sitting in an outdoor café in Buenos Aires. Using the *presente progresivo*, describe what you see from your table.

> **MODELO** una chica / escribir una carta
> Una chica está escribiendo una carta.

1. otra chica / dibujar
2. el mesero / poner una mesa
3. un muchacho / hablar por el celular
4. el niño / mirar a sus padres
5. un padre y una madre / comer con sus hijos
6. unos señores / jugar al ajedrez
7. tú / salir

Capítulo 7 *doscientos ochenta y tres* **283**

283

Notes **Comparisons.** Explain to students that in Spanish the present progressive is not used as frequently as it is in English. Rather, the present tense is normally used. The present progressive is reserved for stating more emphatically that the action is currently going on.

Comparisons. You may wish to note for students that in Spanish, present participles cannot be used as nouns as they are in English (Learning is fun). In Spanish, the noun form of the verb is the infinitive. This point will be explained later in the lesson.

✦ Comunicación

 25 Estoy...

Working in pairs, imagine you are in the following places: *una cafetería, Buenos Aires, una tienda de videos, una fiesta para tu cumpleaños, una clase de español, la sala de la casa, el museo, la calle, el parque.* Pretend you are talking on the phone with a friend and discuss what you are doing right now. Add to the conversation by asking such things as who you are with, where each place is located, etc.

MODELO **A:** ¿Qué estás haciendo?
B: Estoy tomando café en una cafetería.
A: ¿Dónde está la cafetería?
B: Está en La Boca.

 26 Están ocupados

With a classmate, pretend you are calling one another trying to reach various people on the phone. The person answering must apologize and say the person you are trying to reach is not home and, then, say what the person is doing. Be creative!

MODELO **A:** Hola. ¿Puedo hablar con Eduardo por favor?
B: Lo siento. Eduardo está paseando por la calle ahora mismo.

Estrategia

Clarifying meaning by asking questions
If you hear a new word in a conversation but do not understand what it means, do not be afraid to ask someone to fill you in. Many words in Spanish have different uses depending on the region or country where they are used. So the next time you hear a word or expression you are unsure of, do not be embarrassed; ask someone to explain it to you.

Repaso rápido: direct object pronouns

You have already learned to use direct objects to show the person or thing in a sentence that receives the action of the verb. Do you remember the direct object pronouns?

los pronombres de complemento directo

me	*me*	**nos**	*us*
te	*you (tú)*	**os**	*you (vosotros,-as)*
lo	*him, it, you (Ud.)*	**los**	*them, you (Uds.)*
la	*her, it, you (Ud.)*	**las**	*them, you (Uds.)*

*No **la** veo.*
I do not see **her.**
I do not see **it.** (*la lista de las películas nuevas*)

*Nunca **lo** veo.*
I never see **him.**
I never see **it.** (*el programa*)

Estructura

Using the present progressive with direct object pronouns

You have already seen that direct object pronouns usually precede conjugated verbs. However, direct object pronouns may be attached to an infinitive.

Lo *voy a alquilar.*
*Voy a alquilar***lo.**

I am going to rent **it.** *(el DVD)*

Similarly, you may choose to attach an object pronoun to the end of a present participle. When doing so, however, you must add an accent mark to the present participle in order to maintain the original pronunciation of the present participle without the pronoun.

La *estamos leyendo.*
*Estamos leyéndo***la.**

We are reading **it.** *(la revista)*

 ## Práctica

27 Lo estamos haciendo

Tell what the following people are doing right now, using direct object pronouns.

1. la señora Herrera / empezar / un viaje a Venezuela
2. Uds. / escribir / la lista de películas nuevas
3. nosotros / leer / un libro sobre Buenos Aires ahora
4. yo / escuchar / la radio ahora
5. Pilar / buscar / el control remoto

Estamos tomando mate.

28 Haciéndolo

Imagine you and your friend are watching television and commenting on various characters and programs. Working in pairs, take turns asking and answering questions using the provided cues. Follow the model, attaching direct object pronouns to the verbs in each sentence.

MODELO los hermanos / leer el diario de la hermana
    A: ¿Están leyendo los hermanos el diario de la hermana?
    B: Sí, están leyéndolo.

1. tú / buscar el programa
2. el cantante / cantar una canción de amor
3. Julia / escuchar la radio
4. nosotros / ver esta telenovela
5. Mónica / dibujar un mapa en la servilleta
6. mi equipo favorito / jugar un partido importante

Capítulo 7

doscientos ochenta y cinco **285**

Teacher Resources

 Activities 27–28

 Activity 13

 Activity 6

 Activity 14

Answers

27 1. La señora Herrera lo está empezando.
2. Uds. la están escribiendo.
3. Nosotros lo estamos leyendo.
4. Yo la estoy escuchando.
5. Pilar lo está buscando.

28 1. ¿Estás buscando...?/...estoy buscándolo.
2. ¿Está cantando...?/...está cantándola.
3. ¿Está escuchando...?/...está escuchándola.
4. ¿Estamos viendo...?/ ...estamos viéndola.
5. ¿Está dibujando...?/...está dibujándolo.
6. ¿Está jugando...?/...está jugándolo.

Activities

Expansion
The present progressive tense can be made negative by placing a negative expression such as *no* before the conjugated form of *estar: estoy dibujando (no estoy dibujando)*. Practice this point by having students make these sentences negative: *(No) Estoy jugando al ajedrez.; ¿(No) Estás viendo televisión?*

Notes Write on the board several sentences that demonstrate the use of the present progressive tense with direct object pronouns. Remind students that the direct object answers the question (subject + verb +) **who?** or **what?**

Mate (shown in the photograph) is a hot beverage similar to tea. It is very popular in Argentina. It is customarily served in a wooden cup called a *mate* and sipped through a metal straw (the best of which are silver) called a *bombilla*.

Refer to the list of Teacher Resources at the top of the page to find ancillaries for practicing the present progressive with direct object pronouns.

285

29 Otra vez

Redo activity 27 by attaching the direct object pronouns to the end of the present participle. Make any other appropriate changes.

30 Conexión con otras disciplinas: estadística

Prepare a list of at least eight pastimes in Spanish *(ir al cine, jugar al voleibol)*. Then ask five people to rank the pastimes, with *1* being their favorite and *8* being their least favorite activity. Prepare a written summary of your findings in Spanish. Follow the model.

MODELO ¿Qué pasatiempos de mi lista son tus favoritos, en una escala del uno al ocho?

¡Extra!

Comparando inglés y español

You have learned to combine the present tense of *estar* with a present participle *(gerundio)* of a verb in Spanish to describe what is going on right now. This verb form is comparable to the *-ing* form of a verb in English. Notice, however, that words ending in *-ing* in English may require an infinitive in Spanish if the English word functions as a noun instead of a verb. Compare the following:

Me gusta **jugar** al voleibol.	I like **playing** volleyball. *(noun)*
Nadar es divertido.	**Swimming** is fun. *(noun)*

but:

Estoy **jugando** al voleibol.	I am **playing** volleyball. *(verb)*
¿Estás **nadando**?	Are you **swimming**? *(verb)*

¿Qué pasatiempos de mi lista son tus favoritos, en una escala del uno a ocho?

1. Me gusta leer revistas. 1 2 3 4 5 6 7 8
2. Me gusta escuchar la radio. 1 2 3 4 5 6 7 8

31 Mirando y haciendo

Mira a cuatro o cinco personas desde donde tú estás ahora. ¿Qué están haciendo?

MODELO El profesor está ayudando a un estudiante.

Notes Activity 30 offers a cross-curricular connection to mathematics (specifically, statistics).

Have students share the results of their surveys with the class. Ask a volunteer to write each new activity on the board.

Follow up activity 31 with a class discussion reviewing everyone's activities in the classroom.

Comunicación

32 Los pasatiempos

Write the names in Spanish of at least five or six of your favorite pastimes. Next to the list, add columns telling where you participate in the activity, how long you have done the activity and with whom you do the activity. Then, working with a partner, take turns asking and answering questions about each other's pastimes.

Juego al voleibol en la playa.

MODELO
A: ¿Cuál es tu pasatiempo favorito?
B: Mi pasatiempo favorito es jugar al voleibol.
A: ¿Dónde juegas al voleibol?
B: Juego en la playa.
A: ¿Cuánto tiempo hace que tienes este pasatiempo?
B: Hace dos años que tengo este pasatiempo.

33 El tiempo libre

In small groups, talk about the activities and pastimes you enjoy during school breaks and vacation. Make sure each of you describes at least two activities/pastimes. Have a group member make a list of all the activities and pastimes you talk about and share the information with the class.

¡Nuestro pasatiempo favorito es el fútbol!

Capítulo 7

doscientos ochenta y siete **287**

Answers

34 1. El fútbol es el deporte más popular de Argentina./El juego del pato es el deporte nacional de Argentina.
2. Hace más de 400 años que se originó el juego del pato.
3. Originalmente, los gauchos jugaban al pato con un pato vivo.
4. En 1822 fue prohibido el juego del pato.
5. Hoy, el juego del pato se juega entre ocho jinetes.

35 Answers will vary.

Activities

Multiple Intelligences (linguistic)
Ask individuals to research Argentina and then report their findings to the class. Possible topics: compare and contrast the Argentine *gaucho* with the American cowboy; discuss the Argentinean economy; compare what Evita Perón was really like to the image presented in the movie *Evita*.

Spanish for Spanish Speakers
Students write a short composition in Spanish in which they discuss something they know about Argentina. Expand the activity by having students seek out additional information about Argentina at the library or on the Internet.

Lectura cultural

El juego del pato

*E*n Argentina, el deporte más popular es el fútbol, pero el deporte nacional es el juego del pato[1]. Éste es un deporte hípico[2] similar al polo que se originó hace más de 4 siglos entre los gauchos[3] de Argentina.

Originalmente, jugaba con un hacia arriba[5] y atropellaban[7] unos a otros, trágicos que

el juego del pato se pato vivo[4] que se arrojaba dos grupos de jinetes[6] se para capturarlo y pasarlo Había tantos resultados fue prohibido en 1822.

En 1937, el juego del pato volvió, reglamentado[8] y modernizado. Ya no se juega con un pato sino con una pelota blanca con seis asas[9]. Dos equipos de cuatro jugadores cada uno juegan en un campo de 220 metros por 90 metros. El objetivo del juego es pasar la pelota—a la que se llama pato—por un aro[10] que tiene un metro de diámetro. Los jugadores, a caballo, deben recoger[11] el pato y lanzarlo con la mano derecha. Es un deporte de fuerza[12] y habilidad, y aunque no es muy popular, es el deporte más tradicional de Argentina.

Pasando la pelota por el aro.

El juego del pato, el deporte nacional de la Argentina.

[1]the duck game [2]equine [3]Argentinian cowboys [4]live duck [5]thrown into the air [6]horsemen
[7]would trample each other [8]regulated [9]handles [10]hoop [11]pick up [12]strength

34 ¿Qué recuerdas?

Correct these false statements.

1. El juego del pato es el deporte más popular de Argentina.
2. Hace más de 40 años que se originó el juego del pato.
3. Originalmente, los gauchos jugaban al pato con una pelota blanca.
4. En 1953 fue prohibido el juego del pato.
5. Hoy, el juego del pato se juega entre dos jinetes.

> • Why do you think *el juego del pato* is not very popular today among Argentines? Do you think it could become popular in the United States if it were introduced here? Explain.

35 Algo personal

1. ¿Cuál crees que es el deporte nacional de Estados Unidos?
2. ¿Qué deporte practican los *cowboys* de Estados Unidos?
3. ¿A qué deporte es el juego del pato similar? Explica.
4. ¿Te gustaría aprender a jugar al pato? ¿Por qué sí o por qué no?

288 *doscientos ochenta y ocho* **Lección A**

Notes The *Lectura cultural* has been recorded and is available in the Audio CD Program along with activities 34 and 35. You may wish to help students with the reading and then assign the reading and the questions as homework. After reviewing the contents of the *Lectura cultural*, play the recording and allow students to read along silently. Then play the audio CD of the activities, pausing after each question and calling on students to provide an answer.

¿Qué aprendí?

Visit the web-based activities at www.emcp.com

Autoevaluación

As a review and self-check, respond to the following:

1. What are your favorite leisure activities?
2. Name a sport that is very popular in Argentina.
3. Ask in Spanish if a friend can play volleyball tomorrow.
4. How long have you been studying Spanish?
5. Say four things people around you are doing right now.
6. A friend asks if you have your Spanish book. Answer by saying that you are looking for it.
7. What do you know about Argentina?

Palabras y expresiones

Pasatiempos
- los aeróbicos
- el ajedrez
- el básquetbol
- las cartas
- las damas
- el equipo
- el fútbol americano
- hacer aeróbicos
- el pasatiempo
- el programa
- la telenovela
- el videojuego
- el voleibol

Otras expresiones
- ahora mismo
- antes de
- ¿Cuánto *(+ time expression)* hace que *(+ present tense of verb). . .*?
- después de
- esta noche
- hace *(+ time expression)* que
- el minuto
- mismo
- *(number +)* vez/veces al/a la *(time expression)*

- por la (mañana, tarde, noche)
- el segundo
- el siglo
- todavía

Verbos
- alquilar
- apagar
- costar (ue)
- dar
- dibujar
- dormir (ue, u)
- jugar (ue)
- permitir
- poder (ue, u)
- recordar (ue, u)
- volver (ue, u)

Expresiones y otras palabras
- americano,-a
- casi
- el control remoto
- estupendo,-a
- la lista
- mismo,-a
- remoto,-a
- el televisor
- la vida

Estoy buscando un programa.

El control remoto.

Notes **Comparisons.** Remind students that in Spanish, present participles cannot be used as gerunds as they are in English (Learning is fun). In Spanish the noun form of the verb is the infinitive: *Me gusta cantar* (I like singing); *Bailar es divertido* (Dancing is fun).

Teacher Resources

Activity 14

Information Gap Activities
Postcard Activities
Funciones de Comunicación

Answers

Autoevaluación
Possible answers:
1. Answers will vary.
2. El fútbol es muy popular en (la) Argentina.
3. ¿Puedes jugar al voleibol mañana?
4. Hace un año que estudio español.
5. Mi amigo está escribiendo ahora...
6. Estoy buscándolo.
7. Large cattle ranches there are called *estancias*.

Activities

Multiple Intelligences (bodily-kinesthetic/linguistic)
Assign students to read *The House of the Spirits* by Isabel Allende. Then have them write their own copy for a book jacket. They should include pictures, line drawings, type design, a blurb about the book and a sketch of the author.

Technology
Check with your media center or ask your students if they have access to a Spanish-speaking station on their cable network or from a satellite dish. Have them tape a segment of a Sunday afternoon soccer match and bring it in to share with the rest of the class.

Las estaciones en Chile

 Activity 1

 Activity 50

 Activities 1–3

 Activity 1

 Activities 1–2

Content reviewed in *Lección B*
- **months and seasons of the year**
- **expressing likes and dislikes**
- **present progressive tense**
- **sports**

Activities

Prereading Strategy
Conduct a discussion about the activities students enjoy during each of the four seasons. Then have students look through the scenes quickly to find cognates and words they recognize.

Spanish for Spanish Speakers
Call on students to state in Spanish activities people like to do during different seasons in their country of origin.

Lección B

Chile

Vocabulario I
Las estaciones en Chile

¡Este lugar es excelente!

Hace frío.

esquiar

No hace mucho calor.

patinar sobre hielo

montar en patineta

el invierno

el otoño

la primavera

el verano

hace sol

llover

dar un paseo por la playa

la flor

Hay flores por todos lados.

290 *doscientos noventa*

Lección B

Notes When speaking informally, native Spanish speakers occasionally abbreviate words. For example, *la bicicleta* may be referred to as *la bici* and *la televisión* may be called *la tele*. Ask students to think of similar abbreviations in English or Spanish.

Remind students that an infinitive can act as a noun in Spanish: *Esquiar es mi deporte favorito.*

No me gusta esquiar, pero en cambio me gusta ver televisión.

Sí, pero ya estoy lista.

¿Todavía continúas en la computadora?

La chica envía un correo electrónico a Juan. Ella copia la dirección de Juan en su cuaderno. Ella pone los papeles en su lugar.

1 Las estaciones

Escoge la estación correcta, según lo que oyes.

la primavera

el otoño

el verano

el invierno

2 Las estaciones en Chile

Contesta las siguientes preguntas.

1. ¿En qué estación pueden patinar sobre hielo en Chile?
2. ¿En qué meses hay flores en Chile?
3. ¿En qué meses están esquiando en Chile?
4. ¿Qué estación es en abril y mayo en Chile?
5. ¿Qué estación es en enero y febrero en Chile?
6. ¿Qué estación es en junio y julio en Chile?

¡Extra!

¿Cuándo es verano?

In the Southern Hemisphere, the seasons are the reverse of the seasons in the Northern Hemisphere. For this reason, people ski in Chile from June to August because it is winter there. Similarly, the summer months in Chile are December, January and February.

Teacher Resources

 Activities 1–2

Answers

1 1. el invierno; 2. la primavera; 3. el verano; 4. el otoño

2 1. Pueden patinar sobre hielo en Chile en el invierno.
2. Hay muchas flores en los meses de septiembre, octubre y noviembre.
3. Están esquiando en junio, julio y agosto.
4. Es otoño.
5. Es verano.
6. Es invierno.

Activities

Pronunciation (*las letras* m, n, ñ)
Review the sound of *m (mucho, tiempo, minutos, menos, primavera, mes)*, n *(cuestan, cuánto, verano, nuevas, tengo, poner)* and ñ *(año, cumpleaños, mañana, niño, otoño, cariñosa)*. Then pronounce the following carefully, having students say the sentence several times before writing what they hear: *Mañana es el primer día del invierno, que nos gusta mucho en Chile, pero que al señor Núñez no le gusta.* Ask students if they understand the meaning of the sentence.

TPR
Using TPR, introduce or review expressions that name various pastimes: *dar un paseo, montar en bicicleta, nadar, ver televisión, jugar al fútbol, jugar al tenis, esquiar, patinar.*

Notes Tell students that although the infinitives *poner* and *dar* were introduced earlier, the present-tense forms of these verbs are taught in *Capítulo 7, Lección B*.

Your students may find it interesting that the school year in many South American countries begins in February or March.

Activity 1 is intended for listening comprehension practice. Play the audio CD of the activity that is part of the Audio CD Program or use the transcript that appears in the ATE Introduction if you prefer to read the activity yourself.

¡Vamos a esquiar!
Activities 3–5

Answers

3 1. Diego quiere dar un paseo por la playa.
2. Porque hace mucho calor.
3. Prefiere montar en patineta.
4. Quiere ir a esquiar.
5. A Pablo le gusta el invierno.
4 Answers will vary.
5 All answers begin with *Puedo* and end with an appropriate activity for the indicated season.

Activities

Critical Listening
Play the audio CD recording of the dialog as students cover the words and listen to the conversation. Then ask several individuals to state what they believe the conversation is about.

Expansion
Additional questions (*Algo personal*): *¿Qué tiempo hace en tu ciudad en primavera/verano/otoño/ invierno?*; *¿Qué te gusta hacer en la primavera/el verano/el otoño/el invierno?*; *¿Vas a la playa en el verano? ¿A qué playa?*; *¿Qué otros pasatiempos te gustan?*

Prereading Strategy
Instruct students to cover up the dialog with one hand and look at the photographs. Ask them to look through the dialog quickly to find cognates and words they recognize.

Diálogo I

¡Vamos a esquiar!

DIEGO: ¿Vamos a dar un paseo por la playa?
PABLO: No, gracias. Hace mucho calor.
ELENA: Yo prefiero montar en patineta.

PABLO: ¡Vamos a esquiar!
ELENA: ¡En enero no podemos esquiar en Chile!
PABLO: No, aquí, no. ¡Vamos a Colorado!

ELENA: ¡Qué tonto eres!
PABLO: Me gusta el invierno.
ELENA: ¡Ya está bien! Vamos a tomar un refresco.

3 ¿Qué recuerdas?

1. ¿Quién quiere dar un paseo por la playa?
2. ¿Por qué no quiere Pablo ir a la playa?
3. ¿Qué prefiere hacer Elena?
4. ¿Qué quiere hacer Pablo?
5. ¿A quién le gusta el invierno?

4 Algo personal

1. ¿Cuál es tu estación favorita? Explica.
2. ¿Qué te gusta hacer en tu estación favorita?
3. ¿Qué deportes practicas donde tú vives en la primavera? ¿Y en el verano? ¿Y en el otoño? ¿Y en el invierno?

5 ¿Qué actividades puedes hacer?

 Escucha la información y di qué actividad o actividades puedes hacer.

MODELO Puedo montar en patineta en el parque.

Montamos en patineta.

Notes Explain that the articles *el* and *la* may be omitted after *en* and after forms of the verb *ser: hace sol en (el) verano; mi estación favorita es (la) primavera.*

This dialog and activities 3, 4 and 5 have been recorded by native speakers and are included in the *Navegando* Audio CD Program. Have students cover up the dialog on page 292 and look at the photographs as you play the dialog. Then discuss the contents of the dialog to evaluate what students have understood.

Cultura viva

La Isla de Pascua.

Chile

Mainland Chile is located along the western coast of South America between the Andes Mountains and the Pacific Ocean. The country also has many interesting islands, including the *Juan Fernández Islands,* where Robinson Crusoe lived for four years, and Easter Island *(Isla de Pascua),* an island with a mysterious past which is inhabited by people of Polynesian ancestry. Most Chileans live in urban areas, like the capital, Santiago. The

La región de los lagos (southern lakes region), Chile.

population is well educated and the country has a strong literary tradition: Chileans are very proud of their two Nobel Prize-winning poets, Gabriela Mistral and Pablo Neruda. Since much of Chile's population has European origins, it is not uncommon to encounter people of Italian, English, German, Irish or Polish ancestry, or to see street signs with names that are obviously not of Spanish origin. Indeed, the southern city of Puerto Montt was for many years a German colony and the liberator and first ruler of Chile was Bernardo O'Higgins.

When you visit, you will discover that Chile is a country of magnificent contrasts offering everything, from large cosmopolitan cities with the latest in modern-day conveniences and skyscrapers *(rascacielos)* that reach to the sky to the beautiful rustic countryside of the southern lakes region. Just a short distance away from cosmopolitan Santiago, ski resorts like Portillo or Farellones in the Andes Mountains and resort beaches near Viña del Mar offer an escape from the pressures of modern life.

Los rascacielos de Santiago.

6 Chile

Contesta las siguientes preguntas sobre Chile.

1. ¿Está Chile en América del Sur o en América del Norte?
2. ¿Qué montañas están en Chile?
3. ¿Qué océano está al oeste de Chile?
4. ¿En qué isla vive gente de ancestro polinesio?
5. ¿Cuál es la capital del país?
6. ¿Quién es una persona famosa de Chile?
7. ¿Adónde puede uno ir a esquiar? ¿Y a nadar en la playa?

7 Conexiones con otras disciplinas: geografía

Use an encyclopedia or search the Internet for information about Chile. Then list four or five interesting details about places mentioned in the *Cultura viva* (e.g., Juan Fernández Islands, Isla de Pascua, Viña del Mar, etc.).

Capítulo 7   *doscientos noventa y tres*   **293**

Answers

8 1. esquían
2. copia
3. continúas
4. envían
5. esquiamos
6. continúo
7. ve
8. patina
9. envía

Activities

Students with Special Needs
Model a second sentence for activity 8.

Idioma

Estructura

Verbs that require special accentuation

Sometimes verbs that end in *-uar* or *-iar* (*esquiar, enviar* and *continuar,* for example) require a written accent mark to indicate that a vowel should be stressed for all present-tense forms except for *nosotros.* You will have to learn which verbs follow this pattern since some verbs that end in *-uar* or *-iar* may not follow this pattern (such as the verb *copiar*).

> esquiar: esquío, esquías, esquía, esquiamos, esquiáis, esquían
> enviar: envío, envías, envía, enviamos, enviáis, envían
> continuar: continúo, continúas, continúa, continuamos, continuáis, continúan

but:

> copiar: copio, copias, copia, copiamos, copiáis, copian

Práctica

8 Todos hacen algo

Indica qué hacen estas personas cuando tienen tiempo libre.

MODELO Yo (esquiar) con mis padres.
Yo esquío con mis padres.

1. Eva y Luis (esquiar) en Portillo.
2. Claudia (copiar) canciones de la internet.
3. Tú (continuar) dando paseos por el parque.
4. Sara y Paz (enviar) correos electrónicos a sus amigos.
5. Nosotros (esquiar) en Farillones.
6. Yo (continuar) montando en patineta, mi actividad favorita.
7. Alberto (ver) DVDs.
8. Victoria (patinar) sobre hielo.
9. Mamá (enviar) cartas a mis abuelos.

Yo esquío con mis padres.

Notes You may wish to mention that *mandar* is a synonym for *enviar.*

Syllabification and accentuation are explained in the Appendices.

Some other verbs that require an accent when conjugated are *criar* (to raise, breed); *fiar* (to confide); *guiar* (to lead); *telegrafiar* (to telegraph); *desafiar* (to challenge); *extraviar* (to lose).

9 ¿Qué pasa?

Read the following statements and indicate where there are missing accent marks. Then identify the letter of the illustration that best matches each statement.

1. Hace calor y juegan al básquetbol.
2. Esquiamos todos los días.
3. Ellos continuan patinando sobre hielo.
4. Ella copia el número de teléfono.
5. Continua haciendo sol.
6. Él envia una carta.
7. Está nublado.
8. Ellos esquian ahora mismo.

A

B

✿ Comunicación

10 Un correo electrónico

Imagine you have a key pal in Chile. Write an e-mail telling him or her about your home and school life. You may want to say, for example, that you like to ski during the winter, that you and your family ski once a month, that you would like to go to Portillo, that you continue studying Spanish at school and that you are sending pictures of you and your family with the e-mail. Add any other details you would like.

Yo envío un correo electrónico a Chile.

Notes Inform students that a key pal (or pen pal) in Spanish is *amigo/amiga por correspondencia.*

Have students apply strategies they have already learned in previous chapters as they complete activity 10.

Estructura

Present tense of *dar* and *poner*

The verbs *dar* and *poner* have irregular present-tense *yo* forms. In addition, the verb *dar* has an irregular *vosotros,-as* form. Other verbs that are regular in the present tense except for the *yo* form of the verbs: *hacer (yo hago), saber (yo sé), ver (yo veo), salir (yo salgo)*.

dar	
doy	damos
das	**dais**
da	dan

poner	
pongo	ponemos
pones	ponéis
pone	ponen

 Práctica

11 ¿Dan un paseo a pie o en carro?

Create logical sentences using the expression *dar un paseo* and either *a pie* or *en carro*, according to what makes the most sense.

MODELO Enrique / por el parque
Enrique da un paseo por el parque a pie.

1. yo / por la playa
2. tú / por la ciudad
3. nosotros / por el centro
4. Marta y Esperanza / por la calle
5. mi amigo / por la Avenida de la Independencia
6. mis padres / por la plaza

Ellas dan un paseo a pie. (Bariloche, Argentina.)

12 ¡Ponen todo en su lugar!

Completa las oraciones con la forma apropiada del verbo *poner*.

MODELO Elena pone la patineta en su cuarto.

1. Paz __ las flores en la mesa del comedor.
2. Yo __ los papeles en el escritorio.
3. Carlos y Paula __ sus bicicletas en el garaje.
4. Mi padre __ el televisor en la sala.
5. Tú __ la leche en el refrigerador.
6. Todos nosotros __ los cubiertos sucios en el lavaplatos.

Notes The verb *poner* is sometimes used in place of *encender* when you are talking about turning on an appliance: *Voy a encender (poner) el televisor.*

Review the various uses of *poner*: *poner* (to put), *poner el televisor* (to turn on), *poner la mesa* (to set the table).

13 ¡Me gusta la primavera!

Completa el siguiente párrafo con la forma apropiada de *comer, poner, dar, salir* y *ver* para saber por qué Sara dice que le gusta la primavera.

En la primavera yo siempre (1) con mi madre los domingos por la mañana a buscar flores. Yo (2) flores por toda la casa. Casi todas las mañanas yo (3) paseos por el parque con mi hermana y por la tarde alquilamos películas en una tienda cerca de la casa para verlas por la noche. Mi padre siempre me (4) dinero para alquilarlas. Claro, a veces, nosotros no las (5) porque (6) a dar un paseo por la noche y entonces no hay tiempo para verlas. Ahora mis hermanos y yo (7) la mesa para la comida. Hoy vamos a (8) en el patio porque no hace calor y no llueve. ¡Me gusta la primavera!

Pongo flores por toda la casa.

Comunicación

14 Preguntas personales

 En parejas, alternen en hacer y contestar las siguientes preguntas en español.

1. ¿Qué haces cuando tienes tiempo libre?
2. ¿Te gusta dar paseos? ¿Dónde?
3. ¿Dan tu familia y tú paseos en carro los fines de semana? ¿Adónde van?
4. ¿Cómo das paseos en el verano? ¿En carro? ¿A pie? ¿En bicicleta?
5. ¿Dan tus amigos y tú paseos en el verano? ¿Adónde?
6. ¿En qué estación del año te gusta más dar paseos? ¿Por qué?
7. ¿Adónde vas de viaje con tu familia en el verano? ¿En la primavera? ¿En el otoño? ¿En el invierno?
8. ¿Quién pone las maletas en el carro cuando vas de viaje con tu familia?
9. ¿Pones flores en tu casa en la primavera? ¿Quién las pone?
10. ¿Dónde pones tu mochila en las vacaciones, cuando no hay clases?

15 ¿Qué actividades haces?

 Working in small groups, talk about the activities you enjoy during different times of the year according to the season. Include activities such as going for a walk, taking rides, skiing, ice-skating, watching television or any other favorite pastimes. Include details such as when and with whom you do an activity, what the weather is like at that time of year and why you like or dislike the activity.

MODELO **A:** ¿Qué actividades haces en el verano?
   B: En el verano doy paseos por las playas de Viña del Mar todos los fines de semana. Siempre voy con mi padre y caminamos por una hora.

Teacher Resources

 Activity 14

Answers

13 1. salgo
2. pongo
3. doy
4. da
5. vemos
6. salimos
7. ponemos
8. comer
14 Answers will vary.
15 Creative self-expression.

Activities

Expansion
After completing activity 15, have a member of each group summarize what members of their group discussed.

Students with Special Needs
Provide a model for activities 13 and 14.

Notes Complete one or two answers as a class before assigning activity 13.

You may wish to have students write out the answers for activity 14 before pairing up with a classmate. As an alternative, after doing the activity orally in pairs, have students write their answers to be sure they understand and can retain what they practiced.

Teacher Resources

 El tiempo

 Activity 4

 Activity 51

 Activities 9–11

 Activity 4

 Activities 6–9

Activities

Critical Thinking

Play the audio CD of *Vocabulario II* as students observe and consider the following: what is happening in each scene; where and when each scene takes place; what the people are saying. Finally, have students guess what they believe is the main theme of each scene.

Language through Action

Using overhead transparency 51, have students come to the front of the class and point to the different scenes as you describe them randomly in Spanish.

Notes Encourage students to obtain current weather information in Spanish via the Internet:

The Weather Channel
http://espanol.weather.com/

It may help some students to know that it is also possible to ask for the temperature using the expressions *¿Cuál es la temperatura?* or *¿A cuánto está la temperatura?*. The answers could be *Es de* (number) *grados* or *Está a* (number) *grados*.

el corredor

	Corredor Nº
primero	1º	208
segundo	2º	103
tercero	3º	501
cuarto	4º	931
quinto	5º	002
sexto	6º	321
séptimo	7º	711
octavo	8º	600
noveno	9º	820
décimo	10º	030

16 ¿Quién es?

Selecciona la foto de la persona apropiada.

A   **B**   **C**   **D**   **E**   **F**

17 El tiempo

Contesta las siguientes preguntas en español.

1. ¿En qué estación hace mucho frío?
2. ¿En qué mes llueve mucho?
3. ¿Cuándo hace mucho calor?
4. Cuando va a llover, ¿cómo está el día?
5. ¿Qué tiempo hace en primavera? ¿Y en verano? ¿Y en otoño? ¿Y en invierno?

18 ¿Qué tiempo hace?

 In small groups, take turns describing the weather during one of the seasons without naming the season. Others then try to guess which season you are describing.

Notes Using overhead transparencies 51 and 52, present and practice the vocabulary on pages 298 and 299.

Expand the presentation of weather-related vocabulary by providing the class with the following words and phrases: *huracán, ciclón, relámpago, trueno; hace fresco; hay neblina.*

Expand activity 18 by extending the discussion to the entire class.

Teacher Resources

 Activities 16–17

 Activity 52

Answers

16 1. C
2. E or F
3. A
4. D
5. B
6. E

17 Possible answers:
1. Hace frío en el invierno.
2. Llueve mucho en la primavera.
3. Hace mucho calor en el verano.
4. Está nublado.
5. Answers will vary.

18 Creative self-expression.

Activities

Expansion
Have students answer the following questions in relation to the weather where they live: *¿Qué tiempo hace en el invierno?; ¿Cuándo hace mucho frío y nieva?; ¿Cuándo hace mucho calor?; ¿Cuándo hace un poco de frío y viento?; ¿Cuándo hay muchas flores?; ¿Nieva en tu ciudad? ¿Hay mucha nieve o poca?; ¿Cuándo hay mucha nieve?; Cuando hace sol, ¿qué te gusta hacer?; ¿Cómo sabes cuando va a llover?; ¿Te gusta caminar o correr en la lluvia?; ¿Qué haces cuando llueve?*

Answers

19 1. Dice que hace calor. Hace treinta y cinco grados.
2. Quiere jugar al básquetbol.
3. Pablo es un buen esquiador.
4. Pueden ir a Portillo.
5. Pablo va a ser el primero en terminar el refresco.

20 Answers will vary.

21 1. F; 2. C; 3. D; 4. A; 5. B; 6. E

Activities

Critical Thinking
Remind students that in the Southern Hemisphere the seasons are the reverse of the seasons in the Northern Hemisphere. Check student understanding of weather expressions by asking several questions. For example, ask questions about the weather north and south of the equator: *En los Estados Unidos es invierno, ¿qué tiempo hace en Chicago? ¿Qué tiempo hace en Santiago? ¿Hace mucho frío en el sur de Chile?; En los Estados Unidos es primavera, ¿qué tiempo hace en Virginia? ¿Qué tiempo hace en Buenos Aires? ¿Hace mucho viento en Chile?; En los Estados Unidos es verano, ¿qué tiempo hace en Missouri? ¿Está nevando en el sur de Chile? ¿Hace calor en Buenos Aires?; En los Estados Unidos es otoño, ¿está lloviendo en Michigan? ¿Está nublado en Chile? ¿Está soleado en Argentina?*

Diálogo II
¿Qué temperatura hace?

DIEGO: ¡Qué buen refresco!
PABLO: ¿Qué temperatura hace?
ELENA: Hace calor. Hace treinta y cinco grados.

DIEGO: ¡Vamos a jugar al básquetbol!
PABLO: Soy mal jugador de básquetbol.
ELENA: Eres un buen basquetbolista.
PABLO: No, soy un buen esquiador.

ELENA: En julio podemos ir a esquiar a Portillo.
DIEGO: ¿Quién va a ser el primero en terminar el refresco?
PABLO: ¡Yo! Y el segundo vas a ser tú.

19 ¿Qué recuerdas?

1. ¿Dice Elena que hace calor o hace frío?
2. ¿A qué quiere jugar Diego?
3. ¿Quién es un buen esquiador?
4. ¿Adónde pueden ir a esquiar en julio?
5. ¿Quién va a ser el primero en terminar el refresco?

20 Algo personal

1. ¿Qué temperatura hace ahora?
2. ¿Qué tiempo hace?
3. ¿Te gusta cuando hace mucho calor? ¿Y cuando hace frío?

21 ¿Qué tiempo hace?

 Selecciona la ilustración que corresponde con lo que oyes.

A   **B**   **C**

D   **E**   **F**

Notes Using the recorded version of the dialog, ask students to cover the words and try to figure out what Diego, Pablo and Elena are saying to one another.

You may choose whether to have students do activities 19 and 20 orally or in writing since they are recorded and included in the *Navegando* Audio CD Program.

Activity 21 has been provided for listening comprehension practice. A recorded version of the activity is included in the Audio CD Program. A reproducible answer sheet for the activity has been provided at the end of the Audio CD Program Manual should you wish to have students use it.

Cultura viva

¿Fahrenheit o centígrados?

Whereas in the United States most people generally refer to the temperature in degrees Fahrenheit *(grados Fahrenheit),* throughout most of the world the temperature is given in degrees centigrade, also referred to as degrees Celsius *(grados centígrados o grados Celsius).* To ask for and understand the temperature in Spanish, you must know more than just the words that tell the temperature. You must be able to use degrees centigrade. For example, the temperature at which water freezes is

Hace mucho calor.

Hace -5 grados centígrados.

0 in degrees centigrade and 32° in degrees Fahrenheit. You can make conversions using the following formula:

$$\frac{°C}{5} \times 9 + 32 = °F$$

2/2 Conexión con otras disciplinas: matemáticas

Cambia las temperaturas de grados centígrados a grados Fahrenheit para las siguientes ciudades en Chile.

> MODELO   La Serena 12°C
> Hace 53.6°F.

1. Iquique	28°C
2. Arica	25°C
3. Concepción	20°C
4. Santiago	35°C
5. Balmaceda	30°C
6. Puerto Montt	18°C
7. Temuco	15°C
8. Punta Arenas	9°C

¿Qué temperatura hace en Santiago?

2/3 Pronóstico del tiempo

Present a weather forecast to your class in Spanish using any props, charts and maps you wish or ones that you create. Make believe you are an actual meteorologist reporting for the ten o'clock news.

Answers

2/2
1. Hace 82.4 grados.
2. Hace 77 grados.
3. Hace 68 grados.
4. Hace 95 grados.
5. Hace 86 grados.
6. Hace 64.4 grados.
7. Hace 59 grados.
8. Hace 48.2 grados.

2/3 Creative self-expression.

Activities

Cooperative Learning
Divide the class into small groups and ask each group to choose one of the countries featured in *Navegando.* The groups should each prepare a country-specific weather report to share with the class.

Technology
Have students do an Internet search for the five-day forecast for Santiago, Chile. They should then print out a copy of the report to share with the class.

Notes   When converting Fahrenheit to centigrade, you may wish to use the following formula:

$$\frac{5(°F - 32)}{9} = °C$$

Note that metric measurements are commonly used in the Spanish-speaking world. For example, distances are measured in *kilómetros* and weight is given in *kilogramos* or simply *kilos.*

Select several students each day to present weather forecasts.

Answers

24 1. Es futbolista.
2. Es patinadora.
3. Somos deportistas.
4. Es tenista.
5. Son esquiadores.
6. Soy basquetbolista.
7. Eres beisbolista.
8. Soy corredor(a).

Activities

Communities
Have students name several well-known athletes (past or present) from your state. They should then call on a classmate who must describe the person as a *corredor, corredora,* etc.

Students with Special Needs
Model a second sentence for activity 24.

Idioma

Estructura

Describing people using *-dor* and *-ista*

You can identify someone who participates in a particular sport or activity by changing the ending on the sport to *-dor (-dora)* in some cases or *-ista* in others (which remains the same for males or females).

patinar	– el patina**dor** /la patina**dora**	el tenis	– el/la ten**ista**
esquiar	– el esquia**dor**/la esquia**dora**	el básquetbol	– el/la basquetbol**ista**
correr	– el corre**dor**/la corre**dora**	el fútbol	– el/la futbol**ista**
jugar	– el juga**dor**/ la juga**dora**		

Note: The accent mark is not used on the newly formed word when these endings are added.

Práctica

24 ¿Qué son?

Describe a estas personas usando las siguientes palabras: *basquetbolista, beisbolista, corredor(a), deportista, esquiador(a), futbolista, nadador(a), patinador(a), tenista.*

MODELO Mis primas nadan en la piscina.
Son nadadoras.

1. Juan está jugando al fútbol.
2. Beatriz está patinando sobre hielo.
3. Nosotros tenemos práctica de deportes.
4. Marta está jugando al tenis.
5. Jorge e Iván esquían muy bien.
6. Estoy jugando al básquetbol.
7. Tú estás listo para jugar al béisbol.
8. Estoy corriendo en el parque.

Juan está jugando al fútbol.

Notes Take a few minutes to review the meaning of the new terms created by adding the endings *-dor* and *-ista*. Ask students, for example, if they can figure out the meaning of *patinador/patinadora, esquiador/esquiadora, corredor/corredora, tenista, basquetbolista* and *futbolista.* Finally, ask if students can guess what a *deportista* is.

25 ¿Qué deportes practican?

Di qué deportes practican las personas de las fotografías.

MODELO Es beisbolista.

1

2

3

4

5

6

Comunicación

26 Mis deportistas favoritos

In small groups, talk about your favorite athletes. Try to include the names of one or two Spanish-speaking athletes, if possible. Say the person's name, sport and where the person is from (if you know). If the person plays with a team, name the team. Be as specific and detailed as you can, and add any information you can to your classmates' descriptions.

MODELO **A:** Mi deportista favorito es Sammy Sosa. Es beisbolista y es de la República Dominicana.
B: Juega con Chicago, ¿verdad?
A: Sí. Juega con Chicago.
C: Pues, mi deportista favorito es un basquetbolista. Se llama Pau Gasol.

¡Oportunidades!

El español y los deportes
You probably are familiar with a number of Spanish-speaking sports figures who learned English either before becoming famous or while traveling internationally as they participated in their sport. Knowing another language has helped them communicate with people they have met in their travels. What opportunities do you think might occur for you if you participate in sports and become really good? How might knowing Spanish help you if you are an athlete? Can you think of ways Spanish might help if you were a member of a sports team that competes internationally?

Capítulo 7   *trescientos tres* **303**

Notes Sports are important in countries throughout the world, the Spanish-speaking world included. In addition to baseball, soccer, bicycling and boxing, several other sports are very popular.

A popular sport in some Spanish-speaking countries is *jai alai,* a form of handball for singles or doubles competition played on a court with one or three walls. Players use a curved wicker basket *(cesta)* for returning the ball. The sport originated in the Basque region of Spain.

Estructura

Using ordinal numbers

You use ordinal numbers to place things in order (first, second, third, etc.). In Spanish, only the first ten ordinal numbers are used often. They generally follow definite articles and precede nouns. Like other adjectives in Spanish, the ordinal numbers agree in gender (masculine/feminine) and number (singular/plural) with the noun they modify.

*¿Cuáles son los **primeros** corredores en terminar?*

When *primero* and *tercero* appear before a masculine singular noun, they are shortened to *primer* and *tercer*.

*Francisco es el **primer** corredor en terminar.*
*Lorenzo es el **tercer** corredor en terminar.*

You can abbreviate ordinal numbers ending in *-o, -a, -os, -as* or *-er* by placing those letters at the upper right-hand side of the number: *primero → 1º, primera → 1ª, primeros → 1ᵒˢ, primeras → 1ᵃˢ, primer → 1ᵉʳ, tercer → 3ᵉʳ.*

 ## Práctica

27 **La competencia anual del colegio**

El Colegio San Ignacio de Santiago tiene una competencia de esquí en Portillo todos los años. Completa los resultados de la competencia de este año con el número ordinal apropiado.

MODELO Ingrid fue la <u>décima</u> esquiadora en terminar.

Competencia Anual			
1ª	Olga	6º	Javier
2º	Edgar	7ª	Paula
3º	Hugo	8ª	Paz
4ª	Natalia	9º	Alfonso
5º	Enrique	10ª	Ingrid

1. Javier fue el __ esquiador en terminar.
2. Paula fue la __ esquiadora en terminar.
3. Alfonso fue el __ esquiador en terminar.
4. Paz fue la __ esquiadora en terminar.
5. Hugo fue el __ esquiador en terminar.
6. Olga fue la __ esquiadora en terminar.
7. Edgar fue el __ esquiador en terminar.
8. Natalia fue la __ esquiadora en terminar.
9. Enrique fue el __ esquiador en terminar.
10. Ingrid fue la __ esquiadora en terminar.

Ingrid fue la décima esquiadora en terminar.

Notes Inform students that ordinal numbers are usually placed before a noun.

Point out the similarity in the spelling of the words *cuatro* (number four) and *cuarto* (fourth, room).

Note for students that the noun sometimes is omitted when using ordinal numbers:

Nosotros somos los primeros (corredores) en terminar.

Tell students that it is common to use the abbreviated forms of the ordinal numbers. For example, such abbreviations are very common in addresses (street and avenue names, floor numbers, etc.).

28 ¡El pasatiempo nacional!

Irene loves soccer and would like to find out the standings for her favorite Chilean teams. Use the information provided in the chart to update her.

Tabla de posiciones

Equipos	PJ	PG	PE	PP	Pts.
1. Palestino	38	32	2	4	66
2. Everton	38	30	4	4	64
3. Colo Colo	38	27	5	3	59
4. Cobresal	38	24	3	11	51
5. Concepción	38	23	2	13	48
6. La Española	38	20	5	13	45
7. O'Higgins	38	18	6	14	42
8. La Católica	38	15	10	13	40
9. Cobreloa	38	12	5	21	29
10. La Serena	38	9	7	22	25

PJ: Partidos jugados; PG: Partidos ganados; PE: Partidos empatados; PP: Partidos perdidos; Pts.: Puntos

1. El Cobresal es el __ equipo.
2. El O'Higgins es el __ equipo.
3. El Colo Colo todavía es el __ equipo.
4. El Concepción es el __ equipo.
5. La Serena es el __ equipo.
6. La Católica es el __ equipo.
7. El Everton es el __ equipo.
8. El Palestino es el __ equipo.
9. El Cobreloa es el __ equipo.
10. La Española es el __ equipo.

Comunicación

29 ¿Quién fue el primero en terminar la carrera?

Working in pairs, talk about the final results of the girls' and boys' cross-country race.

MODELO A: ¿Quién fue el octavo en terminar?
B: Gerardo fue el octavo en terminar.

¿Quién va a ser el primero en terminar?

muchachos		muchachas	
1º	Jorge	1ª	Ana
2º	Pedro	2ª	Marta
3º	Carlos	3ª	Susana
4º	Ramiro	4ª	Paula
5º	Juan	5ª	Julia
6º	Javier	6ª	Luisa
7º	Alejandro	7ª	Yolanda
8º	Gerardo	8ª	Raquel
9º	Rogelio	9ª	Carlota
10º	Victor	10ª	Paz

Capítulo 7

trescientos cinco **305**

Notes Before beginning activity 29, check to be sure that students know the meaning of the preterite-tense form *fue,* which they learned in *Capítulo 5.*

Point out that in everyday language only cardinal numbers are used after *décimo.* Therefore, Alfonso the Thirteenth is *Alfonso XIII (trece).*

Follow up activity 29 by asking students to write out their answers.

30 Los deportes en familia

 David and Teresa are fraternal twins, so they have a lot in common. However, they like to participate in totally different sports. Working in pairs, talk about the information provided here depicting their activities during various times during the year. You may want to talk about what each person is doing, what the season is, what the weather is like or anything else you can say in Spanish. Correct any information your partner says that you think is wrong.

1   **2**

3

MODELO   **A:** En el primer dibujo es otoño.

         B: No, no es otoño, es primavera. Hace viento. El chico está jugando al básquetbol.

         A: Sí, y la chica está jugando al tenis.

Notes Chile offers many impressive ski resorts in addition to Portillo and Farellones (see page 293). Valle Nevado near Santiago is the largest ski resort in South America. It has 50 ski lifts and 22,000 acres of Andean ski slopes. Some runs are 10 miles long and 17,908 feet high.

31 En el verano

In groups of three, each of you should list five summer activities in order from most to least favorite, using ordinal numbers. Then discuss your preferences.

> 1º ir a la playa
> 2º dar paseos por el parque
> 3º jugar al fútbol

MODELO　**A:** Primero, me gusta ir a la playa en el verano. Hace sol y es muy divertido. Segundo, me gusta dar paseos por el parque.
> **B:** Bueno, primero me gusta dormir.
> **C:** A mí, primero, me gusta montar en patineta.

Una playa en Chile.

Answers

31 Creative self-expression.

Activities

Multiple Intelligences (bodily-kinesthetic)
Borrow a soccer ball from the physical education department. Call out one of the ordinal numbers and throw the ball to a student, who must call out the next ordinal number in the sequence before catching the ball. You may vary the drill by having the students say the previous ordinal number to the one you call out before catching the ball.

Notes Spanish-speaking countries have won medals in several popular sports in the Olympics, including boxing *(boxeo)*, swimming and diving *(natación y clavado)*, weight lifting *(levantamiento de pesas)* and equestrian sports *(equitación)*.

Your students may find it interesting to learn that Chile was the first Spanish-speaking country to participate in the Olympics in 1896.

Just as *Estados Unidos* is abbreviated EE.UU., the abbreviation for *Juegos Olímpicos* is *JJ.OO.*

Answers

32 1. Carlos es de Chile. Él practica el andinismo.
2. Desde Santiago de Chile se puede ver la Cordillera Sur de los Andes.
3. El Monumento Natural de El Morado es una montaña en un parque a hora y media de Santiago. Está cerrado en el invierno porque hay mucha nieve.
4. El primer día, Carlos va a dar un paseo por la laguna El Morado.
5. El segundo día, va a hacer mucho frío.

33 Answers will vary.

Activities

Spanish for Spanish Speakers
Have students write a short composition in Spanish, summarizing what they know about Chile. Expand the activity by having students seek additional information about Chile in the library or via the Internet.

Lectura personal

Cantantes y grupos musicales

Dirección http://www.emcp.com/músico/ola/e.diario-6.htm ▲ Archivo Edición Ver Favoritos Herramientas Ayuda

página principal · miembros · e-diario

Grupo musical La OLA

Nombre: Carlos Cubillas Lorca
Edad: **19 años**
País natal: **Chile**
Su estación favorita: **verano**

Un glaciar.

¡Otro excelente concierto en Santiago de Chile! Saben amigos, estoy muy contento de estar en mi país después de tantos meses. Eché de menos[1] mis montañas. Chile tiene 4200 kilómetros (2260 millas) de cordillera[2]. Desde casi cualquier[3] lugar de la capital se puede ver la majestuosa Cordillera Sur de los Andes. Cuando no toco la guitarra con el grupo La Ola, practico el andinismo: deporte de escalar[4] montañas, específicamente los Andes. ¡Me gusta mucho el andinismo! Después de enviar este mensaje, voy a ir al Monumento Natural de El Morado con un buen amigo (y excelente esquiador).

El Morado está a sólo hora y media de Santiago. El parque está cerrado entre[5] los meses de mayo y septiembre porque hay mucha nieve, pero estamos en otoño, entonces está bien. El primer día vamos a dar un paseo por la laguna[6] El Morado. Probablemente va a hacer fresco. El segundo día, en cambio, va a hacer mucho frío. Ese día pensamos escalar en hielo por el glaciar de San Francisco. A pesar de las bajas temperaturas, la falta[7] de oxígeno y el viento, vale la pena[8] visitar este lugar para poder presenciar[9] la magia de las montañas, mis montañas chilenas.

[1] I missed [2] mountain chain [3] any [4] climb [5] between [6] lagoon [7] lack [8] it is worthwhile [9] to witness

32 ¿Qué recuerdas?

1. ¿De dónde es Carlos? ¿Qué deporte practica?
2. ¿Qué se puede ver desde Santiago de Chile?
3. ¿Qué es el Monumento Natural de El Morado? ¿En qué estación está cerrado? ¿Por qué?
4. ¿Adónde va a dar un paseo Carlos el primer día?
5. ¿Qué tiempo va a hacer el segundo día?

• From what you can infer from the reading, what is Chile's geography and climate like? Compare it with the geography and climate of the state in which you live.

33 Algo personal

1. ¿Hay montañas donde vives? ¿Cómo se llaman?
2. ¿Te gustaría escalar El Morado? ¿Por qué sí o por qué no?
3. ¿Qué estación es buena para practicar el andinismo?

Notes Encourage students to find out more about Chile by going to the following Web sites:

Chile http://www.chile.com/
LanChile http://www.lanchile.com
general travel information
http://www.expedia.com

¿Qué aprendí?

Autoevaluación
As a review and self-check, respond to the following:

Visit the web-based activities at www.emcp.com

1. Name a favorite activity during each of the seasons.

2. What is the weather like where you live in the spring? Summer? Fall? Winter?

3. How would you ask what the temperature is today in Santiago, Chile?

4. Ask a friend how to send an e-mail letter and where you should put the address.

5. Imagine you are recording finishing times at a school track meet and it is your job to rank the runners as they finish. Using the ordinal numbers, count the first ten runners to cross the line in order to tell each runner where they are ranked.

6. What do you know about Chile?

Palabras y expresiones

El tiempo
el cambio
está nublado,-a/
    soleado,-a
la estación
el fresco
el grado
hace (+ weather expression)
hay neblina/sol
el hielo
el invierno
la lluvia
máximo,-a
mínimo,-a
la neblina
la nieve
nublado,-a
el otoño
la primavera
¿Qué tiempo/
    temperatura hace?

el sol
soleado,-a
la temperatura
el tiempo
el viento
Para describir
buen
cuarto,-a
décimo,-a
excelente
listo,-a
mal
noveno,-a
octavo,-a
quinto,-a
segundo,-a
séptimo,-a
sexto,-a
tercero (tercer),-a
todavía

Deportistas
el basquetbolista,
    la basquetbolista
el corredor, la
    corredora
el deportista, la
    deportista
el esquiador, la
    esquiadora
el futbolista, la
    futbolista
el jugador, la jugadora
el patinador, la
    patinadora
el tenista, la tenista

Verbos
continuar
copiar
enviar
esquiar
llover (ue)
montar en patineta
nevar (ie)
patinar sobre hielo
Expresiones y otras palabras
dar un paseo
en cambio
la flor
el lugar
el paseo
la patineta
por
por todos lados

Teacher Resources

📝 Activity 16

💬 **Information Gap Activities**
Postcard Activities
Funciones de Comunicación

Answers

Autoevaluación
Possible answers:
1. Me gusta montar en patineta en la primavera....
2. En la primavera hace viento....
3. ¿Qué temperatura hace hoy en Santiago de Chile?
4. ¿Cómo envío mi carta por correo electrónico y dónde pongo la dirección?
5. Primero, segundo, tercero, cuarto, etc.
6. Two writers from Chile, Gabriela Mistral and Pablo Neruda, have won Nobel Prizes.

Activities

Multiple Intelligences (logical-mathematical)
Ask students to give the Fahrenheit equivalent of several temperatures: 39°C (102.2°F), 100°C (212°F) and so on.

Spanish for Spanish Speakers
As an alternative to one of the *Autoevaluación* activities, ask students to read one or two poems by Pablo Neruda and summarize the themes presented (either orally or in writing).

Notes The name Chile comes from the indigenous word *Tchili* meaning **the deepest point of the earth.**

In 1980, Chile initiated an intensive literacy campaign. The rate of adult literacy rose from 89 percent in 1980 to 93.4 percent in 1990.

Chile is a country of young people, with over half of the population under the age of twenty. The country has one of the lowest rates of population growth in South America, roughly 1.5 percent a year.

309

¡Viento en popa!

Tú lees

Estrategia

Previewing

Before starting to read, try various activities that will help you preview what the reading is about. For example, you will understand more and enjoy what you are about to read on this page if you quickly skim the first and last paragraph of the following reading.

Previewing Activities

Read the title.
Look for cognates.
Skim the first paragraph.
Skim the last paragraph.
Look at information in accompanying charts.
Ask yourself what the main points are.

Preparación

Contesta las siguientes preguntas como preparación para la lectura.

1. ¿Cuál es el tema principal de esta lectura?
2. ¿Cuál es el deporte más popular del mundo hispano?
3. Identifica cinco cognados en la lectura *El mundo de los deportes*.

El mundo de los deportes

Los deportes son populares e importantes en el mundo hispano, y el fútbol es sin duda alguna[1] el deporte favorito de todos. Miles de personas ven los partidos de fútbol todas las semanas y la Copa Mundial[2] de fútbol es el evento más importante del mundo deportivo. Millones de personas en todo el mundo miran los partidos de la Copa Mundial y se contagian de la fiebre del "¡Gol!"[3]. La Copa Mundial sólo se juega una vez cada cuatro años y países de todo el mundo participan en este gran espectáculo del deporte.

El béisbol es otro deporte muy popular en el Caribe, especialmente en Cuba, la República Dominicana y Puerto Rico. También es muy popular en algunas regiones de México y en

Futbolistas de Inglaterra y Argentina en la Copa Mundial.

Notes The first Hispanic Olympic medal winner was Ramón Fonst, from Cuba, in 1900. The first Olympic Games to be held in a Spanish-speaking country took place in Mexico in 1968. The most recent Spanish-speaking nation to host the Olympics was Spain (Barcelona, 1992). The Spanish-speaking country with most gold medal winners for one sport is Uruguay, which has eight athletes with two medals each in soccer. Cuba is the country that has won the most gold medals.

Many of most famous soccer players in the world have come from Argentina and Uruguay.

Estos chicos juegan al jai alai.

Venezuela. Muchos jugadores de estos países juegan en las grandes ligas de los Estados Unidos. Algunos[4] de los jugadores más famosos de todos los tiempos son hispanos, como Pedro Martínez y Sammy Sosa (de la República Dominicana) y Roberto Clemente (de Puerto Rico).

El boxeo (también llamado[5] el deporte de las narices chatas[6]) el frontón[7], el jai alai y el ciclismo son también deportes populares en los países hispanos. Estos dos últimos también son muy populares en España, junto con[8] el básquetbol (también llamado baloncesto).

En el mundo hispano se practican muchos otros deportes y desde hace décadas los hispanos, al igual que[9] el resto del mundo, practican deportes no sólo como pasatiempo, sino también para mantener buena salud[10] y una vida activa.

[1]Without a doubt [2]World Cup [3]they all catch "goal" fever [4]Some [5]called [6]flat noses [7]a sport similar to squash or handball [8]along with [9]just as [10]good health

El ciclismo es popular en los países hispanos.

A ¿Qué recuerdas?

1. ¿Cómo son los deportes en el mundo hispano?
2. ¿Qué ven miles de personas cada semana?
3. ¿Cuál es el evento más importante en el fútbol?
4. ¿Qué deporte es muy popular en la región del Caribe?
5. ¿Qué otros deportes son populares en el mundo hispano?

B Algo personal

1. ¿Haces alguno de estos deportes? ¿Cuál? ¿Dónde? ¿Con quién?
2. ¿Cuál es tu deporte favorito?
3. ¿Cuánto tiempo hace que haces ese deporte?
4. ¿Sabes algo de los deportes en el mundo hispano? ¿Qué sabes?
5. ¿Ves muchos deportes en la televisión? ¿Cuáles?

Nuestro deporte favorito es el béisbol.

Capítulo 7   *trescientos once*   **311**

Teacher Resources

 Activities A–B

Answers

A 1. Los deportes en el mundo hispano son populares e importantes.
2. Ven los partidos de fútbol.
3. El evento más importante es la Copa Mundial de fútbol.
4. El béisbol es muy popular en la región del Caribe.
5. Otros deportes populares son el boxeo, el frontón, el ciclismo, el básquetbol, el jai alai.

B Answers will vary.

Activities

Critical Listening
Describe a celebrity without stating his/her name and ask the students to identify the person described. As a follow-up activity, have students work in pairs to prepare and present similar descriptions.

Notes   Discuss with the class what students know about some of the people mentioned in the reading. Pedro Martínez is one of the best pitchers in baseball. Sammy Sosa received international attention in 1998 during his race with Mark McGwire to break the single season home-run record. Roberto Clemente was a batting champion four times during his career playing right field for the Pittsburgh Pirates. His career ended with his untimely death in a plane crash on his way from Puerto Rico to Managua, Nicaragua, to help victims of a devastating earthquake on Christmas Eve of 1972.

Tú escribes

Answer the questions that follow in order to generate ideas for writing on the theme *Mi tiempo libre*. Then select some of the ideas that you like and write a paragraph about your free time. Remember to incorporate some transition words *(en cambio, entonces, pero)* to tie your ideas together and make your composition flow smoothly.

1. ¿Cuáles de estas actividades te gustan?

montar en patineta	practicar deportes
ver la tele	escuchar música
leer revistas	esquiar
ir a un concierto	ir a partidos de béisbol, fútbol, etc.
hacer ejercicios	montar a caballo
montar en bicicleta	hacer un picnic
ir al cine	trabajar con la computadora
ir de compras	tocar un instrumento musical
patinar sobre hielo	ir a fiestas con amigos
dar un paseo	hablar por teléfono

2. ¿Qué otras actividades te gusta hacer?
3. Completa estas frases pensando en lo que te gusta hacer.
   A. En el verano, me gusta....
   B. En el invierno, me gusta....
   C. Cuando hace mal tiempo, yo....
   D. Cuando estoy enfermo/a, prefiero....
   E. Si estoy aburrido/a, yo....
   F. Cuando estoy solo/a, me gusta....
   G. Cuando estoy con mi familia, prefiero....
   H. Cuando estoy con mis amigos....
   I. Si tengo dinero, me gusta....
   J. Cuando no tengo dinero, prefiero....

Proyectos adicionales

A Comunidades

Using the Internet, the newspaper, information from family and friends, etc., find out what you can about five well-known athletes in your local community or state (try to find at least one person who speaks Spanish). Try to find out where they are from, where they live, whether they speak Spanish, what they do when they have free time or anything else that interests you. Then write two or three statements describing each person.

B Comparisons

Compare sports where you live with what you know about sports in Spanish-speaking countries. Are the same sports popular? Does the weather have an effect on the sports being practiced? Are the sports played at the same time of the year? During the same season?

C Conexión con la tecnología

Using the Internet, visit a Web site that gives weather information for different cities around the world. Find the current weather conditions for several Spanish-speaking countries. Then write several paragraphs in Spanish to summarize what you find. Be sure to include the following information: identify the different symbols used to represent weather conditions, describe today's weather in several cities, give the current temperature, tell what season it is and predict what people are doing now due to the weather.

Santiago 22.7 ºC (73 ºF)
Valparaiso 17.6 ºC (64 ºF)

Santiago 9 ºC (48 ºF)
Valparaiso 11.4 ºC (53 ºF)

ANNUAL AVERAGE
Santiago 384 mm (15.1 inches)
Valparaiso 462.6 mm (18.2 inches)

Teacher Resources

 Trabalenguas

Activities

Connections
Have students draw a map of Argentina that shows major cities, rivers, mountains and surrounding countries. They may add any other geographical features they wish.

Spanish for Spanish Speakers
Assign the book *El jardín de senderos que se bifurcan* by Jorge Luis Borges. Next, students must write a 50–100-word summary of the contents printed on colored paper. Then have students design a poster to promote the story by combining the summary with illustrations and appropriate lettering to create a visually attractive poster.

Repaso

Now that I have completed this chapter, I can...	Go to these pages for help:
talk about leisure time activities	270
discuss sports	271
say what someone can do	274
discuss length of time	280
describe what is happening	282
talk about the seasons and weather	290, 298
indicate order	304

I can also...

talk about life in Argentina and Chile.	273, 293
talk about television and renting movies.	276
convert temperatures from centigrade to Fahrenheit.	301
understand a weather forecast in Spanish.	313

Trabalenguas

Es primavera: ¡Cuántas flores florean en el florido campo!

Notes Chile is the only Spanish-speaking Latin American country with two Nobel Prize winners in literature. Gabriela Mistral received the prize in 1945 and Pablo Neruda in 1971.

Argentina has long been noted for the high quality of its intellectual life and for its many artistic influences. Among its modern literary figures of international reputation are Jorge Luis Borges, Julio Cortázar, Ernesto Sábato and Manuel Puig.

Loose translation of the *Trabalenguas:* It is spring. How many flowers blooming in the flowery field!

Vocabulario

los **aeróbicos** aerobics 7A
ahora mismo right now 7A
el **ajedrez** chess 7A
alquilar to rent 7A
americano,-a American 7A
antes de before 7A
apagar to turn off 7A
el **básquetbol** basketball 7A
el **basquetbolista, la basquetbolista** basketball player 7B
buen good 7B
el **cambio** change 7B
las **cartas** playing cards 7A
casi almost 7A
continuar to continue 7B
el **control remoto** remote control 7A
copiar to copy 7B
el **corredor, la corredora** runner 7B
costar (ue) to cost 7A
¿Cuánto (+ time expression) **hace que** (+ present tense of verb) ... ? How long ... ? 7A
cuarto,-a fourth 7B
las **damas** checkers 7A
dar un paseo to go for a walk, to go for a ride 7B
dar to give 7A
décimo,-a tenth 7B
el **deportista, la deportista** athlete 7B
después de after 7A
dibujar to draw, to sketch 7A
dormir (ue, u) to sleep 7A
en cambio on the other hand 7B
enviar to send 7B
el **equipo** team 7A
el **esquiador, la esquiadora** skier 7B
esquiar to ski 7B
esta noche tonight 7A
está nublado,-a/soleado,-a it's cloudy, it's sunny 7B
la **estación** season 7B

estupendo,-a wonderful, marvelous 7A
excelente excellent 7B
la **flor** flower 7B
el **fresco** cool 7B
el **fútbol americano** football 7A
el **futbolista, la futbolista** soccer player 7B
el **grado** degree 7B
hace (+ time expression) **que** (time expression +) ago 7A
hace (+ weather expression) it is (+weather expression) 7B
hacer aeróbicos to do aerobics 7A
hay neblina/sol it is misting/it is sunny 7B
el **hielo** ice 7B
el **invierno** winter 7B
el **jugador, la jugadora** player 7B
jugar (ue) to play 7A
la **lista** list 7A
listo,-a ready 7B
llover (ue) to rain 7B
la **lluvia** rain 7B
el **lugar** place 7B
mal bad 7B
la **maquinita** little machine, video game 7A
máximo,-a maximum 7B
mínimo,-a minimum 7B
el **minuto** minute 7A
mismo,-a same 7B
montar en patineta to skateboard 7B
la **neblina** mist 7B
nevar (ie) to snow 7B
la **nieve** snow 7B
noveno,-a ninth 7B
nublado,-a cloudy 7B
octavo,-a eighth 7B
el **otoño** autumn 7B
el **pasatiempo** pastime, leisure activity 7A
el **paseo** walk, ride, trip 7B
el **patinador, la patinadora** skater 7B

patinar sobre hielo to ice-skate 7B
la **patineta** skateboard 7B
permitir to permit 7A
poder (ue, u) to be able to 7A
por la mañana in the morning 7A
por la noche at night 7A
por la tarde in the afternoon 7A
por todos lados everywhere 7B
por by 7B
la **primavera** spring 7B
el **programa** program 7A
¿Qué temperatura hace? What is the temperature? 7B
¿Qué tiempo hace? How is the weather? 7B
quinto,-a fifth 7B
recordar (ue, u) to remember 7A
remoto,-a remote 7A
el **segundo** second 7A
segundo,-a second 7B
séptimo,-a seventh 7B
sexto,-a sixth 7B
el **siglo** century 7A
el **sol** sun 7B
soleado,-a sunny 7B
la **telenovela** soap opera 7A
el **televisor** television 7A
la **temperatura** temperature 7B
el **tenista, la tenista** tennis player 7B
tercero (tercer),-a third 7B
el **tiempo** weather 7B
todavía yet 7A
todavía still 7B
(number +) **vez/veces al/a la** (time expression) (number +) time (s) per (+ time expression) 7A
la **vida** life 7A
el **viento** wind 7B
el **voleibol** volleyball 7A
volver (ue, u) to return, to go back, to come back 7A

Capítulo 7

trescientos quince **315**

Notes Remind students that the *ue* or *u* shown in parentheses after infinitives listed in *Navegando* help students remember how these verbs are formed, for example, *costar (ue)* and *jugar (ue)*.

Spanish is the official language of Argentina. However, it is a distinctly Argentine Spanish, characterized by special words, expressions and pronunciation. A dialect called Spanish *Lunfardo,* which developed in Buenos Aires before 1900, with many borrowed words from Italian and Portuguese, has had a significant impact on the Spanish that is spoken in the capital.

◯onnections with Parents

Try to encourage parents and guardians to have a larger role in their child's classroom education. In *Capítulo 8*, students will be learning vocabulary associated with chores and helping around the house. As you begin the new chapter, encourage students to talk with their parents or guardians about what they are learning in class. Consider having students ask if they may prepare a dish at home using a recipe from a Spanish-speaking country. A recipe for *paella* appears on page 341. Students might also find a recipe on the Internet, or you may prefer to provide a different favorite one of your own.

Capítulo **8**

Mis quehaceres

Objetivos

❖ **talk about household chores**

❖ **say what just happened**

❖ **ask for and offer help**

❖ **talk about the past**

❖ **identify and describe foods**

❖ **discuss food preparation**

❖ **make comparisons**

Visit the web-based activities at www.emcp.com

316 *trescientos dieciséis*

Notes Communicative objectives are provided on page 316 to prepare students for the chapter they are about to begin. A checkoff list of the functions appears on page 360, along with additional objectives, that students use as a self-check to evaluate their own progress.

España

Nombre oficial: **Reino de España**
Población: **40.100.000**
Capital: **Madrid**
Ciudades importantes: **Barcelona, Valencia, Sevilla**
Unidad monetaria: **el euro**
Fiesta nacional: **12 de octubre, Día de la Hispanidad**
Gente famosa: **Antonio Banderas (actor), Pablo Picasso (pintor), Enrique Iglesias (cantante), Penélope Cruz (actriz)**

Activities

Critical Thinking

Have students look at the photos at the start of the chapter. Ask if students can guess which country they will be studying in this chapter. Then call on several students to say what they think they will be learning about in this chapter.

trescientos diecisiete **317**

Notes The cultural focus of this chapter is Spain.

Take some time reviewing the contents of these two pages. First, point out and call on students to read the objectives shown on page 316. Then ask questions about what students see in the photographs. For example, ask if students can figure out where the people are in the large photograph. Ask what students think the people in the small photograph are doing (washing dishes).

Spain is the only Spanish-speaking country with a monarchy. *Juan Carlos de Borbón* has been king and his wife, *Sofía,* queen since 1975.

Teacher Resources

 Los quehaceres

 Activity 1

 Activities 53–54

Activity 1

Activity 1

 Activities 1–2

Content reviewed in *Lección A*
- rooms in a house
- family
- direct object pronouns
- present progressive
- objects in a kitchen

Activities

Prereading Strategy
Ask students to identify cognates and any known vocabulary in *Vocabulario I*.

Lección A

España

Vocabulario I
Los quehaceres

colgar la ropa

doblar la ropa

hacer la cama

Quizás debo sólo adornar esta pared.

cocinar/preparar la comida

limpiar

adornar

el abrigo

Ramón sube algo al primer piso.
Él le sube una camisa a su hermano.

En la familia García hay mucha gente.
Ellos son nueve personas.
Juntos hacen los quehaceres de la casa.

El abuelo acaba de llegar y deja su abrigo en la sala.

Notes Use a variety of *Navegando 1* support materials to teach and reinforce the vocabulary presented on pages 318–319. For example, support for the content of these pages is available in the Audio CD Program, the Listening Activities Manual, Overhead Transparencies, Workbook, Grammar and Vocabulary Exercises Manual and Quizzes.

Tell students that another common way of saying **to cook** is *hacer la comida*.

trabajar en el jardín

1 Julia
  1. adornar la sala
  2. cocinar el pollo
  3. trabajar en el jardín
  4. hacer la cama
  5. limpiar la cocina
  Enrique
  6. adornar la sala
  7. preparar la ensalada
  8. doblar la ropa
  9. hacer la cama
  10. limpiar la cocina

2 Possible answers:
  1. El abuelo acaba de llegar.
  2. Deja el abrigo en la sala.
  3. Ramón le sube un abrigo a su hermano.
  4. Sí, hay mucha gente en la familia García. Son nueve personas.
  5. Sí, hacen juntos los quehaceres.

3 Answers will vary.

1 ¿Qué tienen que hacer?

Write the names Julia and Enrique. Next, listen and list under each of their names what chores *(quehaceres)* each of them has to do. Then circle any items on the lists that they both have to do. The first one has been done for you.

MODELO

Julia   Enrique
adornar la sala

2 La familia García

Contesta las siguientes preguntas según la información en el Vocabulario I.

1. ¿Quién acaba de llegar?
2. ¿Dónde deja el abrigo el abuelo?
3. ¿Qué le sube Ramón a su hermano?
4. ¿Hay mucha gente en la familia García? ¿Cuántas personas son?
5. ¿Hacen juntos los quehaceres?

3 Tu familia

Haz una lista de los quehaceres que hacen en tu casa según lo que aprendiste en el Vocabulario I. Luego, di quién hace cada uno de esos quehaceres en tu familia.

hacer las camas   mi hermana
limpiar la sala   yo
limpiar la cocina   mi padre y mi madre

Estrategia

Increasing your vocabulary

When reading or learning new vocabulary in Spanish, you can figure out the meaning of a new word by relating it to your knowledge of other words that are spelled similarly. Such groups of similar words are called "word families." All the "members" of a word family share a common, easily recognizable root. Can you see how the verb *cocinar* (to cook) and the noun *cocina* (kitchen) are related in this way since people cook in a kitchen? Recognizing word families can help you expand your Spanish vocabulary and can make learning new words easier.

Activities

Prereading Strategy
Ask students to discuss the chores they are expected to do at home. Then instruct students to cover up the words in *Vocabulario I* with their hands and look only at the illustrations. Ask them to imagine what is taking place. Finally, have students look through the text bubbles and boxes quickly to find cognates and words they recognize.

Capítulo 8   *trescientos diecinueve*   **319**

Notes Remind students they have already learned that cognates *(cognados)* are words that are similar in English and Spanish. Words that appear the same but that are not cognates are considered false cognates *(cognados falsos)* because their meaning or usage is different in the two languages. Have students give the meaning for the cognate that appears on page 318, *preparar,* and the false cognates *sacar, ropa* and *aprender,* all of which students have already seen in previous chapters.

¿Me ayudas?

INÉS: Víctor, ¿qué haces?
VÍCTOR: Hago unos quehaceres.

INÉS: ¡Qué aburrido! ¿Por qué no vamos al cine?
VÍCTOR: Tengo que terminar de limpiar la casa. ¿Me ayudas?
INÉS: Sí, dejo mi abrigo aquí y te voy a limpiar la cocina.

INÉS: Bueno, la cocina ya está limpia. Hola, señora Zea.
SRA. ZEA: Hola, Inés. Hola, Víctor. ¡Qué casa tan limpia!
VÍCTOR: Gracias, mamá. Ahora voy al cine con Inés.

4 ¿Qué recuerdas?

1. ¿Qué hace Víctor?
2. ¿Adónde quiere ir Inés?
3. ¿Qué tiene que terminar Víctor primero?
4. ¿Qué limpia Inés?
5. ¿Qué dice la Sra. Zea?

5 Algo personal

1. ¿Cómo ayudas con los quehaceres en casa?
2. ¿Piensas que hacer los quehaceres es aburrido? Explica.
3. ¿Te gusta ir al cine?

6 ¿Me ayudas?

 Mira las tres fotos que van con el diálogo y di si lo que oyes va con la primera, la segunda o la tercera foto.

MODELO Va con la tercera foto.

Todos ayudan en la cocina.

Cultura viva

España: país multicultural

Spain's culture and diverse population today reflect the influence of people from many different ethnic groups and races over thousands of years. For example, cave paintings indicate people lived in an area *(Altamira)* of northern Spain between 25,000 and 10,000 B.C. Over 4,000 years ago the Iberians *(íberos)* invaded the area

Granada, España.

that would later be named the Iberian Peninsula *(Península Ibérica)* and that is shared today by Spain and Portugal. In 1100 B.C., the Phoenicians *(fenicios)* from present day Lebanon founded cities where *Cádiz* and *Málaga* are located. Blue-eyed, blond Celts *(celtas)* traveled from northern Europe south to Spain between 800 and 700 B.C., which explains why many Spaniards have those features today. The Greeks *(griegos)*, who arrived between 800 and 700 B.C., along with the Phoenicians, brought with them olive trees and grapevines. As a result, both olives *(aceitunas)* and grapes *(uvas)* are important products in Spain's economy today. Many other people

Córdoba es una ciudad bonita.

arrived later: the Carthaginians *(cartagineses)* from the area known today as Tunisia; the Romans *(romanos)*, who introduced Latin, which evolved into Spanish; the Visigoths *(visigodos)* from Germany; and the Arabs from northern Africa, also called Moors *(moros)*, who introduced the cultivation of rice *(arroz)* and oranges *(naranjas)* and turned *Córdoba* and *Granada* into important and prestigious cities. By the time the Moors were defeated in Granada and removed from power in 1492 by the Catholic monarchs Ferdinand *(Fernando)* and Isabella *(Isabel)*, many elements in contemporary Spain had taken root and are still evident today.

Los Reyes Católicos, Isabel y Fernando.

7 Conexiones con otras disciplinas: historia y ciencias sociales

Conecta la información de las dos columnas de una manera lógica.

1. los griegos y los fenicios
2. los moros
3. los celtas
4. los romanos
5. los fenicios
6. 25,000–10,000 B.C.

A. el latín
B. Altamira
C. el arroz y las naranjas
D. Cádiz y Málaga
E. las aceitunas y las uvas
F. rubios

Capítulo 8

trescientos veintiuno 321

Answers

8 1. Alfredo las está buscando./Alfredo está buscándolas.
2. María y Fernando la están preparando./Están preparándola.
3. Lo estamos adornando./Estamos adornándolo.
4. Carlos la está limpiando./Está limpiándola.
5. Mis hermanos las están haciendo./Mis hermanos están haciéndolas.
6. Yo los estoy colgando./Yo estoy colgándolos.
7. Los estamos haciendo juntos./Estamos haciéndolos juntos.

Activities

Multiple Intelligences (linguistic/spatial)
Divide students into groups of three or four and assign one-third of the groups to make a visual image of the direct object pronoun located to the left of the conjugated verb. Another third of the groups must make a visual image of the direct object pronoun attached to the infinitive. The final third must make a visual image of the direct object pronoun attached to the present participle.

Idioma

Repaso rápido: direct object pronouns

You have already learned that direct object pronouns can precede conjugated verbs, attach to the end of an infinitive or attach to the end of a present participle.

me	nos
te	os
lo/la	los/las

Remember to add an accent mark to the present participle in order to maintain the original pronunciation of the present participle without the pronoun.

Marta está limpiando la cocina.
*Marta **está limpiándola.*** *Marta **la está limpiando.***

---

8 Todos están haciendo quehaceres

Sigue el modelo para decir la misma oración de forma diferente, usando un pronombre de complemento directo.

MODELO Yo estoy doblando *la ropa.*
Yo la estoy doblando./Yo estoy doblándola.

1. Alfredo está buscando *las tazas.*
2. María y Fernando están preparando *la comida.*
3. Estamos adornando *el cuarto.*
4. Carlos está limpiando *la cocina.*
5. Mis hermanos están haciendo *las camas.*
6. Yo estoy colgando *los abrigos.*
7. Estamos haciendo juntos *los trabajos de la casa.*

El verbo *colgar*

The present tense of *colgar* (to hang) follows the pattern of other verbs that require the change *o → ue: cuelgo, cuelgas, cuelga, colgamos, colgáis, cuelgan.*

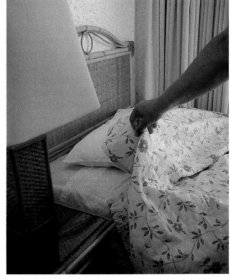

Está haciendo la cama.

Notes Remind students that they can find the direct object in a sentence by answering the question (subject + verb +) **who?** or **what?**
Use the following examples as you review direct object pronouns: *La voy a terminar* (before a conjugated verb); *Voy a terminarla* (attached to the end of an infinitive); *Estoy terminándola* (attached to the end of a present participle).

See if students can remember any other verbs with the *o → ue* change: *poder, dormir,* etc.

Estructura

Indirect object pronouns

An indirect object indicates **to whom** or **for whom** something is said or done. An indirect object pronoun (*pronombre de complemento indirecto*) may replace an indirect object. You have already learned to use indirect object pronouns with the verb *gustar*. They look the same as direct object pronouns except for *le* and *les*.

los pronombres de complemento indirecto			
me	to me, for me	**nos**	to us, for us
te	to you, for you (tú)	**os**	to you, for you (vosotros,-as)
le	to you, for you (Ud.) to him, for him to her, for her	**les**	to you, for you (Uds.) to them, for them

Indirect object pronouns follow the same rules for placement in a sentence that you learned for the direct object pronouns:

- They usually precede the conjugated form of the verb, but they also may follow and attach to an infinitive or a present participle. (Add an accent mark to the present participle in order to maintain the original pronunciation of the present participle.)

  *Pilar **me** va a preparar una ensalada.*
  Pilar va a prepararme una ensalada.   Pilar is going make a salad **for me.**

  Te estoy escuchando.
  Estoy escuchándote.   I am listening **to you.**

- Place negative expressions (e.g., *nunca*) before the indirect object pronouns.

  ***Nunca nos** hacen la cama.*   They **never** make the bed **for us.**

Add the word *a* plus a pronoun or noun to a sentence in order to clarify the meaning of *le* and *les*, or in order to add emphasis.

Le escribo   *a ella.*
      a María.
      a mi hermana.

Les escribo   *a ellas.*
      a María y a Mario.
      a mis primos.

Le escribo a María.

Teacher Resources

 Activities 3–4

 Activities 4–6

 Activity 2

 Activities 4–7

Activities

Expansion
Ask the class for sample sentences using direct object pronouns.

Language through Action
Expand the discussion of the indirect object pronouns using gestures as you walk around the room and give objects to students. Tell students what you are giving them as you hand the object to a person: *Te estoy dando un libro; Le doy un lápiz a Jorge.* You can vary the verb forms, but use indirect object pronouns in your sentences. As a second step in this activity, have students repeat your sentences after you. Finally, call on a few volunteers to demonstrate the transfer of knowledge, asking several students to make a statement using an indirect object pronoun while performing an action.

Multiple Intelligences (musical)
Play music from Spain as you explain to your students the use of *vosotros/vosotras* to give students an auditory connection to help them remember that this subject pronoun is used in Spain.

Notes Show the class they can locate the indirect object in a sentence by asking themselves the following question: (subject + verb +) **to whom** or **for whom?**

Point out that in English sentences using an indirect object or indirect object pronoun, the word **to** is commonly understood: I'm writing **(to)** him.

Activities

Critical Thinking
Ask students for an alternative way of saying the sentences for activity 9, placing the object pronouns after the infinitives.

Students with Special Needs
Provide a second model for activity 11.

 Práctica

9 Antes de ir de vacaciones

Pablo y su familia van de vacaciones y unos amigos van a ayudar a la familia a prepararse para el viaje. Completa tus oraciones con *me, te, le, nos* o *les*, diciendo qué van a hacer.

MODELO   Marta <u>nos</u> va a limpiar las ventanas (a nosotros).

1. Raúl __ va a buscar las maletas (a mí).
2. Marta __ va a doblar la ropa (a mi madre).
3. La Sra. Martínez __ va a preparar la comida (a mis padres).
4. El Sr. Martínez __ va a colgar los abrigos (a mi padre).
5. Raúl y Marta __ van a hacer las camas (a nosotros).

10 De otra manera

Estás hablando de los quehaceres de la casa con unos amigos. ¿Cómo puedes decir la misma oración de otra manera *(another way)*?

MODELO   ¿*Me* estás colgando la ropa?
¿Estás colgándo*me* la ropa?

1. Él nunca *le* puede limpiar la casa.
2. Quizás Carlos *te* puede poner la mesa.
3. ¿No *me* quieres preparar la comida?
4. Quizás *te* debo escribir una lista de quehaceres.
5. *Les* estamos colgando la ropa.
6. ¿No *nos* está Ud. adornando el cuarto?

11 ¿Me ayudas?

 In pairs, take turns asking one another for help with the indicated tasks. The person responding may agree or refuse to help.

MODELO   colgar los abrigos
A: ¿Me cuelgas los abrigos?
B: Sí, (No, no) te cuelgo los abrigos.

1. limpiar el patio
2. doblar las servilletas
3. limpiar la mesa del comedor
4. buscar la sal
5. encender las luces del comedor
6. hacer las camas
7. poner la mesa
8. subir la ropa a mi cuarto

¿Me estás colgando la ropa?

Notes   You may wish to remind students that in the fifth sentence of activity 11, the verb *encender* requires the stem change *e → ie.*

If you are teaching *vosotros/vosotras,* give students several sentences that practice the direct and indirect object pronoun *os.* You can easily accomplish this by modifying one or two of the sentences for each activity.

12 Ayudando en casa

Las personas de la ilustración están ayudándote en las tareas de la casa.
Describe lo que hace cada una de las personas.

MODELO Marta

Marta me está limpiando la mesa./Marta está
limpiándome la mesa.

1. Antonio y Carlota   2. Ernesto   3. Cristóbal   4. Julia

✦ Comunicación

13 ¿Qué haces?

Make a list of your household chores and another list of what you do to help
specific members of your family. Then talk with a classmate about what you do
to help around the house and who you help with the household duties.

MODELO A: ¿Qué haces para ayudar en tu casa?
B: Doblo mi ropa y la subo a mi cuarto. ¿Y tú? ¿Ayudas a tus padres?
A: Sí. Le pongo la mesa a mi madre.

14 ¿Me ayudas?

A group of exchange students from Spain will be staying with families in your
community. With a classmate, take turns asking one another when each of
you will be able to help with various chores to prepare for their visit.
Answers should indicate if and when the person answering will be able to
help with the indicated tasks.

MODELO A: ¿Cuándo me puedes limpiar la cocina?
B: Quizás te puedo limpiar la cocina por la tarde./Quizás puedo limpiarte la
cocina por la tarde.

Capítulo 8   *trescientos veinticinco*   **325**

Notes Before beginning activity 12,
remind students that the direct and
indirect object pronouns may be used
before the form of *estar* (or other verb
helper) or after and attached to the
present participle.

15 ¿Qué les gusta hacer?

In small groups, discuss your most favorite and least favorite household chores. Each person should make a list of at least three chores you all like to do and a second list of three chores that you do not like to do. Each member of your group should then talk with members of other groups to find out how your lists compare. Finally, one person from each group should summarize the findings for the class.

MODELO **A:** ¿Les gusta cocinar la comida?
B: Sí, nos gusta cocinarla.
A: A nosotros también nos gusta.

Nos gusta	No nos gusta
cocinar	poner la mesa

Estructura

Saying what just happened with *acabar de*

You can say what has just happened using a form of the verb *acabar* (to finish, to complete, to terminate) followed by *de* and an infinitive.

acabar de + infinitive

Acabo de llegar. — I just arrived.
Mi padre acaba de poner la mesa. — My father just set the table.

Práctica

16 ¡Gracias por la ayuda!

Francisco tiene muchos quehaceres y muchos buenos amigos. A sus amigos les gusta ayudar con sus quehaceres. Contesta las preguntas para decir quién acaba de hacer cada quehacer, usando las pistas entre paréntesis.

MODELO ¿Los platos? (Alicia / limpiar)
Alicia acaba de limpiarlos.

1. ¿Las camisas? (Ana / doblar)
2. ¿Las camas? (Pedro y Pablo / hacer / ahora mismo)
3. ¿El cuarto? (Alejandro y yo / limpiar / juntos)
4. ¿La sala? (Elena / adornar)
5. ¿Los abrigos? (yo / colgar)
6. ¿Las ventanas? (Ángel / limpiar / hace media hora)

Alicia acaba de limpiar los platos.

Notes The verb *acabar* is always followed by the preposition *de* before an infinitive because it refers to actions that have already happened or that are coming to an end.

Other verbs like *acabar* are *alegrarse*, *arrepentirse*, *dejar* and *terminar*.

17 La fiesta de despedida

 You and a friend are organizing the farewell party for the Spanish exchange students who just spent the last week with families in your community. Take turns asking and answering questions to find out what everyone has just done to help out.

MODELO Uds. / limpiar la cocina
> **A:** ¿Qué acaban de hacer Uds.?
> **B:** Acabamos de limpiar la cocina.

1. Ana / poner la mesa
2. Andrés y Rosa / adornar las paredes
3. tú / limpiar las ventanas
4. Jaime y Cristina / preparar la comida
5. Mercedes / llegar con la comida
6. yo / leer la lista de quehaceres

 ## Comunicación

18 ¿Qué acabas de hacer?

Imagine it is Saturday at noon and you are talking on the phone with a friend. Discuss some things each of you did just recently and what you are going to do later in the day. You may want to include in your conversation something interesting that someone in your family or a friend did recently, too.

MODELO **A:** ¿Qué haces?
> **B:** Bueno, yo acabo de poner la mesa. ¿Y tú?
> **A:** Pues, yo acabo de terminar mi tarea. Mis padres dicen que puedo salir. ¿Quieres hacer algo?

Acabo de poner la mesa.

Capítulo 8 | *trescientos veintisiete* **327**

 # Teacher Resources

Activity 17

Answers

17 1. ¿...acaba de...?/Acaba de....
2. ¿...acaban de...?/Acaban de....
3. ¿...acabas de...?/Acabo de....
4. ¿...acaban de...?/Acaban de....
5. ¿...acaba de...?/Acaba de....
6. ¿...acabo de...?Acabas de....

18 Creative self-expression.

Activities

Critical Listening
Tell students that they will hear several statements that give impressions of recent travels in the Spanish-speaking world. They should listen to each statement and use *acabar de* to say where the speaker has recently traveled or visited. Possible statements include: *Madrid es una ciudad muy bonita; Me gusta mucho el Parque de Chapultepec; Caracas es grande y moderna; En San Juan y toda la isla el béisbol es muy popular; Me encantan las playas de Viña del Mar pero también me gusta esquiar en las montañas.* As closure, review what students have learned about different countries in *Navegando 1*.

¡Oportunidades!

Estudiante de intercambio
It is becoming more and more popular for language students to spend time overseas as exchange students. After you have studied Spanish for a couple of years, it would be a great opportunity for you to become an exchange student in Spain or in another Spanish-speaking country. What you learn at school will be very valuable to you. Living within the culture in a different country, practicing the language you have learned with native speakers, developing life long friendships, and gathering first hand experience will be very rewarding and exciting.

Teacher Resources

 Más quehaceres

 Activity 6

 Activities 55–56

 Activity 8

 Activity 3

 Activities 9–10

Activities

Language through Action
In advance, write the expressions from *Vocabulario II* and other household chores students have learned on separate pieces of paper. Have individuals each select one of the pieces of paper at random. Then call on them to act out the expressions while classmates guess what the expressions are in Spanish.

Vocabulario II
Más quehaceres

lavar las ollas

barrer

dar de comer al perro

recoger la mesa

arreglar el comedor

¡Pedro, Pedro! ¿No me oyes? ¡Qué listo eres!

poner las cosas en su lugar

pasar la aspiradora

La familia Gutiérrez arregla la casa hoy. Trabajaron mucho ayer también.

Notes Other *Navegando 1* components that practice and reinforce the vocabulary presented on pages 328 and 329 include the Audio CD Program, the Listening Activities Manual, Overhead Transparencies, Workbook, Grammar and Vocabulary Exercises Manual and Quizzes. The Teacher Resources listed at the top of the page indicate the specific numbered activities coordinated to the content of these pages for your convenience. Use any of the other ancillaries you feel will help you to tailor the content to your teaching style.

Yo traigo el pan y la leche.

sacar la basura

Él va a buscar leche y pan a la tienda.

19 Los quehaceres

Selecciona la foto de la persona que corresponda con lo que oyes.

A **B** **C** **D**

20 ¡Más quehaceres!

Di qué quehaceres debes hacer, según las ilustraciones.

MODELO Debo poner la mesa.

1

2

3

4

5

6

Notes Play the audio CD of *Vocabulario I* to provide students with pronunciation practice before they try to figure out the meaning of the new words and expressions on pages 328 and 329.

Activity 19 is intended for listening comprehension practice. Play the audio CD of the activity or use the transcript that appears in the ATE Introduction if you prefer to read the activity yourself.

Answers

19 1. C
   2. A
   3. D
   4. B
20 1. ...pasar la aspiradora.
   2. ...lavar las ollas.
   3. ...dar de comer al perro.
   4. ...sacar la basura.
   5. ...lavar la ropa.
   6. ...preparar la comida.

Activities

Cooperative Learning
Have students bring in pictures from magazines or newspapers of people performing household chores that were taught in the lesson. They should also bring in a picture of a household chore not taught in this lesson, learn the term and teach it to a classmate. Then have students work in pairs or small groups, pretending they are doing the chore shown in each picture. Use Spanish sentences as models, if necessary: *¿Arreglas el cuarto?/Sí (No, no) arreglo el cuarto.* You can extend the activity by having students review the present progressive with the same pictures: *¿Qué estás haciendo ahora?/Estoy arreglando el cuarto.*

Diálogo II

Hay mucho por hacer

SRA. ZEA: Ayer trabajasteis mucho, pero hoy hay quehaceres también.
VÍCTOR: Pues, yo voy a recoger la mesa y lavar las ollas.
SRA. ZEA: Entonces, David puede pasar la aspiradora.

SRA. ZEA: ¿Quién va a la tienda a buscar leche?
DAVID: ¿Qué?
SRA. ZEA: ¿No me oyes? ¡Qué listo!

SRA. ZEA: ¿Puedes ir a buscar leche a la tienda?
DAVID: ¿Y por qué yo? ¿Por qué no va Víctor?
SRA. ZEA: Porque él va a lavar las ollas. ¿Quieres hacer eso?

21 ¿Qué recuerdas?

  1. ¿Quiénes trabajaron mucho ayer?
  2. ¿Qué va a hacer Víctor?
  3. ¿Quién pasa la aspiradora?
  4. ¿Quién es listo?
  5. ¿Qué no quiere hacer David?

22 Algo personal

  1. ¿Qué quehaceres haces en casa?
  2. ¿Eres listo/a?
  3. ¿Te gusta ir a la tienda a buscar leche o pan? Explica.
  4. ¿Quién saca la basura en tu casa? ¿Quién pasa la aspiradora?

23 ¿Vais a hacer un quehacer o a hacer un deporte?

 Las siguientes personas van a hablar de sus actividades de hoy. Di si lo que oyes es *un quehacer* o *un deporte*.

¡Extra!

El cambio de g → j

You have learned to use several verbs that are regular in the present tense except for a minor stem change *(poder, jugar)* or a spelling change. These changes do not affect the verb's present-tense endings. For verbs that end in *-ger* (such as *recoger*) the letter *g* changes to *j* before the letters *a* and *o* to maintain pronunciation: *Yo recojo la mesa muchas veces.*

Notes Ask students if they recognize the verb form *trabajasteis*, which appears in the dialog. Then ask what the infinitive form of the verb is *(trabajar)*. This would be a good time to review this cultural and linguistic point with students. Remind them that many Spaniards (especially in the south) use this plural informal form of the verb. Note that the verb form may be accompanied by the subject pronouns *vosotros* or *vosotras* when the subject is not clear. Finally, practice conjugating several verbs using *vosotros* and *vosotras*.

Tell the class that they will remember the spelling change for *-ger* and *-gir* verbs if they think of them as the *yo-jo* verbs *(recojo)*.

330

Cultura viva

Los quehaceres en una casa española

Do you like doing chores? Helping with the household chores is a long-standing tradition in many homes throughout the world. In Spain, young people generally help with chores starting at an early age, and everyone helps out with the

Limpiando un suelo.

cleaning *(la limpieza)* and upkeep of the home. Spanish houses do not, as a general rule, have wall-to-wall carpeting *(alfombra, moqueta)*. Instead, floors often consist of uncovered tile *(losa)*, marble *(mármol)* or wood *(madera)* and they are usually washed every day. If there are teenagers in the house, they usually are the ones chosen to perform this chore. The laundry is another household task that must

Ropa en el tendedero (Almeria, España).

be performed nearly every day. Dryers *(secadoras de ropa)* are not common in Spanish homes because of the high cost of energy, so laundry *(lavado de ropa* or *colada)* in many instances must be washed daily or every other day, and clothes are left to hang from lines to dry *(tender la ropa en el tendedero)*. Both girls and boys often have to hang the laundry, take it down and fold it. In addition, boys are often required to run errands *(hacer recados)* for their parents, while girls, traditionally, help with cooking.

How do you help with the cleaning and maintenance of your home? Regardless of your answer, one thing you have in common with young people in Spain and throughout the world: Although you may accept that they are an integral part of living together as a family, nobody seems to like doing chores!

24 Los quehaceres en una casa española

¿Es cierto o falso? Si es falso, di lo que es cierto.

1. Es tradicional empezar a ayudar con los quehaceres de casa cuando uno es joven en España.
2. Sólo los padres hacen la limpieza en las casas españolas.
3. Muchas casas tienen alfombra o moqueta en los pisos.
4. Hay muchas secadoras porque la energía no cuesta mucho en España.
5. Las muchachas y los muchachos cuelgan la ropa y la doblan.

25 Comparando

Make two lists of chores, one with what you and your friends do and another one with the chores you know young people in Spain do. Do you see any differences? Are there similarities? In what other ways do you think young people in Spain help around the home?

Capítulo 8   *trescientos treinta y uno* 331

Answers

26 1. oyen
2. oye
3. oye
4. oyen
5. oímos
6. oigo
7. oyendo
8. oyes

Activities

Critical Thinking
Inquire whether students remember other verbs that have -go in the *yo* form (*vengo, tengo, pongo, salgo, hago*).

Expansion
Practice these two new irregular verbs by asking the following questions: *¿Qué traes a la escuela en un día típico?; ¿Qué traes a la clase de español?; ¿Qué trae el maestro/la maestra a la clase?; ¿Oyen Uds. anuncios en la escuela? ¿Cuándo?*

Idioma

Estructura

Present tense of *oír* and *traer*

The verbs *oír* (to hear, to listen) and *traer* (to bring) are irregular.

oír	
oigo	oímos
oyes	oís
oye	oyen
gerundio: oyendo	

traer	
traigo	traemos
traes	traéis
trae	traen
gerundio: trayendo	

Práctica

26 A todos nos gusta oír la radio

Completa el siguiente párrafo con las formas correctas del verbo *oír*.

A toda mi familia le gusta oír la radio. Mis primos (1) las noticias todas las noches. Son muy listos. Mi tía (2) un programa de música española por las tardes. Mi hermano (3) los deportes, cuando no puede verlos en la televisión. Si mi abuelo y mi padre están trabajando en el garaje, (4) música popular y cantan. Mamá y yo siempre (5) el pronóstico del tiempo para saber si va a llover. Yo (6) la radio cuando escribo e-mails y también siempre estoy (7) música cuando hago la tarea. Y tú, ¿cuándo (8) la radio?

A mi hermano le gusta oír la radio.

Notes Note the use of *vosotros/vosotras* in the verb paradigm on page 332. Remind students that *vosotros/vosotras* is used in Spain, the country featured in *Capítulo 8.* If you are requiring students to learn the *vosotros/vosotras* form of verbs, be sure to practice the verbs *oír* and *traer* in sentences that contain either *vosotros* or *vosotras.*

27 ¿Qué trae cada uno?

 Unos amigos vienen a una fiesta en tu casa y cada persona tiene que traer algo diferente. Trabajando en parejas, alterna con tu compañero/a preguntando y contestando qué trae cada persona.

MODELO el Sr. y la Sra. Lorenzo
A: ¿Qué traen el Sr. y la Sra. Lorenzo?
B: El Sr. y la Sra. Lorenzo traen el pollo.

1. Paloma   **2.** Enrique y Tomás   **3.** mi amiga y yo

4. Alberto   **5.** Blanca y Graciela   **6.** Pedro

❋ Comunicación

 ## 28 En mi casa

 Working in pairs, talk about how your families and friends balance fun and work, describing some of your families' and your friends' favorite pastimes and telling how everyone helps when organizing activities or when doing chores. Mention which of the activities people like a lot or do not like. You may wish to use some of these activities to get started.

oír la radio	cocinar	buscar la leche y el pan
mirar la televisión	lavar las ollas	limpiar la cocina
tener una fiesta	traer CDs	arreglar el cuarto

MODELO **A:** En mi familia nos gusta hacer quehaceres los sábados y, luego, algunas veces tenemos una fiesta con los amigos y la familia. Mis primos siempre traen la música para bailar.
B: Yo siempre oigo música y arreglo mi cuarto los fines de semana.

Capítulo 8   *trescientos treinta y tres* **333**

Notes Students will find it interesting that in addition to the use of *vosotros*, the pronunciation of certain letters and words heard in Spain has certain unique features. For example, most Spaniards pronounce the soft *c* and the letter *z* with a sound that is similar to the English sound *th*, as in the words *gracias* and *feliz*.

Walk around the room as students are doing activity 28 and listen in on conversations. Offer help when needed.

Activity 8

Activity 11

Activity 6

Activity 13

Answers

29
1. llegaron
2. cociné
3. limpió
4. ayudó
5. pasó
6. sacaste
7. trabajaron
8. hablaron
9. lavó
10. bailamos

Activities

Students with Special Needs
Practice conjugating several verbs with students using *vosotros/vosotras*. First, try several verbs in the present tense. Then, after presenting the preterite tense of regular *-ar* verbs, practice conjugating some verbs in the preterite tense. Verb charts present forms throughout the book and the Appendices offer examples for reference.

TPR
The preterite can be introduced through TPR. Give students the commands: *Cierra la puerta* and *Abre la puerta.* Then have them restate the action: *Él/Ella cerró la puerta y luego la abrió.*

334

Estructura

Talking about the past: preterite tense of *-ar* verbs

Use the preterite tense when you are talking about actions or events that were completed in the past. Form the preterite tense of a regular *-ar* verb by removing the last two letters from the infinitive and attaching the endings shown.

lavar					
yo	lav**é**	I washed	nosotros nosotras	lav**amos**	we washed
tú	lav**aste**	you washed	vosotros vosotras	lav**asteis**	you washed
Ud. él ella	lav**ó**	you washed he washed she washed	Uds. ellos ellas	lav**aron**	you washed they washed they washed

Note: Regular verbs that end in *-car (buscar, explicar, sacar, tocar)*, *-gar (apagar, colgar, jugar, llegar)* and *-zar (empezar)* require a spelling change in the *yo* form of the preterite in order to maintain the original sound of the infinitive.

infinitivo			pretérito
bus**car**	*c*	→	*qu* yo bus**qué**
apa**gar**	*g*	→	*gu* yo apa**gué**
empe**zar**	*z*	→	*c* yo empe**cé**

 Práctica

29 Ayer en la casa de Pilar

Completa las siguientes oraciones con la forma correcta del pretérito de los verbos entre paréntesis para decir lo que pasó ayer en la casa de Pilar.

1. Mis amigos *(llegar)* temprano.
2. Yo *(cocinar)* desde las nueve.
3. Daniel *(limpiar)* el piso del comedor.
4. Ángela me *(ayudar)* mucho también.
5. Ella *(pasar)* la aspiradora por la sala.
6. Tú *(sacar)* la basura antes de comer.
7. Uds. *(trabajar)* todo el día ayudándome.
8. Todos *(hablar)* bien de la comida.
9. Después de comer, Paco me *(lavar)* los platos.
10. Luego, nosotros *(bailar)* en la sala.

Notes Review some of the handy time expressions students can add to a sentence when they are talking about the past: *ayer, anoche, la semana pasada, el año pasado.* Ask students if they can add any other expressions to the list.

Do the first sentence of activity 29 as a class.

30 ¿Qué cocinaste?

Completa el siguiente párrafo con la forma apropiada del pretérito de los verbos entre paréntesis.

Yo *(1. cocinar)* una sopa ayer en mi casa para toda la familia. Mi hermana me *(2. ayudar)*. Yo *(3. empezar)* a preparar todo muy temprano. Primero yo *(4. buscar)* los ingredientes. Luego *(5. lavar)* la olla grande y *(6. sacar)* los cubiertos. Después *(7. preparar)* unos refrescos. Al terminar de cocinar, *(8. apagar)* la estufa y *(9. arreglar)* los cubiertos en la mesa. Entonces, *(10. llamar)* a todos a comer.

31 ¿Qué hiciste?

 In pairs, take turns asking whether your classmate has completed the indicated chores. Your partner should say that he or she did not do each task because someone else already did it.

MODELO comprar el pan / Roberto
    A: ¿Compraste el pan?
    B: No, yo no compré el pan porque Roberto ya lo compró.

1. buscar los platos / Ernesto
2. apagar la estufa / Miguel
3. sacar la basura / Pedro
4. colgar los abrigos / Alfonso y Ana
5. preparar la comida / Jorge y Luisa
6. lavar la olla grande / Isabel

✦ Comunicación

32 Mini-diálogos

 Working in pairs, discuss some of the things that needed to be done around the home recently and whether or not either of you has done any of them. Some suggested chores and activities are provided to get you started.

MODELO **A:** ¿Preparaste la comida?
    B: Sí, (No, no) la preparé.

preparar la comida   sacar la basura   arreglar el cuarto
pasar la aspiradora
colgar la ropa en tu cuarto   comprar la leche   lavar las ollas

33 Todos en mi familia ayudaron

 Talk about what everyone in your family did last week to help around the house.

Teacher Resources

 Activity 31

Answers

30 1. cociné; 2. ayudó; 3. empecé; 4. busqué; 5. lavé; 6. saqué; 7. preparé; 8. apagué; 9. arreglé; 10. llamé

31 1. ¿Buscaste...?/No, yo no busqué los platos porque Ernesto ya los buscó.
2. ¿Apagaste...?/No, yo no apagué la estufa porque Miguel ya la apagó.
3. ¿Sacaste...?/No, yo no saqué la basura porque Pedro ya la sacó.
4. ¿Colgaste...?/No, yo no colgué los abrigos porque Alfonso y Ana ya los colgaron.
5. ¿Preparaste...?/No, yo no preparé la comida porque Jorge y Luisa ya la prepararon.
6. ¿Lavaste...?/No, yo no lavé la olla grande porque Isabel ya la lavó.

32 Possible answers:
1. ¿Lavaste las ollas?/Sí, (No, no) las lavé.
2. ¿Pasaste la aspiradora?/Sí, (No, no) la pasé.
3. ¿Colgaste la ropa en tu cuarto?/Sí, (No, no) la colgué.
4. ¿Sacaste la basura?/Sí, (No, no) no la saqué.
5. ¿Compraste la leche?/Sí, (No, no) la compré.
6. ¿Arreglaste el cuarto?/Sí, (No, no) no lo arreglé.

33 Creative self-expression.

Notes Set a time limit for activities 31, 32 and 33.

To extend activities 32 and 33, have students write out a summary of what they discussed. As an alternative, have students make a list of the chores they will be discussing before assigning students to work with a partner.

Hold students accountable for their work and provide additional practice speaking by calling on several individuals to summarize the results of their discussions for activities 32 and 33.

Activities

Expansion

The *Lectura cultural* offers a good opportunity for you to conduct a class discussion or have a debate about who does what around the house. Be sure to review the conjugation of *deber* and *tener que* before starting the activity.

Lectura cultural

¿Quién lo hace?

En España, mientras la participación de las mujeres[1] en el mercado laboral incrementa cada día (40% de mujeres trabajan), la desigualdad[2] entre los sexos todavía existe en las tareas domésticas. Las mujeres dedican siete horas y veintidós minutos cada día a los quehaceres. Los hombres, en cambio, dedican tres horas y diez minutos. Si nos referimos a quehaceres específicos de la casa (lavar, planchar, barrer, etc.), las mujeres dedican cinco veces más tiempo que los hombres.

Entre los jóvenes de 15–17 años, son las mujeres, otra vez, las que hacen más labores domésticas.

En el año 2000, la Unión Europea recomendó a los estados miembros (España es uno) la inclusión en la escuela de una asignatura de trabajo doméstico. Quizás, esta nueva asignatura ayude a establecer la igualdad[3] en los quehaceres. Después de todo, la democracia empieza en casa.

	Mujeres	Hombres
Total	7 h 22'	3 h 10'
Trabajo de la casa	3 h 58'	0 h 44'
Mantenimiento	0 h 27'	0 h 55'
Cuidado de la familia	1 h 51'	0 h 51'
Compras	0 h 53'	0 h 26'
Servicio	0 h 13'	0 h 14'

Fuente: Encuesta sobre "Usos del tiempo", Instituto de la Mujer, 2001.

Porcentaje de jóvenes que no hacen nunca o sólo en ocasiones los siguientes quehaceres

	Mujeres 15–17años	Hombres 15–17años
Cuidar a los niños	57,1%	65,7%
Limpiar la casa	50,6%	75,8%
Hacer la cama	32,2%	49,5%

Fuente: INJUVE, Informe Juventud en España, 2000.

[1]women [2]inequality [3]equality

34 ¿Qué recuerdas?

¿Sí o no?

1. 40% de las mujeres en España trabajan en casa.
2. Las mujeres españolas pasan siete horas y veintidós minutos todos los días en los quehaceres de la casa.
3. En España, 75,8% de los hombres entre quince y diecisiete años limpian la casa.
4. En España, 67,8% de las mujeres entre quince y diecisiete años hacen las camas.
5. La Unión Europea quiere que las escuelas enseñen trabajo doméstico.

35 Algo personal

1. ¿Qué tareas domésticas tienes que hacer en casa?
2. ¿Crees que las mujeres y los hombres deben compartir *(share)* todos los quehaceres? Explica.
3. ¿Piensas que todos los estudiantes deben tomar una asignatura de trabajo doméstico? ¿Por qué sí o por qué no?

• Complete a survey of your classmates like the one in the article. Find out the percentage of girls and boys that never or only occasionally take care of younger siblings, clean the house and make their beds. Compare yourselves with the fifteen- to seventeen-year-old Spaniards surveyed. In your group, is there more or less equality among who does the chores?

Notes Remind students that when talking about numbers, a comma is used in Spanish where a period would be used in English (75,8%).

Help students with reading the tables that accompany the *Lectura cultural.*

¿Qué aprendí?

Autoevaluación

As a review and self-check, respond to the following:

1. What do you do to help around the house?

2. Name two things you have just done in the last week.

3. Your family is having a party at your house and you are in charge of getting the house ready for guests. Ask your sister or brother to do three or four things to help with preparations.

4. List three or four things you did to help your parents.

5. State something you learned in this lesson about Spain.

Visit the web-based activities at www.emcp.com

Palabras y expresiones

En casa
- el abrigo
- la aspiradora
- la basura
- la cama
- la gente
- el jardín
- la leche
- la olla
- pasar la aspiradora
- la persona
- el quehacer
- recoger la mesa

Verbos
- acabar
- adornar
- arreglar
- barrer
- cocinar
- colgar (ue)
- doblar
- dejar
- lavar

- limpiar
- llegar
- oír
- preparar
- recoger
- sacar
- subir
- trabajar
- traer

Expresiones y otras palabras
- acabar de (+ *infinitive*)
- algo
- dar de comer
- junto,-a
- listo,-a
- quizás
- sólo
- el trabajo

Él está sacando la basura.

Ella está limpiando la cocina.

Capítulo 8   *trescientos treinta y siete*   **337**

Teacher Resources

Activity 12

Information Gap Activities
Postcard Activities
Funciones de Comunicación

Answers

Autoevaluación
Possible answers:
1. Arreglo mi cuarto.
2. Acabo de preparar la comida y trabajar en el jardín.
3. ¿Me puedes colgar la ropa? ¿Puedes ayudarme a preparar la comida? ¿Puedes sacarme la basura?
4. Saqué la basura todos los días la semana pasada. Preparé la comida, barré, y colgé la ropa.
5. Spain's population is diverse and its history consists of a variety of ethnic groups and races, including the Iberians *(los íberos)*, the Phoenicians *(los fenicios)* and the Moors *(los moros)*.

Activities

Multiple Intelligences (interpersonal)
Ask students to work in small groups discussing how they feel about doing various household chores. They should use *gustar, molestar* and other verbs to discuss their likes and dislikes. Each group should then select one member to summarize the results of this informal discussion in front of the class.

Notes Tell the class that in Spain the Spanish language is commonly called *castellano* (the language of Castilla). Other regional languages include *gallego, catalán* and *vasco/euskera*.

Spain occupies most of the Iberian Peninsula, which is at the southwestern corner of the European continent.

Mainland Spain is divided into autonomous regions that make up 98 percent of the national territory. Other *autonomías* include the Balearic Islands, in the Mediterranean Sea, and the Canary Islands, 650 miles southwest of the mainland, off the coast of Africa.

Teacher Resources

 El supermercado

 Activity 1

 Activities 57–58

 Activities 1–2

 Activity 1

 Activities 1–5

> **Content reviewed in *Lección B***
> • jobs around the house
> • numbers
> • preterite tense of regular *-ar* verbs
> • celebrations

Activities

Critical Thinking
Before playing the audio CD for *Vocabulario I,* ask students if they can guess where the people are. Then ask what they are probably discussing.

Prereading Strategy
Have students find cognates and other words they know in *Vocabulario I.*

Lección **B**

España

Vocabulario I
El supermercado

¿Me prestas la receta de la paella?

Sí, claro.

De esta receta nos hace falta el ingrediente más importante, el arroz.

¡Ay, olvidamos añadirlo! La paella sin arroz no es paella.

Verduras

el guisante
la cebolla
el ajo
los peores tomates
el tomate
el pimiento
los mejores tomates
el aguacate
el arroz
la lata
la lechuga

No todos los tomates están frescos.
Algunos parecen muy maduros.
Los chicos van a escoger los mejores tomates.
A ellos les importa llevar tomates maduros.

Notes The word *receta* has two primary uses in Spanish: It may refer to a **recipe** for cooking or a **medical prescription** *(una receta médica).* Context will make the meaning clear.

Explain to students that the verb *escoger* is conjugated like the verb *recoger,* which students learned to use in *Lección A* of this chapter.

1 En el supermercado

))) Selecciona la ilustración que corresponde con lo que oyes.

A   **B**   **C**   **D**   **E**   **F**

2 De compras en el supermercado

Di lo que *le(s) gusta, le(s) hace falta, le(s) parece* o *le(s) importa* a estas personas, usando las pistas y las ilustraciones y añadiendo los artículos indefinidos apropiados.

> **¡Extra!**
>
> ### Hacer falta, importar y parecer
>
> The expressions *hacer falta* (to need), *importar* (to matter) and *parecer* (to seem) often require an indirect object pronoun and follow a pattern like the one you learned for the verb *gustar: Me gusta el ajo; Me hace falta un aguacate; No me importa si el tomate no es maduro; Me parece buena la receta.*

MODELO   a mí / parecer bien / llevar unos
         A mí me parece bien llevar unos tomates.

1. a Uds. / hacer falta / llevar una

2. a los chicos / hacer falta / llevar un

3. a la Sra. Herrera / gustar / los

4. a Pedro y a Julio / importar / comprar las mejores

5. a Rodrigo / hacer falta / comprar el

6. a Santiago / gustar / comprar mucho

7. a mí / importar / llevar los mejores

8. a Elena / no importar / llevar una

Capítulo 8   *trescientos treinta y nueve*   **339**

Notes It is common for Spaniards to shop either at a supermarket (*supermercado*) or at small specialty shops, such as a *panadería*.

Shopping patterns vary from one country to another. Many Spaniards tend to shop for produce, meat and fish on a daily basis to have the freshest food possible for each meal.

Activities

Cooperative Learning
After discussing the content of the dialog, have students practice it in pairs. Circulate and assist with pronunciation and intonation.

Critical Listening
Play the audio CD recording of the dialog as students cover the words and listen. Ask several individuals to state what they believe the main theme of the conversation is.

Expansion
Additional questions (*¿Qué recuerdas?*): *¿Necesitan más pollo?*; *¿Los tomates son para la paella?*

Additional questions (*Algo personal*): *¿Te gusta el pollo?*; *¿Te gusta el arroz?*; *¿Te gustan los tomates?*

Diálogo I

¿Qué nos hace falta comprar?

INÉS: ¿Tienes la receta de la paella?
VÍCTOR: Sí, aquí la tengo.
INÉS: ¿Qué nos hace falta comprar?

VÍCTOR: Ayer compramos el pollo. Todavía necesitamos arroz, tomates y pimientos.
INÉS: Vamos primero a las verduras.
VÍCTOR: ¡Ah, mira! ¿Qué te parecen estos tomates?
INÉS: No parecen muy frescos.

VÍCTOR: ¿Y estos? ¿Qué te parecen?
INÉS: Algunos parecen muy maduros.
VÍCTOR: ¿Por qué no escoges los tomates y yo escojo los pimientos? Me llaman el Sr. Pimiento.
INÉS: ¡Qué loco!

3 ¿Qué recuerdas?

1. ¿Quién tiene la receta de la paella?
2. ¿Qué les hace falta comprar?
3. ¿Cuándo compraron el pollo?
4. ¿Cómo parecen los tomates?
5. ¿Qué busca Víctor?
6. ¿Cómo llaman a Víctor?

4 Algo personal

1. ¿Te gusta ir de compras al supermercado? Explica.
2. ¿Qué verduras te gustan?
3. ¿Cuáles son los ingredientes de tu receta favorita?

5 ¿Qué les hace falta?

 Di la letra de la ilustración que identifica lo que les hace falta comprar a las siguientes personas, según lo que oyes.

A   **B**   **C**   **D**   **E**   **F**

Notes The word *paella* is related to the pan in which the food is prepared—a *paellera*—which comes from the Latin word for **pan**. The *paellera* is a round, wide, shallow receptacle made of metal with two or more handles and a depth varying from 1 1/2 to 3 inches. This utensil remains a legacy of the combined influence of the Romans and the Moors.

The Romans introduced this type of pan, and the Arabs are credited with first having brought rice to Spain.

Activity 5 has been recorded as part of the Audio CD Program.

ꡡꡡ Cultura Viva ꡡꡡ

La paella (ingredientes para seis personas)

1 pollo en pedazos[1]	1 cebolla, troceada[6]	1 taza de
1/2 kg. de gambas[2]	2 dientes[7] de ajo, troceados	guisantes
1/2 kg. de langostinos[3]	2 zanahorias, limpias y cortadas[8]	5 hilos de azafrán[9]
1/4 kg. de mejillones[4]	2 tomates grandes	4 tazas de agua
1 lata de almejas[5] (200 gramos)	1 pimiento verde, troceado	5 cucharadas de aceite de oliva
2 tazas de arroz	1 lata de pimientos rojos, troceados	sal y pimienta

En una sartén[10] grande o paellera (sartén especial para la paella), poner el aceite y añadir el pollo, la cebolla troceada, el ajo y el pimiento verde; freír[11] hasta que se empiece a dorar—diez minutos. Luego, añadir el tomate, la zanahoria y media taza de guisantes. Cubrir[12] y dejar freír durante diez minutos. Después, añadir el arroz y el agua, los pimientos, el azafrán, sal y pimienta, y cocinar por otros quince minutos. Luego, añadir las gambas, los langostinos, los mejillones y las almejas y cocinar, con la sartén cubierta[13] otros diez minutos. Para terminar, adornar con la otra mitad de los guisantes, otra lata de pimientos (opcional) y un poco de perejil. Dejar que repose la paella durante quince minutos antes de servirla.

[1]pieces [2]shrimp [3]prawns [4]mussels [5]clams [6]diced [7]cloves [8]cut [9]saffron strings [10]frying pan [11]fry [12]cover [13]covered

6 La paella

Contesta las siguientes preguntas.

1. ¿Cuánto langostino tiene esta paella?
2. ¿Cuáles de los ingredientes en esta receta no son frescos?
3. ¿Qué verduras tiene la paella?
4. ¿Con qué puedes adornar la paella?
5. ¿Te gustaría preparar una paella? ¿Por qué?
6. ¿Hay un restaurante en tu ciudad con paella en el menú? ¿Cuál?

7 Conexión con otras disciplinas: matemáticas

Cambia los pesos (weights) a libras u onzas, según la pista entre paréntesis.

1. 2 kilos de aguacates (libras)
2. 200 gramos de pollo (onzas)
3. 1,5 kilos de tomates (libras)
4. 750 gramos de judías (libras)
5. 1/2 kilo de pimientos (onzas)
6. 1/4 kilo de arroz (onzas)

¡Extra!

¿Cuánto pesa?

1 kilogram, kg. (kilo, kg.)	=	2.2 pounds, lbs. (libras, lbs.)
1 kilogram	=	1000 grams, gr. (gramos, gr.)
1 ounce, oz. (onza, oz.)	=	28.35 grams

8 ¿Puedes preparar una paella?

Prepara una paella en tu casa y cuéntale la experiencia a la clase.

Capítulo 8 · trescientos cuarenta y uno **341**

Teacher Resources

 La paella
Activity 6

 Activity 2

Answers

6 1. Tiene medio kilo.
2. Los pimientos rojos, los guisantes, y las almejas no son frescos.
3. Tiene pimientos, cebolla, ajo, guisantes, zanahorias y tomates.
4. Puedo adornar la paella con guisantes, pimientos y perejil.
5. Answers will vary.
6. Answers will vary.

7 1. 4.4 lbs. de aguacates
2. 7.05 oz. de pollo
3. 3.3 lbs. de tomates
4. 1.65 lbs. de judías
5. 17.6 oz. de pimientos
6. 8.8 oz. de arroz

8 Creative self-expression.

Activities

Communities
Find a restaurant in your community that serves *paella*. Arrange a trip or have students meet there after school to taste this typical Spanish dish.

Multiple Intelligences (bodily-kinesthetic)
Have students find a simple recipe in a cookbook of Spanish cuisine, prepare it and share it with the class. Students should also explain the recipe and its history.

Notes The word for **shrimp** in Spain is *la gamba.*

As an alternative to or extension of activity 8, ask students to bring the ingredients from home and arrange with the Family and Consumer Science Department in your school to prepare and serve the dish in class.

Activity 7 offers a cross-curricular connection to mathematics in which students must perform calculations to convert the weights and measurements indicated to ounces or pounds. This is good preparation for actually having to perform the same conversions when traveling in Spain.

341

Activities

Expansion

Review the terms used to name classroom objects. Then have students compare the sizes of objects as you or other students hold up the items in the air: *El libro es más grande que el lápiz.*

Idioma

Estructura

Making comparisons

You can use the following patterns when making comparisons in Spanish:

> **más/menos + noun/adjective/adverb + que**

*Hay **más/menos ajo que** sal.* — There is **more/less (fewer)** garlic **than salt.**

> **tanto, -a, -os, -as + noun + como**

*Hay **tanto** pescado **como** verduras en esa paella.* — There is **as much** fish **as** vegetables in that paella.

> **tan + adjective/adverb + como**

*Estos aguacates no están **tan maduros como** esos aguacates.* — These avocados are not **as ripe as** those avocados.

> **verb + tanto como**

*Pedro **cocina tanto como** Pilar.* — Pedro **cooks as much as** Pilar.

> **verb + más que/menos que**

*Pedro **cocina más que** Tomás.* — Pedro **cooks more than** Tomás.

You can also make comparisons by singling out a person, group, object or attribute as the best, most or least by using the following patterns:

> **definite article (+ noun) + más/menos + adjective**

*El ajo es **el ingrediente más importante**.* — Garlic is **the most important ingredient.**

> **verb + lo + más/menos + adverb + posible**

*Debes lavarla **lo más** pronto **posible**.* — You should wash it **as early as possible.**

Use *más de* or *menos de* and a number for stating there are "more than" or "fewer than" the number of items or people indicated.

*Veo **más de/menos de** cinco cebollas.* — I see **more than/fewer than** five onions.

Notes Point out that *mayor, menor, mejor* and *peor* are usually placed in front of the word they modify: *Es el/la mejor (peor) estudiante....*

Explain that the adjectives in comparisons must agree in gender and number with the items they describe: *El tomate es más fresco que la lechuga. La cebolla es más madura que el aguacate.*

The following adjectives and adverbs have irregular comparative forms:

better	–	*mejor*
worse	–	*peor*
older	–	*mayor*
younger	–	*menor*

*Esos aguacates son **buenos,** pero aquellos aguacates son **mejores** y estos aguacates son **los mejores de todos.***

Those avocados are **good,** but those avocados over there are **better** and these avocados **are the best of all.**

Note: When referring to quantity, the comparative forms of *pequeño* and *grande* are *menor* (lesser, smaller, fewer) and *mayor* (greater, larger).

*Hay un **menor (mayor)** número de pimientos en lata que de pimientos frescos.*

There are **fewer** canned bell peppers than fresh bell peppers.

 Práctica

9 En el supermercado

Estás haciendo compras en el supermercado. Completa estas comparaciones.

MODELO Estas cebollas son <u>más grandes</u> que esas cebollas. (grande)

1. Estos tomates están __ que esos tomates. (fresco)
2. Este pollo es __ que el otro. (pequeño)
3. Ese aguacate está __ que este aguacate. (maduro)
4. Estas lechugas son __ que esas lechugas. (pequeño)
5. Aquellos pimientos están __ que esos pimientos. (maduro)

¡Estos tomates son los mejores de todos!

Teacher Resources

Activities 10 and 12

10 Possible answers:
1. Javier (Clara) tiene tanto arroz como Clara (Javier).
2. Las lechugas del supermercado Día no son tan grandes como las lechugas del supermercado Hypercor.
3. Ana (Alberto) va al supermercado tanto como Alberto (Ana).
4. No hay tantos guisantes como pescado en una paella valenciana./Hay menos guisantes que pescado en una paella valenciana./Hay más pescado que guisantes en una paella valenciana.
5. Teresa y Armando compran tantas latas de tomates como de guisantes.
6. Alfonso no tiene tantas recetas como Belén.

11 1. tantas/como; 2. menos/que; 3. tantos/como; 4. más/que; 5. tantas/como

12 1. ...lo mejor posible.
2. ...lo más pronto posible.
3. ...lo más rápidamente posible.
4. ...lo mejor posible.
5. ...lo mejor posible.
6. ...lo más pronto posible.
7. ...lo más tarde posible.

---

10 Comparando

Use the information provided to make as many comparisons as you can.

> **MODELO** **Información:** Ana puede ir de compras al supermercado en una hora pero yo necesito dos horas para ir de compras al supermercado.
> **Comparación 1:** No puedo ir de compras al supermercado tan rápidamente como Ana.
> **Comparación 2:** Ana puede ir de compras al supermercado más rápidamente que yo.
> **Comparación 3:** Yo puedo ir de compras al supermercado menos rápidamente que Ana.

1. Javier tiene dos kilos de arroz y Clara tiene dos kilos de arroz.
2. Las lechugas del supermercado Día son pequeñas pero las lechugas del supermercado Hypercor son grandes.
3. Alberto va al supermercado tres veces al mes y Ana va al supermercado tres veces al mes.
4. Hay mucho pescado en una paella valenciana pero no hay muchos guisantes.
5. Teresa y Armando compran dos latas de tomates y dos latas de guisantes.
6. Belén tiene cincuenta recetas y Alfonso tiene sólo cinco recetas.

11 ¿Cuánto necesitas?

You are preparing a paella valenciana, using the recipe in the *Cultura viva*. Complete these sentences, saying what you will need and compare whether you will need more, less or the same amount of each of the listed ingredients.

> **MODELO** Necesito <u>tanto</u> pimiento verde <u>como</u> cebolla.

1. Necesito __ latas de almejas __ latas de pimientos rojos.
2. Necesito __ mejillones __ gambas.
3. Necesito __ tomates __ zanahorias.
4. Necesito __ agua __ aceite de oliva.
5. Necesito __ gambas __ langostinos.

¿Qué necesitas para hacer una paella?

12 ¡Deben hacer lo siguiente!

If you were the owner of a restaurant, what instructions might you give your employees during the week?

> **MODELO** abrir el restaurante / temprano
> Debes abrir el restaurante lo más temprano posible.

1. preparar las recetas / bien
2. hacer las comidas / pronto
3. recoger las mesas / rápidamente
4. barrer el suelo / bien
5. limpiar la cocina / bien
6. sacar la basura / pronto
7. cerrar el restaurante / tarde

Notes Discuss activity 10 with the class to be sure students know what to do. Offer a second model if students have trouble.

Tell students they will need to look at the *Cultura viva* on page 341 for the recipe for paella to complete activity 11.

13 ¡Dos supermercados!

Compara lo que ves en las ilustraciones de estos dos supermercados, según las pistas.

MODELO aguacates / ser grande

Los aguacates del supermercado Día son más grandes que los aguacates del supermercado Hypercor.

1. lechugas / ser pequeñas
2. tomates / ser mejores
3. los ajos / costar menos
4. las cebollas / ser grandes
5. los guisantes / costar más
6. los pimientos / ser peores
7. el señor / ser joven
8. la señora / ser vieja

13 Possible answers:
1. Las lechugas del supermercado Día son más pequeñas que las lechugas del supermercado Hypercor.
2. Los tomates del supermercado Día son mejores que los tomates del supermercado Hypercor.
3. Los ajos del supermercado Hypercor cuestan menos que los ajos del supermercado Día.
4. Las cebollas del supermercado Día son más grandes que las cebollas del supermercado Hypercor.
5. Los guisantes del supermercado Hypercor cuestan más que los guisantes del supermercado Día.
6. Los pimientos del supermercado Día son peores que los pimientos del supermercado Hypercor.
7. El señor del supermercado Día es más joven que el señor del supermercado Hypercor.
8. La señora del supermercado Día es más vieja que la señora del supermercado Hypercor.

Notes This exercise uses metric measurements and the currency used by most European Union countries (the euro).

14 ¡Más comparaciones!

**Mira las ilustraciones de la actividad 13 y completa estas comparaciones con
la palabra apropiada.**

MODELO Hay más <u>de</u> una persona en los dos supermercados.

1. El supermercado Hypercor tiene más tomates __ el supermercado Día.
2. Hay menos __ cinco lechugas en el supermercado Hypercor.
3. Hay menos cebollas en el supermercado Hypercor __ en el supermercado Día.
4. El supermercado Día tiene más __ tres pimientos.
5. Los aguacates en el supermercado Hypercor cuestan tanto __ los aguacates en
   el supermercado Día.

15 ¿Lo hacen tanto como tú?

**Compare how much you help doing chores with how much your friends and
family help around the house. You may make up any of the names you wish.**

MODELO pasar la aspiradora
Mi hermano pasa la aspiradora tanto como yo.
Yo paso la aspiradora más que Julio.

1. cocinar
2. hacer las camas
3. trabajar en el jardín
4. limpiar la cocina
5. poner la mesa
6. ayudar en casa

16 En tu opinión

 **Trabajando en parejas, alterna con tu
compañero/a preguntando y contestando según
las pistas.**

¿Pasas la aspiradora tanto como yo?

MODELO el mejor supermercado de la ciudad donde vives
A: ¿Cuál es el mejor supermercado de la ciudad donde vives?
B: El mejor supermercado de la ciudad donde vivo es. . . .

1. el supermercado más grande de la ciudad donde vives
2. el supermercado más pequeño de la ciudad donde vives
3. el supermercado más nuevo de la ciudad donde vives
4. el supermercado más viejo de la ciudad donde vives
5. el ingrediente más importante de tu receta favorita
6. la mejor receta de tu mamá/papá

Notes When doing activity 15, point
out that students should use the word *yo*
when referring to themselves after *tanto
como, más que* or *menos que: Ella cocina
tanto como yo* (She cooks as much as I).

Comunicación

Answers

17 Creative self-expression.
18 Creative self-expression.
19 Creative self-expression.

 17 Me gusta la comida

Trabajando en parejas, hagan preguntas para comparar comidas diferentes y saber cuál les gusta más.

> MODELO **A:** ¿Te gusta la lechuga tanto como el tomate?
> **B:** Sí, (No, no) me gusta la lechuga tanto como el tomate.

 18 Lo que más comes

Working in pairs, talk about what you eat and drink. Include in your conversation what you eat or drink, and tell which are your most and least favorite foods and beverages.

> MODELO **A:** ¿Qué te gusta comer?
> **B:** Como más pollo que pescado, pero la paella es la mejor comida.

 19 En el supermercado

Imagine you are at a supermarket in Spain shopping for ingredients to make *paella*. Working with a partner, take turns playing the roles of two clients. Remember to make comparisons of quality, size and price for items in the store.

El señor compra ingredientes para hacer una paella.

Capítulo 8   *trescientos cuarenta y siete* **347**

Activities

Expansion
As a follow-up to activity 16, have students ask and answer questions to identify the following items: *el deporte más interesante, la clase más difícil, el mejor/el peor programa de televisión, el estado más bonito, el país hispanohablante más interesante.* After working in pairs, the students should share their opinions with the class.

Pronunciation *(la letra o)*
The sound of *o* in Spanish is similar to the sound of **o** in English, but shorter. It is usually pronounced much like the **o** in the word **row.** Model several words for students: *yo, como, cocinar, cómodo, jamón, colgar, loco.* In addition, the letter *o* is a strong vowel, just like *a* and *e*. When a strong vowel joins a weak vowel *(i* or *u)*, the strong vowel is normally stressed: *Mario, rubio, voy, hoy, nervioso, gimnasio, novio, limpio.* If the weak vowel is stressed, it bears an accent mark: *frío, tío, Eloísa, envío.* Many words end in *-ión*. Note for students that the *o* bears an accent mark because last syllables are not normally stressed in Spanish: *lección, canción, pronunciación, opinión, conversación.*

Notes Set a time limit for activities 17, 18 and 19.

After completing activity 18 orally in pairs, have students write out the list of foods and beverages that they included as their most and least favorite.

You may wish to have students make a list of their most and least favorite foods and beverages before asking them to work orally in pairs.

Hold students accountable for their work by calling on several pairs to present their dialogs in front of the class for activity 19.

348

Notes Tell students that the words *papa* and *patata* both mean **potato.** In Spain, both terms are commonly heard; in other Spanish-speaking countries, the preferred word is *papa*.

el chorizo

el jamón

la carne

20 En el mercado

🔊 Selecciona la ilustración que corresponde con lo que oyes.

A **B** **C** **D** **E** **F**

21 Fuera de lugar

Say which food item does not belong in each of the following groups.

1. maíz	habichuela	zanahoria	chocolate
2. queso	mantequilla	jamón	leche
3. huevo	manzana	fresa	naranja
4. café	cebolla	pimiento	zanahoria
5. carne	pescado	pollo	papa
6. fresa	maíz	uva	plátano

22 Una dieta equilibrada

Trabajando en parejas, escriban una dieta equilibrada *(balanced)* con todas las comidas básicas para cinco días de la semana. La dieta debe incluir el desayuno *(breakfast)*, el almuerzo y la cena *(dinner)*.

Capítulo 8   *trescientos cuarenta y nueve*   **349**

Diálogo II

Comprando chorizo

INÉS: Ayer estuve con Víctor en el supermercado.
EVA: ¿Y qué compraste?
INÉS: Compramos los ingredientes para hacer paella.

EVA: Entonces, ¿qué venimos a hacer al mercado?
INÉS: Quiero comprar chorizo. El chorizo del supermercado no me gusta.
EVA: Bueno, este mercado es el mejor mercado de la ciudad.

INÉS: Señora, ¿a qué precio tiene el kilo de chorizo?
SEÑORA: El chorizo está a € 4,00 el kilo.
INÉS: De acuerdo, llevo un kilo por favor.

23 ¿Qué recuerdas?

1. ¿Qué compró Inés ayer en el supermercado?
2. ¿Qué quiere comprar Inés en el mercado?
3. ¿Es bueno el mercado donde están las chicas?
4. ¿A qué precio está el kilo de chorizo?
5. ¿Compra Inés el chorizo?

24 Algo personal

1. ¿Hay un mercado en tu ciudad? ¿Dónde está?
2. ¿Prefieres ir al mercado o al supermercado? Explica.
3. ¿Cuál es el mercado o supermercado más grande de tu ciudad?

25 ¿Qué comprendiste?

Escucha lo que dicen las personas del diálogo *Comprando chorizo* y di si lo que oyes es cierto o falso. Corrige lo que no es cierto.

¡Extra!

El euro

The symbol for the European euro is €, which became the common currency of most European Union countries in 2002. Spain is a member of the European Union and adopted the euro as its currency, making the Spanish currency, *la peseta*, obsolete.

Lección B

Cultura viva

¡Cómo se come en España!

Spain's cuisine is as diverse as its people are. Learning about the different regional cuisines will allow you to choose what you would like to try during a trip there. For example, *paella valenciana,* which you learned about earlier in the chapter, is a popular rice dish originally from the Mediterranean coast in the region of Valencia. It combines seafood, meat, chicken or pork. On the northern coast of Spain, in the region called Galicia, you might want to try *pulpo a la gallega,* a cooked and marinated octopus dish. In the north central and northeastern regions of Spain that border the Pyrenees, you might try the hearty Basque cuisine by ordering

Madrid is also famous for its sheep and goat cheeses, like *manchego,* and its many and delicious varieties of pork or blood sausages called *chorizos* and *morcillas.*

The southern part of Spain is well known for its vegetables and fish. Vegetables are used in the preparation of a cold soup called *gazpacho.* Gazpacho is popular in part because of its thirst-quenching qualities on hot summer days in sunny *Andalucía.* The region is also known for its ham *(jamón serrano)* and marvelous fresh sardines and smelt, fished right out of the Mediterranean Sea.

As you can see, Spaniards have plenty to choose from when it comes to meals!

Gazpacho.

Bacalao al pilpil.

cod prepared the "Basque way" *(bacalao al pilpil),* or Catalán cuisine, which is known for its delicious oxtail in *diabla* sauce and *butifarra con alubias* (beans with sausage).

Madrid, the capital, is famous for its *callos* (beef tripe). The area around

Callos a la madrileña.

26 ¿Cómo se come en España?

Make a list of dishes mentioned in the *Cultura viva.* Then choose one that you would like to try, and find the recipe for it, using sources such as the Internet, cookbooks, etc.

 Activity 9

Activity 4

Answers

26 Answers will vary.

Activities

Critical Thinking
Ask small groups of students to develop logical comparisons involving the following items: *la comida española/la comida mexicana; la comida italiana/ la comida china; los restaurantes/ las cafeterías; los supermercados/ los mercados.* Other possibilities not related to food include comparisons of classes, sports and music. The results should be shared with the class.

Expansion
As an additional activity, have students draw a map of Spain, separating the country into provinces and/or regions and placing the names of dishes given in the text in the corresponding regions.

Spanish for Spanish Speakers
Have students prepare a report in Spanish about the foods that the New World gave to Spain and how those were integrated into Spanish cuisine (e.g., the potato).

Notes Using a map, point out where the places mentioned in *Cultura viva* are located.

Tell the class that many people in the United States have a mistaken impression about what food is like in Spanish-speaking countries. For example, although some people may think of *tacos* and *tortillas* when they are talking about Spanish foods, *tacos* are considered Mexican fast food and *tortillas* are corn- or flour-based pancake-like shells that are filled with other ingredients or that serve as a substitute for bread in Mexico. Point out that if students ask for a *tortilla* in Spain, they will be served a Spanish omelet.

351

Activity 27

 Activity 7

 Activities 10–12

 Activity 5

 Activities 14–15

Answers

27 1. ...compramos....
2. ...buscó....
3. ...busqué....
4. ...trabajó....

28 1. Daniel y Gloria estuvieron esta mañana.
2. Mi tía estuvo el mes pasado.
3. Los chicos estuvieron el fin de semana pasado.
4. Mis primas estuvieron anteayer.
5. Ud. estuvo el viernes.
6. Yo estuve el sábado pasado.
7. Uds. estuvieron ayer.
8. Tú estuviste el jueves.

Idioma

Repaso rápido: preterite tense of regular *-ar* verbs

Do you remember how to form the preterite tense of a regular *-ar* verb? Remove the last two letters from the infinitive and add the indicated endings.

hablar	
habl**é**	habl**amos**
habl**aste**	habl**asteis**
habl**ó**	habl**aron**

Note: Regular verbs that end in *-car* (*buscar, explicar, sacar, tocar*), *-gar* (*apagar, colgar, jugar, llegar, pagar*) and *-zar* (*empezar*) require a spelling change in the *yo* form of the preterite.

27 El diario de Marta

Marta siempre escribe en su diario por la noche. Haz oraciones completas con las pistas que se dan para saber lo que escribe esta noche.

1. nosotros / comprar zanahorias
2. mi madre / buscar el pollo
3. yo / buscar mi receta favorita
4. mi padre / trabajar todo el día

Estructura

Preterite tense of *dar* and *estar*

The verbs *dar* and *estar* are irregular in the preterite tense.

dar	
di	dimos
diste	disteis
dio	dieron

estar	
estuve	estuvimos
estuviste	estuvisteis
estuvo	estuvieron

28 Estuvieron en el mercado

Di cuándo las siguientes personas estuvieron en el mercado.

MODELO Enrique / el martes pasado
Enrique estuvo el martes pasado.

1. Daniel y Gloria / esta mañana
2. mi tía / el mes pasado
3. los chicos / el fin de semana pasado
4. mis primas / anteayer
5. Ud. / el viernes
6. yo / el sábado pasado
7. Uds. / ayer
8. tú / el jueves

Notes Review the spelling changes that are required in the first-person preterite tense for verbs that end in *-car* (change *c* to *qu*), *-gar* (change *g* to *gu*), *-zar* (change *z* to *c*). Then practice conjugating some of the verbs listed in the *Repaso rápido* before assigning activity 27.

Práctica

29 Todos ayudaron

 Last week your school held a food drive. In pairs, take turns reporting what food items people donated. Follow the model.

MODELO tú
A: ¿Qué diste tú?
B: Yo di unas frutas.

1. yo
2. el Sr. y la Sra. García

3. tú y yo
4. la profesora
5. Pedro
6. los hermanos Jiménez

30 Mi fiesta de cumpleaños

Completa el siguiente párrafo con la forma apropiada del pretérito de los verbos entre paréntesis.

El sábado pasado mi hermano mayor *(1. dar)* una fiesta para mi cumpleaños. Muchos de mis amigos *(2. estar)* allí. Mi amigo Pedro no *(3. estar)* y mis mejores amigas, Clara y Elvira, tampoco *(4. estar)*. Nosotros *(5. estar)* muy contentos. Mi hermano me *(6. dar)* un regalo que me *(7. gustar)* mucho. Luego, mis amigos Carlos y Gabriel *(8. dar)* un concierto muy bueno. Carlos *(9. cantar)* cinco canciones y Gabriel las *(10. tocar)* en su guitarra. Yo *(11. estar)* muy contento porque mis amigos *(12. estar)* muy contentos. Todos le *(13. dar)* las gracias a mi hermano por la fiesta tan buena.

Comunicación

31 ¿Dónde estuvieron?

 Working in pairs, discuss where you and people you know were last weekend, adding any details you wish.

MODELO A: ¿Dónde estuviste el fin de semana pasado?
B: Estuve con mi madre en el mercado.

32 ¿Qué dieron?

 In pairs, talk about your last birthday celebration. Discuss, among other things, when your birthday was, where it took place, what kind of food was served and the gifts that were given to you. Make up any information you want.

Capítulo 8

trescientos cincuenta y tres 353

Notes After completing activities 31 and 32 orally in pairs, consider asking students to summarize their work for either one or both activities.

353

Answers

33
1. La Tomatina.
2. En Buñol, un pueblo de Valencia, el último miércoles de cada agosto.
3. Participan aproximadamente treinta mil personas y se tiran 68.000 kilos de tomates.
4. Se tiran tomates en las calles.
5. Todos paran de tirar tomates y los residentes limpian las calles.
6. El agua la traen de un acueducto romano que está cerca.

34 Answers will vary.

Activities

Spanish for Spanish Speakers
Have students prepare a report on the Tomatina.

Lectura personal

Cantantes y grupos musicales

Dirección ▸ http://www.emcp.com/músico/ola/e.diario-7.htm ▲ Archivo Edición Ver Favoritos Herramientas Ayuda

página principal   miembros   e-diario

Grupo musical La OLA

Nombre: **Yadira Torres Ortega**
Edad: **15 años**
País natal: **México**
Verdura favorita: **lechuga**
Postre favorito: **helado de arroz**

Ayer miércoles fue un día que nunca voy a olvidar. Acabábamos[1] de dar un concierto en Madrid, la capital de España, y estábamos[2] en ruta a Valencia para otro concierto. Al mediodía, paramos en un pueblo llamado Buñol. Al bajar del camión, miles de personas en las calles estaban tirándose[3] tomates maduros los unos a los otros. ¡Fue la pelea[4] de comida más grande del mundo! Parece que lo hacen todos los años. Se llama la Tomatina, un festival popular, divertido y—debo añadir—para personas a las que no les importa estar sucios[5]. El último miércoles de cada agosto, entre las 11:00 de la mañana y la 1:00 de la tarde, treinta mil personas se tiran[6] tomates: 68.000 kilos de tomates, para ser exacta. ¡Imaginen el desastre! Las calles parecen ríos de sopa de tomate. Cuando suena[7] una sirena, todos paran[8] y los residentes empiezan a barrer las calles y lavarlas con enormes mangueras[9]. (El agua la traen de un acueducto romano que está cerca.) En unas pocas horas, las calles de Buñol están limpias, sin evidencia de que hubo[10] más tomates que en ninguna otra parte del mundo.

[1]we just finished   [2]we were   [3]were throwing at each other   [4]fight   [5]dirty   [6]they throw at each other   [7]blows   [8]stop   [9]hoses   [10]there were

33 ¿Qué recuerdas?

1. ¿Cuál es la pelea de comida (*food fight*) más grande del mundo?
2. ¿Dónde y cuándo es?
3. ¿Aproximadamente cuántas personas participan? ¿Cuántos tomates usan?
4. ¿Qué hacen los participantes entre las 11 A.M. y la 1 P.M.?
5. ¿Qué hacen los residentes cuando suena una sirena (*a siren blows*)?
6. ¿De dónde traen el agua?

- Although people know that the Tomatina began in the 1940s, nobody knows for sure how it started. How do you think it all started? Compare your theory with those of your classmates.

34 Algo personal

1. ¿Has participado alguna vez en una pelea de comida?
2. En lugar de tomates, ¿qué otra fruta crees que es buena para una pelea de comida?
3. Imagina que vas a ir a la Tomatina. ¿Qué ropa llevas? ¿Por qué?

354 *trescientos cincuenta y cuatro*   **Lección B**

Notes The *Lectura personal* and activities 33–34 are recorded and available on audio CD as part of the Audio CD Program.

Have students pair up and take turns asking the questions for activities 33–34. Then have students write the answers to the two activities to turn in for a grade.

¿Qué aprendí?

Autoevaluación

As a review and self-check, respond to the following:

Visit the web-based activities at www.emcp.com

1. Name some foods found in a supermarket. Which ones might you also find at an outdoor market *(mercado al aire libre)*?

2. Name some of the ingredients and how much of each is needed in a recipe to make *paella valenciana* for six people.

3. Compare several foods you like and dislike.

4. Name two or three things that are the most, the best or the worst possible.

5. Imagine you keep a journal and every day you write where you went, where you were and other interesting information about what you did during the day. Make a brief list of five things that you would write about today in your journal.

6. What are two things you have learned about Spain in this lesson?

Palabras y expresiones

En el mercado
- el aguacate
- el ajo
- el arroz
- el café
- la carne
- la cebolla
- el chocolate
- el chorizo
- la fresa
- la fruta
- el guisante
- la habichuela
- el helado
- el huevo
- el ingrediente
- el jamón
- el kilo

- la lata
- la lechuga
- el maíz
- la manzana
- el mercado
- la papa
- el pimiento
- el plátano
- el precio
- el queso
- el supermercado
- el tomate
- la uva
- la verdura
- el vinagre
- la zanahoria

Para describir
- fresco,-a
- maduro,-a
- mayor
- mejor
- menor
- peor

Verbos
- añadir
- escoger
- importar
- olvidar
- parecer

Expresiones y otras palabras
- el/la/los/las (+ *noun*) más/menos (+ *adjective*)
- el/la/los/las mejor/ mejores/peor/ peores (+ *noun*)
- hacer falta
- lo más/menos (+ *adverb*) posible
- más/menos (+ *noun/adjective/ adverb*) que
- la paella
- la receta
- sin
- tan (+ *adjective/adverb*) como
- tanto como
- tanto,-a (+ *noun*) como

Frutas y verduras *(fruits and vegetables)*.

Capítulo 8 · *trescientos cincuenta y cinco* · **355**

Notes Mention to students that the authentic *paella valenciana* was cooked outdoors over a wood fire. The classic way of eating *paella* is for everyone to sit in a circle and eat directly from the pan. Each person would have an intricately carved boxwood spoon for eating, and exact triangles would be marked out as portions for each person.

One interesting aspect of preparing *paella* is that in Valencia the dish has traditionally been prepared by males in the family. This may be due in part to the fact that making *paella* is a social event that takes place in the open air, away from the kitchen.

Teacher Resources

📝 **Activity 13**

💬 **Information Gap Activities Postcard Activities**
Funciones de Comunicación

Answers

Autoevaluación
Possible answers:
1. En un supermercado puedo comprar una cebolla, unos tomates y una lata de guisantes. En un mercado al aire libre puedo comprar una cebolla y unos tomates.
2. un pollo, medio kilo de gambas, medio kilo de langostinos, una taza de guisantes, dos tazas de arroz
3. Me gustan los tomates más que los aguacates.
4. Aprender el español es lo más importante para mí.
5. Fui al colegio esta mañana. Estuve allí todo el día. Hablé con mis amigos para hacer planes para el sábado.
6. Answers will vary.

Activities

Cooperative Learning
Have students imagine they are at an outdoor market doing grocery shopping for different foods. Then, working in pairs, they should take turns playing the roles of the vendor and the client.

355

Answers

Preparación
1. D
2. A

Activities

Critical Thinking
The reading presents a very different meal schedule and work schedule from what is common in the United States. Ask students their opinion of the schedules in each country and to consider the advantages and disadvantages of each.

¡Viento en popa!

Tú lees

Estrategia

Gathering meaning from context
When reading in another language, you will often encounter words you do not know. Before looking in a dictionary, look for clues that tell you what a word means. For example, you have already learned to recognize some unknown words because they are cognates (e.g., *familia*) or because they are related to words you have already learned (e.g., *baile/bailar*). At other times it may be necessary to look at the words before and after an unknown word (the context) in order to guess its meaning. Looking for these contextual clues will help improve your reading skills and will also make reading more enjoyable because you will spend less time looking up words in a dictionary.

Preparación

¿Qué quieren decir las palabras *tertulia* y *tapas* en las siguientes oraciones?

1. Un pasatiempo español es la **tertulia** con amigos en un café o un restaurante.
   A. comer empanadas
   B. ir de compras
   C. tomar café
   D. reunirse y conversar con amigos
2. A los españoles les gusta comer **tapas** con sus amigos antes de ir a casa para comer.
   A. comida pequeña antes de una comida principal
   B. pan con mantequilla
   C. frutas y verduras
   D. comida grande con carne y pescado

Ir de tapas y a merendar

Hay un par de pasatiempos que son muy populares entre la gente en España: ir de tapas e ir a merendar.[1] Ir de tapas es reunirse[2] con amigos o parientes para conversar y tomar aperitivos[3] antes de ir a casa para comer con la familia. Durante la conversación (o tertulia) las personas hablan de todo y comen tapas muy diversas (aceitunas, jamón serrano, patatas bravas[4], diferentes quesos, empanadas[5], etc.). Hay restaurantes y bares que sólo tienen tapas. Los grupos de amigos o familia pueden ir a tres o cuatro lugares diferentes para comer las tapas típicas de ese lugar. Hay dos

Aquí sirven tapas.

Notes One style of *tapa* called *banderillas* (named after the colorful darts used in bullfights) consists of skewering various ingredients onto toothpicks. They should be eaten by putting the entire contents of each *banderilla* into the mouth at once so that the tastes of the various ingredients blend together.

razones para comer tapas en España: la primera es que los españoles toman el almuerzo muy tarde (a las 2:00 o a las 3:00 de la tarde) y también cenan[6] muy tarde (a las 9:00 o a las 10:00 de la noche), y la segunda, la verdadera[7] razón, es que a los españoles les gusta mucho hablar y pasar tiempo con sus amigos y familia.

Merendar es otra forma de pasar tiempo con amigos y familia en donde los españoles salen para hablar y comer. En España la gente puede merendar en cafeterías, en merenderos[8] o en casa. Merendar, o la merienda, consiste de café para los adultos y de leche o chocolate para los jóvenes, además de[9] pasteles[10] y dulces. La merienda se come entre las cinco y las seis de la tarde, tres o cuatro horas antes de la cena[11], o ¡una hora antes de las tapas!

Unas tapas ricas.

[1]to have an afternoon snack   [2]to get together   [3]appetizers   [4]spicy potatoes   [5]bread dough filled with meat or fish   [6]eat dinner   [7]real   [8]places to have *merienda*   [9]in addition to   [10]pastries and cakes   [11]supper

A ¿Qué recuerdas?

1. ¿Qué es ir de tapas?
2. ¿Qué es merendar?
3. ¿Qué tapas comen los españoles?
4. ¿Adónde puede ir la gente para merendar?
5. ¿Por qué salen los españoles de tapas y meriendas?

B Algo personal

1. ¿Te gustan los aperitivos? ¿Cuáles te gustan?
2. ¿Qué te gustaría más, ir de tapas o ir a merendar?
3. ¿Qué te gustaría comer de tapas?
4. ¿Qué te gustaría comer de merienda?

Ellas meriendan.

Notes How to prepare *banderillas:* Your students can prepare *banderillas* by skewering four or five of the following ingredients on a toothpick: pitted green Spanish olives, pitted ripe black olives, pearl onions, small marinated mushrooms, pieces of canned pimento, chunks of solid white tuna, boiled shrimp, hard-boiled egg, marinated artichoke heart and pieces of bell pepper.

Teacher Resources

 Activities A–B

Answers

A 1. Ir de tapas es reunirse con amigos o parientes para conversar y tomar aperitivos antes de ir a casa para comer.
2. Merendar es salir con amigos y familia para hablar y comer.
3. Comen aceitunas, jamón serrano, patatas bravas, diferentes quesos y empanadas.
4. La gente puede ir para merendar en cafeterías, merenderos o en casa.
5. Salen de tapas y meriendas porque toman el almuerzo y cenan muy tarde y porque les gusta salir con amigos y familia.

B Answers will vary.

Activities

Language through Action
Have your students prepare some *tapas* from home to bring to school and share with the class. As an alternative, arrange with the consumer science department to prepare *banderillas* as a fun class project.

Tú escribes

Estrategia ◆◆◆◆◆◆◆◆◆◆◆◆◆◆◆◆◆◆◆◆◆◆◆◆◆◆◆◆◆◆

Using graphic organizers
It is useful to brainstorm ideas about your topic before actually beginning to write. If the subjects you are going to write about are related in some way, a graphic organizer such as a Venn diagram will help you visualize different aspects of your theme.
A Venn diagram, consisting of two intersecting circles, is especially good when your writing includes a comparison of what two subjects (such as people, places or events) have in common.

◆◆◆◆◆◆◆◆◆◆◆◆◆◆◆◆◆◆◆◆◆◆◆◆◆◆◆◆◆◆◆◆◆◆◆◆◆

A Imagine you are going to celebrate a special event by having a special dinner with friends. First, write the name of the event you are celebrating (e.g., *cumpleaños de mi amigo Julio, viaje de mi amiga Elena*), and the date and the time the dinner will begin. Next, draw two intersecting circles (a Venn diagram). In one circle, list in Spanish the things you plan to do. In the second circle, list the things your friends plan to do. In the shared space, list the activities that the two of you plan to do together. Place each activity you think of in the appropriate area of the graphic. Be sure to include the *quehaceres* that must be completed both before and after the dinner.

B Underneath the circles of the Venn diagram you prepared, write a paragraph in Spanish describing the dinner you are planning, who is invited and who is responsible for carrying out the preparations.

Notes Note for students that eating in Spain may be unlike anything they are accustomed to. Meals and snacks are planned throughout the day and offer coveted opportunities for socialization. With regard to the meal times mentioned in the reading *Ir de tapas y a merendar* (pages 356–357), note that typical business hours in Spain are 9:00–2:00 and 5:00–8:00.

Inform students whether you want them to work individually or in pairs to do activities A and B.

Proyectos adicionales

A Conexión con la tecnología

Search the Web for sites about Spanish cuisine using key words (cuisine, food, Spanish, paella, etc.). How many different recipes *(recetas)* can you find? For example, how many ways can *paella* be prepared? How are the recipes different? List the ingredients. Can you locate any restaurants that serve *paella*? How much does it cost? Share your findings with the class.

La comida española.

B Comparaciones

 Working with three or four classmates, compare your food habits. For example, ask your classmates if they eat more often at home or in restaurants; talk about the location and names of restaurants where members of the group eat; find out what foods your classmates think are the best at home and in each of the restaurants they name; and find out what foods each person prepares at home (and ask whether it is better or worse than the same food at a restaurant or when someone else prepares it. Take notes and report your findings to the class.

MODELO **A:** ¿Comes más en restaurantes que en tu casa?
B: No, como más en mi casa que en restaurantes.

C Conexión cultural

What comes to mind when you think about Spain? Prepare a list of at least ten Spanish words that convey what you associate with Spain. Try to include words that relate to Spain's history as well as to modern Spain. Then, based on the words in your list, create a poster using pictures, art and other graphics to depict the images you have of Spain. Finally, display the poster and tell the class about your project. Be creative!

La Feria de abril (Sevilla, España).

Teacher Resources

Situation Cards

P *Capítulo 8*

Answers

A Creative self-expression.
B Creative self-expression.
C Creative self-expression.

Activities

Communities
Have students visit the school or city library and prepare a report on any Spaniards who explored your state. Students should report what influences those visits have had on life in your state today.

Critical Thinking
Discuss with students the images they associate with Spain. Then ask what images they think of in relation to the United States. Do any of the responses overlap?

Multiple Intelligences (musical)
Play flamenco music for students and have them compare it to the rhythms of rap.

Spanish for Spanish Speakers
Have students prepare a report on the origins of flamenco music and dancing.

Notes The Spaniards heard about Aztec chocolate and took it to Spain in 1520. They added sugar, an important contribution, and later, cinnamon and vanilla. Spain zealously guarded the secret of chocolate production as long as it could and maintained a monopoly on the supply of cocoa, which came from its American colonies. *Chocolate a la española* is the thickest hot chocolate possible.

Teacher Resources

 Trabalenguas

Activities

Connections

Give students a recipe for preparing *churros con chocolate a la española* in Spanish. Read it in class, and using TPR, have students demonstrate how to prepare these fun snacks. You may ask students to prepare them at home and then bring them to class to share.

Critical Thinking

Ask students to name ten foods and compare them: *Me gustan las zanahorias tanto como las manzanas; no me gusta el chorizo tanto como el pollo.*

Repaso

Now that I have completed this chapter, I can...

	Go to these pages for help:
talk about household chores.	318
say what just happened.	318
ask for and offer help.	323
talk about the past.	334
identify and describe foods.	338
discuss food preparation.	338
make comparisons.	342

I can also...

talk about Spain's past.	321
talk about life in Spain today.	331
use survival skills.	341
name foods from different regions of Spain.	351

Trabalenguas

Pepe Pecas pica papas con un pico,
con un pico pica papas Pepe Pecas.

Notes A custom that coincides with the tradition of *tapas* is the *paseo*, an afternoon or evening stroll with family or friends. The *paseo* provides a bit of exercise but is primarily a social activity.

Through the *Repaso*, students can measure their own progress in learning the main elements of the chapter.

Loose translation of the *Trabalenguas*: Pepe Pecas chops potatoes with a pickax, with a pickax chops Pepe Pecas potatoes.

A popular breakfast in Spain is *churros con chocolate*. *Churros* consist of a fried batter of flour and water. It is also customary to end the evening by eating *churros con chocolate* at a *churrería*.

Vocabulario

el **abrigo** coat *8A*
  acabar to finish, *8A*
  acabar de *(+ infinitive)* to have just *8A*
  adornar to decorate *8A*
el **aguacate** avocado *8B*
el **ajo** garlic *8B*
  algo something, anything *8A*
  añadir to add *8B*
  arreglar to arrange, to straighten, to fix *8A*
el **arroz** rice *8B*
la **aspiradora** vacuum cleaner *8A*
  barrer to sweep *8A*
la **basura** garbage *8A*
el **café** coffee *8B*
la **cama** bed *8A*
la **carne** meat *8B*
la **cebolla** onion *8B*
el **chocolate** chocolate *8B*
el **chorizo** sausage *(seasoned with red peppers) 8B*
  cocinar to cook *8A*
  colgar (ue) to hang *8A*
  dar de comer to feed *8A*
  dejar to leave *8A*
  doblar to fold *8A*
  escoger to choose *8B*
la **fresa** strawberry *8B*
  fresco,-a fresh, chilly *8B*
la **fruta** fruit *8B*
la **gente** people *8A*
el **guisante** pea *8B*
la **habichuela** green bean *8B*
  hacer falta to be necessary, to be lacking *8B*

el **helado** ice cream *8B*
el **huevo** egg *8B*
  importar to be important, to matter *8B*
el **ingrediente** ingredient *8B*
el **jamón** ham *8B*
el **jardín** garden *8A*
  junto,-a together *8A*
el **kilo (kg.)** kilogram *8B*
la **lata** can *8B*
  lavar to wash *8A*
la **leche** milk *8A*
la **lechuga** lettuce *8B*
  limpiar to clean *8A*
  listo,-a smart *8A*
  llegar to arrive *8A*
  llevar to take, to carry *5A*
  maduro,-a ripe *8B*
el **maíz** corn *8B*
la **manzana** apple *8B*
  más *(+ noun/adjective/adverb)* **que** more *(+ noun/adjective/adverb) 8B*
  mayor older, oldest *8B*
  mejor better, *8B*
  menor lesser, least *8B*
  menos *(+ noun/adjective/adverb)* **que** less *(+ noun/adjective/adverb) 8B*
el **mercado** market *8B*
la **olla** pot, saucepan *8A*
  olvidar to forget *8B*
  oír to hear, to listen *8A*
la **paella** paella *(traditional Spanish dish with rice) 8B*
la **papa** potato *8B*
  parecer to seem *8B*
  pasar la aspiradora to vacuum *8A*
  peor worse *8B*
  peor/peores *(+ noun)* the worst *(+ noun) 8B*

la **persona** person *8A*
el **pimiento** bell pepper *8B*
el **plátano** banana *8B*
el **precio** price *8B*
  preparar to prepare *8A*
  prestar to lend *8B*
el **quehacer** chore *8A*
el **queso** cheese *8B*
  quizás perhaps *8A*
la **receta** recipe *8B*
  recoger to pick up *8A*
  recoger la mesa to clear the table *8A*
  sacar to take out *8A*
  sin without *8B*
  sólo only, just *8A*
  subir to climb, to go up, to go upstairs, to take up, to bring up, to carry up *8A*
el **supermercado** supermarket *8B*
  tan *(+ adjective/adverb)* **como** *(person/item)* as *(+person/item)* as *8B*
  tanto como as much as *8B*
  tanto,-a *(+ noun)* **como** *(person/item)* as many/much *(+noun)* as *8B*
el **tomate** tomato *8B*
  trabajar to work *8A*
el **trabajo** work *8A*
  traer to bring *8A*
la **uva** grape *8B*
la **verdura** greens, vegetables *8B*
el **vinagre** vinegar *8B*
la **zanahoria** carrot *8B*

El jamón.

¡Hay buen chorizo! ¿Cuántos kilos quiere?

Teacher Resources

Module 3

Episode 8

Testing/ Assessment

Test Booklet
Portfolio Assessment

Activities

Multiple Intelligences (spatial/linguistic)
Have students create a map of Spain, detailing the locations and names of important cities, rivers, mountains, regions, etc. As an alternative, have students write a short composition about an aspect of Spain that interests them.

Spanish for Spanish Speakers
Have students write a composition in Spanish summarizing what they know about Spain. Expand the activity by having students seek out additional information about Spain at the library or via the Internet.

Notes Remind students that the words and expressions listed here are provided for easy reference and consist of all vocabulary they must know from *Capítulo 8*. Students should review and test themselves over the content of the *Vocabulario* in preparation for the chapter test and for future chapters in *Navegando 1*.

Connections
Have students name some cities in Ecuador and Panama. Then ask if anyone in class has visited or knows someone who has visited either country. Ask what students know about these countries.

Critical Thinking
Use the visuals that appear at the start of the chapter to discuss the functions, cultural setting and themes of the chapter ahead. For example, ask students to answer the following: 1) Where are the people shown in these photographs?; 2) What are the people doing?; 3) What do students think they will be studying in the chapter?; 4) Can they guess which countries the chapter features?; 5) What similarities or differences do they note between shopping in the United States and shopping as it is depicted on these pages?

Capítulo 9
La ropa

Objetivos

❖ **describe clothing**

❖ **identify parts of the body**

❖ **express disagreement**

❖ **talk about the past**

❖ **discuss size and fit**

❖ **discuss price and payment**

Visit the web-based activities at www.emcp.com

362 *trescientos sesenta y dos*

Notes The communicative objectives are provided here to help prepare students for what they will be learning in *Capítulo 9*. Spend a few moments discussing the objectives with the class.

A checkoff list of these functions, along with additional objectives, appears on page 408 so students can evaluate their own progress.

Contexto cultural

Panamá
Nombre oficial: **República de Panamá**
Población: **2.845.000**
Capital: **Ciudad de Panamá**
Ciudades importantes: **San Miguelito, Colón, David**
Unidad monetaria: **el balboa**
Fiesta nacional: **3 de noviembre, Separación de Panamá de Colombia**
Gente famosa: **Rubén Blades (cantante, actor), Ómar Torrijos (ex-presidente)**

Ecuador
Nombre oficial: **República del Ecuador**
Población: **13.183.000**
Capital: **Quito**
Ciudades importantes: **Guayaquil, Cuenca, Machala**
Unidad monetaria: **el sucre**
Fiesta nacional: **10 de agosto, Primer Grito de la Independencia de Quito**
Gente famosa: **Jorge Enrique Adum (escritor), Oswaldo Guayasamin (pintor)**

trescientos sesenta y tres **363**

Notes Talk with the class about the contents of pages 362 and 363. The large photograph depicts shopping in Panama at a retail clothing store; the small photograph shows an open-air market in Quito, Ecuador.

In this chapter students will be learning how to use Spanish when shopping for clothing and gifts. They will also learn to evaluate their own shopping tastes. Finally, students will learn what it is like to go shopping in Panama and in Ecuador and what they might find in stores and markets if they travel to one of these Spanish-speaking countries in Central and South America.

En la tienda por departamentos

Activity 1

Activities 61–62

Activities 1–3

Activity 1

Activities 1–4

Content reviewed in *Lección A*
- colors
- preterite tense of regular *-ar* verbs
- preterite tense of *ser*
- negation

Activities

Prereading Strategy

Using overhead transparencies 61 and 62, introduce the lesson vocabulary. Say the words and have students repeat after you to practice individual words and to begin to become familiar with the new words. Be sure to include both the articles of clothing and colors. Then follow up by practicing the vocabulary, asking students to identify and spell the words you indicate.

Lección A

Panamá

◆Vocabulario I
En la tienda por departamentos

Departamento de ropa para hombres

la corbata

el pijama

la camisa de algodón

la ropa interior

el traje de baño

el traje

Departamento de ropa para mujeres

la blusa de seda

morada

marrón

rosada

anaranjada

el vestido

el traje de baño

el pijama

la ropa interior

las medias

el cuerpo

la cabeza

la bota

el dedo

el brazo

la mano

la pierna

el pie

el dedo

el zapato bajo

el zapato de tacón

Notes Ask students what they know about Panama. Most students are familiar with the Panama Canal, which is discussed on page 367. Ask for student volunteers to create a bulletin board or travel brochure about this Spanish-speaking Central American country.

Have students find cognates and words they already know in *Vocabulario I*. Quickly check student comprehension of the descriptions that accompany the illustrations on these two pages.

¿Prefieres la camisa roja o la verde?

Prefiero la roja. Yo le pedí una roja a mis padres para mi cumpleaños, pero me dieron una azul.

1 1. B
2. F
3. D
4. E
5. A
6. C

2 1. El vestido es verde.
2. Las botas son marrones.
3. El pijama es azul.
4. La corbata es morada.
5. La blusa es rosada.
6. El traje de baño es anaranjado.

3 1. la cabeza
2. el brazo
3. la mano
4. el dedo
5. la pierna
6. el pie
7. el dedo

1 Comprando ropa

))) Selecciona la ilustración que corresponde con lo que oyes.

A   **B**   **C**   **D**   **E**   **F**

2 ¿De qué color son?

Describe la ropa de la actividad anterior, usando los colores.

1. el vestido
2. las botas
3. el pijama
4. la corbata
5. la blusa
6. el traje de baño

3 El cuerpo

Nombra (name) las partes del cuerpo.

Activities

Critical Thinking
Ask individuals about the *Vocabulario I* illustration using simple questions with **yes** or **no** for answers: *¿Es roja la corbata?* Then gradually begin to ask questions that require more elaborate answers: *¿De qué color es el vestido?* Finally, personalize the questions: *¿De qué color son tus zapatos?*

Notes Activity 1 is intended for listening comprehension practice. Play the audio CD of the activity or use the transcript that appears in the ATE Introduction if you prefer to read the activity yourself. A reproducible answer sheet for the activity can be found at the end of the Audio CD Program Manual.

You may want to have students write answers for activities 2 and 3.

Use overhead transparencies 61 and 62 to present and practice the new words and expressions in *Vocabulario I.*

Diálogo I
¿Cuál prefieres?

ROCÍO: ¿Dónde está el departamento de ropa para mujeres?
PEDRO: ¿Qué buscas?
ROCÍO: Busco un vestido de seda para la fiesta del sábado.

ROCÍO: Aquí hay unos vestidos. ¿Cuál prefieres?
PEDRO: Prefiero el vestido rosado. Y no cuesta mucho.
ROCÍO: ¿El rosado? No me gusta ni un poquito. Prefiero el morado.

PEDRO: Con el rosado puedes llevar unas medias verdes.
ROCÍO: ¿Una medias verdes? ¡Estás loco!
PEDRO: Sí, te vas a ver muy bonita, como una flor.

4 ¿Qué recuerdas?

1. ¿Qué busca Rocío?
2. ¿Qué vestido prefiere Pedro?
3. ¿Cuesta mucho el vestido rosado?
4. ¿Le gusta el vestido rosado a Rocío?
5. ¿Qué vestido prefiere Rocío?
6. Según Pedro, ¿con qué puede llevar Rocío el vestido rosado?

5 Algo personal

1. ¿Cuál es tu color favorito?
2. ¿Tienes un color favorito para la ropa?
3. ¿Qué ropa te gustaría comprar?
4. ¿Qué colores te gusta llevar juntos?
5. ¿Te gusta ayudar a tus amigos/as a comprar ropa? Explica.

¡Extra!

¿Recuerdas?

Do you remember learning the following colors?

amarillo negro
azul rojo
blanco verde
gris

6 ¿Cuál prefieres?

 Selecciona la letra de la ilustración que corresponde con lo que las siguientes personas prefieren.

A   **B**

Notes This dialog and activities 4, 5 and 6 have been recorded by native speakers and are included in the *Navegando* Audio CD Program.

Teenagers are often fairly fashion conscious, but they also recognize that how they dress represents only one aspect of who they are. With that in mind, your students may enjoy learning a proverb in Spanish that says it is not the clothes you wear that are important, but rather who you are: *Aunque la mona se vista de seda, mona se queda* (Even though it may be wearing silk, the monkey is still a monkey).

Cultura Viva

La ciudad de Panamá.

Panamá, el cruce del mundo

Although small by comparison with many Spanish-speaking countries, Panama serves as an important crossroads for the world due to its geographic location and physical features. You are probably familiar with the canal (el Canal de Panamá) that divides the country in two. This valuable international travel route took years to build and many people died during its construction. Today the canal serves a critical function connecting the Atlantic and the Pacific oceans, shortening the time and energy required to transport goods from one part of the world to another.

Panama's people (los panameños) have a varied background. When Rodrigo de Bastidas, Juan de la Cosa and Vasco Nuñez de Balboa arrived in Panama in 1501, followed by Columbus in 1502, the land was inhabited primarily by natives of two indigenous groups, the kuna and the chocó. Panama's citizens today are descendants of these and other indigenous groups, Spanish conquistadors, African slaves and workers from China (who were involved in constructing the railroad in the mid-1800s), among others. Direct descendants of the kuna and chocó people still inhabit the San Blas archipelago.

Most Panamanians prefer to live in cities along the canal. For example, Panama City (la Ciudad de Panamá), the capital and largest city, is located along the canal. Panama City has become an important financial center, with more than ninety banks from throughout the world registered to do business.

El canal de Panamá.

7 Panamá, el cruce del mundo

Di si lo siguiente es *cierto* o *falso*.

1. Panamá es un país pequeño.
2. La capital de Panamá es San José.
3. El Canal de Panamá va del Océano Pacífico al Atlántico.
4. La capital es la ciudad más grande del país.
5. Bastidas, de la Cosa y Balboa llegaron a Panamá en 1905.
6. Descendientes de los kuna y los chocó viven en el archipiélago de San Blas.

8 Conexión con otras disciplinas: arquitectura e historia

Working in small groups, research the history of the Panama Canal. Try to find information regarding its construction, how long the project took, etc. Share your findings with the class.

Notes The Kuna Indians who live on the San Blas archipelago are famous for their *molas*—colorful reverse appliqués—made of several layers of colorful cotton fabric.

Connections. Activity 8 makes the cross-curricular connection to architecture and history.

Teacher Resources

 Activity 7

 Activity 2

 Activity 4

Answers

7 1. Cierto.
   2. Falso.
   3. Cierto.
   4. Cierto.
   5. Falso.
   6. Cierto.
8 Creative self-expression.

Activities

Connections (Social Studies)
Have students prepare a report about President Theodore Roosevelt's involvement in Panama's independence from Colombia.

Spanish for Spanish Speakers
Encourage interested students to study the development and operation of the Panama Canal, using the Internet and library resources. Then have students prepare a report about the canal and explain its construction to the class.

Answers

9 Answers will vary.
10 1. el
2. el
3. —
4. los
5. —
6. —
7. la
8. El

Activities

Students with Special Needs
Remind students that for agreement in gender and number, color words and other adjectives ending in -o have four forms; those ending in -e or a consonant have two forms. Practice the point by choosing a color such as *negro* or *rosado* and then say several nouns to which students may respond individually when you call on them or in chorus. Do the same with *verde* and then with an adjective ending in a consonant such as *gris* or *azul*.

Idioma

Estructura

Adjectives as nouns

Although a definite article is not usually needed when a color describes an object (because the color is an adjective), a definite article is required when naming colors in Spanish (because they are considered nouns).

Pedí un pantalón negro de cumpleaños. I asked for black pants for my birthday.

but:

Prefiero el (color) rojo. I prefer red.

In addition, sometimes a word being described may be omitted in order to avoid repeating a noun. In such cases the article remains and the adjective must agree with the noun that was omitted.

¿Te gusta el vestido azul o el (vestido) gris? Do you like the blue dress or **the grey one?**
Compré la camisa blanca, no la verde. I bought the white shirt, not **the green one.**

 Práctica

9 Los colores de mi ropa

Completa las oraciones con el adjetivo apropiado para describir algunos artículos de ropa en tu cuarto.

MODELO   Tengo un pantalón rojo.

1. Tengo mucha ropa __.
2. Tengo unas botas __.
3. Tengo unos zapatos __.
4. Tengo un pijama __.
5. Tengo una camisa __.
6. Tengo un traje de baño __.

10 Los gustos personales

Tengo un pantalón rojo.

Completa las siguientes oraciones con un artículo definido si lo necesitan.

1. A Marta le gusta __ color verde.
2. El color favorito de Enrique es __ morado.
3. A mi prima le gustaría comprar un impermeable __ amarillo.
4. ¿Elena prefiere los calcetines verdes o __ rojos?
5. Mi madre tiene una blusa de seda __ rosada porque es su color favorito.
6. A Pedro le gustan sus botas __ negras.
7. Esperanza compró la ropa interior azul ayer, no __ blanca.
8. __ anaranjado es mi color favorito.

Notes You may want to share with students the following additional color names: *la violeta* (violet), *el azul marino* (navy blue), *el verde claro* (light green), *el rojo vivo* (bright red).

Practice using color names as nouns before assigning activity 10.

11 ¡Vamos de compras!

Imagina que tienes $300.00. Haz una lista de la ropa que te gustaría comprar este sábado, añadiendo los colores y los materiales que te gustan.

Comunicación

12 ¿Cuánto cuesta?

Trabajando en parejas, un estudiante hace de cliente *(customer)* y el otro de vendedor(a) *(salesperson)*. Alternen en regatear los precios de los artículos en las ilustraciones.

MODELO

A: ¿Cuánto cuestan las botas?
B: Las botas cuestan $80.
A: Le doy $70.
B: No puedo. Se las doy por $75.

Estrategia

Developing language survival skills: *regatear*

Most shops and stores in Spanish-speaking parts of the world have a fixed price *(precio fijo)*, and trying to negotiate a lower price would be inappropriate. However, in some instances negotiating *(regatear)* the price for an item is a common and accepted practice. For example, street vendors selling clothing, baskets, jewelry, etc. in Panama City would expect you to negotiate with them on prices.

How might knowing Spanish help you negotiate a price while visiting a Spanish-speaking country? Do you feel confident enough with your Spanish skills to be able to negotiate a price?

¡Oportunidades!

Regatear
Is there a flea market where you live? Go there and practice bargaining for items. Learning how to bargain will be beneficial if you travel to a Spanish-speaking country where you can combine your ability to bargain with your ability to speak Spanish.

1   **2**

3   **4**   **5**   **6**

Answers

13 Creative self-expression.
14 Answers will vary.

Activities

Expansion
Review the present-tense forms of these verbs with students before teaching the preterite tense. Then compare the present-tense stem changes with the preterite-tense stem changes.

---

 13 ¿Qué ropa ves?

 Trabajando en parejas, habla con tu compañero/a sobre la ropa de la tienda del Vocabulario I. Miren el dibujo y señalen *(point out)* con el dedo los artículos de ropa.

> **MODELO** **A:** ¿Qué te gustaría comprar en la tienda?
> **B:** Me gustaría comprar los zapatos negros, los marrones no me gustan.

14 ¿Qué ropa llevan?

Discuss what clothing people around you are wearing. Begin by saying who is wearing the article of clothing. Your partner then must describe the material or color. Each student must name and describe at least five articles of clothing.

> **MODELO** **A:** Estoy mirando el pantalón de Julia.
> **B:** Su pantalón es azul y es de algodón.

Estructura

Talking about the past: preterite tense of -*er* and -*ir* verbs

Form the preterite tense of regular -*er* and -*ir* verbs by removing the last two letters from the infinitive and adding the same set of endings for either type of verb.

correr	
corr**í**	corr**imos**
corr**iste**	corr**isteis**
corr**ió**	corr**ieron**

escribir	
escrib**í**	escrib**imos**
escrib**iste**	escrib**isteis**
escrib**ió**	escrib**ieron**

*¿Quién **corrió** a la tienda?*   Who **ran** to the store?
*¿Le **escribió** Julia una carta a su prima?*   **Did** Julia **write** a letter to her cousin?

Note: Stem changes that occur in the present tense for -*ar* and -*er* verbs do not occur in the preterite tense. However, -*ir* verbs that have a stem change in the present tense require a different stem change in the preterite tense for *Ud., él, ella, Uds., ellos* and *ellas*. This second change is shown in parentheses after infinitives in this book. Some verbs that follow this pattern include *dormir (ue, **u**), mentir (ie, **i**), pedir (i, **i**), preferir (ie, **i**), repetir (i, **i**)* and *sentir (ie, **i**)*. The stem changes do not interfere with the verb endings.

dormir	
dormí	dormimos
dormiste	dormisteis
d**u**rmió	d**u**rmieron

pedir	
pedí	pedimos
pediste	pedisteis
p**i**dió	p**i**dieron

preferir	
preferí	preferimos
preferiste	preferisteis
pref**i**rió	pref**i**rieron

Notes Review the preterite tense of -*ar* verbs before beginning the *Estructura* on -*er* and -*ir* verbs.

Be sure to practice conjugating several -*er* and -*ir* verbs so students are clear about what they need to do for the activities that follow.

Práctica

15 **¿Lo hiciste ayer o no?**

Use each of the verbs shown to state ten things you did or did not do yesterday.

> *abrir*
> **recoger**   comer
> aprender
> correr
> **escribir**   dormir   barrer
> *mentir*   **salir**   repetir

MODELO recoger
Recogí unas fotos ayer.

¿Corriste ayer?

¿Aprendieron mucho en la clase?

Capítulo 9   *trescientos setenta y uno* **371**

16 En la tienda de ropa

 Working in pairs, one person plays the part of the owner of a clothing store who has returned from vacation and one person plays the part of an employee who has been managing the store during the owner's absence. What might the conversation sound like, based upon the provided cues?

MODELO recoger las corbatas nuevas
   A: ¿Recogiste las corbatas nuevas?
   B: Sí, (No, no) las recogí.

1. aprender a arreglar los pantalones
2. barrer siempre el suelo de la tienda por la mañana
3. pedir las camisas
4. escoger las corbatas para los clientes
5. subir la ropa nueva a la oficina

17 ¿Qué hicieron ayer?

Usa elementos de cada columna para hacer siete oraciones completas y decir lo que pasó ayer.

MODELO Yo pedí tres corbatas.

I	II	III
tú y yo	pedir	al departamento de ropa para hombres
Uds.	estar	comprarte unas botas nuevas
la profesora	dormir	toda la tarde
Ud.	correr	ropa interior blanca
los chicos	preferir	en la tienda por departamentos
tú	repetir	tres corbatas
yo		los trajes de baño
		el precio dos veces

Estuvimos en el centro comercial ayer.

Notes Review direct object pronouns and their position in sentences before beginning activity 16.

Consider completing one or two of the sentences in activity 17 with students to be sure they understand what they are to do.

18 En la tienda por departamentos

En parejas, hablen Uds. de lo qué pasó en la tienda por departamentos ayer, según las pistas y las ilustraciones.

MODELO

Belén/pedir ver

A: ¿Qué pidió ver Belén?

B: Belén pidió ver unas botas marrones.

1. Jorge y Edgar/ pedir ver

2. Manuel/escoger

3. Alfonso y su hermano/ volver para comprar

4. la amiga de Ernesto/ correr a comprar

5. Carmen y su mamá/escoger

6. Pedro/preferir comprar

✿ Comunicación

19 La semana pasada

Make a list of some things you did in the past week. Then, in small groups, talk about the activities on everyone's list. One person starts by mentioning something he or she did. Then others in the group ask questions such as when and with whom you did each activity. You may wish to include some of the following activities: *escribir un correo electrónico, dormir tarde, comer en un restaurante, salir con amigos,* etc.

MODELO **A:** Escribí un correo electrónico.
  B: ¿A quién lo escribiste?
  A: Lo escribí a un amigo en Panamá.
  C: ¿Cuándo escribiste el correo?
  A: Lo escribí anteayer.

Capítulo 9

trescientos setenta y tres **373**

Notes Have students find cognates and words they already know in *Vocabulario II*. Quickly check student comprehension of the text boxes and bubbles that accompany the illustrations on these two pages.

Use overhead transparency 63 to present and practice the new words and expressions in *Vocabulario II*.

An *abrigo* is called a *gabán* in Argentina and a *tapado* in Uruguay.

Answers

20 1. guantes
2. abrigo
3. chaqueta
4. impermeable
5. suéter
6. pantalón
21 1. botas
2. traje de baño
3. zapatos
4. chaqueta
5. sombrero
6. traje
22 Answers will vary.

Activities

Critical Listening

As an extension of activity 22, select and read aloud the names of articles of clothing from both lists, having students raise their left hand if the item is worn on the beach or their right hand if the item is used when snow skiing.

Expansion

As a follow-up to activity 22, ask students what items besides clothing they would take on a ski trip or to the beach.

20 ¿Qué es?

Escribe el artículo de ropa que oyes.

MODELO el <u>sombrero</u>

1. los __   2. un __   3. una __   4. un __   5. tu __   6. el __

21 ¿Qué llevo?

Escoge la palabra apropiada para completar lógicamente las siguientes oraciones.

MODELO Si hace frío llevo un (ropa interior, <u>abrigo</u>, blusa).

1. Ay, está nevando y no tengo (corbata, amarillo, botas).
2. Hace sol y calor. Debo llevar mi (suéter, traje de baño, falda) a la playa.
3. Me gusta caminar por la playa sin (zapatos, seda, gris).
4. No quiero llevar una (chaqueta, corbata, camisa) porque no hace frío.
5. Hace mucho viento y no debo llevar el (sombrero, camisa, suéter).
6. El pantalón del (rosado, traje, falda) está sucio.

22 La ropa que usas

Haz una lista de la ropa que necesitas para esquiar en la nieve y otra lista para pasar un día en la playa.

Notes Activity 20 is intended for listening comprehension practice. Play the audio CD of the activity or use the transcript that appears in the ATE Introduction if you prefer to read the activity yourself. A reproducible answer sheet for the activity can be found at the end of the Audio CD Program Manual.

Consider allowing students to do activity 22 in pairs. For example, students might ask one another what they need to ski (*¿Qué necesitas par esquiar en la nieve?*) or what they need to spend a day at the beach (*¿Qué necesitas para pasar un día en la playa?*). Follow up by having students list on paper the clothing they need for each activity.

Diálogo II

Un vestido de seda

ROCÍO: ¿Hay alguien a quien preguntar por otros vestidos?
PEDRO: Sí, allí. Señora, ¿nos puede ayudar?
SEÑORA: Sí, cómo no.

ROCÍO: Busco un vestido de seda.
SEÑORA: ¿No le gusta ninguno de aquí?
ROCÍO: No, ninguno. Bueno, este azul, pero no me queda bien.

SEÑORA: Bueno, aquí hay otros pero son de lana.
ROCÍO: No, los vestidos de lana no me gustan nada.
SEÑORA: Le gustaría ver algo más, ¿guantes, abrigos, faldas?

23 ¿Qué recuerdas?

1. ¿Hay alguien a quien preguntar por otros vestidos?
2. ¿Le gustan los vestidos de seda a Rocío?
3. ¿Qué vestidos no le gustan a Rocío?
4. ¿Qué más puede ver Rocío?

24 Algo personal

1. ¿Prefieres los vestidos de lana o los de seda?
2. ¿Qué color de ropa te queda bien?
3. ¿Qué ropa compras cuando vas de vacaciones?

¿Qué vestido prefieres?

25 ¿Cuándo?

 Listen carefully to statements made by several people. Indicate whether each sentence you hear is in the past *(pretérito)* or in the present *(presente)*.

376 *trescientos setenta y seis*

Lección A

376

Cultura viva

También se dice

[A]s you have seen many times now, words that [a]re used to name items in Spanish often vary a [gr]eat deal as you travel from one country or [re]gion to the next. Even common articles of clothing are referred to in many different ways. For example, the item you know as a *falda* may be called a *saya* in the Caribbean or a *pollera* in parts of South America. However, in Panama the term *pollera* refers to the national dress, which consists of a brightly colored blouse that is connected to a full skirt. In the Caribbean, *zapatos de tacón* are sometimes called simply *tacones*. In addition, an *abrigo* may be called a *sobretodo* in Chile, and many people use *almacén* instead of *tienda de ropa* to refer to the place where they shop for clothing.

Tiene ojos castaños.

Words used to refer to some colors vary, too, as you travel from one Spanish-speaking part of the world to another. For instance, there are many different words to refer to the color brown. In countries that have been influenced by the French many people favor the word *marrón* for **brown.** In the Caribbean, *carmelita* and the expressions *color café* or *color tabaco* are used. In some countries the word for brown varies according to what is being described. For example, the word *castaño* describes brown hair or brown eyes.

Un tacón de color café.

26 Juego: ¿Quién es?

In small groups, play this game: Take turns describing what someone in the class is wearing, one article of clothing at a time, without looking directly at the person; next, ask *¿Quién es?* and have one member of the group answer after the piece of clothing has been described. If the person does not guess correctly who the person is, describe another article of clothing and continue. The winner is the person that correctly identifies the classmate who is wearing the clothing being described.

MODELO   **A:** Lleva una camisa blanca. ¿Quién es?
        B: Es Carlos.

Lleva un abrigo rosado. ¿Quién es?

Capítulo 9

trescientos setenta y siete **377**

Teacher Resources

☑ **Activity 5**

Answers

26 Creative self-expression.

Activities

Spanish for Spanish Speakers
Pair bilingual and nonbilingual students for activity 26.

Technology
Have students search the Internet using the word *pollera*. (See the ATE Introduction for suggestions on using the Internet for searches.) Students will find many different Web pages that discuss *polleras*. Ask students to find Web pages that discuss *polleras* in Panama. Follow up and ask students if they found any sites written in Spanish. Students should print pages from a Spanish-language site, skim it for phrases that they recognize and then share it with the class. You may also want students to summarize what they found on any English-language sites as additional support for a class discussion.

Activities

Multiple Intelligences (linguistic/spatial)
Have students think of a memory device and make a visual representation to depict the forms of *ser* and *ir* in the preterite. Share their ideas with the rest of the class and display the best ones on a bulletin board.

Idioma

Estructura

Preterite tense of *ir* and *ser*

You have already seen forms of the preterite tense of *ser*. The irregular preterite-tense forms of *ir* (to go) and *ser* (to be) are identical.

ir/ser	
fui	fuimos
fuiste	fuisteis
fue	fueron

¿Quién **fue** al centro comercial ayer? Who **went** to the mall yesterday?
¿**Fueron** ellos al centro comercial? **Did** they **go** to the mall?

but:

¿Qué día **fue** ayer? What day **was** yesterday?
Esos días **fueron** fantásticos. Those days **were** fantastic.

¿Fueron ellos al centro comercial?

Notes The preterite tense of *ser* was introduced briefly in *Capítulo 5* so students could talk about the days of the week.

Remember to select from the Teacher Resources indicated at the top of the page to find support materials for teaching from the pages of the textbook. For example, you will find activities that practice and reinforce the preterite tense of *ir* and *ser* in the Listening Activities Manual, Workbook and Grammar and Vocabulary Exercises Manual.

8

Práctica

27 ¿Adónde fueron ayer?

 Indica adónde fueron estas personas, según las ilustraciones.

MODELO

Ana y Pablo
Ana y Pablo fueron al cine ayer.

1. yo

2. tú

3. Julia

4. mis padres

5. mi amigo y yo

6. Raúl e Inés

28 Haciendo compras en la isla Contadora

Completa el siguiente párrafo con el pretérito de los verbos indicados para decir qué ropa compraron Juanita y sus dos hermanas en la isla Contadora.

Primero yo *(1. escoger)* un traje de baño porque el que tengo no me queda bien. Lo *(2. comprar)* por poco dinero. Mis hermanas también *(3. comprar)* en la misma tienda unos vestidos de algodón muy bonitos. Cuando nosotras *(4. volver)* al centro comercial, yo *(5. ir)* a buscar otro traje de baño para mí. Ese día en la tienda, los dependientes *(6. vender)* todos los trajes de baño rápidamente. Nosotras *(7. comprar)* el último. Me gustaría tener dos. Luego, mi tía Julia *(8. ir)* con nosotras de compras. Ella *(9. prometer)* comprarme ropa para mi cumpleaños y yo le *(10. pedir)* unos zapatos bajos, de color marrón. ¡Qué bonitos son! Nosotras *(11. estar)* comprando todo el día y *(12. llegar)* tarde al hotel, ¡cansadas pero contentas!

Capítulo 9 *trescientos setenta y nueve* **379**

Teacher Resources

 Activity 27

Answers

27 Possible answers:
1. Yo fui a la Ciudad de Panamá ayer.
2. Tú fuiste al parque ayer.
3. Julia fue al centro comercial ayer.
4. Mis padres fueron a la playa ayer.
5. Mi amigo y yo fuimos a un restaurante ayer.
6. Raúl e Inés fueron al concierto ayer.

28
1. escogí
2. compré
3. compraron
4. volvimos
5. fui
6. vendieron
7. compramos
8. fue
9. prometió
10. pedí
11. estuvimos
12. llegamos

Activities

Students with Special Needs
Before assigning activity 27, have students identify the sites in the illustrations.

379

29 Fueron y compraron lo siguiente

Imagina que tus amigos y tú fueron de compras al centro comercial el sábado pasado. Di lo que las siguientes personas fueron a comprar. Sigue el modelo.

MODELO Andrés
Andrés fue a comprar un suéter verde.

1. Marta   2. Lola y Rita   3. tú   4. nosotros   5. yo

✦ Comunicación

30 Haciendo cosas

 With a partner, talk about where family and friends went yesterday, last week, last month or last year. Include in your discussion how the people named went to each place, whom they went with and what they did. Take notes as you talk. Then share the most interesting bit of information you learned with the class.

MODELO **A:** ¿Fueron tú y tu familia a un buen restaurante la semana pasada?
B: Sí. Fuimos a un restaurante nuevo en el centro comercial.
A: ¿Te gustó?
B: Sí, me gustó mucho.

31 Una encuesta

 Haz una investigación sobre las actividades que hacen tus compañeros(as) de clase. Prepara una lista de actividades (quehaceres, deportes, pasatiempos, etc.) y trata de encontrar una persona que haya hecho *(has done)* cada actividad y pregúntale cuándo la hizo durante la semana pasada. Puedes usar las siguientes frases para completar la investigación: *dormir tarde, escribir un correo electrónico, ir al centro comercial, ir a un buen restaurante, ir al cine, ir a la playa, ir al parque.*

MODELO **A:** ¿Dormiste tarde la semana pasada?
B: Sí, dormí tarde el jueves.

Actividad	Nombre	Día
dormir tarde		jueves
escribir un correo electrónico		

Estructura

Affirmative and negative words

You have learned to make a sentence negative by placing *no* before a verb.

No veo la chaqueta.   I do **not** see the jacket.

Unlike English, in Spanish it is sometimes possible to use two negative expressions in the same sentence. The following chart contains a list of common negative expressions along with their affirmative counterparts.

Expresiones afirmativas	Expresiones negativas
sí *(yes)* **Sí,** ella habla español. Él dice que **sí.**	**no** *(no)* **No,** él **no** habla español. Ella dice que **no.**
algo *(something, anything)* ¿Quieres comprar **algo**? ¿Compraste **algo** ayer?	**nada** *(nothing, anything)* **No** quiero comprar **nada.** **Nada** me gustó.
alguien *(somebody, anybody)* ¿Lo sabe **alguien**? **Alguien** debe saberlo.	**nadie** *(nobody, anybody)* **No** lo sabe **nadie.** **Nadie** lo sabe.
algún, alguna, -os, -as *(some, any)* ¿Le gusta **algún** abrigo? ¿Le gusta **alguna** blusa? ¿Compras **algunos** calcetines? ¿Buscas **algunas** corbatas?	**ningún, ninguna, -os, -as** *(none, not any)* No, **ningún** abrigo me gusta. No, **ninguna** me gusta. No, **no** compro **ningunos** calcetines. No, **no** busco **ningunas** corbatas.
o...o *(either... or)* Puedes comprar **o** un abrigo **o** un sombrero.	**ni... ni** *(neither... nor)* **No** voy a comprar **ni** un abrigo **ni** un sombrero.
siempre *(always)* Él **siempre** lleva botas.	**nunca** *(never)* Ella **no** lleva botas **nunca.** Ella **nunca** lleva botas.
también *(also, too)* Ella viene hoy **también.** Ella **también** viene hoy.	**tampoco** *(neither, either)* Él **no** viene mañana **tampoco.** Él **tampoco** viene mañana.

Note: The words *alguno,-a* (some, any) and *ninguno,-a* (none, not any) sometimes are used as pronouns.

*¿Va **alguno** o **alguna** de Uds.*   *No, **ninguno** de nosotros va al*
al centro comercial ahora?   *centro comercial ahora.*

Activities

Expansion
Call on several students to give examples of sentences that use these affirmative and negative expressions.

Students with Special Needs
Return to previously studied dialogs and readings and ask students to find examples of affirmative and negative expressions.

Notes Tell the class that the plural negative words *ningunos* and *ningunas* are used very little. In most cases, the singular words *ningún* and *ninguna* are preferred.

Inform students that *algún* and *ningún* are shortened forms of *alguno* and *ninguno.*

When combining negative expressions in one sentence in Spanish, it is often possible to use one of the negative expressions before the verb and another negative expression (and sometimes even more than one) after the verb. However, *no, nada, nadie, nunca, tampoco* and forms of *ninguno* may be used alone, before the verb, without the word *no*.

No voy **nunca** al centro. **Nunca** voy al centro.	I **never** go downtown.
No estoy comprando **nada tampoco**. **Tampoco** estoy comprando **nada**.	I am **not** buying **anything either**.

When *nadie* or a form of *ninguno* are direct objects referring to people they require the personal *a*.

No veo **a nadie** aquí.	I don't see **anyone** here.
No veo **a ningún** amigo aquí.	I don't see **any** friends here.

✿ Práctica

32 A completar

Completa estos mini-diálogos lógicamente, usando una de las siguientes palabras: *algo, alguien, nada o nadie.*

1. __ debe ir con Uds.
No queremos ir con __.
2. __ te llama por teléfono.
Marta te quiere decir __.
3. ¿Va __ con Uds.?
Sí, Isabel va con nosotras porque quiere comprar __.
4. ¿Ves a __ en esa tienda de ropa?
No, no veo a __.
5. ¿Quieres comprar ___?
No, no me gusta __.

33 ¡No!

Contesta las preguntas en forma negativa.

MODELO ¿Qué quieres mirar?
No quiero mirar nada.

1. Yo no voy a la tienda de ropa. ¿Y tú?
2. ¿Con quién fueron Uds. de compras ayer?
3. ¿Prefieres las botas anaranjadas o las verdes?
4. ¿Viste alguna falda de algodón?
5. ¿Ves a algún amigo del colegio?
6. ¿Compraron Uds. el suéter rojo o el suéter azul?
7. ¿Sus padres siempre les dan dinero para ir de compras?
8. ¿Te gustaría vender ropa interior o carros?
9. ¿Siempre van Uds. de compras al centro?
10. ¿Quiénes de Uds. son de Panamá?

¿Compraron el suéter rojo?

Notes Model several sentences that use the negative expressions before assigning the activities on pages 382 and 383.

Ask students to pair up before starting activity 33. Follow up by having students write their answers.

34 ¡Estoy enfermo/a y no quiero hacer nada!

Estás de mal humor porque estás enfermo/a y tus padres te hacen muchas preguntas. Trabajando en parejas, alternen en hacer las siguientes preguntas y en dar respuestas negativas a cada una.

MODELO A: ¿Piensas ir de compras o vas a estudiar?
　　　　　B: No, no pienso ni ir de compras ni estudiar.

1. ¿Qué vas a hacer hoy?
2. ¿Quién te va a visitar en casa?
3. ¿Siempre juegas con el perro cuando estás enfermo/a?
4. ¿Quieres comer algo?
5. ¿Vas a hablar con alguien por teléfono?
6. ¿Quieres ver alguna película en DVD?
7. ¿Te puedo comprar algo?

✤ Comunicación

35 No se hace

Trabajando en parejas, hablen Uds. de lo que nadie hace nunca y hagan una lista de siete u ocho cosas que nadie hace nunca. Luego, deben leer las mejores frases de la lista a la clase.

MODELO Nadie va al centro comercial sin zapatos.

36 ¿Qué llevas mucho?

Talk with a classmate about the clothing you like to wear and when. Include in your discussion how often you wear various articles of clothing, the colors you prefer, when and where you went shopping and whether or not you purchased something, which articles of clothing each of you purchased last week/month/year (naming a specific time) and anything else you wish.

MODELO A: ¿Qué ropa te gusta llevar mucho?
　　　　　B: Me gusta llevar este suéter anaranjado casi todos los días.
　　　　　A: ¿Dónde lo compraste?
　　　　　B: No lo compré, me lo regaló mi hermano.

Me gusta llevar mi vestido rojo y azul.

Teacher Resources

　Activity 34

Answers

34 Possible answers:
1. No voy a hacer nada hoy.
2. Nadie me va a visitar en casa.
3. No, nunca juego con el perro cuando estoy enfermo/a.
4. No, no quiero comer nada.
5. No, no voy a hablar con nadie por teléfono.
6. No, no quiero ver ninguna película en DVD.
7. No, no me puedes comprar nada.

35 Creative self-expression.
36 Creative self-expression.

Activities

Critical Listening

Tell students that they will hear a series of erroneous statements with affirmative or negative words. For each statement given, the students should state the opposite to provide the correct information. Possible statements: *La clase de español siempre empieza tarde; Tenemos clase el sábado y el domingo también; En esta clase no tenemos ningún examen; El profesor/la profesora no conoce a nadie en (país); Para mañana no tenemos que hacer nada.*

Notes Activities 34, 35 and 36 can be repeated. Have students work on each activity with one partner. Then have them switch partners and try the activity again.

Set time limits for the paired activities on page 383 and keep a brisk pace.

Remember to circulate around the room as students complete these activities to keep students on task and to offer help as needed.

Activity 36 serves as a good starting point for a composition on a favorite teen topic: clothing.

Teacher Resources

Las molas: símbolo de la cultura kuna
Activity 37

Answers

37 1. Los kunas viven en el archipiélago de San Blas a 200 millas de la costa de Panamá.
2. El traje tradicional de las mujeres kunas consiste en faldas coloridas, blusas decoradas con molas y anillos de oro en las narices.
3. Las molas se hacen con telas de diferentes colores.
4. Usan las molas para decorar las blusas.

38 Answers will vary.

Activities

Multiple Intelligences (spatial)
Have students make *molas* out of construction paper.

Lectura cultural

Las molas: símbolo de la cultura kuna

En el mar[1] Caribe, a 200 millas de la costa de Panamá, está el archipiélago de San Blas *(Kuna Yala)*. En estas islas tropicales viven los indios kuna. Uno de los elementos más conocidos de los indios kuna es su vestimenta tradicional[2] que es espectacular: las mujeres llevan anillos de oro[3] en la nariz, faldas coloridas y blusas decoradas con las famosas molas. Las molas son paneles de intricados diseños[4] cosidos a mano[5]. Las mujeres kuna observan, transforman y representan el mundo que ven y su medio ambiente y los convierten en estas obras de arte usando aguja, hilos y telas de colores vivos[6].

Los paneles adornan la parte delantera y trasera de las blusas y los diseños pueden ser muy antiguos, con piezas geométricas y animales sagrados, relativos a la vida diaria de las mujeres. Las molas son apreciadas piezas de arte indígena y pueden encontrarse en museos y colecciones privadas. Las molas pueden alcanzar un precio muy elevado, dependiendo del número de capas, los detalles y el mérito artístico del diseño.

[1]sea [2]traditional clothing [3]gold [4]designs [5]hand-sewn [6]threads and fabrics of bright coloring

37 ¿Qué recuerdas?

1. ¿Dónde viven los kunas?
2. ¿Cómo es el traje tradicional de las mujeres kunas?
3. ¿Cómo se hacen las molas?
4. ¿Para qué usan las molas?

38 Algo personal

1. En tu opinión, ¿son las molas ropa, arte o los dos? Explica.
2. Imagina que vas a crear una mola. Describe el diseño y los colores de tu mola.

- Compare and contrast the molas of the Kuna Indians with a traditional piece of clothing of another culture. Are they worn just by women? Are they sold as art pieces? Are they made of cotton? Do they have colorful designs?

384   *trescientos ochenta y cuatro*   **Lección A**
384   *trescientos ochenta y cuatro*   **Lección A**

Notes The *mola* designs come from the body paintings of Kuna ancestors who didn't wear clothes until French Huguenot settlers introduced clothing in the mid-nineteenth century. The Kuna simply transposed the body paintings onto cotton fabrics.

Connections. This *Lectura cultural* makes the cross-curricular connections to art, history and geography.

384

¿Qué aprendí?

Autoevaluación
As a review and self-check, respond to the following:

Visit the web-based activities at www.emcp.com

1. Describe three of your favorite clothing items, saying what color they are and what they are made of.

2. Imagine you are deciding either to take a vacation to Panama to enjoy warm weather or go to Chile for a winter ski trip. List at least three articles of clothing you will need to take with you for each vacation choice.

3. State three things you did yesterday.

4. Name two places you went yesterday.

5. Make two affirmative and two negative statements about something that happened yesterday.

6. Name two things you have learned about Panama.

Palabras y expresiones

Para describir
algún, alguna
anaranjado,-a
marrón
morado,-a
ningún, ninguna
rosado,-a

Pronombres
algo
alguien
alguno,-a
nada
nadie
ninguno,-a

La ropa
la bota
la chaqueta
la corbata
el guante
el impermeable
las medias
el pijama
la ropa interior
el sombrero
el suéter
el traje (de baño)
el vestido
el zapato (bajo/de tacón)

Partes del cuerpo
el brazo
la cabeza
el cuerpo
el dedo
la mano
el pie
la pierna

Verbos
combinar
contar (ue)
prometer
quedar
vender

Expresiones y otras palabras
el algodón
el centro comercial
el departamento
el hombre
la lana
la mujer
ni... ni
o... o
quedarle bien a uno
la seda
las vacaciones

Unas botas marrones.

Un traje de baño rosado.

Un traje de baño azul.

Capítulo 9

trescientos ochenta y cinco **385**

Teacher Resources

Activity 14

Information Gap Activities
Postcard Activities
Funciones de Comunicación

Answers

Autoevaluación
Possible answers:
1. Answers will vary.
2. Necesito llevar una chaqueta y mis botas./Necesito traer el traje de baño y una camisa de algodón.
3. Compré unas botas nuevas....
4. Fui al centro comercial.
5. Escribí algunas cartas./Nunca salí con mis amigos.
6. La capital es la Ciudad de Panamá....

Activities

Cooperative Learning
Have students work in pairs to play guessing games. Students take turns describing an object in the classroom (being certain to use the colors) while the partner guesses what the object is.

Notes **Communities.** Ask if students know who Rubén Blades is. Explain that he is from Panama and is a well-known actor and singer.

Students may find it interesting that although the monetary unit in Panama is the *balboa*, in larger cities the U.S. dollar is also widely used.

Tell students that the Panama Canal is not only important to Panama, it is also vital to international trade, because it allows ships to pass from one ocean to another in a matter of hours.

Panama wasn't established as a nation until November 3, 1903. Before that date, Panama was part of Colombia.

Teacher Resources

 Regalos

 Activity 1

 Activities 64–65

 Activity 1

Activity 1

GV Activities 1–3

Content reviewed in *Lección B*
- clothing
- family
- adjective-noun agreement
- talking about the past
- prepositions
- places in a city

Activities

Prereading Strategy
Play the audio CD recording of the vocabulary and have students repeat the words while showing them overhead transparency 64.

Notes Have students find cognates and words they already know in *Vocabulario I*. Quickly check student comprehension of the descriptions that accompany the illustrations on these two pages.

Ask students what they know about Ecuador. Most students are probably familiar with the Galapagos Islands, which are discussed on page 389. Ask for student volunteers to create a bulletin board or travel brochure about this Spanish-speaking South American country.

Inform students that they are about to study the country that was named for the equator: *Ecuador*.

la escalera mecánica

el ascensor

el regalo

el paraguas

1 ¿Qué les gustaría recibir de regalo?

 Selecciona la letra de la ilustración que corresponde con lo que oyes.

A

B

C

D

E

F

2 Hablando de los artículos de la tienda

Contesta las siguientes preguntas en español.

1. ¿Qué puede ser de cuero?
2. ¿Qué puede ser de plata?
3. ¿Qué puede ser de perlas?
4. ¿Te gusta usar perfume? Explica.
5. ¿Cuándo llevas pañuelo?
6. ¿Cuándo llevas bufanda?
7. ¿De qué materiales puede ser un bolso?
8. ¿Qué joyas te gusta llevar?

3 Regalos para todos

Trabajando en parejas, preparen tres listas de regalos, una para hombres, otra para mujeres y otra para hombres y mujeres. Cada lista debe tener tres o cuatro regalos en cada columna.

Para hombres	Para mujeres	Para hombres y mujeres
?	?	?

Capítulo 9

trescientos ochenta y siete 387

Notes Use overhead transparencies 64 and 65 to present and practice the new words and expressions in *Vocabulario I*.

Activity 1 is intended for listening comprehension practice. Play the audio CD of the activity that is included in the Audio CD Program or use the transcript that appears in the ATE introduction if you prefer to read the activity yourself. A reproducible answer sheet for the activity can be found at the end of the Audio CD Program Manual.

Teacher Resources

  Activity 1

Activities 2–3

Answers

1 1. D; 2. F; 3. A; 4. C; 5. B; 6. E
2 Possible answers:
1. Pueden ser de cuero un cinturón, un bolso o una billetera.
2. Pueden ser de plata unos aretes, una pulsera, un collar o un anillo.
3. Pueden ser de perlas un collar, una pulsera o unos aretes.
4. Answers will vary.
5. Answers will vary.
6. Llevo bufanda cuando hace frío.
7. Un bolso puede ser de material sintético o de cuero.
8. Answers will vary.
3 Answers will vary.

Activities

Expansion
Use overhead transparencies 64 and 65 to introduce the new words and expressions in *Vocabulario I*. Begin by showing students transparency 64 and point to one of the items in the store and identify it in Spanish. Students should repeat after you. Continue with the next item and repeat the process. As a second step, show students transparency 65. Once again identify the objects in Spanish, allowing students to see how each word is spelled.

387

Answers

4 1. Busca un regalo.
2. Busca un regalo bueno, bonito y barato.
3. Busca algo para una mujer.
4. No.
5. Le parece perfecto el perfume.

5 Answers will vary.

6 1. A; 2. A; 3. B; 4. A; 5. B; 6. B

Activities

Critical Listening
Play the audio CD recording of the dialog. Instruct students to cover up the words as they listen to the conversation. Have students look at the photographs and ask several individuals to state what they believe is the main theme of the conversation.

Expansion
Additional questions *(Algo personal): ¿Te gusta comprar regalos?; ¿Prefieres comprar regalos en el centro comercial o en las tiendas?; ¿Para quién compras regalos más caros, para la familia o para los amigos?; ¿Por lo general, ¿qué compras para regalos—ropa, artículos personales, aparatos eléctricos, discos compactos?*

Prereading Strategy
Instruct students to cover up the dialog with one hand and to look at the photographs. Ask them to imagine where the conversation takes place and what the people are saying to one another.

Diálogo I
Busco un regalo

DANIEL: Busco un regalo, bueno, bonito y barato.
SEÑORA: ¿Para hombre o para mujer?
DANIEL: Para mujer.

SEÑORA: ¿Qué le parece una pulsera de oro?
DANIEL: No. Ella dijo que joyas no.

SEÑORA: Entonces, ¿qué le parece este perfume?
DANIEL: El perfume es perfecto.

4 ¿Qué recuerdas?

1. ¿Qué busca Daniel?
2. ¿Qué tipo de regalo busca?
3. ¿Para quién busca algo Daniel?
4. ¿Va a comprar Daniel una pulsera de oro?
5. ¿Qué le parece perfecto?

5 Algo personal

1. Cuando buscas un regalo, ¿lo buscas bueno, bonito y barato? Explica.
2. ¿Piensas que es más fácil comprar un regalo para un hombre o una mujer?
3. En tu opinión, ¿qué regalos piensas son para hombres? ¿Y para mujeres?

¡Extra!

En otras palabras

el anillo	*la argolla, la sortija*
los aretes	*los zarcillos, los aros, los pendientes*
el bolso	*la cartera, la bolsa, el monedero*
el material sintético	*el plástico, el acrílico*
el paraguas	*la sombrilla*
el pijama	*el payama/el piyama*
la pulsera	*el brazalete*

6 Bueno, bonito y barato

 Selecciona la letra de la ilustración que corresponde con lo que buscan las siguientes personas.

A   **B**

Notes This dialog and activities 4, 5 and 6 have been recorded by native speakers and are included in the *Navegando* Audio CD Program. A reproducible student answer sheet for activity 6 is available at the end of the Audio CD Program Manual.

Cultura viva

Ecuador, país de maravillas naturales

Ecuador is located southwest of Colombia and north of Peru. The equator *(ecuador)*, which is located high in the Andes Mountains, cuts through the country just a few miles north of the nation's capital, Quito. A monument here marks the dividing point between the Northern and the Southern Hemisphere.

Quito, Ecuador.

Soy de las Islas Galápagos.

Ecuador was once part of the Incan Empire. When he died in the sixteenth century, the Incan emperor Huayna Cápac divided the empire between two sons: Atahualpa ruled the portion that was based in Quito, and Huáscar ruled the portion that was based in Cuzco, Peru. Huayna Cápac did not know, however, that the division would weaken the empire and lead to its rapid conquest by the Spanish conquistadors. Ecuador remained Spanish until becoming the first South American nation to declare its independence in 1809.

Remains of Ecuador's colorful past are still evident throughout the nation today. Along with historical reminders of the past, Ecuador offers visitors compelling natural wonders, as well. One of these, the *Archipiélago de Colón,* also known as the Galapagos Islands *(Islas Galápagos),* is located off the coast of Ecuador in the Pacific Ocean. The islands were formed by volcanic eruptions. Today they have become a national park *(parque nacional)* consisting of more than 600 miles of coastline, where an interesting mix of tropical and cold-climate animals *(animales)* and plants *(plantas)* live that cannot be found in any other part of the world.

---

7 Conexión con otras disciplinas: geografía

Completa las frases de la izquierda con una de las frases de la derecha, según la información en la Cultura viva.

1. El ecuador divide...
2. La capital del Ecuador...
3. El Ecuador formó parte...
4. El Ecuador declaró su independencia...
5. Al Archipiélago de Colón se le llama también...
6. Las Islas Galápagos están...
7. En las Galápagos hay...

A. ...en el Océano Pacífico.
B. ...en 1809.
C. ...el mundo en norte y sur.
D. ...un parque nacional con plantas y animales.
E. ...es Quito.
F. ...las Islas Galápagos.
G. ...del imperio inca.

Capítulo 9   *trescientos ochenta y nueve*   **389**

Notes **Connections.** Activity 7 makes the cross-curricular connection to geography.

It is noteworthy that the word *galápagos* is a Spanish term that refers to the large tortoises that live on the islands.

Connections. The six Galapagos Islands are also called *Las Islas Encantadas.* Charles Darwin's observations of life on the islands led to his theory of evolution, which he explained in his book *On the Origin of Species.*

Teacher Resources

 Activity 2

 Activity 4

Answers

7 1. C
2. E
3. G
4. B
5. F
6. A
7. D

Activities

Connections
Show students where Ecuador is located, using the maps in the book or the transparencies that are part of this program.

Expansion
Have a class discussion about Ecuador. You may choose to ask the following questions to stimulate other student questions: *¿Cómo se llama el inca que dividió el imperio entre sus dos hijos?; ¿Cómo se llaman los dos hijos?; ¿Existen los incas hoy?; ¿Existe la cultura india en Ecuador hoy?*

389

Answers

8 1. el bolsito
2. la billeterita
3. el cinturoncito
4. el pañuelito
5. la bufandita
6. el collarcito
7. las botitas
8. los guantecitos
9. el suétercito

9 1. la chaqueta
2. el zapato
3. las joyas
4. el traje
5. la puerta
6. el sombrero
7. la corbata
8. el jardín
9. el hijo

10 Creative self-expression.

Activities

Critical Thinking
Ask students to give the original form of several words: *chiquita (chica), Sarita (Sara), hermanito (hermano).* Then see if students can give diminutive forms for several words: *casa (casita), regalo (regalito), muchacha (muchachita).*

Idioma

Estructura

Diminutives

Indicate affection or convey the idea that something is small by replacing the final vowel of a noun with the endings *-ito, -ita, -itos* and *-itas: Ana (Anita)*. For nouns that end in a consonant, add the endings *-cito, -cita, -citos* or *-citas* to the complete word: *collar (collarcito)*. Additional diminutive endings you may encounter include *-illo, -illa, -uelo, -uela, -ico* and *-ica*. Other words may require a spelling change: *poquito (poco)*.

Although many exceptions exist for the diminutive forms, most are easily recognized: *hotelito (hotel), Daniel (Danielito)*. It is best to learn the variations as you encounter them since they can vary from country to country and even from one person to another within countries.

 Práctica

 8 Todo es pequeñito

Cambia las siguientes palabras al diminutivo.

1. el bolso
2. la billetera
3. el cinturón
4. el pañuelo
5. la bufanda
6. el collar
7. las botas
8. los guantes
9. el suéter

 9 ¿De dónde vienen?

Indica la palabra original.

MODELO el regalillo → el regalo

1. la chaquetilla
2. el zapatico
3. las joyitas
4. el trajecillo
5. la portezuela
6. el sombrerito
7. la corbatica
8. el jardincito
9. el hijuelo

Los guantes.

Comunicación

10 Comprando un regalo con mucho cariño

Imagine you and a close friend are in a department store shopping for a birthday gift for someone you like a lot. Create a conversation using the diminutive to refer to the objects you are considering buying and to convey your affection for the person for whom you are shopping.

MODELO **A:** Mira estas joyitas tan lindas para tu mamita. Me gustan mucho.
B: No me gustan mucho. Me gusta más este bolsito.
A: El bolsito no está mal, pero prefiero aquel collarcito de perlitas.

Notes Explain that the diminutive of *poco* is *poquito*. This spelling change occurs to maintain the original sound of the *c* in *poco*. Ask if students recall any other words that change their spelling from *c* to *qu: buscar → busqué*.

Some adverbs that use the diminutive form include the following: *ahora (ahorita), despacio (despacito)*.

Estructura

Preterite tense of *leer, oír, ver, decir, hacer* and *tener*

The verbs *leer, oír, ver, decir, hacer* and *tener* all have irregularities in the preterite tense. For example, for *leer* and *oír,* an *i* between two vowels changes to a *y.* Both *leer* and *oír* require additional accent marks to separate vowel sounds and to indicate how these words are pronounced. The preterite tense of the verb *ver* uses the regular *-er* verb endings, but without any accent marks.

leer	
leí	leímos
leíste	leísteis
leyó	leyeron

oír	
oí	oímos
oíste	oísteis
oyó	oyeron

ver	
vi	vimos
viste	visteis
vio	vieron

Learning the irregular preterite-tense stem of *decir (dij),* *hacer (hic)* and *tener (tuv)* and the endings *-e, -iste, -o, -imos, -isteis* and *-ieron* will help you when you wish to use the preterite tense of these three irregular verbs.

Note: The *c* in the preterite-tense stem for *hacer* changes to *z* in *hizo; dijeron* is also an exception to the above because no *i* is required for the preterite ending.

decir	
dije	dijimos
dijiste	dijisteis
dijo	dijeron

hacer	
hice	hicimos
hiciste	hicisteis
hizo	hicieron

tener	
tuve	tuvimos
tuviste	tuvisteis
tuvo	tuvieron

 Práctica

11 ¡No oí!

Imagina que estás en una tienda comprando ropa con tu familia y todos te dicen algo al mismo tiempo y no oyes algunos de los comentarios. ¿Qué debes decir?

MODELO mi mamá
¿Qué dijo mi madre? No la oí.

1. tú
2. la Sra. de la tienda
3. mis hermanos
4. mi padre
5. mis hermanas
6. mi prima y mi tío

¿Qué dijo mi madre?

Notes Review the regular preterite tense forms for *-ar, -er* and *-ir* verbs and the preterite tense of *ir* and *ser.* Model and ask for students to give several examples of verbs they already know how to conjugate in the preterite tense before introducing the new irregular preterite tense verbs that appear here.

Review the use of the direct object pronouns before assigning activity 11.

Teacher Resources

 Activity 4

 Activities 6–10

 Activity 3

 Activities 5–8

Answers

11
1. ¿...dijiste...? ...te....
2. ¿...dijo...? ...la....
3. ¿...dijeron...? ...los....
4. ¿...dijo...? ...lo....
5. ¿...dijeron...? ...las....
6. ¿...dijeron...? ...los....

Activities

Cooperative Learning
Give each student an index card to use in a verb drill. Have them choose five different verbs that are irregular in the preterite tense. Include *ser* and *ir* if you want to recycle them as well. Vary the subjects for each verb and write the correct preterite form of each infinitive to agree with its subject: *leer (tú)* = *leíste* (you read), *hacer (nosotros)* = *hicimos* (we did; we made), etc. When finished, students may exchange cards to look for errors and make corrections. Then pair students to drill each other with their verb cards. Collect the cards, double-check for errors and save them to use another time for a quick review before a quiz or when there are a few minutes left in the class period.

12 ¿Qué le(s) gustaría recibir?

Di qué dijeron las siguientes personas que les gustaría recibir de regalo para su cumpleaños, según las ilustraciones.

MODELO

mi padre
Mi padre dijo que le gustaría recibir unos pañuelos.

1. yo   2. mis primos   3. mi tía   4. mi mamá

5. mi hermano   6. nosotros   7. tú   8. Uds.

13 ¿Qué hice?

Di cuáles de las siguientes cosas hiciste o no hiciste ayer.

MODELO leer un libro
Sí, leí un libro ayer./No, no leí un libro ayer.

1. tener que ir a la tienda para comprar pan y leche
2. oír un CD de mi cantante favorito
3. ver televisión
4. hacer la tarea de español
5. decir una mentira
6. comprar un regalo para alguien
7. tener un examen
8. leer una revista

14 Todos hicieron algo

 En parejas, hablen de lo que hicieron las siguientes personas, usando las pistas que se dan.

MODELO tu amigo: leer un libro / y / oír un disco compacto
A: ¿Qué hizo tu amigo?
B: Mi amigo leyó un libro y oyó un disco compacto.

1. Uds.: tener que comprar un regalo / y / hacerlo por la internet
2. tus amigos: hacer la tarea / y / ir a jugar al fútbol con sus amigos
3. tu hermana: tener que comprar unos zapatos cómodos / e / hacer unos quehaceres
4. tú: leer un libro muy interesante / y / ver una película divertida en DVD
5. tu madre: tener que ir a trabajar / y luego / volver a casa a hacer la comida
6. tus tías: hacer un viaje a las Islas Galápagos / pero / olvidar llevar sus trajes de baño

Notes Before doing activity 12, ask students to identify the articles that people would like to receive as gifts. Also, remind students how to use *gustaría:* they should not change the verb form, only the indirect object pronoun that precedes *gustaría.*

Follow up activity 13 with a class discussion of what members of the class did or did not do yesterday.

15 En la tienda por departamentos

Di lo que hicieron algunas personas el fin de
semana en la tienda, según las ilustraciones
y los verbos indicados.

MODELO comprar
Algunas personas compraron paraguas.

1. oír

2. hacer

3. tener

4. arreglar

5. ver

6. leer

✦ Comunicación

16 ¿Qué hicimos?

Trabajando con un/a compañero/a de clase, hablen de lo que hicieron el fin
de semana pasado.

MODELO
A: ¿Qué hiciste el sábado?
B: Leí un libro fascinante.

A: ¿Y qué más hiciste?
B: El sábado oí música por la mañana,
luego tuve que .... Y tú, ¿qué hiciste?

17 ¿Qué tuviste que hacer?

Imagine you and a classmate work at a department store. Yesterday was a very
busy day at the store and you each had to do too many things. Make up activities
and talk with your classmate about all the things each of you had to do.

MODELO
A: Ayer tuve muchas cosas que hacer en la tienda.
B: ¿Qué tuviste que hacer?
A: Para empezar, tuve que llegar muy temprano. Luego, otra persona y yo
tuvimos que arreglar las billeteras, los cinturones y las bufandas en la
sección de regalos antes de abrir. Luego, tuve que....

393

En la caja

 Activities 5–6

 Activity 66

 Activities 11–12

 Activity 4

 Activities 9–10

Activities

Prereading Strategy
Have students look through *Vocabulario II* quickly to find cognates and other words they recognize.

TPR
Ask students to do things with clothing and colors. For example, say *Toca algo azul (rojo, verde,* etc.) and observe to see that students respond appropriately. You may choose to bring in a bag of old clothing, especially items that are out of style, awful colors or unusual sizes as a humorous way to allow students to find and point out colors and items of clothing that you name or describe. As an alternative, you may use paper doll clothing and have students merely touch the item to show comprehension. Use commands such as *toca, ponte, quítate, guarda.*

Vocabulario II
En la caja

Notes Quickly check student comprehension of the text bubbles and boxes that accompany the illustrations on these two pages.

Note the pronunciation of *ahorrar* in *Vocabulario II* by reminding students that the *h* is silent and the *rr* is trilled.

18 ¿Cuál es la respuesta correcta?

 Escoge la letra de la respuesta correcta a lo que oyes.

A
Sí, es una seda
muy buena.

B
Necesita el recibo.

C
Pago con tarjeta
de crédito.

D
No, está en oferta.

E
Son tres dólares con
cincuenta.

F
Sí, voy contigo.

19 Lo opuesto

Completa las siguientes oraciones para decir lo opuesto de las palabras indicadas.

MODELO No compré el anillo *caro,* preferí el anillo <u>barato</u>.

1. No compré ningún perfume *de mala calidad,* compré un perfume __.
2. No pagué *a crédito,* pagué __ en una de las cajas.
3. No me gustó el bolso *de tamaño pequeño,* me gustó el bolso __.
4. No vi los aretes *caros,* vi los aretes __.
5. No vi cinturones *cortos,* sólo vi cinturones demasiado __.
6. No le pagué *al dependiente,* le pagué __.
7. No me gusta ir de compras *contigo,* porque a ti no te gusta ir de compras __.

Notes Activity 18 is intended for listening comprehension practice. Play the audio CD of the activity that is included in the Audio CD Program or use the transcript that appears in the ATE Introduction if you prefer to read the activity yourself.

A reproducible answer sheet for the activity can be found at the end of the Audio CD Program Manual.

Teacher Resources

Activity 18

Answers

18 1. C
2. F
3. B
4. E
5. A
6. D
19 1. de buena calidad
2. en efectivo
3. de tamaño grande
4. baratos
5. largos
6. a la dependienta
7. conmigo

Activities

Expansion
Use overhead transparency 66 to introduce and practice the new words and expressions in *Vocabulario II.*

Prereading Strategy
Play the audio CD recording of the vocabulary and have students repeat the words while showing them overhead transparency 66.

Spanish for Spanish Speakers
Ask students to write a dialog between two friends who want to go shopping in a mall. Make sure they include a variety of stores they want to go to and the things they want to buy.

Students with Special Needs
Model a second sentence for students in activity 19.

Answers

20 1. El perfume está en oferta.
2. Cuesta treinta dólares.
3. Va a pagar en efectivo.
4. El cambio es de diez dólares.
5. Le da el recibo.
21 Answers will vary.
22 1. Sí.
2. No. ...barato.
3. No. ...tarjeta de crédito/en efectivo.
4. No. Muchas gracias.
5. Sí.

Activities

Cooperative Learning
Pair bilingual and nonbilingual students to invent a dialog in which they discuss things they would like to buy at the mall.

Expansion
Additional questions: *¿Qué está haciendo Daniel?; ¿Con una oferta especial el precio es más barato o más caro que el precio normal?; ¿Compras algo en oferta especial si no te gusta?; ¿Te gusta ir de compras solo/sola o con los amigos o la familia?; ¿Tienes una tarjeta de crédito?*

Diálogo II

¿Cómo va a pagar?

DANIEL: ¿Cuánto cuesta el perfume?
SEÑORA: Está en oferta. Cuesta treinta dólares.
DANIEL: Sí, no está caro. Lo llevo.

SEÑORA: ¿Cómo va a pagar? ¿En efectivo o a crédito?
DANIEL: Voy a pagar en efectivo.

SEÑORA: Aquí tiene diez dólares de cambio y su recibo.
DANIEL: Muchas gracias.

20 ¿Qué recuerdas?

1. ¿Qué está en oferta?
2. ¿Cuánto cuesta el perfume?
3. ¿Cómo va a pagar Daniel?
4. ¿Cuánto es el cambio?
5. ¿Qué más le da la señora a Daniel?

21 Algo personal

1. ¿Qué compras en oferta?
2. ¿Prefieres pagar a crédito o en efectivo? Explica.
3. ¿Te gusta dar regalos caros o baratos? Explica.
4. ¿Qué haces con el dinero que recibes de cambio?

22 ¿Sí o no?

¿Son lógicos los diálogos? Corrige lo que no es lógico.

¿Cuánto cuesta el perfume?

Compro camisetas en oferta.

Notes This dialog and activities 20, 21 and 22 have been recorded by native speakers and are included in the *Navegando* Audio CD Program. A reproducible answer sheet for activity 22 is available for your convenience at the end of the Audio CD Program Manual.

Tell students that the adjective *caro* normally is used with the verb *ser*. Here Daniel uses the verb *estar* to emphasize a special sale price.

Cultura viva

De compras en Guayaquil

Para hacer compras en Ecuador, debes ir a Guayaquil. Para las compras modernas está en Guayaquil el Mall del Sol, el centro comercial más grande del Ecuador con más de 187 tiendas, veinticinco restaurantes de comida rápida, cinco bancos, un supermercado grande (Megamaxi), nueve cines, cibercafés, discotecas, tiendas de souvenirs, parques y estacionamiento (parking) para más de 2.000 carros. Es un centro comercial supergigante y muy divertido.

Si te gustan las compras menos modernas y más de artesanía, y no te gustan los centros comerciales, puedes ir al Mercado Artesano de Guayaquil. En el Mercado Artesano hay 280 exhibiciones y puestos de venta (sales stands) donde trabajan sólo

Unos chicos ecuatorianos en el mall.

Una artesana vendiendo su arte.

Unos chalecos (vests) en el Mercado Artesano.

artesanos (las personas que hacen artesanía) creando y vendiendo su arte. Al dar un paseo por las exhibiciones puedes escuchar música ecuatoriana a la vez que admiras los diferentes estilos de los artistas del país.

Como puedes ver, tanto si te gusta la compra moderna y dinámica, como la más tranquila y tradicional, Guayaquil te ofrece infinitas posibilidades.

23 Comparando

Compara el centro comercial Mall del Sol en Guayaquil con un centro comercial de tu ciudad.

Centro comercial Mall del Sol	Centro comercial de tu ciudad
1. 187 tiendas	1. 150 tiendas
2.	2.
3.	3.

Capítulo 9

trescientos noventa y siete 397

Teacher Resources

De compras en Guayaquil

Activity 5

Activities

Expansion

As a follow-up to this reading and to activity 23, tell students that you recently bought a present for a friend and their task is to find out what it is. They may ask a maximum of twelve yes/no questions in trying to identify the mystery gift. The first student to correctly name the gift should then think of another present and the activity is repeated.

Notes You may wish to have students create Venn diagrams for activity 23. See the section *Tú escribes* (page 358) at the end of *Capítulo 8*.

Note that this *Cultura viva* is written in Spanish. Unknown words have been translated and the content has been edited to be interesting and of an appropriate reading level so students will find it enjoyable. All the *Cultura viva* readings in *Navegando 2* are in Spanish.

Answers

24 1. en, sobre
2. de
3. con
4. en
5. para
6. desde
7. sin
8. por

Activities

Critical Thinking
Review the prepositions by asking students to generate original sentences about their school and city (e.g., *Uds. estudian en la biblioteca con amigos; La biblioteca está cerca de/lejos de la cafetería*).

Multiple Intelligences (linguistic/spatial)
Have students think of a memory device and make a visual representation to depict the meanings of the prepositions. For example, a drawing of a male stick figure standing beside a house with the words "There is a lad beside the house" could represent *al lado de*. Ask students to share their ideas with the rest of the class and display the best representations on a bulletin board.

Idioma

Repaso rápido: prepositions

How many of the following prepositions *(preposiciones)* in Spanish do you remember?

preposiciones

a	de	para	con	desde
por	en	sin	hasta	sobre

24 Unos aretes para mi mamá

Completa las siguientes oraciones, escogiendo una palabra apropiada de la lista.

con	de	desde	en
para	por	sin	sobre

1. ¿Cuánto cuestan los aretes que están (1) aquella mesa?
2. Los aretes son (2) plata y cuestan veinte dólares.
3. ¿Va a pagarlos (3) tarjeta de crédito?
4. No, voy a pagarlos (4) efectivo.
5. Los aretes son (5) mi mamá.
6. Mi madre usa aretes (6) pequeña.
7. Ella nunca sale a la calle (7) aretes.
8. Muchas gracias (8) su compra.

Estructura

Using prepositions

You have already learned to use prepositions with prepositional pronouns. For example, prepositional pronouns are sometimes used in combination with the preposition *a* to add emphasis or to clarify the meaning of a sentence: *A mí me gusta comprar todo lo que está en oferta.* The following prepositional pronouns also may be used with the other prepositions you have learned.

los pronombres después de las preposiciones			
sin mí	*without me*	sin nosotros,-as	*without us*
sin ti	*without you*	sin vosotros,-as	*without you*
sin Ud.	*without you*	sin Uds.	*without you*
sin él	*without him*	sin ellos	*without them*
sin ella	*without her*	sin ellas	*without them*

398 *trescientos noventa y ocho* — **Lección B**

Notes Remind students that prepositions connect verbs, nouns and adjectives with their complements. English, like Spanish, uses prepositions as linking words. However, the two languages do not always use the same preposition to convey the same meaning.

Explain that prepositional pronouns are the same as subject pronouns with the exception of *yo* and *tú*, which become *mí* and *ti* after most prepositions. Let students know that *mí* has an accent to distinguish it from the possessive *mi* (my). The pronoun *ti*, however, does not need a written accent.

Two exceptions are the words *conmigo* (with me), which is used instead of *con* followed by *mí*, and *contigo* (with you), which is used instead of *con* followed by *ti*.

¿Quieres ir de compras **conmigo**?   Do you want to go shopping **with me**?
Sí, me gusta ir de compras **contigo**.   Yes, I like to go shopping **with you**.

 ## Práctica

 25 **Un regalo para mi tío**

Completa este correo electrónico con palabras de la lista. Puedes usar las palabras más de una vez.

| conmigo | contigo | ella | él | mí | nosotros | ti |

E-Mail

Archivo   Ver   Mensajes   Ayuda

A...   Amparo
Cc...
Asunto: Regalo para el tío Gonzalo

Hola, prima,
Como tú sabes, el próximo fin de semana es el cumpleaños del tío Gonzalo y quiero ir al centro comercial a comprar un regalo para (1). Te llamé a casa pero parece que estás en la internet. Bueno, sólo quiero saber si quieres venir (2). Me gustaría mucho ir (3) porque tú sabes más sobre (4) que yo. Si voy (5) puedo comprar algo más rápido y va a ser más fácil para (6). ¿Puedes escribirme un correo electrónico ahora mismo para decirme si puedes venir (7)? Sin (8) voy a tomar horas comprando el regalo. Voy a estar en la computadora una hora más. Si no me contestas en una hora, voy sin (9).

Anabel

26 **¿Puedes venir conmigo?**

Trabajando con un(a) compañero/a de clase, alternen en hacer las invitaciones indicadas y en dar excusas para cada invitación.

MODELO al cine
  A: ¿Puedes venir conmigo al cine?
  B: No, no puedo ir contigo porque no tengo dinero.

1. el banco
2. a comprar unos zapatos que están en oferta
3. la tienda de artículos electrónicos
4. la tienda por departamentos
5. el centro comercial
6. a cambiar un cinturón que compré y ahora no me gusta

Capítulo 9   *trescientos noventa y nueve*   **399**

27 En la tienda por departamentos

Da conclusiones apropiadas para las siguientes situaciones, usando las preposiciones y pronombres apropiados. Sigue las indicaciones entre paréntesis.

 Situación: Yo llegué a la tienda a las cuatro de la tarde, tu amigo llegó a las cuatro menos diez y tú llegaste allí a las tres y media. (yo/después de)

Conclusión: (Yo) llegué después de Uds.

1. **Situación:** Tú llegaste primero porque vives más cerca de la tienda que yo. (yo/lejos de)
2. **Situación:** Tu amigo me dijo que vive en la Calle 128, N° 171, y mi familia y yo vivimos en la Calle 128, N° 173. (él/cerca de)
3. **Situación:** Son las cinco de la tarde y mi amigo y yo estamos mirando cinturones en el departamento para hombres y tú y tu amigo están mirando perfumes en el mismo departamento. (Uds./al lado de)
4. **Situación:** Mi amigo y yo nos compramos regalos el uno para el otro. Yo compré un regalo para mi amigo. (él/para)
5. **Situación:** Yo voy a recibir un bolso de mi amigo y tú también vas a recibir un bolso de tu amigo. (nosotras/de)

28 ¿Qué hiciste?

Trabajando con un(a) compañero/a de clase hagan mini-diálogos, tomando elementos de cada columna para hablar de lo que hiciste en días pasados.

MODELO **A:** ¿Adónde fuiste después de las clases?
B: Fui a la biblioteca.

A: ¿Quién fue contigo?
B: Mi hermano Pedro.

A	**B**	**C**
antes de venir aquí	la tienda por departamentos	mis padres
ayer por la noche	de compras	nadie
después de las clases	la tienda de artículos electrónicos	mi hermano/a
el domingo por la mañana	el cine	mi tío/a
el sábado por la noche	el centro comercial	mis abuelos
el viernes por la tarde	la biblioteca	mi primo/a
la semana pasada	el parque	mi amigo/a

¿Fuiste al cine?

Notes Point out the abbreviation N^o (for *número*) in activity 27.

Activity 27 develops higher-order thinking skills.

Comunicación

29 Fuimos de compras

Trabajando con un(a) compañero/a de clase, hablen de la última vez que fueron de compras. Pueden hablar de lo que compraron, para quién lo compraron y con quién fueron.

MODELO **A:** ¿Cuándo fue la última vez que fuiste de compras?
B: Fui el sábado pasado.

A: ¿Qué compraste y para quién?
B: Compré unos aretes para mi mamá.

A: ¿Con quién fuiste?
B: Fui contigo.

Fui de compras el sábado pasado.

30 De compras

Trabajando con un(a) compañero/a de clase, preparen un diálogo de cinco o seis oraciones sobre un día de compras. Uno de Uds. puede preguntar si la otra persona quiere ir contigo o no. Luego, pueden hablar de lo que van a comprar, el precio, la calidad, el tamaño y cómo van a pagar. Recuerden usar en forma apropiada las preposiciones.

MODELO **A:** ¿Te gustaría ir de compras conmigo al centro comercial?
B: Sí, claro, voy contigo. ¿Vas con tu hermana?
A: No, voy sin ella.
B: ¡Qué lástima! ¿Qué vas a comprar?

31 Seguimos de compras

In groups of six to eight, form concentric circles so three or four students in an inside circle face the same number of students in an outside circle. Then the opposing pairs of students should take turns asking and answering what each of you bought the last time you went shopping and what each of you would like to buy when you return there. Take notes as your partner speaks. Then students in the outer circle move one to the right and begin a similar conversation with the new partner. Continue until you have spoken with everyone in the other circle. One person from each circle should report the findings to the class.

MODELO **A:** ¿Qué compraste la última vez que fuiste de compras?
B: Compré un bolso de material sintético para mí.

Lectura personal

Cantantes y grupos musicales

Dirección http://www.emcp.com/músico/ola/e.diario-9.htm ▲ Archivo Edición Ver Favoritos Herramientas Ayuda

página principal   miembros   e-diario

Grupo musical La OLA

Nombre: Xavier Rodríguez Guerra
Edad: 18 años
País natal: Estados Unidos
Artículo de ropa favorito: sombreros
Artículo de ropa que nunca usa: pantalones de cuero

Estamos en Ecuador, un país muy lindo. Después del concierto, el grupo se fue de compras a Quito. Yo también me fui de compras pero no a una tienda por departamentos con escaleras mecánicas y todo eso. Yo me fui en avión a la provincia de Manabi, que está en el centro de las costas ecuatorianas. Manabi tiene playas lindas, pero ésa no es la razón por la cual fui. Estuve en el pueblo[1] colonial de Montecristi, para comprar un sombrero "panamá" para mi nuevo *"look"*. Grandes personajes como Humphrey Bogart, Gary Cooper y Winston Churchill han usado sombreros "panamá". Creo

Hacen sombreros "panamá" en Ecuador.

que se ven muy elegantes. Saben, el sombrero "panamá" no es de Panamá; es un producto de Ecuador. Ecuador empezó a exportar estos sombreros en los años 1800s. En los años 40, era el producto de exportación número uno de Ecuador. Como se vendían[2] en los puertos[3] de Panamá, se les llamó sombreros "panamá", pero su verdadero[4] nombre es sombrero de jipijapa o sombrero de Montecristi. Montecristi produce los mejores sombreros "panamá" del mundo llamados "superfinos". Están hechos con la planta Carludovica palmata, que se hierve[5], se seca[6] y luego se teje[7]. Tardan tres meses en hacer un sólo sombrero. Son bastante caros, pero también son muy *"cool"*, ¿no creen?

[1]town [2]were sold [3]ports [4]real [5]boil [6]dry [7]weave

32 ¿Qué recuerdas?

Identifica cada uno.

1. el producto de exportación número uno de Ecuador en los cuarenta
2. sombrero de jipijapa
3. Manabi
4. Montecristi
5. Carludovica palmata

33 Algo personal

1. En tu opinión, ¿son los sombreros "panamá" elegantes? ¿Por qué sí o por qué no?
2. Donde tú vives, ¿hay un centro de producción de ropa? ¿Qué artículos de ropa hacen o venden?
3. Imagina que quieres tener un nuevo "look". Describe tu nueva ropa.

• Panama hats are really from Ecuador. Can you think of other products (such as foods) that have a country in their names even though they did not originate from that country? How do you think this happens?

¿Qué aprendí?

Visit the web-based activities at www.emcp.com

Autoevaluación

As a review and self-check, respond to the following:

1. Name at least three items sold in a mall department store.
2. Name something that can be made of gold, silver or pearl.
3. Imagine you are buying a gift for your best friend. Describe the item you purchased.
4. Say at least three things you read, heard or saw yesterday.
5. The last time you made a purchase, did you pay cash or did you use credit?
6. Imagine you are shopping in a Spanish-speaking country. How would you ask how much an item costs and if it is on sale?
7. Say two things you learned about Ecuador.

Palabras y expresiones

Para describir
barato,-a
bastante
caro,-a
corto,-a
demasiado
largo,-a
lindo,-a
perfecto,-a
sintético,-a

En la tienda
el anillo
el arete
el ascensor
la billetera

el bolso
la bufanda
la caja
la calidad
el cambio
el cinturón
el collar
el crédito
el cuero
el dependiente,
   la dependienta
el efectivo
la escalera mecánica
la joya
el material

mecánico,-a
la oferta
el oro
el pañuelo
el paraguas
el perfume
la perla
la plata
la pulsera
el recibo
el regalo
el tamaño
la tarjeta (de crédito)

Verbos
ahorrar
cambiar
pagar
recibir
usar

Expresiones y otras palabras
a crédito
conmigo
contigo
en efectivo

Venden aretes, collares y otras joyas.

Un paraguas negro.

Notes Encourage students to find out more about Ecuador by going to the following Web sites:

Organization of American States
http://www.oas.org
Embassy of Ecuador
http://www.ecuador.org

general travel information
http://www.expedia.com
Virtual Countries, Inc.
http://www.ecuador.com/macie.html

Teacher Resources

Activity 14

Information Gap Activities
Postcard Activities
Funciones de Comunicación

Answers

Autoevaluación
Possible answers:
1. las bufandas, las billeteras, los paraguas
2. Un anillo puede ser de oro.
3. Le compré unos guantes de cuero.
4. Leí el periódico....
5. Pagué en efectivo por las cosas que compré.
6. ¿Cuánto cuesta? ¿Está en oferta especial?
7. La capital del Ecuador es Quito....

Activities

Pronunciation (*el sonido* ch)
In Spanish, *ch* sounds like the English *ch* in **church.** It never sounds like the combination *ch* in **machine** or in **chemistry.** Model these words with students: *archipiélago, chisme, chica, chorizo, Conchita, muchacho.*

Spanish for Spanish Speakers
Ecuador is one of the OPEC nations. Have students investigate and prepare a report on the impact that petroleum had on the Ecuadorean economy during the 1970s.

Preparación
1. A
2. C
3. B

Activities

Critical Thinking
To further reinforce the importance of visual organization to content, ask students to describe the typical format and related information for the following items: a job application, a recipe, a movie poster.

Multiple Intelligences (logical-mathematical)
Have students find out the value in dollars for the *balboa* (Panamanian currency) and for the *sucre* (currency of Ecuador). Sources for currency exchange rates include the business section of the local paper, the *Wall Street Journal,* other newspapers or the Internet. The school media specialist may be able to help students find other sources for exchange rates as well.

¡Viento en popa!

Tú lees

Estrategia

Using visual format to predict meaning
Visual details of printed information such as the style and format of printed media can tell you a lot about its probable content. For instance, the format of a letter will indicate whether it is for business or if it is personal. Similarly, cartoons are easily recognized by the style of the illustration and the way the contents appear on the page. Advertisements and brochures can differ greatly from one another depending on the intended population. Before starting to read, look at the layout, the artwork, the pictures, the titles and the format of the writing for hints about its content and meaning.

Preparación

Observa el título, el arte y la forma de esta lectura y contesta las siguientes preguntas.

1. ¿Qué tipo de lectura es ésta?
   A. Es un anuncio *(ad)*.
   B. Es un artículo *(article)* de periódico.
   C. Es una encuesta *(survey)*.
2. ¿Qué venden?
   A. Venden artículos electrónicos.
   B. Venden frutas y verduras.
   C. Venden ropa y servicios.
3. ¿Para quién es lo que venden?
   A. Para hombres.
   B. Para hombres, mujeres y jóvenes.
   C. Para mujeres.

Las rebajas de Danté

Las fabulosas rebajas de Danté te ofrecen grandes ahorros en ropa casual para todos. Tenemos grandes rebajas del 20%, 30%, 40% y hasta el 50%. Aquí puedes conseguir la ropa que necesitas para ir al cine, las fiestas y al colegio. Tenemos todos los estilos que te gustan en todas las marcas y colores.

Servicios generales

❖ Sastrería
❖ Pedidos especiales de vestidos
❖ Sorteos

❖ Danté Café
❖ Abrimos los domingos
❖ Tarjeta de crédito Danté

Notes *Almacenes Danté* is a large department store in Panama. You may wish to inform your students that they can visit the Web site for the store by searching the term *Almacenes Danté* in the search box of any browser. (See the *Navegando 1* ATE Introduction for suggested browsers or use one of your choosing.)

ESPIRAL
CENTRO COMERCIAL

SHOPPING CENTER

CENTRO COMERCIAL
ESPIRAL

Un centro comercial en Quito, Ecuador.

¿Adónde vas de compras con más frecuencia?

A ¿Qué recuerdas?

1. ¿En qué tipo de ropa puedes ahorrar dinero si la compras en esta tienda?
2. ¿De cuánto son las rebajas en esta tienda?
3. ¿Para ir a qué tipo de lugares puedes comprar ropa en Danté?
4. ¿Qué servicios tiene esta tienda?

B Algo personal

1. ¿Qué piensas del anuncio?
2. ¿Para qué tipo de personas piensas que es este anuncio?
3. ¿Buscas anuncios con rebajas antes de ir de compras? Explica.
4. ¿Qué tipo de anuncios te gustan?
5. ¿Adónde vas de compras con más frecuencia?

Capítulo 9

cuatrocientos cinco **405**

Tú escribes

Estrategia

Indicating sequence
You have already learned to use transition words to make your writing flow smoothly. When writing about past activities or events, transition words can indicate the sequence in which actions occurred. Some sequence words you may want to use in your writing include the following: *primero* (first), *luego* (later, then), *antes de* (before), *después de* (after), *finalmente* (finally).

Shopping centers and malls are more than just convenient places to shop. Going to a *centro comercial* often turns into a social event that offers shoppers an opportunity to spend time with friends and to meet new people. What does shopping at the mall mean to you? Write a short composition telling about your last visit to the mall *(Mi última visita al centro comercial)*. Include when you went, with whom you went, what places you visited, if you visited a *tienda por departamentos*, what you did, whom you met, what you bought and any other information you wish. Be sure to use connecting words for making smooth transitions and for telling the sequence of events.

Compré una bolsa de cuero en la tienda por departamentos.

Notes Explain that when shopping in most Hispanic countries, shoppers will notice that the clerk who waits on the customer does not usually collect the money for the purchase. Instead, the clerk gives a copy of the bill to the customer. Another copy of the bill, along with the item being purchased, is given by the clerk to the cashier. The customer then stands in line at the cashier's register to pay for and receive the item purchased. Students should be aware that shopping in a store in Ecuador and in other Spanish-speaking countries may take more time and require more waiting in line.

Proyectos adicionales

A Conexión con la tecnología

You learned how to create a dialog journal in the *Tú escribes* activity in the *¡Viento en popa!* section of *Capítulo 2*. Create an electronic dialog journal entry to send to your teacher. Write about your last trip to a *tienda por departamentos* to shop for something special (e.g., clothing for yourself, a gift). You may wish to tell about where and with whom you went shopping, what you purchased and how much you paid. Include any other information you would like and e-mail the journal entry to your teacher.

B Conexión con otras disciplinas: arte y diseño

Imagine you work for an advertising agency. Cut out advertisements and pictures of different clothing items from fashion magazines and newspapers and design a poster-sized advertisement for clothing. Include in your collage various types of clothing in different colors and sizes. Then, working with a classmate, talk about fashion and clothing styles in the advertisement, including what the people are wearing, the colors of each article of clothing and whether you like the item or not. For what type of occasions is the clothing shown appropriate? What age and gender are you targeting with your advertisement?

C Comunidades

How do people in your community dress? Write a short composition describing how young people dress during a specific season of the year. What are the most popular colors and materials? What statement do you think they wish to convey by how they dress?

Unas mujeres en Otavalo, Ecuador.

Unos niños Amish en Ohio.

Teacher Resources

 Situation Cards

 Capítulo 9

Answers

A Creative self-expression.
B Creative self-expression.
C Creative self-expression.

Activities

Connections
Students can learn about both Spanish and science by investigating and preparing a report on the impact of ecotourism on the Galapagos Islands. Ask them to determine and justify whether ecotourism is good or bad for the islands.

Multiple Intelligences (bodily-kinesthetic)
Produce a fashion show. Divide the class into groups and have each group choose one or two students to be *los modelos*. The entire group writes a description of the style, articles of clothing and colors the models are wearing; then, one or two people in the group read the description as the model or models walk into the classroom. Videotape the production and save it to show as a model for future classes.

Notes For further practice with transition words, assign a composition about a real or imaginary trip to Panama or Ecuador. Students should include information on where they went and things that they did.

Connections. Activity B makes the cross-curricular connection to art and design.

Activities

**Multiple Intelligences
(spatial/linguistic)**
Have students prepare a travel
brochure about the Galapagos
Islands. Brochures should include
what visitors can see, how to get
there, lodging, etc. Students can
use their own drawings or cut
pictures from magazines.

Spanish for Spanish Speakers
Ask students to write an essay
describing their favorite gift and
stating who gave it to them and
on what occasion (e.g., their
birthday) they received it.

Repaso

Now that I have completed this chapter, I can...	Go to these pages for help:
describe clothing.	364
identify parts of the body.	364
express disagreement.	374
talk about the past.	374
discuss size and fit.	386
discuss price and payment.	394

I can also...	
talk about life in Panama and Ecuador.	367, 389
ask questions when I do not understand something.	368
talk about personal taste in clothing.	374
use affirmative and negative expressions in conversations.	381
use diminutives to express affection or that something is small.	390

Trabalenguas

Venancio vendía bonitas boinas, bonitas, baratas, embalaba
baberos, bolillos, botas bellas y boinas buenas.

Notes Review the functions and other
objectives in the *Repaso* and assign the
activities and answer questions so students
can prepare for the Chapter Test. Follow
up by reviewing the activities as a class.

Loose translation of the *Trabalenguas:*
Venancio sold pretty berets, pretty cheap;
he packed bibs, bobbins, beautiful boots
and good berets.

Vocabulario

ahorrar to save *9B*

algo something, anything *9A*

el **algodón** cotton *9A*

alguien someone, anyone, somebody, anybody *9A*

algún, alguna some, any *9A*

alguno,-a some, any *9A*

anaranjado,-a orange (color) *9A*

el **anillo** ring *9B*

el **arete** earring *9B*

el **ascensor** elevator *9B*

barato,-a cheap *9B*

bastante rather, fairly, sufficiently, enough, sufficient *9B*

la **billetera** wallet *9B*

el **bolso** purse *9B*

la **bota** boot *9A*

el **brazo** arm *9A*

la **bufanda** scarf *9B*

la **cabeza** head

la **caja** cashier's desk *9B*

la **calidad** quality *9B*

cambiar to change, to exchange *9B*

el **cambio** change *9B*

caro,-a expensive *9B*

el **centro comercial** shopping center, mall *9A*

la **chaqueta** jacket *9A*

el **cinturón** belt *9B*

el **collar** necklace *9B*

combinar to combine *9A*

conmigo with me *9B*

contar (ue) to tell (a story) *9A*

contigo with you *9B*

la **corbata** tie *9A*

corto,-a short (not long) *9B*

el **crédito** credit *9B*

a crédito on credit *9B*

el **cuero** leather *9B*

el **cuerpo** body *9A*

el **dedo** finger *9A*

demasiado too (much) *9B*

el **departamento** department *9A*

el **dependiente, la dependienta** clerk *9B*

el **efectivo** effective *9B*

en efectivo in cash *9B*

la **escalera mecánica** escalator *9B*

estar en oferta to be on sale *9B*

el **guante** glove *9A*

la **joya** jewel *9B*

el **hombre** man *9A*

el **impermeable** raincoat *9A*

la **lana** wool *9A*

largo,-a long *9B*

lindo,-a pretty *9B*

la **mano** hand *9A*

marrón brown *9A*

el **material** material *9B*

las **medias** pantyhose, nylons *9A*

morado,-a purple *9A*

la **mujer** woman *9A*

nada nothing *9A*

nadie nobody *9A*

ni... ni neither... nor *9A*

ningún, ninguna none, not any *9A*

ninguno,-a none, not any *9A*

o... o either... or *9A*

la **oferta** offer *9B*

el **oro** gold *9B*

pagar pay *9B*

el **pañuelo** handkerchief, hanky *9B*

el **paraguas** umbrella *9B*

perfecto,-a perfect *9B*

el **perfume** perfume *9B*

la **perla** pearl *9B*

el **pie** foot *9A*

la **pierna** leg *9A*

el **pijama** pajamas *9A*

la **plata** silver *9B*

prometer promise *9A*

la **pulsera** bracelet *9B*

quedar to remain, to stay *9A*

quedarle bien a uno to fit, to be becoming *9A*

recibir to receive *9B*

el **recibo** receipt *9B*

el **regalo** gift *9B*

la **ropa interior** underwear *9A*

rosado,-a pink *9A*

la **seda** silk *9A*

sintético,-a synthetic *9B*

el **sombrero** hat *9A*

el **suéter** sweater *9A*

el **tamaño** size *9B*

la **tarjeta (de crédito)** credit card *9B*

el **traje (de baño)** swimsuit *9A*

usar to use *9B*

las **vacaciones** vacation *9A*

vender to sell *9B*

el **vestido** dress *9A*

el **zapato bajo** flat shoe *9A*

el **zapato de tacón** high-heeled shoe *9A*

Llevamos las corbatas a la escuela.

Venden ropa interior para mujeres.

Capítulo 9 — *cuatrocientos nueve* **409**

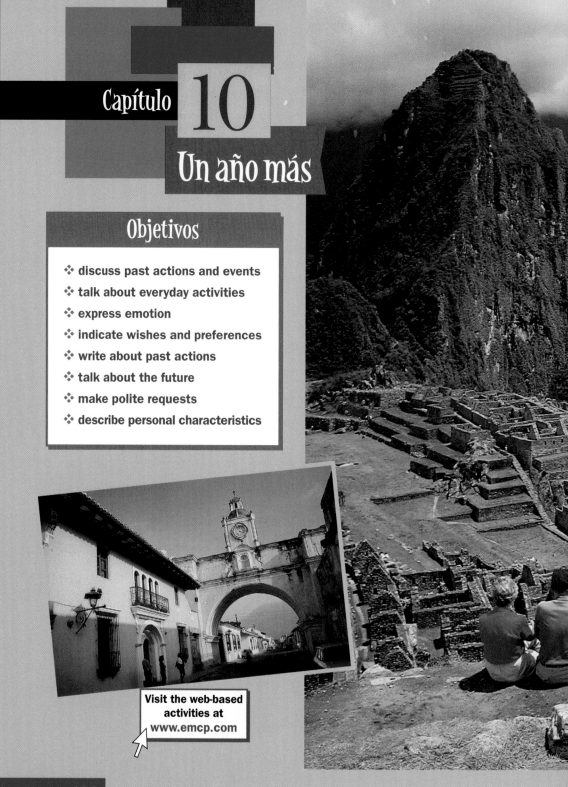

Capítulo 10
Un año más

Objetivos

❖ **discuss past actions and events**

❖ **talk about everyday activities**

❖ **express emotion**

❖ **indicate wishes and preferences**

❖ **write about past actions**

❖ **talk about the future**

❖ **make polite requests**

❖ **describe personal characteristics**

Visit the web-based activities at www.emcp.com

Notes *Capítulo 10* offers a broad review of the content of *Navegando 1*. This final chapter contains no new vocabulary or grammar. Therefore, select specific content you would like to review (e.g., the preterite tense, comparisons, expressions or vocabulary), complete the entire chapter or stop using the book after *Capítulo 9*. The authors have left the choice up to you to decide, according to time constraints and your own particular curricular needs.

The large photograph is of Machu Picchu in Peru. This interesting remain of a past civilization is discussed in greater detail on page 416. The smaller photograph shows the colonial architecture typical of Antigua, Guatemala.

Perú
Nombre oficial: **República del Perú**
Población: **27.483.000**
Capital: **Lima**
Ciudades importantes: **Arequipa, Trujillo**
Unidad monetaria: **el nuevo sol**
Fiesta nacional: **28 de julio, Día de la Independencia**
Gente famosa: **Mario Vargas Llosa, César Vallejo (escritores)**

Guatemala
Nombre oficial: **República de Guatemala**
Población: **12.974.000**
Capital: **Ciudad de Guatemala**
Ciudades importantes: **Antigua, Chichicastenango, Quetzaltenango**
Unidad monetaria: **el quetzal**
Fiesta nacional: **15 de septiembre, Día de la Independencia**
Gente famosa: **Rigoberta Menchú (líder popular)**

Activities

Connections
Using the maps at the front of the book, the *Navegando 1* transparencies or a wall map, conduct a class discussion about some of the geographical features of Peru and Guatemala.

cuatrocientos once 411

Notes If you decide to use this chapter, you may skip activities or expand your review of a particular topic, according to the time you have available and according to student needs. *Capítulo 10* offers your students an opportunity to do interesting projects in which they talk about the past year (what they have learned, what they have done, what some of their favorite classes were). They also will have an opportunity to consider careers, future travel, relationships and other topics that are challenging and enjoyable.

Teacher Resources

 Fue un año divertido
Activities 1–3

 Activities 1–2

 Activity 67

 Activity 1

 Activities 1–2

GV **Activity 1**

Content reviewed in *Lección A*

- talking about the past
- school
- leisure activities
- talking about the future
- *gustar*

Answers

1 1. No hay más tareas.
2. Mario estudió mucho.
3. Le gustó más jugar al fútbol y las clases de historia.
4. Le gustó más la clase de biología.
5. No le gusta la biología.
6. Silvia tiene amigos en el equipo de voleibol.

2 Answers will vary.

3 1. Falso. ...divertido.
2. Cierto.
3. Falso. ...biología.
4. Cierto.

Diálogo

Fue un año divertido

MARIO: ¡Un año más! No hay más tareas por unos meses.
SILVIA: ¡Qué bueno! Fue un año divertido.
MARIO: Estudié mucho.

SILVIA: ¿Qué fue lo que más te gustó?
MARIO: ¡Jugar al fútbol y las clases de historia!
SILVIA: A mí me gustó más la clase de biología.

MARIO: A mí la biología no me gusta.
SILVIA: Sí, yo sé. Bueno, también hice nuevos amigos.
MARIO: ¿Tus amigos del equipo de voleibol?
SILVIA: Sí, y voy a verlos ahora. Adiós.

1 ¿Qué recuerdas?

1. ¿Qué no hay por unos meses?
2. ¿Quién estudió mucho?
3. ¿Qué fue lo que más le gustó a Mario?
4. ¿Qué le gustó más a Silvia?
5. ¿Qué no le gusta a Mario?
6. ¿Quién tiene amigos en el equipo de voleibol?

2 Algo personal

1. ¿Fue tu año divertido? Explica.
2. ¿Te gusta hacer tareas? ¿Por qué?
3. ¿Qué fue lo que más te gustó del colegio este año?
4. ¿Qué deporte jugaste más este año?

3 ¡Fue un año divertido!

 Di si lo que oyes es cierto o falso, según el Diálogo I. Si es falso, corrige la información.

Notes *Capítulo 10* offers you the choice of whether to teach the contents to the entire class or to individuals based upon their interests, abilities or needs. For example, graduating seniors may benefit from some of the topics covered as they prepare for college, work or travel. Gifted and highly motivated students may enjoy doing portions of the chapter independently. In addition, you may have one or two students in class who are planning a trip to Peru or Guatemala and would like to learn about those countries.

Cultura **viva**

El Perú, centro del imperio inca

Peru formed the center point of the Incan Empire *(el imperio inca)*. Located on the Pacific Ocean along the western shores of South America, and situated between Ecuador and Chile, Peru, with its rich gold and silver deposits, quickly attracted many Spanish explorers in the sixteenth century. Although the Spaniards introduced their language and religion, the influence of the Inca civilization is evident throughout the modern-day culture of Peru. Descendants of the Incas still populate the Andean *(Andes)* highlands and

Somos del Perú.

the eastern jungles *(selvas del este)*. Many of them do not speak Spanish and they continue to live as their ancestors did centuries ago. In direct contrast to Peru's indigenous past is the country's contemporary capital, Lima, where 30 percent of Peru's population lives and works. Lima is the most important area of development in the country. However, remnants of the past can be found even in this modern city. One example is the University of San Marcos, which is one of the oldest universities in the world.

Descendientes de los incas viven en Perú.

La iglesia Santo Domingo en Cuzco, Perú.

4 El Perú

Contesta las siguientes preguntas sobre el Perú.

1. ¿De qué imperio fue Perú el centro?
2. ¿Por qué vinieron los exploradores españoles al Perú?
3. ¿En qué zona del Perú viven todavía los descendientes de los incas?
4. ¿Cómo se llama la capital del Perú?
5. ¿Cómo se llama una de las universidades más viejas del mundo?

5 ¡A viajar!

Imagina que te gustaría visitar Perú para practicar tu español. ¿Qué te gustaría ver o hacer allí? Busca información sobre Perú en la internet. Luego, haz un itinerario con fechas, hoteles, restaurantes, lugares interesantes para visitar, precios, etc. Prepara un póster de viaje sobre el lugar y presenta la información a la clase.

¡Oportunidades!

En otro país

Have you ever visited another country? What did you see? What did you do there? After studying Spanish for a year, you probably realize the many opportunities that are available to you to use your language skills. Have you ever considered attending school in a different country for a year? Studying and living in a Spanish-speaking country could increase the Spanish skills you acquired this year.

Capítulo 10   *cuatrocientos trece* **413**

Teacher Resources

 Activity 4

 Activity 3

 Activities 2–4

Answers

4
1. Fue el centro del imperio inca.
2. Vinieron por el oro y la plata.
3. Viven todavía en las zonas de los Andes y las selvas del este del Perú.
4. Se llama Lima.
5. Se llama la universidad de San Marcos.

5 Creative self-expression.

Activities

Cooperative Learning
Have students work in pairs preparing a dialog in which two people are talking about a trip one of them has just taken to Peru.

Expansion
Ask the following questions for discussion: *¿Qué países conoces?; ¿Qué hiciste en ese país/esos países?; ¿Qué lugares visitaste?; ¿Qué país(es) te gustaría visitar? ¿Por qué?; ¿En qué país te gustaría estudiar? ¿Por qué?; ¿Por qué es importante el español?*

Multiple Intelligences (musical)
Play Andean music to students and have them compare it to their favorite music.

Notes Founded in 1551, the University of San Marcos is the oldest university in South America.

Peru's indigenous peoples comprise nearly half of the population. Peru has more indigenous people than any other country in South America. Most indigenous people live in Peru's *Altiplano*, all areas of the Andes above 6,500 feet.

Activity 4

 Activities 5–7

 Activity 3

 Activities 2–3

Answers

6 Creative self-expression.
7 Creative writing practice.
8 Answers will vary. You may also want to conduct the poll again with groups composed of all males and all females. Then compare the results to those of the mixed groups.

Activities

Cooperative Learning
After completing activity 8, have students conduct a similar survey on an issue of interest in your school.

Expansion
Select several students to summarize for the class what they learned about their partner in activity 6.

Spanish for Spanish Speakers
Pair bilingual and nonbilingual speakers for activity 6.

 Proyectos

 6 Una entrevista para el periódico del colegio

Prepara una entrevista para hacerla a un(a) compañero/a de clase para saber sobre sus experiencias y actividades durante este año. Pregúntale sobre las cosas más importantes que hizo, las más divertidas, las más aburridas, lo que más le gustó del año, lo que menos le gustó, algo interesante que le pasó y cualquier otra información de su vida en el colegio o en su casa. Luego, escribe un artículo en español de una página y preséntalo a la clase.

7 Tus experiencias

Escribe un ensayo (*essay*) en español de uno o dos párrafos sobre algo especial que te pasó durante tu vida escolar este año. En tu composición puedes hablar por ejemplo sobre alguien interesante que conociste, una actividad importante que hiciste, una clase que te gustó mucho, un deporte que hiciste o un evento al que fuiste. Añade detalles (*details*) importantes que rodearon (*surrounded*) el hecho (*event*), como por ejemplo, la fecha en que pasó, el lugar, el tiempo que hizo, lo que pasó antes y lo que pasó después, etc.

> ### Estrategia
> **The importance of reviewing**
> It is important to review what you have learned. No one remembers everything they have studied. You have made progress this year with Spanish, and reviewing will help keep everything fresh in your mind.

8 Encuesta estudiantil

 Haz la siguiente encuesta a diez compañeros(as) de clase para averiguar (*to find out*) cuáles fueron las clases favoritas de tus compañeros(as) este año. Primero, completa la encuesta en cualquier clase que no sea la de español y hazte la encuesta a ti mismo y luego a tus compañeros(as) de español del grupo, compartan los resultados. Finalmente, reporten los resultados del grupo a la clase.

Encuesta sobre las clases favoritas del año

Por cada una de las siguientes clases di el número que representa mejor tu opinión.

1. el arte	0	1	2	3	4
2. las ciencias (biología, química, etc.)	0	1	2	3	4
3. la computación	0	1	2	3	4
4. la educación física	0	1	2	3	4
5. el español	0	1	2	3	4
6. los estudios sociales	0	1	2	3	4
7. la historia	0	1	2	3	4
8. el inglés	0	1	2	3	4
9. las matemáticas (álgebra, geometría, etc.)	0	1	2	3	4
10. la música (banda, orquesta, coro, etc.)	0	1	2	3	4
11. (¿otras?) _____	0	1	2	3	4

0 = No sé. No tengo una opinión.
1 = Fue horrible. Me disgustó (*disliked*) mucho.
2 = Fue aburrida. No me gustó mucho.
3 = Fue buena. Me gustó.
4 = Fue excelente. Me gustó mucho.

Notes **Review.** Review the preterite tense with students before assigning activity 6.

Before assigning activity 7, review some of the writing strategies students have learned over the course of the year. Tell students they should apply as many of these strategies as possible when writing their essay.

Review classes and the use of *gustar* before assigning activity 8.

9 Encuesta electrónica

Prepara un e-mail o una página de la Web con una encuesta como la que hiciste en la actividad anterior sobre las clases favoritas. Envíala a otra clase (de tu colegio, de cualquier otro colegio del país o de un país de habla hispana), pidiendo a los estudiantes contestarla también por la internet. Comparte los resultados con la clase, comparando y contrastando los resultados de la encuesta.

10 Un país hispanohablante

Crea un collage que represente al país hispanohablante que encontraste *(found)* más interesante durante tu año de clases de español. Luego, muéstralo a la clase y da una corta explicación del collage.

Un collage de fotos de la Argentina.

11 Tu poesía

Escribe un poema o una canción en español sobre algún tema que aprendiste este año. Después, puedes leer tu poema o cantar tu canción a la clase.

Estoy escribiendo un poema.

Answers

9 Creative self-expression.
10 Creative self-expression.
11 Creative self-expression.

Activities

Cooperative Learning
Tell the class that it is time for a role-reversal: Instead of answering the teacher's questions or a partner's questions, it is their opportunity to ask questions of the teacher. The students should work in pairs to develop appropriate questions; the interview session follows.

Multiple Intelligences (musical)
Ask for volunteers to teach the class a song they know in Spanish. The song may be traditional or contemporary. As an alternative, ask if anyone in class would like to recite the poem or perform the song they wrote for activity 11.

Notes Activity 10 is meant to provide an additional opportunity for visual and artistic learners to excel and show what they have learned during the year.

Ask permission of students to place some of the better collages and poems on the wall or in a public display in the school.

You may also wish to contact the editor and supervisor of the school newspaper to arrange to print one or two of the poems.

Answers

12 1. no
2. sí
3. sí
4. sí
5. no
13 Answers will vary.

Activities

Expansion
Have students look in the media center for pictures of Machu Picchu and bring them in to share with the class.

Lectura cultural

Machu Picchu

Miles de turistas visitan este sitio arqueológico cerca de Cuzco, Perú. ¿Por qué?

Belleza[1]...

Los incas construyeron[2] Machu Picchu entre dos picos[3] altos. Las construcciones de piedra[4] parecen desplegarse[5] sobre la montaña. Abajo, el torrencial río[6] Urubamba corre por la selva amazónica. Es un lugar mágico.

Historia...

Machu Picchu fue construida[7] en el siglo XV cuando el imperio inca se extendía desde Ecuador a Argentina. Se la conoce como la Ciudad Perdida porque permaneció[8] escondida[9] hasta 1911 cuando Hiram Bingham la descubrió[10] intacta.

Misterio...

Machu Picchu, en quechua, quiere decir "Cima[11] Vieja" pero su verdadero nombre no se conoce. Tampoco se sabe la historia o la función de esta ciudad fortificada inca. Algunos creen que fue un monasterio pero como los incas no tenían escritura[12], este lugar estará siempre rodeado[13] de misterio.

Respeto...

La perfección de las paredes de Machu Picchu sorprende[14]. No usaron argamasa[15], y sin embargo[16], la unión entre las piedras es tan perfecta que no se puede introducir ni la hoja[17] de un cuchillo. La construcción de Machu Picchu—con sus paredes perfectas, acueductos, terrazas, observatorios, reloj solar—es evidencia de la sabiduría[18] de los incas.

[1]Beauty [2]built [3]peaks [4]stone [5]unfold [6]river [7]built [8]remained [9]hidden [10]discovered [11]Peak [12]writing [13]surrounded
[14]amazes [15]mortar [16]however [17]blade [18]wisdom

12 ¿Qué recuerdas?

¿Sí o no?

1. Machu Picchu fue la capital secreta del imperio inca en el siglo XV.
2. Hiram Bingham descubrió las ruinas de Machu Picchu en 1911.
3. La geografía de Machu Picchu incluye montañas y selva.
4. La construcción de las paredes de Machu Picchu es perfecta.
5. Los incas sabían escribir y leer.

• Compare and contrast the architecture and landscape of Machu Picchu with that of the city in which you live.

13 Algo personal

1. ¿Qué más sabes sobre Machu Picchu? Comparte algunos datos con la clase.
2. ¿Por qué crees que nadie, ni los conquistadores españoles, descubrieron Machu Picchu hasta 1911? ¿Cuál crees que fue la función de esa ciudad inca?

416 *cuatrocientos dieciséis*   **Lección A**

Notes Before beginning the *Lectura cultural* have students identify cognates and known words.

The Incas were the rulers of the largest native empire of the Americas. At the time of their demise, the Incas consisted of and ruled an estimated twelve million people in much of what is now Peru and Ecuador, as well as in large parts of Chile, Bolivia and Argentina.

¿Qué aprendí?

Autoevaluación

As a review and self-check, respond to the following:

Visit the web-based activities at www.emcp.com

1. Use the preterite tense to state six things you did this year.
2. State four things you learned about Peru.
3. Name two opportunities you have because you know Spanish.
4. Why is it important to review what you have learned?
5. Summarize the results of the surveys you did about favorite classes for activities 8 and 9.
6. State two things you learned about Machu Picchu.

Lima, la capital de Perú.

Unas paredes en Machu Picchu.

¡Aprendimos mucho este año!

Capítulo 10 · *cuatrocientos diecisiete* **417**

Notes Students can find out more about Cuzco and Machu Picchu by visiting these Web sites:

Cuzco http://www.peru.com/cuzco/
Machu Picchu general information
http://www.machupicchu.org

Teacher Resources

Activity 10

Activities 4–5

**Information Gap Activities
Postcard Activities**
Funciones de Comunicación

Answers

Autoevaluación
Answers will vary.

Activities

Pronunciation *(las letras l e y, y el sonido ll)*

The sound of *l* in Spanish is similar to the sound of *l* in English, but shorter. Model several words for students: *la, lavar, limpiar, lista, lugar, el, abril, telenovela.* In Spanish, *ll* has a sound that is similar to the English *y* as in **yet.** Have students practice the sound by having them pronounce the following words: *ella, paella, silla, olla, llueve, cuchillo, llegan, Guillermo, vainilla.* The letter *y* in Spanish is similar to the English *y* in **yet,** when preceding a vowel: *ayudar, ya, yo, mayo, playa, oyendo, leyendo.* When following a vowel, the Spanish *y* sounds like an *i.* This usually happens at the end of the word: *soy, estoy, hoy, hay, doy, voy, muy.*

Lección B

Guatemala

Diálogo

¿Adónde van de vacaciones?

LUIS: Hola, Inés.
INÉS: Hola, Luis. ¿Qué hiciste el sábado?
LUIS: Tuve que ayudar a mis padres.

INÉS: ¿Van a ir de vacaciones?
LUIS: Vamos a ir a las ruinas de Tikal.
INÉS: Fui a Tikal el año pasado. Me gustó mucho.

LUIS: Y tú, ¿qué vas a hacer en las vacaciones?
INÉS: No sé. Me gustaría ir a California a la casa de mi tía, o trabajar en la tienda de mi padre.
LUIS: Pienso que debes ir a California. Va a ser más divertido.

1 ¿Qué recuerdas?

1. ¿Qué hizo Luis el sábado pasado?
2. ¿Adónde va Luis de vacaciones?
3. ¿Adónde fue Inés el año pasado?
4. ¿Adónde le gustaría a Inés ir de vacaciones?

2 Algo personal

1. ¿Qué hiciste el sábado pasado?
2. ¿Qué vas a hacer en las vacaciones?
3. ¿Adónde te gustaría ir de vacaciones?
4. ¿Piensas que trabajar durante las vacaciones es una buena idea?

3 ¿Quién dijo qué?

 ¿Quién dijo lo siguiente, Inés o Luis?

¡Extra!

Me gustaría

Remember to use *gustaría* combined with *me, te, les, nos* and *les* in order to make a request, to politely express a wish or to ask about another person's wishes.

Me gustaría ir a California.
¿Te gustaría ir de vacaciones?

Notes Before beginning the dialog, review the preterite tense, family vocabulary, the use of *tener que*, the *futuro próximo* and adjective-noun agreement.

Cultura viva

Guatemala, tierra maya

Tikal, Guatemala.

One aspect of Guatemala that fascinates anyone who visits the country is that Guatemala is the land of the Maya Indian civilization. Although the ancient Mayan civilization disappeared mysteriously, traces of the advanced Mayan culture remain today. The Mayans had an extensive knowledge of astronomy, mathematics and architecture. Tikal, one of the most well-known Mayan cities, was founded around 700 B.C. The Mayan languages (mainly *quiché*) and traditions are still very much alive among the Mayans in today's Guatemala. The colors and patterns of the traditional ceremonial costumes that many Mayan descendants wear are visible evidence of one tradition that has been passed on for many years from one generation to the next.

The cities of *Antigua, Chichicastenango, Huehuetenango* and *Quetzaltenango* still contain remnants of the Spanish colonial period, which started in 1524. The capital, Guatemala City *(Ciudad de Guatemala)*, was founded in 1776, and in 1821 the region declared its independence from Spain.

Today Guatemala offers a mix of old and new, rustic and urban. The modern capital is the commercial, industrial, educational and governmental center of the country. However, Guatemala's rich farmland serves as the main source of income for the country's 14 million inhabitants, just as it has for centuries.

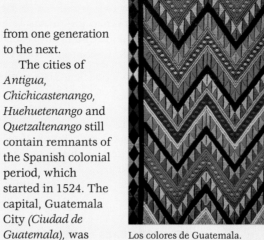

Los colores de Guatemala.

Unas chicas mayas.

4 Guatemala, tierra maya

Di si las siguientes oraciones sobre Guatemala son ciertas o falsas.

1. Guatemala es un centro de la civilización maya.
2. Los mayas estudiaron astronomía, matemáticas y biología.
3. La ciudad más famosa del imperio maya es Tikal.
4. La lengua maya es el español.
5. Antigua es una ciudad muy moderna.
6. La capital de Guatemala es la Ciudad de Guatemala.

Activity 4

Activity 4

Activity 3

Answers

4 1. Cierta.
2. Falsa.
3. Cierta.
4. Falsa.
5. Falsa.
6. Cierta.

Activities

Expansion
Assign students to research and write a report on the work of Nobel Peace Prize winner Rigoberta Menchú.

Spanish for Spanish Speakers
Students should write a short composition in Spanish summarizing what they know about Guatemala. Expand the activity by having students seek out additional information about Guatemala on the Internet and at the library.

Technology
Ask students to search the Internet for pictures of the sites mentioned here. They should print them out on a color printer and bring them in to share with the class. Display the best ones on a bulletin board.

Notes Belize, situated to the east of Guatemala, is the only English-speaking country in Central America.

Antigua's Spanish colonial architecture, particularly its churches, is a major tourist attraction. A major earthquake struck the city in 1976.

Tell students that numerous Mayan ruins are located in Mexico's Yucatan Peninsula near Cancún. They include Chichén Itzá, Uxmal and Tulum.

Chichicastenango is known for its colorful market held every Sunday and Thursday. The market is described later in this chapter in the *Lectura personal*.

Answers

5 Answers will vary.
6 Creative writing practice.
7 Answers will vary.

Activities

Cooperative Learning
As follow-up to activity 6, ask students to make predictions about their lives in ten to fifteen years: *¿Qué carreras van a tener?*; *¿Dónde van a vivir y trabajar?*; *¿Van a usar el español en sus carreras?*

Multiple Intelligences (linguistic/spatial)
Have students do a variation on the theme for activity 6 by assigning a composition in the past tense to tell what they did last summer. Have them attach a picture or a visual to make their paragraph more interesting and display their work on a bulletin board.

 Proyectos

 5 Otra entrevista para el periódico del colegio

Trabajando con un(a) compañero/a de clase, hazle las siguientes preguntas en combinación con cinco preguntas originales para saber sobre sus planes para el verano. Después de la entrevista, escribe un artículo de uno o dos párrafos sobre los planes de tu compañero/a y léelo a la clase.

1. ¿Cuál de los trabajos de la lista te gustaría hacer este verano?
2. ¿Qué otro trabajo de la lista te gustaría hacer?
3. ¿Tienes experiencia en alguno de estos trabajos? ¿En cuál? ¿Cuánta experiencia tienes?
4. ¿En cuáles de los trabajos de la lista no te gustaría trabajar? Explica.
5. ¿Vas a viajar durante tus vacaciones? ¿Adónde?
6. – 10. ¿...?

- cuidar a niños
- ser salvavidas de una piscina o de una playa
- hacer trabajos de jardinería
- trabajar en un restaurante
- limpiar casas
- trabajar en un supermercado
- pintar casas
- trabajar en una oficina
- reparar autos
- trabajar en una tienda

6 Tus vacaciones de verano

Escribe un ensayo en español de uno o dos párrafos sobre tus planes para las vacaciones. Di qué actividades piensas hacer, con quién las piensas hacer, cuál es la actividad que más te gusta hacer durante el verano, etc. Añade detalles relevantes asociados con cada actividad, como por ejemplo, cuándo piensas hacer la actividad, en dónde, por cuánto tiempo, etc.

 7 Otra encuesta

Haz la siguiente encuesta a diez compañeros(as) de clase para averiguar cuáles son las actividades favoritas de tus compañeros(as) durante el verano. Hazte la encuesta a ti mismo y luego a tus compañeros(as). Añade otras actividades a la encuesta si es necesario. Después, en grupos de cuatro o cinco estudiantes compartan los resultados. Finalmente, reporten los resultados del grupo a la clase.

Encuesta sobre las actividades favoritas durante el verano				
Por cada una de las siguientes actividades di el número que representa mejor tu opinión.				
dormir	0 1	2	3	4
hacer deportes	0 1	2	3	4
hacer quehaceres	0 1	2	3	4
ir a la playa	0 1	2	3	4
ir al centro comercial	0 1	2	3	4
ir al cine	0 1	2	3	4
jugar a videojuegos	0 1	2	3	4
leer	0 1	2	3	4
nadar en una piscina	0 1	2	3	4
navegar en la internet	0 1	2	3	4
ver la televisión	0 1	2	3	4
viajar	0 1	2	3	4
(¿otras?) _____	0 1	2	3	4

0 = No sé. No tengo una opinión.
1 = Es horrible. Me disgusta mucho.
2 = Es aburrida. No me gusta mucho.
3 = Es buena. Me gusta.
4 = Es excelente. Me gusta mucho.

Notes **Communities.** Activities 5, 10 and 11 provide the basis for a class discussion about career options and work opportunities that students have available to them because of their Spanish skills.

8 Las próximas vacaciones

Trabajando en los mismos grupos de la actividad anterior, creen un collage que represente las actividades favoritas del grupo durante las vacaciones y luego, preséntenlo a la clase.

9 Un proyecto en la internet

Trabajando en grupos de tres a cinco estudiantes, busquen información en la internet sobre algún lugar en un país hispanohablante adonde les gustaría ir de vacaciones. Luego, preparen un póster sobre el lugar, indicando las principales actividades que se pueden hacer allí y creando un slogan para decir por qué creen Uds. que este lugar es el mejor para ir de vacaciones. Finalmente, presenten el póster a la clase.

10 ¿Qué te gustaría ser?

Numera del 1 al 12 las siguientes profesiones en el orden de tu preferencia, siendo la número 1 la que más te gusta y la número 12 la que menos te gusta. Luego, en grupos de tres, compara los resultados de cada persona. Explica por qué crees que ciertas carreras y profesiones son más populares que otras, considerando el salario, los beneficios, las condiciones de trabajo, el horario, etc. Reporta los resultados de tu grupo a la clase.

agricultor/a	hombre/mujer
arquitecto/a	de negocios
artista	ingeniero/a
banquero/a	maestro/a
cocinero/a	médico/a
enfermero/a	programador/a
	veterinario/a

¡Oportunidades!

Pensando en el futuro, las carreras y el español
You are already aware that knowing how to communicate in a foreign language can enhance your career *(carrera)* opportunities. The following are some interesting careers requiring foreign language expertise that you may want to consider investigating:

border patrol agent	journalist
court interpreter	language
customer service representative	teacher
foreign broadcaster	lawyer
foreign diplomat	travel
hotel sales manager	agent
imported clothing merchandiser	

11 Tu futuro

Escribe uno o dos párrafos en español sobre la carrera que te gustaría estudiar. En tu composición, debes decir por qué te gustaría estudiar esa carrera y qué características piensas que tienes y son importantes para poder trabajar en esa profesión.

Teacher Resources

 Activities 5–6

 Activities 4–5

 Activities 6–7

Answers

- **8** Creative self-expression.
- **9** Creative self-expression.
- **10** Creative self-expression.
- **11** Creative writing practice.

Activities

Communities
Suggest to students that they talk with their parents about ways they may use Spanish and communication skills they have developed during the year to volunteer in the community. Over the summer, students may decide to volunteer at the local library, using Spanish with Spanish-speaking customers. Start a class discussion of other ways students may be able to participate in community service.

Multiple Intelligences (interpersonal/intrapersonal/linguistic)
Begin a discussion about how students intend to use Spanish in the future. Ask questions and let them express thoughts about places they would like to visit, careers they are now considering and contributions they will be able to make to their community because they know Spanish.

Notes Extend activities 8 and 9 by having students summarize their work in writing.

Communities. Try to locate someone in your community who uses Spanish in his or her job and ask the person to speak to the class. Be sure to have students prepare questions in advance to keep the discussion going.

Review some of the writing strategies students have learned over the course of the year. Encourage students to apply as many of these strategies as possible in the composition for activity 11.

Answers

12
1. En Guatemala viven 6 millones de mayas.
2. El libro sagrado de los mayas quichés se llama el Popol Vuh.
3. La blusa que usan las mujeres mayas se llama el huipil.
4. Los días de mercado en Chichicastenango son los jueves y los domingos.
5. El mercado de Chichicastenango es interesante porque se presencia la cultura maya: los trajes coloridos, las diferentes lenguas, los rituales.

13 Answers will vary.

Activities

Expansion

Ask students to summarize what they have learned to date about Guatemala. Then conduct a class discussion about places in Guatemala and elsewhere in the Spanish-speaking world that they would like to visit.

Lectura personal

Cantantes y grupos musicales

Dirección http://www.emcp.com/músico/ola/e.diario-10.htm ▲ Archivo Edición Ver Favoritos Herramientas Ayuda

página principal   miembros   e-diario

Grupo musical La OLA

Nombre: **Ceci Eugenia Madrigal**
Edad: **18 años**
País natal: **Uruguay**
Pasatiempos: **dormir, comer, escuchar música**

Mercado de Chichicastenango.

Iglesia de San Tomás, Chichicastenango.

El domingo, tempranito por la mañana, tomamos un bus de la Ciudad de Guatemala a Chichicastenango. Nosotros hemos viajado[1] mucho este año y hemos visto[2] muchos mercados pero ninguno como el mercado de Chichicastenango. Es más que un mercado: es un impresionante espectáculo de colores, sonidos y aromas. Miles de indígenas de la región llegan al mercado cada jueves y domingo a vender, comprar, hablar, comer, reír, regatear. Chichicastenango se distingue por sus tejidos[3], particularmente el huipil, blusa femenina de los mayas. Yo me compré una muy colorida y después fui a la plaza. Allí está la iglesia[4] de San Tomás, construída[5] en 1540. Fue en esta iglesia donde un español vio por primera vez el Popul Vuh, el libro sagrado[6] de los mayas quichés. Aunque[7] es una iglesia católica, muchas de las ceremonias y los rituales son mayas. En las escaleras, vi a un hombre maya quemar[8] incienso[9]. En Guatemala viven 6 millones de mayas y hablan 20 lenguas mayas. Presenciar[10] la cultura maya fue una gran manera de concluir nuestra gira mundial.

[1]have traveled [2]have seen [3]weavings [4]church [5]built [6]sacred [7]Although [8]burn [9]incense [10]To witness

12 ¿Qué recuerdas?

1. ¿Cuántos mayas viven en Guatemala?
2. ¿Cómo se llama el libro sagrado de los mayas quichés?
3. ¿Cómo se llama la blusa que usan la mujeres mayas?
4. ¿Cuáles son los días de mercado en Chichicastenango?
5. ¿Por qué es el mercado de Chichicastenango interesante?

• Compare the market in Chichicastenango with a place in your town where people go to buy, talk, eat, laugh. What are the similarities? What are the differences?

13 Algo personal

1. ¿Hay un mercado en tu comunidad? ¿Qué venden allí?
2. ¿Existe una cultura indígena en tu comunidad? ¿Cómo es su traje tradicional?
3. ¿Cuándo fue la última vez que oliste incienso? ¿Dónde fue?

422 *cuatrocientos veintidós* **Lección B**

Notes **Connections.** This activity makes cross-curricular connections to geography and history.

The embroidered garments that are worn by the Maya today have a signature pattern that identifies them as members of a particular community. Each village has a characteristic woven or embroidered design. Often these ornate designs form a cross when the blouse or shirt is open and flat. The cross shape represents eternal life and the four cardinal points, the four winds and the four phases of the moon.

¿Qué aprendí?

Autoevaluación
As a review and self-check, respond to the following:

Visit the web-based activities at www.emcp.com

① Where is Tikal?

② State four things you learned about Guatemala.

③ Tell what you are going to do this summer. Say where you are going to go, whom you are going to be with and what you are going to do there.

④ Summarize the results of the survey you did about favorite summer activities for Activity 7.

⑤ Name a place in a Spanish-speaking country you would like to go for vacation. Why would you like to go there?

⑥ Name three careers that may be open to you because you know Spanish.

⑦ What do you know about Chichicastenango?

Tikal, Guatemala.

Venden artesanías en Guatemala.

Mercado de Chichicastenango, Guatemala.

Capítulo 10 *cuatrocientos veintitrés* **423**

Teacher Resources

Activities 6–8

Activities 4–5

Information Gap Activities
Postcard Activities
Funciones de Comunicación

Answers

Autoevaluación
Possible answers:
1. Está en Guatemala.
2–7. Answers will vary.

Activities

Pronunciation *(las letras* d y t)
The letter *d* is similar in Spanish and in English, but in Spanish the tip of the tongue touches the inside of the upper front teeth, not the palate. Have students try these words: *damas, deber, décimo, deportista, desde, día, dibujar, donde.* After a vowel, *d* is pronounced much like the *th* in the English word **mother.** Have students practice the sound by saying these words: *nublado, poder, rápidamente, todavía, vida, usted.* The Spanish *t* is also formed by touching the tip of the tongue to the inside of the upper front teeth. The sound is much like the *t* in the English word **stop.** Students can practice the sound by saying the following words: *continuar, estación, carta, tener, tiempo, tonto.*

Notes Rigoberta Menchú and Miguel Ángel Asturias are two well-known Guatemalans. Menchú is an advocate for the indigenous people of her country and the winner of the 1992 Nobel Peace Prize; Asturias received the Nobel Prize in literature in 1967.

The currency of Guatemala is the *quetzal,* which is also a typical bird of the region.

¡Viento en popa!

Tú lees

Conexión con otras disciplinas: música

Estrategia

Strategy summary
You have learned several ways of understanding different types of Spanish narratives. You know how to use cognates, you have learned to anticipate possible vocabulary and you have learned to gather information by skimming the content before starting to read. Use these techniques to read *Es sólo una cuestión de actitud* sung by La Ola.

Preparación
Contesta las siguientes preguntas como preparación para la lectura de la canción.

1. ¿Qué crees que quiere decir el título de la canción?
2. ¿Cuál es el tema principal de la canción?

Es sólo una cuestión[1] de actitud

Por Fito Páez

Es sólo una cuestión de actitud,
si lo cuentas no se cumple el deseo[2].
Es sólo una cuestión de actitud,
caballero, ¿me podría[3] dar fuego[4]?

Es sólo una cuestión de actitud
atreverse[5] a desplazarse[6] en el tiempo.
Es sólo una cuestión de actitud
entender[7] lo que está escrito en el viento.

Es sólo una cuestión de actitud
ir con taco aguja[8] en pista de hielo[9].
Es sólo una cuestión de actitud
recibir los golpes[10], no tener miedo.

Es sólo una cuestión de actitud
y no quejarse[11] más de todo, por cierto.
Es sólo una cuestión de actitud
atreverse a atravesar[12] el desierto[13].

Notes The song *Es sólo una cuestión de actitud* has been recorded and is included in the Audio CD Program. Consider playing the recording as students follow the words in the *Tú lees*.

Hay un pozo profundo[14] en la esquina[15] del sol,
si caés[16], la vida te muele a palos[17].

Tengo rabia[18], que todo se pase y adiós
mis peleas[19] por estar a tu lado.

Cuando vos decidís elegir[20] la razón
yo prefiero siempre un poco de caos.

Soy tu rey[21], soy tu perro, soy tu esclavo[22]
y soy tu amor,

soy tu espejo[23] mirando el otro lado.

Es sólo una cuestión de actitud
reírse[24] del fracaso[25] y del oro.

Es sólo una cuestión de actitud
no tener nada y tenerlo todo.

Es sólo una cuestión de actitud
y nunca nadie sabe nunca nada,
para colmo[26].

Es sólo una cuestión de actitud,
espada[27], capa[28], torero[29] y toro[30].

[1]It's only a matter of [2]the wish will not come true [3]could [4]light [5]to dare [6]to travel [7]understand [8]stiletto heels [9]ice arena [10]receive a beating [11]not complain [12]to cross [13]the desert [14]deep well [15]corner [16]if you fall [17]life gives you a beating [18]I am mad [19]fights [20]to choose [21]king [22]slave [23]mirror [24]to laugh [25]failure [26]to top it all off [27]sword [28]cape [29]bullfighter [30]bull

A ¿Qué recuerdas?

Completa las frases de la izquierda con una de las frases de la derecha, según la canción *Es sólo una cuestión de actitud*.

1. si lo cuentas...
2. caballero,...
3. atreverse a...
4. entender...
5. recibir los golpes,...
6. Tengo rabia,...
7. soy tu espejo...
8. reírse...

A. ...¿me podría dar fuego?
B. ...lo que está escrito en el viento
C. ...mirando el otro lado
D. ...que todo se pase y adiós
E. ...no se cumple el deseo
F. ...desplazarse en el tiempo
G. ...del fracaso y del oro
H. ...no tener miedo

B Algo personal

1. ¿Qué piensas de esta canción? ¿Te gusta? Explica.
2. ¿Piensas que en la vida todo es cuestión de actitud? Explica.
3. ¿Qué actitud puedes cambiar hoy para hacer tu vida mejor?
4. ¿Te gustan las canciones con mensajes para pensar? ¿Por qué sí? ¿Por qué no?

Answers

A 1. E; 2. A; 3. F; 4. B;
   5. H; 6. D; 7. C; 8. G
B Answers will vary.

Activities

Pronunciation (*las letras* ca, co, cu, que y qui)
Practice the sound of the letter combinations *ca, co, cu, que* and *qui* by noting for students that the English sound of the consonant *k*, just like the sound of *p*, is explosive: that is, if you hold your hand over your mouth when you pronounce them, you will feel a slight puff of air. Note, however, that in Spanish this does not occur. Have students say and compare the English words **café, capital, card, kiss** and **quality** with the Spanish words *cada, cocina, cuarto, que* and *quince*, which begin with a similar sound, but without the puff of air that occurs in the English words. To help students who are experiencing difficulty avoiding the explosive burst of air, have them repeat *tatatata*, then *cocococo*, until they are able to say *taco* without the puff of air. Then have students practice the following sentences: *¿Quién está comiendo en el comedor?; No sé, pero Carlota está comiendo coco en la cocina.*

Notes Rodolfo "Fito" Páez (born in Rosario, Argentina) is the composer of this song. He is very famous throughout the Spanish-speaking world. Fito started his first rock band (Staff) during his teen years. His songs and lyrics have been popular for more than thirty years and both new and old Hispanic rock bands often borrow his materials.

Tú escribes

Estrategia

Defining your purpose for writing
Before you begin a writing assignment, it is a good idea to identify your purpose. Then keep your purpose in mind throughout the writing process as you brainstorm your topic, formulate your rough draft and edit your finished product.

The purpose of this writing assignment is to describe yourself, using the format of an acrostic poem. In an acrostic poem, certain letters of each line spell out the letters of a specific word the author has in mind.

Use the letters of your name or nickname, in their correct order, as your acrostic word. Design the pattern for placing a letter of your name in each line. For instance, you might choose to highlight the first letter of each line, the first letter of the last word in each line, etc.

Then, in the lines, include some personal information you have learned this year to describe your personality, your appearance and your preferences. Also, work in some information about what you are going to do in the future. Be sure to make the letters of your acrostic word stand out in the poem (as was done in the poem on this page). Finally, you may wish to accompany your poem with artwork or graphics to make it more visually appealing.

> Juego al fútbol, al básquetbol, y mucho más.
> Soy un jugador, fuerte y rápido.
> Quiero jugar al fútbol profesional algún día.
> Las matemáticas, no me gustan ni un poquito.

Proyectos adicionales

A Conexión con la tecnología

Prepare an electronic survey about favorite careers or jobs, using an e-mail or a Web page similar to the surveys you completed in this chapter. Ask another class (preferably in a different state or country) to complete the survey and send the results back to you via Internet. Share the information with your classmates, comparing and contrasting the results of your survey.

B Conexión con otras disciplinas: música

Working in pairs, find a song in any language you like. Using the music for the song, create lyrics in Spanish about some aspect of your life (school, vacations, family, etc.). Sing the song to the class.

C Conexión cultural

In groups of three to five students, research a group or culture that is native to your state or region. Find out the name of the group, where they lived, their social activities, number of inhabitants and where any ruins or remains may be found. Share the results with another group of students (a class in another region of the world, for example) and request the same information about civilizations that inhabited their region of the world.

Un indígena de North Dakota.

Ruinas de un pueblo de los Anasazi, indígenas de norteamérica.
(Mesa Verde National Park, Colorado, U.S.A.)

Teacher Resources

 Situation Cards

 Capítulo 10

Answers

A Creative self-expression.
B Creative self-expression.
C Creative self-expression.

Activities

Critical Thinking
Have students complete a culture project in which they look back on the countries studied this year and make a collage that reflects what they have learned about one or more of the nations. A possible theme for the collage is *Mirando hacia el pasado*.

Multiple Intelligences (interpersonal/linguistic/logical-mathematical/spatial)
In groups of four, students should decide what are the main contributions of the Mayas, Aztecs and Incas. Then have them create posters showing the contributions.

Notes Activities A, B and C provide opportunities in keeping with the philosophy and goals of *Navegando 1* for students as they become lifelong learners. These activities encourage students to learn about communities in the world where Spanish is spoken and to begin to make comparisons between the student's background knowledge and the reality of life in the Spanish-speaking world. In addition, students are invited to use what they have learned in Spanish class to establish connections with their neighborhood and with the larger world community.

Activities

Expansion

Review adjective-noun agreement by having students write a composition describing a favorite relative. The composition should address the person's personality, appearance and typical activities. Encourage students to include a photo or drawing of the relative as well.

Repaso

Now that I have completed this chapter, I can...

	Go to these pages for help:
discuss past actions and events.	412
talk about everyday activities.	412
express emotion.	418
indicate wishes and preferences.	418
write about past actions.	418
talk about the future.	421
make polite requests.	421
describe personal characteristics.	426

I can also...

talk about Peru and Guatemala.	413, 419
research a topic in the library and on the Internet.	413
name some personal benefits to learning Spanish.	413
recognize some benefits to reviewing what I have already learned.	414
recognize the importance of reviewing what I have learned.	414
talk about Machu Picchu and Chichicastenango.	416, 422
identify some careers that use Spanish.	421
express myself artistically about what I have learned.	426

Trabalenguas

Pedro Pérez pide permiso para partir para París, para ponerse peluca postiza porque parece puerco pelado.

Notes Students can find out more about Peru by visiting these Web sites:

Organization of American States
http://www.oas.org
Peru Gateway
http://www.peru-explorer.com
PromPerú   http://www.peru.org.pe

general information
http://www.expedia.com

Loose translation of the *Trabalenguas:* Pedro Pérez asks for permission to leave for Paris, to get a wig since he looks like a hairless pig.

¡Vamos a esquiar!

Café de Colombia.

El Angelito, México, D.F.

INSTITUTO PANAMEÑO DE TURISMO

El Morro, San Juan, Puerto Rico.

Teacher Resources

El viaje a Guatemala

Module 4

Episode 10

Testing/ Assessment
Test Booklet
Portfolio Assessment

Activities

Communities
Ask students if they know people who use a foreign language in their professions. Encourage students to interview these individuals and share their findings with the class.

Expansion
Ask students personalized questions that require them to practice forms of *tener que* (they may make up any answers they wish): *¿Qué tienes que hacer hoy?; ¿Qué tienes que hacer mañana?; ¿Qué tienes que hacer este fin de semana?*

Spanish for Spanish Speakers
Have students write a short composition in Spanish summarizing what they know about Peru. Expand the activity by having students seek out additional information about the country on the Internet and at the library.

Notes Students can find out more about Guatemala by visiting these Web sites:

Organization of American States
http://www.oas.org
Visita Guatemala
http://www.terra.com.gt/turismogt/
general information
http://www.expedia.com/

Appendices

Appendix A

Definite articles

	Singular	Plural
Masculine	el	los
Feminine	la	las

Indefinite articles

	Singular	Plural
Masculine	un	unos
Feminine	una	unas

Adjective/noun agreement

	Singular	Plural
Masculine	El chico es alto.	Los chicos son altos.
Feminine	La chica es alta.	Las chicas son altas.

Pronouns

Singular	Subject	Direct object	Indirect object	Object of preposition
1st person	yo	me	me	mí
2nd person	tú	te	te	ti
	Ud.	lo/la	le	Ud.
3rd person	él	lo	le	él
	ella	la	le	ella
Plural				
1st person	nosotros	nos	nos	nosotros
	nosotras	nos	nos	nosotras
2nd person	vosotros	os	os	vosotros
	vosotras	os	os	vosotras
3rd person	Uds.	los/las	les	Uds.
	ellos	los	les	ellos
	ellas	las	les	ellas

Interrogatives

qué	*what*
cómo	*how*
dónde	*where*
cuándo	*when*
cuánto, -a, -os, -as	*how much, how many*
cuál/cuáles	*which (one)*
quién/quiénes	*who, whom*
por qué	*why*
para qué	*why, what for*

Demonstrative adjectives

Singular		Plural	
Masculine	**Feminine**	**Masculine**	**Feminine**
este	esta	estos	estas
ese	esa	esos	esas
aquel	aquella	aquellos	aquellas

Possessive adjectives

Singular	Singular nouns	Plural nouns
1st person	mi hermano mi hermana	mis hermanos mis hermanas
2nd person	tu hermano tu hermana	tus hermanos tus hermanas
3rd person	su hermano su hermana	sus hermanos sus hermanas

Plural	Singular nouns	Plural nouns
1st person	nuestro hermano nuestra hermana	nuestros hermanos nuestras hermanas
2nd person	vuestro hermano vuestra hermana	vuestros hermanos vuestras hermanas
3rd person	su hermano su hermana	sus hermanos sus hermanas

Appendix B

Verbs

Present tense (indicative)

Regular present tense		
hablar *(to speak)*	hablo hablas habla	hablamos habláis hablan
comer *(to eat)*	como comes come	comemos coméis comen
escribir *(to write)*	escribo escribes escribe	escribimos escribís escriben

Preterite tense (indicative)

hablar *(to speak)*	hablé hablaste habló	hablamos hablasteis hablaron
comer *(to eat)*	comí comiste comió	comimos comisteis comieron
escribir *(to write)*	escribí escribiste escribió	escribimos escribisteis escribieron

Present participle

The present participle is formed by replacing the *-ar* of the infinitive with *-ando* and the *-er* or *-ir* with *-iendo*.

hablar	hablando
comer	comiendo
vivir	viviendo

Progressive tenses

The present participle is used with the verbs *estar, continuar, seguir, andar* and some other motion verbs to produce the progressive tenses. They are reserved for recounting actions that are or were in progress at the time in question.

Present tense of stem-changing verbs

Stem-changing verbs are identified in this book by the presence of vowels in parentheses after the infinitive. If these verbs end in -*ar* or -*er*, they have only one change. If they end in -*ir*, they have two changes. The stem change of -*ar* and -*er* verbs and the first stem change of -*ir* verbs occur in all forms of the present tense, except *nosotros* and *vosotros*.

cerrar (ie) *(to close)*	e → ie	cierro cierras cierra	cerramos cerráis cierran

Verbs like **cerrar:** calentar *(to heat)*, comenzar *(to begin)*, despertar *(to wake up)*, despertarse *(to awaken)*, empezar *(to begin)*, encerrar *(to lock up)*, nevar *(to snow)*, pensar *(to think)*, recomendar *(to recommend)*, sentarse *(to sit down)*

contar (ue) *(to tell)*	o→ ue	cuento cuentas cuenta	contamos contáis cuentan

Verbs like **contar:** acordar *(to agree)*, acordarse *(to remember)*, almorzar *(to have lunch)*, colgar *(to hang)*, costar *(to cost)*, demostrar *(to demonstrate)*, encontrar *(to find, to meet someone)*, probar *(to taste, to try)*, recordar *(to remember)*

jugar (ue) *(to play)*	u → ue	juego juegas juega	jugamos jugáis juegan

perder (ie) *(to lose)*	e → ie	pierdo pierdes pierde	perdemos perdéis pierden

Verbs like **perder:** defender *(to defend)*, descender *(to descend, to go down)*, encender *(to light, to turn on)*, entender *(to understand)*, extender *(to extend)*, tender *(to spread out)*

volver (ue) *(to return)*	o → ue	vuelvo vuelves vuelve	volvemos volvéis vuelven

Verbs like **volver:** devolver *(to return something)*, doler *(to hurt)*, llover *(to rain)*, morder *(to bite)*, mover *(to move)*, resolver *(to resolve)*, soler *(to be in the habit of)*, torcer *(to twist)*

pedir (i, i) *(to ask for)*	e → i	pido pides pide	pedimos pedís piden

Verbs like **pedir:** conseguir *(to obtain, to attain, to get)*, despedirse *(to say good-bye)*, elegir *(to choose, to elect)*, medir *(to measure)*, perseguir *(to pursue)*, repetir *(to repeat)*

sentir (ie, i) (to feel)	e → ie	siento sientes siente	sentimos sentís sienten

Verbs like **sentir**: advertir *(to warn)*, arrepentirse *(to regret)*, convertir *(to convert)*, convertirse *(to become)*, divertirse *(to have fun)*, herir *(to wound)*, invertir *(to invest)*, mentir *(to lie)*, preferir *(to prefer)*, requerir *(to require)*, sugerir *(to suggest)*

dormir (ue, u) (to sleep)	o → ue	duermo duermes duerme	dormimos dormís duermen

Another verb like **dormir**: morir *(to die)*

Present participle of stem-changing verbs

Stem-changing verbs that end in *-ir* use the second stem change in the present participle.

dormir (ue, u)	durmiendo
seguir (i, i)	siguiendo
sentir (ie, i)	sintiendo

Preterite tense of stem-changing verbs

Stem-changing verbs that end in *-ar* and *-er* are regular in the preterite tense. That is, they do not require a spelling change, and they use the regular preterite endings.

pensar (ie)		volver (ue)	
pensé	pensamos	volví	volvimos
pensaste	pensasteis	volviste	volvisteis
pensó	pensaron	volvió	volvieron

Stem-changing verbs ending in *-ir* change their third-person forms in the preterite tense, but they still require the regular preterite endings.

sentir (ie, i)		dormir (ue, u)	
sentí	sentimos	dormí	dormimos
sentiste	sentisteis	dormiste	dormisteis
sintió	sintieron	durmió	durmieron

Verbs with irregularities

The following charts provide some frequently used Spanish verbs with irregularities.

buscar *(to look for)*	
preterite	busqué, buscaste, buscó, buscamos, buscasteis, buscaron
Similar to:	explicar *(to explain)*, sacar *(to take out)*, tocar *(to touch, to play an instrument)*

dar *(to give)*	
present	doy, das, da, damos, dais, dan
preterite	di, diste, dio, dimos, disteis, dieron

decir *(to say, to tell)*

present	digo, dices, dice, decimos, decís, dicen
preterite	dije, dijiste, dijo, dijimos, dijisteis, dijeron
present participle	diciendo

enviar *(to send)*

present	envío, envías, envía, enviamos, enviáis, envían
Similar to:	esquiar *(to ski)*

estar *(to be)*

present	estoy, estás, está, estamos, estáis, están
preterite	estuve, estuviste, estuvo, estuvimos, estuvisteis, estuvieron

hacer *(to do, to make)*

present	hago, haces, hace, hacemos, hacéis, hacen
preterite	hice, hiciste, hizo, hicimos, hicisteis, hicieron

ir *(to go)*

present	voy, vas, va, vamos, vais, van
preterite	fui, fuiste, fue, fuimos, fuisteis, fueron
present participle	yendo

leer *(to read)*

preterite	leí, leíste, leyó, leímos, leísteis, leyeron
present participle	leyendo

llegar *(to arrive)*

preterite	llegué, llegaste, llegó, llegamos, llegasteis, llegaron
Similar to:	colgar *(to hang)*, pagar *(to pay)*

oír *(to hear, to listen)*

present	oigo, oyes, oye, oímos, oís, oyen
preterite	oí, oíste, oyó, oímos, oísteis, oyeron
present participle	oyendo

poder *(to be able)*

present	puedo, puedes, puede, podemos, podéis, pueden
preterite	pude, pudiste, pudo, pudimos, pudisteis, pudieron
present participle	pudiendo

poner *(to put, to place, to set)*

present	pongo, pones, pone, ponemos, ponéis, ponen
preterite	puse, pusiste, puso, pusimos, pusisteis, pusieron

querer (to love, to want)

present	quiero, quieres, quiere, queremos, queréis, quieren
preterite	quise, quisiste, quiso, quisimos, quisisteis, quisieron

saber (to know)

present	sé, sabes, sabe, sabemos, sabéis, saben
preterite	supe, supiste, supo, supimos, supisteis, supieron

salir (to go out, to leave)

present	salgo, sales, sale, salimos, salís, salen

ser (to be)

present	soy, eres, es, somos, sois, son
preterite	fui, fuiste, fue, fuimos, fuisteis, fueron

tener (to have)

present	tengo, tienes, tiene, tenemos, tenéis, tienen
preterite	tuve, tuviste, tuvo, tuvimos, tuvisteis, tuvieron

traer (to bring)

present	traigo, traes, trae, traemos, traéis, traen
preterite	traje, trajiste, trajo, trajimos, trajisteis, trajeron
present participle	trayendo

venir (to come)

present	vengo, vienes, viene, venimos, venís, vienen
preterite	vine, viniste, vino, vinimos, vinisteis, vinieron
present participle	viniendo

ver (to see, to watch)

present	veo, ves, ve, vemos, veis, ven
preterite	vi, viste, vio, vimos, visteis, vieron

Appendix C

Numbers

Cardinal numbers 0–1.000

0—cero	13—trece	26—veintiséis	90—noventa
1—uno	14—catorce	27—veintisiete	100—cien/ciento
2—dos	15—quince	28—veintiocho	200—doscientos,-as
3—tres	16—dieciséis	29—veintinueve	300—trescientos,-as
4—cuatro	17—diecisiete	30—treinta	400—cuatrocientos,-as
5—cinco	18—dieciocho	31—treinta y uno	500—quinientos,-as
6—seis	19—diecinueve	32—treinta y dos	600—seiscientos,-as
7—siete	20—veinte	33—treinta y tres, etc.	700—setecientos,-as
8—ocho	21—veintiuno	40—cuarenta	800—ochocientos,-as
9—nueve	22—veintidós	50—cincuenta	900—novecientos,-as
10—diez	23—veintitrés	60—sesenta	1.000—mil
11—once	24—veinticuatro	70—setenta	
12—doce	25—veinticinco	80—ochenta	

Ordinal numbers

1—primero,-a (primer)	6—sexto,-a
2—segundo,-a	7—séptimo,-a
3—tercero,-a (tercer)	8—octavo,-a
4—cuarto,-a	9—noveno,-a
5—quinto,-a	10—décimo,-a

Appendix D

Syllabification

Spanish vowels may be weak or strong. The vowels *a, e* and *o* are strong, whereas *i* (and sometimes *y*) and *u* are weak. The combination of one weak and one strong vowel or of two weak vowels produces a diphthong, two vowels pronounced as one.

A word in Spanish has as many syllables as it has vowels or diphthongs.

> al gu nas
> lue go
> pa la bra

A single consonant (including *ch, ll, rr*) between two vowels accompanies the second vowel and begins a syllable.

> a mi ga
> fa vo ri to
> mu cho

Two consonants are divided, the first going with the previous vowel and the second going with the following vowel.

> an tes
> quin ce
> ter mi nar

A consonant plus *l* or *r* is inseparable except for *rl, sl* and *sr*.

> ma dre
> pa la bra
> com ple tar
> Car los
> is la

If three consonants occur together, the last, or any inseparable combination, accompanies the following vowel to begin another syllable.

> es cri bir
> som bre ro
> trans por te

Prefixes should remain intact.

> re es cri bir

Appendix E

Accentuation

Words that end in *a, e, i, o, u, n* or *s* are pronounced with the major stress on the next-to-the-last syllable. No accent mark is needed to show this emphasis.

> octubre
> refresco
> señora

Words that end in any consonant except *n* or *s* are pronounced with the major stress on the last syllable. No accent mark is needed to show this emphasis.

> escribir
> papel
> reloj

Words that are not pronounced according to the above two rules must have a written accent mark.

> lógico
> canción
> después
> lápiz

An accent mark may be necessary to distinguish identical words with different meanings.

> dé/de
> qué/que
> sí/si
> sólo/solo

An accent mark is often used to divide a diphthong into two separate syllables.

> día
> frío
> Raúl

Vocabulary Spanish / English

All active words introduced in *NAVEGANDO 1* appear in this end vocabulary. The number and letter following an entry indicate the lesson in which an item is first actively used. Additional words and expressions are included for reference and have no number. Obvious cognates and expressions that occur as passive vocabulary for recognition only have been excluded from this end vocabulary.

Abbreviations:
d.o. direct object
f. feminine
i.o. indirect object
m. masculine
pl. plural
s. singular

A

a to, at, in *2B; a caballo* on horseback *3A; a crédito* on credit *9B; a pie* on foot *3A; a propósito* by the way *1A; ¿a qué hora?* at what time? *2B; a veces* sometimes, at times *5B; a ver* let's see, hello (telephone greeting)
abierto,-a open *4A*
abran: see *abrir*
el **abrazo** hug *6B*
abre: see *abrir*
la **abreviatura** abbreviation
el **abrigo** coat *8A*
abril April *5B*
abrir to open *5A; abran (Uds. command)* open; *abre (tú command)* open
la **abuela** grandmother *4A*
el **abuelo** grandfather *4A*
aburrido,-a bored, boring *4B*
acabar to finish, to complete, to terminate *8A; acabar de (+ infinitive)* to have just *8A*
el **aceite** oil *6A*
la **aceituna** olive
el **acento** accent *1A*
la **acentuación** accentuation
aclarar to make clear, to explain
la **actividad** activity *5A,* exercise
el **acuerdo** accord; *de acuerdo* agreed, okay *3B*
adiós good-bye *1A*
el **adjetivo** adjective; *adjetivo posesivo* possessive adjective

¿adónde? (to) where? *3A*
adoptar to adopt
adornar to decorate *8A*
el **adverbio** adverb
los **aeróbicos** aerobics *7A*
el **aeropuerto** airport
la **agencia** agency; *agencia de viajes* travel agency
agosto August *5B*
el **agricultor** farmer
el **agua** *f.* water *3B; agua mineral* mineral water *3B*
el **aguacate** avocado *8B*
ahora now *3B; ahora mismo* right now *7A*
ahorrar to save *9B*
el **ajedrez** chess *7A*
el **ajo** garlic *8B*
al to the *3A; al lado de* next to, beside *6B*
alegre happy, merry, lively
el **alfabeto** alphabet
el **álgebra** algebra
algo something, anything *8A*
el **algodón** cotton *9A*
alguien someone, anyone, somebody, anybody *9A*
algún, alguna some, any *9A*
alguno,-a some, any *9A*
allá over there *6A*
allí there *2B*
la **almeja** clam
el **almuerzo** lunch *2B*
aló hello (telephone greeting) *2B*
alquilar to rent *7A*

alterna alternate (*tú* command)
alternen alternate (*Uds.* command)
alto,-a tall, high *4B*
amable kind, nice *4A*
amarillo,-a yellow *2B*
ambiguo,-a ambiguous
la **América** America; *América Central* Central America; *América del Sur* South America
americano,-a American *7A; el fútbol americano* football *7A*
el **amigo,** la **amiga** friend *2A; amigo/a por correspondencia* pen pal
el **amor** love *5A*
anaranjado,-a orange (color) *9A*
andino,-a Andean, of the Andes Mountains
el **anillo** ring *9B*
anteayer the day before yesterday *5B*
anterior preceding
antes de before *7A*
añade: see *añadir*
añadir to add *8B; añade (tú command)* add
el **año** year *5B; Año Nuevo* New Year's Day *5B; ¿Cuántos años tienes?* How old are you? *1A; tener (+ number) años* to be (+ number) years old *5A*
apagar to turn off *7A*
el **apartamento** apartment
el **apellido** last name, surname
el **apodo** nickname

aprender to learn
apropiado,-a appropriate
apunta: see *apuntar*
apuntar to point; *apunta (tú* command) point (at); *apunten (Uds.* command) point (at)
apunten: see *apuntar*
apurado,-a in a hurry *4A*
aquel, aquella that (far away) *6A*
aquellos, aquellas those (far away) *6A*
aquí here *1A; Aquí se habla español.* Spanish is spoken here.
el **árbol** tree; *árbol genealógico* family tree
el **arete** earring *9B*
la **Argentina** Argentina *1A*
arreglar to arrange, to straighten, to fix *8A*
arroba (@) at *(the symbol (@) used for e-mail addresses) 2B*
el **arroz** rice *8B*
el **arte** art *2B*
el **artesanía** handicrafts, artisanry
el **artículo** article *5A*
el **artista** artist
el **ascensor** elevator *9B*
la **asignatura** subject
la **aspiradora** vacuum *7A; pasar la aspiradora* to vacuum *8A*
el **Atlántico** Atlantic Ocean
la **atracción** attraction
aunque although
el **autobús** bus *3A*
la **avenida** avenue *3B*
aventurero,-a adventurous
el **avión** airplane *3A*
¡ay! oh! *2A*
ayer yesterday *5B*
la **ayuda** help
ayudar to help *6A*
el **azafrán** saffron
los **aztecas** Aztecs
el **azúcar** sugar *6A*
azul blue *2B*

bailar to dance *4B*
bajo,-a short (not tall), low *4B; planta baja* floor level *6B*
balanceado,-a balanced
el **baloncesto** basketball
el **banco** bank *3A*
el **baño** bathroom *6B; traje de*

baño swimsuit *9A*
barato,-a cheap *9B*
el **barco** boat, ship *3A*
barrer to sweep *8A*
el **barril** barrel
basado,-a based
el **básquetbol** basketball *7A*
el **basquetbolista, la basquetbolista** basketball player *7B*
bastante rather, fairly, sufficiently; enough, sufficient *9B*
la **basura** garbage *8A*
la **bebida** drink
el **béisbol** baseball *4B*
la **biblioteca** library *3A*
la **bicicleta** bicycle, bike *3A*
bien well *1B*
bienvenido,-a welcome
la **billetera** wallet *9B*
la **biología** biology *2B*
blanco,-a white *2B*
la **blusa** blouse *2B*
la **boda** wedding
el **bolígrafo** pen *2A*
Bolivia Bolivia *1A*
el **bolo** ball; *jugar a los bolos* to bowl
el **bolso** handbag, purse *9B*
bonito,-a pretty, good-looking, attractive *4A*
borra: see *borrar*
el **borrador** eraser *2A*
borrar to erase; *borra (tú* command) erase; *borren (Uds.* command) erase
borren: see *borrar*
la **bota** boot *9A*
el **brazo** arm *9A*
buen good (form of *bueno* before a *m., s.* noun) *7B*
bueno well, okay (pause in speech) *3B*; hello (telephone greeting)
bueno,-a good *4B; buena suerte* good luck; *buenas noches* good night *1B; buenas tardes* good afternoon *1B; buenos días* good morning *1B*
la **bufanda** scarf *9B*
buscar to look for *5A*

el **caballero** gentleman
el **caballo** horse *3A; a caballo* on

horseback *3A*
la **cabeza** head *9A*
cada each, every *5A*
el **café** coffee *8B*
la **cafetería** cafeteria
la **caja** cashier's desk *9B*
el **calcetín** sock *2B*
el **calendario** calendar
la **calidad** quality *9B*
caliente hot *4A*
la **calle** street *3B*
el **calor** heat *6B; hace calor* it is hot *7B; tener calor* to be hot *6B*
calvo,-a bald *4B*
la **cama** bed *8A*
el **camarón** shrimp
cambiar to change, to exchange *9B*
el **cambio** change *9B; en cambio* on the other hand *7B*
caminar to walk *3A*
el **camión** truck *3A*; bus (Mexico); *en camión* by truck *3A*
la **camisa** shirt *2B*
la **camiseta** jersey, polo, t-shirt *2B*
la **canción** song *5A*
canoso,-a white-haired *4B*
cansado,-a tired *4A*
el **cantante, la cantante** singer *3B*
cantar to sing *4B*
la **cantidad** quantity
la **capital** capital *1A*
el **capitán** captain
el **capítulo** chapter
la **cara** face
la **característica** characteristic, trait; *características de personalidad* personality traits; *características físicas* physical traits
¡caramba! wow! *5A*
cariñoso,-a affectionate *4A*
el **carnaval** carnival
la **carne** meat *8B*
caro,-a expensive *9B*
la **carrera** career, race
el **carro** car *3A; en carro* by car *3A*
la **carta** letter *6B*, playing card *7A*
la **casa** home, house *4A; en casa* at home
el **casete** cassette *5A*
casi almost *7A*
catorce fourteen *1A*
el **CD** CD (compact disc) *2B*
la **cebolla** onion *8B*
celebrar to celebrate *5B*

el **censo** census

el **centavo** cent

el **centro** downtown, center 3B; *centro comercial* shopping center, mall 9A

cerca (de) near 3A

cero zero 1A

cerrado,-a closed 4A

cerrar (ie) to close 6A; *cierra (tú* command) close; *cierren (Uds.* command) close

el **cesto de papeles** wastebasket 2A

chao bye

la **chaqueta** jacket 9A

charlando talking, chatting

la **chica** girl 2A

el **chico** boy 2A, man, buddy

Chile Chile 1A

el **chisme** gossip 6B

el **chocolate** chocolate 8B

el **chorizo** sausage (seasoned with red peppers) 8B

el **ciclismo** cycling

cien one hundred 1B

la **ciencia** science

ciento one hundred (when followed by another number) 5B

cierra: see *cerrar*

cierren: see *cerrar*

cinco five 1A

cincuenta fifty 1B

el **cine** movie theater 3A

el **cinturón** belt 9B

la **ciudad** city 3A

la **civilización** civilization

el **clarinete** clarinet

¡claro! of course! 3A

la **clase** class 2A

el **clima** climate

el **coche** car; *en coche* by car

la **cocina** kitchen 6A

cocinar to cook 8A

el **cognado** cognate

el **colegio** school 2B

colgar (ue) to hang 8A

el **collar** necklace 9B

Colombia Colombia 1A

la **colonia** colony

el **color** color 2B

combinar to combine 9A

el **comedor** dining room 6A

comer to eat 3B; *dar de comer* to feed 8A

cómico,-a comical, funny 4B

la **comida** food 3B, dinner

como like, since, as

¿cómo? how?, what? 1A; *¿Cómo?* What (did you say)? 2B; *¿Cómo está (Ud.)?* How are you (formal)? 1B; *¿Cómo están (Uds.)?* How are you (pl.)? 1B; *¿Cómo estás (tú)?* How are you (informal)? 1B; *¡Cómo no!* Of course! 3B; *¿Cómo se dice...?* How do you say...? 2A; *¿Cómo se escribe...?* How do you write (spell)...? 1A; *¿Cómo se llama (Ud./él/ella)?* What is (your/his/her) name? 1A; *¿Cómo te llamas?* What is your name? 2A

comodidad comfort

cómodo,-a comfortable 6B

el **compañero,** la **compañera** classmate, partner 5A

comparando comparing

la **competencia** competition

completa: see *completar*

completar to complete; *completa (tú* command) complete

la **compra** purchase 4B; *ir de compras* to go shopping 4B

comprar to buy 4B

comprender to understand 2A; *comprendo* I understand 2A

comprendo: see *comprender*

la **computadora** computer (machine) 2B

la **computación** computer science 2B

común common

con with 1A; *con (mucho) gusto* I would be (very) glad to 1B; *con permiso* excuse me (with your permission), may I 1B

el **concierto** concert 3B

la **conjunción** conjunction

conmigo with me 9B

conquistar to conquer

conseguir (i, i) to obtain, to attain, to get

la **contaminación** contamination, pollution; *contaminación ambiental* environmental pollution

contar (ue) to tell (a story) 9A; *cuenta (tú* command) tell; *cuenten (Uds.* command) tell; to count

contento,-a happy, glad 4A; *estar contento,-a (con)* to be satisfied (with) 4A

contesta: see *contestar*

contestar to answer 4B; *contesta (tú* command) answer; *contesten (Uds.* command) answer

contesten: see *contestar*

el **contexto** context

contigo with you (*tú*) 9B

continúa: see *continuar*

continuar to continue 7B; *continúa (tú* command) continue; *continúen (Uds.* command) continue

continúen: see *continuar*

la **contracción** contraction

el **control remoto** remote control 7A

copiar to copy 7B

la **corbata** tie 9A

correcto,-a right, correct

el **corredor,** la **corredora** runner 7B

el **correo** mail; *correo electrónico* e-mail 2B

correr to run 6B

la **cortesía** courtesy

corto,-a short (not long) 9B

la **cosa** thing 6A

la **costa** coast

Costa Rica Costa Rica 1A

costar (ue) to cost 7A

crear to create

el **crédito** credit 9B; *a crédito* on credit 9B; *la tarjeta de crédito* credit card 9B

creer to believe

el **crucero** cruise ship

cruzar to cross

el **cuaderno** notebook 2A

¿cuál? which?, what?, which one? *(pl. ¿cuáles?)* which ones? 2B

la **cualidad** quality

cualquier any

cuando when 6B

¿cuándo? when? 3A

¿cuánto,-a? how much? 2B *(pl. ¿cuántos,-as?)* how many? 2B; *¿Cuántos años tienes?* How old are you? 1A; *¿Cuánto (+ time expression) hace que (+ present tense of verb)...?* How long...? 7A

cuarenta forty *1B*

el **cuarto** quarter *1B*, room, bedroom *6B*; *cuarto de baño* bathroom; *menos cuarto* a quarter to, a quarter before *1B*; *y cuarto* a quarter after, a quarter past *1B*

cuarto,-a fourth *7B*

cuatro four *1A*

cuatrocientos,-as four hundred *5B*

Cuba Cuba *1A*

los **cubiertos** silverware *6A*

la **cuchara** tablespoon *6A*

la **cucharita** teaspoon *6A*

el **cuchillo** knife *6A*

cuenta: see *contar*

cuenten: see *contar*

el **cuero** leather *9B*

el **cuerpo** body *9A*

cuidar to take care of

el **cumpleaños** birthday *5B*; *¡Feliz cumpleaños!* Happy birthday! *5B*

cumplir to become, to become (+ number) years old, to reach *5B*; *cumplir años* to have a birthday *5B*

la **dama** lady

las **damas** checkers *7A*

dar to give *7A*; *dar de comer* to feed *8A*; *dar un paseo* to go for a walk, to go for a ride *7B*; *dé* (*Ud.* command) give

de from, of *1A*; *de acuerdo* agreed, okay *3B*; *¿de dónde?* from where? *1A*; *¿De dónde eres?* Where are you from? *1A*; *de la mañana* in the morning, A.M. *1B*; *de la noche* at night, P.M. *1B*; *de la tarde* in the afternoon, P.M. *1B*; *de nada* you are welcome, not at all *1B*; *de todos los días* everyday *6A*; *¿de veras?* really? *5B*; *¿Eres (tú) de...?* Are you from...? *1A*

dé: see *dar*

deber should, to have to, must, ought (expressing a moral duty) *6A*

décimo,-a tenth *7B*

decir to tell, to say *6B*; *¿Cómo se dice...?* How do you say...?

2A; *di* (*tú* command) say, tell; *díganme* (*Uds.* command) tell me; *dime* (*tú* command) tell me; *¿Qué quiere decir...?* What is the meaning (of)...? *2A*; *querer decir* to mean *6B*; *quiere decir* it means *2A*; *se dice* one says *2A*

el **dedo** finger, toe *9A*

dejar to leave *8A*

del of the, from the *3A*

delgado,-a thin *4B*

demasiado too (much) *9B*

la **democracia** democracy

el **dentista**, la **dentista** dentist *3A*

el **departamento** department *9A*

el **dependiente**, la **dependienta** clerk *9B*

el **deporte** sport *5A*

el **deportista**, la **deportista** athlete *7B*

desaparecido,-a missing

el **desastre** disaster

el **desayuno** breakfast

describe (*tú* command) describe

descubrir to discover

desde since, from *6B*

desear to wish

el **deseo** wish

la **despedida** farewell

después afterwards, later, then *6A*; *después de* after *7A*

di: see *decir*

el **día** day *2B*; *buenos días* good morning *1B*; *de todos los días* everyday *5A*; *todos los días* every day *5A*

el **diálogo** dialog

diario,-a daily

dibuja: see *dibujar*

dibujar to draw, to sketch *7A*; *dibuja* (*tú* command) draw; *dibujen* (*Uds.* command) draw

dibujen: see *dibujar*

el **dibujo** drawing, sketch *6B*

diciembre December *5B*

el **dictado** dictation

diecinueve nineteen *1A*

dieciocho eighteen *1A*

dieciséis sixteen *1A*

diecisiete seventeen *1A*

diez ten *1A*

la **diferencia** difference

diferente different

difícil difficult, hard *4B*

diga hello (telephone greeting)

dígame tell me, hello (telephone greeting)

díganme: see *decir*

dime: see *decir*

el **dinero** money *5A*

la **dirección** address *2B*; *dirección de correo electrónico* e-mail *2B*

el **director**, la **directora** director

dirigir to direct

el **disco** disc *2B*; *disco compacto (CD)* compact disk *2B*

disfrutar to enjoy

diskette diskette *2B*

divertido,-a fun *4A*

doblar to fold *8A*

doce twelve *1A*

el **doctor**, la **doctora** doctor

el **dólar** dollar

domingo Sunday *2B*; *el domingo* on Sunday

don title of respect used before a man's first name

donde where *6B*

¿dónde? where? *1A*

doña title of respect used before a woman's first name

dormir (ue, u) to sleep *7A*

dos two *1A*

doscientos,-as two hundred *5B*

Dr. abbreviation for *doctor*

Dra. abbreviation for *doctora*

durante during

el **DVD** DVD (digital video disc) *5A*; *el reproductor de DVDs* DVD player *5A*

e and (used before a word beginning with *i* or *hi*) *6B*

la **ecología** ecology

el **Ecuador** Ecuador *1A*

la **edad** age

el **edificio** building *3B*

la **educación física** physical education

el **efectivo** cash *9B*; *en efectivo* in cash *9B*

egoísta selfish *4B*

el **ejemplo** example; *por ejemplo* for example

el the *(m., s.)* *2A*

él he *2A;* him (after a preposition) *4B; Él se llama....* His name is.... *2A*

eléctrico,-a electric

electrónico,-a electronic *2B*

El Salvador El Salvador *1A*

ella she *2A;* her (after a preposition) *4B; Ella se llama....* Her name is.... *2A*

ellos,-as they *2A;* them (after a preposition) *4B*

empatados: see *empate*

el **empate** tie; *los partidos empatados* games tied

empezar (ie) to begin, to start *6A*

en in, on, at *2A; en* (+ vehicle) by (+ vehicle) *3A; en cambio* on the other hand *7B; en casa* at home; *en efectivo* in cash *9B; en resumen* in short

encantado,-a delighted, the pleasure is mine *3A*

encender (ie) to light, to turn on (a light) *6A*

encontrar (ue) to find

la **encuesta** survey, poll

enero January *5B*

el **énfasis** emphasis

el **enfermero,** la **enfermera** nurse

enfermo,-a sick *4A*

la **ensalada** salad *3B*

enseñar to teach, to show

entero,-a whole

entonces then *6A*

entrar to go in, to come in *5A*

entre between, among

la **entrevista** interview

enviar to send *7B*

el **equipo** team *7A; equipo de sonido* sound system, stereo *5A*

equivocado mistaken; *número equivocado* wrong number *2B*

eres: see *ser*

es: see *ser*

escalar to climb

la **escalera** stairway, stairs *6B; escalera mecánica* escalator *9B*

la **escena** scene

escoger to choose *8B; escogiendo* choosing

escogiendo: see *escoger*

escriban: see *escribir*

escribe: see *escribir*

escribir to write *6B; ¿Cómo se escribe...?* How do you write (spell)...? *1A; escriban (Uds.* command) write; *escribe (tú* command) write; *se escribe* it is written *1A*

el **escritorio** desk *2A*

escucha: see *escuchar*

escuchar to listen (to) *4B; escucha (tú* command) listen; *escuchen (Uds.* command) listen

escuchen: see *escuchar*

la **escuela** school *3A*

ese, esa that *6A*

eso that (neuter form)

esos, esas those *6A*

el **espacio** space

España Spain *1A*

el **español** Spanish (language) *2B*

español, española Spanish

especial special *6A*

especializado,-a specialized

el **espectáculo** showcase

la **esposa** wife, spouse *4A*

el **esposo** husband, spouse *4A*

el **esquiador,** la **esquiadora** skier *7B*

esquiar to ski *7B*

está: see *estar*

establecieron settled down

la **estación** season *7B*

el **estadio** stadium

el **Estado Libre Asociado** Commonwealth

los **Estados Unidos** United States of America *1A*

están: see *estar*

estar to be *2B; ¿Cómo está (Ud.)?* How are you (formal)? *1B; ¿Cómo están (Uds.)?* How are you (pl.)? *1B; ¿Cómo estás (tú)?* How are are you (informal)? *1B; está nublado,-a* it's cloudy *7B; está soleado,-a* it's sunny *7B; están* they are *1B; estar contento,-a (con)* to be satisfied (with) *4A; estar en oferta* to be on sale *9B; estar listo,-a* to be ready *7B; estás* you (informal) are *1B; estoy* I am *1B*

estás: see *estar*

este well, so (pause in speech)

este, esta this *6A; esta noche* tonight *7A*

el **estéreo** stereo

estos, estas these *6A*

estoy: see *estar*

la **estructura** structure

estudia: see *estudiar*

el **estudiante,** la **estudiante** student *2A*

estudiar to study *2B; estudia (tú* command) study; *estudien (Uds.* command) study

estudien: see *estudiar*

el **estudio** study

la **estufa** stove *6A*

estupendo,-a wonderful, marvellous *7A*

el **examen** exam, test *2B*

excelente excellent *7B*

el **éxito** success

explica: see *explicar*

la **explicación** explanation

explicar to explain; *explica (tú* command) explain

el **explorador,** la **exploradora** explorer

la **exportación** exportation

exportador, exportadora exporting

expresar to express

la **expresión** expression

la **extensión** extension

fácil easy *4B*

la **falda** skirt *2B*

falso,-a false

la **familia** family *4A*

famoso,-a famous

fantástico,-a fantastic, great *3A*

el **favor** favor; *por favor* please *1B*

favorito,-a favorite *3B*

febrero February *5B*

la **fecha** date *5B*

felicitaciones congratulations

feliz happy *(pl. felices) 5B; ¡Feliz cumpleaños!* Happy birthday! *5B*

femenino,-a feminine

feo,-a ugly *4B*

el **ferrocarril** railway, railroad

la **fiesta** party *3A*

la **filosofía** philosophy

el **fin** end *5A; fin de semana* weekend *5A*

la **física** physics *6A*

la **flauta** flute

la **flor** flower *7B*

la **florcita** small flower

la **forma** form

la **foto(grafía)** photo *4A*

la **frase** phrase, sentence

el **fregadero** sink *6A*

la **fresa** strawberry *8B*

el **fresco** cool *7B; hace fresco* it is cool *7B*

fresco,-a fresh, chilly *8B*

los **frijoles** beans *3B*

el **frío** cold *4A; hace frío* it is cold *7B; tener frío* to be cold *6B*

frío,-a cold *4A*

la **fruta** fruit *8B*

fue: see *ser*

fuerte strong

el **fútbol** soccer *4B; fútbol americano* football *7A*

el **futbolista,** la **futbolista** soccer player *7B*

el **futuro** future

la **gana** desire *6B; tener ganas de* to feel like *6B*

ganados: see *ganar*

ganar to win; *los partidos ganados* games won

el **garaje** garage *6B*

el **gato,** la **gata** cat *5A*

el **género** gender

generoso,-a generous *4B*

la **gente** people *8A*

la **geografía** geography

la **geometría** geometry

el **gerundio** present participle

el **gesto** gesture

el **gimnasio** gym

la **gira** tour

el **gobernador,** la **gobernadora** governor

gordo,-a fat *4B*

la **grabadora** tape recorder *5A*

gracias thanks *1B; muchas gracias* thank you very much *1B*

el **grado** degree *7B*

gran big (form of *grande* before a *m., s.* noun)

grande big *3B*

gris gray *2B*

el **grupo** group; *grupo musical* musical group

el **guante** glove *9A*

guapo,-a good-looking, attractive, handsome, pretty *4A*

Guatemala Guatemala *1A*

el **guía,** la **guía** guide

Guinea Ecuatorial Equatorial Guinea *1A*

el **guisante** pea *8B*

la **guitarra** guitar

gusta: see *gustar*

gustar to like, to be pleasing to *4B; me/te/le/nos/vos/les gustaría...* I/you/he/she/ it/we/they would like... *6B*

gustaría: see *gustar*

el **gusto** pleasure, delight, taste *3A; con (mucho) gusto* I would be (very) glad to *1B; el gusto es mío* the pleasure is mine *3A; ¡Mucho gusto!* Glad to meet you! *1A; Tanto gusto.* So glad to meet you. *3A*

la **habichuela** green bean *8B*

la **habitación** room, bedroom

el **habitante,** la **habitante** inhabitant

habla: see *hablar*

hablar to speak *2B; habla (tú* command) speak; *hablen (Uds. command)* speak; *Se habla español.* Spanish is spoken.

hablen: see *hablar*

hace: see *hacer*

hacer to do, to make *3B; ¿Cuánto (+ time expression) hace que (+ present tense of verb)...?* How long...? *7A; hace buen (mal) tiempo* the weather is nice (bad) *7B; hace fresco* it is cool *7B; hace frío (calor)* it is cold (hot) *7B; hace (+ time expression) que* ago *7A; hace sol* it is sunny *7B; hace viento* it is windy *7B; hacer aeróbicos* to do aerobics *7A; hacer falta* to be necessary, to be lacking *8B; hacer un viaje* to take a trip *5A; hacer una pregunta* to ask a question *3B; hagan (Uds. command)* do, make; *haz (tú* command) do, make; *haz el papel* play the part; *hecha* made

hagan: see *hacer*

el **hambre** hunger *6B; tener hambre* to be hungry *6B*

hasta until, up to, down to *1A; hasta la vista* so long, see you later; *hasta luego* so long, see you later *1A; hasta mañana* see you tomorrow *1B; hasta pronto* see you soon *1B*

hay there is, there are *2A; hay neblina* it is misting *7B; hay sol* it is sunny *7B*

haz: see *hacer*

hecha: see *hacer*

el **helado** ice cream *8B*

la **hermana** sister *4A*

el **hermano** brother *4A*

el **hielo** ice *7B; patinar sobre hielo* to ice skate *7B*

la **hija** daughter *4A*

el **hijo** son *4A*

hispano,-a Hispanic

hispanohablante Spanish-speaking

la **historia** history *2B*

la **hoja** sheet; *hoja de papel* sheet of paper; leaf

hola hi, hello *1A*

el **hombre** man *9A*

Honduras Honduras *1A*

la **hora** hour *1B; ¿a qué hora?* at what time? *2B; ¿Qué hora es?* What time is it? *1B*

el **horario** schedule *2B*

el **horno microondas** microwave oven *6A*

horrible horrible *4B*

el **hotel** hotel *3A*

hoy today *3B*

el **huevo** egg *8B*

la **idea** idea *5B*

ideal ideal *4B*

ignorar to not know

imagina: see *imaginar*

la **imaginación** imagination

imaginar to imagine; *imagina (tú* command) imagine

el **impermeable** raincoat *9A*

importante important *4B*

importar to be important, to matter *8B*

la **impresora (láser)** (laser) printer *2B*

los **incas** Incas

incluir to include

indefinido,-a indefinite

la **independencia** independence

indica: see *indicar*

la indicación cue

indicado,-a indicated

indicar to indicate; *indica* (*tú* command) indicate

indígena native

el informe report

el inglés English (language) 2B

el ingrediente ingredient 8B

inicial initial

inmenso,-a immense

la inspiración inspiration

inteligente intelligent 4B

interesante interesting 4B

interrogativo,-a interrogative

el invierno winter 7B

la invitación invitation

invitar to invite

ir to go 3A; *ir a* (+ infinitive) to be going to (do something) 3B; *ir de compras* to go shopping 4B; *¡vamos!* let's go! 3A; *¡vamos a* (+ infinitive)! let's (+ infinitive)! 3B; *vayan* (*Uds.* command) go to; *ve* (*tú* command) go to

la isla island

el jamón ham 8B

el jardín garden 8A

la jirafa giraffe

los jeans jeans, blue jeans 2B

joven young 5B

la joya jewel 9B

el juego game

jueves Thursday 2B; *el jueves* on Thursday

el jugador, la jugadora player 7B

jugar (ue) to play 4B, *jugar a* (+ sport/game) 4B

el jugo juice 3B

julio July 5B

junio June 5B

junto,-a together 8A

el kilo (kg.) kilogram 8B

la the (*f., s.*) 2A; her, it, you (*d.o.*) 5A; *a la...* at...o'clock 2B

el lado side 6B; *al lado (de)* next to, beside 6B; *por todos lados* everywhere 7B

la lámpara lamp 6A

la lana wool 9A

la langosta lobster

lanzar to throw

el lápiz pencil (*pl. lápices*) 2A

largo,-a long 9B

las the (*f., pl.*) 2A; them, you (*d.o.*) 5A; *a las...* at...o'clock 2B

la lástima shame; *¡Qué lástima!* What a shame! 5A

la lata can 8B

el lavaplatos dishwasher 6A

lavar to wash 8A

le (to, for) him, (to, for) her, (to, for) it, (to, for) you (formal)(*i.o.*) 3A

lean: see *leer*

la lección lesson

la leche milk 8A

la lechuga lettuce 8B

la lectura reading

lee: see *leer*

leer to read 3B; *lean* (*Uds.* command) read; *lee* (*tú* command) read

lejos (de) far (from) 3A

la lengua language

lento,-a slow 4B

les (to, for) them, (to, for) you (*pl.*)(*i.o.*) 3A

la letra letter

levantarse to get up, to rise; *levántate* (*tú* command) get up; *levántense* (*Uds.* command) get up

levántate: see *levantarse*

levántense: see *levantarse*

la libertad liberty, freedom

la libra pound

libre free 4A

la librería bookstore 5A

el libro book 2A

el líder leader

limitar to limit

limpiar to clean 8A

limpio,-a clean 4A

lindo,-a pretty 9B

la lista list 7A

listo,-a ready 7B, smart 8A; *estar listo,-a* to be ready 7B; *ser listo,-a* to be smart 8A

la literatura literature

llama: see *llamar*

llamar to call, to telephone 5A; *¿Cómo se llama (Ud./él/ella)?* What is (your/his/her) name?

2A; *¿Cómo te llamas?* What is your name? 1A; *llamaron* they called (preterite of *llamar*); *me llamo* my name is 1A; *se llaman* their names are; *te llamas* your name is 1A; (*Ud./Él/Ella) se llama....* (Your [formal]/His/Her) name is.... 2A

llamaron: see *llamar*

llamas: see *llamar*

llamo: see *llamar*

llegar to arrive 8A; *llegó* arrived (preterite of *llegar*)

llegó: see *llegar*

llevar to wear 2B; to take, to carry 5A

llover (ue) to rain 7B

la lluvia rain 7B

lo him, it, you (*d.o.*) 5A; *lo que,* that which 6B; *lo siento* I am sorry 1B

loco,-a crazy 4A

lógicamente logically

lógico,-a logical

los the (*m., pl.*) 2A; them, you (*d.o.*) 5A

luego then, later, soon 1A; *hasta luego* so long, see you later 1A

el lugar place 7B

lunes Monday 2B; *el lunes* on Monday

la luz light (*pl. luces*) 6A

la madrastra stepmother

la madre mother 4A

maduro,-a ripe 8B

el maestro teacher, master; *La práctica hace al maestro.* Practice makes perfect.

el maíz corn 8B

mal badly 1B; bad 7B

la maleta suitcase 5A

malo,-a bad 4B

la mamá mother, mom

la manera manner, way

la mano hand 9A

el mantel tablecloth 6A

la mantequilla butter 6A

la manzana apple 8B

mañana tomorrow 1B; *hasta mañana* see you tomorrow 1B; *pasado mañana* the day after tomorrow 5B la **mañana** morning *1B; de la mañana* A.M., in the morning *1B; por la mañana* in the morning *7A*

el **mapa** map *2A*

la **maravilla** wonder, marvel

mariachi popular Mexican music and orchestra

el **marisco** seafood, shellfish

marrón brown *9A*

martes Tuesday *2B; el martes* on Tuesday

marzo March *5B*

más more, else *4A; el/la/los/las (+ noun) más (+ adjective)* the most *(+ adjective) 8B; lo más (+ adverb) posible* as *(+ adverb + noun)* as possible *8B; más (+ noun/adjective/adverb) que* more *(+ noun/adjective/adverb)* than *8B*

masculino,-a masculine

las **matemáticas** mathematics *2B*

el **material** material *9B*

máximo,-a maximum *7B*

maya Mayan

los **mayas** Mayans

mayo May *5B*

mayor older, oldest *5B,* greater, greatest *8B*

la **mayúscula** capital letter *1A*

me (to, for) me *(i.o.) 4B;* me *(d.o.) 5A; me llaman* they call me; *me llamo* my name is *1A*

mecánico,-a mechanic *9B; la escalera mecánica* escalator *9B*

la **medianoche** midnight *1B; Es medianoche.* It is midnight. *1B*

mediante by means of

las **medias** pantyhose, nylons *9A*

el **médico,** la **médica** doctor *3A*

medio,-a half; *y media* half past *1B*

medio tiempo (trabajo) part-time (work)

el **mediodía** noon; *Es mediodía.* It is noon. *1B*

mejor better *8B; el/la/los/las mejor/mejores (+ noun)* the best *(+ noun) 8B*

menor younger, youngest *5B,* lesser, least *8B*

menos minus, until, before, to (to express time) *1B,* less *8B; el/la/los/las (+ noun) menos (+ adjective)* the least *(+ adjective + noun) 8B; lo menos (+ adverb) posible* as *(+ adverb)* as possible *8B; menos (+ noun/adjective/adverb) que* less *(+ noun/adjective/adverb)* than *8B; por lo menos* at least

mentir (ie, i) to lie

la **mentira** lie *6B*

el **menú** menu *3B*

el **mercado** market *8B*

el **merengue** merengue (dance music)

el **mes** month *5B*

la **mesa** table *6A; poner la mesa* to set the table *6A; recoger la mesa* to clear the table *8A*

el **mesero,** la **mesera** food server *3B*

el **metro** subway *3A*

mexicano,-a Mexican

México Mexico *1A*

mi my *2A; (pl. mis)* my *4A*

mí me *4B;* (after a preposition) *4B*

el **miedo** fear *6B; tener miedo de* to be afraid of *6B*

el **miembro** member, part

mientras que while

miércoles Wednesday *2B; el miércoles* on Wednesday

mil thousand *5B*

mínimo,-a minimum *7B*

la **minúscula** lowercase *1A*

el **minuto** minute *7A*

mío,-a my, mine; *el gusto es mío* the pleasure is mine *3A*

mira: see *mirar*

mirar to look (at) *4B; mira (tú* command) look *2B;* hey, look (pause in speech); *miren (Uds.* command) look; hey, look (pause in speech)

miren: see *mirar*

mismo right (in the very moment, place, etc.) *7A; ahora mismo* right now *7A*

mismo,-a same *7A*

el **misterio** mystery

la **mochila** backpack *2A*

el **modelo** model

moderno,-a modern

el **momento** moment *3B*

el **mono** monkey

montar to ride *5A; montar en patineta* to skateboard *7B*

morado,-a purple *9A*

moreno,-a brunet, brunette, dark-haired, dark-skinned *4B*

la **moto(cicleta)** motorcycle *3A*

la **muchacha** girl, young woman *1A*

el **muchacho** boy, guy *1A*

muchísimo very much, a lot

mucho much, a lot of, very much *4A*

mucho,-a much, a lot of, very *3B; (pl. muchos,-as)* many *3B; con (mucho) gusto* I would be (very) glad to *1B; muchas gracias* thank you very much *1B; ¡Mucho gusto!* Glad to meet you! *1A*

la **mujer** woman *9A*

el **mundo** world; *todo el mundo* everyone, everybody

la **muralla** wall

el **museo** museum *3B*

la **música** music *2B*

muy very *1B*

N

la **nación** nation

nacional national

nada nothing *9A; de nada* you are welcome, not at all *1B*

nadar to swim *4B*

nadie nobody *9A*

la **naranja** orange *3B*

natal birth

la **Navidad** Christmas *5B*

la **neblina** mist *7B; hay neblina* it is misting *7B*

necesitar to need *2B*

negativo,-a negative

el **negocio** business; *el hombre de negocios* businessman; *la mujer de negocios* businesswoman

negro,-a black *2B*

nervioso,-a nervous *4A*

nevar (ie) to snow *7B*

ni not even *5B; ni...ni* neither...nor *9A*

Nicaragua Nicaragua *1A*

la **nieta** granddaughter *4A*

el **nieto** grandson *4A*

la **nieve** snow *7B*

ningún, ninguna none, not any *9A*

ninguno,-a none, not any *9A*

niño,-a child

no no *1A*

la **noche** night *1B; buenas noches* good night *1B; de la noche* P.M., at night *1B; esta noche* tonight *7A; por la noche* at night *6B*

el **nombre** name

el **norte** north

nos (to, for) us *(i.o.) 4B;* us *(d.o.) 5A*

nosotros,-as we *2A;* us (after a preposition) *4B*

la **nota** grade

la **noticia** news

novecientos,-as nine hundred *5B*

noveno,-a ninth *7B*

noventa ninety *1B*

la **novia** girlfriend

noviembre November *5B*

el **novio** boyfriend

nublado,-a cloudy *7B; está nublado* it is cloudy *7B*

nuestro,-a our *4A*

nueve nine *1A*

nuevo,-a new *2A; el Año Nuevo* New Year's Day *5B*

el **número** number *2B; número de teléfono/de fax/de teléfono celular* telephone/fax/cellular telephone number *2B, número equivocado* wrong number *2B*

nunca never *4A*

o or *2B; o...o* either...or *9A*

la **obra** work, play

ochenta eighty *1B*

ocho eight *1A*

ochocientos,-as eight hundred *5B*

octavo,-a eighth *7B*

octubre October *5B*

ocupado,-a busy, occupied *4A*

ocupar to occupy

la **odisea** odyssey

la **oferta** sale *9B; estar en oferta* to be on sale *9B*

oficial official

la **oficina** office *3A*

oigan hey, listen (pause in speech)

oigo hello (telephone greeting)

oír to hear, to listen *8A; oigan* hey, listen (pause in speech); *oigo* hello (telephone greeting); *oye* hey, listen (pause in speech) *3B*

la **olla** pot, saucepan *8A*

olvidar to forget *8B*

la **omisión** omission

once eleven *1A*

el **opuesto** opposite

la **oración** sentence

el **orden** order

la **organización** organization

el **órgano** organ

el **oro** gold *9B*

os (to, for) you (Spain, informal, *pl., i.o.*), you (Spain, informal, *pl., d.o.*)

el **otoño** autumn *7B*

otro,-a other, another *(pl. otros,-as) 4A; otra vez* again, another time *6A*

oye hey, listen (pause in speech) *3B*

el **Pacífico** Pacific (Ocean)

el **padrastro** stepfather

el **padre** father *4A; (pl. padres)* parents

la **paella** paella (traditional Spanish dish with rice, meat, seafood and vegetables) *8B*

pagar to pay *9B*

la **página** page *2A*

el **país** country *1A*

la **palabra** word *2A; palabra interrogativa* question word; *palabras antónimas* antonyms, opposite words

el **pan** bread *6A*

Panamá Panama *1A*

la **pantalla** screen *2B*

el **pantalón** pants *2B*

el **pañuelo** handkerchief, hanky *9B*

la **papa** potato *8B*

el **papá** father, dad

los **papás** parents

el **papel** paper *2A,* role; *haz el papel* play the role; *la hoja de papel* sheet of paper

para for, to, in order to *3A*

el **paraguas** umbrella *9B*

el **Paraguay** Paraguay *1A*

parecer to seem *8B*

la **pared** wall *2A*

la **pareja** pair, couple

el **pariente,** la **pariente** relative *4A*

parientes políticos in-laws

el **parque** park *3A*

el **párrafo** paragraph

la **parte** part

el **partido** game, match *4B; partidos empatados* games tied; *partidos ganados* games won; *partidos perdidos* games lost

pasado,-a past, last *5B; pasado mañana* the day after tomorrow *5B*

pásame: see *pasar*

pasar to pass, to spend (time) *5A,* to happen, to occur; *pásame* pass me *6A; pasar la aspiradora* to vacuum *8A; ¿Qué te pasa?* What is wrong with you?

el **pasatiempo** pastime, leisure activity *7A*

la **Pascua** Easter

el **paseo** walk, ride, trip *7B; dar un paseo* to go for a walk, to go for a ride *7B*

el **patinador,** la **patinadora** skater *7B*

patinar to skate *4B; patinar sobre ruedas* to in-line skate *4B; patinar sobre hielo* to ice skate *7B*

la **patineta** skateboard *7B*

el **patio** courtyard, patio, yard *6B*

pedir (i, i) to ask for, to order, to request *6B; pedir perdón* to say you are sorry *6B; pedir permiso (para)* to ask for permission (to do something) *6B; pedir prestado,-a* to borrow *6B*

la **película** movie, film *5A*

pelirrojo,-a red-haired *4B*

la **pelota** ball

pensar (ie) to think, to intend, to plan *6A; pensar de* to think about (i.e., to have an opinion) *6A; pensar en* to think about (i.e., to focus one's thoughts on) *6A; pensar en* (+ infinitive) to think about (doing something)

peor worse *8B*; **el/la/los/las peor/peores** (+ noun) the worst (+ noun) *8B*

pequeño,-a small *6B*

perder (ie) to lose; *los partidos perdidos* games lost

perdidos: see *perder*

perdón excuse me, pardon me *1B*; *pedir perdón* to say you are sorry *6B*

perezoso,-a lazy

perfecto,-a perfect *9B*

el **perfume** perfume *9B*

el **periódico** newspaper *2A*

el **periodista**, la **periodista** journalist, reporter

el **período** period

la **perla** pearl *9B*

el **permiso** permission, permit *7A*; *con permiso* excuse me (with your permission), may I *1B*; *pedir permiso (para)* to ask for permission (to do something) *6B*

permitir to permit *7A*

pero but *3B*

el **perro**, la **perra** dog *5A*

la **persona** person *8A*

personal personal; *el pronombre personal* subject pronoun

el **Perú** Peru *1A*

el **pescado** fish *3B*

el **petróleo** oil

el **piano** piano *4B*

el **pie** foot *9A*; *a pie* on foot *3A*

la **pierna** leg *9A*

el **pijama** pajamas *9A*

la **pimienta** pepper (seasoning) *6A*

el **pimiento** bell pepper *8B*

pintar to paint

la **pirámide** pyramid

la **piscina** swimming pool *6B*

el **piso** floor *6B*; *el primer piso* first floor *6B*

la **pista** clue

la **pizarra** blackboard *2A*

la **planta** plant *6B*; *planta baja* ground floor *6B*

la **plata** silver *9B*

el **plátano** banana *8B*

el **plato** dish, plate *6A*; *plato de sopa* soup bowl *6A*

la **playa** beach *4A*

la **plaza** plaza, public square *3B*

poco,-a not very, little, few *6B*; *un poco* a little (bit) *5A*

poder (ue) to be able *7A*

políticamente politically

el **pollo** chicken *3B*

poner to put, to place *6A*; to turn on (an appliance); *poner la mesa* to set the table *6A*

popular popular *4A*

un **poquito** a very little (bit)

por for *4A*, through, by *6B*, in *7A*, along *7B*; *por ejemplo* for example; *por favor* please *1B*; *por la mañana* in the morning *7A*; *por la noche* at night *6B*; *por la tarde* in the afternoon *7A*; *por teléfono* by telephone, on the telephone *6B*; *por todos lados* everywhere *7B*; *por lo general* generally

¿por qué? why? *3A*

porque because *3A*

la **posibilidad** possibility

la **posición** position, place

el **póster** poster

el **postre** dessert *6A*

la **práctica** practice *5A*; *La práctica hace al maestro.* Practice makes perfect.

el **precio** price *8B*

preferir (ie, i) to prefer *6A*

la **pregunta** question *3B*; *hacer una pregunta* to ask a question *3B*

preguntar to ask *3B*

el **premio** award, prize

la **preparación** preparation

preparar to prepare *8A*

el **preparativo** preparation

la **preposición** preposition

presenciar to witness

la **presentación** introduction

presentar to introduce, to present; *le presento a* let me introduce you (formal, *s.*) to *3A*; *les presento a* let me introduce you (*pl.*) to *3A*; *te presento a* let me introduce you (informal, *s.*) to *3A*

presente present

presento: see *presentar*

prestado,-a on loan *6B*; *pedir prestado,-a* to borrow *6B*

prestar to lend *8A*

la **primavera** spring *7B*

primer first (form of *primero* before a *m., s.* noun) *6B*; *el primer piso* first floor *6B*

primero,-a first *5B*

primero first (adverb) *5A*

el **primo**, la **prima** cousin *4A*

principal main

la **prisa** rush, hurry, haste *6B*; *tener prisa* to be in a hurry *6B*

el **problema** problem *3A*

produce produces

el **producto** product

el **profesor**, la **profesora** teacher *2A*; *el profe* teacher

el **programa** program, show *7A*

prometer to promise *9A*

el **pronombre** pronoun; *pronombre personal* subject pronoun

el **pronóstico** forecast

pronto soon, quickly *1B*; *hasta pronto* see you soon *1B*

la **pronunciación** pronunciation

el **propósito** aim, purpose; *A propósito* by the way *1A*

próximo,-a next

la **publicidad** publicity

público,-a public

la **puerta** door *2A*

Puerto Rico Puerto Rico *1A*

pues thus, well, so, then (pause in speech) *3B*

la **pulsera** bracelet *9B*

el **punto** point, dot *(term used in Internet addresses)* *2B*

la **puntuación** punctuation

el **pupitre** desk *2A*

que that, which *5A*; *lo que* what, that which *6B*; *más* (+ noun/adjective/adverb) *que* more (+ noun/adjective/adverb) than *8B*; *que viene* upcoming, next *5A*

¡qué (+ adjective)! how (+ adjective)! *4A*

¡qué (+ noun)! what a (+ noun)! *5A*

¿qué? what? *2A*; *¿a qué hora?* at what time? *2B*; *¿Qué comprendiste?* What did you understand?; *¿Qué hora es?*

What time is it? *1B; ¿Qué quiere decir...?* What is the meaning (of)...? *2A; ¿Qué tal?* How are you? *1B; ¿Qué te pasa?* What is wrong with you?; *¿Qué temperatura hace?* What is the temperature? *7B; ¿Qué (+ tener)?* What is wrong with (someone)? *6B; ¿Qué tiempo hace?* How is the weather? *7B*

quedar to remain, to stay *9A; quedarle bien a uno* to fit, to be becoming *9A*

el **quehacer** chore *8A*

el **quemador de discos compactos (CDs)** compact disc (CD) burner *5A*

querer (ie) to love, to want, to like *6A; ¿Qué quiere decir...?* What is the meaning (of)...? *2A; querer decir* to mean *6B; quiere decir* it means *2A; quiero* I love *4A;* I want *3A*

querido,-a dear *6B*

el **queso** cheese *8B*

¿quién? who? *2A; (pl. ¿quiénes?)* who? *3A*

quiere: see *querer*

quiero: see *querer*

la **química** chemistry

quince fifteen *1A*

quinientos,-as five hundred *5B*

quinto,-a fifth *7B*

quisiera would like

quizás perhaps *8A*

la **radio** radio (broadcast) *4B; el radio* radio (apparatus)

rápidamente rapidly *5B*

rápido,-a rapid, fast *4B*

el **rascacielos** skyscraper

el **ratón** mouse (pl. *ratones*) *2B*

la **razón** reason

real royal

la **realidad** reality

la **receta** recipe *8B*

recibir to receive *9B*

el **recibo** receipt *9B*

recoger to pick up *8A; recoger la mesa* to clear the table *8A*

recordar (ue) to remember *7A*

redondo,-a round

el **refresco** soft drink, refreshment *3B*

el **refrigerador** refrigerator *6A*

el **regalo** gift *9B*

regañar to scold

regatear to bargain, to haggle

la **regla** ruler *2A*

regresar to return, to go back

regular average, okay, so-so, regular *1B*

relacionado,-a related

el **reloj** clock, watch *2A*

remoto,-a remote *7A*

repasar to reexamine, to review

el **repaso** review

repetir (i, i) to repeat *6B; repitan (Uds. command)* repeat; *repite (tú command)* repeat

repitan: see *repetir*

repite: see *repetir*

reportando reporting

el **reproductor** player *5A; reproductor de CDs* CD player *5A; reproductor de DVDs* DVD player *5A; reproductor de MP3* MP3 player *5A*

la **República Dominicana** Dominican Republic *1A*

resolver (ue) to resolve, to solve

responder to answer

la **respuesta** answer

el **restaurante** restaurant *3A*

el **resultado** result

el **resumen** summary; *en resumen* in short

la **reunión** meeting

la **revista** magazine *2A*

rico,-a rich

el **riel** rail

el **río** river

el **ritmo** rhythm

rojo,-a red *2B*

la **ropa** clothing *2B; ropa interior* underwear *9A*

rosado,-a pink *9A*

rubio,-a blond, blonde *4B*

la **rutina** routine

sábado Saturday *2B; el sábado* on Saturday

saber to know *3B; sabes* you know *3B; sé* I know *2A*

sabes: see *saber*

el **sacapuntas** pencil sharpener *2A*

sacar to take out *8A; sacar fotos* to take photographs

la **sal** salt *6A*

la **sala** living room *6B*

salir to go out *4A*

la **salsa** salsa (dance music)

la **salud** health

el **saludo** greeting

el **salvavidas** lifeguard

la **sangre** blood

el **santo** saint's day; *Todos los Santos* All Saints' Day

el **saxofón** saxophone

se *¿Cómo se dice...?* How do you say...? *2A; ¿Cómo se escribe...?* How do you write (spell)...? *1A; ¿Cómo se llama (Ud./él/ ella)?* What is (your/his/her) name? *2A; se considera* it is considered; *se dice* one says *2A; se escribe* it is written *1A; Se habla español.* Spanish is spoken.; *se llaman* their names are; *(Ud./Él/Ella) se llama....* (Your [formal]/His/Her) name is.... *2A*

sé: see *saber*

sea: see *ser*

la **sed** thirst *6B; tener sed* to be thirsty *6B*

la **seda** silk *9A*

seguir (i, i) to follow, to continue, to keep on; *sigan (Uds. command)* follow; *sigue (tú command)* follow

según according to

el **segundo** second *7B*

segundo,-a second *7A*

seguro,-a safe

seis six *1A*

seiscientos,-as six hundred *5B*

selecciona select (*tú* command)

la **selva** jungle; *selva tropical* tropical rain forest

la **semana** week *5A; el fin de semana* weekend *5A; Semana Santa* Holy Week

sentarse (ie) to sit (down); *siéntate (tú command)* sit (down); *siéntense (Uds. command)* sit (down)

sentir (ie, i) to be sorry, to feel sorry, to regret *6A; lo siento* I am sorry *1B*

señalar to point to, to point at, to point out; *señalen (Uds. command)* point to

señalen: see *señalar*

el **señor** gentleman, sir, Mr. *1B*

la **señora** lady, madame, Mrs. *1B*

la **señorita** young lady, Miss *1B*

septiembre September *5B*

séptimo,-a seventh *7B*

ser to be *2A; eres* you are *1A; ¿Eres (tú) de...?* Are you from...? *1A; es* you (formal) are, he/she/it is *1B; es la una* it is one o'clock *1B; Es medianoche.* It is midnight. *1B; Es mediodía.* It is noon. *1B; fue* you (formal) were, he/she/it was (preterite of *ser*) *5B; ¿Qué hora es?* What time is it? *1B; sea* it is; *son* they are *1B; son las* (+ number) it is (+ number) o'clock *1B; soy* I am *1A*

serio,-a serious

la **servilleta** napkin *6A*

sesenta sixty *1B*

setecientos,-as seven hundred *5B*

setenta seventy *1B*

sexto,-a sixth *7B*

si if *5A*

sí yes *1A*

siempre always *3B*

siéntate: see *sentarse*

siéntense: see *sentarse*

siento: see *sentir*

siete seven *1A*

sigan: see *seguir*

el **siglo** century *7A*

los **signos de puntuación** punctuation marks

sigue: see *seguir*

siguiente following; *lo siguiente* the following

la **silabificación** syllabification

el **silencio** silence

la **silla** chair *2A*

el **símbolo** symbol

similar alike, similar

simpático,-a nice, pleasant *3A*

sin without *8B*

sintético,-a synthetic *9B*

la **situación** situation

sobre on, over, on top of *2B*, about; *patinar sobre hielo* to ice skate *4B; patinar sobre ruedas* in-line skate *4B*

la **sobrina** niece *4A*

el **sobrino** nephew *4A*

el **sol** sun *7B; hace sol, hay sol* it is sunny *7B*

solamente only

soleado,-a sunny *7B; está soleado* it is sunny *7B*

solo, -a alone

sólo only, just *8A*

el **sombrero** hat *9A*

son: see *ser*

el **sondeo** poll

el **sonido** sound; *equipo de sonido* sound system *5A*

la **sopa** soup *6A*

la **sorpresa** surprise *5A*

soy: see *ser*

Sr. abbreviation for *señor 1B*

Sra. abbreviation for *señora 1B*

Srta. abbreviation for *señorita 1B*

su, sus his, her, its, your *(Ud./Uds.)*, their *4A*

suave smooth, soft

el **subdesarrollo** underdevelopment

subir to climb, to go up, to go upstairs, to take up, to bring up, to carry up *8A*

el **suceso** happening

sucio,-a dirty *4A*

el **sueño** sleep *6B; tener sueño* to be sleepy *6B*

el **suéter** sweater *9A*

el **supermercado** supermarket *8B*

el **sur** south

el **sustantivo** noun

tal such, as, so; *¿Qué tal?* How are you? *1B*

el **tamal** tamale

el **tamaño** size *9B*

también also, too *3A*

el **tambor** drum

tampoco either, neither *2B*

tan so *5A; tan* (+ adjective/adverb) *como* (+ person/item) as (+ adjective/adverb) as (+ person/item) *8B*

tanto,-a so much *3A; tanto,-a* (+ noun) *como* (+ person/item) as much/many (+ noun) as (+ person/item) *8B; tanto como* as much as *8B; Tanto gusto.* So glad to meet you. *3A*

la **tapa** tidbit, appetizer

la **tarde** afternoon *1B; buenas tardes* good afternoon *1A; de la tarde* P.M., in the afternoon *1B; por la tarde* in the afternoon *7A;* late

la **tarea** homework *4B*

la **tarjeta** card *9B; tarjeta de crédito* credit card *9B*

el **taxi** taxi *3A*

la **taza** cup *6A*

te (to, for) you *(i.o.) 3A;* you *(d.o.) 5A; ¿Cómo te llamas?* What is your name? *1A; te llamas* your name is *1A*

el **teatro** theater *3B*

el **teclado** keyboard *2B*

el **teléfono** telephone *2B; el número de teléfono* telephone number *2B; por teléfono* by the telephone, on the telephone *6B*

la **telenovela** soap opera *7A*

la **televisión** television *4B; ver la televisión* to watch television *4B*

el **televisor** television set *7A*

el **tema** theme, topic

la **temperatura** temperature *7B; ¿Qué temperatura hace?* What is the temperature? *7B*

temprano early *5B*

el **tenedor** fork *6A*

tener to have *5A; ¿Cuántos años tienes?* How old are you? *1A; ¿Qué* (+ *tener*)? What is wrong with (person)? *6B; tener calor* to be hot *6B; tener frío* to be cold *6B; tener ganas de* to feel like *6B; tener hambre* to be hungry *6B; tener miedo de* to be afraid *6B; tener* (+ number) *años* to be (+ number) years old *5A; tener prisa* to be in a hurry *6B; tener que* to have to *6A; tener sed* to be thirsty *6B; tener sueño* to be sleepy *6B; tengo* I have *1A; tengo* (+ number) *años* I am (+ number) years old *1A; tiene* it has; *tienes* you have *1A*

tengo: see *tener*

el **tenis** tennis *4B*

el **tenista,** la **tenista** tennis player *7B*

tercer third (form of *tercero* before a *m., s.* noun) *7B*

tercero,-a third *7B*

terminar to end, to finish *2B*
ti you (after a preposition) *4B*
la **tía** aunt *4A*
el **tiempo** time *4A*, weather *7B*, verb tense; *Hace buen (mal) tiempo.* The weather is nice (bad). *7B; ¿Qué tiempo hace?* How is the weather? *7B*
la **tienda** store *3B*
tiene: see *tener*
tienes: see *tener*
el **tío** uncle *4A*
típico,-a typical
el **tipo** type, kind
la **tiza** chalk *2A*
toca: see *tocar*
tocar to play (a musical instrument) *4B*, to touch; *toca (tú command)* touch; *toquen (Uds. command)* touch
todavía yet *7A*, still *7B*
todo,-a all, every, whole, entire *4A; de todos los días* everyday *6A; por todos lados* everywhere *7B; todo el mundo* everyone, everybody; *todos los días* every day *5A*
todos,-as everyone, everybody
tolerante tolerant
tomar to take *3A*, to drink, to have *3B*
el **tomate** tomato *8B*
tonto,-a silly *4B*
el **tópico** theme
toquen: see *tocar*
trabajar to work *8A; trabajando en parejas* working in pairs
el **trabajo** work *8A*
traer to bring *8A*
el **traje** suit *9A; traje de baño* swimsuit *9A*
el **transporte** transportation *3A*
tratar (de) to try (to do something)
trece thirteen *1A*
treinta thirty *1B*
el **tren** train *3A*
tres three *1A*
trescientos,-as three hundred *5B*
triste sad *4A*
el **trombón** trombone

la **trompeta** trumpet
tu your (informal) *2B; (pl. tus)* your (informal) *4A*
tú you (informal) *1A*
la **tumba** tomb
el **turista,** la **turista** tourist

u or (used before a word that starts with o or ho) *6B*
Ud. you (abbreviation of *usted*) *1B;* you (after a preposition) *4B; Ud. se llama….* Your name is…. *2A*
Uds. you (abbreviation of *ustedes*) *1B;* you (after a preposition) *4B*
último,-a last
un, una a, an, one *2A*
único,-a only, unique *4A*
unido,-a united
la **universidad** university
uno one *1A*
unos, unas some, any, a few *2A*
el **Uruguay** Uruguay *1A*
usar to use *9B*
usted you (formal, *s.*) *1B;* you (after a preposition) *4B*
ustedes you *(pl.)* *1B;* you (after a preposition) *4B*
la **uva** grape *8B*

las **vacaciones** vacation *9A*
Vallenato a combination of African, European and Colombian folkloric sounds
¡vamos! let's go! *3A; ¡vamos a (+ infinitive)!* let's *(+ infinitive)!* *3B*
varios,-as several
el **vaso** glass *6A*
vayan: see *ir*
ve: see *ir*
veinte twenty *1A*
veinticinco twenty-five *1B*
veinticuatro twenty-four *1B*
veintidós twenty-two *1B*
veintinueve twenty-nine *1B*
veintiocho twenty-eight *1B*
veintiséis twenty-six *1B*
veintisiete twenty-seven *1B*

veintitrés twenty-three *1B*
veintiuno twenty-one *1B*
vender to sell *9A*
Venezuela Venezuela *1A*
vengan: see *venir*
venir to come *5B; vengan (Uds.* command) come
la **ventana** window *2A*
ver to see, to watch *3B; a ver* let's see, hello (telephone greeting); *ver la televisión* to watch television *4B*
el **verano** summer *4A*
el **verbo** verb
verdad true
la **verdad** truth *6B*
¿verdad? right? *3A*
verde green *2B*
la **verdura** greens, vegetables *8B*
ves: see *ver*
el **vestido** dress *9A*
la **vez** time *(pl. veces)* *5B; a veces* at times, sometimes *5B;* (number +) *vez/veces al/a la* (+ time expression) (number +) time(s) per (+ time expression) *7A; otra vez* again, another time *6A*
viajar to travel *6A*
el **viaje** trip *5A; hacer un viaje* to take a trip *5A; la agencia de viajes* travel agency
la **vida** life *7A*
el **videojuego** video game *7A*
viejo,-a old *5B*
el **viento** wind *7B; hace viento* it is windy *7B*
viernes Friday *2B; el viernes* on Friday
el **vinagre** vinegar *8B*
la **vista** view; *hasta la vista* so long, see you later
vivir to live *4A*
el **vocabulario** vocabulary
la **vocal** vowel; *vocales abiertas* open vowels; *vocales cerradas* closed vowels
el **voleibol** volleyball *7A*
volver (ue) to return, to go back, to come back *7A*
vosotros,-as you (Spain, informal, *pl.*) *1B*

vuestro,-a,-os,-as your (Spain, informal, *pl.*)

y and *1A; y cuarto* a quarter past, a quarter after *1B; y media* half past *1B*

ya already *6A; ¡ya lo veo!* I see it!

yo I *1A*

la **zanahoria** carrot *8B*

el **zapato** shoe *2B; zapato bajo* flats *9A; zapato de tacón* high-heel shoe *9A*

ocabulary English / Spanish

A

a un, una *1B*; *a few* unos, unas *1B*; *a lot (of)* mucho *4B*, muchísimo
about sobre
accent el acento *1A*
activity la actividad *5A*
to add añadir *8B*
address la dirección *2B*
to adopt adoptar
aerobics los aeróbicos *7A*; *to do aerobics* hacer aeróbicos *7A*
affectionate cariñoso,-a *4A*
afraid asustado,-a; *to be afraid of* tener miedo de *6B*
after después de *7A*
afternoon la tarde *1B*; *good afternoon* buenas tardes *1A*; *in the afternoon* de la tarde *1B*; por la tarde *7A*
afterwards después *7A*
again otra vez *6A*
age la edad
agency la agencia; *travel agency* agencia de viajes
ago hace (+ *time expression*) que *7A*
agreed de acuerdo *3B*
airplane el avión *3A*; *by airplane* en avión *3A*
airport el aeropuerto
algebra el álgebra
all todo,-a *4A*
almost casi *7A*
alone solo,-a
along por *7B*
already ya *6A*
also también *3A*
alternate alterna (tú *command*); alternen (Uds. *command*)
although aunque
always siempre *3B*
American americano,-a *7A*
an un, una *2A*

and y *1A*; e *(used before a word beginning with i or hi)* *6B*
another otro,-a *2A*; *another time* otra vez *4B*
answer la respuesta
to answer contestar *4B*
any unos, unas *2A*; alguno,-a, algún, alguna *8A*, cualquier
anybody alguien *9A*
anyone alguien *9A*
anything algo *9A*
apartment el apartamento
apple la manzana *8B*
April abril *5B*
Argentina la Argentina *1A*
arm el brazo *9A*
to arrange arreglar *8A*
to arrive llegar *8A*
art el arte *2B*
article el artículo *5A*
artist el artista, la artista
as tal *1B*, como; *as (+ adverb) as possible* lo más/menos (+ *adverb*) posible *8B*; *as (+ adjective/adverb) as (+ person/ item)* tan (+ *adjective/adverb*) como (+ *person/item*) *8B*; *as much/many (+ noun) as (+ person/item)* tanto,-a (+ *noun*) como (+ *person/item*) *8B*; *as much as* tanto como *8B*
to ask preguntar *3B*; *to ask a question* hacer una pregunta *3B*; *to ask for* pedir (i, i) *6B*; pedir permiso (para) *to ask for permission (to do something)* *6B*
at en; (@) *symbol for e-mail address* arroba *2B*; *at home* en casa *9B*; *at night* de la noche *1B*, por la noche *6B*; *at... o'clock* a la(s)... *2B*; *at times* a veces *5B*; *at what time?* ¿a qué hora? *2B*
athlete el deportista, la deportista *7B*
to attain conseguir (i, i)

attractive bonito,-a, guapo,-a *4A*
August agosto *5B*
aunt la tía *4A*
autumn el otoño *7B*
avenue la avenida *3B*
average regular *1B*
avocado el aguacate *8B*
award el premio

B

backpack la mochila *2A*
bad malo,-a *4B*
bald calvo,-a *4B*
ball pelota, bola; *to bowl* jugar a los bolos
banana el plátano *8B*
bank el banco *3A*
to bargain regatear
baseball el béisbol *4B*
basketball el básquetbol *7A*, el baloncesto; *basketball player* el basquetbolista, la basquetbolista *7B*
bathroom el baño *6B*, el cuarto de baño
to be ser *2A*; *to be able to* poder (ue) *7A*; *to be afraid of* tener miedo de *6B*; *to be hot* tener calor *6B*; *to be hungry* tener hambre *6B*; *to be important* importar *8B*; *to be in a hurry* tener prisa *6B*; *to be lacking* hacer falta *8B*; *to be necessary* hacer falta *8B*; *to be (+ number) years old* tener (+ *number*) años *5A*; *to be pleasing to* gustar *4B*; *to be ready* estar listo,-a *7B*; *to be satisfied (with)* estar contento,-a (con) *4A*; *to be sleepy* tener sueño *6B*; *to be smart* ser listo,-a *8A*; *to be sorry* sentir *6A*; *to be thirsty* tener sed *6B*
beach la playa *4A*
beans los frijoles *3B*
because porque *3A*

to become cumplir *5B; to become (+ number) years old* cumplir *(+ number)* años *5B*
bed la cama *8A*
bedroom el cuarto *6B*, la habitación
before antes de *7A*
to begin empezar *(ie) 6A*
to believe creer
belt el cinturón *9B*
beside al lado (de) *6B*
best mejor *8B; the best (+ noun)* el/la/los/las mejor/mejores *(+ noun) 8B*
better mejor *8B*
between entre
bicycle la bicicleta *3A*
big grande *3B*, gran *(form of grande before a m., s. noun)*
bike la bicicleta *3A*
biology la biología *2B*
birthday el cumpleaños *5B; Happy birthday!* ¡Feliz cumpleaños! *5B; to have a birthday* cumplir años *5B*
black negro,-a *2B*
blackboard la pizarra *2A*
blond, blonde rubio,-a *4B*
blouse la blusa *2B*
blue azul *2B; blue jeans* los jeans *2B*
boat el barco *3A*
body el cuerpo *9A*
Bolivia Bolivia *1A*
book el libro *2A*
bookstore la librería *5A*
boot la bota *9A*
bored aburrido,-a *4B*
boring aburrido,-a *4B*
to borrow pedir prestado,-a *6B*
boy el chico *2A*, el muchacho *1A*
boyfriend el novio
bracelet la pulsera *9B*
bread el pan *6A*
breakfast el desayuno
to bring traer *8A*
to bring up subir *8A*
brother el hermano *4A*
brown marrón *9A*
brunet, brunette moreno,-a *4B*
building el edificio *3B*
bus el autobús *3A*
busy ocupado,-a *4A*
but pero *3B*
butter la mantequilla *6A*
to buy comprar *4B*

by por *4A; by (+ vehicle)* en *(+ vehicle) 3A; by telephone* por teléfono *6B; By the way* A propósito; *by means of* mediante

C

cafeteria la cafetería
calendar el calendario
to call llamar *5A*
can la lata *8B*
capital la capital *1A*
car el carro *3A*, el coche; *by car* en carro *3A*, en coche
card la tarjeta *9B; credit card* tarjeta de crédito *9B; playing card* la carta *7A*
carrot la zanahoria *8B*
to carry llevar *5A; to carry up* subir *8A*
cash el efectivo *9B; in cash* en efectivo *9B*
cash register la caja *9B*
cassette el casete *5A*
cat el gato, la gata *5A*
CD el CD, el disco compacto *2B; CD player* el reproductor de CDs *5A; CD burner* el quemador de CDs *5A*
to celebrate celebrar *5B*
census el censo
center el centro *3B; shopping center* centro comercial *9A*
century el siglo *7A*
chair la silla *2A*
chalk la tiza *2A*
change el cambio *9B*
to change cambiar *9B*
cheap barato,-a *9B*
checkers las damas *7A*
cheese el queso *8B*
chemistry la química
chess el ajedrez *7A*
chicken el pollo *3B*
child niño,-a
Chile Chile *1A*
chilly fresco,-a *7B*
chocolate el chocolate *8B*
to choose escoger *8B*
chore el quehacer *8A*
Christmas la Navidad *5B*
city la ciudad *3A*
clam la almeja
clarinet el clarinete
class la clase *2A*
classmate el compañero, la compañera *5A*

clean limpio,-a *4A*
to clean limpiar *8A*
clerk el dependiente, la dependienta *9B*
to climb subir *8A; escalar*
clock el reloj *2A*
to close cerrar *(ie) 6A*
closed cerrado,-a *4A*
clothing la ropa *2B*
cloudy nublado,-a *7B; it is cloudy* está nublado *7B*
coat el abrigo *8A*
coffee el café *8B*
cold frío,-a *4A*; el frío *4A; it is cold* hace frío *7B; to be cold* tener frío *6B*
Colombia Colombia *1A*
color el color *7B*
to combine combinar *9A*
to come venir *5B; to come back* volver *(ue) 7A; to come in* entrar *5A*
comfort comodidad
comfortable cómodo,-a *6B*
comical cómico,-a *4B*
common común
compact disc el disco compacto (CD) *2B; CD player* el reproductor de discos compactos (CDs) *5A; CD burner* el quemador de discos compactos (CDs) *5A*
competition la competencia
to complete completar, acabar *8A*
computer la computadora *2B*
computer science la computación *2B*
concert el concierto *3B*
congratulations felicitaciones
to conquer conquistar
to continue continuar *7B*, seguir *(i, i)*
to cook cocinar *8A*
cool el fresco *7B; it is cool* hace fresco *7B*
to copy copiar *7B*
corn el maíz *8B*
to cost costar *(ue) 7A*
Costa Rica Costa Rica *1A*
cotton el algodón *9A*
to count contar
country el país *1A*
couple la pareja
courtyard el patio *6B*
cousin el primo, la prima *4A*
crazy loco,-a *4A*

to create crear
credit el crédito *9B; credit card* la tarjeta de crédito *9B; on credit* a crédito *9B*
to cross cruzar
Cuba Cuba *1A*
cup la taza *6A*
cycling ciclismo

dad el papá
to dance bailar *4B*
dark obscuro,-a; *dark-haired, dark-skinned* moreno,-a *4B*
date la fecha *5B*
daughter la hija *4A*
day el día *2B; every day* todos los días *6A; the day after tomorrow* pasado mañana *5B; the day before yesterday* anteayer *5B*
dear querido,-a *5B*
December diciembre *5B*
to decorate adornar *8A*
degree el grado *7B*
delighted encantado,-a *3A*
dentist el dentista, la dentista *3A*
department el departamento *9A*
desire la gana *6B*
desk el escritorio, el pupitre *2A*
dessert el postre *6A*
difficult difícil *4B*
dinner la comida
to direct dirigir
director el director, la directora
dirty sucio,-a *4A*
disaster el desastre
disc el disco *2B; compact disc (CD)* el disco compacto *2B; CD player* el reproductor de discos compactos (CDs) *5A; CD burner* el quemador de discos compactos (CDs) *5A*
to discover descubrir
dish el plato *6A*
dishwasher el lavaplatos *6A*
diskette el diskette *2B*
to do hacer *3B; to do aerobics* hacer aeróbicos *7A*
doctor el médico, la médica *3A,* el doctor, la doctora
dog el perro, la perra *5A*
dollar el dólar

Dominican Republic la República Dominicana *1A*
door la puerta *2A*
dot punto *2B*
downtown el centro *3B*
to draw dibujar *7A*
drawing el dibujo *6B*
dress el vestido *9A*
drink el refresco *3B,* la bebida
to drink tomar *3B*
drum el tambor
during durante
DVD el DVD *5A; DVD player* el reproductor de DVDs *5A*

e-mail correo electrónico *2B*
each cada *5A*
early temprano *5B*
earring el arete *2B*
Easter la Pascua
easy fácil *4B*
to eat comer *3B*
Ecuador el Ecuador *1A*
egg el huevo *8B*
eight ocho *1A*
eight hundred ochocientos, -as *5B*
eighteen dieciocho *1A*
eighth octavo,-a *7B*
eighty ochenta *1B*
either tampoco *2B; either...or* o...o *9A*
electric eléctrico,-a *6A*
electronic electrónico,-a *2B*
elevator el ascensor *9B*
eleven once *1A*
El Salvador El Salvador *1A*
else más *4A*
end el fin *5A*
to end terminar *2B*
English el inglés *(language) 2B*
to enjoy disfrutar
enough bastante *9B*
to erase borrar
eraser el borrador *2A*
escalator la escalera mecánica *9B*
every todo,-a *4A,* cada *5A; every day* todos los días *5A*
everybody todo el mundo, todos,-as
everyday de todos los días *5A*
everyone todo el mundo, todos,-as
everywhere por todos lados *7B*

exam el examen *5A*
example el ejemplo; *for example* por ejemplo
excellent excelente *7B*
to exchange cambiar *9B*
excuse me perdón, con permiso *1B*
expensive caro,-a *9B*
to explain explicar, aclarar
explanation la explicación

face la cara
fairly bastante
family la familia *4A; family tree* el árbol genealógico
famous famoso,-a
fantastic fantástico,-a *3A*
far (from) lejos (de) *3A*
fast rápido,-a *4B*
fat gordo,-a *4B*
father el padre *4A*
favorite favorito,-a *3B*
fear el miedo *6B; to be afraid of* tener miedo de *6B*
February febrero *5B*
to feed dar de comer *8A*
to feel like tener ganas de *6B*
to feel sorry sentir *(ie) 6A*
few poco,-a *6A*
fifteen quince *1A*
fifth quinto,-a *7B*
fifty cincuenta *1B*
film la película *5A*
to find encontrar *(ue)*
finger el dedo *9A*
to finish terminar *2B,* acabar *8A*
first primero,-a *5B,* primer *(form of primero before a m., s. noun) 6B,* primero *(adverb) 5B; first floor* el primer piso *6B*
fish el pescado *3B*
to fit quedarle bien a uno *9A*
five cinco *1A*
five hundred quinientos,-as *5B*
to fix arreglar *8A*
floor el piso *6B; first floor* el primer piso *6B; ground floor* la planta baja *6B*
flower la flor *7B*
flute la flauta
to fold doblar *8A*
to follow seguir *(i, i); the following* lo siguiente
food la comida *3B; food server* el mesero, la mesera *3B*

foot el pie *9A*; *on foot* a pie *3A*

football el fútbol americano *7A*

for por, para *3A*; *for example* por ejemplo *1B*

to forget olvidar *8B*

fork el tenedor *6A*

forty cuarenta *1B*

four cuatro *1A*

four hundred cuatrocientos, -as *5B*

fourteen catorce *1A*

fourth cuarto,-a *7B*

free libre *4A*

fresh fresco,-a *8B*

Friday viernes *2B*; *on Friday* el viernes

friend el amigo, la amiga *2A*

from de *1A*, desde *6B*; *from the* de la/del (de + el) *3A*; *from where?* ¿de dónde? *1A*

fruit la fruta *8B*

fun divertido,-a *4A*

funny cómico,-a *4B*

game el partido *4B*, el juego

garage el garaje *6B*

garbage la basura *8A*

garden el jardín *8A*

garlic el ajo *8B*

generally generalmente

generous generoso,-a *4B*

geography la geografía

geometry la geometría

to get conseguir *(i, i)*

to get together reunir

gift el regalo *9B*

girl la chica *2A*, la muchacha *1A*

girlfriend la novia

to give dar *7A*

glad contento,-a *2A*; *Glad to meet you!* ¡Mucho gusto! *1A*; *I would be glad to* con (mucho) gusto *1A*; *So glad to meet you.* Tanto gusto. *1A*

glass el vaso *4B*

glove el guante *9A*

to go ir *3A*; *let's go!* ¡vamos! *3A*; *to be going to (do something)* ir a (+ *infinitive*) *3B*; *to go back* regresar, volver *(ue)* *7A*; *to go in* entrar *5A*; *to go out* salir *4A*; *to go shopping* ir de compras *4B*; *to go up* subir *8A*; *to go upstairs* subir *8A*

gold el oro *9B*

good bueno,-a *4B*, buen (*form of* bueno *before a m., s. noun*) *7B*; *good afternoon* buenas tardes *1B*; *good luck* buena suerte; *good morning* buenos días *1B*; *good night* buenas noches *1B*

good-bye adiós *1A*

good-looking guapo,-a *4A*, bonito,-a *4A*

gossip el chisme *6B*

grade la nota, la calificación

granddaughter la nieta *4A*

grandfather el abuelo *4A*

grandmother la abuela *4A*

grandson el nieto *4A*

grape la uva *8B*

gray gris *2B*

great fantástico,-a *3A*

greater mayor *8B*

greatest mayor *8B*

green verde *2B*

green bean la habichuela *8B*

greens la verdura *8B*

group el grupo; *musical group* grupo musical

Guatemala Guatemala *1A*

guitar la guitarra

guy el muchacho *1A*

gym el gimnasio

half medio,-a; *half past* y media *1B*

ham el jamón *8B*

hand la mano *9A*; *on the other hand* en cambio *7B*

handbag el bolso *9B*

handkerchief el pañuelo *9B*

handsome guapo,-a *4A*

to hang colgar *(ue)* *8A*

to happen pasar

happy contento,-a *4A*, feliz (*pl.* felices) *5B*, alegre; *Happy birthday!* ¡Feliz cumpleaños! *5B*

hard difícil *4B*

hat el sombrero *9A*

to have tomar *3B*, tener *5A*; *to have a birthday* cumplir años *5B*; *to have just* acabar de (+ *infinitive*) *8A*; *to have to* deber, tener que *6A*

he él *2A*

head la cabeza *9A*

health la salud

to hear oír *8A*

heat el calor *6B*

hello hola *1A*; *hello (telephone greeting)* aló *2B*, diga, oigo

help la ayuda

to help ayudar *6A*

her su, sus *4A*; la *(d.o.)* *5A*; le *(i.o.)* *1A*; *(after a preposition)* ella *4B*

here aquí *1A*

hey mira, miren, oye, oigan

hi hola *1A*

him lo *(d.o.)* *5A*; le *(i.o.)* *3A*; *(after a preposition)* él *4B*

his su, sus *4A*

hispanic hispano,-a

history la historia *2B*

hockey el hockey

home la casa *4A*; *at home* en casa

homework la tarea *4B*

Honduras Honduras *1A*

horrible horrible *4B*

horse el caballo *3A*; *on horseback* a caballo *3A*

hot caliente *4A*; *it is hot* hace calor *7B*; *to be hot* tener calor *6B*

hotel hotel *3A*

hour la hora *1B*

house la casa *4A*

how? ¿cómo? *1A*; *How are you?* ¿Qué tal? *1B*; *How are you (formal)?* ¿Cómo está (Ud.)? *1B*; *How are you (informal)?* ¿Cómo estás (tú)? *1B*; *How are you (pl.)?* ¿Cómo están (Uds.)? *1B*; *How do you say...?* ¿Cómo se dice...? *2A*; *How do you write (spell)...?* ¿Cómo se escribe...? *1A*; *How is the weather?* ¿Qué tiempo hace? *7B*; *How long...?* ¿Cuánto (+ *time expression*) hace que (+ *present tense of verb*)...? *7A*; *how many?* ¿cuántos,-as? *2B*; *how much?* ¿cuánto,-a? *2B*; *How old are you?* ¿Cuántos años tienes? *1A*

how (+ adjective)! ¡qué (+ *adjective*)! *4A*

hug el abrazo *6B*

hunger el hambre *f.* *6B*

hungry: to be hungry tener hambre *6B*

hurry la prisa *6B*; *in a hurry* apurado,-a *4A*; *to be in a hurry* tener prisa *6B*

husband el esposo *4A*

I

I yo *1A*
ice el hielo *7B*; *to ice skate* patinar sobre hielo *7B*
ice cream el helado *8B*
idea la idea *5B*
ideal ideal *4B*
if si *5A*
to **imagine** imaginar
important importante *4B*
in en *2A*, por *4A*
in-laws los parientes políticos
ingredient el ingrediente *8B*
in order to para *3A*
intelligent inteligente *4B*
to **intend** pensar *(ie) 6A*
interesting interesante *4B*
to **introduce** presentar *3A*; *let me introduce you (formal, s.) to* le presento a *3A*; *let me introduce you (informal, s.) to* te presento a *3A*; *let me introduce you (pl.) to* les presento a *3A*
invitation la invitación
to **invite** invitar
island la isla
it la *(d.o.)*, lo *(d.o.) 5A*
its su, sus *4A*

J

jacket la chaqueta *9A*
January enero *5B*
jeans los jeans *2B*
jersey la camiseta *2B*
jewel la joya *9B*
juice el jugo *3B*
July julio *5B*
June junio *5B*
just sólo

K

to **keep on** seguir *(i,i)*
keyboard el teclado *2B*
kilogram el kilo (kg.)
kind amable *4A*, el tipo
kitchen la cocina *6A*
knife el cuchillo *6A*
to **know** saber *3B*

L

lady la señora, Sra. *1B*, la dama; *young lady* la señorita *1B*
lamp la lámpara *6A*
language la lengua, el idioma
last pasado,-a *5B*, último,-a

late tarde
later luego *1A*, después *6A*; *see you later* hasta luego *1A*, hasta la vista
lazy perezoso,-a
to **learn** aprender
leather el cuero *9B*
to **leave** dejar *8A*
leg la pierna *9A*
to **lend** prestar *8B*
less menos *8B*; *less (+ noun/adjective/adverb) than* menos (+ *noun/adjective/adverb*) que *8B*; *the least (+ adjective + noun)* el/la/los/las (+ *noun*) menos (+ *adjective*) *8B*
let's (+ infinitive)! ¡vamos a (+ *infinitive*)! *3B*
let's go! ¡vamos! *3A*
letter la carta *6B*, la letra; *capital letter* la mayúscula *1A*; *lowercase letter* la minúscula *1A*
lettuce la lechuga *8B*
library la biblioteca *3A*
lie la mentira *6B*
to **lie** mentir *(ie, i)*
life la vida *7A*
light la luz *(pl. luces) 6A*
to **light** encender *(ie) 6A*
like como
to **like** gustar *4B*; querer *6A*; *I/you/he/she/it/we/they would like...* me/te/le/nos/vos/les gustaría... *6B*
list la lista *7A*
to **listen (to)** escuchar *4B*
little poco,-a *6B*; *a little (bit)* un poco *5A*; *a very little (bit)* un poquito
to **live** vivir *4A*
living room la sala *6B*
lobster la langosta
long largo,-a *9B*
to **look (at)** mirar *4B*; *to look for* buscar *3A*
to **lose** perder *(ie)*
love el amor *5A*
to **love** querer *6A*
lunch el almuerzo *2B*

M

magazine la revista *2A*
to **make** hacer *3B*
mall el centro comercial *9A*
man el hombre *9A*
many mucho,-a *3B*

map el mapa *2A*
March marzo *5B*
market el mercado *8B*
match el partido *4B*
material el material *9B*
mathematics las matemáticas *2B*
to **matter** importar *8B*
maximum máximo,-a *7B*
May mayo *5B*
me me *(i.o.) 4B*; me *(d.o.) 5A*; *they call me* me llaman; *(after a preposition)* mí
to **mean** querer decir *6B*; *it means* quiere decir *2A*; *What is the meaning (of)...?* ¿Qué quiere decir...? *2A*
meat la carne *8B*
mechanic mecánico,-a *9B*; la escalera mecánica *9B*
menu el menú *3B*
Mexico México *1A*
microwave oven horno microondas *6A*
midnight la medianoche *1B*; *It is midnight.* Es medianoche. *1B*
milk la leche *8A*
mine mío,-a; *the pleasure is mine* el gusto es mío *3A*
minimum mínimo,-a *7B*
minus menos *1B*
minute el minuto *7A*
Miss la señorita, Srta. *1B*
mist la neblina *7B*
mistaken equivocado
modern moderno,-a
mom la mamá
moment el momento *3B*
Monday lunes *2B*; *on Monday* el lunes
money el dinero *5A*
month el mes *5B*
more más *4A*; *more (+ noun/adjective/adverb) than* más (+ *noun/adjective/adverb*) que *8B*
morning la mañana *1B*; *good morning* buenos días *1B*; *in the morning* de la mañana *1B*, por la mañana *7A*
most: the most (+ adjective + noun) el/la/los/las (+ *noun*) más (+ *adjective*) *8B*
mother la madre *4A*
motorcycle la moto(cicleta) *3A*

mouse ratón (*pl.* ratones) *2B*

movie la película *5A*; *movie theater* el cine *3A*

Mr. el señor, Sr. *1B*

Mrs. la señora, Sra. *1B*

much mucho,-a, mucho *4B*; *very much* muchísimo

museum el museo *3B*

music la música *2B*

must deber *6A*

my mi *2A*, *(pl. my)* mis *4A*; *my name is* me llamo *1A*

N

name el nombre; *last name* el apellido; *my name is* me llamo *1A*; *their names are* se llaman; *What is your name?* ¿Cómo te llamas? *2A*; *What is (your/his/her) name?* ¿Cómo se llama (Ud./él/ella)? *1A*; *(Your [formal]/His/Her) name is....*(Ud./Él/Ella) se llama.... *2A*; *your name is* te llamas *1A*

napkin la servilleta *6A*

near cerca (de) *3A*

necklace el collar *9B*

to **need** necesitar *2B*

neither tampoco *2B*; *neither...nor* ni...ni *9A*

nephew el sobrino *4A*

nervous nervioso,-a *4A*

never nunca *4A*

new nuevo,-a *2A*; *New Year's Day* el Año Nuevo *5B*

news la noticia

newspaper el periódico *2A*

next próximo,-a, que viene *5A*; *next to* al lado (de) *6B*

Nicaragua Nicaragua *1A*

nice simpático,-a *3A*, amable *4A*; *the weather is nice* hace buen tiempo *7B*

nickname el apodo

niece la sobrina *4A*

night la noche *1B*; *at night* de la noche *1B*, por la noche *6B*; *good night* buenas noches *1B*

nine nueve *1A*

nine hundred novecientos, -as *5B*

nineteen diecinueve *1A*

ninety noventa *1B*

ninth noveno,-a *7B*

no no *1A*

nobody nadie *9A*

none ninguno,-a, ningún, ninguna *9A*

noon el mediodía; *It is noon.* Es mediodía. *1B*

north el norte

not: not any ninguno,-a, ningún, ninguna *9A*; *not even* ni *5B*; *not very* poco,-a *6B*

notebook el cuaderno *2A*

nothing nada *9A*

November noviembre *5B*

now ahora *2B*; *right now* ahora mismo *7A*

number el número *2B*; *telephone/fax/cellular telephone number* número de teléfono/ de fax/de teléfono celular *2B*; *wrong number* número equivocado *2B*

O

to **obtain** conseguir *(i, i)*

occupied ocupado,-a *4A*

to **occur** pasar

October octubre *5B*

of de *1A*; *of the* de la/del (de + el) *1A*

of course! ¡claro! *3A*, ¡Cómo no! *3B*

office la oficina *3A*

official oficial

oh! ¡ay! *2A*

oil el aceite *6A*, el petróleo

okay de acuerdo *3B*, regular *1B*; *(pause in speech)* bueno *3B*

old viejo,-a *5B*; *How old are you?* ¿Cuántos años tienes? *1A*; *to be (+ number) years old* tener (+ number) años *5A*

older mayor *5B*

oldest el/la mayor *5B*

on en *2A*, sobre *2B*; *on credit* a crédito *9B*; *on foot* a pie *3A*; *on loan* prestado,-a *6B*; *on the other hand* en cambio *7B*; *on the telephone* por teléfono *6B*

one un, una, uno *2A*

one hundred cien *1B*; *(when followed by another number)* ciento *5B*

onion la cebolla *8B*

only único,-a *4A*, sólo *8A*, solamente

open abierto,-a *4A*

to **open** abrir *5A*

or o *2B*, u *(used before a word that starts with o or ho)* *6B*; *either...or* o...o *9A*

orange la naranja *3B*; anaranjado,-a *(color)* *9A*

to **order** pedir *(i, i)* *6B*

organ el órgano

other otro,-a *4A*

ought deber *6A*

our nuestro,-a *4A*

over sobre *2B*; *over there* allá *6A*

P

paella la paella *8B*

page la página *2A*

pair la pareja

pajamas el pijama *9A*

Panama Panamá *1A*

pants el pantalón *2B*

pantyhose las medias *9A*

paper el papel *2A*; *sheet of paper* la hoja de papel

Paraguay el Paraguay *1A*

pardon me perdón *1B*

parents los padres *2A*, los papás

park el parque *3A*

part-time (work) medio tiempo (trabajo)

partner el compañero, la compañera *5A*

party la fiesta *3A*

to **pass** pasar *5A*; *pass me* pásame *6A*

past pasado,-a *5B*; *half past* y media *1B*

pastime el pasatiempo *7A*

patio el patio *6B*

to **pay** pagar *9B*

pea el guisante *8B*

pearl la perla *9B*

pen el bolígrafo *2A*

pencil el lápiz *(pl.* lápices) *2A*; *pencil sharpener* el sacapuntas *2A*

people la gente *8A*

pepper la pimienta *(seasoning)* *6A*; *bell pepper* el pimiento *8B*

perfect perfecto,-a *9B*

perfume el perfume *9B*

perhaps quizás *8A*

permission el permiso *7A*; *to ask for permission (to do something)* pedir permiso (para) *6B*

permit el permiso *7A*

to **permit** permitir *7A*

person la persona *7A*
personal personal
Peru el Perú *1A*
philosophy la filosofía
photo la foto(grafía) *4A*
physics la física *6A*
piano el piano *4B*
to pick up recoger *8A*
pink rosado,-a *9A*
place el lugar *7B*, la posición
to place poner *6A*
to plan pensar *(ie)* *6A*
plant la planta *6B*
plate el plato *6A*
to play jugar *(ue)* *4B; (a musical instrument)* tocar *4B; (+ a sport/game)* jugar a *4B*
player: el jugador, la jugadora *7B; CD player* el reproductor de CDs *5A; DVD player* el reproductor de DVDs *5A; MP3 player* el reproductor de MP3 *5A*
playing card la carta *7A*
plaza la plaza *3B*
pleasant simpático,-a *3A*
please por favor *1B*
pleasure el gusto *3A; the pleasure is mine* encantado,-a, el gusto es mío *3A*
plural el plural
point el punto
to point apuntar; *to point to (at, out)* señalar
politically políticamente
pollution la contaminación ambiental
polo la camiseta *2B*
popular popular *4A*
pot la olla *8A*
potato la papa *8B*
pound la libra
practice la práctica *5A*
to prefer preferir *(ie, i)* *6A*
to prepare preparar *8A*
pretty bonito,-a *2A*, guapo,-a *2A*, lindo,-a *8B*
price el precio *8B*
printer (laser) la impresora (láser) *2B*
problem el problema *3A*
program el programa *7A*
to promise prometer *9A*
public público,-a; *public square* la plaza *3B*
Puerto Rico Puerto Rico *1A*

purchase la compra *4B*
purple morado,-a *9A*
purpose el propósito
purse el bolso *9B*
to put poner *6A*

quality la calidad *9B*
quarter el cuarto *1B; a quarter after, a quarter past* y cuarto *1B; a quarter to, a quarter before* menos cuarto *1B*
question la pregunta *3B; to ask a question* hacer una pregunta *3B*
quickly pronto *1B*

radio (broadcast) la radio *4B;* el radio
rain la lluvia *7B*
to rain llover *(ue)* *7B*
raincoat el impermeable *9A*
rapid rápido *4B*
rapidly rápidamente *5B*
rather bastante *9B*
to reach cumplir *5B*
to read leer *3B*
reading la lectura
ready listo,-a *7B; to be ready* estar listo,-a *7B*
really? ¿de veras? *5B*
receipt el recibo *9B*
to receive recibir *9B*
recipe la receta *8B*
red rojo,-a *2B*
red-haired pelirrojo,-a *4B*
refreshment el refresco *3B*
refrigerator el refrigerador *2B*
to regret sentir *(ie,i)* *6A*
regular regular *1B*
relative el pariente, la pariente *4A*
to remain quedar *9A*
remains restos
to remember recordar *(ue)* *7A*
remote remoto,-a *7A; remote control* el control remoto *7A*
to rent alquilar *7A*
to repeat repetir *(i, i)* *6B*
report el informe
reporter el periodista, la periodista
to request pedir *(i,i)* *6B*
to resolve resolver *(ue)*
restaurant el restaurante *3A*

to return volver *(ue)* *4A*, regresar
to review repasar
rice el arroz *8B*
ride el paseo *7B; to go for a ride* dar un paseo *7B*
to ride montar *5A*
right correcto,-a; *right now* ahora mismo *7A*
right? ¿verdad? *3A*
ring el anillo *9B*
ripe maduro,-a *8B*
river el río
room el cuarto *6B; dining room* el comedor *6A; living room* la sala *6B*
ruler la regla *2A*
to run correr *6B*
runner el corredor, la corredora *7B*
rush la prisa *6B*

sad triste *4A*
safe seguro,-a
saint's day el santo; *All Saints' Day* Todos los Santos
salad la ensalada *3B*
sale la oferta *9B; to be on sale* estar en oferta *9B*
salt la sal *6A*
same mismo,-a *7A*
satisfied: *to be satisfied (with)* estar contento,-a (con) *4A*
Saturday sábado *2B; on Saturday* el sábado
saucepan la olla *8A*
sausage el chorizo *(seasoned with red peppers)* *8B*
to save ahorrar *9B*
saxophone el saxofón
to say decir *6B; How do you say...?* ¿Cómo se dice...? *2A; one says* se dice *2A; to say you are sorry* pedir perdón *6B*
scarf la bufanda *9B*
schedule el horario *2B*
school el colegio *2B*, la escuela *3A*
science la ciencia
to scold regañar
screen la pantalla *2B*
season la estación *7B*
second el segundo *7B*; segundo,-a *7A*
to see ver *3B; I see it!* ¡ya lo veo!; *let's see* a ver; *see you later*

hasta la vista, hasta luego *1A*;
see you soon hasta pronto *1B*;
see you tomorrow hasta
mañana *1B*; *you see* ves
to seem parecer *8B*
selfish egoísta *4B*
to sell vender *9A*
to send enviar *7B*
sentence la oración, la frase
September septiembre *5B*
settled down establecieron
seven siete *1A*
seven hundred setecientos,-as
5B
seventeen diecisiete *1A*
seventh séptimo,-a *7B*
seventy setenta *1B*
several varios,-as
shame la lástima; *What a
shame!* ¡Qué lástima! *5A*
she ella *2A*
sheet la hoja; *sheet of paper*
hoja de papel
ship el barco *3A*
shirt la camisa *2B*
shoe el zapato *2B*; *high-heel
shoe* zapato de tacón *9A*;
low-heel shoe zapato bajo *8A*
short bajo,-a *(not tall)* *4B*,
corto,-a *(not long)* *9B*; *in short*
en resumen
should deber *6A*
show el programa *7A*
to show enseñar
shrimp el camarón
sick enfermo,-a *4A*
side el lado *6B*
silk la seda *9A*
silly tonto,-a *4B*
silver la plata *9B*
silverware los cubiertos *6A*
since desde *6B*, como
to sing cantar *4B*
singer el cantante, la cantante *3B*
sink el fregadero *6A*
sir el señor, Sr. *1B*
sister la hermana *4A*
six seis *1A*
six hundred seiscientos,-a *5B*
sixteen dieciséis *1A*
sixth sexto,-a *7B*
sixty sesenta *1B*
size el tamaño *9B*
to skate patinar *4B*; *to ice skate*
patinar sobre hielo *7B*; *to in-line
skate* patinar sobre ruedas *4B*

skateboard la patineta *7B*
to skateboard montar
en patineta *7B*
skater el patinador, la
patinadora *7B*
sketch el dibujo *6B*
to sketch dibujar *7A*
to ski esquiar *7B*
skier el esquiador, la
esquiadora *7B*
skirt la falda *2B*
skyscraper el rascacielos
sleep el sueño *6B*
to sleep dormir *(ue, u)* *7A*
slow lento,-a *4B*
small pequeño,-a *6B*
smart listo,-a *8A*; *to be smart*
ser listo,-a *8A*
smooth suave
snow la nieve *7B*
to snow nevar *(ie)* *7B*
so tal, tan *5A*
soap opera la telenovela *7A*
soccer el fútbol *4B*; *soccer
player* el futbolista, la
futbolista *7B*
sock el calcetín *2B*
soft suave; *soft drink*
el refresco *3B*
so long hasta luego *1A*
to solve resolver *(ue)*
some unos, unas *2A*; alguno,-a,
algún, alguna *9A*
somebody alguien *9A*
someone alguien *9A*
something algo *9A*
sometimes a veces *5B*
son el hijo *4A*
song la canción *5A*
soon luego *1A*, pronto *1B*;
see you soon hasta pronto *1B*
sorry: *I am sorry* lo siento *1B*;
to feel sorry sentir *(ie, i)* *6A*;
to say you are sorry pedir
perdón *6B*
so-so regular *1B*
sound system el equipo de
sonido *5A*
soup la sopa *6A*; *soup bowl* el
plato de sopa *6A*
south el sur
Spain España *1A*
Spanish el español *(language)*
2B, español, española;
Spanish-speaking
hispanohablante

to speak hablar *2B*
special especial *6A*
to spend (time) pasar *5A*
sport el deporte *5A*
spouse el esposo,
la esposa *4A*
spring la primavera *7B*
stadium el estadio
stairway la escalera *6B*
to start empezar *(ie)* *6A*
to stay quedar *9A*
stepfather el padrastro
stepmother la madrastra
stereo el estéreo
still todavía *7B*
store la tienda *3B*
stove la estufa *6A*
to straighten arreglar *8A*
strawberry la fresa *8B*
street la calle *3B*
strong fuerte
student el estudiante, la
estudiante *2A*
study el estudio
to study estudiar *2B*
subject la asignatura *8A*
subway el metro *3A*
such tal
sufficient bastante *9B*
sufficiently bastante
sugar el azúcar *6A*
suit el traje *9A*
suitcase la maleta *5A*
summer el verano *4A*
sun el sol *7B*
Sunday domingo *2B*; *on
Sunday* el domingo
sunny soleado,-a *7B*; *it is sunny*
está soleado *7B*, hay sol *7B*,
hace sol *7B*
supermarket el supermercado
8B
surprise la sorpresa *5A*
sweater el suéter *9A*
to sweep barrer *8A*
to swim nadar *4B*
swimming pool la piscina *6B*
swimsuit el traje de baño *9A*
synthetic sintético,-a *9B*

T

table la mesa *6A*; *to clear the
table* recoger la mesa *8A*; *to set
the table* poner la mesa *6A*
tablecloth el mantel *6A*
tablespoon la cuchara *6A*

to take tomar *3A*, llevar *5A*; *take turns* alterna (*tú command*); alternen (*Uds. command*); *to take a trip* hacer un viaje *5A*; *to take out* sacar *8A*; *to take up* subir *8A*

tall alto,-a *4B*

tape recorder la grabadora *5A*

taste gusto

to taste probar

to teach enseñar

teacher el profesor, la profesora *2A*

team el equipo *7A*

teaspoon la cucharita *6A*

telephone el teléfono *2B*; *by the telephone, on the telephone* por teléfono *6B*; *telephone number* el número de teléfono *2B*; *cellular telephone number* número de teléfono celular

to telephone llamar *5A*

television la televisión *4B*; *to watch television* ver la televisión *4B*

television set el televisor *7A*

to tell decir *6B*; *(a story)* contar *(ue) 9A*; *tell me* dígame (*Ud. command*)

temperature la temperatura *7B*; *What is the temperature?* ¿Qué temperatura hace? *7B*

ten diez *1A*

tennis el tenis *4B*

tennis player el tenista, la tenista *7B*

tenth décimo,-a *7B*

to terminate acabar *8A*

test el examen *2B*

than: more (+ noun/ adjective/adverb) than más (+ *noun/adjective/adverb*) que *8B*

thanks gracias *1B*; *thank you very much* muchas gracias *1B*

that que *5A*, ese, esa *6A*, *(far away)* aquel, aquella *6A*, *(neuter form)* eso; *that which* lo que *6B*

the el *(m., s.) 2A*, la *(f., s.) 2A*, las *(f., pl.) 2A*, los *(m., pl.) 2A*; *to the* al *3A*

theater el teatro *3B*

their su, sus *4A*

them les *(i.o.) 3A*; los/las *(d.o.) 5A*; *(after a preposition)* ellos,-as *4B*

theme el tema, el tópico

then luego *1A*, después *6A*, entonces *6A*; *(pause in speech)* pues *3B*

there allí *2A*; *there is, there are* hay *2A*; *over there* allá *6A*

these estos, estas *6A*

they ellos,-as *2A*; *they are* son *2A*; *they were* fueron

thin delgado,-a *4B*

thing la cosa *6A*

to think pensar *(ie) 6A*; *to think about (i.e., to have an opinion)* pensar de *6A*; *to think about (i.e., to focus one's thoughts)* pensar en *6A*; *to think about (doing something)* pensar en (+ *infinitive*)

third tercero,-a,tercer *(form of tercero before a m., s. noun) 7B*

thirst la sed *6B*; *to be thirsty* tener sed *6B*

thirteen trece *1A*

thirty treinta *1B*

this este *(m., s.)*, esta *(f., s.) 6A*

those esos, esas *6A*, *(far away)* aquellos, aquellas *6A*

thousand mil *5B*

three tres *1A*

three hundred trescientos,-as *5B*

through por *6B*

to throw lanzar

Thursday jueves *2B*; *on Thursday* el jueves

thus pues *3B*

tie la corbata *9A*

time el tiempo *4A*, la vez (pl. veces) *5B*; *at times, sometimes* a veces *5B*; *at what time?* ¿a qué hora? *2B*; *(number +) time(s) per (+ time expression) (number +)* vez/veces al/a la (+ *time expression) 7A*; *What time is it?* ¿Qué hora es? *1B*

tired cansado,-a *4A*

to a *2B*

today hoy *3B*

toe el dedo *9A*

together junto,-a

tomato el tomate *8B*

tomorrow mañana *1B*; *see you tomorrow* hasta mañana *1B*; *the day after tomorrow* pasado mañana *5B*

tonight esta noche *7A*

too también *3A*, *too (much)* demasiado *9B*

to touch tocar

train el tren *3A*

transportation el transporte *3A*

to travel viajar *6A*

tree el árbol; *family tree* árbol genealógico

trip el paseo *7B*, el viaje *5A*; *to take a trip* hacer un viaje *5A*

trombone el trombón

truck el camión

trumpet la trompeta

truth la verdad *6B*

to try (to do something) tratar (de)

t-shirt la camiseta *2B*

Tuesday martes *2B*; *on Tuesday* el martes

to turn off apagar *7A*

to turn on encender *(ie) 6A*, poner

twelve doce *1A*

twenty veinte *1A*

twenty-eight veintiocho *1B*

twenty-five veinticinco *1B*

twenty-four veinticuatro *1B*

twenty-nine veintinueve *1B*

twenty-one veintiuno *1B*

twenty-seven veintisiete *1B*

twenty-six veintiséis *1B*

twenty-three veintitrés *1B*

twenty-two veintidós *1B*

two dos *1A*

two hundred doscientos,-as *5B*

typical típico, -a

U

ugly feo,-a *4B*

umbrella el paraguas *9B*

uncle el tío *4A*

to understand comprender *2A*; *I understand* comprendo *2A*

underwear la ropa interior *9A*

unique único,-a *4A*

united unido,-a

United States of America los Estados Unidos *1A*

university la universidad

until hasta *1A*, *(to express time)* menos *1B*

upcoming que viene *5A*

Uruguay el Uruguay *1A*

us nos *(i.o.)* 4B; nos *(d.o.)* 5A; *(after a preposition)* nosotros 4B
to use usar 9B

vacation las vacaciones 9A
vacuum la aspiradora 7A; *to vacuum* pasar la aspiradora 8A
vegetable la verdura 8B
Venezuela Venezuela 1A
verb el verbo
very muy, mucho,-a 3B; *very much* mucho, muchísimo 4A; *not very* poco,-a 6B
video game el videojuego 7A
vinegar el vinagre 8B
volleyball el voleibol 7A

walk el paseo 7B; *to go for a walk* dar un paseo 7B; *to walk* caminar 3A
wall la pared 2A, la muralla
wallet la billetera 9B
to want querer 6A
to wash lavar 8A
wastebasket el cesto de papeles 2A
watch el reloj 2A
to watch ver 3B; *to watch television* ver la televisión
water el agua *f.* 4B; *mineral water* agua mineral 3B
way la manera; *By the way* A propósito 1A
we nosotros 2A
to wear llevar 2B
weather el tiempo 7B; *How is the weather?* ¿Qué tiempo hace? 7B; *the weather is nice (bad)* hace buen (mal) tiempo 7B
Wednesday miércoles 2B; *on Wednesday* el miércoles
week la semana 5A
weekend el fin de semana 5A
welcome bienvenido,-a; *you are welcome* de nada 1B
well bien 1B; *(pause in speech)* bueno, este, pues 3B

what a (+ noun)! ¡qué (+ noun)! 5A
what? ¿qué? 2A, ¿cuál? 2B; *at what time?* ¿a qué hora? 2B; *What is the meaning (of)...?* ¿Qué quiere decir...?* 2A; *What is the temperature?* ¿Qué temperatura hace? 7B; *What is wrong with (someone)?* ¿Qué (+ tener)? 6B; *What is wrong with you?* ¿Qué te pasa?; *What is your name?* ¿Cómo te llamas? 2A; *What is (your/his/her) name?* ¿Cómo se llama (Ud./él/ella)? 1A; *What time is it?* ¿Qué hora es? 1B
when cuando 6B
when? ¿cuándo? 3A
where donde 6B
where? ¿dónde? 1A; *from where?* ¿de dónde? 1A; *(to) where?* ¿adónde? 3A
which que 5A; *that which* lo que 6B
which? ¿cuál? 2B; *which one?* ¿cuál? 2B; *which ones?* ¿cuáles? 2B
white blanco,-a 2B
white-haired canoso,-a 4B
who? ¿quién? 2A, *(pl.)* ¿quiénes? 3A
whole entero,-a
why? ¿por qué? 3A
wife la esposa 4A
to win ganar; *games won* los partidos ganados
wind el viento 7B; *it is windy* hace viento 7B
window la ventana 2A
winter el invierno 7B
to wish desear
with con 1A; *with me* conmigo 9B; *with you* (tú) contigo 9B
without sin 8B
to witness presenciar
woman la mujer 9A
wonderful estupendo,-a 7A
wool la lana 9A
word la palabra 2A
work el trabajo 8A, la obra

to work trabajar 8A
world el mundo
worse peor 8B
worst: the worst (+ noun) el/la/los/las peor/peores 8B
wow! ¡caramba! 5A
to write escribir 6B; *How do you write...?* ¿Cómo se escribe...? 1A; *it is written* se escribe 1A

yard el patio 6B
year el año 5B; *New Year's Day* el Año Nuevo 5B; *to be (+ number) years old* tener (+ number) años 5A
yellow amarillo,-a 8A
yes sí 1A
yesterday ayer 5B; *the day before yesterday* anteayer 5B
yet todavía 7A
you tú *(informal)* 1A, usted (Ud.) *(formal, s.)* 1B, ustedes (Uds.) *(pl.)* 1B, vosotros,-as *(Spain, informal, pl.)* 1B; *(after a preposition)* ti 4B, usted (Ud.), ustedes (Uds.), vosotros,-as 1B; la, lo, *(d.o.)* 5A, las, los, *(d.o.)* 5A, te *(d.o.)* 6A, os *(Spain, informal, pl., d.o.)*, le *(formal, i.o.)*, les *(pl., i.o.)* 1A, os *(Spain, informal, pl., i.o.)*, te *(i.o.)* 3A; *Are you from...?* ¿Eres (tú) de...? 1A; *you are* eres 1A; *you (formal) are* es 1B; *you (pl.) were* fueron
young joven 5B; *young lady* la señorita 1B; *young woman* la muchacha 3A
younger menor 5B
youngest el/la menor 5B
your tu *(informal)* 2B, tus *(informal, pl.)* 4A, su, sus (Ud./Uds.) 4A, vuestro,-a,-os, -as *(Spain, informal, pl.)*

zero cero 1A

Index

Credits

Acknowledgments

The authors wish to thank the many people of the Caribbean Islands, Central America, South America, Spain, and the United States who assisted in the photography used in the textbook and videos. Also helpful in providing photos and materials were the National Tourist Offices of Argentina, Chile, Costa Rica, Colombia, Ecuador, Guatemala, the Dominican Republic, Honduras, Mexico, Nicaragua, Panamá, Perú, Puerto Rico, Spain, and Venezuela.

We would like to thank the Bilingual Press/Editorial Bilingüe, Arizona State University, Tempe, AZ, for permission to reprint *Coplas 1* and *9* from *Puentes y Fronteras/Bridges and Borders* (1996) by Gina Valdés, appearing on page 82 of this textbook.

We would also like to thank the following institutions for permission to reproduce the paintings by Frida Kahlo on page 127 (*Autorretrato con mono,* 1938, and *Raíces,* 1943):

Banco de México Diego Rivera and Frida Kahlo Museums Trust, Av. 5 de Mayo No. 2, Col. Centro, Del. Cuauhtémoc 06059, México, D.F.

Instituto Nacional de Bellas Artes y Literatura, Dirección de Asuntos Jurídicos, Edificio "La Nacional" 8° Piso, Av. Juárez No. 4 esq. Eje Central Lázaro Cárdenas, Col. Centro, 06050, México, D.F.

Photographs of these paintings are © Albright-Knox Art Gallery/CORBIS and © SuperStock, Inc., respectively.

Finally, we would like to thank Nicaraguan artist Rosa Delia López and her representatives, Americas' Arts L.L.C. [P.O. Box 4404, Gettysburg, PA, 17325], for permission to reproduce her painting *La Gritería* (© 1997), which appears on page 180.

Photo Credits

Anderson, Jennifer J.: 105 (#2), 185 (r), 219 (l, c), 301 (tl), 362 (l), 389 (tl), 407 (l, c)
AFP/CORBIS: xx (bl)
AP / Wide World Photos: v (t), xxi (br), xxii (tl), 15 (Penélope Cruz), 46 (Shakira), 78 (b), 82, 85 (Pablo Picasso), 132 (San Juan, Puerto Rico), 151 (Salma Hayek), 168 (Juan Pablo Montoya), 172 (Sammy Sosa), 174 (Pedro Martínez), 175 (t: Ramón Martínez; b: Ramón and Pedro Martínez), 211 (tl), 220, 310, 354 (c, r), 407 (r)
Arruza, Tony / CORBIS: 170 (#2)
Azzara, Steve / CORBIS: 170 (Jennifer López)
Bechara Baruque, Omar; Eye Ubiquitous / CORBIS: 247 (tl)
Béjar Latonda, Mónica: 30 (l, r), 58 (l), 80 (l), 92 (tl, tc, tr), 102 (tl, tc, tr), 112 (l, c, r), 118 (l, c, r), 124 (l), 172 (l), 216 (l), 228 (tl, tc, tr), 236 (tl, tc, tr), 246 (l, c, r), 254 (l, c, r), 260 (l), 272 (l, c, r), 278 (l, c, r), 292 (l, c, r), 300 (l, c, r), 308 (l), 320 (l, c, r), 330 (l, c, r), 331 (l), 340 (l, c, r), 341, 350 (l, c, r), 354 (l), 366 (l, c, r), 376 (l, c, r), 388 (l, c, r), 396 (tl, tc, tr), 402 (l), 422 (l), 424, 425
Bettmann / CORBIS: 126 (Frida Kahlo)
Charlier, Claude / CORBIS: 320 (b)
Chilean Ministry of Tourism (Ministerio de Turismo de Chile): x (t), 293 (tr)

Colita / CORBIS: 147 (Gabriel García Márquez)
Corbis Royalty-Free: vi (l), x (b), xxv (br), 7, 11 (tr), 23 (Activity 10, #2; Activity 11, #3), 47 ("Alicia," "tú," "Pablo"), 56 (tr), 56 (#8), 59 (l, r), 64, 65, 70, 74, 78 ("Josefina, Kathy, y yo"), 88–89, 99 (c), 100 ("en bicicleta"), 142, 148 (#2), 155 (A, B, C, E, F), 156 (b), 165 (#2, #6, #8), 171 (br), 189 (#2, #3, #4, #6), 193 (frog), 195 (t), 196, 204, 207 (bl, br), 223 (l, r), 228 (bl, bc, br), 229 (pearl in shell), 243 (l, r), 263 (l, r), 268–269, 271 (A, E), 275 (#1, #2), 277, 280, 281 (t), 287 (t), 289 (r), 292, 293 (tl), 297, 299 (A, B, E), 303 (Modelo, #3, #5, #6), 304, 327, 329 (Activity 19, C), 332, 336, 337 (l, r), 344, 346, 367 (b), 377 (tr), 384 (r), 396 (c), 401, 403 (r), 415 (b), 417 (b), 427 (l, r)
Corporación Nacional de Turismo-Colombia: xxvi (tr), 247 (tr)
Creatas Images: 10 (Modelo, #1, #2 in Activity 18), 23 (Activity 10, #3; Activity 11, #2), 76 (l), 77 (r), 78 ("Mi tía Sandra"), 81 (r), 165 (#7), 193 (r), 377 (tl)
Cummins, Jim / CORBIS: 302
Dias, Mark: 216 (r)
Digital Stock: 215
DigitalVision: 272 (b)
Duomo / CORBIS: 299 (D)
Dydynski, Krzysztof / Lonely Planet Images: xxvi (bl)